Social Forces and Aging

Also by Robert C. Atchley

Aging: Continuity and Change

Of Related Interest from Wadsworth

Margaret Huyck and William Hoyer, *Adult Development and Aging*

Morris Rockstein and Marvin Sussman, *Biology of Aging*

James H. Schulz, *The Economics of Aging, Third Edition*

Jay Sokolovsky, *Growing Old in Different Societies: Cross-Cultural Perspectives*

John R. Weeks, *Aging, Concepts and Social Issues*

Of Related Interest from Brooks/Cole

Janet K. Belsky, *Aging: A Psychological Approach*

Irene Burnside, *Working with the Elderly: Group Process and Techniques, Second Edition*

Nancy Eustis, Jay Greenberg, and Sharon Patten, *Long-Term Care for Older Persons: A Policy Perspective*

Richard Kalish, *Death, Grief, and Caring Relationships, Second Edition*

Richard Kalish, *Late Adulthood, Second Edition*

Richard Kalish, *The Later Years: Social Applications of Gerontology*

Carol Lium O'Brien, *Adult Day Care: A Practical Guide*

Wilbur H. Watson, *Aging and Social Behavior: An Introduction to Social Gerontology*

Diana Woodruff and James Birren, *Aging: Scientific Perspectives and Social Issues*

Fourth Edition

Social Forces and Aging

An Introduction to Social Gerontology

Robert C. Atchley

Scripps Foundation Gerontology Center, Miami University

Wadsworth Publishing Company
Belmont, California
A Division of Wadsworth, Inc.

Gerontology Editor: Sheryl Fullerton
Production Editor: Robin Lockwood,
    Bookman Productions
Designer: Leigh McLellan
Copy Editor: Elliot Simon
Technical Illustrator: Carl Brown

The design on the cover is a *Shou*, a Chinese symbol for longevity.

Printed in the United States of America

1 2 3 4 5 6 7 8 9 10—89 88 87 86 85

0-534-04338-0

Library of Congress Cataloging in Publication Data
Atchley, Robert C.
    Social forces and aging.

    Rev. ed. of: The social forces in later life.
3rd ed. c1980.
    Bibliography: p.
    Includes index.
    1. Gerontology.   2. Aged—United States.
3. Retirement—United States.   I. Atchley, Robert
C. Social forces in later life.   II. Title.
HQ1061.A78 1985   305.2′6′0973   84-20942
ISBN 0-534-04338-0

Contents

Preface

The goal of this book is to provide a brief but comprehensive introduction to social gerontology—the emerging social science discipline dealing with human aging. Since the first edition, published in 1972, the book has gradually been expanded, deepened, and refined. This fourth edition represents a major reorganization and expansion. It contains four new chapters: The Demography of Aging, The History of Aging in America, Deviance and Social Control, and Health and Social Services. Because the scope of the book was broadened to include middle age as well as later life and because the focus has been expanded to include more effects of an aging population on society, the title has been changed from *The Social Forces in Later Life* to *Social Forces and Aging*.

The statistics reported have been updated to reflect the most recent data possible, including the 1980 U.S. Census. The earlier editions' research illustrations have been dropped from this edition for two reasons. First, both the text and the bibliography have been lengthened considerably, which means that space is at a premium. Second, singling out particular research as exemplary is less appropriate now than it was in 1972, for the volume of high-quality research has increased dramatically, as the bibliography reflects. Students and teachers who want to review good original research are encouraged to use the chapter cross-references in the bibliography to identify supplementary reading.

I am excited about the fourth edition. The new chapters and reorganized order of presentation seem to me to accurately reflect the maturing of social gerontology. Keeping in touch with the changes in any field of study is challenging, but in social gerontology—where the subject matter ranges from physiology to societal institutions to human development—the task is enormous. I have reviewed over 500 new additions to the gerontology literature for this edition, and I believe I have succeeded in integrating the best of the new literature into a much more serviceable framework, as the table of contents shows.

In preparing this revision I was helped by a number of people. The new chapter on The Demography of Aging was reviewed by Kay Phillips, Richard V. Smith, Sue Adlon, and Sheila J. Miller. Charles F. Longino, Jr., provided useful unpublished material on migration, Cynthia Taeuber provided unpublished census material, and Jacob Siegel generously provided an advance copy of his latest demographic work on the older population. The new chapter on The History of Aging in America was reviewed by Andrew Achenbaum, Brian Gratton, and Terri Premo. The new chapter on Deviance and Social Control was reviewed by Richard Troiden and Sherry L. Corbett. The new chapter on Health and Social Services was reviewed by Mildred M. Seltzer.

The entire third edition was reviewed and suggestions for revision were made by Tom Hickey, University of Michigan; Martha Storandt, Washington University; Linda K. George, Duke University Medical Center; Karen C. Holden, University of Wisconsin; Frederick R. Eisele, Pennsylvania State University. Also, Mildred Seltzer reviewed all of the revised chapters and made useful comments. Sue Adlon reviewed the revised chapter on The Scope of Social Gerontology, and Mark Dorfman made numerous useful suggestions for the chapter on The Economy.

Robin Lockwood did an excellent job of guiding the book through production. She is a wonderful person to work with, thoroughly professional, warm, and supportive. The book was improved substantially by the hundreds of editorial suggestions made by Elliot Simon.

I want to thank Sheila Miller, Melissa Atchley, and Christopher Atchley for their patience and good humor in the face of a summer sacrificed to this book. I also want to thank my colleagues—Sheila Miller, Sue Adlon, Helena Lopata, Lillian Troll, Linda George, Ted Wagennar, Kay Phillips, Marty Jendrek, Steve Cutler, Powell Lawton, Carroll Estes, Gloria Cavanaugh, Martha Holstein, Tim Brubaker, Bill Cifferi, and Larry Eickhoff—for enriching, challenging, and supporting my work.

I owe special thanks to Dave Lewis, whose devotion to science, social reform, and humanism attracted me to demography and sociology. Fred Cottrell taught me to blend research, teaching, and service and to respect the importance of each. He also taught me that knowledge is worthless unless it is in a form that can be used for the betterment of people's lives. Millie Seltzer taught me the incredible power of unwavering support. Sheila Miller taught me the value of having a true partner in life. And from Carl Adlon I learned who is using all this knowledge. I have been truly blessed by each of these people.

I also owe tremendous thanks to the office staff of the Scripps Foundation: Debbie Rumpler, Joan McLaughlin, and Thelma Carmack. Their dedication, competence, and goodness are contagious.

Social Forces and Aging

PART I

Setting the Stage

This book is an introduction to *social gerontology*, the scientific discipline devoted to the study of the nonphysical aspects of human aging. As you will see, social gerontology covers a wide range of topics. Most of the book deals with up-to-date, factual information and current perspectives on aging. Part I, consisting of three chapters, provides a context for this material.

Chapter 1 describes the *scope* of social geron-

tology: the general subjects included in social gerontology, how aging and the aged are defined, and some of the broad issues involved in the study of aging. Chapter 2 presents the *demography* of aging. It covers how aging becomes widespread in a population and how population aging is measured. It then considers the growth of the older population in the United States as well as its size, composition,

1

geographic distribution, mobility, and life expectancy. It also discusses the nature of population projections and their uses in serving the older population. Chapter 3 is a *historical overview* of aging in America, from Colonial times to the present. Because aging today is often contrasted with aging in earlier times, it is important that such comparisons be based on fact rather than myths about "the good old days." A knowledge of history also helps us to better understand how contemporary society works. Together, these three chapters provide the background needed for the study of present-day social gerontology.

Chapter 1

The Scope of Social Gerontology

So far as we know, the process of **aging*** has been around as long as life itself. Provided, of course, that illness or violence does not end life before its genetically programmed span, all living organisms pass through three broad stages from conception to death: maturation, maturity, and aging. And even though the *average* length of human life in most societies did not extend into "old age" until the 20th century, there have been old people on earth for thousands of years.

Although biology forms the primary basis of aging, the *significance* of aging is largely social. Physical changes associated with aging such as declining eyesight or graying hair have little significance except as they relate to what is expected of people. For example, declining eyesight is only a problem if (1) it cannot be corrected and (2) it interferes with a person's ability to function normally. And gray hair is significant only because it is used to put people into a particular social category. Thus, it is not only a matter of what aging does to us but also —and more importantly—what we do with aging.

Aging also influences how a society or group is itself viewed. We speak of an "aging society" when the average age of its members is increasing. "The graying of America" is not about individuals who are aging but about the United States as a whole.

Aging affects everyone because nearly everyone has the potential to grow old and because all of the groups in which we live have older members. But although aging has always been a part of human life, the systematic study of aging, especially its social aspects, is relatively young. For example, the Gerontological Society of America—an organization of researchers, practitioners, and educators interested in aging— was not founded until 1946. However, since 1960 research on aging has expanded so rapidly that in 1984 there were research and education

---

*All boldfaced terms are defined in the Glossary.

programs on aging in over 300 colleges and universities.

What Is Gerontology?

Gerontology is defined as "the scientific study of the processes and phenomena of aging" (Funk and Wagnalls, 1963). It includes the results of research on aging from all academic disciplines and fields of professional practice. Biologists study the effect of age on the body's immunity to disease. Physicians search for effective ways to treat disease in older people whose immunity has been reduced. Psychologists study changes in bodily coordination with age. Occupational therapists search for ways to retrain older people whose coordination is impaired. Economists study income requirements of middle-aged and older people. Retirement counselors gather information about how to stretch retirement income. Sociologists study how aging affects social roles. Recreation workers develop ways to help older people get involved in new roles. The list goes on. Almost every area of study or practice that deals with people or their needs has a branch that is devoted to aging. And all these branches of all these fields come together under the label of *gerontology*.

There are four interrelated aspects to the study of aging: physical, psychological, social psychological, and social. The study of *physical aging* examines the causes of the body's declining capacity to renew itself, the physical effects of bodily aging, and the means for preventing, treating, or compensating for conditions caused by physical aging or related to it. The study of *psychological aging* focuses on sensory processes, perception, coordination, mental capacity, human development, personality, and coping ability as they are affected by aging. *Social psychological aging* means the interaction of the individual with his or her environment, and includes such topics as attitudes, values, beliefs,

social roles, self-image, and adjustment to aging. *Social aging* refers to the nature of the society in which individual aging occurs, the influence that that society has on its aging individuals, and the impact aging individuals have on their society. All four aspects of aging are so interrelated in everyday life that it is often difficult to distinguish one from another. Yet subdividing gerontology is useful for the scientific study of aging.

Social Gerontology

Social Gerontology is the subfield of gerontology that deals primarily with the *nonphysical* side of aging. Physical aging is of interest to social gerontologists only as it influences the ways individuals and societies adapt to one another. Yet, because physical aging is at the root of all aspects of aging, social gerontologists need to understand as much as they can about it.

Society as used here is not a single thing. The word refers to the shared ideas and common actions of the residents of a nation, and it includes messages in the mass media, common beliefs, typical ways that people solve problems, laws and regulations, administrative procedures, ideologies, and a host of other factors. Society does *not* act as a unit but rather as a loose structure of individuals, each of whom has a slightly different view of reality, truth, and goodness. Resist the trap of thinking of society as a single entity capable of single-minded action.

What Is Human Aging?

Aging is a broad concept that includes *physical changes* in our bodies over adult life, *psychological changes* in our minds and mental capacities, and *social changes* in how we are viewed, what we can expect, and what is expected of us.

It is common to describe the human life cycle in terms of three broad periods: (1) *maturation,* in which the person develops, (2) *full maturity,* in which the person exercises full powers, and (3) *aging,* in which the person gradually declines. This view, based as it is on the biological characteristics of life in animals and plants, is actually too simplistic.

Biological, Psychological, and Social Aging

Biological aging is the result of numerous processes, most of which do not progress at the same rate. For example, the kidneys typically show diminished functioning much earlier than does the skin. In addition, different physical functions reach maturity at different ages. For instance, sexual maturity is usually reached biologically several years before we attain full height. To complicate matters, most physical functions vary quite a bit from person to person at all stages of life. As an illustration, diastolic blood pressure ranges from 45 to 105 even in men age 18 to 24 (80 is considered "normal") (Gordon, 1964).

When we examine *psychological aging* in adulthood we find that certain dimensions diminish with age while others increase or remain relatively constant. For example, problem-solving ability generally declines with age, vocabulary usually increases, and habits tend to remain relatively constant. Variability is as great for psychological aging as it is for physical aging.

Social aging, on the other hand, is largely an arbitrary process of defining what is appropriate to or expected of people of various ages, usually not based on information about what people of various ages are typically capable of. Thus, school begins at age six, even though most children are quite capable of beginning sooner (and many do). Airline pilots must retire at age 60 even though most can still fly a plane. Ideas about when a person is old enough to marry vary from age 13–16 in Appalachia to age 25 to 30 in Chinatown. Thus, social aging adds yet another level of variability to an already complex issue.

The Two Faces of Aging

Aging is not one process, but many, and it has many possible outcomes, some positive and some negative. On the one hand, increasing age brings greater experience and expanded opportunities for wisdom or skill at subtle arts and crafts, ranging from politics to music. Wisdom and experience can give an older person the kind of long-range perspective that is invaluable in an adviser. Older people can also be keepers of tradition. They know about many unrecorded events that have taken place over the years in families, at workplaces, in communities, and in the nation. Aging can also bring a personal peace and mellowing. Later life can be a time of extraordinary freedom and opportunity once the responsibilities of employment and child rearing are set aside.

On the other hand, aging is a losing proposition for some people. They may lose physical or mental capacities, good looks, opportunity for employment and income, or positions in organizations to which they belong. They may outlive their spouse and friends. *Aging is neither predictably positive nor predictably negative.* For some it is mainly positive, for others it is mainly negative, and for still others it is somewhere in between.

How aging is viewed by society reflects the two-sided nature of aging. In some realms, such as politics, the advantages of age are stressed. In others, such as industrial employment, the disadvantages are emphasized. In still others, such as in the family, both sides are accepted. The double-edged nature of aging is also reflected in the current literature on the subject. There are those who choose to emphasize the negative when they look at the elderly, focusing on sickness, poverty, isolation, and demoralization. Their theories seek to explain how people arrive at such an unhappy state. They tend to see aging as a problem. Other writers emphasize the positive, viewing most of the elderly as being in good health and in frequent contact with family, and as having at least adequate incomes and a high degree of satisfaction with life. The theories they develop try to explain how aging can have such positive outcomes. For them the problems of aging apply to a minority of the elderly.

Because aging can have both positive and negative outcomes, *neither view is wrong.* Certainly, both kinds of outcomes exist, and understanding both kinds of outcomes is important. However, it is also important to acknowledge that *positive outcomes outnumber the negative by at least two to one.*

The positive-negative nature of aging is further reflected in the fact that aging is both a social problem *and* a great achievement. For a sizable minority of older Americans, the system does *not* work. They have difficulty securing an adequate income, are discriminated against at work and in social programs, lack adequate health care, and need better housing and transportation. That these problems recur regularly represents a significant social problem. Yet, the majority of older Americans do not encounter such problems. For them the system works. They are in good health, have modest but adequate retirement pensions, own their own homes, drive their own cars, and need little in the way of social services. Believing that all of the aged are needy or that all of them are self-sufficient are pitfalls to be avoided. *Both types of people exist!* The fact that most of the elderly do not need assistance makes it possible to do something for those who do.

Defining the Aging and the Aged

Aging begins long before it becomes obvious. But to use age as a social attribute, it is necessary to identify specific *indicators* of aging, such as chronological age, functional capacity, or life stage.

Chronological Age

Chronological age, for which the birth certificate is an unambiguous source, satisfies the need to set a point at which bureaucratic rules and policies can be applied and to also separate people who are eligible for something from those who are ineligible. However, because the relationship between chronological age and the consequences of aging is not strong, all such chronological definitions tend to misclassify some proportion of the population.

For example, age 65, the most common age for classifying people as aged or elderly, is currently the age at which people become eligible for full retirement benefits from **Social Security** as well as for **Medicare.** Since mandatory retirement has most commonly occurred at age 65, this seemed the point at which most people would need such benefits and assistance. Yet thousands of people become unable to work due to poor health *before* age 65 and thousands more continue employment *after* age 65. There is, of course, provision for early retirement at age 62, but workers who elect it must accept a lowered benefit. And those who delay retirement beyond 65 are not given a proportionate benefit increase. Thus, the choice of age 65 to define eligibility for these programs unfairly includes some people (such as the employed) who do not need the programs and excludes others (such as those under 62 and in ill health) who do need the programs' benefits. These are the costs of using chronological age. Sometimes the costs outweigh the advantage of easy administration —ask anyone who would like to work longer so as to earn higher Social Security retirement benefits but can't do so because the program is dominated by the idea that 65 is *the* retirement age.

The problem is compounded by the fact that there are also other chronological ages used to define "older." A worker is defined as "older" by the U.S. Department of Labor at age 40. At age 62, people become eligible to live in housing for the elderly. Under Social Security, widows become eligible for survivor benefits at age 60. And this is only in a few of the government's programs. The range in age for *all* government as well as local community agencies is amazing, resulting in a confusing hodgepodge of definitions that reveal no consensus about when "old age" begins. Nonetheless, age 65 remains dominant as the *legal* definition of when a person becomes "older"; it also dominates as the most-used research demarcation point for *aged*, *older*, and *elderly*.

Functional Age

Definitions of **functional age** rely on observable individual attributes to assign people to age categories. Physical appearance, mobility, strength, coordination, and mental capacity are examples of such functional attributes. Commonly-used general criteria for categorizing people as old include gray hair, wrinkled skin, and stooped posture. Adults who move stiffly, tentatively, and with poor coordination exhibit the physical frailty that we associate with old age. And people who are quite forgetful, sometimes confused, and hard of hearing have some of the psychological frailties associated with old age. Anyone who has all of these attributes is undoubtedly "old" regardless of his or her chronological age. Since only a small percentage of people have even a few of these attributes, classifying people into age categories based on functional attributes is mostly an uncertain process. Functional age definitions also vary from one work environment to another. For example, a pro tennis player usually becomes functionally old as early as age 30 or 35, whereas one can still be a functionally capable judge at age 90. And because functional age definitions are so difficult to assess, they are seldom used in research, legislation, or social programs. Nevertheless, in everyday life such definitions give us a general feeling of where to place people along a continuum of functional age.

Life Stages

Very often we use a combination of physical and social attributes to categorize people into broad **life stages,** such as adolescence, young adulthood, adulthood, middle age, later maturity, and old age.

Middle Age.   **Middle age** is the life stage during which most people first become aware that physical aging has noticeably changed them and that they have less energy. During middle age, people often begin to seek less physically demanding activities. Recovery from exertion takes longer. Chronic illness becomes more prevalent. Vision and hearing begin to decline.

What else typically happens during middle age? Job careers often reach a plateau of routine performance. Children leave their parents' households to establish their own. Married couples often grow closer. People sometimes make midcareer job changes. Women who have raised children often rejoin the workforce. More and more people retire in middle age with no continuation of employment. Middle age is also a time when people experience the death of those close to them, usually but not exclusively parents. Women (more than men) sometimes lose a spouse in middle age.

Middle age is a stage marked primarily by social transitions—at home, on the job, in the family. Significant physical transitions usually come later. For most people, middle age is an exciting time, for many of its transitions lead to a more satisfying, sometimes less hectic life. For a few, however, middle age brings irreplaceable loss.

Chronologically, middle age usually begins around age 40, although this varies a great deal depending on when people or those around them perceive that they are *symptomatically* middle-aged. Still, middle age is the stage at which people become part of the *aging* population (as opposed to the *aged* population).

Later Maturity.   The declines in physical functioning and energy availability that begin in middle age continue in **later maturity** (usually considered to begin in the early sixties). Chronic illness becomes more common. Activity limitations become more prevalent, although most people continue to be relatively active. Mortality begins to take its toll among family and friends, with most of these deaths associated not with long sieges of chronic illness but instead with acute episodes of cardiovascular disease. Such deaths often bring home the fact of one's own mortality.

As with middle age, the major changes associated with later maturity are social. Retirement typically occurs during this stage. For most people this is a welcome and beneficial change, but one that usually brings a reduction in income. By contrast, a sizable percentage of women become widows during this stage, and while most manage to adjust to widowhood, it is seldom easy. Deaths of friends and relatives begin to reduce noticeably the size of the everyday social environment.

Despite the aura of loss that typifies later maturity, most people retain a fair measure of physical vigor, which, coupled with freedom from responsibilities, makes this one of the most open and free periods of the life course for those prepared to take advantage of it.

Old Age.   **Old age** is characterized by extreme physical frailty. Chronologically, the onset of old age typically occurs in the late seventies (although many people in their eighties show no signs of it). Mental processes slow down; organic brain disease becomes more common. People spend a lot of time thinking about themselves and their pasts, trying to find meaning in the lives they have led. The individual in old age feels that death is near. Activity is greatly restricted. Social networks have become decimated by the deaths of friends and relatives and by the individual's own disabilities. Institutionalization is common. This stage of life is apt to be unpleasant, at least externally. While middle

age and later maturity are defined mainly by social factors such as the empty nest or retirement, old age is defined more in terms of the physical frailty that accompanies it. Most people die before they reach this stage of extreme disability.

The stages of later life are based on sets of characteristics that seem to be related in many cases, though seldom will a particular individual show each and every characteristic typical of a given stage. Also, these categories are not based on chronological age. Different people show characteristics of old age at different chronological ages—one person could be in old age at 55 while another might still be in later maturity at 85.

In this book we will use the terms *midlife* and *middle age* to refer to people in their forties, fifties, and early sixties. *Aged, elderly,* and *older people* will be used interchangeably for people 65 and over. These chronological definitions misclassify some people, but they are necessary in order to summarize information and make comparisons. Just remember that we are using them for convenience; their value in helping us relate to *specific individuals* is limited.

Gerontology Is a Unique Field of Study

Many of the concepts, theoretical perspectives, factual information, and research issues in social gerontology are unique to gerontology, and are largely unknown in other disciplines. To be sure, gerontology shares a great deal of its vocabulary, ideas, perspectives, and research techniques with other social sciences, but it also has some of its own. In addition, many of the tools borrowed from other social sciences must be modified, sometimes substantially, before they can be utilized effectively in the study of aging. A few examples may be helpful here.

The term **self,** as used in sociology, social psychology, and other social sciences, refers to ideas about oneself that are developed in interaction with others, a view that is useful in explaining how young people develop a sense of self. However, in gerontology we much more often study people whose self-concept is already solid and not very sensitive to outside influence. Thus, to be of use to gerontologists, the concepts and theories about the self that come from general social science literature must be modified and extended. For gerontology the issue is more often how individuals maintain or defend their self-concept than how the self-concept develops.

A great deal of what passes for "fact" about aging or the aged is actually the perpetuation of false stereotypes. For example, the literature on the family tends to treat as "fact" that the transition from a rural, agrarian society to an urban, industrial one caused families to become more mobile and to lose their capacity for including or caring for their elderly members. However, the view of this issue in the gerontology literature is quite different. After two decades of careful historical and survey research, it is clear that families in general do include their older members, have not abandoned them, are in frequent contact with them, and when necessary provide physical, financial, and emotional support to them. Despite the remarkable consistency of this gerontological finding, it has been slow to make its way into the general social science literature (Shanas, 1979).

A final difference between social gerontology and most other social sciences is that gerontology covers a much broader portion of the human life cycle. As a result, research that follows the same individuals or categories over an extended period of time (longitudinal research) is much more prevalent and important in gerontology.

These examples don't mean that social gerontology is in any way superior to other social sciences but only that its special focus on aging gives social gerontology perspectives and information that are unique and that are probably most accurate and detailed *as they apply to aging*.

Concepts and Perspectives

Concepts are created by humans to organize thought, observation, and communication. Like all tools, concepts must be precise if they are to be effective. In social gerontology, you will encounter some new concepts as well as familiar ones with new meanings. You may also need to modify or reject some of your existing concepts. One of the major goals of this book is to provide a sound conceptual basis for thinking, observing, and communicating about aging.

Concepts are usually grouped into classifications and theories. In this book you will encounter numerous classifications, from types of physical changes that accompany aging to types of human services for the elderly. These classifications help to put specific observations in an appropriate context and they aid in identifying valid points of comparison.

Theoretical perspectives help us understand not only *what* is happening but *how* and *why*. Table 1-1 shows some of the major concepts and explanatory perspectives you will encounter in social gerontology and how they relate to one another. It is obvious from the table that social gerontology is loaded with theories and perspectives. This runs contrary to the notion that gerontology is atheoretical. Don't be concerned if many of these concepts and theories are unfamiliar now. By the time you finish this book, they will seem like long-time acquaintances.

Remember, concepts and theoretical perspectives are merely *tentative*—always in need of verification. Of course, there are some theories (such as the theory of gravity) that have been reconfirmed so many times they hardly seem tentative. But we must *always* be alert to change. (People were once certain that the earth was flat.)

Another point to remember is that perspectives are seldom mutually exclusive. For instance, we can say, "People cope with role loss by consolidating their efforts within their remaining roles," *and* we can say, "People cope with role loss by withdrawing." Since some

TABLE 1-1　Concepts and perspectives in social gerontology

The Aging Individual			
Physical Aging	**Mental Aging**	**Social Aging**	**Individual Adjustment to Aging**
Physiological structure	Senses	Social roles	Compensation
Genetic mutations	Structural change	Social attributes	Habituation
Genetic errors	Thresholds	Self-concept	Continuity
Wear and tear		Self-esteem	Conflict management
Cross-links	Perception	Life course	Coping with loss
	Trace effects	Age norms	Substitution
Physiological systems		Age grading	Consolidation
Immune system	Motor capacity	Age stratification	Withdrawal
Auto-immunity	Central processes	Social support	Relative appreciation
Homeostasis	Motivation	Exchange theory	Selective interaction
Neurotransmitters	Body structure		Discounting
			Selective perception
	Mental ability		Denial
	Decrement		Escape
	Increment		
	Terminal drop		
	Interference		
	Cohort differences		
	Personality		
	Human development		
	Stage theories		
	Process theories		
	Social learning theory		
	Personality traits		
	Coping ability		

Aging and Society			
Aging Society	**Social Status of the Elderly**	**Aged Response as Category**	**Care of the Aged**
Political economy	Age discrimination	Aged as subculture	Medical care model
Retirement institution	Societal disengagement	Aged as minority group	Social care model
Health care system	Modernization theory	Aged voluntary associations	Filial responsibility
Elderly services	Age stratification	Advocacy groups	Continuum of care

people follow one pattern and some the other, the real question is not which perspective is true and which false but rather, What *proportion* of people who experience role loss fit into *each* perspective (and why do some people withdraw while others don't)?

Factual Information

Factual information about aging needs to be *representative*. Most of us get quite a bit of information from our everyday experience, information that is often correct as far as it goes. Unfortunately, we are seldom exposed to a complete cross section of people or situations. For example, suppose someone asks, "Do people have difficulty adjusting psychologically to retirement?" And suppose we have a group of four experts respond. The first is a psychiatrist (who, after all, should know a lot about psychological adjustment). She says, "Yes. I see many people who are highly distressed about retirement." The second respondent is director of a planned retirement community (who has lots of experience with retired people). He says, "No. In my ten years at Covebrook Center, I have seen only two people who had a significant problem in adjusting to retirement." The third to respond is director of a senior center: "Yes. Many of the people who come to my center are quite anxious. They feel cut adrift and unsure of what to do." The fourth person, another senior center director, says, "That's interesting. At my center the people are all retired from Xenon Corporation and they're all delighted with retirement." Who is one to believe? The difficulty here is that the experience of each of these experienced people is *selective*. The psychiatrist has little experience with well-adjusted people—they don't need her services. The retirement community staffer sees people who are healthy, wealthy, and committed to an active life style. The two senior center directors' conflicting views reflect the fact that senior centers differ in the social, ethnic, occupational, re-

gional, and community backgrounds of their clientele.

Information collected via scientific research has at least three major advantages over information gathered from everyday experience. First, social science research examines samples of people or situations whose representativeness can be evaluated, thus giving us a basis for weighing evidence from various sources. A second advantage of scientific data is that the procedures used to collect the information and arrive at conclusions are explicit, thus providing another tool for weighing evidence. Weighing evidence is a skill that requires experience and practice. The facts seldom speak for themselves. They need to be interpreted and put into context. A third advantage of scientific research is the existence of a body of standards by which to judge research adequacy. For example, statistical tests of significance allow us to assess the probability that particular research results are merely chance occurrences rather than meaningful and repeatable.

Research Issues

With only minor modification, most of the research methods of the other social sciences are applicable to social gerontology. For example, the statistical techniques that students learn in undergraduate psychology, sociology, geography, and so on are essentially the same as those used by social gerontologists. But in social gerontology, there are certain areas where the emphasis differs from that of the other social sciences: the logic of research, the mix of types of research, sampling, and measurement.

Logic of Research. Much social science research involves making comparisons among groups or categories, or examining relationships among variables measured at the same moment in time. If we wanted to know the effect of race on income, for example, we might examine the average incomes of various racial categories in a given year. But if we are to learn about aging, we cannot simply compare people of different ages at a single point in time. We need also to observe how the same people change over time. In addition, historical period can influence the effect of being a particular age. In gerontology, we call these different concepts age differences, age changes, and period effects.

Age differences result from comparisons of people who are different ages at the same moment in time. For example, in the United States in 1977 the median income of men age 55 to 64 was $14,865 while for men age 65 and over it was only $8,035 (U.S. Bureau of the Census, 1979). From these data, one might conclude that aging causes income to go down, which may indeed be the case. But it is also true that the median number of years of school completed by men age 55 to 64 was 8.6 compared with only 6.3 for men 65 and over. Should we conclude that aging causes level of education to drop? Of course not. This illustrates a problem: There are factors other than aging that can cause age differences. The preceding age difference in education was not caused by aging but by two other factors: (1) The two age categories (called **cohorts**) received their educations at different historical times, and (2) ideas about how much education is appropriate and society's capacity to provide education both change over time. Even in the income example above, aging is probably responsible for only part of the age difference; part is also probably the result of a higher average wage when the younger cohort began employment.

Age changes occur in the same individual over time. For example, when Bob was 19, he had 20/20 vision, but by age 40 it was 20/40, good enough to drive legally without glasses and to perform all the tasks required in his everyday life. Nevertheless, he had experienced an age change in visual acuity.

Period effects are always with us and they interact with aging. For instance, one of the major transitions to adulthood is getting a full-time job, which most people go through be-

tween the ages of 18 and 22. But the nature and quality of this transition is very much affected by the climate of the times in which it occurs. Those who first sought employment during the Great Depression generally had a tough time and may have had to settle for a much less desirable job than they were qualified for. Those who entered the labor market in the mid-1960s generally found good jobs readily available, provided they were not drafted for the Vietnam War. In the late 1970s, economic recession, along with large numbers of young adults from the baby boom, created an extremely tight job market.

The effect of a time period on an individual depends on how old the person is when he or she experiences that period. At the onset of the Great Depression, for example, the suicide rate increased among white males in America, and the amount of increase went up for each successive five-year cohort. From 1925 to 1930, the suicide rate of white males age 30 to 34 went up 38 percent, for those 40 to 44 the increase was 49 percent, and for those 50 to 54, 51 percent (Atchley, 1980).

Whether period effects, age changes, and cohort differences can be completely disentangled is questionable (Palmore, 1978; Feinberg and Mason, 1978; George, Siegler, and Okun, 1981). Nevertheless, social gerontologists must be aware of these different types of effects and design research that tries to control and separate them as much as possible.

Types of Research.   Social scientists use several types of research to gather information, including direct observation in the field, analysis of existing statistics or records, experiments, and social surveys. Social gerontologists use these same types of research, but not necessarily in the same proportions as in other social sciences. A comparatively large number of social gerontology topics are still in exploratory stages, which affects the types of research being done.

When research into a new field begins, it is

much like an explorer charting unknown territory. Ideas about the new territory are vague and maps are crude. As we gradually explore the territory more fully we are able to identify major routes and important locations. For example, research in cognitive psychology has progressed to the point where tight experiments can be designed to answer detailed questions about such topics as how aging affects intelligence, memory, or problem solving. On the other hand, research on how aging affects marriage is still mainly descriptive, trying to identify the major facts, issues, and perspectives that will produce useful research. Social gerontology, being a relatively new specialty within social science, does research that is necessarily more descriptive. Thus, small-scale field studies and pilot surveys are more numerous than in other fields.

Ralph Waldo Emerson defined a scholar as a person in the process of hard thinking (Emerson, 1867). In this context, research means gathering information and then reflecting on it. It also follows that the more methods the scholar uses to gather information, the more likely it is that the results of reflection will be accurate. In my own studies of retirement, I have observed retired people in their homes and in their communities, interviewed them, examined survey data from over 10,000 retired people, read the research results of dozens of others who have studied retirement, and looked at various kinds of demographic data. After more than 15 years of such work, I am just now beginning to feel that I really know something about retirement. The point is that *every* type of research is necessary in order to gain an understanding of the social world. Unfortunately, most research fields experience fads—this or that type of research being favored. Such fads are worth resisting. They ebb and flow like the sands on a desert and hardly provide a sound basis for knowledge. In the social sciences right now, large national sample surveys are in vogue, justified in part by the contention that they are more representative than small-scale surveys.

Yet careful analysis for various regions of the country reveals that local response rates to these large surveys are sometimes as low as 20 percent, certainly an inadequate representation. This in turn means that such surveys, though national in scope, are not as representative as they might appear to be. National surveys are certainly useful, but they also benefit from cross-checking with the results of other types of research. And there are important research questions that do not lend themselves to national surveys.

In addition, the mystique of the large national sample by implication casts a shadow on the value of community-based studies. Yet for many purposes, community-based studies are superior to national surveys. For example, in any study of the effect of retirement on leisure activities, it would be important to hold constant the availability of recreational programs and facilities. This would be vastly easier to do in a study of a single community than in a national survey of people in hundreds of communities.

Sampling. Because older people constitute only a little over 10 percent of the population, sampling the elderly is sometimes difficult, particularly if we are looking for something that occurs in only a minority of older people. For example, mental health professionals cite cases of depression associated with retirement. However, in studies that have followed representative samples of people through retirement, only a tiny fraction experienced depression associated with it. This means that if one wants to study those who become depressed as a result of retirement, finding an adequate sample would be difficult indeed. There are no lists one could use, and going door-to-door would be too expensive. Unfortunately, gerontologists must often settle for the samples they can get rather than the samples they would like to have. And while this is true some of the time in any field, it is true more often in social gerontology.

Measurement.   Measurement involves translating observations into meaningful numbers. The adequacy of the procedures we use to measure social variables is judged by two important criteria, validity and reliability. The term **validity** refers to the correspondence between what is supposed to be measured and what is actually measured. The closer the correspondence, the more valid the measure. Validity can be assessed by comparing the results of the measure in question with an already accepted measure, but often the researcher must settle for measures that only *appear* to most observers to be valid, without real proof. Since validity often cannot be established concretely, the investigator must be constantly on the alert for impressions of validity.

The term **reliability** refers to the extent to which a given measure gives results that are stable over successive trials. In the *test-retest method* of assessing reliability, a test is given to the same people more than once and the results compared. Note: A measure can be reliable without being valid, but it can never be valid without being reliable.*

Questions of validity and reliability are important for gerontological research because many of the measures we want to use were established for young research subjects, not for older ones. It is quite possible for a test to be valid and reliable for college students but not for retired professors. The investigator who wants to use an already-established measure will ordinarily want to reestablish the validity and reliability of the measure when it is tried with older people. Gerontological researchers have paid too little attention to this problem.

These and many other methodological issues related to the study of aging are covered in more detail by Nelson and Starr (1972), Nesselroade and Reese (1973), and Herzog and Rodgers (1981).

---

*For a detailed discussion of validity and reliability, see Kidder, 1981, and Baltes, Reese, and Nesselroade, 1977.

Despite some methodological difficulties, social gerontology has made enormous strides over the past two decades. As you will see, we know quite a bit about aging; much of what we know has been found repeatedly, so we can be relatively confident about it. But, as in any field, knowledge is constantly changing, which should keep us on our toes.

Some Important Gaps in Knowledge

While most aspects of later life have been researched far more than one might expect, there are nevertheless two very important gaps in our present knowledge: the lack of cross-national data and the lack of data on older minority group members. Since aging becomes a visible social problem primarily in industrialized societies, there has been very little research on social gerontology in the nonindustrialized nations of the world. In addition, the data for industrialized nations are quite variable, with the United States by far the most widely researched. Thus, the body of knowledge we call *social gerontology* is heavily biased in terms of the American situation; this book of necessity reflects this bias.

Moreover, despite the fact that older Americans have been researched far more than any other older population in the world, less is known about significant subgroups of older Americans. Not only are there individual differences that produce heterogeneity in the older population, but there also are subgroup differences in culture and behavior that create diversity among older people. Sixty-five-year-old Americans cannot be understood apart from their earlier lives; if they are minority group members, their experience has probably been quite different from that of most of their fellow older Americans. Thus, older people who also happen to be black, poor, Appalachian, foreign-born, or members of an ethnic minority probably face an old age that is different from that of the majority of the older population. Although research on aging among minorities is much more prevalent now than a decade ago, much of what we have to say about older people in this book still may not necessarily apply to older members of minority groups.

Summary

Although aging has its roots in the nature of humans as biological organisms, the significance of aging is often defined socially. Aging not only affects what people are capable of doing, but it also influences what they are expected to do, allowed to do, or prohibited from doing. Large increases in the proportion of the population that is aged also influence the issues that societies must resolve, and lead us to speak of "aging societies."

Gerontology is a relatively new field devoted to the scientific study of aging. It includes knowledge about aging from all academic disciplines and fields of professional practice, as well as that developed within gerontology itself. Social gerontology is a social science discipline that deals with the nonphysical side of aging. It includes the psychological, social psychological, and social aspects of aging.

Human aging is not one process, but many. Even at the biological level there is great variety within a single individual as to when aging begins in a particular organ or system and the rate at which it progresses. Psychologically, some functions decline with age, some remain relatively stable, and some improve. Social aging brings both advantages and disadvantages for the aging individual. Because aging varies both within and between individuals and because it can have both positive and negative results, the consequences of aging for a particular individual are not predictable. The two faces of aging —positive and negative—are reflected in society's treatment of older people, in the literature on aging, and in our theories about aging and the aged.

To study aging, we must know whom to study. We can define aging by chronological age, functional age, or life stage. Each type of definition has advantages and limitations. Because chronological definitions are the easiest to use, they dominate aging research and social policy about aging. Chronologically, middle age begins at about age 40 in most cases. Age 65 is the most common demarcation age for when a person becomes aged, elderly, or older, although different age markers are used in numerous governmental laws and regulations, as well as in a great deal of research into aging.

As a field of study, social gerontology shares concepts, theoretical perspectives, classifications, factual knowledge, and research methods with the other social sciences, but it also has developed some that are uniquely its own. Theories are numerous in social gerontology, and most of them are relatively unknown in the other social sciences.

Science is the main method used to collect factual information in social gerontology because, compared with everyday observation, scientific information is usually more representative, easier to evaluate, and can rely on a set of rules and conventions for making decisions about whether something is true or not.

Research methods in social gerontology differ from those in the other social sciences in the attention paid to differentiating age differences from age changes and period effects. Age differences derive from comparing individuals of different ages at a given point in time and can result from a number of factors other than aging. Age changes are changes in a given individual over time. Period effects result from variations in social conditions over time. Age and period effects interact so that the consequences of being a particular age depend somewhat on when in history one experiences that age.

Social gerontology, like any new discipline, needs an abundance of research to explore new territory. This means a larger proportion of small-scale pilot research than in more established disciplines. Nevertheless, social gerontology, like all disciplines, benefits from research of all types. Researchers in social gerontology are often frustrated by difficulties in sampling—particularly for relatively rare events, characteristics, or processes—in what is already a relatively small segment of the total population. As a result, less than ideal samples are more common in gerontology than in some other disciplines. Researchers in social gerontology also have to beware of measuring the elderly with instruments that were developed for use with other age groups. It is important to reestablish the validity and reliability of such measures for use with older people.

Chapter 2

The Demography of Aging

One of the main forces behind social gerontology is the aging of the population, that is, the increasing proportion of older people in many countries of the world. This chapter discusses how the aging of a population is measured and what demographic forces produce it, the nature of population projections and their uses, and the details about the composition of the older population of the United States. Together, these topics allow us to understand demographic factors as an important *context* for both societal and individual adjustment to aging. The chapter also illustrates how population issues can influence society's institutions as they relate to the elderly.

Measuring Age Structure

In order to understand the age structure of a society, we need some means of summarizing it. After all, in 1980 the United States population was made up of over 226 million individuals. One effective way to summarize the age structure of America is to classify the population into 5-year age categories and then compute the percentage of the population in each category. Because the number of males relative to the number of females at any age can also be important, percentages are usually compiled by gender for each age category.

Table 2-1 shows the percentage distribution of the 1980 U.S. population, by age and sex. From it we can determine that older persons then represented 11.3 percent of the population and that older women outnumbered older men by about 3 to 2. Another 24.8 percent of the population was between the ages of 40 and 64. Thus, using the common chronological definitions, about 35 percent of the U.S. population was middle-aged or older in 1980.

Population Pyramids

A better way to visualize the age and sex structure of a population is to convert the percentage

TABLE 2-1   Population of the United States, by age and sex: 1980

Age (years)	Total Number (in millions)	Percent	Males Number (in millions)	Percent	Females Number (in millions)	Percent
0–4	16.348	7.2	8.362	3.7	7.986	3.5
5–9	16.700	7.4	8.539	3.8	8.161	3.6
10–14	18.242	8.1	9.316	4.1	8.926	3.9
15–19	21.168	9.3	10.755	4.7	10.413	4.6
20–24	21.319	9.4	10.663	4.7	10.655	4.7
25–29	19.521	8.6	9.705	4.3	9.816	4.3
30–34	17.561	7.8	8.677	3.8	8.884	3.9
35–39	13.965	6.2	6.862	3.0	7.104	3.1
40–44	11.669	5.2	5.708	2.5	5.961	2.6
45–49	11.090	4.9	5.388	2.4	5.702	2.5
50–54	11.710	5.2	5.621	2.5	6.089	2.7
55–59	11.615	5.1	5.482	2.4	6.133	2.7
60–64	10.088	4.5	4.670	2.1	5.418	2.4
65–69	8.782	3.9	3.903	1.7	4.880	2.2
70–74	6.798	3.0	2.854	1.3	3.945	1.7
75–79	4.794	2.1	1.848	0.8	2.946	1.3
80–84	2.935	1.3	1.019	0.4	1.916	0.8
85+	2.240	1.0	0.682	0.3	1.559	0.7
Total	226.546	100.2%*	110.053	48.5%	116.493	51.2%
65+	25.549	11.3	10.304	4.6	15.245	6.7

*Due to rounding error, percent columns add to more or less than 100 percent.

Source: U.S. Bureau of the Census, initial tabulation, May 6, 1983.

distribution into a **population pyramid.** Figure 2-1 is a population pyramid constructed from the data in Table 2-1.* The figure shows better than the table the effect of the post–World War II "baby boom" and the subsequent drop in birth rates. We will return to the age structure of the United States later.

Population pyramids are useful for making comparisons between age and sex categories within a single population and also for making comparisons between populations, including populations of very different sizes. For example, Figure 2-2 shows population pyramids for Pakistan and Sweden in 1975. From these graphs we can see that Pakistan had a very high percentage of children and a relatively low percentage of older people, while Sweden had a very high percentage of older people and a relatively low percentage of children. The reason for these differences will be dealt with later in the chapter. For now it is enough to note the value of population pyramids in making comparisons between societies' age-sex structures.

*This type of chart is called a pyramid because at the time it was first devised, most population age and sex structures resembled a pyramid—there were a great many young children and a steady erosion of numbers because death rates were high at all ages.

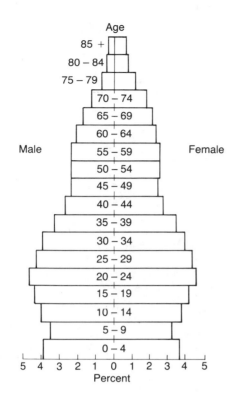

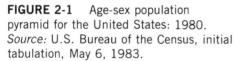

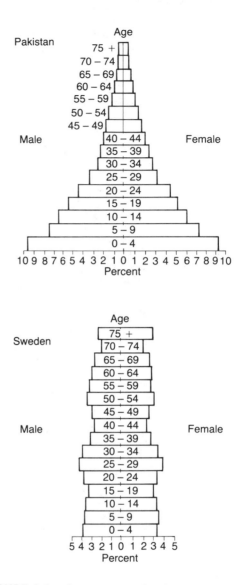

FIGURE 2-1   Age-sex population pyramid for the United States: 1980. *Source:* U.S. Bureau of the Census, initial tabulation, May 6, 1983.

Sometimes we want to compare many different societies or to compare the same society at many different points in time. To do so using population pyramids or percentage distributions is too cumbersome. We need instead a single summary measure of the degree of population aging. The three most commonly used measures are the percent of the population age 65 and over, the aged dependency ratio, and life expectancy at birth.

Proportion of Older People

The **proportion of older people in the population** is simple to compute and based on data readily available for most countries of the

FIGURE 2-2   Age-sex pyramids for Pakistan and Sweden: 1975. *Source:* Adapted from Weller and Bouvier, 1981: 44.

world. It is also readily available for nearly all subdivisions of the United States, which allows us to compare the United States with other countries and to compare subdivisions of the United States. Table 2-2 shows the percentage of persons age 65 and over in selected countries, and it indicates that the United States, along

TABLE 2-2   Population percentage of persons age 65 and over, and dependency ratios: selected countries, 1979

Country	Percent 65 & Over	Youth Dependency Ratio	Aged Dependency Ratio	Total Dependency Ratio
Liberia	2	.73	.06	.79
Morocco	2	.88	.05	.93
Niger	3	.82	.09	.91
Mexico	3	.79	.07	.86
Brazil	3	.73	.05	.78
Iran	3	.85	.06	.91
India	3	.70	.06	.76
Pakistan	3	.88	.07	.95
Thailand	3	.75	.06	.81
Malaysia	4	.71	.06	.77
South Korea	4	.60	.05	.65
Syria	4	1.07	.08	1.15
Chile	5	.57	.08	.65
Canada	8	.36	.13	.49
Japan	8	.34	.13	.47
U.S.S.R.	9	.63	.09	.72
U.S.A.	11	.34	.17	.51
Netherlands	11	.34	.17	.51
Hungary	13	.32	.20	.52
Denmark	14	.32	.22	.54
France	14	.32	.22	.54
Norway	14	.22	.20	.42
West Germany	15	.27	.24	.51
Sweden	15	.31	.24	.55

Source: Computations by the author based on data from: Population Reference Bureau, 1979; United Nations, 1979.

with most of Europe, has a relatively high proportion of older people in its population. Canada, Japan, and the U.S.S.R. are in an intermediate position, and the remainder have relatively low percentages of older people. (The dependency-ratio columns of Table 2-2 will be considered shortly.)

When we look at population data within the United States (Figure 2-3), we see obvious variations among the states in the percentage of older people. For example, the elderly population ranges from 2.9 percent in Alaska, through Utah, next lowest at 7.5 percent, to 17.3 percent in Florida. We can easily see that older people make up a relatively small part of the populations of several mountain states of the west and a relatively large part of the farm states of the midwest and Florida. We will discuss this distribution in more detail in a later section of this chapter. For now it is enough to realize that

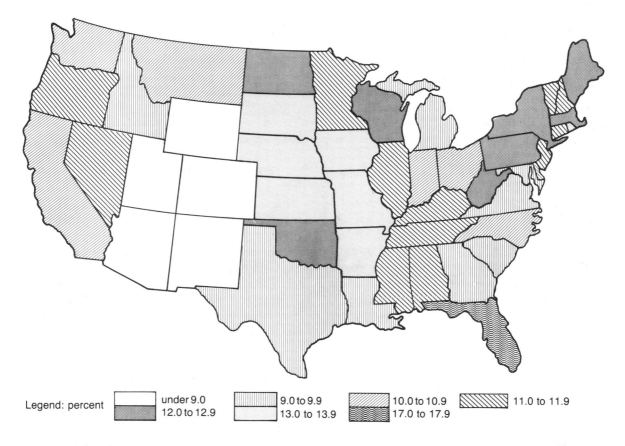

FIGURE 2-3   Percent of state population age 65 and over: 1980. *Source:* U.S. Senate Special Committee on Aging, 1981: 31.

the percentage of older people is an effective statistical tool for looking at population aging cross-nationally and within the United States.

Dependency Ratios

The **aged dependency ratio** is another common measure of population aging. It is the ratio of the number of older people in the population to the population in the age categories most closely associated with employment (usually 15 to 64) and is designed to give a very rough index of the size of the older population in comparison with the size of the population that could be expected to pay taxes to support benefits for the elderly. Obviously, the aged dependency ratio misclassifies a large number of older people who are employed and a large number of people age 15 to 64 who are not. For this reason, the aged dependency ratio is a much-less-than-perfect indicator of what it was designed to show. Nevertheless, it is widely used, so you need to be familiar with it.

The aged dependency ratio is often used in conjunction with the **youth dependency ratio,** that is, the ratio of the number of youths under age 15 to the total number of employable age (15–64). The youth and aged dependency ratios combined together, form a **total dependency ratio,** or the total "dependent" population (youth and the aged) relative to the "working-age" population.

Table 2-2 shows the youth, aged, and total dependency ratios for selected countries in 1979. Notice how the youth dependency ratio fluctuates much more than the aged dependency ratio. Once again, the United States is among the countries with a high ratio of older people. Notice also that countries with high aged dependency ratios tend to have relatively low youth dependency ratios. This means, at least hypothetically, that those countries with high demand for services for the elderly should also have lower demand for services for the young.

There has been much written recently about the "burden of dependency" that an aging population brings. However, Table 2-2 makes it absolutely clear that the United States population could age considerably (so it resembled Sweden in its age-sex structure) without altering the total dependency ratio very much. Indeed, countries that have the highest "dependency burden" are also those with high youth dependency ratios. Thus, high birth rates, not aging populations, translate into high total dependency ratios.

Table 2-2 also lets us compare the proportion of the population that is older with the aged dependency ratio as indicators of population aging. Notice that the table is in rank order by proportion of older people in the population. We see that while aged dependency ratios generally parallel the increases in percent aged, there are some exceptions. The reason for these exceptions relates to "abnormal" age distributions. For example, in the U.S.S.R. the aged dependency ratio is relatively low because large numbers of Russians died during W.W.II and thus did not survive to become part of the older population. Which of these measures to use depends mainly on convenience, since both are effective. I prefer the proportion of older people in the population because it is more readily available and is less subject to misinterpretation. Although the aged dependency ratio has

an appealing logic, because of the misclassification problem mentioned earlier it really does not measure economic dependency, and this in turn raises the potential for misinterpretation.

Life Expectancy

Life expectancy, or the average number of years an age category is expected to live given the base-year mortality rates, can be computed for any age category, but life expectancy at birth is the one most commonly used. As an index of aging, life expectancy at birth shows the average length of life a cohort is expected to live given the mortality rates in the year of its birth. For example, in 1979, life expectancy at birth was 73.7 for the entire United States population—69.9 for men and 77.6 for women. For white males it was 70.6 and for white females, 78.2. For other races, male life expectancy was 65.5 compared to 74.2 for females (U.S. Bureau of the Census, 1982a).

Because the mortality rates from which it is computed are among the most widely available population statistics, life expectancy has the advantage of allowing comparisons across a wide range of societies. The main disadvantage is that life expectancy at birth is very sensitive to infant mortality rates, which do not necessarily parallel mortality rates at other ages. As Table 2-3 shows, life expectancy at birth fluctuates much more from country to country than does life expectancy at age 65. As a result, life expectancy at birth is a highly imprecise indicator of population aging.

In addition to life expectancy, **life tables** contain other data that could be used to measure population aging, particularly the proportion of babies born in the base year expected to live to age 40 or to age 65. For example, as Table 2-4 shows, 93.8 percent of boys and 96.8 percent of girls born in the United States in 1979 are expected to survive to age 40. Of the boys, 71.8 percent are expected to live to age 65, compared to 84.5 percent of the girls. In Mexico by contrast, only 78.4 percent of the boys born in 1979

TABLE 2-3 Life expectancy at birth and at age 65, by sex: selected countries, latest available year

Country (year)	Life Expectancy			
	At Birth		At Age 65	
	Male	Female	Male	Female
Liberia (1971)	45.8	44.0	12.3	13.1
Syria (1970)	54.5	58.7	11.9	13.1
Iran (1974)	57.6	57.4	13.0	14.6
Chile (1970)	60.5	66.0	12.6	14.6
Mexico (1975)	62.8	66.6	14.7	15.0
Malaysia (1975)	65.4	70.8	13.2	16.5
Hungary (1974)	66.5	72.4	12.2	14.8
West Germany (1975)	68.3	74.8	12.3	15.7
U.S.A. (1975)	68.7	76.5	13.7	18.0
France (1974)	69.0	76.9	13.2	17.2
Canada (1971)	69.3	76.4	13.7	17.5
Denmark (1976)	71.1	76.8	13.7	17.1
Netherlands (1973)	71.2	77.2	13.6	16.9
Norway (1974)	71.9	78.1	14.1	17.4
Sweden (1974)	72.1	77.8	14.0	17.2

Source: Compiled from the Demographic Yearbook, 1977.

TABLE 2-4 Percentage expected to survive to selected ages, by sex: United States, 1979; Mexico, 1975

	Percentage Expected to Survive			
	To Age 40		To Age 65	
	Male	Female	Male	Female
United States	93.8	96.8	71.8	84.5
Mexico	78.4	82.0	53.9	62.3

Source: U.S. Bureau of the Census, 1979a:71; 1979b:8.

are expected to reach age 40 and only 53.9 percent to reach age 65, while 82 percent of the girls born that year are expected to reach age 40 and 62 percent to reach age 65 (U.S. Bureau of the Census, 1979b). The comparison of the United States and Mexico in Table 2-4 reflects the difference in degree of population aging inherent in prevailing mortality rates much more than does the comparison of life expectancies in Table 2-3. Unfortunately, data on the proportions who survive to various ages are scarce for many countries and for the states and local areas of the United States. In addition, the life-table survival values are hypothetical ones based on the assumption that mortality rates will remain unchanged for a hundred years.

Perhaps the most significant limitation of life-table statistics as indicators of population aging is that they do not take into account *fertility rates* in a population. For a population to grow older, the number of older people must increase at a faster rate than the number of children entering the population. If the birth rate is high, there can be a substantial reduction in mortality at older ages yet little change in the proportion of older people. Thus, a valid measure of population aging must not only indicate the prevalence of older people in the population but also give some indication of the relationship between the size of the older population compared to other age categories. Both the proportion who are 65 and over and the aged dependency ratio satisfy this criterion; life expectancy does not.

How Populations Age

The demographic forces behind population aging are straightforward. As human societies gain the ability to control disease, death is postponed for more and more people. And many societies have responded to this change by also lowering their birth rate. The result is a larger number of survivors moving into the older ages and a smaller number of infants entering the population, which of course results in an aging population.

Control of disease began with the discovery that clean water and sewage control can reduce the spread of infectious diseases. Disease control was furthered by the development of national systems of transportation, which reduced the effects of local famine, and of sanitary food-processing and storage methods. Finally, the introduction of antibiotics and immunization processes ended centuries of terror associated with diseases such as smallpox, tuberculosis, typhoid, cholera, polio, hepatitis, plague, and a host of others. In most countries, death rates went down gradually, followed some time later by a fall in the birth rate.

When the birth rate is higher than the death rate, the population increases. For example, assuming no migration, a population with a birth rate of 37 per 1,000 per year and a death rate of 9 per 1,000 per year has an annual rate of natural increase of $(37 - 9)/1,000$, or 2.8 percent. If this does not seem like much, remember that populations increase geometrically (2, 4, 8, 16), so that a population increasing at 2.8 percent per year would *double* its size in just 25 years!

Thus, the falling death rates that began in Europe in the late 1600s produced extremely high population increases until birth rates also began to fall. Today in most countries of Europe and in the United States, population growth is low because death rates and birth rates are both low. And in East Germany in 1980, the population was aging even faster than in the rest of Europe because the death rate (11.5 per 1,000) was higher than the birth rate (10.0 per 1,000).

Low death rates mean that more people survive to enter old age; combined with low birth rates this means that the number of children born into a population is not substantially different from the number of people dying. For example, in 1979 Sweden had a birth rate of 11.6 and a death rate of 11.0 (United Nations, 1979). The eventual result (assuming no migration) is an age structure such as Sweden's (see Figure 2-2), whose population is quite evenly distributed across the various age categories. By contrast, high birth rates and death rates produce an age structure like Pakistan's (Figure 2-2), in which a very large proportion of the population is under 15 and a very small proportion survives to age 65. Thus, we say that Swe-

den has a relatively "old" population and Pakistan a relatively "young" one.

Population aging can also occur *within* an older population, usually the result of lowered death rates at the older ages, but possibly also the result of entry into the older population of a relatively small birth cohort. For example, during the Depression years of the 1930s, birth rates in the United States were lower than in the preceding decades. In 1995, when that cohort enters the older population, the average age of the older population will go up even if death rates and the proportion of older people in the population remain the same.

Population Projections

Population projections are used mainly for planning. They involve making assumptions about what will happen to birth rates, death rates, and migration patterns and then projecting the current population into the future based on those assumptions. Projections are usually made by age and sex, and give the age-sex distribution of a presumed future population. The U.S. Bureau of the Census periodically publishes population projections for the total United States and for the individual states.

Accurate projections of total population are difficult to make. Birth rates can fluctuate widely and are often hard to anticipate. Also, in recent years death rates have fallen faster than anticipated. For states and local areas the problem is further compounded by the enormous difficulty of measuring migration. For births and deaths we at least have current vital statistics; but we have very little information from which to estimate current migration, much less to make predictions about the future.

Population projections are useful and are available for most parts of the United States, but keep in mind when using them that they are essentially educated guesses about the future. In particular, pay attention to the assumptions underlying the projections. Do they seem sensible? If not, the projections will be of little value.

Growth of the Older Population

When the first United States Census was taken in 1790, about 50,000, or 2 percent, of the 2.5 million Americans were 65 or older. A hundred years later, the older population had grown to 2.4 million and comprised just under 4 percent of the population. As Figure 2-4 shows, from 1890 to 1920 the older population grew relatively slowly, but from 1920 the rate of increase accelerated, so that by 1980 there were 25.5 million older Americans—11.3 percent of the population.

Figure 2-4 also includes projections of the older population to the year 2030, projections made under the conservative assumptions that birth rates would remain low and death rates would not decline much. Since mortality declines have consistently been greater than anticipated, these projections probably underestimate

the number of older people in the future. Of course, assumptions about the birth rate do not affect projections of the older population in 2030 because everyone who will be part of that older population has already been born. The 51.6 million older people projected for 2030 represents 20.9 percent of the total population projected for that year.

Composition of the Older Population

The older population is often thought of in the public mind as a relatively homogeneous category, but nothing could be further from the truth. As we shall see in this section, there are wide variations in age, racial and ethnic differences, differences in education and income, wide variations in living arrangements, and other differences. What we have is an older population that is very diverse and becoming more so.

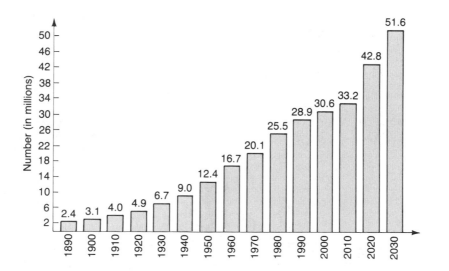

FIGURE 2-4   Older population (in millions): United States, 1890–2030 (actual and projected). *Source:* U.S. Bureau of the Census, 1975b; 1977c.

Age and Sex

The older population is itself growing older. And as it does so, older women increasingly outnumber older men. If we divide the older population into the *young-old* (age 65–74), the *middle-old* (age 75–84), and the *old-old* (age 85 and over), the effects of aging within the older population can be seen more clearly. As Table 2-5 shows, in 1960 nearly two-thirds of the older population was under age 75, but by the year 2000 the young-old will have dropped to 55.7 percent of the older population. At the same time, the old-old will have increased from 6 percent of the older population in 1960 to 10.4 percent in 2000. In absolute numbers, the entire older population will nearly double over the 40-year period, while the number of old-old will triple!

The **sex ratio** is the number of males per 100 females. Aging of the older population will cause the overall sex ratio in the older population to drop from 82 men per 100 women in 1960 to only 65 men per 100 women in 2000 (see Table 2-6). In the old-old population the

TABLE 2-5 Changing age composition of the older population: United States, 1960–2000

Age Category	1960	1970	1980	1990[c]	2000[c]
Young-Old					
(65–74)N[a]	11.0	12.4	15.6	17.5	17.1
Percent[b]	66.2	62.3	60.7	60.6	55.7
Middle-Old					
(75–84)N	4.6	6.1	7.8	8.9	10.3
Percent	27.7	30.7	30.4	30.9	33.2
Old-Old					
(85+)N	1.0	1.4	2.3	2.5	3.2
Percent	6.0	7.0	8.9	8.6	10.4

[a]Number (in millions)
[b]Percent of the older population
[c]Projected

Source: Compiled from U.S. Bureau of the Census, 1982a, 1977c.

TABLE 2-6 Changing sex ratios in the older population: United States, 1960–2000

Age Category	Sex Ratio				
	1960	1970	1980	1990	2000
Young-Old					
(65–74)	86	77	77	75	76
Middle-Old					
(75–84)	76	65	59	59	58
Old-Old					
(85+)	67	56	43	39	39

Source: Compiled from U.S. Bureau of the Census, 1982a; 1977c.

drop in sex ratio is even more dramatic, from 67 men per 100 women at age 85 and over in 1960 to only 39 men per 100 women at that age in the year 2000. The reason behind this shift in the sex ratio is the well-known difference in mortality rates for men and women. As Table 2-7 indicates, women have a substantially lower probability of dying at every age. The underlying reason for this difference is unknown, but our best guess is that about half is due to sex differences in environment and social roles and about half to genetic differences (Palmore, 1980).

Race

Race is difficult to define precisely. Theoretically it refers to a scientific classification of major biologically different subdivisions of humanity. But in practice race is difficult to define biologically because there has been so much intermingling of various groups throughout history. In the U.S. Census, race is self-rated.

The major racial groups in the U.S. are Caucasian (white), black, Asian, and American Indian. In 1980, 90.3 percent of the older population was white, 8.7 percent was black, 0.5 percent was Asian, and 0.3 percent was American Indian. The remaining 0.2 percent was undefined.

TABLE 2-7 Probability of dying during selected age intervals: United States, 1977

Age	Males	Females
55–59	.07	.04
60–64	.12	.06
65–69	.16	.08
70–74	.24	.13
75–79	.34	.21
80–84	.44	.31

Source: Vital statistics of the U.S., 1977: 5–11.

The proportion of blacks in the older population is growing, the proportion of whites is declining, and the proportion of other races is remaining about the same. However, in the future there will be large numbers of Asian refugees who will enter the older population, and when they do, the proportion of Asians will increase. While these people will still represent a very small minority of the elderly, they will present unique problems in service delivery as a result of differences in cultural background and language.

Racial differences in the older population are considered again, in detail, in Chapter 14, "Social Inequality."

Ethnicity

Ethnic groups share a common language and culture. In the United States, although blacks, Asians, and American Indians all have characteristics of ethnic groups, in the demographic literature, it is their racial character that is given priority. The major purely ethnic subdivision in America is that of "Spanish origin"; for many in this category, Spanish is their first language. People of Spanish origin may be of any race, but a majority classify themselves as white. In 1980, nearly 3 percent of the older population was of Spanish origin, an increase of nearly one

percent over 1970. Although we tend to think of the category of Hispanic Americans as relatively homogeneous, in fact it is comprised of a number of economically and culturally distinct subgroups: Mexican Americans in the southwest, Puerto Ricans in the northeast, and Cuban Americans in the southeast. (More details on the Hispanic older population are included in Chapter 14.)

Marital Status

Three-fourths of older men are married, while more than half of older women are widowed. Even among those age 75 and over, nearly 70 percent of men have spouses living with them. On the other hand, at age 75 and over, two-thirds of women are widows (see Table 2-8). Being a widower is more common among blacks and Hispanic elderly than among whites, and a smaller proportion of minority older men are married. These data have far-reaching implications for social support—advice, approval, and care-giving. Most older men have spouses to rely on, while most older women must find other sources of social support.

Education

The number of years of formal education varies considerably within the older population. In 1979, the median education of the United States population age 14 and over was 12.4 years. But within the older population, nearly 600,000 (2.6 percent) had no formal education whatever and another 1.5 million (6.6 percent) had less than a fifth-grade education. By contrast, nearly 2 million older people (8.5 percent) were college graduates. There are substantial age differences in education within the older population, as well as differences by sex, race, and ethnicity (See Tables 2-9 and 2-10). Compared to the total older population; the young-old and women are better educated, and blacks and Hispanic older people tend to have less education.

TABLE 2-8   Percent marital status, by age and sex, for total, white, black, and Hispanic populations: United States, 1981

	Age					
	55–64		65–74		75+	
Marital Status	Male	Female	Male	Female	Male	Female
Total						
Never married	5.1	4.2	4.9	5.4	3.5	6.2
Married, spouse present	81.2	67.1	80.6	48.3	69.7	21.8
Married, spouse absent	3.1	3.2	2.4	1.7	2.2	1.4
Widowed	4.0	18.4	8.2	40.1	22.1	68.2
Divorced	6.1	7.1	3.9	4.4	2.4	2.3
White						
Never married	5.0	4.1	4.4	5.5	3.5	6.3
Married, spouse present	83.4	69.6	82.7	49.8	70.9	22.5
Married, spouse absent	2.4	2.4	1.8	1.3	1.6	1.2
Widowed	3.6	17.0	7.5	39.2	21.6	67.8
Divorced	5.7	6.8	3.6	4.2	2.3	2.2
Black						
Never married	7.2	5.3	6.5	4.9	2.6	5.4
Married, spouse present	62.6	43.9	62.7	33.5	58.0	14.4
Married, spouse absent	10.9	11.1	7.7	6.2	6.8	4.5
Widowed	8.9	29.5	16.3	48.6	28.7	72.2
Divorced	10.4	10.2	6.8	6.8	3.8	3.5
Hispanic						
Never married	6.9	5.8	5.4	7.5	4.1	8.3
Married, spouse present	78.6	55.6	74.2	43.0	58.8	27.3
Married, spouse absent	6.8	10.3	5.8	5.5	2.8	0.2
Widowed	2.4	17.9	8.5	36.9	29.5	62.7
Divorced	5.3	10.5	6.1	7.0	4.8	1.4

Source: Compiled from U.S. Bureau of the Census, 1982c.

Projecting educational attainment into the future reveals that the older population will become more like the general population, that the gap between older blacks and whites will be reduced substantially, and that older women will lose their educational advantage over older men. Older Hispanics will still be at a decided educational disadvantage compared to the total older population, but the gap will be smaller. Figure 2-9 shows that by the year 2009, nearly a fifth of the older population will be college graduates, compared to only about 10 percent now. However, a much smaller proportion of older blacks will have college degrees.

These trends in educational attainment have implications for the employment potential of the older population and for the politics of aging. In the future, the older population is much less likely to be hampered in the job market by lack of education than it is today. In addition,

TABLE 2-9 Median number of years of school completed, by age and sex, for total, black, and Hispanic older populations: United States, 1979–2009

| | 1979 | | 1989 | | 1999 | | 2009 | |
Age	Male	Female	Male	Female	Male	Female	Male	Female
Total								
65–69	10.7	11.5	12.4	12.3	12.5	12.4	12.8	12.6
70–74	9.8	10.7	12.1	12.2	12.4	12.4	12.7	12.5
75 +	8.7	8.9	9.8	10.7	12.1	12.2	12.4	12.4
Black								
65–69	7.6	8.5	8.9	9.7	11.8	11.7	12.5	12.5
70–74	6.3	7.6	8.2	8.8	9.7	10.9	12.0	12.3
75 +	5.1	7.3	6.3	7.6	8.2	8.8	9.9	11.0
Hispanic								
65–69	6.7	6.6	8.6	8.1	9.7	9.6	10.5	11.0
70–74	5.4	5.3	8.5	8.2	9.9	8.8	10.3	11.9
75 +	4.2	5.1	5.4	5.3	8.5	8.2	9.9	8.8

Overall median, 1979 = 12.4

Source: 1979 base-line data from the U.S. Bureau of the Census, 1980; projections by the author.

as the older population becomes more like the general population in its educational background, older people may well become more vocal in the political arena.

These data on education are revealing, but they are also deceptive. What we tend to forget is that many older people are self-educated and that their desire to learn on their own can offset their lack of formal education. Another factor to consider is that when most people went to school for only eight years, more basic education was crammed into those years. As the amount of time young people were expected to stay in school increased, more subjects were included and the pace for basic subjects such as language and mathematics was stretched out. Thus, many people who went only as far as eighth grade in 1920 learned more math and English than many people receiving high school diplomas today. In short, it would be a mistake to assume that an older person's level of education tells you much about what he or she has learned or is capable of as compared with today's youth.

Income

Although most older people have an adequate income, a substantial minority does not. Income is one of the most variable characteristics within the older population. The incomes of older men, even those who work full time, are lower than incomes of men age 45 to 64 (see Table 2-11). Older women in general also have lower incomes than younger women, but older women who work full time have incomes on a par with those of full-time women workers age 45 to 64.

Some of the age difference in income stems from real reductions in income related to retirement and to job dislocations. For example, Parnes and King (1977), who studied a large number of middle-aged men who became unemployed during the period 1966 to 1976, found that most were successful in getting an-

TABLE 2-10 Percent college graduates, by age and sex, for total and black older populations: United States, 1979–2009

Age	1979		1989		1999		2009	
	Male	Female	Male	Female	Male	Female	Male	Female
Total								
65–69	10.1	8.8	16.0	8.0	21.5	11.3	26.2	16.2
70–74	9.1	8.1	12.1	8.3	18.1	9.9	22.3	13.5
75+	9.2	6.5	9.1	8.1	12.1	8.3	18.1	10.0
Black								
65–69	2.5	3.9	4.0	4.7	8.2	9.7	11.5	7.1
70–74	1.0*	3.6	4.7	4.6	5.7	5.0	6.6	6.9
75+	2.4	0.8	2.0*	3.6	4.7	4.6	5.7	5.0

Total population age 14 and over = 13.3% in 1979

*estimated

Source: 1979 base-line data from the U.S. Bureau of the Census, 1980; projections by the author.

other job, but usually at a much lower wage. In addition, retirement reduces income by 40 percent on average. But even for those employed full time, the incomes of older workers do not increase as fast as those of the middle-aged. In making its income projections, the U.S. Bureau

of the Census (1980b) assumes that income growth for older people will be 10 percent lower than for people 45 to 64.

Only a very small proportion of the older population has income from employment and property only and no retirement income (see Table 2-12). Nearly half of families with an older head have earnings from employment in addition to retirement income, while just over half have retirement income only. We will look at sources of retirement income shortly. For individuals who do not live in families, nearly 85 percent have retirement income only, and only 14.2 percent have earnings from employment as well as retirement income. The median incomes for these various categories differ substantially.

When we look at the sources of retirement income for those who have retirement income only, two points stand out (see Table 2-13). First, most retired people have income in addition to Social Security. This is a marked change from the situation just 20 years ago, when 60 percent of older Americans lived solely on Social Security or Old Age Assistance (Atchley,

TABLE 2-11 Median money income of individuals, by age and sex, for total population and full-time workers: United States, 1980

Age	Total Population		Working Full time	
	Male	Female	Male	Female
45–49	20,424	6,755	22,413	11,973
50–54	19,269	5,974	22,221	12,250
55–59	18,348	5,320	21,825	11,851
60–64	13,532	4,627	19,714	12,070
65–69	8,952	4,378	17,531	12,683
70+	6,544	4,167	16,711	11,868

Source: U.S. Bureau of the Census, 1981b: 22.

TABLE 2-12   Income sources for the older population: United States, 1979

	Persons in Families			Persons Not in Families		
	Number (in millions)	Percent	Median Income	Number (in millions)	Percent	Median Income
Total Number	8.773			7.609		
Earnings from employment and assets	0.060	0.7	$27,926	0.066	0.9	$4,652
Retirement income plus earnings	3.914	44.6	$15,820	1.080	14.2	$7,640
Retirement income only	4.799	54.7	$8,957	6.463	84.9	$4,399

Source: Compiled from U.S. Bureau of the Census, 1981c.

1972: 140). Second, retired couples are substantially better off financially than the unmarried retired. The reason for this is twofold: Social Security benefits rise considerably because of the 50 percent spouse-benefit that is available to couples. And most single retired people are women, whose earnings tended to be low, which in turn translates into lower benefits, both Social Security and private pensions. In addition, most retired women were never covered by private pensions on the job.

The poverty level in 1979 was defined by the Census Bureau as $3,585 for a single older person and $4,480 for an older couple. The median income of the minority who lived on Social Security alone was just above poverty for couples and well below the poverty level for single people. The benefit cuts imposed by Congress in 1983 will mean even further hardship for these people.

The incidence of poverty is much greater among older people than it is among other age categories, especially in minority groups (see Table 2-14). In 1980, there were 3.9 million older Americans with incomes below the poverty level—15.7 percent of the older population. We can take some consolation from the fact that this figure is down considerably from the 35.2 percent of older people below the poverty level in 1959. However, there are categories within the older population with very high rates of poverty: 38.1 percent of older blacks; 42.6 percent of older black women; 34.4 percent of Hispanic older women. These people were no doubt somewhat skeptical when the Secretary of the Department of Health and Human Services told the North American Technical Conference on Aging in June of 1981 that poverty was not a problem among older Americans. It is a fact that most older Americans are not poor, but that is little consolation to the millions who are.

We will return to income, particularly its personal implications, in Chapter 8, "Needs and Resources."

TABLE 2-13   Sources of retirement income: United States, 1979

Source	Older Families			Older Single Individuals		
	Number (in thousands)	Percent	Median Income	Number (in thousands)	Percent	Median Income
Social Security only	429	8.9	$4,775	969	15.0	$3,136
Pension only	8	0.2	—*	19	0.3	—
Pension + assets	58	1.2	—	130	2.0	7,949
Social Security + Supplemental Security Income	34	0.7	—	17	0.3	—
Social Security + assets	1,347	28.1	8,133	2,285	35.4	4,604
Social Security + pension	248	5.2	8,276	219	3.4	4,554
Social Security + Pension + assets	1,709	35.7	11,936	1,212	18.8	7,606
Other combinations	466	20.0	7,058	1,612	24.8	3,546
Total	4,799	100.0	8,957	6,463	100.0	4,399

*Number too small to report median income.

Source: Compiled from U.S. Bureau of the Census, 1981c.

Implications

The older population forms a very heterogeneous category. It varies widely on all of the demographic characteristics we have examined so far: age, sex ratio, race, ethnicity, marital status, education, and income. This variability means that planning to meet the needs of this heterogeneous population is a difficult task. Heterogeneity stands in the way of legislators, administrators, and the public when they try to get a picture of "older Americans." On the other hand, this diversity of the older population has its advantages. Since many older people have adequate educational and financial resources, their need for benefits and services is minimal. This eases the financial and administrative job involved in assisting those in need.

We will return to this theme in Chapter 17, "Politics and Government."

Geographic Distribution of the Older Population

The geographic distribution of the older population in America is similar to that of the general population. The most populous states—California, New York, Texas, Pennsylvania, Illinois, Ohio, Florida, Michigan, and New Jersey—are also the states with the largest populations of older people (see Figure 2-5 and Table 2-15).

The concentration of older people in the population is another matter, because it depends on the size of the older population com-

TABLE 2-14 Poverty rate,* by age, sex, race, and Spanish origin: United States, 1980

| | Total | | | |
Age	Total	White	Black	Spanish
22–44	10.2%	8.2%	24.5%	19.5%
45–54	7.8	6.1	21.4	18.9
55–59	8.6	6.6	27.6	16.3
60–64	10.4	8.4	30.9	19.4
65 +	15.7	13.6	38.1	30.8
	Males			
22–44	7.9%	6.6%	17.7%	15.5%
45–54	6.5	5.4	15.2	15.2
55–59	6.4	4.8	22.3	12.7
60–64	7.8	6.2	24.6	19.1
65 +	10.9	9.0	31.5	26.8
	Females			
22–44	12.4%	9.8%	30.2%	23.1%
45–54	8.9	6.7	26.3	22.4
55–59	10.6	8.2	31.8	19.5
60–64	12.6	10.3	35.8	19.6
65 +	19.0	16.8	42.6	34.4

Poverty rate is the percentage with income below the poverty level.

Source: Compiled from U.S. Bureau of the Census, 1981b.

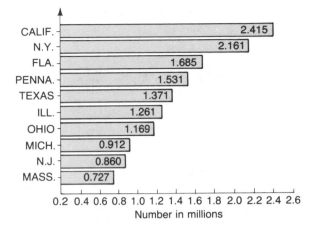

FIGURE 2-5 Population aged 65 and older, top ten states: 1980. *Source:* U.S. Senate Special Committee on Aging, 1981: 32.

in metropolitan areas are more likely to live in the inner city. In rural areas, older people are more likely to live in small towns. More than a quarter of the elderly live in counties with no town with a population of over 25,000 and no city with a population of 50,000 or more in any adjacent county. What this means is that a large minority of older Americans live in areas that are likely to lack extensive facilities and services. Another quarter of the elderly live in inner-city neighborhoods where fear of crime and urban decay present major problems (see Table 2-16).

Living Arrangements

At age 55 to 64, over 80 percent of men and over 65 percent of women live with their spouses (see Figure 2-7). At age 65 to 74, those living with spouse still comprise around 80 percent for men, but less than 50 percent for women. Even at age 75 and over, nearly 70 percent of men are still living with a spouse, while only 20 percent of women are. This is an effect of the sex difference in the death rate referred to earlier as well as the fact that men on the aver-

pared to that of other age categories. Figure 2-6 shows the top ten states in proportion of older people. Figure 2-3 also shows the concentration of older people by state. As we saw earlier, high concentrations of older people occur primarily in Florida, the Northeast, and in the Midwest. Low concentrations occur primarily in the western mountain states.

Locally, older people are less likely than the general population to live in metropolitan areas, particularly the suburbs, and those who do live

TABLE 2-15   Number and percent of each state's total population age 65 and over, 1980 census count (Apr. 1)

[Numbers in thousands]

| State | All Ages | | 65 + | | | | Percent Increase 1970–1980 |
	Number	Rank	Number	Rank	Percent	Rank	
Alabama	3,890	22	440	19	11.3	24	35.8
Alaska	400	51	12	51	2.9	51	71.4
Arizona	2,718	29	307	28	11.3	25	90.7
Arkansas	2,286	33	312	27	13.7	2	31.6
California	23,669	1	2,415	1	10.2	34	34.8
Colorado	2,889	28	247	33	8.6	46	32.1
Connecticut	3,108	25	365	26	11.7	18	26.7
Delaware	595	48	59	48	10.0	36	34.1
District of Columbia	638	47	74	46	11.6	20	5.7
Florida	9,740	7	1,685	3	17.3	1	71.1
Georgia	5,464	13	517	16	9.5	41	41.6
Hawaii	965	39	76	45	7.9	49	72.7
Idaho	944	41	94	41	9.9	37	40.3
Illinois	11,418	5	1,261	6	11.0	29	15.8
Indiana	5,490	12	585	13	10.7	31	18.9
Iowa	2,913	27	387	24	13.3	4	10.9
Kansas	2,363	32	306	29	13.0	8	15.5
Kentucky	3,661	23	410	21	11.2	27	22.0
Louisiana	4,204	19	404	22	9.6	39	32.5
Maine	1,125	38	141	36	12.5	11	23.7
Maryland	4,216	18	396	23	9.4	42	32.9
Massachusetts	5,737	11	727	10	12.7	10	14.8
Michigan	9,258	8	912	8	9.8	38	21.8
Minnesota	4,077	21	480	18	11.8	17	17.9
Mississippi	2,521	31	289	31	11.5	21	30.8
Missouri	4,917	15	648	11	13.2	5	16.1
Montana	787	44	85	43	10.7	32	25.0
Nebraska	1,570	35	206	35	13.1	7	12.6
Nevada	799	43	66	47	8.2	47	113.0
New Hampshire	921	42	103	40	11.2	28	32.1
New Jersey	7,364	9	860	9	11.7	19	23.9
New Mexico	1,300	37	116	38	8.9	45	65.7
New York	17,557	2	2,161	2	12.3	13	10.8
North Carolina	5,874	10	602	12	10.2	35	46.1
North Dakota	653	46	80	44	12.3	14	21.2
Ohio	10,797	6	1,169	7	10.8	30	17.7
Oklahoma	3,025	26	376	25	12.4	12	25.8
Oregon	2,633	30	303	30	11.5	22	34.1
Pennsylvania	11,867	4	1,531	4	12.9	9	20.8
Rhode Island	947	40	127	37	13.4	3	22.1
South Carolina	3,119	24	287	32	9.2	44	51.1
South Dakota	690	45	91	42	13.2	6	13.8
Tennessee	4,591	17	518	15	11.3	26	35.6
Texas	14,228	3	1,371	5	9.6	40	38.8
Utah	1,461	36	109	39	7.5	50	41.4
Vermont	511	49	58	49	11.4	23	23.4
Virginia	5,346	14	505	17	9.4	43	38.7
Washington	4,130	20	431	20	10.4	33	31.7
West Virginia	1,950	34	233	34	12.2	15	22.7
Wisconsin	4,705	16	564	14	12.0	16	19.7
Wyoming	471	50	38	50	8.0	48	66.7

Source: U.S. Senate Special Committee on Aging, 1981:30.

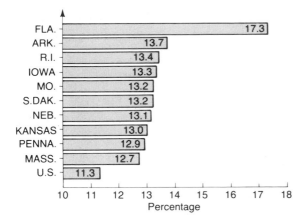

FIGURE 2-6   Percentage of total population age 65 and older: top ten states, 1980. *Source:* U.S. Senate Special Committee on Aging, 1981: 33.

TABLE 2-16   Distribution of population, by residence location and age: United States, 1979

Residential Category	Age Under 65 (percent)	Age 65+ (percent)
Total	100.0	100.0
Metropolitan Areas	68.1	63.4
Central cities	27.8	30.5
Suburbs	40.3	33.0
Nonmetropolitan Areas	31.9	36.6
Counties with no city of 25,000 or more	24.0	28.3
Counties with a city of 25,000 or more	12.4	13.4

Source: U.S. Bureau of the Census, 1982a.

age are about two years older than their wives. Older women are more likely than men to live with relatives other than their spouse (usually an unmarried adult son or daughter), especially after age 75. And for obvious reasons, women are more likely to live alone.

Some assume that older people are forced to live alone because their families do not want them, but research on this issue has shown that older people prefer the independence of living alone as long as they are financially and physically able to do so. In addition, when older people need assistance, family members are by far the most likely to provide it. Only a small percentage of in-home care for the elderly is provided by social agencies (Shanas, 1979).

About 4 percent of the older population lives in some sort of group housing—2 percent in boarding homes, rest homes, or homes for the aged, and 2 percent in nursing homes. However, as might be expected, the proportion living in such situations increases with age. Among people age 85 and over, most of whom are women, 50 percent live independently, 25 percent live with family members, and 25 percent live in institutions.

Population Processes and the Older Population

The processes that change any population include fertility, mortality, migration, and social mobility. All of these affect the older population, too, but the effects are often different from the effects on the general population. Discussing all of the possible interrelationships among these forces and population size, composition, and distribution is well beyond the scope of this book. Instead, we will look only at some of the more obvious and significant relationships. We will first consider the influence of past fluctuations in birth rates on the age and sex composition of the older population. We will then look at changes that are occurring in death rates at the older ages and the implications of these changes. We will next consider migration and its influence on the geographic distribution and concentration of the older population. Finally, we will conclude the chapter with a look at social mobility and how it affects the older population.

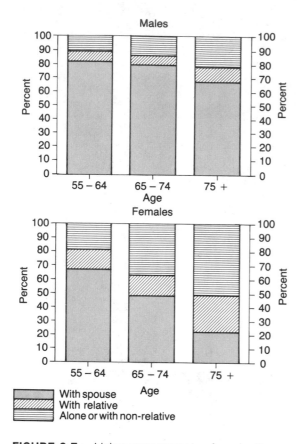

FIGURE 2-7 Living arrangements of noninstitutionalized persons, by age and sex: United States, 1980. *Source:* U.S. Senate Special Committee on Aging, 1981: 15–16.

Fluctuating Birth Rates

Most Americans are familiar with the "baby boom"—the period of very high birth rates that occurred in the United States between 1947 and 1967. What most people do not realize is that birth rates have fluctuated periodically over the nation's entire history. Let's look at the relative size of several birth cohorts: the relatively small cohort born in the Depression years of 1931 to 1940, the large baby-boom cohort born between 1956 and 1965, and the relatively small "baby-bust" cohort born between 1971 and 1980. Figure 2-8 shows six population pyramids that fol-

low these cohorts from 1985 to the year 2050.*

The first thing worth noting about Figure 2-8 is that the Depression cohort (age 45–54 in 1985) is smaller than the cohorts either before or after it. This was probably advantageous to the members of the cohort as they grew up because they had fewer age peers to compete with for opportunities in education and employment. And when this cohort retires, probably between 1990 and 2005, the baby-boom cohort will be there to help provide retirement income. The Depression cohort will also have less competition for scarce services to the elderly than the cohorts just ahead of it. As was pointed out earlier, when the Depression cohort enters the older population, the average age of the older population will increase because of the relative smallness of the Depression cohort.

In contrast, the baby-boom cohort (age 20–29 in 1985) will have experienced more competition for opportunities in education and employment than the cohorts either before or after it. However, because it is a large cohort and because the Depression cohort is small, the pressure on the baby-boom cohort to provide retirement income will be lower than for most cohorts, other things being equal. Yet when the baby-boom cohort retires, probably between 2015 and 2030, it will have to rely on the relatively small baby-bust cohort to help provide retirement income. The result may well be pressures to raise the retirement age. In fact this is exactly the reasoning used by the President's Commission on Pension Policy in recommending that retirement age under Social Security be gradually raised to 68 by the year 2002 (The Commission, 1981). Also, when the baby-boom cohort enters its later years, the average age of the older population will drop.

The baby-bust cohort (age 5–14 in 1985) will also have less competition among age peers for

---

*These population pyramids show actual population numbers instead of percentages. Although percentages are generally more useful, actual numbers are better for the kind of comparisons we want to make here.

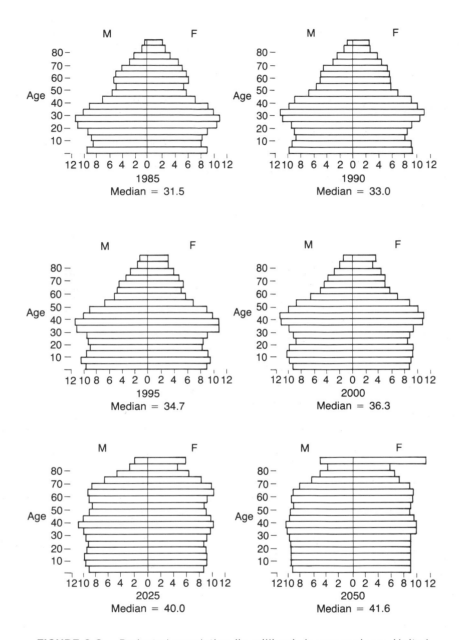

FIGURE 2-8 Projected population (in millions), by age and sex: United States, 1985–2050. *Source:* U.S. Bureau of the Census (1982d).

opportunities, especially in comparison with the baby-boom cohort. However, it may be taxed more in order to provide for the baby-boom cohort when it reaches old age. And when the baby-bust cohort itself reaches age 65, the large baby-boom cohort will be competing with them for facilities and services for the elderly. Obviously, both the size and age structure of the older population will be affected by both the Depression cohort and the baby-boom cohort.

TABLE 2-17   Death rates, life expectancy, and projections, by sex and age: United States, 1976 and 2000

	Sex					
	Male			Female		
Age	1976[b]	2000	Percent Change	1976[b]	2000	Percent Change
	Number of Deaths per 1,000 Resident Population			Number of Deaths per 1,000 Resident Population		
All ages[c]	9.99	9.42	−5.7	7.44	6.75	−9.3
Under 1 year	18.96	15.04	−20.7	14.92	11.74	−21.3
1–4 years	0.79	0.71	−10.1	0.64	0.55	−14.1
5–9 years	0.43	0.40	−7.0	0.30	0.27	−10.0
10–14 years	0.47	0.45	−4.3	0.28	0.25	−10.7
15–19 years	1.49	1.55	4.0	0.55	0.53	−3.6
20–24 years	2.04	2.13	4.4	0.66	0.63	−4.5
25–29 years	1.90	1.95	2.6	0.77	0.72	−6.5
30–34 years	2.06	2.08	1.0	1.01	0.94	−6.9
35–39 years	2.74	2.68	−2.2	1.64	1.52	−7.3
40–44 years	4.16	3.94	−5.3	2.44	2.26	−7.4
45–49 years	6.82	6.41	−6.0	3.74	3.44	−8.0
50–54 years	10.31	9.64	−6.5	5.49	5.03	−8.4
55–59 years	16.27	15.17	−6.8	8.24	7.57	−8.1
60–64 years	24.94	23.14	−7.2	12.35	11.18	−9.5
65–69 years	36.52	34.18	−6.4	17.78	16.05	−9.7
70–74 years	55.04	51.78	−5.9	29.97	27.14	−9.4
75–79 years	81.86	77.37	−5.5	49.82	44.80	−10.1
80–84 years	114.14	109.11	−4.4	78.83	70.45	−10.6
85 years and over	183.61	183.20	−0.2	151.71	149.52	−1.4
	Remaining Life Expectancy (in years)			Remaining Life Expectancy (in years)		
At birth	68.7	69.6	1.3	76.1	77.4	1.7
1 year	69.0	69.6	0.9	76.2	77.3	1.4
5 years	65.2	65.8	0.9	72.4	73.5	1.5
10 years	60.3	60.9	1.0	67.5	68.6	1.6
20 years	50.9	51.5	1.2	57.8	58.8	1.7
30 years	41.8	42.4	1.4	48.2	49.2	2.1
40 years	32.7	33.3	1.8	38.7	39.7	2.6
50 years	24.2	24.8	2.5	29.8	30.7	3.0
60 years	16.8	17.3	3.0	21.5	22.3	3.7
65 years	13.7	14.2	3.6	17.7	18.5	4.5
70 years	11.0	11.3	2.7	14.1	14.8	5.0

[a]Data are based on intercensal estimates and national vital registration system

[b]The 1976 death rates and expectation of life were estimated by the Social Security Administration; when the Social Security Administration study was underway, the 1976 figures were not final and were estimated by adjusting the 1974 rates.

[c]Age-adjusted rate computed by the direct method and standardized to the United States population in 1970 using 19 age groups.

Source: Compiled from Bayo, Shiman, and Sobus, 1977 and National Center for Health Statistics, 1980.

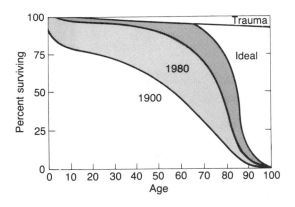

FIGURE 2-9 The increasingly rectangular survival curve. *Source:* Adapted from Fries, 1980: 131.

Thus, fluctuations in past fertility can be an important force in the composition of the older population.

Changes in Mortality

Mortality rates in the United States are already quite low. In 1976, the age-adjusted death rate was only 6.3 per 1,000 per year. Nevertheless, further declines in mortality are expected by the year 2000 (see Table 2-17). Fries (1980) estimated that by the year 2045 we will have reached the maximum possible survival curve, at which point 95 percent of all deaths will occur between the ages of 77 and 93, with the average age at death (for those who do not die from trauma such as accidents or violence) approaching 85. Figure 2-9 shows the survival curves in 1900 and 1980, along with Fries' definition of the hypothetical ideal. Although Fries' analysis is controversial, particularly his idea that age 85 is a significant limit to the average length of life, further reductions in mortality are quite likely. Further reductions in mortality will increase the proportion of people surviving *to* old age as well as the proportion surviving *in* old age. The result will be a further squaring off of the population pyramid. Who knows, soon we may have to rename such figures population "boxes," at least for the developed countries.

As more progress is made in preventing premature death from heart disease and related disorders of the circulatory system, more of the older population will live out their lives in better health, especially in the later years. On the other hand, we will also have larger numbers of people reaching the point of frailty associated with advanced old age. These old-old people will require more assistance even in their own homes compared to the relatively young older population of today. We will discuss this in more detail in Chapter 4, "Physical Aging."

Migration

By and large, migration is a phenomenon of youth. The highest interstate migration rates occur between the ages of 23 and 32, when about 15 percent moves from one state to another during any given 5-year period. By contrast, at age 65 or older, only about 4 percent makes interstate moves in a 5-year period (see Figure 2-10).

Some older people move in connection with retirement, but the volume of retirement-related migration is so small that it does not show up in age-categorized migration data for the total population. Although only 25 percent of men who make interstate moves between ages 45 and 64 are no longer in the labor force, 88 percent of men who do so at 65 or older are out of the labor force. But this is more because people who move at age 65 or over are retired rather than because those who retire move.

Figure 2-11 shows the major streams of interstate migration of the elderly for the period 1975 to 1980. Most people were moving away from the Northeast and into Florida and California. However, most residential moves by the elderly are between communities within the same geographic area. While 20 percent of the elderly changed residence between 1975 and 1980, 15 percent of them did so within the same community. In contrast, while 76 percent of

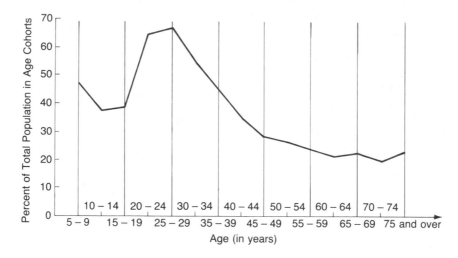

FIGURE 2-10   Residential mobility rates by age: United States, 1965–1970.
Source: Adapted from Wiseman, 1978: 19.

those age 25 to 29 moved, 49 percent of that age group did so within the same community. At the same time, there were much smaller streams of return migration from Florida and California (see Figure 2-12). Longino (1980) found that, in contrast to migrants to full-service retirement communities or public housing projects for the elderly, migrants to the sun belt tended to resemble people on extended vacations. Most were married and in excellent health. Longino predicted that when this population grows older and more in need of assistance, many individuals would return to their communities of origin, where their potential informal support networks are more likely to be. Figure 2-12 documents this trend.

Residential mobility *redistributes* the older population less than it does the young. Migration streams are smaller and less numerous, even as a proportion of the elderly population. The major exception to this is Florida, whose older population has very definitely been swelled by in-migration of the elderly from many other states. This is because older people are more likely than other age groups to move to Florida. On the other hand, although many elderly migrate to California, this migration has not increased the concentration of elderly because California is a popular migration destination among all age groups.

Migration of the young also affects the *concentration* of older people. Such states as Iowa, Missouri, Nebraska, and South Dakota have large proportions of older people because of out-migration of the young rather than in-migration of the old. In states such as Montana the proportion of older persons increased very little from 1970 to 1980 because of large in-migrations of young workers. Out-migrations of the young have likewise increased the concentration of the elderly in inner cities.

Thus, while migration is a major factor in both the distribution and the concentration of the elderly, it is mainly the migration of the young rather than of the elderly that exerts the influence. What course will migration take in the future? Over the next two decades we will probably see a continuation of migration out of the Northeast. This should decrease the concentration of elderly there. But exactly where these migrants will go is unclear. In addition, return migration streams can be expected to increase.

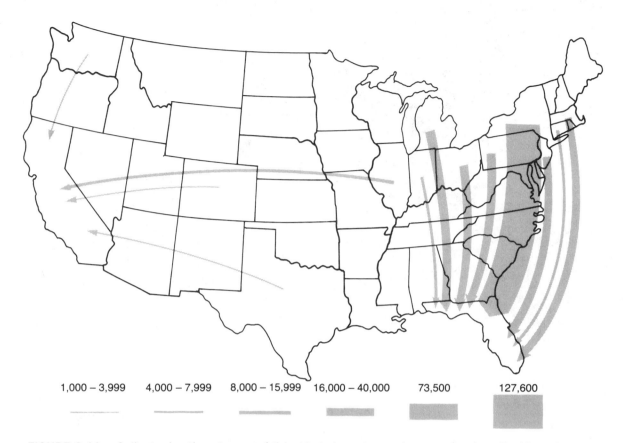

FIGURE 2-11   Salient migration streams of the elderly from noncontiguous states into Florida and California, 1975–1980. *Source:* Adapted from an unpublished figure prepared by Charles F. Longino, Jr., Robert F. Wiseman, Cynthia Flynn, and Jeanne C. Biggar.

Social Mobility

Social mobility refers to a change in social status, usually measured by characteristics such as occupation, income, and education. Aging can change status charcteristics, and thereby alter the characteristics of a cohort moving into the older population. For example, retirement changes one's occupational status and, usually, income as well.

Studies of the relative status of the elderly compared to other adult age categories have generally shown the elderly to have lower status (Palmore and Whittington, 1971; Palmore and Manton, 1974), mainly due to the effects of retirement on occupation and income. However, it would be a mistake to conclude that these changes also bring lower esteem for the elderly or a compression in the range of social prestige *among* the elderly. Henretta and Campbell (1976) found that the same mechanisms that were operating in the preretirement period also explained differences in income during retirement. The key to understanding this situation is remembering that status characteristics are important only as *indicators* of a person's relative social position. Since aging alters the *appropriateness* of occupation and money income

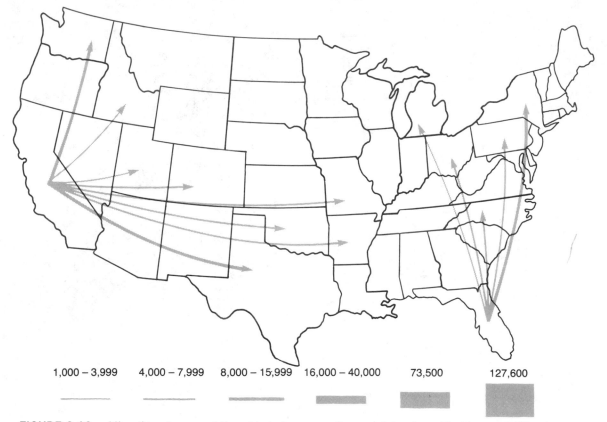

FIGURE 2-12   Migration streams of the elderly to noncontiguous states from Florida and California, 1975–1980. *Source:* Adapted from an unpublished figure prepared by Charles F. Longino, Jr., Robert F. Wiseman, Cynthia Flynn, and Jeanne C. Biggar.

as indicators, it actually seldom changes people's social position relative to their age peers.

Summary

This chapter has covered a lot of ground, including how to measure age structure, how populations age, how population projections are made, and a detailed portrait of the older population in the United States.

Age structure can be measured in a number of ways: by simple percent distributions of the population, classified by sex and age categories; by population pyramids; or by summary indicators such as the proportion of the population that is older. Indicators such as life expectancy at birth and the aged dependency ratio can also be used, but each of these has more liabilities than does the simple proportion of older people in the population.

Populations age as a result of low death rates and low birth rates. Low death rates mean that more people survive to enter the older population and low birth rates mean that the proportion of children born into the population is not very different from the proportion dying.

Population projections begin with a set of assumptions about the future course of fertility, mortality, and migration rates, which are then applied to the existing age-sex structure of the population to derive projections of future population. Projections are available for the entire United States and for most individual states. How useful they are depends on how good the assumptions are that underlie them. Projections generally tend to underestimate the number of older people in the future.

The older population of the United States has grown rapidly in this century and will grow even more rapidly over the next 50 years. By 2030, there will be over 50 million older Americans, representing over 20 percent of the total population.

The older population is quite heterogeneous and includes a great range of ages. The male-to-female sex ratio drops substantially in each successively older age cohort, a result of death rates that are much lower for women than for men. In the future, older women will outnumber older men even more than they do now. The older population is 90 percent white, nearly 9 percent black, and 1 percent other races. About 3 percent of the older population is of Spanish origin. Compared to whites, older blacks and other minorities are more likely to have low income, little education, and to be widowed or divorced.

Three-fourths of older men are married, while more than half of older women are widowed. At age 75 and over, two-thirds of women are widows. Education varies widely in the older population: about 9 percent have very little or no formal education while nearly 9 percent are college graduates. The gap between the education of the elderly and that of the general adult population is closing. In addition, many older people are self-educated. Most older Americans have adequate incomes, yet 15 percent of the total older population is living in poverty and as many as 40 percent of the elderly in some minority categories are in poverty. The key to financial adequacy in retirement is having several sources of income in addition to Social Security. The great variation within the older population on nearly every population characteristic represents a challenge to planners and policy makers.

The older population is evenly distributed throughout the United States, with Florida being the only state to have a very heavy concentration of older people (17.3 percent). Older people are more likely than other age groups to live in small towns and rural areas, and in inner cities as well. They are less likely to live in suburbs.

Only about 4 percent of the elderly live in institutions, half of these in nursing homes. Among those not in institutions, 80 percent of men and just under half of women live with a spouse. Women are much more likely than men to be widowed and living alone. Women above the age of 75 are much more likely than men in the same age group to live with a relative other than a spouse. Older people generally live alone because they prefer to do so. There is little evidence of desertion or abandonment of the elderly by their adult offspring.

Fluctuations in the birth rate in the past have caused ebbs and flows in the age structure of the population and in the relative size of the older population compared to other age categories. Death rates will continue to drop over the next 50 years, resulting in more survivors in old age as well as more survivors to old age. Migration influences the concentration of older people in various parts of the country, primarily through out-migration of the young rather than by in-migration of the old. Migration is not common among older people, and those residential moves they do make tend to be local moves within the same community.

Social mobility refers to a change in social position, either up or down. Social position is usually indicated by occupation, education, and income. Since the level of these indicators often drops at retirement, some people think that the social position of the elderly declines, too. But another explanation is that the appropriateness of the indicators changes with age.

Chapter 3

The History of Aging in America

A common misconception about older people is that they had it better in "the good old days," but it is important to separate the rhetoric and ideology of aging from the realities. Indeed, ideas about aging and the realities of growing older have probably always had both positive and negative elements. Certainly, this has been the case in Western civilization. For example, Aristotle had the following to say about elderly men:

> They have lived many years; they have often been taken in and often made mistakes; and life on the whole is a bad business. The result is that they are sure about nothing and under-do everything. They "think," but they never "know"; and because of their hesitation they always add a "possibly" or a "perhaps," putting everything this way and nothing positively. They are cynical; that is, they put the worse construction on everything. . . . They are small-minded, because they have been humbled by life: their desires are set upon nothing more exalted or unusual than what will help them keep alive (McKee, 1982:11).

In contrast, Cicero said:

> Those, therefore, who allege that old age is devoid of useful activity adduce nothing to the purpose, and are like those who would say that the pilot [navigator] does nothing in the sailing of the ship, because, while others are climbing the masts, or running about the gangways, or working the pumps, he sits quietly in the stern and simply holds the tiller [which steers the ship]. He may not be doing what younger members of the crew are doing, but what he does is better and much more important. It is not by muscle, speed, or physical dexterity that great things are achieved, but by reflection, force of character, and judgement; in these qualities old age is not only not poorer, but is even richer (McKee, 1982:26).

And Plato said:

> [A]t the age of 50 those who have survived the tests and proved themselves altogether the best in every task and form of knowledge must be brought at last to the goal. We shall require them to turn upward the vision of their souls and fix their gaze on that which sheds light on all, and

when they have thus beheld the good itself they shall use it as a pattern for the right ordering of the state and the citizens and themselves throughout the remainder of their lives . . . (McKee, 1982:53).

In truth, aging is not predictable. It is sometimes a positive force and sometimes a negative one, even in the same individual. For thousands of years, writers and orators have sometimes emphasized the positive qualities that aging can bring and sometimes the negative. So it is with culture. For example, Simmons (1945), in his extensive review of aging in 71 cultures, found that in some cultures the aged were revered and in others they were not. As we shall see, Americans have always been ambivalent about aging. And because both positive and negative elements of aging are always present, in any era either could be emphasized. But what factors influenced the weight of emphasis? Was it the realities of aging, or was it our untested beliefs and ideologies, or both? This is the main issue we will address in this chapter.

Fortunately, the volume of historical material about aging in the United States has increased dramatically in recent years. Fischer (1978), Achenbaum (1978, 1983), Haber (1983), and Graebner (1980), in particular, have assembled a great deal of evidence about the history of aging in America, and this chapter is based mainly on these five resources.

Modernization Theory

The interpretation of historical materials must always be guided by theories that provide frameworks around which various fragments of history can be organized. In the case of aging, modernization has been the most frequently used concept for organizing ideas about how aging and treatment of the aged may have changed over the past 200 years. The central thesis of **modernization theory** is that the processes that cause societies to evolve from rural and agrarian social and economic systems to urban and industrial ones also cause change in the positions that older people occupy in the society and the esteem afforded to the aged. And usually the direction of change is assumed to be for the worse.

Simmons (1945) was probably one of the first to address the issue of modernization's effect on the elderly. Based on a cross-cultural study of 71 societies, he concluded that in relatively stable agricultural societies, the aged usually occupy positions of favor and power, owing mainly to the concept of seniority rights. But when the rate of change increases, Simmons said, the aged lose their advantaged status. He did not specify how or why this happened.

Cottrell (1960b) viewed modernization as a result of the growing use of fossil fuels and technology to increase human productivity. To him, the most significant aspect of the historical shift from agrarian to high-energy industrial forms of production was its effect on the organization of society. Agrarian societies revolved around the village, which itself was a collection of families. The power of elderly men, and occasionally elder women, in the agrarian system stemmed from their positions as heads of families, which in turn admitted them to the council of elders that ran the community. In addition, tradition was the main way that people decided issues in agrarian societies, which gave elders value as keepers of knowledge and tradition. Heads of families made decisions in all realms of life: economic, political, religious, and social.

With the growing use of wind, water, steam, and electric power, the relationship between human effort and the volume of goods produced weakened. Because production depended less on land and more on technology, decision-making power shifted from many landowners to relatively fewer factory owners and merchants, which eroded the power of family patriarchs. In addition, as the volume of scientific and technical knowledge grew beyond the capacity of any one human to know it all, the value of the elders as keepers of knowledge diminished (Cottrell, 1960b).

Fischer (1978:108–112) advanced the notion that in order for the new egalitarian type of society to emerge, the traditional hierarchical type had to be undercut. And in the process, because the aged were usually in control of traditional societies, as a category they became the targets for attack by those who wanted to change the system. Thus, it was not their capabilities or lack of them that caused the aged to lose their advantaged positions, but rather the fact that they were symbols of an outdated social order.

All these are plausible explanations of why the aged may have lost their hold on the privileged positions in industrialized society. But they did not merely become equal to everyone else, they became less valued than other age categories. Why? Cowgill (1972, 1974b) developed a theory to explain why the elderly were devalued by the process of modernization (see Figure 3-1). He felt that several factors associated with modernization combined to reduce the desirability of the aged participants in society. First, as we saw in Chapter 2, demographic trends produced a higher proportion of older people in the population of the United States. This, coupled with a lower demand for workers because of the increased use of technology, heightened the competition between the old and

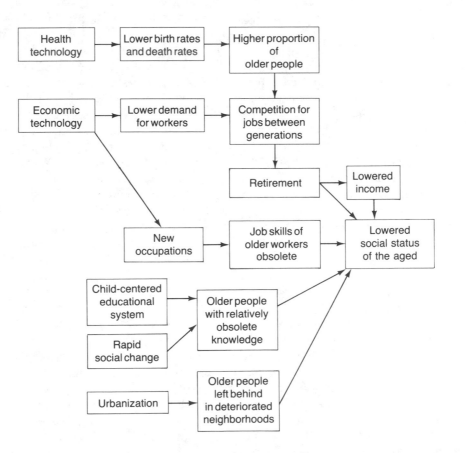

FIGURE 3-1   Pressures toward lowered social status of the aged. *Source:* Adapted and revised from Cowgill, 1974b: 14—1.

the young for jobs. In addition, the growing number of new kinds of jobs reduced the value of experience and practiced skills, which were the elderly's main ways of offsetting their relative lack of physical dexterity. Retirement lowered the value of the aged because it was based on the assumption that they were no longer capable and because it dropped them into a less desirable income category. Rapid social change and child-centered education outside the family made obsolete much of the knowledge that had formerly been a foundation of esteem for the elderly. Finally, urbanization often left the elderly behind, causing them to be viewed as "backward." For these reasons, the elderly presumably lost a great deal of power and prestige in the process of modernization.

Some analysts contend that the decline in the social position of the aged occurred *before* many of the effects cited by Cowgill became obvious (Fischer, 1978; Achenbaum, 1978). If so, then the aspects of modernization cited by Cowgill could not be responsible for lowering the status of the elderly. However, this does not necessarily discredit modernization as the primary cause, simply those aspects suggested by Cowgill. If we consider that modernization might first and foremost be a revolution of *ideas*, then we might see both industrialization and the changing position of the aged as being caused by the same shift in ideas. The central point here is that modernization is not merely the result of more people or greater use of technology or of bureaucratic organization. Efforts to assist today's third world nations to modernize have amply illustrated that new ways of *thinking* must also be present if new forms of economic and social organization are to take root.

Let us examine these ideas about modernization and the elderly in the context of a brief review of the history of aging in America, beginning with the period before the American Revolution and proceeding to the present. We will not consider every period of American history but only significant happenings that influenced aging or the aged.

Aging in Colonial America

Summarizing American life in any time period is risky because we are and always have been a diverse people. The Colonial settlers came from a variety of backgrounds and made their livings in a variety of ways. In the 1600s the dominant economic activity was trade—in furs and skins, salted fish, and wood for England's growing fleets of ships. Settlements were small, and work organizations, though numerous, were also small. Life was organized around the community. By the mid-1700s, farming had eclipsed logging and trapping as a major economic activity in the New World. In 1770, for example, tobacco, wheat and flour, dried fish, and rice were the leading export commodities (U.S. Bureau of the Census, 1975b:1183–1184).

The social heritage of the Colonies was primarily British. In 1790, nearly 80 percent of the population of the new United States claimed one of the countries in the British Isles as their nationality (U.S. Bureau of the Census, 1975b:1168). As mentioned in Chapter 2, older people were relatively rare in the New World, comprising only about two of every hundred people. Yet those who did survive to old age often occupied an advantaged position, partly because position was tied to an age hierarchy.

The cornerstones of life in the New World were religion, politics, family, agriculture, and trade. And in each of these arenas, older people had distinct advantages over their younger counterparts.

The sacred scriptures' many references to respect for elders were translated in the pulpit and in popular literature into an ethic of veneration of the elderly. This ethic was based in the belief in both Puritan and Calvinist Protestantism that God was in control of every detail of life: someone favored with a long life must be morally superior. Thus, in a society dominated by concern with demonstrating one's moral worth, aging elevated people to a revered and exalted position.

However, it would be a mistake to assume

that this veneration was an unmixed blessing for the elderly. The distance that the hierarchical moral order imposed between family generations sometimes stood in the way of friendship and affection between older parents and their offspring. In addition, the demand that the elderly continually set a moral example for the young was seen by many as a hindrance to getting any fun out of life.

In agriculture, power and control then—as now—were based on land ownership. Older men in Colonial America were often in control of if and when management of family lands would pass to the younger generation. In practical terms this meant that adult men could be denied economic independence by their fathers until well into adulthood.

Colonial elders also had an advantage in trade. But in this setting it was based on skill developed through experience in trading. Skillful trading required wide knowledge of the relative worth of the objects being traded, as well as wisdom in dealing with people. Experience was a very distinct advantage in this system. In addition, young people learned how to trade by watching their elders. The lore of the period is filled with stories illustrating the poor performance of youth against the wisdom of age in the marketplace.

Because of the veneration of the elderly, the importance of age in acquiring position, and the importance of experience in the market, it was probably natural that the colonists turned to the elders for leadership in times of crisis. For example, Fischer recounts the story of Deacon Josiah Haynes who on his eightieth birthday

> . . . turned out with the rest of the Minutemen of his town of Sudbury and marched eight miles to Concord bridge with blood in his eye and a long stride that left his younger neighbors puffing and struggling behind him (Fischer, 1978:50).

Haynes took leadership of his company from a young man who was less eager to fight.

> Twenty-one elite companies of British infantry fled down the Boston road with an infuriated eighty-year-old Congregational deacon close at their heels—so close, in fact, that Josiah Haynes was shot and killed while reloading his musket, and another "grey champion" entered New England's folklore (Fischer, 1978:50).

Fischer goes on to say that "the grey champion" was not just a cultural myth. In times of crisis, older men joined the ranks of Selectmen and Revolutionary Committeemen even before younger men left for the army. The grey champion was institutionalized as "Uncle Sam" and had become a popular symbol of the new United States of America by the 1830s (Achenbaum, 1978:25).

Traditional societies also have a unique approach to training their members to make decisions. David Riesman (1950) developed a classification scheme based on how people make decisions: Those who emphasize tradition as a way of deciding he called *tradition-directed*, those who emphasize their own internal principles he said were *inner-directed*, and those who base their decisions on what their contemporaries consider proper he labeled *other-directed*. Riesman contended that different economic and demographic eras require different human qualities and therefore create a differential emphasis among these various ways to come to decisions. He also believed that the predominant mode of decision making in any period has strong effects on how parents rear their children. In Riesman's framework, Colonial America emphasized tradition even in the midst of rapid and sometimes chaotic social change. In the traditional society,

> . . . the parents train the child to succeed *them*, rather than to succeed by rising in the social system. Within any given social class, society is age-ranked, so that a person rises as a cork does in water: it is simply a matter of time, and little *in him* needs change (Riesman, 1950:39; italics in the original).

In such societies, the family is the major force shaping the individual's approach to life, imitation is the major process through which people learn to cope, and older family members tend to run the family.

Obviously, then, aging had certain advantages in Colonial America; but it would be a mistake to assume that these advantages were widely realized or automatic. Indeed, even though many people did live to become old, age was seldom used to suddenly elevate a person's social position. More often, age simply added a bit more prestige to people who already had earned the respect of their families and communities. In addition, the chronological point at which age brought status was not clear-cut, since legislative definitions of old age did not exist and role changes that could be used to define old age were less common (Haber, 1983).

From the Revolution to the Civil War

At the time of the American Revolution, there was underway a great expansion of wealth in the Colonies, due primarily to the growth of markets and systems of exchange (Fischer, 1978:110). And with this increase in wealth came an increase in the range of income inequality: More wealth was concentrated in the hands of a few (who were often older).

During the years following the Revolution, the population of the new country expanded very rapidly, from just under 4 million in 1790 to nearly 13 million in 1830! Such a large increase in population has several effects on a society (Mott, 1965). As the size and density of a population increase, pressures are exerted for more specialization within society, roles tend to become more formalized, and wider variations tend to develop in what is considered proper behavior. Population expansion also tends to increase the number of levels of influence and authority, the number of prestige and influence hierarchies, and the potential for friction and conflict.

Ideologically, the Revolution marked an acceleration of emphasis on individual achievement, religious secularism, equality, and the free market. These ideological shifts, along with economic and demographic forces, were setting the stage for the evolution of a new type of society, an evolution in which hierarchical relations of family and position were slowly replaced by social relationships based on achievement. These new relationships were held together not by loyalty to family or community but by contract. These changes took away the advantages of age, but they did not leave the aged at a disadvantage—yet.

As guiding principles, the ideals of liberty and equality gained ground steadily in the new United States, replacing traditional hierarchical ideas of social position. As Fischer states:

> There was a radical expansion of the idea of equality—not equality of possessions but equality of condition, equality of legal status, equality of social obligation, equality of cultural manners, equality of political rights. . . .

> American society became a world in which "Liberty" (now a singular noun and capitalized) was itself a prior condition for most men (women, slaves, and paupers excepted). The growth of that idea destroyed the authority of age by dissolving its communal base, for the powers of elders in early America had rested upon a collective consciousness—upon the submergence of individuality in the family, the town, the church (Fischer, 1978:109).

Between 1790 and 1830 the land area of the United States more than doubled. This, coupled with rapid population growth and increased wealth, encouraged a great deal of geographic mobility. Many adult offspring no longer remained in the communities in which they had grown up. The relatively isolated communities of the mid-1700s began to expand and overlap one another.

The legitimacy of the traditional hierarchy was further eroded by religious changes in the New World. In the late 1700s, Methodist, Baptist, and Presbyterian doctrines—with their denial of predestination and belief in individual salvation as a possibility for all—injected egalitarian and individualistic thought into the religious sphere (Furnas, 1969:323–325). In these new ideologies, long life was not necessarily evidence of moral superiority, nor were the elders necessarily superior guides for religious life. To be sure, these new religious ideologies did not predominate during this period, but their influence began then. And they stood in stark opposition to the prevailing religious ideologies, which held that the elderly were morally superior because of their vast experience and their opportunity for a lifetime of self-improvement (Achenbaum, 1978:35).

Authority in the traditional society was based on the aristocratic and religious hierarchical standards of the times. To establish a new republic in the new egalitarian society, some new form of legitimacy was required, one that established the "rightness" of authority among free and equal men. The ideology of *the social contract,* given shape by John Locke in the late 1600s, provided the needed legitimacy. Authority came not from on high, but from the consent of the governed through the social contract. As Klapp has pointed out,

> [T]he idea of the social contract has unique advantages as a legitimizing device. . . . It provides a natural and reasonable explanation for getting together to set up an authority over free men (Klapp, 1973:136).

Because it is based on the theory that men are "endowed by their creator with certain inalienable rights," the social contract, although revocable, has ultimate authority. It is an ideal device to serve as a social bond among people who are not kin (Klapp, 1973:136). Under the social contract, the elders have neither more nor fewer rights than anyone else.

While the Declaration of Independence set forth the ideology of the social contract, Adam Smith's *The Wealth of Nations,* also published in 1776, set forth the free market as an ideal way of determining the social order. The concept of the free market includes

> . . . any competitive offering which leads to the fixing of a value by collective response, which al-

locates resources, and which commits people to action and organization as the result of their willingness to "buy" (Klapp, 1973:162).

Self-interest, not moral principles, could be depended upon to provide the balance that would produce an effective social system. As Smith put it:

> It is not from the benevolence of the butcher, the brewer, or the baker that we expect our dinner, but from their regard for their own interest. . . . I have never known much good done by those who affected to trade for the public good. It is an affectation, indeed, not very common among merchants, and very few words need be employed in dissuading them from it. . . . The natural effort of every individual to better his own condition, when suffered to exert itself with freedom and security, is so powerful a principle, that it is alone and without any assistance, not only capable of carrying on the society to wealth and prosperity, but of surmounting a hundred impertinent obstructions with which the folly of human laws too often incumbers its operations (Smith, 1776:151).

In other words, once free of meddling by government and church, individual selfish interest would lead us all to a better world because each person would look out for his or her interests. This is individualism in its most basic economic form. Yet so long as the market was dominated by old-fashioned trade, the elders held on to the advantages of experience. As we shall see, it was only in the late 19th century that the ideal of the free market became coupled with faith in progress through technology and efficiency, thus putting the aged at a disadvantage.

The growing trend toward individualism, the westward movement of large numbers of young adults, and the growing complexity of economic, political, religious, and social life in America also changed the emphasis on how people made decisions. In Riesman's (1950) terms, the emphasis shifted from tradition-directed to inner-directed decision making. In a pluralistic world,

> . . . the growing child soon becomes aware of

competing sets of customs—competing paths of life—from which he is, in principle, free to choose. And while parentage and social origins are all but determinative for most people, the wider horizon of possibilities and of wants requires a character which can adhere to rather generalized and more abstractly defined goals. . . . A society in which many people are internally driven—and are driven toward values, such as wealth and power, which are by their nature limited—contains in itself a dynamic of change by the very competitive forces it sets up. Even those who do not care to compete for higher places must do so in order not to descend in the social system, which has become a more open and less age-graded and birth-graded one (Riesman, 1950:40–41).

In this inner-directed mode, the parent is

> . . . not satisfied with mere behavioral conformity . . . but demands conformity of a more subtle sort, conformity as evidence of characterological fitness and self-discipline (Riesman, 1950:42).

In such a system, ethics and work performance depend not so much on external punishments and pressures, but are

> . . . instilled as a drive in the individual, and tremendous energies are unleashed toward the alteration of the material, social, and intellectual environment and toward the alteration of the self (Riesman, 1950:43).

Thus, parents retained essential character-molding functions. They more than anyone were responsible for creating internalized standards and principles that would see their children through an unpredictable future.

As we pointed out earlier, there was little in the new ideologies that inherently put the elderly at a disadvantage. However, because many held exalted positions in the old order, which had to be undercut to make way for the new one, older people became the target of social disapproval, and less positive traits of age (such as physical infirmity), which earlier had been glossed over, were used to discredit elderly officials. It was not that every characteristic of the elderly had become negative. Indeed, what is more likely is that a more realistic balance was

perceived between the advantages and liabilities of aging, compared to the overly positive viewpoint of the early 1700s.

Civil War to 1900

The last half of the 19th century is an important interval for modernization theory, since this is the time when modernization took hold in America. If modernization theory is correct, then the 19th century is a period in which the elderly lost their ability to secure or retain positions. We will examine this issue in detail.

There were numerous changes that occurred in the 19th century. Most important among them were the rise of the scientific method; the development of an ideology of progress through efficiency, technology, and bureaucracy; the emergence of retirement as a social institution; and massive immigration from Europe. As we shall see in this section, *it was ideological change, not change in objective circumstances or increases in the proportion of older people in the population, that gave rise to both industrialization and age discrimination.* Thus, modernization theory needs to be revised to take account of these ideological components.

The Rise of Science

The first and perhaps most sweeping of the changes of the 19th century was the rise of science as a method of knowing. In the scientific method, observation replaces tradition as the source of ideas about the world and how it works. What this new method proposed

> . . . was to produce a rigorously purified, value-free body of information for society, screened by the scientific method rather than by censors. Such reliable information would presumably allow any society to adapt most rapidly to whatever problems it had to face (Klapp, 1973:47).

Science caught on quickly in a society bent on progress as its highest priority. Unfortunately, science generated new information much faster than society could develop the decision rules or values needed to sort out this new information. As we shall see shortly, the image of the elderly was one of the first casualties of science.

Scientists working in Europe advanced the notion that one could understand diseases in old age only by clinically investigating and localizing specific diseases. By the 1880s, American medicine had progressed to the point that research using this approach was practical. This led to a detailed documentation of the physical decrepitude associated with aging in most of the body's organs and systems. There was almost total concern with age differences in *average* levels of functioning. No consideration was given to variety *within* given age categories. And, of course, there was no information on the extent to which the effects of these changes could be alleviated. For example, declines in eyesight are practically insignificant as long as they can be offset by wearing corrective eyeglasses.

Researchers looking at the effects of aging on mental capacities came to similar negative conclusions. Achenbaum (1978:46) cites the work of George Beard in the 1860s and 1870s, which concluded that mental abilities were at their peak between the ages of 30 and 45, after which they declined. William James, the pioneering psychologist, contended that as people age they become set in their mental ways and unable to keep up with the changing times (Achenbaum, 1978:46).

Thus was born the scientific variant of the long-standing theory of aging as inevitable decline, which held that people go through a period of maturation, a period of maturity during which their powers are greatest, and a period of aging in which both physical and mental resources are diminished. As in most fledgling fields of study, the initial facts were sparse and so the conclusions drawn from them were sometimes great fanciful leaps rather than carefully taken scientific steps. It was not until the 1960s that alternatives to the theory of aging as inevitable decline, such as activity theory and continuity theory, began to find wide support in the scientific literature. Thus, for nearly a hundred years the theory of aging as decline was the dominant scientific model of the physical and mental effects of aging.

The Ideology of Material Progress

The same optimistic and pragmatic urges that gave rise to science also gave rise to a new economic ideology of material progress through efficiency, technology, and bureaucracy. Human effort was seen as the key to progress. Achievement in science and technology and in the organizing of effort was seen as leading to a better lot for humankind. Many of the evils of social inequality that appeared at the beginnings of industrialization, such as child labor, would naturally disappear through the increasing material well-being that would arise from the application of technology in a free market. Another key concept in the formula for progress was efficiency: Only by making the most efficient use of both people and machines could the material growth necessary for an affluent society be achieved.

Numerous practical offshoots of this ideology of progress appeared in the late 19th century. First, there was a dramatic rise in demand for achievement from the individual. Second, a new type of work organization arose—the bureaucracy. Third, there was growth in technology. Each of these changes set the stage for massive age discrimination.

Individual Achievement.   Individual achievement was an important aspect of the new organization of work. Although it is often thought that America has always been a land of rugged individualists, this has not always been the case. As we saw earlier in the chapter, early America emphasized community effort to solve community problems. Fitting in and doing one's assigned job was not related to individual achievement or creativity but rather to conformity. Although the move toward achievement standards began in the 1700s, it accelerated dramatically after the Civil War. For example, de Charms and Moeller (1961) sampled every third page of four representative children's reading texts for each 20-year interval from 1800 to 1960. They calculated the frequency with which individual achievement imagery occurred in these texts (see Figure 3-2). They found that achievement imagery was uncommon prior to 1850, but multiplied sharply after 1850, reaching a peak in 1890 and declining thereafter. This shows very clearly that the rise in achievement imagery occurred *before* industrialization began to dominate the American economy (about 1890).

Bureaucracy.   When the focus of social standards becomes individual achievement rather than group achievement, competition increases and every individual in a work organization is expected to produce to a certain level. But in organizations where everyone works together, such comparisons are often difficult to make. However, after the Civil War there was a sharp

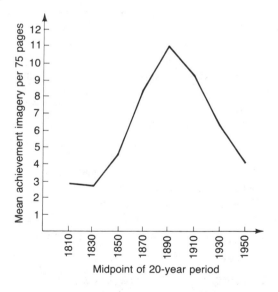

FIGURE 3-2   Mean frequency of achievement imagery in children's readers: United States, 1800–1960. *Source:* Adapted from de Charms and Moeller, 1961: 139.

increase in the size of work organizations and a rise in the use of bureaucratic principles. The main features of bureaucracy are: a highly specialized division of labor, formal rules, impersonal personnel procedures, hierarchical chain of command, and centralized authority. The job standardization that accompanied bureaucracy created ideal standards against which the achievement of each employee could be measured.

The growth of bureaucracy and the rationalization of jobs did not immediately affect the elderly in the workforce. For one thing, bureaucracy increased the levels of authority in organizations, giving older workers more managerial slots. For another, there was still a spirit of community among those who worked in these new bureaucratic organizations, just as there is today. Supervisors were very reluctant to discharge long-time employees even when they were obviously unable to perform (Graebner, 1980:90). The lack of provisions for either public or private retirement pensions meant that to force someone to retire was to force them into poverty. Finally, older people were still a very small percentage of the population, which meant that the number of infirm older workers that had to be accommodated in growing organizations was relatively small.

The Beginnings of Retirement

Although age discrimination was not common before 1900, the beginnings of a retirement institution began to emerge in the late 19th century. The most significant thing about the emergence of pensions and mandatory retirement policies is that they had little to do with aging. The forerunner of modern private retirement pensions was instituted by the Baltimore and Ohio Railroad in 1884. The plan stipulated that at age 65, retirement was compulsory and workers with at least ten years of service were entitled to a pension. Pensions were paid entirely by the company and the monthly amount was 1 percent of the worker's final wage, multiplied by number of years of service (Fischer, 1978: 166). Between 1885 and 1900, eight other companies instituted pension programs. Pensions tended to follow the "railroad formula," but minimum retirement age, length of service requirements, and mandatory age rules varied. Some plans required employee contributions while others did not (Achenbaum, 1978).

Private pensions were developed to discourage workers from changing jobs, not to provide old age income security. There was a great deal of labor mobility in the early days of industrialization. Pensions, with their length-of-service requirements, were established to make changing from one job to another unprofitable. In the words of one official,

> The pension operates as an incentive to hold men between the ages of 40 and 50 when they have acquired the experience and skill which makes them especially valuable and prevents their being tempted away by slightly increased wages (Haber, 1978:83).

During the period from the Civil War to the turn of the century, industrial unions were trying to gain management acceptance of the idea of seniority as the basis for layoffs or cutbacks. Seniority rules in effect established a property right to a job, with the most senior (and usually the oldest) workers having the greatest right to job security. Compulsory retirement developed as a way to limit the protection provided by seniority rules. Management opposition to seniority was based on two factors: senior workers were usually more costly, and seniority created problems in dealing with workers whose age made them no longer able to perform. Mandatory retirement solved both problems. It limited the protection given by seniority and relieved the employer from having to confront workers too infirm to continue. The unions were willing to trade mandatory retirement for seniority because at the time few workers lived to reach mandatory retirement age, especially compared to the huge numbers who would benefit from seniority (Haber, 1978).

Immigration

A final factor operating to change the situation for the elderly was massive migration into the United States from southern and eastern Europe. Of the 76 million residents of the United States in 1900, nearly 12 percent (9 million) had entered the country after 1880! Unlike immigrants from earlier eras, these people did not settle primarily in the rural frontiers; they settled in the cities and competed for jobs in the nation's growing manufacturing industries. And they often worked for wages much lower than native workers would accept. To employers looking for profits, the contrast between the wages of senior workers and the wages of immigrant workers was a gold mine.

1900 to 1929

From the turn of the century to the Great Depression, the pace of industrialization quickened substantially. The prosperity of the period was reflected in Herbert Hoover's campaign promise of "a chicken in every pot and two cars in every garage." The ideology of progress through technology and efficiency in the free market seemed to be working. From the point of view of social gerontology, the most important developments during this period were the continued high rate of immigration from Europe, the acceleration of the use of fossil fuels in industry, the introduction of more and more machine technology, the rise of "scientific management" as a means of managing work, growing age discrimination in the work force, increasing numbers of older people in poverty, and the development of early ways of coping with the problems of the aged.

Changing Ways to Do Work

From 1900 to 1930, the use of fossil fuels in industrial production tripled; a rate far higher than at any time before or since (U.S. Bureau of the Census, 1954; 1978). And these increased energy resources were used to run machines.

Using the printing industry as an example, Graebner (1980) traced the impact of technology on the older worker. In 1885, printing was a craft industry in which type was set by hand in numerous small shops. But in 1884, Mergenthaler invented the Linotype—a machine that allowed direct setting of lines by operating a typewriter-like keyboard. By 1895 the Linotype had swept the printing industry. Between 1895 and 1915, age discrimination resulted in the displacement of many older workers in the printing industry. But why were older workers at such a disadvantage in an industry in which skill and experience still played a large part? Graebner attributed it to three primary factors: a speedup in the pace of work, the theory of aging as decline, and principles of "scientific management."

The speedup of work was the combined result of labor agitation for a shorter work day and management concern for getting a full, productive return on money invested in machinery. Unions pressed for a reduction in the work day from ten hours to nine by offering to work faster; the success of their plan placed many workers—older workers, in particular—at a disadvantage. Graebner (1980:23) reports that those affected

> ... understood that not the machine but the demands placed on its operator by the shop owner were behind "the grind the old boy has to undergo today in order to hold his job." Although printers agreed that good eyesight and supple fingers were requisites of Linotype operation, ...

the "unnatural pace" of the work was held responsible for the difficulties older workers had in performing satisfactorily.

While labor unions accepted work speedups as a trade-off for shorter working hours, management's motives for them involved both efficient return on investment and new ideology about the ideal industrial worker. "Scientific management" was not really scientific. Rather,

it was merely systematic and logical. Many of its tenets were developed by deduction from untested assumptions about human performance. Nonetheless, as a body of ideas about how to organize work, scientific management influenced decisions in the workplace. For our purposes, the most important principle had to do with what sort of worker industry was looking for. One key to successful management was "the rejection of ordinary workmen and the employment only of unusual ones" (Graebner, 1980:32). Thus, the speedup in work was justified in part by the principle that only exceptionally fast operators should be operating the machinery in the first place.

Age Discrimination and Poverty

In selecting employees in an age of technology, the manager is always faced with the problem of screening applicants so that only those who stand a reasonable chance of filling the bill will be seriously considered. It was in this way that the theory of aging as inevitable decline did its damage; it identified older workers as a category that justifiably could be ruled out for hiring and singled out for firing or layoff. However, even with all of these pressures, many older workers were successful in keeping their jobs. The exclusion of the elderly from the workforce was gradual rather than sudden. Nevertheless, by 1929 there were substantial numbers of older people without jobs and without pensions. The majority of residents of the "poor house" in most communities were old, and avoiding the "poor house" became a major security goal of Americans who grew up in the 1920s and saw older people relegated there. Many of the elderly who were not on any form of welfare were desperately poor. Thus, it was not the physical or mental effects of individual aging that made aging a social problem but the economic effects of age discrimination in the absence of adequate retirement pensions. Even as late as 1920, less than 1 percent of the elderly were eligible for pensions (Achenbaum, 1978:83).

The approach to solving the social problems posed by a growing population of elderly poor was to assign the responsibility first to the family and then to the community (either a locality or a labor union). The community solution was the old-age home. Between 1875 and 1919, more than 800 benevolent homes for the aged were founded. These local institutions catered to the elderly members of religious denominations or nationality groups (Achenbaum, 1978:82). Also during this period, most U.S. counties built homes for the indigent, and more than two-thirds of the residents of these institutions were elderly. But by 1929 it was clear that the older population in general, and the population of elderly poor in particular, was growing too fast to be handled by building more institutions. In addition, "old folks homes" had become dreaded institutions, so the climate for expanding their availability was bad.

The ideological climate of the period from the turn of the century to the Depression fostered three conflicts that still pervade the politics of aging: age discrimination, old age financial insecurity, and retirement. Of these, however, age discrimination and financial insecurity in old age were the most intense.

The Great Depression

The 1930s was an awful decade for America and for the rest of the industrialized world. But bad as it was, the Depression set in motion social forces that eventually shifted the status of the elderly from desperate to more hopeful. The main elements of this shift were attempts to reform the image of aging, a changing definition of the causes of poverty, the collapse of many private pension schemes, the inability of benevolent homes and alms houses to cope with the rising numbers of elderly poor, political pressure from organizations of older people, the emergence of a clear federal role in public welfare, and the advent of Social Security.

Beginning in the 1920s, popular books began to appear with titles like *Life Begins at Forty*, books intended to foster more positive identities and constructive life styles for aging people. In addition, scientists were developing an alternative to the theory of inevitable decline with age. In particular, Dr. I. L. Nascher stressed the body's ability to renew itself and encouraged physicians to see the possibilities for good health in later life rather than to accept disease as a normal part of aging (Achenbaum, 1978:118–119). But despite these early attempts, the negative images of aging prevailed in the 1930s, no doubt in large part because so many older people were poor.

The Spread of Poverty

Prior to the Depression, poverty had seemed immoral to most Americans. If a person was poor in his or her old age, it was assumed that this was because the individual had failed to save money. The prevailing ideology also held that people could achieve anything if they only had will power. If people were poor, it was because they chose to be poor. Therefore, those who were poor deserved to be poor. Part of the justification of the stark conditions of the alms houses was that they would motivate people to choose not to be poor. There was little recognition that our beliefs about the relative worth of individual attributes like age, race, gender, ethnic group, and social class were being used as discriminatory screening devices in the labor market and that these same biases severely limited the occupational success that individual achievement could bring.

The Depression challenged the common conceptions of the causes of poverty and made people acknowledge the role of social forces. Too may people who had faithfully followed the prescription of industry, prudence, and thrift nonetheless lost their jobs, saw their pensions disappear, lost their life savings in failed banks, lost their homes to foreclosure, and so on. Too many "decent" people were on relief. It was finally obvious that something beyond individual failure was at work, and that "something" was society's institutions.

The Depression greatly worsened the situation of many retired people. As a result of capital losses, thousands of business failures, collapsed banks, and a host of other economic disasters, most private pension plans were disrupted. Many plans curtailed benefits, and 100,000 workers lost pension coverage altogether. In 1930, the New York Old Age Security Commission reported that most private pensions were practically insolvent (Achenbaum, 1978:129).

The New Deal

The Depression also called into question the long-standing assumption that a free market would automatically set society on the right course. After all, the free market had produced the Depression. But what could replace the free market in guiding national development? The New Deal was essentially a government-guided national effort to lift the country out of the Depression. In accepting it, the public accepted for the first time a role for the federal government as provider for the well-being of the American public. Government leadership was to replace the invisible hand of the free marketplace.

One of the major social problems of the Depression was the steady growth in the numbers of older people in poverty. By 1940, a substantial proportion of the nation's 9 million older people were on some form of relief (Fischer, 1978:174) and unemployment among older men approached 30 percent (Achenbaum, 1978:128). This situation gave rise to several national organizations pressing for some sort of government intervention on behalf of the elderly, the most well known of which was the *Townsend Movement*. Francis Townsend was a California physician who proposed that everyone over the age of

60 be given an old age pension of $200 a month, with the stipulation that they refrain from employment and spend the pension within 30 days (Achenbaum, 1978:129). The plan was to be financed through a sales tax (Fischer, 1978:180). By the mid-1930s, Townsend claimed over 3 million followers. Although Townsend's was the largest such organization, there were numerous others also agitating for some sort of old age security.

The Social Security Act.   In 1934, President Roosevelt's Committee on Economic Security began drafting the legislation that would become the *Social Security Act of 1935*. It was a broad-based social insurance plan designed to address two of the main evils of the day—old age income insecurity and unemployment.* We will concern ourselves only with the old age security aspects of the program.

Title I of the Social Security Act provided for a federal–state program of public assistance specifically for the aged. Called *Old Age Assistance*, this program was for the aged poor, regardless of employment history. It imposed national standards on states that were to receive federal funds. For example, a state could not require local communities to carry all of the state's share of the program; some of the funds had to come directly from the state. The state also had to centrally administer its program, with a guaranteed right to appeal for those denied assistance (Achenbaum, 1978:134).

Title II of the Social Security Act set up a national social insurance system to provide pensions for retired workers, disabled workers, and (in 1939) survivors of workers. One had to have worked at a job covered by the program for a specified length of time in order to be eligible for retirement benefits at age 65. Initially, the Title II program did not cover farm laborers,

*Accounts differ as to whether this was primarily humanitarian legislation or an example of shrewd political manipulation. (See Achenbaum, 1983:47–48; Graebner, 1980.)

domestics, government employees, or the self-employed. In 1939, the act was amended to provide spousal and other dependents' benefits in addition to the worker's retirement pension. Eligibility for full benefits required that, after retirement, the worker restrict earnings from employment to less than $15 per month.

The funding mechanisms chosen for Old Age Assistance and retirement/disability/survivors benefits reflect their very different purposes. Old Age Assistance was to be funded from general tax revenues, whereas retirement, disability, and survivor benefits were to be financed through a payroll tax, half from the employee and half from the employer. The primary difference between the two programs was the nature of the social contract. The Title I contract involved a direct federal–state partnership for providing assistance to those who were both old and poor. The Title II social contract was quite different: In return for workers' contributing to the Social Security system, the U.S. government was obligated to provide them the pensions to which they were entitled. The level of retirement or disability benefits was tied to the level of contributions over the working years.

Rather than establish an individual insurance-type savings account for every participant in the system, tax contributions from current workers were to be used to pay benefits to those who had already retired. This format was selected for at least two reasons. First, there was stiff opposition from business leaders to putting such a large amount of insurance capital under the control of the federal government. Second, several European systems had already tried the insurance-capital approach and had found it lacking: reserve funds were too susceptible to erosion from inflation. Thus, the solvency of the Social Security retirement-disability-survivor system does not depend on money in individual accounts. Its solvency derives completely from the formula used to collect the needed tax contributions. As we shall see later, the mistaken contention among many of today's journalists and politicians that Social Security is "going

broke" has seriously eroded public confidence in the system. The capacity of the U.S. government to fulfill its Social Security obligations is not in doubt; the debate is over how high benefits should be and how they should be financed, not over whether the government has the resources to do it.

The Social Security Act of 1935 was a small step in the direction of income security for the aged, but because it was founded on the premise that the aged would not be employed, it has inadvertently supported the ideology of age discrimination. Indeed, one of the major benefits New Deal politicians saw coming from Social Security was a reduction in unemployment brought about by changing the status of many older people from unemployed to retired.

1942 to 1965

From 1942 to 1965 there were numerous changes that affected the aged; the most important ones being the rapid aging of the population, steady improvements in retirement income, new attitudes toward consumption and leisure, lower retirement ages, and efforts to improve both the image and the circumstances of the aged.

Although the growth of the older population was outweighed by the "baby boom" that followed the Second World War, the fact is that from 1940 to 1960 the older population nearly doubled! During the war, older people stayed on the job. The government developed screening programs that brought older people back into the labor force, and people who were eligible to retire did not. The result was a slowdown in the rate at which older people were leaving the labor force (see Figure 3-3).

Growth of Programs for the Elderly

The war also strengthened the nation's willingness to put its faith in the federal government. The postwar period saw rapid growth in federal

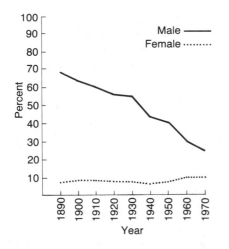

FIGURE 3-3   Percentage of persons over age 65 in the labor force: United States, 1890–1970. *Source:* Adapted from Achenbaum, 1978: 96.

economic policy. The federal government assumed more and more of the primary responsibility for the well-being of the population. As a result, increases in coverage and adequacy of benefits under Social Security were enacted.

Court cases improved the coverage of private pensions. By 1950, corporations were allowed business deductions for their contributions to private pension plans. In addition, unions were allowed to include pensions in collective bargaining with management. From 1945 to 1955 the number of private pension plans rose from 7,400 covering 5 million workers to 23,000 covering more than 15 million workers (Atchley, 1982d:272). Such expansion did little for those already retired, but it laid the foundation for adequate retirement incomes for those who were to retire in the 1970s.

Inequities amid Affluence

Achenbaum (1983:55) has pointed out that "statistics barely capture the surge in productivity and prosperity that ensued as the economy readjusted to peacetime needs." From 1945 to 1960 the gross national product more than dou-

bled, and except for three short recessions, the period from 1945 to 1970 was the "longest segment of uninterrupted prosperity this country has ever enjoyed." The economic prosperity of the period had many effects. It allowed the standard of living of the American worker to rise to unprecedented heights while also allowing an ever-increasing volume of profits for business. The accelerated use of technology led to shorter work weeks and earlier retirement. High income and easy credit stimulated desires for more and more consumer goods. Even retirement was marketed as a commodity, and eventually many people came to think of it as prepaid leisure. The growing amount of time over which the individual had discretion and the general affluence of the period led to a new kind of individualism. For many, survival was assured, and so they turned to developing the skills and knowledge needed for a satisfying life.

Yet within this general aura of prosperity, there was an undertow of discontent (Achenbaum, 1983:66–83). Galbraith (1958) decried the lavish spending on selfish consumption in the absence of America's willingness to use some of its vast wealth to improve public institutions for the common good. Whyte's *The Organization Man* (1956) and Mills' *White Collar* (1951) pointed to problems of overconformity and alienation from work. Riesman (1950) wrote about other-direction, in which internal direction gives way to social chameleons capable of adopting any ethic demanded by their compatriots.

In 1961, the White House Conference on Aging drew attention to the majority of older Americans who were poor in the midst of plenty. In the 1972 edition of this book, I wrote that 60 percent of older people in 1965 had incomes below, at, or very near the poverty level and that 80 percent of them had no income whatever apart from Social Security (Atchley, 1972:139). These dismal figures for the older population in 1965 were even worse for older members of minorities, particularly blacks. In addition, there was no means available to pay for medical care for needy older people. In short, neither the aged nor minority groups participated much in the surge of affluence in America from 1942 to 1965.

The Civil Rights movement of the early 1960s raised the nation's consciousness about massive injustice beneath the aura of the "affluent society." At the root of this movement was a doctrine of social justice through law, and an assertion of individual rights and entitlements. The elderly were among several disadvantaged categories identified as in special need.

1965 to 1980

Between 1955 and 1965, America had become aware of the massive injustice lying beneath the gloss of prosperity. From 1965 to 1975 it tried to do something about it, chiefly through federal legislation entitling the elderly to a wide variety of supports and services and protecting them from discrimination.

Legislation on Behalf of the Elderly

In 1965, Congress passed the *Older Americans Act*. The act established an Administration on Aging as part of the Department of Health, Education and Welfare, and authorized grants for planning, coordination of services, and training. *Medicare* was also established in 1965 to provide financing for many types of health services for the elderly. The *Age Discrimination in Employment Act* of 1967 prohibited the use of age as a criterion for hiring, firing, discriminatory treatment on the job, and referral by employment agencies. It also prohibited job advertisements reflecting age preferences, age discriminatory pressures by labor unions, and retaliation against workers who asserted their rights under the act.

In the 1970s the legislative onslaught on problems of the elderly continued. In 1972, the Older Americans Act was amended to provide

for a national network of agencies serving the elderly. Old Age Assistance was replaced by *Supplemental Security Income,* which established a more adequate floor of income under the elderly poor in *all* of the states. In 1974, the *Employees Retirement Income Security Act* imposed federal standards on private pension plans and set up a National Pension Benefit Guarantee Corporation to insure that private pension promises would be kept. In 1978 the Age Discrimination in Employment Act was amended to raise the age at which retirement could be made mandatory for most workers from 65 to 70.

The 1970s also saw rapid membership growth in organizations of older people. By the mid-1970s the American Association of Retired Persons/National Retired Teachers Association (AARP/NRTA) claimed a membership of over 6 million; the National Council of Senior Citizens claimed 3 million (H. Pratt, 1974). The combined membership of these organizations represented at least a third of the entire older population. It would be a mistake to assume that political advocacy was the major goal motivating older people to join such organizations. Some joined to take part in group purchasing programs for commodities and services such as drugs, travel, and insurance. Some joined for purely social purposes. Still, their large number of members allowed these groups to do at least two things of historical consequence. First, magazines such as *Modern Maturity* were produced that emphasized a positive view of aging. Second, these organizations had the resources to employ skilled lobbyists to protect the legislative gains of 1965 to 1975. We will return to this subject in Chapter 17, "Politics and Government."

Research on Aging

On the scientific front, evidence was being amassed that contradicted the theory of aging as inevitable decline, at least in terms of aging's effect on social functioning. In 1961, Cumming and Henry published *Growing Old: The Process of Disengagement*. In it they argued that society's abandonment of older people and the elderly's corresponding withdrawal from social life was necessary, inevitable, and desired by individuals as well as society.* This book ran directly against the "keep active" school of successful aging, and the conflict between the two views sparked an unprecedented volume of research. The results of this research showed that the vast majority of the elderly were capable people who remained integrated in social networks and that disengagement was mainly a result of age discrimination.

The Older Americans Act also marked the beginning of systematic government support for research on aging and for programs to train specialists in the field of aging. In 1974, the National Institute on Aging was added to the National Institutes of Health and given the charge of setting priorities and funding basic research on aging.

We will not go into more detail on these developments here; they are covered in the remainder of the book. Suffice it to say that the period from 1965 to 1980 was one of unprecedented growth in concern for the general well-being of the elderly and in the number of programs designed to promote it.

The 1980s

The beginning of the 1980s was marked by a full assault on the gains made on behalf of older Americans in the previous 15 years. The Reagan Administration went all out to convince the American public that older Americans had been lifted out of poverty and no longer needed government assistance; it chose to ignore that this assistance was exactly *why* the situation of the elderly had improved. The president promised that program cuts would be fairly shared by all

Americans, but in fact he proposed severe cuts in assistance to the very neediest of older people —the poor, the disabled, the institutionalized— while providing enormous tax cuts for the well-to-do.

These changes in support levels were not made on the basis of age prejudice; indeed, the elderly fared better in the budget-cutting than many other categories of Americans. The cuts were the result of a change in ideology about the appropriate role of the federal government in providing for the well-being of the population. Ronald Reagan stood for political conservatism, which many felt answered the need to curb alarming levels of inflation. Reagan's solution to the problems of old age dependency was to minimize federal responsibility and call on families, communities, and private charity to assume the burden and at the same time to continue paying high federal taxes to support programs that benefitted mainly the economic elite, on the presumption that this would eventually benefit the entire population through increased employment. This expectation was exceedingly unrealistic because families and communities had already assumed the lion's share of caring for the elderly.

Reagan's solution to the problem of financing Social Security was to propose that the elderly take a cut rather than increasing taxes. This cut was accomplished by increasing the retirement age (which lowers the total amount of benefits throughout the individual's years of retirement) and by postponing cost-of-living increases (which means a loss in real income—purchasing power) for those already retired. This conservative solution shifted the burden to the individual, regardless of capacity to bear it and regardless of the fact that the entire society benefits from the reduction in unemployment that retirement represents.

The debate over Social Security will not be settled by the time this book is published because it reflects some very deep divisions within American society about how best to deal with an aging population. These divisions are based

---

*See Chapters 12 and 13 for discussions of disengagement theory.

on differing views of the realities of aging, the appropriate role of government, the capacity of individuals and families to fend for themselves without federal tax relief, and a host of other issues. Somehow we must find a way to resolve these conflicting views if we are to avoid severe problems as our older population increases in both proportion and age.

Summary

The fact that human aging can produce both positive and negative results has been reflected in our ideas about aging since at least the time of the Greeks. It can bring wisdom or senile dementia, perspective or anxiety, skill or infirmity. This basic duality is reflected in the ideas about aging contained in most cultures. But as we have seen in this chapter, social ideologies have often had more influence on how the aged were viewed and treated than have the objective circumstances of the aged.

Modernization is the theoretical perspective traditionally used in historical research to account for changes in the treatment afforded older people. It begins with the notion that in preindustrial societies the elderly have certain advantages, which they lose in the process of industrialization. In Colonial America, seniority rights gave elders first claim to important social positions, and the communal and hierarchical nature of preindustrial society also gave the elderly a moral as well as a social advantage that was embodied in the ethic of veneration of the elderly. In addition, elders controlled the family, which in turn led to control of the community. All of these perspectives lead to a view that at one time Americans who were in the "proper" social category (that is, free, white, male, and from the appropriate class) could expect their social status to rise with age. For the poor, aging could be a miserable lot.

Modernization—the processes by which societies move from rural, agrarian economic and social systems to urban, industrial ones—is thought by most analysts to cause a loss of position for the elderly as a social category, even though some elderly people might succeed in retaining power and privilege. Several factors have been advanced as possible causes of this loss of status, but the status of the elderly did not suddenly change. Nor did it change as a result of a single factor.

Before the American Revolution, the image of the elderly was probably overly positive, for it tended to underplay the negative aspects of aging. The social position of the elderly was assured by various social institutions—property law, religious doctrine, trade, and the image of the heroic "gray champion."

It appears that over time the moral and social advantages enjoyed by the elderly were neutralized by a host of factors: increased inequality and expansion of wealth and trade, population increase, egalitarian social ideology, free market ideology, and individualism. But it was not until the late 19th century that the theory of aging as inevitable decline in both physical and mental capacities solidified. Early scientific research detailed countless negative changes, without considering their effects in the context of the whole person or the possibility of compensation.

Industrialization did not spring forth suddenly. Many decades of agricultural and mercantile economic growth provided the wealth necessary for industrialization. Rapid population growth from both natural increase and immigration provided an ample labor force. But new ideas were mainly responsible for the growth of industrialization—ideas about how to organize work, the importance of individual achievement, faith in progress through efficiency in a free market, increased use of technology and less reliance on human energy. These ideological shifts produced a competitive society, and the theory of aging as inevitable decline put the elderly at a disadvantage in the competition.

These shifts occurred in the 1890s, prior to very high levels of industrialization and prior to rapid growth in the older population, but they did not displace large numbers of older workers. Thus, even though the elderly had lost status as workers, it was not until the 1920s, when impersonal bureaucratic personnel procedures replaced the personal, communal approach to hiring and firing that age discrimination became widespread.

Advocates of modernization theory usually assume that underlying economic and demographic factors are the main influences on the status of the elderly. But powerful ideological factors were also at work, often prior to the economic and demographic changes. Thus, modernization theory must include these ideological influences.

In the 1930s, the elderly organized for political action against age discrimination and the resulting enforced poverty, and thereby raised the consciousness of the country and provided impetus for the Social Security Act of 1935. Thus, the explanatory power of modernization theory essentially was negated by 1940. After that, the growth of the federal government's role in public programs became a more important force.

After W.W.II, the United States entered an era of enormous prosperity, an era in which the pre-Depression free market was replaced by a federally regulated market. In addition, social welfare increasingly became a federal responsibility. Accordingly, interest groups vied with one another to influence federal legislation.

The Civil Rights movement advanced an ideology of social justice through law, and the 1961 White House Conference on Aging focused attention on the dire circumstances of most older Americans. By the mid-1970s, prosperity, interest-group politics, social justice ideology, and the large numbers of elderly poor had all combined to produce an impressive array of support, services, and programs for the elderly, those who work with the elderly, and those who study aging.

Thus, modernization had cost the elderly status, and the growth of the responsible national state returned a large measure of it. Recent challenges to these gains.illustrate the vulnerability of the elderly in times of economic hardship. Like the past, what the future holds will no doubt reflect our ideologies. The conditions out of which this future will emerge are detailed in the remainder of this book.

PART II

Individual Aging

This part of the book examines physical, psychological, and social aging and their effects on individuals. It begins with physical aging, its causes, its general physical effects, and its effects on health in particular. It then looks at psychological aging in terms of specific mental functions, human development, and mental illness. Finally, it looks at the extent to which individual aging is influenced by social factors such as the use of age as a social attribute that determines an individual's life chances. All three chapters of Part II are concerned with models and typologies used to diagnose various aspects of aging and with the facts that result from their application in research.

Chapter 4

Physical Aging

Many people are uncomfortable about the subject of aging because aging ultimately leads to death. Since what is noticed about physical aging tends to be decremental, people may also fear that their own aging will entail a lengthy period of physical and mental decline.

It is very important to recognize at the beginning of this discussion of physical aging that although physical aging is inevitable, physical disability or dependency is not. Except for a relatively brief terminal episode of illness, the vast majority of people grow old and die without *ever* experiencing disability. But, you may ask, how can this be true, given that physical aging seems to have affected the appearance, alertness, and agility of older people we see in everyday life?

You have probably misperceived the general effects of aging because we all tend to ignore the healthy, vital older person. For instance, when you're at a department store, you may not notice the healthy older people who are there, for they move about like everyone else, with posture and alertness like those of other adults. But you probably *do* notice those older people who are frail or disabled, for they often move slowly and with difficulty, and may be accompanied by someone who assists them. Because of the relative visibility of the frail elderly, we tend to overestimate their prevalence in the older population; and because of the relative *invisibility* of the able-bodied aged, we underestimate their prevalence. As we shall see, even at age 85 or older a majority of the elderly are still able-bodied.

In our exploration of physical aging, we will first discuss why the body grows old. Then we will look at some of the general influences that aging has on bodily functioning. Finally, we will examine the effects of aging on physical health.

Why Do We Grow Older?

Ideas about physical aging are tied to the concept of the **life span**—the maximum length of life that is biologically possible for a given species. Among animal species there is a wide variation in life span, thought to be a function of the genetic makeup of each species. Human life span is thought to be about 120 years (Shock, 1977a). Of course, since numerous environmental and social factors intervene, the average length of life—life expectancy—is usually much lower than the theoretical maximum, as we saw in Chapter 2.

What is significant about physical aging is what happens to the human body during three broad periods of the lifecycle. We pass first through a period of **maturation,** during which the body grows and develops to its peak level of physical functioning; a period of **maturity,** during which physical functioning remains at peak level; and a period of **aging,** during which the body gradually loses its capacity for peak performance. Each of the body's systems and organs is on a slightly different schedule for maturation, the duration of maturity, and the onset and rate of aging. Indeed, Heron and Chown (1967) concluded that summary measures of aging are not feasible even when functional measures (instead of chronological ages) are used because functions vary so much within individuals.

Because aging is so variable and is not one process but a group of them, biologists have had difficulty separating aging from other phenomena that can also affect the body, such as disease. Strehler (1977) pinpointed several useful criteria in differentiating aging from other biological processes. First, to be a part of the aging process, a phenomenon must be universal; that is, it must eventually occur in all people. This means that the fact that older people are more likely to have a condition does not make that condition a part of aging. For example, older people are more likely than the young to get lung cancer, but since not all older people get it, lung cancer is *not* a part of aging. On the other hand, as people age, they all experience a decline in the ability to fight off disease, which is caused by a decrease in the

effectiveness of the body's immune system. Thus, a decline in bodily immunity *is* a part of aging. Strehler's second criterion of aging says that aging comes gradually from within the body. This rules out environmental factors such as cosmic radiation or situational factors such as accidents, which affect the body but only from outside. This criterion is obviously linked to the genetic basis of aging. Third, says Strehler, aging must have a *negative* effect on the body's functioning, otherwise we would call it maturation (growth) or maturity (no change). Thus, physical aging is something that happens to all people, comes on gradually from within the organism rather than from the external environment, and has a negative effect on physical functioning. To be a part of aging, any physical change must meet *all* of these criteria.

Biologists studying what aging is and why it occurs have looked at every level of physical functioning: genes, cells, molecules, tissues and organs, and physiological systems such as the immune and endocrine systems. Let us now briefly look at some of these areas.*

Genetic Functions

Genetically, aging can be seen either as a preprogrammed result of inherited genes or as a result of gene changes that occur with age. There are two main pieces of evidence that *aging is preprogrammed* in the genes: (1) It has been known for a long time that regardless of social or cultural influences, various animal species differ considerably in life span. (2) Although the rate of aging varies considerably from individual to individual, those with similar heredity show similarities in aging. Thus, there does appear to be a genetic program that sets an upper limit on the life span. However, within a given species, it is also clear that family and environ-

---

*The biology and physiology of aging are extremely complex topics. For a more complete treatment see Finch and Hayflick, 1977.

ment can alter the results of this basic species-wide genetic program (Shock, 1977a:104).

The idea that aging may result from *changes in genetic functioning* has centered on errors that occur as the body synthesizes needed proteins or enzymes according to the genetic code. Presumably, this results in the body's manufacturing proteins and enzymes that are not up to genetic specifications and as a result cannot function properly. As the organism ages, these errors accumulate and eventually result in aging and death of the cell. This notion of erroneous cell production has received some research support, but not consistently, and much more research is necessary to identify the extent of such errors and at what point in the synthesis of proteins and enzymes the errors occur (Shock, 1977a:106).

Another promising line of genetic research involves changes in the capacity of cells to repair damage to their genetic structures. For example, cells from species with long life spans are more likely to repair radiation damage than are cells from species with short life spans (Sinex, 1977).

Cross-Links

Over time, certain molecules in the body develop links, either between parts of a given molecule or between molecules. These cross-links, which are very stable and which accumulate over time, result in physical and chemical changes that affect how the molecules function.

Most of the research evidence on the relationship between cross-links and aging comes from studies of collagen—a substance associated with connective tissue. Cross-links develop in collagen with age, leading to the loss of elasticity in various tissues, including blood vessels and skin. Specific enzymes have been isolated that can break down cross-links in collagen. Other chemicals have been found to inhibit the rate at which cross-links are formed. While this research has not progressed to the point that the

findings can be applied to humans, it remains a very promising line of research (Shock, 1977a).

The Immune System

One of the body's primary defenses, the immune system is geared to recognize and destroy substances from both inside and outside the body that are not part of the "normal" self. Thus, immune cells produce antibodies that attack foreign substances, viruses, germs, and even cancer cells, to keep them from interfering with the body's functioning. The immune system matures in early childhood, remains on an extended plateau into early adulthood, and begins to decline in effectiveness thereafter. Part of the increased vulnerability to disease associated with aging results from this decline in the immune system.

There are two ways that age changes in the immune system influence physical functioning: (1) If the immune system over time loses its capacity to recognize deviations in substances produced within the body, then mutated cells that formerly would have been destroyed by the immune system survive to the potential harm of the organism. This could explain why susceptibility to cancer increases with age. (2) Sometimes the immune system produces antibodies that destroy even normal cells, a process known as *auto-immune reaction*. The prevalence of auto-immune antibodies in the blood increases with age. Auto-immune reactions have also been linked with several age-related diseases, rheumatoid arthritis and late onset diabetes among them. The decline in the body's immune system and auto-immune reactions are both promising areas of research, for they could lead to the identification of ways to influence the rate of immunological decline.

Physiological Controls

Human beings are incredibly complex biological organisms. Our survival requires continual, simultaneous monitoring and control of thousands of systems, structures, and processes within our bodies. In fact, the aging we see in the total human being may result more from a breakdown in integrative mechanisms than from changes in individual cells, tissues, or organs (Shock, 1977b:639). The endocrine glands and the nervous system are the two primary bodily mechanisms for integrative control over homeostasis—the maintenance of a reasonably uniform internal environment, including body temperature, acid-base balance, blood sugar, and blood oxygen.

Endocrine glands, such as the thyroid, pancreas, or pituitary, produce hormones that are transmitted through the bloodstream to organs throughout the body. With aging there is not only a decline in organ response to these controlling hormones, but there is also an increase in the amount of deviation from normal that is required to trigger the production of the hormones needed to restore homeostasis. There are some indications that these declines are the result of age changes in the brain centers for endocrine control and that endocrine declines can be prevented or even reversed to some extent by introducing chemicals that improve the brain's capacity to trigger the production of hormones (Finch, 1977).

Homeostasis also relies on the nervous system, which contains most of the mechanisms for sensing changes that require adjustment as well as the network along which signals to carry out an adjustment must pass. Aging is associated with a noticeable decline in the efficiency of neuromuscular coordination (Shock, 1977a:112). However, there is less evidence about how other aspects of coordination by the nervous system are related to aging (Brody and Vijayashankar, 1977).

The body's control systems, endocrine and nervous, are obviously of prime importance to human survival. But whether they play a central role in physical aging remains to be seen. This is one of the most active and promising areas of current biological research.

In Sum

Physical aging involves a group of processes that reduce the viability of the body and increases its vulnerability to disease. The reduction in viability occurs at all levels—cells, molecules, tissues and organs, and control systems. The increase in vulnerability to disease results mainly from a decline in the functioning of the immune system.

The search for explanations of aging has produced numerous possibilities. Aging may result from:

1. a hereditary genetic program that sets limits on growth, aging, and longevity

2. age changes in the functioning of the genetic program

3. lowered molecular functioning due to an age-related buildup in cross-links

4. age-related lowered efficiency of the immune system in identifying and destroying potentially harmful mutated cells

5. age-related increase in auto-immune reactions in which antibodies are produced that destroy normal cells

6. a decrease with age in the efficiency of endocrine control of various vital functions

7. age decline in the capacity of the nervous system to speedily and efficiently maintain bodily integration and to prevent bodily deterioration

It will be some time before these various explanations are tested and sorted out. It is also likely that they all play some part in the process of aging and that there is no single key that will unlock the mystery of physical aging.

What Are the Physical Consequences of Aging?

Beliefs about physical changes that result from aging are used to develop and justify ideas about appropriate behavior both for the aged themselves and of others toward the aged. Throughout this book, we will be continually trying to establish whether various social patterns exist because of *actual* limitations imposed by age or because of *presumed* limitations that have no basis in fact. At this point, we shall examine basic facts about the consequences of physical aging.

Physical aging affects the functioning of our bodies in many ways: It alters the amount of energy we can mobilize, our stature, mobility, and coordination, our physical appearance, and our susceptibility to illness. As we look in detail at these various kinds of changes, we need to ask three basic questions: (1) What usually happens? (2) Can decrement be prevented, treated, reversed, or compensated for? (3) What are the *social* consequences of the typical change?

Physical Energy

The amount of physical energy that a person has is a function of the capacity of the blood and organs and other bodily systems to deliver oxygen and nutrients throughout the body and to remove waste products, a process that requires complex coordination among the various systems of the body. And because aging reduces both the body's capacity to coordinate its systems and the level of functioning of these systems, aging reduces the supply of physical energy that the body can mobilize. For example, Shock (1977a) reported that the ability to get oxygen into the blood peaks at about age 20, remains relatively high through about age 45, and then steadily declines. At age 80, the volume of oxygen that can be gotten into the blood is only about half as much as at age 40. Accordingly, although muscle strength remains relatively constant through age 70, maximum work output declines steadily after age 40 (Shock and Norris, 1970).

The socially important issue here is the extent to which this decline in physical energy inter-

feres with typical social functioning. Shock (1977b:655) reported that at low to moderate levels of physical work, age does not affect the ability to perform work. The only effect associated with age was the somewhat longer time required to recover from work. Most of the work that adult Americans perform is in the low to moderate range—well within the physical capacities of older adults who have *no* disabling chronic condition (at least 60 percent of the elderly).

Stature, Mobility, and Coordination

Physical activity depends partly on the structure of the body and on its ability to move effectively. As adults grow older, they actually get shorter, partly because bones that have become more porous develop curvature and partly because some older people carry themselves with a slight bend at the hips and knees. A height loss of 3 inches is not uncommon. Older women are especially likely to find themselves too short to reach conveniently in environments designed for the common "adult standard." For instance, standard kitchen cabinets, sinks, and counters tend to be too high and too deep for older women.

The ability to move may also be influenced by aging. For example, we know that with age arthritis increases and that connective tissue in joints stiffens. However, we do not know how these changes influence the ability to flex and extend arms, legs, and fingers. This is a major area in need of research.

We know much more about coordination. Physical coordination is a complex process that involves taking in sensory information, attaching meaning to it through perception, selecting appropriate action based on that perception, transmitting instructions to the various parts of the body that need to act, and initiating action. Coordination depends on several body organs and systems: sensory organs provide information; the nervous system transmits that information to the brain; various parts of the brain handle perception and selection, initiation, and monitoring of action; various muscle groups perform action under the control of the nervous system and the brain. In most cases, these separate functions occur in such rapid succession that the interval between sensation and response action is minute. This rapidity is especially true of practiced skills such as typing, playing a musical instrument, and operating familiar equipment.

Aging can influence coordination through its effects on any of the systems that support physical activity. In fact, however, sensory organs and muscle groups generally perform well into old age. Coordination and performance are much more likely to be influenced by age changes in the brain-based functions, especially by a slowdown in decision making related to performance (Welford, 1959:563).

Physical Appearance

Wrinkled skin, "age spots," gray hair, and midriff bulge are common examples of age changes in appearance. Although it is true that the skin becomes wrinkled with age and is more susceptible to dryness and loss of hair, it is still quite able to perform its protective function much longer than the theoretical life span of 120 years. The significance of aging skin is social rather than functional.

Aging skin, gray hair, and a thicker waistline are significant primarily because they symbolize membership in a less desirable social category—older people. Oil of Olay, Miss Clairol, and Buster's Magic Tummy Tightener enjoy brisk sales not because people want to be young, but because people want to avoid being classified as old. This, in turn, has nothing to do with any genuine physical effects of aging. Instead, it reflects the fact that the aged are often looked down upon and discriminated against.

Age changes in appearance are also feared for what they may do to physical attractiveness. Yet aging does not predictably affect physical attrac-

tiveness. Certainly, if we take a narrow, idealized view of physical beauty, then not very many people fit the bill at any age. But in terms of *practical* attractiveness—the ability to draw positive attention through one's physical appearance—there are plenty of unattractive 25-year-olds. And many people find that they become more attractive as they grow older. Aging rarely transforms a silk purse into a sow's ear. More often it provides interesting facial lines, the image of experience and character. Nevertheless, people tend to fear what aging will do to their appearance, especially if they see attractiveness as one of their major assets. Some people try to surgically alter the effects of aging. The main reasons cited for having cosmetic surgery in middle age or later are job security, marital security, and social attitudes about appearance (Wantz and Gay, 1981:154).

Most people tend to be preoccupied with physical attractiveness and to ignore other attractive features. Yet the secret of many of the most attractive people is their enthusiasm, attention, and personality, characteristics that can improve with age. Still, some people experience aging as a loss of attractiveness, a change they can find difficult to deal with. Fortunately, most of us grow older with mates and friends whose actions reassure us that changes in physical appearance are not nearly as important as we have been led to think they are.

Other Physical Changes

The cessation of menstruation in women is called **menopause**. While it usually occurs in middle age (often between 45 and 50), young women frequently associate menopause with later life. Menopause gradually alters the hormone balance in the body, particularly estrogen. The hot flashes and other physical symptoms thought to be common in menopause are usually receptive to therapy. As for the psychological impact of menopause, Neugarten et al. (1963) discovered that most women find the menopause at worst an unpleasant, brief transition with a beneficial outcome. The majority of postmenopausal women reported feeling better after menopause than they had in years. They also reported feeling calmer and happier.

Two important changes occur in the nervous system as age increases: (1) Hardening of blood vessels may create circulatory problems in the brain. Since adequate blood supply is crucial to an efficiently functioning brain, it is fortunate that most people are not bothered by this problem. (2) Aging reduces the speed with which the nervous system can process information or send signals for action. This decline in the speed of operation of the nervous system is a more widespread problem, even in middle age. Most people begin to notice lagging reflexes and reaction time in their late forties. Changes in the nervous system also influence most psychological processes; these are dealt with in Chapter 5.

Failure of the circulatory system is the most common cause of death for people over 40. Heart disease or interrupted blood flow to the brain or heart are prevalent among older people as a result of reduced cardiac output, reduced elasticity of the large arteries, and general deterioration of the blood vessels. At age 75, the probability of death from cardiovascular disease is 150 times higher than at age 35. Of the major systems and organs in the body, the kidneys show the greatest decline in function with increasing age (Heron and Chown, 1967). The kidneys of people over 80 perform only half as well as those of people in their twenties. The respiratory, digestive, reproductive, and temperature-control systems all decline with age, but while these are among the most common and major effects of aging, only rarely do these systems decline with age enough to produce disability.

Aging and Physical Health

Health is a central factor in everyone's life. Most people are fortunate enough to be able to take good health for granted. Poor health affects life satisfaction, participation in most social roles, and the way we are treated by others. In later life, declining health cuts across all social, political, and economic lines, although disabling illness is more common and occurs at earlier ages among people at the lower socioeconomic levels. Health becomes a major determinant of ability to participate in family, job, community, and leisure pursuits. And health needs absorb a large amount and proportion of older people's incomes. A large proportion of the medical industry's facilities and services are geared toward meeting the needs of people with diseases and infirmities that are most common in old age.

The term *health* is complex in meaning and difficult to define. It refers not merely to the absence of disease or disability, but also to more positive things, such as mental, physical, and social well-being. It is more useful to look at health as a continuum. At one end is complete social, physical, and mental well-being, and at the other end is death. Figure 4-1 shows several stages along the health continuum. Ideally, good health would be measured in terms of social, physical, and mental well-being, but since these conditions are very difficult to measure, good health is usually operationally defined as the absence of disease or infirmity.

A *condition* is defined as a departure from physical or mental well-being. It has its onset when the condition is first noticed by the individual or by a physician. Conditions vary in many important ways. The term **chronic condition** refers to a long-term condition that is permanent, leaves residual disability, requires special training for rehabilitation, or may be expected to require a long period of supervision, observation, or care. Chronic conditions include diseases such as asthma, high blood pressure, diabetes, heart disease, and arthritis, and impairments such as deafness, paralysis, and permanent stiffness in joints. An **acute condition** is expected to be temporary and may be as mild as a bruised foot or as serious as pneumonia. The third and final category of conditions is the

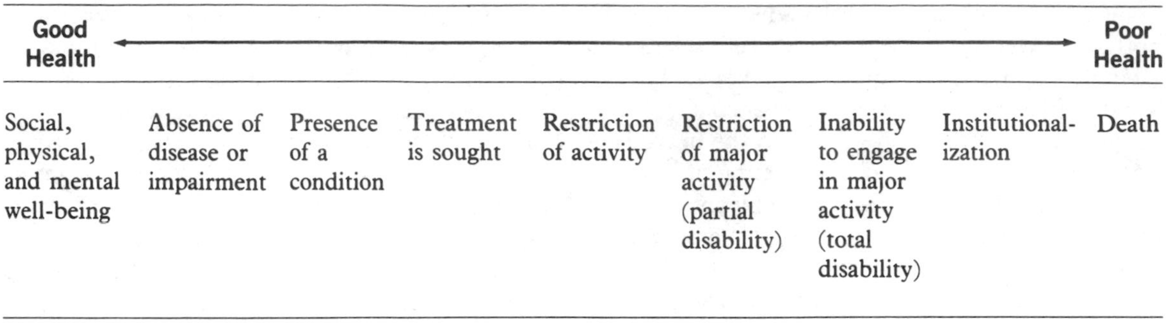

Good Health								Poor Health

←——→

| Social, physical, and mental well-being | Absence of disease or impairment | Presence of a condition | Treatment is sought | Restriction of activity | Restriction of major activity (partial disability) | Inability to engage in major activity (total disability) | Institutional-ization | Death |

FIGURE 4-1   Stages of the health continuum.

injury. Within these categories, conditions can be discussed in terms of *incidence* (number of new cases per year) or *prevalence* (average number of existing cases per year).

Once a condition becomes known, it may simply be ignored. Or the person may *seek treatment,* either self-treatment or professional treatment. The next phase of illness is *restriction of activity,* one that does not, however, prevent the individual from carrying out major activities. A *restriction of major activity* is more serious, since the individual must restrict the most necessary activities, such as job or housework. This phase is commonly called *partial disability.* A person

who is unable to engage in major activities approaches *total disability.* When a condition becomes medically demanding or very serious, or when disability reaches the point at which the individual cannot care for him/herself, the phase of *institutionalization* usually begins. It should be recognized that these phases of illness are quite arbitrary and merely provide a number of useful reference points along a continuum of health that can be used to compare the health of older people with that of younger ones.

On the average, older people are comparatively less often afflicted than the young with

TABLE 4-1   Number of acute conditions per person per year and average duration of restricted activity, by age and sex: United States, 1977–1978

Age	Number of Acute Conditions			Average Number of Days of Restricted Activity		
	Total	Male	Female	Total	Male	Female
0–4	3.9	3.9	3.9	12.2	12.2	12.2
5–14	2.8	2.8	2.8	9.0	8.6	9.5
15–24	2.5	2.2	2.7	10.0	8.6	11.5
25–44	2.1	1.9	2.3	9.2	7.7	10.6
45–64	1.3	1.2	1.6	8.8	7.1	10.3
65+	1.1	0.9	1.2	12.1	9.9	13.6

Source: Ries, 1979.

conditions classified as *acute* (such as infectious disease or the common cold). The elderly are more often afflicted with *chronic* conditions (such as heart disease or deafness) and are more likely to suffer *disability* restrictions on their activity.

The wide variability in the health status of older people definitely shows that poor health is not necessarily associated with aging. But *as a group,* older people do suffer disproportionately from chronic conditions.

Acute Conditions

Acute conditions are illnesses or injuries that are temporary or short-term. The incidence of acute conditions decreases with age. From July

1977 to June 1978, Americans under 5 years of age had an average of 3.9 acute conditions per year, and the incidence decreased with age to a rate of 1.1 acute conditions per year for those age 65 and over. While the incidence of all types of acute conditions decreases with age, the decrease for influenza and accidental injuries is not as pronounced as the decrease for "childhood" diseases, such as mumps and measles, and for the common cold. However, when older people experience acute conditions, they experience more days of restricted activity (see Table 4-1).

There is substantial sex difference with regard to the incidence and duration of acute conditions. Compared to males, females at all *adult* ages show a higher incidence of acute conditions

TABLE 4-2 Percent distribution of persons by chronic condition and activity limitation status, by sex and age: United States, July 1965–June 1967

| Sex and Age | Total Population | Persons with No Chronic Conditions | Persons with One Chronic Condition or More | | |
			Total	No Limitation of Activity	Some Limitation of Activity
Both Sexes					
Under 17	100.0%	77.2%	22.8%	20.9%	1.9%
17–44	100.0	45.9	54.1	46.7	7.4
45–64	100.0	28.9	71.1	51.8	19.3
65 +	100.0	14.4	85.6	39.6	46.0
Male					
Under 17	100.0	75.8	24.2	22.1	2.1
17–44	100.0	47.4	52.6	44.7	8.0
45–64	100.0	30.5	69.5	48.7	6.8
65 +	100.0	15.6	84.4	31.4	53.0
Female					
Under 17	100.0	78.6	21.4	19.5	1.8
17–44	100.0	44.7	55.3	48.5	6.9
45–65	100.0	27.5	72.5	54.7	17.8
65 +	100.0	13.5	86.5	45.9	40.6

Source: Adapted from Wilder, 1971:19.

TABLE 4-3   Persons with limitation of activity due to chronic conditions, by sex and age: United States, 1981

Sex and Age	Total Population	No Limitation of Activity	Some Limitation of Activity	Limitation of Major Activity*
Both Sexes				
Under 17	100.0%	96.2%	3.8%	2.0%
17–44	100.0	91.6	8.4	5.4
45–64	100.0	76.1	23.9	19.1
65 +	100.0	54.3	45.7	39.2
Male				
Under 17	100.0	95.6	4.4	2.4
17–44	100.0	91.1	8.9	5.7
45–64	100.0	75.1	24.9	20.5
65 +	100.0	50.4	49.6	44.7
Female				
Under 17	100.0	96.9	3.1	1.5
17–44	100.0	92.1	7.9	5.1
45–64	100.0	76.9	23.1	17.9
65 +	100.0	56.9	43.1	35.3

Major Activity refers to ability to work, keep house, or engage in school or preschool activities.

Source: National Center for Health Statistics, 1982.

and a longer duration of disability. However, there does not appear to be an increase in this gap in the older age categories (Ries, 1979:20–21).

Chronic Conditions

Chronic conditions are long-term but not necessarily disabling. For example, having no teeth is a chronic condition whose incidence steadily increases with age, and yet it is seldom disabling. As Table 4-2 shows, the percentage of people with no chronic conditions at all during 1965–1967 dropped sharply as age increased and at age 65 and over only 14.4 percent of older people had no chronic conditions. Unfortunately, we have no more recent data on prevalence

of chronic conditions. A key issue is the relationship between chronic conditions and disability or activity limitation. As Table 4-2 also shows, nearly 40 percent of the elderly who had chronic conditions were not limited in any way by them. Nevertheless, the proportion with some limitation of activity increased sharply after age 44.

Table 4-3 shows the most recent data on the degree of activity limitation only *for those who have chronic conditions.* Compared to the data in Table 4-2, the 1981 data in Table 4-3 show that the proportion of older people (65 +) with chronic conditions and *no* limitation of activity increased dramatically, from 39.6 percent in 1965–1967 to 54.3 percent in 1981. Note also that contrary to the pattern for acute conditions, older men are *more* likely than older

TABLE 4-4 Selected chronic conditions causing limitation of activity, according to degree of limitation and age: United States, 1976

Activity Limitation and Age	Number of Persons Limited in Activity	Chronic Condition									
		Arthritis and Rheumatism	Heart Conditions	Hypertension Without Heart Involvement	Diabetes	Mental and Nervous Conditions	Asthma	Impairments of Back or Spine	Impairments of Lower Extremities and Hips	Visual Impairments	Hearing Impairments
		Percent of Persons Limited in Activity Because of Specified Condition									
Limited but Not in Major Activity											
Both sexes, all ages	7,495,791	13.0%	6.7%	5.2%	3.2%	3.4%	7.2%	8.0%	8.2%	6.1%	4.6%
Under 17	1,087,587	1.3	3.0	0.5	1.4	6.1	19.1	5.4	9.3	4.3	5.6
17-44	2,843,947	7.2	3.1	2.9	2.4	3.7	8.2	12.2	10.8	5.6	4.1
45-64	2,264,578	18.4	8.8	7.8	4.9	2.6	3.8	6.9	6.5	4.7	4.2
65+	1,299,679	25.7	14.0	9.6	3.4	1.6	0.9	3.0	4.9	11.2	5.6
Limited in Amount or Kind of Major Activity											
Both sexes, all ages	15,210,160	18.3	16.3	7.8	5.0	4.7	4.6	8.8	5.3	4.2	1.8
Under 17	1,058,928	0.7	1.9	0.2	0.7	7.5	22.6	0.7	4.2	1.7	4.9
17-44	3,721,693	6.8	5.4	4.0	2.3	5.4	4.7	16.5	6.6	3.2	1.8
45-64	5,671,034	20.7	19.9	9.5	6.9	5.3	3.4	9.3	4.8	3.2	1.2
65+	4,758,505	28.4	23.9	10.5	5.9	2.9	1.9	4.1	5.0	6.5	1.7
Unable to Carry on Major Activity											
Both sexes, all ages	7,469,111	17.5	23.4	6.8	7.0	7.0	3.0	4.4	5.6	7.2	1.9
Under 17	120,180	1.7	1.4	—	—	5.7	7.1	4.2	9.0	15.1	3.2
17-44	946,834	5.8	7.5	2.7	1.9	14.5	3.7	8.4	5.3	3.7	1.8
45-64	2,569,077	18.2	26.2	8.7	8.1	9.1	2.9	5.8	6.5	5.0	1.4
65+	3,833,020	20.4	26.1	6.8	7.7	3.6	2.7	2.5	5.0	9.2	2.2

Source: National Center for Health Statistics (1978).

TABLE 4-5   Chronic conditions causing major disability in the middle-aged and elderly: United States, 1976

Age 45–64	Percent Affected	Age 65 and Over	Percent Affected
Heart conditions	26.2	Heart conditions	26.1
Arthritis/Rheumatism	18.2	Arthritis/Rheumatism	20.4
Mental conditions	9.1	Visual impairment	9.2
Hypertension without		Diabetes	7.7
heart involvement	8.7	Hypertension without	
Diabetes	8.1	heart involvement	6.8
Impaired lower body	6.5	Impaired lower body	5.0
Impaired back or spine	5.8	Mental conditions	3.6
Visual impairment	5.0	Asthma	2.7
Asthma	2.9	Impaired back or spine	2.5
Hearing impairment	1.4	Hearing impairment	2.2

Source: National Center for Health Statistics, 1978.

women to experience activity limitations due to chronic conditions.

Table 4-4 shows the types of chronic conditions associated with various degrees of activity limitation, by age, for 1976. For children under 19, asthma was by far the leading cause of activity limitation in general, but blindness was the leading cause of major disability, followed by impairment of the lower body. Impairments of the spine and lower body were the leading causes of all activity limitation in young adulthood, but nervous disorders were the leading cause of major disability. After age 45, arthritis/rheumatism and heart/circulatory conditions became the major limiters of activity for both minor and major disability.

Table 4-5 is a rank order of conditions that caused major disability among the middle-aged and the elderly in 1976. Heart conditions and arthritis/rheumatism were the major disablers in both age groups and they were only slightly more prevalent among the disabled elderly. Mental conditions and hypertension were more likely to be disabling in middle age than in later life. But blindness was much more likely to be

disabling in later life than in middle age. Note that although hearing impairment is common, it is not a major cause of disability or activity limitation in later life or at any other age.

One important implication of the data in Tables 4-4 and 4-5 is that the disabilities that accompany aging are for many people not the result of a normal aging process but the result of pathological conditions that are preventable and treatable. In future years the proportion of older people disabled by heart disease and by arthritis/rheumatism can be expected to fall as our knowledge of these conditions improves.

In 1970, Cantor and Mayer (1976) conducted interviews with a representative sample of 1,552 persons who were 60 or over and who lived in the 26 poorest neighborhoods that make up the inner city of New York. Of these inner city elderly, 49 percent were white, 37 percent were black, and 13 percent were Spanish-speaking, mainly of Puerto Rican origin. Nine out of ten lived in independent households; four out of ten lived alone. There was a wide range of socioeconomic status represented, but at the same time two-thirds were concentrated in the very lowest

TABLE 4-6   Self-rated health, by race and ethnicity (percent)

Self-rated Health	Total	Race and Ethnicity		
		White	Black	Spanish-speaking
Good	34%	41%	29%	23%
Fair	42	38	46	46
Poor	24	21	25	31

Source: Adapted from Cantor and Mayer, 1976.

categories. Most respondents were retired and lived on incomes significantly below the average for older people in New York City as a whole. Nine out of ten interviewed had a primary support system made up of family members and neighbors, but about 8 percent had no personal support system to which they could turn in the event of illness.

In terms of global health assessments, only 34 percent of the inner city elderly rated their health as good, compared with 41 percent for New York City as a whole, 49 percent in New York State, and 52 percent nationally. And certain subgroups among the inner city elderly showed an even lower percentage reporting good health. The sharpest differences were by race and ethnicity (see Table 4-6), differences which appear to be mainly economic in nature, since reports of good health ranged from 24 percent in the lowest income category to 61 percent in the highest.

In terms of functional impairment in tasks of daily living, 50 percent of inner city older people had some impairment, compared to 37 percent nationally. No racial difference in impairment was found, although a disproportionate 62 percent of the Spanish-speaking reported some impairment. Income was again a significant predictor, with 61 percent of those in the lowest income category reporting some impairment compared to only 23 percent in the highest income category. In terms of both global self-assessments and functional impairment, older women reported poorer health than did older men. Functional impairment was more closely related to age than were global self-reports. Finally, health status was significantly related to living arrangements. Global and functional measures each showed couples to have the highest percentage with good health. A slightly lower percentage was found among those who lived alone but independently, and a much lower percentage among those who lived with family. This suggests that very poor health is a primary reason for living with family.

Older people are also much more susceptible to injury from falls than are younger people. Burnside (1981) found falls to be the leading cause of accidental death among people over 75. Older women are especially likely to fall. The most common cause of falls among the elderly is tripping or stumbling over something at home, which is no doubt related to poor coordination and failing eyesight. Falls also occur as a result of dizziness, which is probably related to chronic illnesses such as high blood pressure (hypertension) and to the medications used to treat them.

Many health care professionals, such as physicians and nurses, assume that a certain amount of limiting illness is normal for an aging person, an assumption that is *absolutely untrue.* Yes, limiting chronic conditions are common among older people, but many of these conditions are preventable, most are treatable, and all can be compensated for to some extent. Limiting physical illness is *atypical* of older people at any age.

The social consequences of chronic conditions are of two types: (a) social limits imposed by other people's perceptions of the illness and (b) functional limits imposed by the illness. *Social limits* are often much more severe than the physical limits. For instance, take the case of Dr. T. He suffered a heart attack at age 49 and was disabled for about six months. Still it took him two years to convince his colleagues that he had recovered and that they could refer patients to him. The major *functional limit* caused by illness in later life is in the area of employment. Parnes and Nestel (1981) found that 51 percent of the 2,016 men who retired during their study had retired because of poor health. Poor health also poses by far the greatest limitation on both participation in the community and leisure pursuits, although the proportion of older people affected in nonemployment areas is lower than 20 percent.

Summary

The basic causes of physical aging are still a mystery. The maximum life span of the species is probably genetically determined, and differences in individual longevity are definitely related to differences in heredity. However, these factors do not explain why, even when free of disease, we age as we approach the end of our allotted life span. There are numerous factors that may explain physical aging. Errors in the production of new cells may make these cells less effective and, in turn, create less viable tissues, organs, and physiological systems. Cross-links between certain cell molecules increasingly diminish their functioning. The body's immune system becomes less effective at warding off disease, and it also produces increasing

numbers of auto-immune antibodies that attack normal cells. The endocrine glands become less efficient at maintaining homeostasis. The nervous system's capacity to control and integrate various functions declines. These changes, often cumulative, can all interact with one another.

The consequences of all these physiological changes include reduced capacity to mobilize physical energy, shorter stature, and lessened mobility and coordination. However, in the absence of disease, these changes seldom reduce physical resources below the minimum needed for normal adult functioning.

Physical changes such as wrinkled skin, gray hair, and midriff bulge are functionally unimportant. But, they are important symbolically because they are used to label people as belonging to that less desirable social category—the elderly. Changes in appearance can also be threatening to those who idealize physical attractiveness.

As a cohort grows older, the incidence of acute, short-term illness declines while chronic conditions become more prevalent. But although these changes accompany aging of the *cohort,* they do not necessarily accompany aging for the *individuals* in the cohort. The older a cohort, the larger the percentage in the cohort whose activities are limited by chronic conditions. Nonetheless, the proportion of the elderly with no limitations on activity has actually gone up substantially in recent years, indicating that more people are enjoying a healthy aging. The major causes of activity limitation in later life are mainly heart disease and arthritis/rheumatism, both moderately preventable and treatable now and likely to become more so in the future.

Thus, while physical aging certainly involves loss of capacity, the key question is how much capacity is left. Those aging people who avoid or successfully manage disabling chronic conditions are left with ample physical resources to continue leading enjoyable lives.

Chapter 5

Psychological Aging

Psychology is a vast field of study that includes specific capacities such as vision, memory, thinking, problem solving, intelligence, reaction time, and the like. It also covers the more holistic study of the mind: the nature and content of consciousness, the role of the unconscious, and the relation of mind to behavior. Psychology is also concerned with the interchange between the person and his or her physical and social environments and with the person's adaptation to internal experiences as well as external experiences of the world. In addition, psychology is concerned with mental illness. Aging has been studied in relation to all these concerns of psychology. In this chapter we will review concepts and research findings in three very different areas: (1) the effects of aging on specific psychological functions, (2) aging and human development, and (3) aging and mental health.

In recent years the volume of research in psychology has exploded, especially concerning specific psychological functions, making a thorough review well beyond the scope of this book. We will, however, look at the major findings from each area and refer you to recent, extensive reviews of the literature, three of which are particularly valuable: Birren and Schaie, 1977; Birren and Sloane, 1980; and Busse and Blazer, 1980.

Aging and Specific Psychological Functions

Many of the basic psychological processes, such as sensation, perception, and motor performance, have obvious links to physical aging. As a result, they tend to follow the maturation–maturity–aging model presented in Chapter 4. However, when we begin to examine psychological processes in which experience can play a part, such as intelligence, problem solving, and learning, then the picture is less clear-cut. The more closely a function is tied to physical capacities, particularly physical coordination, the more likely it is to decline with age. The more heavily a function depends on experience, the more likely it will increase and the less likely it will decline with age. In general, practiced skills tend to be maintained to a greater extent than unpracticed ones. In addition, although many laboratory studies show declines in various aspects of cognition, such as memory and learning, data from real-life performance of older adults show much less serious age-related changes. Finally, as with physical functions, the point of onset of psychological aging and the rate of change connected with it vary widely from person to person.

As we examine various psychological functions, keep in mind that we are interested mainly in the effects of age on the social functioning and psychological well-being of the elderly. We are less concerned with levels of statistical significance of laboratory research on these functions.

Sensory Processes

The senses are the means by which the human mind experiences the world outside and inside the body. In order to adapt to and interact with the environment, the individual depends on the senses to gather information about it. Nonetheless, the sensory process is not particularly complex. Sensory organs pick up information about changes in the internal or external environment and pass this information on to the brain, where all of the input from the sensory organs is collected and organized. The subjective result is called *sensory experience*.

The minimum amount of stimulation a sensory organ must experience before sensory information is passed to the brain is called a *threshold:* The higher the threshold, the more stimulus there must be to get information to the brain. Thus, for example, some people have a low threshold for sound and require very little sound to hear, and others have a high sound threshold and require a considerable amount. In studying the operation of the sensory processes as a function of age, we will be concerned not only with changes in threshold that come with advancing age but also with the possible failure of a particular sensory process.*

Vision.   Vision is a particularly adaptable sense. It can receive experience over a wide range of color, intensity, distance, and field angle. The eye has an iris for controlling the amount of light that reaches the optic nerve via the retina, and a lens for bending the light that enters the pupil (the opening in the center of the iris) so as to focus the light pattern on the retina.

In order to focus light from both near and distant objects, the eye lens must change shape. As age increases, the ability of the lens to change shape and thereby focus on very near objects decreases. Hence, many older people need glasses for reading, if for nothing else. The tendency toward farsightedness (presbyopia) increases about ten-fold between age 10 and age 60, but not much more thereafter (Roberts, 1968).

The size of the pupil, which is important because it controls the amount of light that enters the eye, is also influenced by age. In one study, 37 percent of those 65 and over showed no change in pupil size in response to changes in light intensity; 56 percent showed no change in pupil size in response to changes in lens shape (Howell, 1949). Lens shape and pupil size are important because proper focusing of an image on the retina requires both suitable quality of light (controlled by the lens) and the proper amount (controlled by the iris). Since both the lens and the iris show a decline in function with increasing age, vision as a whole gets poorer. The average diameter of the pupil also narrows with age, greatly influencing the amount of

---

*For a more detailed discussion of aging and sensory processes, see Botwinick (1978), Birren and Schaie (1977), and Busse and Glazer (1980).

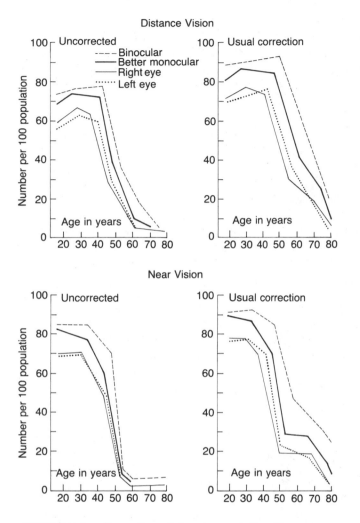

FIGURE 5-1   Proportion of American adults with monocular and binocular visual acuity of 20/20 or better at distance and 14/14 or better at near: United States, 1961–1962. *Source:* Roberts, 1968: 3.

light entering the eye. The eye of the average 60-year-old admits only about one-third as much light as the eye of the average 20-year-old.

Visual acuity is relatively poor for young children but rapidly increases in quality, hitting its peak at about age 30. Thereafter, a marked decline begins. By age 60, few people have normal vision, even with correction. The most common

problem is loss of ability to focus on near objects, which hampers ability to read (Botwinick, 1978:143). However, there are many exceptions to this general trend, because visual acuity is one of the most variable of human senses. Figure 5-1 shows how the percentage of the population with normal vision changes with age.

But this is not all of the story. We are really less interested in peak performance than in ability to perform to a socially defined minimum level of performance. For example, in order to get an unrestricted driver's license in Ohio, an adult must have distance visual acuity of 20/40 or better. As Figure 5-2 shows, the percentage of people with *uncorrected* distance vision of 20/40 or better increases slightly from age 20 to age 40 and then drops sharply until age 70, when it begins to level off. Aging reduces the percentage who are visually qualified to drive from over 90 percent at age 40 to just 30 percent at age 80. However, if we look at *corrected* vision, we see that by age 60, more than 90 percent are still visually qualified for unrestricted driving, and at age 80, 70 percent are still qualified. In addition, people with 20/60 to 20/45 distance vision are qualified by law for a "daytime only" driver's license, which adds another 15 percent —making a total of 85 percent qualified to drive at age 80. Thus, *compensation* allows driver visual qualification at age 80 to increase from 30 percent without compensation to 85 percent with it.

Visual adaptation to dark involves both the speed and the adequacy of adaptation. Older

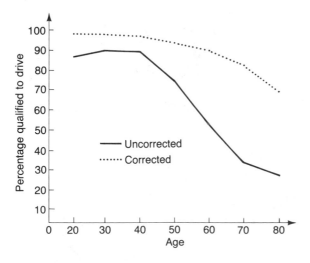

FIGURE 5-2   Percentage of people visually qualified to drive, for corrected and uncorrected vision. *Source:* Adapted from Roberts, 1968: 10.

people seem to adapt about as fast as the young, but their adaptation is not nearly as good (Botwinick, 1978:145). They also find it more difficult to distinguish between levels of brightness. In addition, the stimulus threshold of the optic nerve increases. Color vision also changes as the individual grows older: The lens gradually yellows and thereby filters out violet, blue, and green. The threshold for these colors increases significantly as people grow older, and it is for this reason that older people see yellow, orange, and red more easily than darker colors.

Because of all these changes to the eye, older people need either glasses or large-print books for reading, and close work of all kinds becomes more difficult. General levels of illumination must be significantly higher for older people to get the same visual impact as young people. Older people need more visual contrast compared to young adults (Sekuler and Hutman, 1980). Poor adaptation to darkness means that older people have difficulty driving at night, which does not mean that older people should not drive at night, merely that they must exercise extra care. Finally, changes in color vision mean that for older people to get the same satisfaction from looking at colors as young people, their environment must present more yellow, orange, and red, and less violet, blue, and green.

About 25 percent of people over 70 have cataracts, a clouding of the lens that produces diffusion of light, heightened sensitivity to glare, and impairment of vision (Botwinick, 1978:144). Treatment of cataracts involves surgically removing the natural lens and replacing it with a contact lens.

Only a small percentage of older Americans are blind—2.6 percent at age 65 to 74 compared to 8.3 percent of those 75 or over (National Center for Health Statistics, 1959:9). Yet this represents a large proportion of the total population of the blind. One study found that 55 percent of the blindness in California occurred after age 65, and 85 percent after age 45 (Birren, 1964b:84). Thus, while only a relatively small proportion of old people are blind, blindness is definitely related to age.*

Hearing. Hearing, the second major sense, has many aspects, but the most essential ones are the detecting of the pitch (frequency) of sound, its intensity, and the time interval over which it occurs. As people grow older, their reactions to frequency and intensity change, but there is no evidence to indicate that ability to distinguish time intervals changes significantly with age. Why these changes occur is not clear (A. Weiss, 1959).

Hearing loss begins at about age 20. Very gradually people lose their ability to hear certain frequencies and to discriminate among adjacent frequencies. This type of hearing loss is only slight for low-pitched sounds, but tends to be considerable for high-pitched sounds. Thus, as age increases, higher sounds get relatively harder to hear. About 13 percent of the older population experience severe hearing loss (Corso, 1977). Most loss of hearing involves loss of sensory receptors in the ear and loss of nerve cells in the auditory pathway to the brain (Marsh, 1980).

Intensity threshold also changes with advancing age. There are some frequencies that older people cannot hear no matter how loud, but even within the range of pitch they can hear, the threshold of hearing is higher, particularly for higher pitches (Botwinick, 1978:147).

Botwinick (1978:146) cites certain methodological problems that may lead diagnosticians to overestimate hearing loss. Apparently, older people (1) are more cautious and therefore tend to report hearing things only when fairly sure they have heard them, and (2) have more difficulty concentrating on hearing.

Older people are more susceptible to ear damage than the young. Thus, industrial noise produces greater hearing loss among older workers than among younger ones. Older people, even those with relatively slight hearing loss, have greater difficulty making the fine distinctions required to comprehend speech. After about age 55, there is also a consistent sex difference in hearing ability, which prior to that point is about equal for men and women. After age 55 considerably more men show hearing loss. Botwinick (1978:148) suggests that greater exposure to noise pollution on the job may be the cause.

In summary, as people grow older they have more difficulty hearing high-pitched sounds and sounds of low intensity. That may explain why organ music (rich in low tones) is popular among older people; why older people need to play radio and television louder; and why background noise is more distracting to older listeners (Botwinick, 1978:149).

Impaired hearing is a hearing loss of sufficient magnitude to reduce the individual's capacity to interact successfully with the environment. Loss of hearing does not always impair hearing. For example, the individual with good eyesight can still compensate for hearing loss by reading lips. In addition, hearing loss does not seem to reduce social involvement (Norris and Cunningham, 1981).

Hearing loss can have a major impact on speech communication. Age-related changes in ability to discriminate among sounds make speech more difficult to comprehend, especially when people talk fast, when there is background noise, or when there is distortion or reverberation of sound (Corso, 1977:550). Changes in capacity to make vocal sounds add to speech problems, although these changes can often be offset by retraining (Corso, 1977:551).

Loss of either vision or hearing can be partly compensated for by the other, but when both decline simultaneously, as is so often the case among older people, adaptation to the environment can be a serious problem. Not only is earning ability adversely affected, but those

---

*For greater detail on vision see Marsh (1980).

who deal with such doubly handicapped people must learn to take the limitations into account in order to help them make maximum use of their capabilities and opportunities.

Taste, Smell, and Body Sensations.   The evidence indicates that all four *taste* qualities— sweet, salt, bitter, and sour—show an elevated threshold after age 50. Women remain more sensitive to taste than men; Botwinick (1978:150) suggests that smoking may be a factor in this differential. Not only do individual taste buds become less sensitive with aging, but also the number of functional taste buds drops slightly. People in later life are apt to require more highly seasoned food to receive the same taste satisfactions as when they were 20. They also seem to prefer tart tastes and to show less interest in sweets. Nevertheless, age changes in taste sensitivity tend to be small (Moore, Nielsen, and Mistretta, 1982; Weiffenbach, Baum, and Burghauser, 1982).

Research on the sense of *smell* is sparse, but the weight of the evidence indicates little age change (Engen, 1977:560). Other factors, such as smoking and air pollution, seem to play a much bigger part in changing sensitivity to smell.

Engen (1977:554) points out that the senses of taste and smell are of greater importance than the research evidence indicates. These senses are major components in one's capacity to enjoy. They are also important to one's capacity to survive, for example, in detecting spoiled food, smoke, or natural gas.

The so-called general *body sensations* include touch, pain, muscle movement, and vibration. Sensitivity to touch appears to increase from birth to about age 45, after which the threshold rises sharply. Pain is important in alerting the body to emergency, something within or outside the body that threatens its well-being. Older people appear less sensitive to pain than do young people. However, it is difficult to measure pain because both the feeling and reporting of pain are conditioned by cultural and person-

ality factors. Laboratory data are few, and they often show no age change in pain threshold (Botwinick, 1978:150).

As people grow older, they make more errors in estimating the direction of muscle action. The ability to detect vibrations appears to decline with age only for the lower extremities of the body.

The Perceptual Processes

The senses provide the means for assembling and classifying information, but not for evaluating it. The process of evaluating information gathered by the senses and giving it meaning is called *perception*. Not all sensory input is perceived, for perception is a conscious process and some senses, such as the sense of balance, are mainly nonconscious. But for every sense in which there is consciousness of the stimulus received, there is an evaluative perception. In perception, not all of the information collected may be given equal weight. In visual perception, for example, shape appears to be a more important characteristic than color in evaluating an object.

Older people tend to underestimate the passage of time much more than younger people do. Thus, they are very likely to let time "slip by." They are also less capable of judging the speed of a moving object.

Closure is the ability to come to a decision concerning the evaluation of a stimulus. People are thought to become more cautious and less capable of closure as they grow older. This tendency may partly account for the apparent indecisiveness of some older people. Moreover, people seem to suffer a decline with age in the general speed with which they can organize and evaluate stimuli.

Most research shows an age decrement in perception. One explanation for this is that aging affects the speed with which the nervous system can process one stimulus and make way for the next. The nervous system "trace" of the initial stimulus interferes with perception of subsequent stimuli. This explanation is consistent with a wide variety of research findings that show that with increasing age the time between successive stimuli must be increased in order for accurate perception to occur. Also, certain perceptual illusions are more easily produced in older people. For example, older subjects see a continuous motion picture at about 34 frames per second, while 20-year-olds still see discrete pictures at 39 frames per second (Botwinick, 1978:158).

For many of the sensory and perceptual processes, it would appear, declines in function seldom seriously hamper behavior until after age 70. "Until that time, disease and other unique circumstances would appear to be more relevant than an intrinsic age-related change would be" (Birren, 1964:107).

Psychomotor Performance

The term *psychomotor performance* refers to a complex chain of activity that begins with a sensory mechanism and ends with a reaction, usually muscular. A muscle that acts as a part of a stimulus-response chain is called an *effector*. Between the sense organs and the effectors lies a chain of brain mechanisms called *central processes*. Ideally, psychomotor performance involves sensory input; attaching meaning to that input through perception; incorporating the perceived information into the mind alongside other ideas (integration); making a decision concerning any action required by this new information; sending neural signals to the appropriate effector; and activating the effector (response). This process is much more complex than simple sensation or perception.

Psychomotor performance is limited by the capacities of the various parts of the sensorimotor system.* In most cases, the sensory and

effector mechanisms are quite capable of handling a task. Hence, the limits on performance are usually set by "the central mechanisms dealing with perception, with translation from perception to action, and with the detailed control of action" (Welford, 1959:563). Decision making related to performance is particularly slowed by age (Welford, 1977a).

Performance capacity is a function not only of the available pathways in the brain, but also of the strength of the sensory "signal" and its relative strength compared with other signals entering the brain at the same time. A decline in absolute or relative signal strength can be partially offset by taking more time to integrate incoming data. Such compensation may explain much of the slowness of performance associated with aging. Errors are likely to result if the older individual cannot take the extra time needed—too little information being processed between the moment sensory input is received and the time when action must be taken.

The most serious sensory limitation on psychomotor performance is the general rise in sensory thresholds. Once a sensory response is triggered, however, the senses pose little problem. Research findings suggest that changes in performance would remain even if there were some way to eliminate sensory decline completely (Botwinick, 1978). There is also only a negligible decline in the speed of nerve conduction as age increases.

The effectors usually are not a prime weakness in the psychomotor chain. In fact, any poor muscle performance in old age may be more a result of poor coordination than decline in muscular strength or endurance (Shock and Norris, 1970). Since coordination is under the control of the central processes, any inefficiency of effectors in old age could be considered a result rather than a cause of poor psychomotor performance.

The important limitations on psychomotor performance, then, appear to come from the central processes. But regardless of the cause of

---

*This discussion is drawn mainly from Welford (1959; 1977a).

the limitations, there are definite changes in observed psychomotor performance as the individual ages. The most important changes from the point of view of social functioning are in reaction time, speed and accuracy of response, and ability to make complex responses.

Reaction Time.   Reaction time is usually defined as the period that elapses between the repesentation of a stimulus and the beginning of the response to that stimulus; and traditionally it has been considered a measure of the time used by the central processes.

Reaction time increases with age. Though very slight for simple tasks, this increase becomes greater as tasks grow more complex. The more choices involved in a task, the longer it takes a person to react. The slowing of reactions in older people may result mainly from a tendency toward care and accuracy that seems to characterize this group. Since they tend to spend more than an average amount of time checking results, part of their slowness may be the difference between the time required for *accuracy* and that required for *certainty*.

The slowing of reaction time appears to involve chiefly the central processes. Neither the speed of input nor the speed of output is responsible and, as mentioned, slowing results partly from a desire for certainty rather than a physical inability to act quickly. Botwinick (1978:205) points out, however, that response time does not have a clear influence on higher processes such as cognition. In addition, exercise, increased motivation, and practice can partly counteract the effects of slowed reaction time, and extended practice may eliminate the slowdown completely. Finally, individual differences in reaction time are so great that, even with age changes, very many older people are quicker in response time than many young adults.

Speed and Accuracy.   *Speed* of movement also tends to decrease with age. Again the evidence points to the central processes as the source

rather than to any loss of muscle ability. In fact, when older people try to hurry, their control capabilities are often so poor that their movements appear jerky. The central processes are further implicated because for simple movements the slowing with age is only slight, whereas for complex movements, in which the same muscles must be more controlled, the slowing with age is more marked.

These same observations apply to *accuracy*. Accuracy of movement declines as the individual grows older, unless more time is taken to compensate for the greater difficulty in controlling the response (Welford, 1959:584–599).

Complex Performance.   A complex performance is a series of actions in response to a complex stimulus. It has been found that the brain operates serially on data—that is, it deals with stimuli as they arrive; if one response is not completed before a new stimulus arrives, then the new stimulus must wait its turn. Processing may take older people longer. Certainly, the research data point in this direction. If this hypothesis is true, it could explain why response time increases with age.

Another factor that seems important in producing age differences in complex performance is the strategy used to solve a complex problem. In such a situation, young people, knowing they are capable of quick response, use trial-and-error extensively. Older people, on the other hand, knowing that they cannot respond quickly, tend to think the problem through, hoping to solve it in the fewest possible tries. The result is that, with unlimited time available, older people do about as well as their younger counterparts in solving complex problems. When time is limited, however, and reflection on the problem is not feasible, older people do much worse because they are forced to use trial-and-error. The trial-and-error method is fruitful only with a large number of trials; the slowness of the older person makes such a task very difficult (Welford, 1959:600–602).

In summary, it appears that the psychomotor performance of older people is limited more by the central processes than by any other factor. The central processes can do only a limited amount in a given time. Any loss in capacity can be offset by taking longer, but when this is not possible, a much larger percentage of errors will be observed among older people than among the young. The more complex the integrating and controlling functions must be, the more aging slows down performance. Older people thus shift their emphasis from speed to accuracy.

These various factors in psychomotor performance have important implications. First, factors other than changes in the central processes have relatively little influence on psychomotor response. Also, the central processes are very difficult to offset mechanically, the way glasses or hearing aids can offset sensory loss. Reaction time, speed and accuracy of movement, and organization of complex performance all suffer as a result of the decline in integrating and controlling ability of the central processes in the later years. Yet, whenever and wherever speed is *not* important, age changes in psychomotor performance have little effect on the capacity of older adults to function in typical adult activities such as employment (Welford, 1977a:491).

Mental Functioning

Sensation, perception, and psychomotor performance are all very important for the functioning of the individual, yet in human beings as in no other animal these processes must take a back seat to mental functioning. The term *mental functioning* refers to a large group of complex processes, subdivided for convenience into learning, memory, thinking, problem solving, creativity, and intelligence.

Learning.   *Learning* is the acquisition of information or skills and is usually measured by improvements in task performance. All studies of performance indicate a decline in learning with age. Clearly, however, there are a number of factors other than learning ability that affect performance, including motivation, performance speed, indigence, ill health, and physiological states. In practice, it is extremely difficult to separate these components of performance so as to examine the influence of learning ability, although a number of studies have attempted to do so. What this means is that we are in a poor position to say just what effect age has on learning ability.

Although learning performance tends to decline with age, the decline is not substantial until past age 70 (Arenberg and Robertson-Tchabo, 1980). All age groups *can* learn. Given a bit more time, older people can usually learn anything that other people do. Extra time is required to learn information or skills as well as to demonstrate that learning has occurred. Tasks that are particularly conducive to good performance by older people are those that involve manipulation of concrete objects or symbols, distinct and unambiguous responses, and low interference from prior learning.

Arenberg and Robertson-Tchabo (1980) pointed out that the literature on learning and aging often confuses age changes in learning *ability* with age changes in *competence*. Because everyday environments seldom require people to use their maximum learning capacity, even substantial age changes can occur without affecting social competence. We shall see that this problem is common to much of the research on aging and cognitive ability. In addition, we should not assume that age declines in learning performance can never be modified. For example, Sterns and his colleagues (Sterns et al., 1977) trained older drivers to perform better, improvements that were still there six months later.

Memory.   Memory is intimately related to learning, since to remember is partial evidence of learning. Thus, a person who does not learn has nothing to remember, and conversely, a person who cannot remember shows no sign of having learned.

There are essentially four *types of memory:* short-term, recent, remote, and old. *Short-term* (immediate) *memory* involves recall after very little delay, from as little as 5 seconds up to 30 seconds. *Recent memory* is recall after a brief period, from one hour to several days. *Remote memory* refers to recall of events that took place in one's distant past and that have been recalled frequently throughout the course of a lifetime. *Old memory* means recall of distant personal events that have not been thought of or rehearsed since.

Regardless of type, there are three *stages of memory:* registration, retention, and recall. *Registration* is the "recording" of learning or perceptions, and is analogous to the recording of sound on a tape recorder. *Retention* refers to the ability to sustain registration over time. *Recall* is retrieval of material that has been registered and retained. In all types of memory, a failure at any of these stages results in no *measurable* memory.

It is commonly believed that all kinds of memory decline with advancing age, but it is not clear whether this deficit results from failing memory or from declining ability to learn. There appears to be a greater age loss in short-term and recent memory than in remote or old memory, and the decline with age in memory function is less for rote memory than for logical memory. As age increases, the retention of things heard becomes increasingly superior to the retention of things seen, and use of both gives better results than the use of either separately. However, some older people escape memory loss altogether. People who exercise their memories tend to maintain both remote and recent memory well into old age.

Any attempt to reverse or compensate for a decline in memory functions must obviously depend on some notion of why people forget. None of the several theories about why memory functions decline with age has yet proved effective in identifying the specific cause of the age deficit (Salthouse, 1982:154). Until they do, we

will be in a poor position to intervene in this process.

Thinking.   Via learning and memory, human beings have at their disposal a great many separate mental images. *Thinking, problem solving,* and *creativity* are all terms that apply to the manipulation of ideas and symbols.

Thinking can be defined as the process of developing new ideas. Thinking helps bring order to the chaos of data brought into the mind by learning and perception by differentiating and categorizing these data into what psychologists call *concepts* (Botwinick, 1967:156).

Differentiation occurs at two separate levels. The first is the level of sensation, perception, or learning. Age declines in these functions would serve as effective barriers to concept formation. A second level of differentiation involves a process psychologists call *stimulus generalization.* Stimulus generalization makes different stimuli functionally equivalent, and the more similar the stimuli, the more nearly equal the responses. For example, individual oranges are unique in weight, thickness of skin, number of seeds, number of bumps on their skins, and so on. Yet we have the mental capacity to consider all oranges alike. This capacity is stimulus generalization, and it is an essential prerequisite for the process of *categorization.*

The capacity for stimulus generalization appears to decline with age. When declines in speed are accounted for, most older people produce more specific differentiations, indicating that they are less capable of stimulus generalization than their younger counterparts. Therefore, when not given enough time, older people tend to be confused by tasks that require stimulus generalization. Botwinick (1967:158) advances this as a reason for the cautiousness older people seem to value.

Once mental information has been differentiated, it must be categorized. *Categorization* allows information to be dealt with in general terms, which is much easier than trying to deal with everything in specifics. Thus, when we encounter a stop sign we can deal with it as a member of a class of objects rather than trying to figure out why it is there, who put it there, and so on. The assumptions we make when we encounter a stop sign are the result of stimulus generalization and categorization.

Older people seem to be particularly poor at forming concepts. *Concept formation* often involves making logical inferences and generalizations. Older people have been found to resist forming a higher-order generalization and to refuse choosing one when given the opportunity. All studies seem to agree that as age increases, ability at concept formation and its components declines.

Yet common sense tells us that older people form concepts, and that some do it exceedingly well. What does it mean, then, when we say that older people consistently show a decline in performance on tests of differentiation and categorization? Data from studies where education level was controlled suggest that both level and type of education may modify, but not eliminate, the relationship between age and measured thinking ability (Botwinick, 1967:164). Likewise, studies that have held IQ constant have shown a reduction in the age–thinking association, although not completely. Some studies have also shown that declines in memory function do not account for the age decline in ability to form concepts. Other studies suggest that those who retain the greatest degree of verbal facility in old age are also those who retain the greatest skill in concept formation (Schaie, 1980).

In their entirety, these data suggest that concept formation is not completely independent of other skills such as learning and intelligence, but at the same time is not completely dependent on them either. A substantial part of the decline with age in measured ability to form concepts appears to be genuine, not caused by artifacts of the measurement process or by the influence of intervening variables.

Problem Solving.   Problem solving is the making of choices and decisions through analysis, logic, and thinking. Whereas thinking involves the differentiation and categorization of mental data, problem solving entails making logical deductions about these categories, their properties, and differences among them. Problem solving differs from learning in that learning is the *acquisition* of skills and perceptions, while problem solving is *using* these skills and perceptions to make choices.

Older people are at a disadvantage in solving problems if many items of information must be dealt with simultaneously. They have more difficulty giving meaning to stimuli presented and have more trouble remembering this information later when it must be used to derive a solution. The number of errors made in solving problems rises steadily with age. Older people take a long time to recognize the explicit goal of a particular problem. Their search for information is thus characterized by haphazard questioning rather than by concentration on a single path to the goal. They attain information randomly, have trouble separating the relevant from the irrelevant, and thus tend to be overwhelmed by a multitude of irrelevant facts. They also tend toward repetitive behavior, a tendency that can be disruptive in situations where the nature of problems and their solutions is constantly and rapidly changing, but that can be advantageous in situations that are changing slowly or not at all (Botwinick, 1967: 172–174).

In general, problem solving shows the same trend of decline that has been observed in the other mental processes. Again, although slight decrements occur earlier, socially meaningful decrements seldom take place until the seventies (Seigler, 1980). In addition, Arenberg (1968) found that when abstract problems are presented in familiar, concrete terms older people are better able to solve them. In addition, some of the data on the role of education indicate that older people whose jobs had trained them to use deductive reasoning (for example, physicians) showed deductive ability comparable to younger colleagues (Cijfer, 1966). This finding suggests that there may be sizable cultural and social (cohort) factors operating in the cross-sectional data that have been the mainstay of our knowledge of the relationship between age and problem solving. Indeed, Kesler, Denney, and Whitely (1976) found that what had been presumed to be age effects in problem solving disappeared when education and nonverbal intelligence were controlled.

Creativity.   Creativity is problem solving that is unique, original, and inventive. The biggest problem in studying creativity is deciding how to define the creative person. Colleague ratings and psychological test scores have been used, but the most frequently used method counts how many times the individual has had his or her writing published. H. Lehman (1953) examined historical accounts of major developments in various academic fields and found that the rate of publication declined very gradually through age 70. Clemente and Hendricks (1973) found no correlation between age at receipt of the doctorate and six operational indices of publication output.

More recently, Shin and Putnam (1982) found that the median age of selection for the Nobel Prize or for the post of president of a scientific society ranged from 48.9 to 64.6. Certainly individuals who remain exceptionally creative are prevalent enough in every field, and declines in creativity are gradual enough that one should not assume that older people automatically reach an end to their creativity, particularly at any given chronological age.

A crucial issue in the study of creativity revolves around social supports of creative effort. Zuckerman and Merton (1972) pointed out that within the academic science disciplines the political cards are stacked in favor of older members, who are overrepresented in committee posts, on proposal review committees, among journal referees, and so on. On the other side, however, is the pressure placed on established scholars to move into supervisory and leadership positions, which often takes them away from their own individual work. In addition, the individual seldom gets to be "established" just by virtue of growing old. Crane (1965) suggests that motivation and selection of research topics are both important. Although people in academic competition fall by the wayside and fade into obscurity, it is difficult to experience falling into obscurity unless you live long enough. These points suggest that social factors mediate age differences in raw creativity, but to an unknown extent.

Intelligence.   When we think of intelligence, we usually mean an ability that is both *potential* and *actual*. In practice, however, we always deal with *measured* abilities. Measured intelligence is defined in terms of responses to items on a test. Yet no matter how extensive or well-prepared a test is, there is always a margin of error in its measurement of actual mental ability.

Perhaps the most popular test in studies of adult intelligence and its age-related changes is the *Wechsler Adult Intelligence Scale (WAIS)*. *Intelligence Quotient (IQ)* is a score established by test performance in which the "normal" or average is 100. When the WAIS is used to measure adults aged 20 to 75 and over, there is an age factor built into the determination of what is normal. In Figure 5-3 the heavy black line plots mean raw WAIS score against age. Note that measured performance peaks at about age 25 and declines thereafter, increasingly so after age 65. The shaded area on the graph represents the handicap or advantage that is built into the WAIS IQ score in order to control for age. There could be a 40-point difference between a score at age 25 and one at age 75, yet the IQ score would be the same. The significance of this feature is that the most frequently used test of mental ability *assumes* that a 40-point drop in IQ score from age 25 to age 75 is typical.

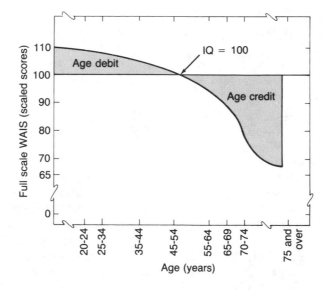

FIGURE 5-3 Full-scale WAIS scores as a function of age. *Source:* Botwinick, 1967: 3. Reprinted by permission.

Because the WAIS is widely used and because cross-sectional data consistently have shown a decline in score with increasing age, it has been widely assumed that aging causes a decline in intelligence. There are several problems with this interpretation, however. To begin with, since the prime use of intelligence tests is to aid in placing people in appropriate academic and job careers, most intelligence tests measure achievement in terms of skills *currently* emphasized by the educational system, not skills that may have been stressed in earlier eras. This bias puts older people at a disadvantage. That intelligence tests put a premium on speed of response also puts older people at a disadvantage compared to younger people with identical mental ability.

Adults vary a great deal in terms of psychological state, educational background, career history, health, and environment, all of which have been shown to influence intelligence test scores. In addition, intelligence is a complex of abilities, not merely a single factor. Baltes and Labouvie (1973), for example, report various studies that considered as many as twenty primary mental abilities. Test scores by age vary depending on which abilities are emphasized. Salthouse (1982) reviewed the results of several studies on selected subtests of the WAIS and found that vocabulary and information scores tended to remain stable or increase with respondent age, whereas series completion and picture completion showed marked decline. Heron and Chown (1967) questioned whether composite or overall scores have much validity.

Another factor that confuses interpretation of IQ scores concerns the effect of mortality. On the one hand, the possibility that people of lower intelligence die sooner leads to an underestimate of the average drop in intelligence. On the other hand, intelligence test scores have been shown to drop significantly just before death (Jarvik and Blum, 1971), a tendency that could lead to an overestimation of the drop.

Finally, quite different results are obtained from cross-sectional and longitudinal studies. Cross-sectional studies generally report significant age decrements in intelligence scores, while longitudinal studies tend to show a variety of age patterns in measured intelligence (Baltes and Labouvie, 1973:168). Disentangling all of these interconnected factors in order to discern age changes in mental functioning is difficult indeed. In 1956 and again in 1963, Nesselroade, Schaie, and Baltes (1972) tested a sample of 301 respondents ranging in age from 21 to 71. They were able to assess the impact of cohort differences as well as age change on mental functioning.

The researchers measures of mental functioning consisted of 13 variables taken from the Primary Mental Abilities Test (Thurstone and Thurstone, 1949) and from the Test of Behavioral Rigidity (Schaie, 1960). Responses to these subtests were factor analyzed separately for 1956 and 1963 and yielded four factors that were stable over the 7-year interval: crystallized intelligence, cognitive flexibility, visuomotor flexibility, and visualization. *Crystallized intelligence* was of especial interest because it related to a particular theory of the development of intelligence (Horn, 1966), according to which crystallized intelligence is a direct result of experience, while fluid intelligence is more biologically determined. Crystallized intelligence as measured in this study was a composite of scores on tests of verbal meaning, reasoning, numbers, word fluency, capitals, and social responsibility. Figure 5-4 presents the results of their data analysis.

The graphs show that, in general, the variations between generations (between groups in the cross-sectional data) tended to be much greater than the variations within specific cohorts (the dotted lines) in the 7-year study period. In fact, cognitive flexibility and visualization showed a persistent cohort difference, but no age decrement at all. The two age changes that did appear went in opposite directions. (1) Visuomotor flexibility showed a decline with

age, which was to be expected, given the evidence on psychomotor performance reviewed earlier in the chapter. (2) Crystallized intelligence showed an increase in performance during the 7 years for all cohorts, but the older cohorts showed the largest increases. In other words, the generation gap in crystallized intelligence narrowed during the 7-year study period. These findings led the investigators to conclude that, for the cohorts they studied, generation was more important than age in explaining performance differentials on the dimensions they studied. They also concluded that historical change influences certain cohorts and ability dimensions more than others.

This study is an interesting example of what can be done to evaluate the impact of various causes of change. A word of caution, however: The 1963 restudy involved only 301 of the 500 original 1956 respondents, and they proved to score higher on all ability dimensions than those who were not restudied; there was no age difference in this bias. This situation illustrates the vulnerability of longitudinal research to participant availability for retest.

Baltes and Labouvie (1973:205–206), in an impressive review of the literature on intelligence, concluded that individual differences in intellectual functioning are great enough to badly erode the predictive value of age and that, in addition, age has a differential impact on various intellectual abilities. In general, age changes in intelligence were "surprisingly small" compared to either generational (cohort) differences or the "terminal drop" (just before death). In addition, studies of intervention suggest that age changes in intelligence can be altered, even in old age. The researchers also conclude that although biological aging undoubtedly influences intellectual functioning, there has been a tendency to underestimate or ignore the impact of environments for older people that are not conducive to "intellectual acquisition and maintenance." Botwinick (1978:230) concluded that education is much more important than age in explaining individ-

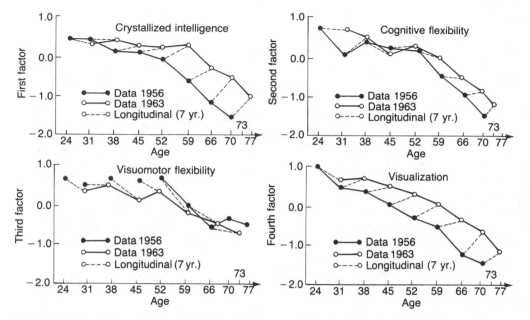

FIGURE 5-4 Differential age functions for four second-order factors of intelligence based on two cross-sectional (1956, 1963) and eight seven-year (1956–63) longitudinal studies. (Reprinted by permission of the publisher, the Gerontological Society, from J. R. Nesselroade, K. W. Schaie, & P. B. Baltes, "Ontogenetic and Generational Components of Structural and Quantitative Change in Adult Cognitive Behavior," *Journal of Gerontology, 27,* 1972. 222–228.)

ual differences in overall intellectual ability. Clearly, the issue of age changes in intelligence is quite controversial and is not likely to be resolved soon.

Practical Implications of Research into Mental Functioning

There are two main behavioral areas for which the practical implications of the foregoing research on aging and mental functioning are of interest: general social functioning and job performance. In terms of general social functioning, it is likely that age-related decrements affect only a small proportion of the population under age 70. This is because there is continuity of life style and habits; that is, most people continue to practice existing skills rather than learning new ones. In addition, for many, free-

dom from job demands means that learning, problem solving, and creative activity can be paced to suit the individual. There is no reason to believe that aging (as opposed to chronic disease or disability or generational differences) significantly limits social functioning. Even among older people who are institutional residents, a large proportion exceed the minimum capacity necessary for adequate social functioning (M. Lawton, 1972a).

Concerning job performance, Fozard and Carr (1972) pointed to the need for functional measures and to the inadequacy of chronological age as an index of potential job performance. Not all pertinent job skills are influenced by age; in those that are, the range of individual differences is too great to give much predictive power to age alone. Belbin and Belbin (1969) found that trainability tests consisting of small work samples were more effective in measuring job potential than were general tests of aptitude or ability. Fozard and Carr (1972) reported that both older workers and their employers consistently overestimated the functional demands of jobs. At the present time, many older workers are being arbitrarily denied jobs on the assumption that beyond a certain chronological age, people cannot perform adequately. The use of job-specific testing could result in better job performance at all ages, although such testing is unlikely as long as there is a labor surplus (McFarland, 1973).

Salthouse (1982:202–3) was impressed with the *absence* of age effects in most normal activities, given the consistent laboratory study findings of decline. He gave several reasons to be cautious when drawing conclusions about everyday life from laboratory results. First, there is a bias against reporting no change because such results often seem less exciting or noteworthy. Second, the variability *within* age groups is usually much greater than variability *between* age groups. Studies have seldom found age differences as high as 50 percent, but differences of this magnitude *within* age groups are not uncommon. Third, most activities of daily living are probably minimally demanding, which means that adults could experience substantial decrements in peak performance and still function well socially. Such performance deficits then become obvious only in emergencies, when time pressure increases, tasks become more complex, and experience is of less help. Fourth, home and job activities of older people have been highly practiced for literally thousands of hours (Salthouse, 1982:203).

Drives, Motives, and Emotions

Thus far we have considered how aging affects the various capabilities necessary for effective functioning. But the individual must also be willing to act. Energy for such action is mobilized by drives, motives, and emotions (Wigdor, 1980). Physical aging appears to increase the level of stimulation required to arouse human drives, motives, and emotions. In addition, age-related social factors such as opportunity for stimulation or boredom can also affect arousal.

Drives. Drives are unlearned bodily states that are frequently experienced as tension or restlessness and that make people want to act. When a person is hungry, for example, feelings of tension and restlessness do not have to be learned, they just appear. The primary drives that have been studied in relation to age changes include hunger, sex, and activity.

Hunger. There has been little systematic study among humans of age changes in hunger, but data from animal studies indicate that older animals are less driven by hunger and can withstand greater food deprivation than younger animals. The literature on the food habits of older people contradicts this picture somewhat. Some older people appear to have less appetite than their younger counterparts, but many older people continue to enjoy eating and do not reduce their food intake appreciably with age.

This seeming enigma raises an interesting point. Past learning associated with the satiation or reduction of drives is frequently overlooked as a factor influencing responses to drives. Certain drives appear regularly, and human culture contains patterns for satisfying them. These cultural patterns become ingrained in the individual as habits, which have a way of acting like drives. A reduction in a physiological state (drive) need not necessarily lead to a change in behavior. Hence, eating habits may persist even though the physiological basis for eating has diminished. When food consumption remains constant or increases with age, it is probably a result more of culture than of the hunger drive.

Another facet of this same question concerns the fact that behavior can serve more than one function. In measuring the hunger drive, for example, we observe only behavior toward food.

However, this behavior can result from habit, from a desire for taste sensation, or from a desire to socialize at mealtime, as well as from hunger. These dilemmas are present in the study of human drives, regardless of which one we study.

Sex.* Although sexual behavior declines with age, it does not disappear. Continued sexual activity in later life is associated with capacity for orgasm, age of partner, and health. Women, once they have discovered the continued capacity for sexual response after the death of a spouse, are apt to seek sexual gratification; the same is true of men; but for men the problem is less acute because at later ages there are many more single women than single men.

As part of their pioneering study of human sexual response, Masters and Johnson (1966) studied in great detail the sexual activity of a small number of older people. In aging women they found that steroid starvation and hormone imbalance following menopause often lead to changes in the sex organs that make coition and orgasm painful. Masters and Johnson considered pain a primary cause of reduced sexual activity in older women; and they contended that hormone therapy succeeds in increasing the sexual capacity of older women primarily because it eliminates pain rather than because it stimulates the sex drive, as had been widely thought. Despite steroid and hormone problems, most older women who have a regular sexual outlet are able to retain a much higher capacity for sexual performance than those who don't.

Male sexual responsiveness wanes with age, found Masters and Johnson. This appears to be true no matter how response is measured. After about age 60, sexual tension and reactive intensity during sexual expression are reduced. Masters and Johnson's data sustain the common notion that the sexual performance of the male

---

*This topic will be considered again in Chapter 7.

declines with age. However, except in cases of drastic physical infirmity, they contend, the greatest causative factor in this change is sociopsychological rather than biological. Mental or physical fatigue, boredom with one's partner, preoccupation with career or economic pursuits, overindulgence in food or drink, physical and mental infirmities, and particularly fear of failure are all held to be more important in the decline of sexual performance in the older male than aging in itself. As in the case of older women, Masters and Johnson found that one of the biggest factors associated with maintenance of effective sexuality in the older male was a continuing, regular outlet for sex.

Beginning in 1954, Duke University conducted a longitudinal study of a small sample of people age 60 and over that was reinterviewed every three years. Part of that study looked at sexual interest and behavior over time (Pfeiffer, 1977). Overall, they found that sexual *interest* tended to decline much less than sexual *behavior*, especially among the men, with declining frequency of sex being much more common than cessation. Interestingly, 25 percent of the older men reported an increase in sexual interest and activity over the 10-year period, compared to a very small percentage of women, and this pattern occurred primarily among unmarried men.

On a more positive note, Starr and Weiner (1981) found that 36 percent of the 800 older people they studied said that sex was better for them currently than when they were younger, 25 percent said it was worse, and 39 percent said it was the same. Most felt that sex should play a large part in an older couple's life. About 80 percent were sexually active, and a majority had intercourse at least once a week. Most experienced an increase in the spontaneity of sexual expression as a result of the empty nest and retirement.

Activity. Most animals appear to have a drive toward undirected, spontaneous activity (sometimes called *curiosity*). Animal studies have found that this drive first increases with age and then decreases. In rats, for example, spontaneous activity increases from birth to puberty, and declines from then on. This drive has not been studied in humans, but at least part of the lethargy to be found in some older people probably results from a decline in the drive toward activity. Nevertheless, the decline in available energy is probably more important than any decline in drive in reducing the spontaneous activity of older people.

In summary, it appears that drives wane as age increases, but because a good many factors intervene between drives and overt behavior, drives probably play a relatively small part in explaining behavior.

Motives.   Motives are closely related to drives. Here's how: Drives are highly generalized dispositions to action. Superimposed on these drives are motives—patterns of learned behavior that give specific direction to these general tendencies to act. Motives are thus specific, goal-directed, and learned. Since motives are learned, even relatively satiated human desires can be aroused, given a sufficient amount of stimulus; motives can also disappear if there is little opportunity to satisfy or reinforce them. As Kuhlen has stated,

> A society or culture decrees in many subtle ways, and in some not subtle, that certain types of stimulation will be brought to bear on certain age groups and largely withheld from those of other ages. . . . Moreover, since the motivational tendencies of people are very largely learned as a result of the reward and punishment systems to which they are exposed during the course of . . . development, it is reasonable to expect that motives may be *changed* during adulthood if the individual is exposed to a new set of punishment and reward patterns (1964a:210–211).

There is some evidence that achievement motivation declines with age, while motivation to exhibit competence may remain unchanged (Atchley, 1980:74; Maehr and Kleiber, 1981). Likewise, competitive urges may give way to

nurturing ones. Since this is a little-researched area, these conclusions are still very tentative.

Elias and Elias (1977:379) raise the important point that too much motivation can be as bad as too little in its effect on performance. Thus, it is important to learn how much motivation is appropriate to specific situations, something that is often socially defined and probably changes with age. This topic is much in need of research.

Emotions.   Emotions—such as fear, anger, anxiety, disgust, grief, joy, and surprise—are powerful mental states, often of an agitated nature. They are frequently accompanied by physiological changes in the gastrointestinal system or in the vasomotor system and are usually a response to an external situation. Emotions often, though not necessarily, lead to observable behavior. There is, however, always an internal state aroused as part of an emotional response.

Studies have shown that as people move into old age, their ability to exhibit emotions declines (Dean, 1962). For example, the expression of irritation and anger is known to decline with age. Yet since older people are frequently under a great deal of social pressure to suppress emotions such as anger, at least part of the observed age decline may be a function of changing social demands rather than changing capacity to experience emotion. This is another area in need of research.

Human Development: Personality and Self

Human development encompasses personality and self across the life span. The **self** is your perception of yourself—what you think you are like, what you think you should or should not be like, and how you feel about the fit between the two. *Personality* is how you appear to others, especially your attitudes, values, beliefs, habits, and preferences. Scholars have looked at personality and self through the life span in terms of stages and in terms of processes. In fact, the literature on human development and aging is overloaded with theories and concepts, so that even just a summary lies beyond the scope of this book. Instead, we will look at prominent examples of two types of theories: stage theories and process theories.

Stage Theories

The idea that people pass through stages of development has been around a long time. Perhaps the most influential stage theory of adult development was formulated by Erik Erikson (1963). Erikson's theory is mainly concerned with how people develop an identity in childhood and adolescence, but it also considers development in old age. To Erikson, identity is built on a foundation of trust, autonomy, initiative, and industry. These qualities, developed in childhood, allow individuals to form a view of themselves as capable, worthwhile, and safe. People who do *not* develop these qualities have difficulty trusting others, have doubts about their abilities, feel guilty about their poor performance, feel inferior to others, and have no confidence in their ability to face the changes of adulthood. Between these two extremes is a continuum along which individual identity can vary considerably.

According to Erikson, the main issue of human growth and development in early adulthood is learning to establish *intimacy*—close personal relationships. Developing intimacy involves learning to unite one's own identity with that of another person. People who do not develop intimacy remain isolated, still relating to others yet lacking a sense of union.

The developmental issue of middle adulthood is *generativity versus stagnation*. Generativity—the ability to support others, particularly one's children and other members of younger generations—involves caring and concern for younger people and also an interest in making a contribution to the world one lives in. Stagnation—when an individual does not learn to contribute to others—is typified by a lack of interest in others, especially the young, a feeling of having contributed nothing, and the appearance of just going through the motions.

To Erikson, the developmental issue of late adulthood is *ego integrity versus despair*. Ego integrity involves being able to see one's life as having been meaningful and to accept oneself as having both positive and negative characteristics, and to be unthreatened by this acceptance. Integrity provides the individual a basis for approaching the end of life with a feeling of having lived completely. Despair is the result of rejecting one's life and oneself and includes the realization that there is not enough time left to alter this assessment. The despairing person is prone to depression and is afraid of dying.

Erikson's stages are both incremental and contingent. That is, life is a process of continuous growth, provided one adequately resolves the life issue at each successive stage. In order to develop intimacy, one must first have developed a positive identity. In order to develop generativity, one must have the capacity for intimacy. And in order to develop integrity, one must feel the connectedness and contribution that come from intimacy and generativity. The progression of human growth in childhood is closely tied to chronological age by the expectations of home and school, but in adulthood the individual is freer to move at his or her own pace. Thus, although generativity may typify middle adulthood, many middle-aged people are still learning to deal with identity or intimacy; thus they feel irritated by demands to exhibit generativity.

Erikson's theory is most useful for what it suggests rather than for any scientific validity. Indeed, many of the theory's concepts, such as integrity and self-acceptance, are so difficult to measure that it may never be possible to test the theory scientifically. Nevertheless, Erikson's framework provides a tool for relating to people. By listening to people, we can get a sense of where they stand on the developmental issues Erikson raised, which in turn may help us understand not only their behavior but also their priorities and their aspirations.

Another stage theory of adult development is that of Levinson et al. (1978). To Levinson, the main work of adulthood is structuring one's life in a way that enhances it. Like Erikson, Levinson acknowledged the importance of intimacy; he also added occupational development as an important issue of early adulthood. Levinson extended Erikson's concept of the generativity of middle adulthood by adding *mentoring*—a relationship in which a middle-aged adult serves as a combination parent figure and friend to a young adult.

Process Theories

For many psychologists, human development does not involve discrete stages but instead is the result of the continuous operation of various developmental processes. Riegel (1975, 1976) contended that human development is a dialectical process that is itself caused by contradictory ideas or actions produced by the constant changes occurring in the person and his or her environment. These contradictions are not deficiencies to be corrected but invitations to a new level of integration. For example, you might notice how at times you are cautious and at other times adventurous. Accepting both parts of yourself as valid is a higher level of integration than putting them in opposition to one another in an effort to make yourself one or the other. "Developmental and historical tasks are never completed. At the very moment when completion seems to be achieved, new questions and doubts arise in the individual and in society" (Riegel, 1976:697). To Riegel, development is a process of resolving the doubts, questions, and contradictions that constantly flow through our consciousness. Riegel's theory is insightful in its focus on the everyday character of development. However, it says very little about the specific mechanisms for achieving the necessary resolution.

Whitbourne and Weinstock (1979) address more specifically the dynamics of continuous development. They argue that adult identity is an integration based on a person's knowledge about his or her physical and mental assets and liabilities, ideas (motives, goals, and attitudes), and social roles.* Identity serves to organize the interpretation of experiences—the assigning of subjective meaning to them. And identity can be modified by experience. The day-to-day contradictions that appear between the identity we bring to experience and the feedback we get from experience can be responded to in a number of ways. If the person is flexible about the content of his or her identity, then identity is a theory of the self that is constantly being tested, modified, and refined through experience (Kelley, 1955). To the extent that one's observations of oneself are honest, one's theory of self gets better as time goes on. That is, the results our identity leads us to expect are the results we get. And the more times our theory works, the greater our confidence in it and the greater our unwillingness to change it.

Sometimes people develop an identity but refuse to test it. They use their identity to decide how to act, but they do not let the results modify their ideas about themselves. Other people never quite develop a firm identity that could be tested; they don't quite know what to expect of themselves in various situations. The result is that they behave in an inconsistent and confused way.

Aging affects the stability of identity in several important ways. First, the longer one has an adult identity, the more times one's theory of self can be tested across various situations. This experience usually results in a stable personal identity that stands up well to the demands of day-to-day living. Second, the reduction in social responsibilities associated with later adulthood can reduce the potential for conflict among various aspects of identity. Third, aging for most people means continuing familiar ac-

---

Social role is defined in detail in Chapter 6.

tivities in familiar environments. Most have long since developed skill and accumulated accomplishments in these arenas. All they need is to maintain them.

The identity perspective also provides a basis for predicting when change might reach crisis proportions. When change in either the individual or the environment is so great that it cannot be integrated without a fundamental reorganization of one's theory of self, an identity crisis results. An identity crisis in these terms means reassessing the very foundations of one's identity. The changes that precipitate the crisis may occur in the individual or in the social situation. Consider these examples.

Mr. F has learned that within six months to a year he will be totally blind.

Mrs. G's husband died six weeks ago. They had been married 47 years.

Mr. M retired from teaching after 41 years.

Mrs. B has become increasingly frail. After 16 years of living alone as a widow, she must move in with her divorced middle-aged daughter.

None of these changes need *automatically* trigger an identity crisis. Whether an identity crisis occurs depends on how central the dimension is to the individual and whether the change was anticipated. Profound physical changes usually have less ambiguous outcomes than social changes. Going blind would be a profound adjustment for most of us. But how much Mrs. G. is affected by her husband's death depends on how her relationship with him has fit into her identity. Whether they were inseparable companions whose selves were completely intertwined or whether theirs had been a marriage of convenience that had endured mainly by force of habit makes a lot of difference to whether his death brings on an identity crisis in his wife. Mr. M may easily be able to give up teaching if he feels he has completed what he set out to do as a teacher and that it is time to move on. He may not be able to leave so easily if he is being

forced to retire when he feels he still has something to contribute. How Mrs. B resolves her dilemma depends on how she feels about being dependent—what it means for her identity—particularly in her relationship with her daughter. An identity crisis is not the product of events alone; it stems from the interpretation of events in the context of a particular identity.

Age Changes in Personality

The term *personality* refers to what the individual typically says and does and how the individual characteristically interacts with his or her physical and social environment. Personality develops out of an interaction between a person's innate dispositions, capacities, and temperament on the one hand and the physical and social environment on the other. The individual actively participates in this process rather than simply being affected by internal or external forces beyond his or her control.*

Personality is difficult to study because it is unique for each individual and because it is made up of hundreds of patterns of thought, motivation, and response. Every theory of personality tends to focus on different aspects of personality, and every person using a personality theory tends to promote his or her focus as the most effective. This difficulty is further compounded by the fact that some theorists are primarily researchers while others are psychotherapists, both of which specialties look at very different samples of people for very different reasons. Another problem in the study of personality is that the object of study—the inner working of the mind—cannot be observed directly (Back, 1976). For all these reasons, the scientific study of personality and aging has advanced very little towards developing a specific profile of age changes in personality (Neugarten, 1977; Fiske, 1974).

---

*For alternative views of and assumptions about personality and how it is affected by aging, see Seigler (1980).

Inner dimensions of personality that have been studied in relation to aging include psychological dependency, dogmatism, cautiousness, ego strength, risk taking, introversion, hopefulness, need for achievement, and creativity, among others (Neugarten, 1977). Two themes emerge from these various studies: (1) there is continuity of personality* in that individual differences in typical thoughts, motives, and emotions tend to be maintained over time, and (2) the *only* internal dimension that changes systematically with age in nearly all studies of personality is introversion—turning one's interest and attention inward on the self rather than toward external objects and actions. Yet this turning inward seems aimed more at self-acceptance and understanding and a yearning for what Erikson called integrity than at social withdrawal.

On the subject of *adaptation patterns,* there is a substantial controversy over whether, when, and how personality changes with age. Vaillant (1977) found numerous changes in men from young adulthood to middle age, changes in the successive life concerns of establishing intimacy, consolidating career, and developing a meaning for life. Florine Livson (1976) found that "traditional" women (nurturant and conventional conformists) showed a steady pattern of personality growth from adolescence to middle age, while "independent" women (ambitious, unconventional, and gaining satisfaction from self-development rather than from attachment to others) found the traditional roles constricting and conflictful in their forties, although by their fifties the social responsibilities of the independent women were more in tune with their personalities. These findings suggest that personality may be adaptable early in adulthood but that it becomes more stable by late middle age. Costa and McCrae (1978; McCrae and Costa, 1982) argue especially strongly that

---

*That there is continuity does *not* mean that there is not also change. The implication is simply that change occurs in the *context* of considerable continuity.

after middle age, stability greatly outweighs personality change.

Consistent with this picture, Neugarten et al. (1964b) found that after middle age, adaptation patterns show no significant change with age. Neugarten concluded that after age 50, changes in health, finances, and marital status were more important influences on social adaptation than were age changes in personality. This pattern of stability in personality after middle age has been confirmed by many investigators (Schaie and Parham, 1976; Neugarten, 1977; Smith and Hall, 1964; Dennis, 1960; Thaler, 1956; Thomae, 1975; McCrae and Costa, 1982). Stability of personality in later adulthood is related to two factors. First, over time there is an "institutionalization" of personality (Neugarten, 1964b), meaning that individuals expect themselves to respond in ways that are consistent with their past histories. Second, they build up around themselves familiar social networks that facilitate dealing with the social world in habitual ways (Streib and Schneider, 1971). Stability is also supported by what happens to the self with advancing age.

Age Changes in the Self

The objective self—the *me* (as contrasted with the subjective self—the *I*) consists of what we think and feel about ourselves. It can be viewed in terms of four components: *Self-concept* is what we think we are like; the *ideal self* is what we think we ought or ought not to be like; *self-evaluation* is a moral self-assessment of how well we live up to our ideal self; and *self-esteem* is whether we like or dislike ourselves, and how much. Both self-concept and ideal self are often tied—more closely early in life—to the social positions we occupy, the roles we play, and the norms associated with personal characteristics such as sex, race, and social class.

How does aging differ from maturation? To answer this question we need to consider how the self works in young adulthood. In young adulthood, we play many roles, and it is often difficult to tell which is the role and which is our self. Part of this difficulty comes from the fact that there are seldom any written or verbal descriptions or rules that dictate what to do in a particular role. Instead, we tend to base our behavior on what we have seen others do—we try to imitate them. The people we imitate are called *role models*. We also watch the reactions of others to our own performance; if we want to improve the impression others have of our performance, we may gradually change the way we play the role. We may attempt to change what others expect of us by introducing personal information about ourselves; at the same time, others may analogously attempt to alter what we expect of them. This taking of roles, finding role models, dropping roles, and transforming roles—all in a wide variety of settings (job, family, community)—is so common in early adulthood that it is often difficult to develop a firm sense of self. The self gets too mixed up with all these roles.

Aging introduces a crucial variable into this confusing situation: *our role relationships increase in duration.* Over time, adults often drop relationships that are not what they want or are unrealistic, given their capacities or interests. With time, we can also become more adept at differentiating self from role, mostly because we are able to view the self across a variety of roles. And the more we know about the self, the more potential we have for avoiding roles that don't suit us. These patterns are not ironclad laws; they are merely tendencies that probably fit the aggregate experience of a large number of people. They are ideas about what can happen when a person is open to learning about the self and using that knowledge to inform life choices. This process need not even be conscious or calculated—it may appear to "just happen."

By the time we reach middle age, we have a huge backlog of evidence about what we are like and should be like in a wide variety of roles and situations and how this self may or may not fluctuate from time to time. While we are trying to separate self from role, messages from others

about our self and personality may greatly influence what we think we are or ought to be. But as time goes by, more and more people develop a firm idea of what they are like. Thus, although the self may be relatively open to outside influence during the process of self-discovery, it tends to be relatively closed to it during the process of self-maintenance.

Self-evaluation and self-esteem always go hand in hand. They are the moral and emotional reactions to self-assessment of the fit between self-concept (what you are) and the ideal self (what you ought or ought not to be). The noted psychologist William James (1890) expressed the relationship as follows:

$$\text{self-esteem} = \frac{\text{success}}{\text{pretensions}}$$

We can rewrite this as:

$$\text{self-evaluation or self-esteem} = \frac{\text{self-concept}}{\text{ideal self}}$$

If this relationship is valid, then self-esteem could be raised by either increasing success (self-concept) or decreasing pretensions (ideal self).

Since the ideal self contains ideas about what one ought to be like as well as ideas about what one ought not to be like, success can be defined in terms of both achieving the "ought's" and avoiding the "ought-not's." If achievement motivation declines with age, then perhaps leading a moral life by avoiding the "ought-not's" assumes more importance in later life compared to early adulthood, when achieving positions and status is stressed by society. In other words, self-esteem in later life may depend more on moral qualities than on social achievement. Although much more research is needed in this area, the theory fits very well the age data on the self.

Many people have low self-esteem in early adulthood. They are unsure of themselves, of what they are capable of, and of what they ought to be capable of. And if one is unsure, it is difficult to bring any of the elements into focus. Over time, self-esteem tends to increase. Bengtson (1983) found that a majority of research studies had observed higher self-esteem among older people than among the young. In one study, the self-esteem scores of older people living independently in the community were nearly double those of high school students (Cottrell and Atchley, 1969; Rosenberg, 1964). This difference can be accounted for in the following way. Once a person has a firm self-concept, then the person can bring the ideal self more in line with the self-concept. Another way to put this is that self-acceptance increases with age. A person is freer to achieve this self-acceptance because of the reduction in role responsibilities (mainly child rearing and employment) that usually occurs around late middle age and because of the increased potential for personalizing role relationships over time. Systems *do* bend to fit people, but this usually takes time. And people can bend to fit systems, again, with time.

For those who experience such a resolution (the majority), the outcome is a solid concept of self that stands up well to the vicissitudes of later life. This continuity in self couples with the continuity of personality to serve as a basis for defense against the assaults of ageism.

Defending the Personality and Self

The gerontology literature is full of assertions that ageism leads to a declining self-image. But numerous studies have shown that most older people do not have a negative self-image and that self-esteem tends to increase with age. This apparent contradiction occurs because the first assertion is incomplete. It should be, *"In the absence of adequate defenses, exposure to ageism erodes the basis for self-esteem."* Fortunately, most people are adequately braced to defend their ideas about themselves and their personalities.

The continuity of personality and self through time means that how we see ourselves involves not only an assessment of our current performance and characteristics but those from the past as well. And people differ a great deal in how much weight they give to the past when making their current assessments of self.

Because the past is available for use in defending the self, roles that a person no longer plays can provide the self with important evidence of past competence and success that is often not apparent to an outsider. Greenwald (1980) has gone so far as to argue that people revise or fabricate their personal histories in ways that virtually guarantee a positive evaluation. First, the past is recalled as a drama in which the self was the leading player. This gives the perception that one had more control and influence than the other actors, even that one was the center of their actions. Were it not for a second process, this tendency might lead to a negative self-evaluation for someone whose earlier roles had many negative results.

But people like to take credit for positive results and to blame outside factors for the negative, as a way of preventing poor results in the past from reaching the current self-image. If this hypothesis is true, then as time goes by one can take a great deal of credit and very little blame. This ability also has important positive implications for the success element in the self-esteem equation.

Greenwald also points out that the self is a very conservative historian, one that insists that new information fit and support the prior view of self. This theory does not imply that the self is impervious to contradictory new information but rather that, as with most ideas, the greater the amount of prior confirmation of self, the greater the amount and credibility of new information that will be needed to change one's existing self-image. For the vast majority of older people the outcome matches what we would expect from Greenwald's theory: most older people have highly positive self-images, quite resistant to disconfirmation (Atchley, 1967).

Individuals can apply the same processes of developing a positive slant to their personal history to evaluating people they love. Thus, close family and friends can often be counted on to support such a fabricated personal history.

Not only are there psychic tools for controlling information about our pasts, but there are also techniques by which we control information about the present. Over time, people tend to conclude that they know themselves better than anyone else does. This tendency can lead us to assign more weight to our own notions about ourselves than to what others say about us. We may also feel that stereotypes about some category we might be assigned to do not apply to us. The gerontology literature has consistently shown that older people can accept the stereotypes about aging and the aged and at the same time consider these stereotypes as having no applicability to themselves.

Continuity of self is reinforced and defended when people remain in familiar environments that allow them to exercise well-practiced skills, providing in turn an experience of competence. Everyday tasks such as housework, driving a car, and shopping can become important symbols of self-sufficiency.

Relative appreciation can also help define a condition or situation as more positive than it might otherwise appear; for example, the older person who acknowledges that aging has reduced the amount of heavy work that he or she can do but who at the same time recognizes that *compared to others of the same age* the decrement has been insignificant. This process is logically opposite to that of *relative deprivation*, in which people feel that they are less fortunate than others. Older people probably show a sizable bias toward relative appreciation over relative deprivation.

The preceding defense techniques are usually effective in insulating us from general stereotypes such as "college student," "professor," or "older person." However, when someone attacks us directly, then another type of defense is needed. We can find something with which to discredit our attacker and thereby discount what they've said. Or we can literally forget such comments. We can also avoid such attacks by interacting selectively, that is, by interacting as much as possible with people who are not so negative. People sometimes avoid negative responses by venturing forth only on days when they are sure their physical appearance will not occasion comment.

People often restrict their interactions to those whom they trust to support a positive moral and emotional self-assessment. In this respect, the freedom from required involvement with people outside one's own circle that often typifies later life is a boon. The more ageist and hostile the environment, the greater the advantage to voluntary involvement.

When Defenses Fail

The defense mechanisms just described are enough to protect about 80 percent of older people most of the time in most everyday situations. Yet the remaining 20 percent has low self-esteem. Why?

To begin with, some older people never develop a solid identity or self-image. These people are defenseless and unsure of themselves their entire lives, and what we see in them currently may have nothing to do with aging. Other older people have the notion that they are *supposed* to be worthless—that a bad self-image is good for them. Ageism gives them more opportunity to accumulate negative credits and they soak up the insults like a sponge, even seeking them out sometimes. These are the masochists in our midst. But probably the biggest category of people with lifelong low self-esteem is made up of those whose expectations for themselves have far outdistanced their capacity for success and whose moral rigidity has prevented the necessary rapprochement. These are the lifelong perfectionists. For all these people, the problem is not a failure to defend self-esteem but a failure to ever develop it. There are also people who don't experience a loss of self-esteem until later life. The key factors responsible for this loss are (1) decline in physical capacity, (2) an already vulnerable self-image, and (3) loss of control over one's physical environment.

A *gradual* decline in physical capacity can be incorporated gradually into the self-concept, and the ideal self can be modified gradually so as to take gradual declines into account. Thus, changes that are *gradual* can sometimes be lived through without loss of self-esteem. One crucial issue here is whether one must simply cut back on an activity or whether one must cut it out altogether. In other words, physical changes that disrupt continuity of preferred activities have a much greater potential for affecting self-concept and self-esteem than do physical changes that allow continuity at a reduced level. For example, a man who sees himself as a capable handyman who can do his own home repairs can continue to hold this image even if he is forced to slow down or get a little help from time to time. But when he wants to repair a loose doorknob and is unable to hold the screwdriver tight enough to do the job, it becomes more difficult to retain the image of current capability. His past accomplishments would still be available as a source of self-esteem, but not his current accomplishments. If being active currently is important to this person's sense of self, then a loss of self-esteem could occur. When activity losses occur gradually, a person can anticipate them, and the results for the self may not be as serious as when the change is sudden and substantial. For example, people with progressive arthritis have much more time to adjust to the idea of cutting down activities than do those who suffer incapacitating strokes.

Some people reach later life with adequate yet vulnerable self-esteem. High vulnerability can arise in several ways, most of which relate to the innumerable human characteristics that form the basis for the ideal self, such as physical ability, mental ability, appearance, roles, activities,

groups one belongs to, personal qualities such as honesty, and relative prestige, honor, or wealth. The vulnerability of self to the changes aging can bring depends largely on the vulnerability of these specific bases for self-image. For example, people who idealize physical appearance are more vulnerable to aging than those whose ideal selves are based mainly on interpersonal qualities such as warmth toward others or trustworthiness. Generally, those whose self-images is based on structural aspects of life such as roles or social position are more highly vulnerable because aging predictably brings role loss and reduction in income.

As already said, most older Americans do not have low self-esteem. Thus, if the foregoing explanation is true, then most older people could be expected to value personal qualities more than positions and roles. Indeed, one study found that the top-ranking personal goals of older people were: being dependable and reliable, having close family ties, and being self-reliant and self-sufficient (Atchley, 1980b:74). The emphasis was on personal qualities and on relationships that one is least likely to lose. Goals such as being prominent in the community or having an important position were ranked at the very bottom. Another study found that adults across all ages tended to stress interpersonal qualities such as honesty, being forgiving, and being helpful over instrumental qualities such as intelligence and imagination (Rokeach, 1973).

People who have a diversified basis for self-esteem are less vulnerable to aging than those whose selves depend on only two or three characteristics. For example, for some people their job is the primary basis for their ideal self, their definition of success, and their self-esteem. Such people are rare, but if they are forced to retire, either because of health or social policy, then the results could be severe. Again, as the research evidence shows, the basis for the self-esteem of most older Americans is a highly diversified pattern of activities, roles, personal qualities, and other characteristics.

Loss of control over one's home or community environment can pose serious problems for maintaining self-image. So long as people remain in a familiar environment, skills and knowledge developed in the past can often compensate for decrements in functioning. But people who move to a new environment can be confronted with changes in their ability to move about or gather and process new information, changes they might not have been aware of before they moved. And if the person has difficulty figuring out the new environment and coping with it, there can be a very unsettling lapse in the person's usual sense of competence. In addition, the person may have left behind a group of friends or family that supported the person's use of past history as a source of self-esteem, a problem that can be aggravated if the person also comes into contact at this time with ageist service providers who think that most older people are helpless or incompetent. Nevertheless, changing environments does not necessarily rob people of all their defenses. They can still attach more weight to their own experiences, discount what others say to them, selectively interact with others, and selectively participate in their new social environment. In addition, only relatively few older people who move to new environments know no one at the new locale. Having friends already there is one of the major factors in selecting a new environment (Longino, 1981).

But entering an institution is another matter. When people enter nursing homes, they are usually at the mercy of the staff, not only for medical and personal care needs but for their sense of self, as well. They usually find themselves among people who do not know their past histories and who cannot be counted on to support this source of self-esteem. They are in an unfamiliar environment, which might be difficult to learn to negotiate even if they are not sick. And in a nursing home it is very difficult to avoid or discount negative responses from others, for the resident is usually not in control of who will be seen, where, and when.

Mental Illness

The line between mental health and mental illness is difficult to identify. Behavior that may be tolerated in one situation may be defined as sick in another. The term *mental illness* implies an impairment in mental functioning. In practice, people are identified as mentally ill if they show progressive or sudden negative changes in mental functions such as memory, cognition, decision making, perception, or emotional response. Mental illness can range from mild to severe, but in this section we will be concerned only with mental illness that impairs the individual's ability to function *socially*. Somewhere under 10 percent of the older population suffers from disabling mental illness, including 3 percent who are institutionalized (Riley and Foner, 1968:363).

One reason why mental illness is difficult to define is that it comes in many forms. Butler and Lewis (1973) listed 131 diagnostic categories of mental illness, and theirs is only a partial listing! Yet it is reasonably feasible and convenient to classify mental illnesses common to later life into three primary categories: mental disorders with no apparent organic cause (usually called **functional mental disorders**), **reversible organic mental disorders,** and **chronic organic mental disorders.** Having reviewed the literature, Butler and Lewis (1973:50) concluded that older people with disabling mental illness are about evenly distributed among these three primary types.

Functional Disorders

Mental disorders that are classified as functional are the psychoses and neuroses. *Psychosis* involves a severe loss of contact with reality. Delusions, hallucinations, strange behavior, and weak impulse control are key symptoms. The main types of psychosis are schizophrenia, affective psychosis, depression, and paranoia. *Neurosis*, thought to be a reaction to acute anxiety, can take many forms, including anxiety states, hysteria, obsessive-compulsive behavior, phobias, hypochondria, and depression (without loss of reality contact). Whether neurotic or psychotic, depression is the most prevalent functional disorder as well as the one most likely to begin in later life (Butler and Lewis, 1973).

Older people with functional mental disorders include those who first became mentally ill early in life and remained so into later life as well as those who first became mentally ill in later life. Those for whom functional disorder begins in later life are primarily people depressed by social or physical losses. Both Busse and Pfeiffer (1969) and Maas and Kuypers (1974) concluded that the people most likely to develop a functional disorder in response to the stresses of aging are those who have had difficulty coping with change earlier in life.

Organic Disorders

Organic mental disorders are typified by mental confusion—loss of memory, incoherent speech, and poor orientation to the environment. They are often accompanied by psychomotor problems, as well. Organic mental disorders can be either reversible or chronic. Because symptoms of both types are similar, diagnosis depends heavily on knowledge of prior health events. For example, before settling on a diagnosis, a doctor seeing a patient with symptoms of organic brain disorder may check for the signs of *reversible organic brain disorder*—malnutrition, drugs the patient may have been taking, and infections or diseases such as diabetes or hyperthyroidism. Reversible brain disorders can also accompany congestive heart failure, alcoholism, or stroke. If none of the causes of reversible organic brain disorders are present, then it is usually assumed that the patient has a chronic brain disorder.

Chronic brain disorders, often called **dementia**, fall into two categories: those caused by a deterioration of brain tissue (Alzheimer's disease) and those caused by cerebral arteriosclero-

sis, which cuts off the blood supply to the brain. All chronic brain disorders involve a gradual deterioration of mental functions, but sometimes they also bring agitated behavior, depression, or delirium. Although not limited to the aged, both types of organic brain disorder increase in prevalence with age and are often assumed, mistakenly, to be a normal part of aging. In addition, organic brain disorders are related to functional depression. No doubt some reversible brain disorders are brought on by environmental factors indirectly through stroke, heart attack, or alcoholism. However, no data on indirect causes of organic brain disorder are yet available. Research is needed in this area.

Busse and Pfeiffer (1969) concluded that there is little increase with age in the proportion of people with mental disorders. However, there is an increase with age in the proportion with *disabling* mental illness, primarily caused by an increase in the prevalence of serious organic mental disorders rather than by any appreciable increase in functional disorders.

As the percentage of the older population that is very old increases, so will the prevalence of chronic organic brain disorders. Kay (1972) reports that above age 75, 90 percent of first admissions to mental hospitals are diagnosed as the result of chronic brain disorders. Shanas and Maddox (1976) report that at age 65 only about 2 percent of the population has chronic organic brain disorders while at age 80 about 20 percent does.

The implications of this rise in the prevalence of chronic organic brain disorders are controversial. Wershow (1977) contends that most of these cases are beyond treatment and that the situation raises some ethical questions.

> Must we be bound to keep alive as long as possible those poor souls who sit tied into their chairs, babbling incoherently, doubly incontinent, whose dining consists of having usually cold food stoked into them as rapidly as possible by overworked aides who must move on and stoke the next bed's prisoner? Is this living, much less living with dignity? (Wershow, 1977:301)

On the other side, Settin (1978) argues that no test exists that is both valid and practical and that can still differentiate treatable organic brain disorders from the untreatable. In addition, Hellebrandt's (1978) observations provide a less stereotypic and more optimistic view of life for people with chronic organic brain disorder who have not reached the level of deterioration described by Wershow. He points out that most people suffering from this condition manage to live at home, cared for by family members and friends. Infections or other complicating diseases usually end life before the individual reaches a "vegetative existence."

Hellebrandt, himself 76, also described life for 16 patients with chronic organic brain disorders who live in a locked ward, part of the convalescent facility of a large retirement village:

> Oblivious to their plight, without apprehension or concern, they move about at will, accepting the locked door with matter-of-fact aplomb on all but the most exceptional occasions. . . . The idea of the locked door may distress a visitor [or the reader] but it is a meaningless concept to virtually all patients deteriorated enough to require segregation in this unit (Hellebrandt, 1978:68).

The average age of these patients is 85. They are generally cooperative and in good general health. They are the most contented residents of the nursing facility.

> They move about freely, often in pairs, showing evidence of concern one for another even though they never address each other by name and cannot identify the person with whom they are walking. . . . They are clean, neat, and groomed appropriately, for the most part. On occasion they may wear two or three dresses at once. . . . The casual visitor would find the group deceptively normal.

> All patients in the locked ward are completely disoriented as to place, time, day, date, year, season, or holidays. They have a poor memory for ongoing events. . . . None know that their behavior is in any way aberrant. Neither do they realize that they have been institutionalized.

This group is classifiable as borderline severe brain damage, according to the Kahn-Goldfarb Mental Status Questionnaire. Yet much of what we consider human still exists in these people—concern for others, friendliness, optimism.

Caring for people who are disoriented is not easy. Student visitors are often upset by patients' inability to remember them from one visit to the next. Many people lack the patience to listen to incoherent ramblings. Incontinence disgusts most people. And it is difficult to regularly face this reality with the knowledge that for those of us who live long enough, there is a one in five chance of experiencing chronic organic brain disorder ourselves.

Summary

Aging produces higher sensory thresholds and lowered sensory acuity. Yet there is a great deal of individual variability in the extent of the decline, and few people experience sensory limits on activity prior to age 75. The evidence with respect to age changes and perception is less clear, but there appears to be a decline with age in various perceptual functions. Age changes in the central processes also seem to limit psychomotor responses, reaction time, and complex performance. However, important social factors may also influence these psychological functions.

The evidence on the relationship between aging and mental functioning is even more confusing. Cross-sectional studies tend to show a drop with age in measured intelligence, while longitudinal studies frequently report stability over time. An important study by Nesselroade et al. (1972) illustrated that intelligence is made up of several dimensions, some of which do not change with age, some of which improve, and some of which decline. In general, age changes in intelligence are minimal in comparison with generational differences or with the decline in intelligence associated with impending death. The evidence on learning is difficult to interpret, but there is no doubt that most older people can learn effectively. Memory declines with age, with the prime problem appearing to be the retrieval function. Aging also seems to reduce ability to categorize and make logical inferences, although these trends may be partly social in origin. The evidence with respect to creativity in older people also suggests that social factors are at least as relevant as psychobiological age changes. Rigidity, perhaps the opposite of creativity, seems to increase with age, but again, social factors are thought to be very important in producing this result.

Drives appear to wane as age increases, but because many factors intervene between drives and behavior, declining drives seem to produce less behavior change with age than might be expected. Motives guide and direct action toward specific goals. There is some indication that as people grow older they become less motivated to grow and expand and more motivated to reduce anxiety and perceived threat. However, motives can be changed, even in older people. The ability to experience emotions apparently also declines with age, and in addition, the meanings and environmental sources of various emotions also change. Again, social factors may also influence emotionality in older people.

Many psychologists might consider the fundamental subject of this chapter to be psychobiology, particularly the early work on aging. In recent years, however, there has been a growing recognition of the important role that social factors play in basic psychological functioning. Throughout this chapter we have repeatedly seen instances where social factors, particularly historical and generational factors, were more important than age changes in producing the cross-sectional relationships between age and various psychological functions. The psychology of aging truly is moving from assuming that unless proved otherwise age differences are a result of psychobiological aging to assuming that unless proved otherwise social factors are at least as important as physical aging. It has also been made clear that the range of individual differences *within* various age categories is usually much greater than the average differences *between* age categories.

From the human development perspective, aging is either a movement through discrete stages or a continuous unfolding. Erikson's stage theory has been the most influential. It assumes that the individual personality is built by confronting a predictable series of life issues that establish capability, worth, and safety. The first life issue of adulthood is intimacy versus isolation, which is usually resolved in early adulthood. The second life issue of adulthood is generativity versus stagnation, which is often an issue of middle adulthood. The final issue, ego integrity versus despair, is usually an issue of later life. Erikson's theory is most useful in helping to identify how far a person has progressed in the developmental process. It is less useful as a means of predicting the central issues of a person's life.

Process theories of human development view aging as a matter of an individual's continuously taking in information about the self, interpreting that information in light of a theory of self, and refining the theory based on experience. The concern here is with individual identity and how it evolves over the life cycle. Aging can solidify one's theory of self by providing a large amount of experience about the self. Reduced job and parenting responsibilities that often accompany aging can lower the potential for conflict among the various aspects of one's identity. Thus, aging is more a matter of identity maintenance than of identity formation. Identity crises result from age changes in the individual or the environment that cannot be accommodated without a complete reorganization of the person's self-concept. No life change predictably causes identity crises. Identity crises result from the individual's interpretation of life events.

After young adulthood, there is more continuity than discontinuity in both self and personality and each becomes more stable with age. This consolidation is a natural consequence of adult development, in which the duration and multiplicity of relationships and environments provide the information needed for the individual to develop a consistent view of his or her personality and self, including a customary strategy for coping with the demands and opportunities of life. Most people enter later life with a stable personality and positive self-esteem.

Coping with aging is usually a matter of defending a positive self-image. Using past successes, discounting messages that do not fit our existing self-concept, refusing to apply general beliefs about aging to ourselves, selectively interacting with others, and selectively perceiving what we are told are all ways to defend ourselves against ageism. But some people develop neither a stable personality nor a positive self-image. And there is little in the situation of older people that is conducive to doing so at that advanced stage.

A person who loses self-esteem in later life tends to do so either (1) because physical changes have become so pronounced that the person is forced to accept what he or she sees as a less desirable self-image, or (2) because the person's self-esteem is precarious or vulnerable as a result of being either too dependent on social positions and roles or too narrow, or (3) because the individual has lost control over his or her home or community environment to such an extent that the person is essentially defenseless. This last possibility is especially likely when a person moves into a nursing home. Most people have the resources and defenses needed to retain or maintain self-esteem into old age, a fact made very clear by the multitude of studies showing that older people living in community settings have a stable, well-defined personality and high self-esteem and that self-esteem increases with age.

Mental illness is best defined as a loss of mental functioning significant enough to either cause the individual concern or impair his or her social functioning. Serious mental illness can be divided into functional disorders (which have no apparent organic basis), reversible organic mental disorders, and irreversible organic mental disorders. About 10 percent of the older population has mental disorders that cause some degree of disability—about evenly split among the three primary types of disorders. Depression is the only functional disorder whose prevalence increases with age, and a substantial proportion of this increase is a result of social losses, such as death of friends and relatives. Reversible organic disorders can arise from medication interactions, alcoholism, heart disease, or diabetes. Chronic organic mental disorders are caused by brain tissue loss or poor circulation. No mental disorder is a normal part of aging. However, the proportion of organic disorders increases from about 2 percent at age 65 to about 20 percent at age 80. Developing effective prevention and treatment measures for organic brain disorder is an important goal if our society is to maintain a high quality of life for the aged.

Chapter 6

Social Aging

Our individual lives are structured by our social environments as well as by our physical and mental capacities. We interact with one another not only as individuals but as role players. And the roles we play are organized sequentially into a life course tied to age or life stage. In addition, social processes such as socialization engage us with our social world. All these aspects of the social environment can be influenced by age.

Social Roles

Social roles have great significance. This is because individuals often define themselves in terms of these roles and because the places of individuals in society are determined by them. A *role* is the expected or typical behavior associated with a position in the organization of a group. Positions, and the roles that go with them, usually have labels such as *mother, teacher, senator, milling machine operator, volunteer, moviegoer*. Obviously, we behave not as isolated role players, but in relation to other players, that is, in *role relationships*. Thus, in the organization of a group, the various positions are related to one another in specified ways *regardless* of who occupies the positions. For example, teachers assign work and evaluate the results, and students do the work and, in the vast majority of cases, aim for a positive evaluation of the work. This much we know in advance without knowing who the actual role players are.

A large part of everyday life consists of human relationships structured at least partially by the social roles and positions of the various actors. But in everyday life the action is much more like improvisational theater, where the characters and dialogue are made up right on stage, than like formal theater, in which the action is predetermined. An example may make this clearer.

Suppose you sign up for a course on aging. When you first meet the professor, you both have general ideas of what to expect from each other. For example, you might expect the professor to already know a lot about aging and to use that knowledge to structure your educational experience. You might also expect the professor to evaluate your progress. The professor might expect that you have relatively little systematic knowledge about aging but are intelligent and interested in the subject and willing to work to improve your knowledge. These general expectations would serve as the background for your initial interactions, but almost immediately the two of you would begin to incorporate *personal* information into your expectations for this *specific* relationship. You might discover, for instance, that the professor is relatively easygoing and has a good sense of humor. The teacher might find you to be conscientious and inquisitive and a good writer. You would each gradually modify and refine your expectations so as to take an increasing amount of personal information into account. The pace of this process would depend on the willingness of each of you to disclose personal information. The longer you kept at this process, the more personalized your relationship would become. Thus, the *duration* of any role relationship is one of its most important features.

Aging Affects Social Roles

When life is filled with relatively new relationships, as in young adulthood, we are uncertain about what to expect from others and what they expect from us. But when life is filled with relationships of long standing, there is a large component of security in knowing what to expect—even if the relationships are not all we might wish them to be. In middle age and later life, most of the role relationships of most people are long standing and highly personalized.

Age is not a position in the structure of a group.* Along with other individual attributes,

---

*There are others who would disagree; see Riley et al. (1972).

such as sex, social class, and race, age is used to determine *eligibility* for various positions, to evaluate the *appropriateness* of various positions for specific people, and to *modify* the expected behavior of an individual in a specific position. Let us look at each of these in turn.

Role Eligibility. In adulthood, advanced age occasionally makes people eligible for valued positions such as *retired person,* but more often it makes them ineligible to hold positions they have valued. Whether we are merely *assigned* to the positions we occupy, whether we must *achieve* them, or whether we have *selected* them, we do not simply occupy or take over or retain positions. Positions are usually available to us as a result of our having met certain criteria. In most societies, different positions, rights, duties, privileges, and obligations are set aside for children, adolescents, young adults, the middle-aged, and the old. In our culture, the primary eligibility criteria are health, age, sex, social class, ethnicity, color, experience, and educational achievement. These criteria may be gradually modified and personalized in some cases, but overall they govern eligibility in prescribed ways.

As we pass through life, the field of positions for which we are eligible keeps changing. A young boy can legitimately be a neighborhood gang member, a pupil, or unemployed—all roles he cannot hold as an adult. As a young man he can be an auto driver, a bar patron, and a voter—all roles he cannot occupy as a child. As an older adult he can be retired, a great-grandfather, or pretend to be deaf—all roles he cannot play as a young adult. Of course, age also works negatively. For example, older people are often prevented from holding a job even if they want one.

Role Appropriateness. In addition to affecting eligibility, age also influences the suitability of particular roles for particular people. For example, Mr. A began competing in local cross-country motorcycle races at age 39. Most of his friends thought he was crazy, and many indicated that *they* would certainly never do anything that dangerous *at his age*. Interestingly, he was encouraged by other racers of all ages, and went on to win a few trophies before he "retired" from competition at age 45. These reactions illustrate that the age standards of society at large may not be adopted by all subgroups. And this tendency, in turn, shows why both older people and younger people often restrict their interactions to subgroups that approve of their role choices.

Role Modification.   Age also serves to modify what is expected of people in particular positions. Young people are often dealt with leniently when they are in adult positions because of their inexperience. For instance, young adults often show too much impatience with others on the job. Such impatient behavior is generally tolerated by supervisors, who attribute it to inexperience rather than to a character flaw. The same amount of impatience from a middle-aged worker would not be tolerated as long or as well. Behavioral standards may be different in old age, as well. For example, an 86-year-old father is allowed to be more dependent in his relationships with his offspring than is a 56-year-old father.

Cumulative Effects

Positions that adults hold or have held provide various degrees of access to advantages such as prestige, wealth, or influence. Highly rewarded positions can be attained either through family background or individual initiative or both. But despite the rhetoric that ours is an open class system in which one can rise from rags to riches, in reality only a tiny minority of people ever move out of the social class into which they are born.

Growing older in an advantaged social position generally means being able to accumulate personal wealth and prestige. People do not become wealthy, revered, or influential just by

becoming old, but by occupying an advantaged position for a number of years. Former President Eisenhower had a great deal of prestige and influence in old age, not because he was old but because he had been both a president and a military chief. A great many of the richest and most influential Americans are old, but their age is not the reason why they are rich or influential. In fact, their wealth and influence *discounts* their age, in that rich and powerful people are much less likely than others to be disqualified from participation purely on account of age. Age disqualification happens mainly to people who are already disadvantaged.

One can also be advantaged by having exceptional skills. Aged great writers, musicians, artists, therapists, diplomats, and others can use their skills to offset their age and to avoid being disqualified from full participation. Pablo Picasso, Carl Jung, and Averell Harriman never had to worry about age discrimination—their talents remained in demand. Other people find that age often offsets ordinary skills and leads to disqualification.

Although part of the disqualifying character of age is related to erroneous beliefs about the predictability of aging effects on performance, part of it is related to the scarcity of leadership positions, the desire for younger people to acquire the positions of leadership that are available, and the willingness of older people to give up their leadership responsibilities.

The Life Course

The **life course** is an idealized and age-related progression or sequence of roles and group memberships that individuals are expected to follow as they mature and move through life. Thus, there is an age to go to school, an age to marry, an age to "settle down," and so forth. For example, Neugarten et al. (1965) found considerable consensus among adults that people should marry in their early twenties and that men should be settled in a career by the time they are 24 to 26.

But the life course in reality is neither simple nor rigidly prescribed. For one thing, various subcultures (whether based on sex, social class, ethnicity, race, or region of the country) tend to develop unique ideas concerning the timing of life course events. For example, male auto workers tend to favor retirement in the mid-fifties while physicians tend to prefer the late sixties. In addition, even within subcultures, there are often several alternatives. For instance, having made a decision to attend college, a young person often has a wide range of types of institutions from which to choose. Thus, like a road map, the abstract concept of the life course in reality is composed of a great many alternative routes to alternative destinations.

As people grow older, their accumulated decisions about various life course options produce increased differentiation among them. Although very late in life the number of options may diminish somewhat because of social and physical aging, the older population is considerably more differentiated than the young. Yet even with the increasing complexity of the life course with age, certain generally accepted standards serve as a sort of master timetable for the entire population. Although there are many exceptions and variations, most Americans start school, finish school, get married, have children, experience the "empty nest," and retire, and each event occurs within a particular chronological age span, that is, an age range during which these events are *supposed* to happen. Most of us spend our lives reasonably on schedule, and when we get off schedule we are motivated to get back on again (Neugarten and Datan, 1973).

The various stages of the life course are made real for the individual in three ways. First, they are related to more specific patterns, such as occupational career and family development. Second, specific expectations or age norms accompany various life stages. And finally, people are forced to make particular types of choices during given phases of the life course.

Dimensions of the Life Course

Figure 6-1 shows, very roughly, how the life course stages are related to chronological age, occupation, the family, and education. More dimensions could be added, but the important point is that various social institutions tend to prescribe their own career cycles and that these cycles are related to the various life stages.

Age Norms

Age norms tell us what people in a given life stage are allowed to do and to be as well as what they are required to do and to be. Some age norms operate very generally to specify dress, personal appearance, or demeanor in a wide variety of social roles. Other age norms govern approach, entry, incumbency, and exit from social roles, groups, or social situations (Atchley, 1975b). Many age norms come down to us through tradition. On the other hand, legal age norms are often the result of compromise and negotiation. A series of assumptions underlies age norms. These assumptions, often uninformed, concern what people in a given life stage are capable of—not just what they *ought to* do, but what they *can* do. Thus, opportunities are limited for both children and older people because others assume that they are not strong enough, not experienced or educated enough, or not capable of adequately mature adult judgments. For instance, older workers are passed by for training opportunities because "you can't teach an old dog new tricks." Older job applicants are passed over on the assumption that people over age 60 have too few years left to work to warrant the investment. By the same token, young adults are passed over because they "don't have enough experience."

Sometimes age norms make useful and valid distinctions. For example, few of us would want

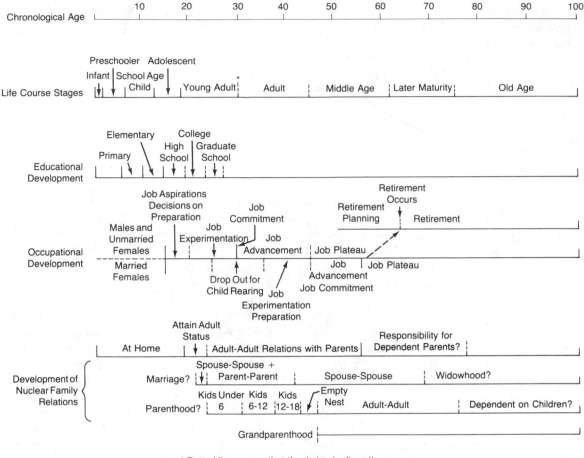

FIGURE 6-1   Various dimensions of the life course.

to drive automobiles if six-year-olds were allowed to take to the roads. But many of the norms for adolescence and beyond become increasingly difficult to justify because of their essentially arbitrary nature. And the greater the gap between the actual level of individual functioning and the level implied by an age norm, the more likely that the age norm will be seen as unjust.

Various mechanisms secure conformity to age norms. For one, people are taught early in life by their parents, teachers, and peers how to apply age norms to themselves. If they do not conform, then friends, neighbors, and associates can be counted on to apply informal pressures. In the formal realm, regulations bring bureaucratic authority to bear. And finally, laws put the full power of the state behind age norms. For example, the idea of retiring by age 70 is supported at every level along this continuum.

Decision Demands

The sometimes chaotic nature of the numerous alternatives presented by various life courses has been mentioned earlier. This chaos is minimized to some degree by age, sex, social class, ethnicity, and so forth. But how do people get into *specific* situations? It is impossible to assign people to each and every niche in a complex, rapidly changing society. **Decision demands** force the individual to work within the system in order to find a slot in the social organization.

Decision demands require that selections be made from an age-linked field of possibilities.* For example, after completing preparatory education, young adults usually enter a period of job experimentation. The field of possibilities expands dramatically immediately after graduation (certification) and continues to expand while the individual gains job experience. But there is an increasing expectation that people will find positions of employment into which they will settle; during this period the field of jobs for which they are eligible may slowly contract. Contraction also occurs as jobs are selected by others of similar age and experience. For many jobs, career tracks are difficult to begin after age 45.** For others, it is difficult to break in after age 35.

Decision demands tend to be concentrated in the first half of the life course. That is, individuals are *required* to make choices and select their "career tracks" in all sorts of areas—education, employment, family, community, voluntary associations, and so on. Life-styles developed before or during middle age tend to persist as long as health and money hold out. Thus, middle-aged people who want to switch tracks or get involved in new areas often must confront the fact that the available slots were taken earlier by their age peers.

On the other hand, those middle-aged people who do retrain and switch careers often find that their new careers develop at an accelerated rate compared to those of younger people starting at the same time. This acceleration is probably due to their greater maturity and general

---

*For a more detailed discussion of decision demands, see Atchley (1975b).

**The term *career* as used here refers to experience in any particular role attached to an ongoing group.

experience plus the underlying notion that a person's position in an organization should match his or her life stage. More research is needed on this phenomenon.

Thus far we have looked primarily at the social structure of life in human groups and how it is affected by aging. We now turn to how aging influences the various social processes through which individuals are incorporated into that structure: socialization, acculturation, anticipation, and adaptation.

Socialization and Acculturation

Socialization is a group of processes through which a group encourages and/or coerces its members to learn, and conform to, its culture—the distinctive way of life of the group. Socialization is society's means for creating capable participants. **Acculturation** is the actual learning of a culture. Much of what we seek to learn through acculturation is aimed at making us more effective role players. Some social scientists use the term *socialization* to refer to both the action initiated by the group toward the individual *and* the individual's response to this action. To the individual, socialization and acculturation are important prerequisites for getting whatever society has to offer. If people know and understand the social system, they can potentially put the system to use. If they do not understand the way of life of the society in which they live, their lives can be confusing and unpredictable. Thus, people are usually motivated to become acculturated.

For society, socialization produces a measure of continuity from one generation to another. After all, society needs new participants, and socialization is a major process through which society attracts, facilitates, and maintains participation. The efforts of the group to help individuals learn the system range from formal, structured programs in which the group is responsible for the outcome, to unstructured, informal processes in which the individual is responsible for the outcome. For example, families are expected to teach children to speak, and schools are expected to teach children to read and write. On the other hand, adults must generally find out on their own how to locate a physician.

Age affects what the individual is expected to know and what he or she needs to know in order to be an effective participant in society. Early in life, the emphasis in socialization is on learning language and customs; then it shifts to preparing for adult social roles. In adulthood, expectations gradually shift toward self-initiated acculturation; that is, adults often recognize their need for knowledge and skills and go after them without waiting to be told (Brim, 1968). At the same time, fewer publicly supported, formal opportunities exist for socialization in adulthood compared to the opportunities that exist for young people.

Rosow (1974) has argued that because norms for the aged do not exist there is nothing to socialize the aged *to*. Although this argument may be accurate in terms of formal socialization, its applicability is questionable in terms of acculturation. Older people often have few required contacts with the general community. They associate primarily with people they know and who know them. In addition, most older people continue to function mainly in roles they have occupied for many years. The point is that most roles older people play are roles they have been socialized to for a long time. Aging often affects primarily the nuances of role playing rather than its basic structure.

Most societies pay little attention to their adult members' needs for maintenance or renewal of their knowledge or skills. In this age of the computer, for example, where do middle-aged or older adults go to learn how to use this new technology for dealing with information? As we shall see later, this pattern seriously hampers the ability of some older members of society to remain an integral part of the society, particularly in terms of the knowledge and skills required for employment. If older people need

information and skills that are necessary for participation in society but that cannot be secured by older people themselves, then the socialization processes in the society are not adequate.

Much adult acculturation comes from experience. For example, Kohlberg (1973a) points out that the moral development of young people is mainly cognitive and symbolic. But in order for the person to develop what Kohlberg calls *principled thinking*—"principles to which the society and the self *ought to be committed*" (1973a:194)—it is not enough merely to "see" the principles. The person must also experience sustained responsibility for the welfare of others and experience having to make irreversible moral choices. A similar process occurs in other areas of life, such as mate selection, career choice, choice of residence, and so on. The adult develops life principles—a philosophy of life—through an interaction between what is known, what is experienced, and his or her personality. And, theoretically at least, the longer one lives, the greater the opportunity for this dialectic to produce refinements in one's approach to living.

For instance, it is one thing to know intellectually that telling lies is wrong, and it is quite another to have experienced the results of having lied. When we are young, it is difficult to believe that all the do's and don'ts we are taught are necessary. As we get older, our experiences give us a fuller understanding of why rules exist. Older people are often more committed to basic moral principles than are the young, not because they are rigid but because life has taught them the value of following the rules.

Anticipation

The process of **anticipation** involves learning the rights, obligations, resources, and outlook of a position one will occupy *in the future*. To the extent that the future position is a general one, it need not represent an unknown. For example, most people understand that in retirement, people are expected to manage their own lives—set goals and form new daily routines. Most also understand that to do so successfully requires financial planning. Through fantasy, it is possible to anticipate what the future will hold, identify potential problems, and make advance preparations (Atchley, 1976b). The role changes common to later life can often be anticipated, thus smoothing out the process of transition.

However, many roles we take up in later life have a degree of vagueness that allows some flexibility in playing them but at the same time hinders anticipation. Such roles are not "packaged," as are roles that young people play. For example, the role of high school student is much more clearly defined than the role of retired person. As a result, older people must often *negotiate* the rights and duties of their positions with significant other people in their environment. Thus, in late adulthood, acculturation—learning or relearning how to function in one's social milieu—depends heavily on the characteristics of others with whom the older person must negotiate. The attitudes of others concerning who the older person is becoming are probably crucial to the content of acculturation in later life. As images of aging become less stereotyped in American culture, the outcome of these negotiations can be expected to become more positive.

Role Adaptation

Social roles, even specific ones such as mother or teacher, tend to be defined in terms that allow room for interpretation. **Adaptation** to roles is a process of fitting role demands to the individual's capabilities. Negotiation—the interpersonal aspect of this adaptation—takes place between role players. This process of tailoring the role to fit the individual and the situation means that it is impossible to describe *the* role of *the* grandfather. We can only describe some of the similarities and differences we find when we look at how grandfathers play their roles and what these similarities or differences are related to.

Thus, through socialization, society tells its members that retirement is normal and that it should occur at around age 65. Through acculturation, an individual comes to *agree* that retirement is normal and that it should occur at around age 65. Through anticipation, the individual identifies potential problems associated with retirement and tries to solve them in advance. Once the individual retires, the process of adaptation involves tailoring the rather vague retirement role to fit the needs of the individual. Part of this process may involve negotiations between spouses about what the retirement role will consist of and how it will influence their life together.

Aging and Changes in Social Context

Writings about later life often give the impression that the aging individual is firmly in the grips of inexorable physical, psychological, and social processes that allow little room for individual or group initiative or maneuvering. It is easy to lose sight of the fact that while our abstractions concerning these processes are built up from individual or group experience, the categories we use are often intellectual conveniences or necessities and are not concrete elements of the social world. Thus, when we read that having a certain social role does this or that to a person, what is really meant is that certain concrete behavior or concrete ideas are more likely to occur in the lives of people who play a given social role. The term *social role* is then merely convenient shorthand for a certain pattern of behavior or particular situation.

An earlier edition of this book stressed role change as the central element of situational change in the later phases of life. Certainly, role changes are important and deserve a good bit of attention. However, roles are not the only important social elements that can change in later life. Moreover, the process of role change itself is governed by how one defines the life course and the age norms associated with it, and by various situational changes.

The term **social situation** is a general one that has been used by social scientists to emphasize that roles, groups, and norms have little meaning for the individual, apart from the particular time and place at which the individual encounters them. The immediate social environment is very important in translating social order in the abstract into concrete reality for the individual. In the following sections we will consider changes in roles, groups, and environments that can accompany aging.

Role Changes

The role changes that we will consider are: launching the children, retirement, widowhood, dependency, disability, institutionalization, and participation in religion, politics, and leisure-time activities.

Launching the Children.   For those who elect to become parents, the launching of their children into adulthood generally occurs early in middle age. For example, people who married in 1955 and had children could expect on the average to see their last child leave home in 1980, at which time the average husband was just over 47 and the average wife about two years younger (Troll et al., 1979:14).

The rhetoric of American society has proclaimed parenting to be reserved mainly for females, and to be a major focus of their lives. Following this supposition to its logical conclusion, it was presumed that the "empty nest" would result in a meaningless existence for most mothers. However, researchers who have put this conventional wisdom to the test have found quite a few surprises.

To begin with, the term *empty nest* is somewhat misleading. It carries the connotation that newly matured people, like newly matured birds, leave the nest once and for all. But Ryder

(1968) found that many newlyweds visited and telephoned their parents often and continued to use their parents' charge accounts, cars, and so on. With delayed marriage becoming more common, *getting* the children to leave home sometimes becomes a bigger problem than *having* them leave.

Lowenthal and Chiriboga (1975) found that the period following the launching of the last child was not stressful. Indeed, middle-aged women who had not yet launched their children reported much less positive self-concepts than those who already had, particularly in terms of those characteristics that influence interpersonal relationships (Chiriboga and Thurnher, 1975:75). Dealing with adolescent or young adult children may be the most difficult task a parent can attempt. The youngsters' inconsistent yearnings and capacities for independence sometimes yield awesome unpredictability. Parents feel the need not only to let their children experiment with assuming responsibility for their own decisions and behavior, but also to supervise them closely enough to avoid potentially drastic errors. This conflict makes parents, too, somewhat unpredictable, for the various conflicting postures create an uneasy situation on both sides and help explain why so few parents feel that they are "a success" at this stage.

Women generally look forward to having their children launched. They see it as a chance for greater freedom and opportunity (Neugarten, 1968). This is less true if motherhood has been the focal point in their life and if they have few other interests (Spence and Lonner, 1971). Men's viewpoints have not been researched.

In summary, then, it would appear that having all of one's children launched into adulthood is not as complete or abrupt as folklore would have it. In addition, this change is one that women look forward to, prepare for, and do not find especially stressful.

Part of the controversy over the effect of the empty nest no doubt results from the fact that researchers have sometimes falsely attributed to the empty nest the consequences of other factors. For example, when the departure of children from the home unmasks an empty marriage, it is the quality of the marriage, not the empty nest, that may lead to divorce. There is no evidence that a solid marital relationship is harmed by an emptied nest. Studies are needed that examine the empty nest as a *transition* and that look at men and women both before and after the last child is launched.

Retirement.   **Retirement** is the institutionalized separation of an individual from his or her occupational position, with entitlement to a continuation of income based on prior years of service. Age is usually the prime consideration in such separation, although health may also be a big factor. Usually a certain latitude is given the individual to choose the point at which he or she retires, sometimes as early as 50 and often as late as 70. Over age 65, about 80 percent of men and about 90 percent of women do not have an occupational position.

When people leave their occupations, many changes occur in their lives regardless of whether retirement was voluntarily or forced. But as we shall see in Chapter 9, retirement means not only giving up a role but also taking up a new one. The self-sufficiency required of retired people is certainly a challenge to most of them. Retirement also influences the other roles an individual plays, although the direction of this influence is unpredictable. For example, some marriages are enhanced by retirement, while others are subverted. Some organizations shun retired members, while others rely heavily on them. To some people, retirement represents a crisis, a world turned upside down. To others, retirement is merely the realization of a long-awaited and well-planned change. Currently it appears that at least two-thirds of those who retire do so with no great difficulty in either giving up their job role or in taking up the retirement role (Atchley, 1976b; 1982b; 1982c).

Widowhood.   Widowhood is another role change that is common among older people. In 1975, more than half the women and 14 percent of the men 65 or over were widows or widowers (U.S. Bureau of the Census, 1976b). For many people, widowhood allows no fulfillment of sexual needs. It also diminishes the possibility of gaining identity through the accomplishments or positions of the spouse. Widowhood also marks the loss of an important type of intimate interaction based on mutual interests. For example, the widow often replaces the one intimate, extensive, and interdependent relationship she had with her husband with several transitory and interdependent relationships with other widows. The case of Mrs. Willoughby illustrates what can happen.

Mrs. Willoughby is having problems adjusting to widowhood and compensating for restrictions in her social, as well as physical, life space after three decades of marriage and joint employment with her husband. Together, they managed an apartment building. She has no children. Today, her most regular contacts are with a younger sister, but there is little comfort in the relationship, for the sister is condescending toward Mrs. Willoughby and her abilities. Mrs. Willoughby feels she thinks too much about herself: "I just think about sitting here and vegetating. I didn't used to have time to think of myself before. I had my husband and we were busy taking care of the apartment house we managed." With the loss of her husband, Mrs. Willoughby's financial situation as well as her health began to deteriorate. She could not continue to manage the apartment building without her husband, and so she is now living on her savings and some Social Security benefits. She would like to work and try to find companionship, perhaps with a man, but her sister has persuaded her she could probably not succeed at either endeavor. She does have misgivings about her sister's wisdom in these things, but not enough self-confidence to act on her own initiative, for she is used to depending on the judgments of others. "I had to do everything my husband said because he was the boss, although I did resent it deeply." In near desperation, she seems to feel there *must* be a way for her to get some of the most pressing needs met; that somewhere, close at hand, there must be a new way of life—if only she could discover it. She would like to make a grasp at it: "I want to do something, but I don't know just what it is or how to go about it." She constantly chides herself for minutes spent in late-morning sleep when she could be doing other things, but she admits frankly she does not know what those things might be (Clark and Anderson, 1967:408).

The role changes that retirement and widowhood bring are not necessarily unwelcome to the individual. Often, people happily give up the responsibilities of work and view retirement as a period of increased fulfillment. Likewise, after the initial shock of grief wears off, many widows enjoy the sense of relief and the freedom from responsibility that come with widowhood. For many, widowhood means a reunion with friends who have been widowed for some time. In fact, a frequent complaint of married older women is that their family obligations shut them out of many of the activities their widowed friends enjoy. Blau (1961) found that this is particularly likely to happen to women over 70. Nevertheless, these changes require the individual to adjust.

Perhaps the most significant factor influencing the adjustment of widows in a given society is the number of other roles available to them. Lopata (1972) found that the more densely settled and the more urbanized the area of residence, the larger the field of available women's roles was and the more freedom widows had in choosing among them.

Dependency.   Perhaps one of the most dreaded role changes accompanying old age is that of **dependency,** the shift from the role of independent adult to that of dependent adult.* Older

---

*While psychologists use the word *dependency* to refer to a psychological state, here it refers to a position and role characterized by the necessity of relying on others, either physically or financially.

people, both in institutions and in the community at large, fear becoming dependent. Whether physical or financial, dependency is a difficult position for most adults to accept. The fear is easy to understand. We are taught from birth to strive to become independent and self-sufficient. This is a deeply ingrained value for most of us, and it is not surprising that we are hostile to the idea of giving up autonomy and becoming dependent on others.

Dependency is all the more difficult to accept because of the changes it brings in other roles. For example, some older people are forced by necessity to fall back on their children. For a number of reasons this necessity strains the parent–child relationship. For one, parents sometimes resist, and often resent, having to depend on their children. They may become angry and frustrated by the changes in interaction brought on by the reversal of positions. They may feel guilty because they believe they should not be dependent. Their children, now adults, may likewise resent having to provide for both their own children and their parents, yet at the same time they may feel guilty for harboring this resentment. And finally, the spouses of the adult children may not willingly accept the diversion of family resources to aged parents.

What makes dependency especially difficult is the set of expectations attached to it: Dependent people in our society are expected to defer to their benefactors, to be eternally grateful for what they receive, and to give up the right to lead their own lives. We demand such deference of our growing children, the poor, or any other dependent group. Is it any wonder, then, that older people, who often have spent as much as 50 years being independent adults, rebel at the idea of assuming a dependent position? Interestingly, while many older Americans find themselves having to ask their children for some kind of help at one time or another, they still tend, on balance, to give as much help as they receive. (See Chapter 7 for additional discussion of this point.)

Disability and Sickness.   Disability is another new role that older people may experience. There are varying degrees of disability, and when it becomes extreme, it usually turns into dependency. But even for the many older people whose disabilities have not reached that extreme, disability still restricts the number of roles they can play, and it also affects other people's reactions. Over a third of the older population of the United States has a disability serious enough to limit their ability to work, keep house, or engage in other major activities (C. Wilder, 1973).

Sickness is similar to disability in that its influence is felt mainly through a limitation of role playing. Good health, or absence of sickness or disability, operates alongside age and sex as a major criterion for eligibility for various positions. Most positions outside the circle of family and friends require activity that is impossible for the severely sick or disabled.

It has long been recognized in our society that sick people occupy a unique position. They are not expected to hold jobs, go to school, or otherwise meet the obligations of other positions, and they are often dependent on others for care. If they play the sick role long enough, they may be permanently excluded from some of their other positions, such as job-holder, officer in voluntary associations, or family breadwinner. Sick people are usually exempt from social responsibilities, are not expected to care for themselves, and are expected to need medical attention. The more serious the prognosis, the more likely they are to find themselves being treated as dependents.

Whether people are defined as sick partly depends on the seriousness and certainty of the prognosis. Even if they have a functional or physical impairment, individuals are less likely to be allowed to play the sick role if the prognosis is known not to be serious. Yet regardless of the prognosis, sick people are often expected to want to get well, and to actually do so (Gordon, 1966). The importance of aging to sickness and

disability is of course that as we age, the probability of disease, illness, or disability becomes greater.

The Role of the Institutional Resident.   When illness and disability become a serious handicap, many older people take up residence in a nursing home or home for the aged. While only about 4 percent of the older population lives in institutional facilities at any one time, those who enter an institution usually face important role changes. In the institutional setting, opportunities for useful or leisure activities, contacts with the outside world, and privacy are all less frequent than they are outside. Coupled with the extremely negative attitude of most older people toward living in an institution, these changes create significant obstacles to continuity of role playing and adaptation. Institutional care is considered in detail in Chapter 18.

Other Important Role Changes.   There are also changes with age in roles that continue from middle age into later life. For example, there is a decline in religious participation. Overall participation in voluntary associations also declines, in terms of both number of memberships held and number of meetings attended. Contacts with friends appear to be maintained until about age 75, after which there is a decline.

Thus far, the changes in position and role that we have found to be associated with aging would be described by most people as changes for the worse. They represent a constriction of individual life space, a diminution in the number of positions such as breadwinner, husband, and employee, and relegation to negatively valued positions such as widow, dependent, and sick person. While these changes have their positive aspects, overall they appear generally negative to most people.

Are there no positive changes in position as one grows older? The answer is, yes, a few. For one thing, people appear to take a stronger interest in politics in their later years. Voting percentages peak at about age 62, and 75 percent of people over 70 vote in presidential elections, as compared with about 60 percent of those age 25. This same pattern exists with regard to party identification, or interest in political affairs. Older people have substantially higher representation among public officials in the United States (both elected and appointed) than among most other occupations. Thus, while only a small fraction of the population engages actively in politics, opportunities for increased political participation seem to be present for a few older people.

Older people may join special groups such as golden age clubs or senior centers. Yet seldom do more than 5 percent of the older people in a given community join such organizations. There appears to be a widespread reluctance on the part of older people to identify themselves as old. One 70-year-old, when asked if she belonged to the local senior center, told me, "Who wants to be with those old fogies all the time?" This reluctance to accept being labeled old is likely to undermine any organization widely promoted as being for older people. Thus, while membership in such clubs opens up to people only as they grow older, it is also a position that many older people reject.

In their later years, people have much more time to devote to leisure-time activities. Most older people spend more time on such activities than on daily grooming, housekeeping, cooking, and the like. Specific activities that increase as people age are watching television, visiting, reading, and gardening. Television watching occupies more of the older person's time than any other single activity, particularly for those who live alone. Older people spend about two hours a day visiting, either inside or outside their own household. Time spent with friends tends to decline from the teens through the fifties, but tends to rise again after age 60. Reading is more important to the old than to the young. Gardening tends to increase from the teens through the sixties. The expansion of lei-

sure time practically forces a change in this area.

Changes in Groups

Much will be said in later chapters about how older people relate to various types of groups. For now, our interest will center on how groups influence the individual's social situation.

Obviously, when people lose jobs through retirement or lose spouses through death, their role changes parallel changes in groups. However, certain role changes do not correspond to changes in position. To begin with, individuals may gain or lose power in a group, even though their position may remain nominally the same. Thus, an older member of a board of directors may experience a change in influence, and a retired executive, having lost an economic power base in the community, may find it difficult to maintain roles in community organizations. Such changes are often subtle, but their impact on the social situation of the individual can be dramatic. Group memberships sometimes interlock in such a way that a change in a relationship to one group will change the individual's relationship to other groups. For example, Atchley (1976b) found that retirement reduced the number of contacts with friends among retired telephone company men because interaction was tied to the workplace, but that retirement increased the contacts with friends among retired men teachers because it was not.

Another important situational issue concerns the fact that certain groups have a finite life span and grow old along with their members. For example, in one small midwestern town, the American Legion Auxiliary was made up of women whose husbands had fought in World War I. In 1971 the organization had five members, all widows, ranging in age from 78 to 84. The group met frequently and the members were close friends who relied on each other heavily for companionship and exchange of small services. A year later, two of the members died, including one who had been a dominant influence on the group. The remaining members found it difficult to carry on community service functions. But more important, they found it difficult to fill their needs for stimulation and companionship within the group. Because new members are not being recruited, this group will eventually disappear.

In groups that recruit new members from upcoming age cohorts, change brings another sort of situational change. Older members of voluntary associations sometimes complain that the goals of the organization have changed or that the type of person being recruited is "not my kind of people." In such cases, nominal continuity of role playing masks some important changes in social situation.

Changes in Environments

People play social roles in particular places, and how they feel about their role performance is partly influenced by the appropriateness of the environment. Aging can potentially bring change to three types of environment: workplace, housing, and community. How people cope with loss of contact with a familiar environment is neglected in gerontological research. However, it is safe to say that some people develop strong feelings about places and the things in them; for these people, environmental change is an important type of situational change.

Retired people often seem to miss a familiar workplace. Even if the work environment was not pleasant, it was mastered, at least in most cases, and this feeling of mastery is important to many people. Also, social scientists tend to neglect the fact that people often develop close relationships with machines—a boat or even a cantankerous furnace may seem like an old friend. In addition, skills associated with work may not be easily exercised in other settings. A retired salesman can use his verbal skills anywhere, but a retired printer cannot easily transfer his skills to other settings.

Few older people change housing in later life,

and even fewer change communities. Those who do may experience dramatic situational change. People become attached to various aspects of their dwellings—the door that has to be opened just so, the pencil marks on the closet door that mark a child's growth, the stain on the carpet from a wedding reception. When a person lives in the same place for a long time, the environment grows rich in associations with the past. Of course, feelings about this past may as easily be negative as positive. In addition, the routines of role playing to some extent also depend on the environment. Being a wife in a high-rise apartment building may be different from being a wife in a single-family home.

It takes time to get to know a new community—how to get around, what facilities are there, who the "good" physicians are, and so on. Older people who change communities often must disconnect themselves from innumerable long-standing relationships, and reestablishing oneself in the new community is always difficult, sometimes impossible. More than anything else, the potentially negative impact of migration on the individual's social situation and level of integration into the community serves to keep older people from changing residences even in the face of strong pressures to do so (Goldscheider, 1971).

Moving into an institution is sometimes necessary in response to the symptoms of physical aging, and as such it is an age-related change in environment, probably the first that comes to mind. However, at most 25 percent of older people actually experiences such a move.*

Life Styles

The life course, age norms, and decision demands combine with other social factors, such as ascription and achievement, to locate people

---

*For further discussion of housing and community, see Chapter 8. For further discussion of institutionalization, see Chapter 18.

in their positions, roles, groups, and environments. This view explains a large measure of the *social* pressures on the individual. But what about pressures from within the individual—pressures that come from his or her preferences, capacities, needs, wants, and fears?

By observing people we can see not only their roles, relationships, group memberships, activities, and environments but also how these elements are forged together by choices, by selective commitments of attention and energy, and by personal mannerisms into a whole life—a *life style*. Even with the restrictions imposed by social class, sex, ethnicity, and age, there are usually many possibilities for mixing one's interests in work, free-time activity, family, friends, creativity, service to others, and a host of other interests into a personal life style. Yet developing a life style is not purely a personal matter.

The *values* that are served by one's life style are determined in part by cultural and subcultural *tradition* and in part by personal *experience*. To a great extent we can expect life style to show large cohort and period influences. For example, in the 1920's it was not unusual for people to select a life style in which marriage played no part. In the 1950's this was practically unheard of. Thus, one era's "traditional" life style can be another's "deviant" life style.

Aging has the potential to alter life style in countless ways. Physical capacities, economic wherewithal, group memberships, activities, and environments are all vulnerable to changes with age. In contrast, aging brings a certain freedom from social restraints that could alter life style more *toward* a person's values than away from them, as might result from physical aging. Since nearly all studies of life style in later life are cross-sectional, it is not possible to assess the impact of age on life style changes. All we can know from these studies is what life styles predominate at various life stages.

In a study of 142 middle-class men and women in their seventies, Maas and Kuypers (1974) found that just over 40 percent of the men had a life style centered on their families

and just over 40 percent had a more solitary life style (all of their male respondents were married) that revolved around hobbies and cursory social contacts. The remainder found their life style dominated by ill health and the consequent dissatisfactions. Women in their seventies were more diverse in life style, owing largely to the fact that half of the women were no longer married. Widowed or divorced women (all of the women respondents had been married at one time) were much more likely than married women to have job-centered life styles (13 percent) or diffuse life styles with no clear-cut focus (22 percent). The life styles of the remaining women paralleled those of the men: about 40 percent had a life style centered on their husband, if married, or visiting with family and friends if not; and there were just over 10 percent each involved in group-centered or illness-centered life styles. Interestingly, although a third of the men were employed, none of them had a job-centered life style.

Williams and Wirths (1965) studied the life styles of 168 men and women over 50 (average age, 65). They found six basic life styles among their respondents, distributed as shown in Table 6-1. The results are generally comparable to those of Maas and Kuypers (1974), cited above, but Williams and Wirths provide no clear-cut data on sex differences. Williams and Wirths found that 65 percent of their subjects were in the "highest" category with respect to being

TABLE 6-1   Focus of life styles in later life

Life Style	Percent
Familism	33
Couplehood	20
World of work	15
Living fully	13
Living alone	12
Minimal involvement	7

Source: Compiled from Williams and Wirths, 1965.

able to adapt to aging successfully within their life style. This was true for all but one life style —minimal involvement, which showed only one-third in the highly successful category. This finding does not support Cumming and Henry's (1961) hypothesis that individual disengagement is a satisfying and successful way to age.

While there are many more questions than answers about the effect of aging on life style, more definitive answers than we already have may not be easy to obtain. The subject of life style is as elusive as that of personality and in addition has been subject to much less development. Yet those researchers who are interested in how "whole lives" change with age cannot avoid the issue of life style.

Summary

Social aging involves society's assigning people to positions and opportunities based on chronological age or life stage. Age is used to determine eligibility, evaluate appropriateness, and modify expectations with respect to various positions in society. Positions in groups and the roles and relationships that go with them largely define the participation of people in their society. As we begin a new role, we tend to play the role rather formally, but the longer we have been in the role the more personalized it becomes and the more comfortable we are in it. Aging is a socially satisfying process to many people because it increases the duration and therefore the security of their role relationships. Holding an advantaged social position for a long time can also result in an accumulation of advantages such as wealth, prestige, and influence. Holding a position for a long time can also lead to the development of exceptional skills that can be used to offset the disqualifying character of older age as an eligibility criterion.

The life course is an ideal sequence of roles a person is expected to play as he or she moves through life. There are many versions of the life course, depending on sex, ethnicity, and social class. The time schedule implied by the life course can also change over historical time, so that, for example, in one era the ideal age to marry may be much older than the ideal age in another era. As people grow older, their accumulated decisions about various life course options increasingly differentiate one person from another. The life course determines the opportunities and limits for people in a given life stage and decision demands require people to make choices from among the options open to them. Generally, the older one gets within a given life stage, the narrower the range of options left. The age norms used to allocate people to positions and roles are based loosely on ideas about what people of various ages are capable of, as well as about what is appropriate for them. The greater the gap between the assumptions about functioning implied by the age norm and the actual level of functioning of the individual to whom the norm is applied, the more likely that the age norm will be seen as unjust.

Society conveys age norms through socialization, and individuals learn them through acculturation. As age increases, opportunities for formal socialization decrease. As adult experience increases, so does appreciation for the value of following rules. Anticipation allows people to prepare for and to smooth out life transitions. Adaptation and negotiation allow people to fit themselves to new roles, and vice versa.

In the previous chapter, we found that aging can have both positive and negative outcomes, that aging is mainly positive for most people, and that it is unpredictable for any given individual. The material in this chapter further illustrates why this is so. Variety among people increases with age as a result of biological, psychological, and social processes that operate differentially. Launching of children, retirement, widowhood, dependency, disability, sickness, and institutionalization are some major role changes that can accompany later life. Taken together, they represent very significant changes in the situations that individuals confront as they grow old. Role change can affect group membership and vice versa. In addition, subtle changes can occur in an individual's relationship to groups even though his or her role may remain essentially the same. The individual's influence may either grow or decline with age, depending on the group. Lost group memberships may influence relationships with other groups. Sometimes groups grow old and die along with their members. In other cases, the group's orientation shifts as the membership changes.

Environment is an important, but neglected, aspect of the social situation. Roles are played in specific places, and people can become quite attached to places and the things in them. Retirement usually brings a loss of relationship to the workplace. Residential mobility creates a new housing situation and sometimes a new community situation, as well. Institutionaliza-tion is without doubt potentially the most dramatic environmental change that people experience in later life.

Life-style choices allow individuals an opportunity to synthesize their personal characteristics with their outward social ties. Aging can cause both positive and negative discontinuities in life style. To the extent that aging brings significant physical decrements, lowered income, reduced social contacts, and so forth, it may force the individual to abandon a satisfying life style. On the other hand, to the extent that aging brings freedom from various social obligations, it may allow the individual to abandon an unsatisfying life style. Of course, some people never quite develop a life style that is suitable for them. Most people try to maintain their customary adult lifestyle throughout their adult lives.

PART III

Aging and the Social Situation

Physical, psychological, and social aging do not occur in the abstract. They occur in the context of specific social situations. Part III considers separate aspects of this context in detail. Chapter 7 examines the influence of aging on social relationships with family and friends and on the need for social support. Chapter 8 looks at how aging affects the ability to satisfy needs: income, housing, health care, transportation, and facilities and services. Chapter 9 deals with employment and retirement. Chapter 10 discusses activities, factors influencing activities, how aging changes activities, and aging in various spheres of activity, such as the workplace, home, and community. Chapter 11, the final one in Part III, examines dying, death, grief, and widowhood. Taken as a whole, the Chapters in Part III provide concepts and information that improve understanding of how aging interacts with everyday social life.

Chapter 7

Family, Friends, and Social Support

People do not cope with aging in isolation. They do it in the company of others who provide social and emotional support and in surroundings that provide a sense of connectedness and belonging. In this chapter we look at how aging influences, and is influenced by, relationships with spouse or mate, parent, child, sibling, relative, friend, and neighbor. In most cases, these are relationships that are intimate, durable, and personal, especially in comparison with other kinds of relationships, such as doctor–patient or social worker–client.

Three Types of Bonds

Relationships are reciprocal connections between people. There are three basic types of such bonds: interdependence, intimacy or affection, and belonging. *Interdependence* brings people together in order to satisfy their needs better than they could acting alone. For example, division of labor reduces the number of things the individual must do or know how to do. Interdependence can also increase the amount of available resources. We can pool our knowledge, financial resources, insights, and encouragement. Bonds of *intimacy* or *affection* allow for the exchange of love, trust, and confidences. Some intimate relationships also allow us to meet our needs for sexual expression. Our confidants' opinions of us and our past histories are important sources of self-respect. Relationships can also be based on a need for *belonging*—the sense of being more than an isolated individual. Relationships of belonging can be a source of companionship, socializing, identity, and safety or security.

These three types of bonds—interdependence, intimacy, and belonging—can exist in combination or in isolation. Given the many possible combinations, it should be clear that relationships can vary a great deal in both quality and purpose. Also, the quality and purpose of relationships are influenced by factors such as sex, social class, and ethnicity, thus insuring that relationships *do* vary a great deal, even within a given social role like that of spouse.

Relationships emerge when people *interact* with one another, usually in the process of playing their various social roles. Interdependence is built into many role relationships, but whether intimacy and/or belonging develop depends more on the specifics of the interaction—whether there is equality, self-disclosure, similarity, acceptance, agreement, trust, or cooperation.

Relationships can also be destroyed or diminished. For instance, relationships can be diminished by permanent geographic separation—a moving apart with no likelihood of return. Interdependence bonds can be weakened if one or both of the participants become less effective. Belonging bonds can be weakened by growing feelings of superiority or inferiority or difference in one or both of the participants. And intimacy bonds can be weakened by selfishness, breaks in trust, or withdrawal by one or both participants.

We will now look at three general types of relationships: family relationships, friendships, and social support.

Family

The family is perhaps the most basic of social institutions.* There are a great many different types of family organizations throughout the world. We will concentrate on the American pattern. Almost everyone is born into a family. Most people spend most of their lives residing with a family group. Most people play several family roles in the course of a lifetime, for example, son, husband, father, grandfather, uncle. For many, the family group is the center of their world, the highest priority in their system of values. Less than 5 percent of the older population are without family.

Just like a person, the family has a life cycle.

The family life cycle begins with marriage—the formation of a couple from two previously unrelated people. There are many ways that families can develop. Some develop intact, others split up, and still others represent a uniting of parts from different split families. What family sociologists call the *family life cycle* is really an ideal representation of the stages in the life of a couple that marries, has children, and stays together until one spouse dies in old age.

Conceptions of the family life cycle vary from simple (Glick and Parke, 1965; Rollins and Feldman, 1970) to complex (Hill and Rodgers, 1964). A relatively simple scheme is sufficient to illustrate the concept.*

Phases of the Family Life Cycle

1. Beginning (couple married 0 to 10 years, without children)
2. Early childbearing (oldest child under 3)
3. Preschool children (oldest child over 3 but under 6)
4. School-age children (oldest child over 5 and under 13)
5. Teenagers (oldest child over 12 and living at home)
6. Launching children (oldest child gone to youngest's leaving home)
7. Middle years (empty nest to retirement)
8. Retirement (one spouse retired to onset of disability)
9. Old age (one spouse disabled to death of one spouse)

Of course, since children and grandchildren usually begin their own family cycles, the chain seldom stops. As we shall see, increasingly it is only the last three phases of the family cycle that occur in later maturity or old age.

The family that produces the relationships of spouse, parent, grandparent, great grandparent,

---

*For a fuller discussion of families in later life, see Troll et al., 1979; Atchley and Miller, 1980.

*The model presented here is adapted from Rollins and Feldman (1970).

and widow(er) is called the *family of procreation;* it is the family within which a person's own procreative behavior occurs. People also belong to a *family of orientation,* usually the family they are born or adopted into. Older people very often carry into their later years the roles from the family of orientation (son, daughter, brother, sister) as well as from the family of procreation. There are also family roles, like cousin, uncle, nephew, brother-in-law, and so on, that derive from the *extended family,* the complex network of kin that parallels both the family of procreation and the family of orientation, usually through a sibling relationship or through the marital bond uniting two separate families of orientation.

Kinship being an extremely complex subject, we will not emphasize extended kinship, but will concentrate on roles in the family of procreation and the family of orientation as they relate to the effects of aging. We will first consider older couples, then we will briefly consider how other marital statuses—never married, widowed, and divorced or separated—influence family relationships. Next we will look at relations with adult offspring, grandchildren, and siblings. Then we will consider friends. The chapter ends with a discussion of social support.

Couples

In the United States, more than 70 percent of older men and 36 percent of older women—comprising more than half the older population—are married and live with a spouse in an independent household. At younger ages, the proportion married is even higher, for example, half of women age 65 to 69 are married. In addition to married couples, there are unmarried couples—heterosexual as well as homosexual—who live together as mates. As male death rates go down, couples will be even more common in middle and later life than they are now.

Although most middle-aged and older couples have been together since early adulthood,

marriage in later life is becoming more common. For example, in 1976 there were nearly 400,000 brides and grooms age 45 or over; of these, 48,000 were 65 or over. Only 5 percent were first-time marriages. Remarriage in middle age or later is much more likely among men than women, for two reasons: women vastly outnumber men of their own or older ages, and men tend to marry women younger than themselves. Grooms 65 or over outnumbered brides in that age category by 2 to 1, and the median age of the grooms of women 65 or over was 67.4, whereas the median age of brides of men 65 or over was 57.6. Even if people married only others their age, there would be no potential mates available for 50 percent of the unmarried women.

Thus, couples are prevalent even among older people. The couple relationship tends to be a focal point in people's lives, especially since the departure of children and retirement have often increased the amount of contact between spouses and perhaps reduced the number of alternative relationships. As the average length of life increases, so does the average number of years a couple can expect to live together after the children leave home.

Marital Satisfaction. Whether the increased focus on the couple is a bane or a blessing depends of course on the quality of the relationship. A happy or satisfied relationship is a blessing. A happy couple relationship is a source of great comfort and support as well as the focal point of everyday life, and satisfied couples usually grow closer as the years go by. Such couples often show a high degree of interdependence, particularly in terms of caring for one another at times of illness. The husband in a strong couple relationship is particularly likely to see the wife as an indispensable pillar of strength. The couple tends to share many activities, and happy couples tend to exhibit greater equality between partners than do unhappy couples, an equality that comes from a gradual loss of sex role boundaries and a decreasing sexual definition of household division of labor. Happy couples tend to remain sexually active into later life (Clark and Anderson, 1967:237–241).

Although most couples are generally happy and satisfied, a small proportion are not. Some people feel their spouse is the cause of all their troubles, and they often wish they could somehow terminate their marriage. People remain in an unhappy marriage for a variety of reasons. For some it is a matter of religious orthodoxy. Some stay rather than confront negative community opinions about divorce. Others remain together because they do not see any other way to economically sustain their life style. Others stay together "for the sake of the kids." Some do so because they *need* the poor relationship in order to continue in their role as martyr. The list could go on and on. Sometimes marriage strains are too much, and people divorce in middle age or later life. In 1976, for example, 168,000 divorces were granted to people age 45 and over in the 29 states that register divorces; of these, 12,000 were granted to people 65 or over.

What happens to marital satisfaction over the life span? From various studies, a consistent picture emerges of high marital satisfaction in early adulthood, a gradual decline in satisfaction through middle age, and a steady increase in marital satisfaction in the period after child rearing. This particular pattern has not been found in all studies, but it has been found often enough that it is probably correct. What appears to happen is that the stresses of marriage become progressively greater from young adulthood and peak in middle age, when often there are teenagers at home, heavy job demands, and high community demands on time and energy. People may also have to care for aging parents during this stage. We might expect the rise in satisfaction after middle age to be related to the breakup of unhappy marriages in middle age, but the data on age at the time of divorce do not support this notion: Of women who divorce, 65 percent do so before age 30 and only 11 percent do so after age 40 (U.S. Bureau of the Census, 1977d). This proportion is not high enough to account for more than a small fraction of the age difference in marital satisfaction between middle-aged adults and older adults that has been observed in many studies.

Part of the reason that marital satisfaction appears to be higher in later life is a shift in the focus of marital expectations. Thurnher (1975) found that among middle-aged respondents, husbands' expectations centered on their wives' performance as housekeeper and mother while wives' expectations centered on their husbands' role as family provider. In the preretirement stage (mean age of 60), both husbands and wives showed greater interest in their spouse's personality, and their descriptions involved more emotional qualities.

Another reason for the greater marital satisfaction of later life relates to goal conflict within some wives. Livson (1976) found that traditional wives tended to be satisfied both in middle age and later, but that women who wanted involvement outside the household felt unhappy and constrained by their roles as wife and as mother. Thurnher (1975) found that unhappiness with their spouses was mainly concentrated among middle-aged women and that there was little difference between middle-aged and preretired men in their satisfaction with their spouses. More than 80 percent of husbands *and* wives had positive feelings about their spouses in the preretirement stage.

For married people, marital satisfaction is a central factor in their overall satisfaction with life. For example, Lee (1978) found that among older married men, only health was a more powerful predictor of their overall life satisfaction than marital satisfaction. For older married women, marital satisfaction was by far the strongest predictor of overall life satisfaction. For both men and women, marital satisfaction was more important than age, education, retirement, or standard of living in predicting life satisfaction. Thus, high marital satisfaction is extremely important to the overall well-being of older couples.

Contributors to Marital Satisfaction. Marital satisfaction does not occur in a vacuum. It is very much tied to other happenings, especially in relation to careers and child rearing. The following scenario shows how various life course factors may interact. But keep in mind that life course factors can vary considerably across social classes and ethnic groups.

Americans typically marry young: Median age at first marriage in 1976 was 21 for women and 23 for men. Early in a marriage, both spouses are likely to be employed. By their late twenties, most couples have completed childbearing. Even though a majority of women nowadays remain in the labor force during their children's preschool years, about 40 percent leave their job and remain out of the labor force through middle age. Once children are born, the roles of the spouses change. Men tend to concentrate on their jobs and economic providing, and women tend to concentrate on housekeeping and child rearing, even if they have jobs. Husband and wife may have little energy and may pay little attention to each other or to their relationship, a situation that may persist for 10 to 15 years. The result is what Cuber and Harroff called the "devitalized" relationship:

> The key to the devitalized [relationship] is the clear discrepancy between middle-aged reality and the earlier years. These people usually characterized themselves as having been "deeply in love" during the early years, as having spent a great deal of time together, having enjoyed sex, and most important of all, having had a close identification with one another. The [middle-age] picture, with some variation from case to case, is in clear contrast—little time is spent together, sexual relationships are far less satisfying qualitatively or quantitatively, and interests and activities are not shared, at least not in the deeper and meaningful way they once were. Most of their time together

now is "duty time"—entertaining together, planning and sharing activities with children, and participating in various kinds of required community responsibilities (1965:45–47).

But whereas jobs and child rearing absorb a couple's energies and attentions to the possible detriment of their marital relationship in early and middle adulthood, changes in these dimensions play an important part in bringing undivorced couples back together. In middle age, a man's career tends to reach a plateau. The job no longer offers prospects for explosive personal growth, advancement, or financial success. Instead, the man settles into a more routine process, continuing to function in a familiar job with only minor increments in status or economic rewards. Maintaining a career can also take less time than making one. The launching of children into adulthood leaves women with a greatly reduced workload and fewer responsibilities at home. A woman may devote more time to her career and may see this as her chance to show what she can do. This shift is made easier if the husband is in a career plateau that allows him to begin to share more of the workload at home. The fact that there are no children to evoke different parental sex roles facilitates a return to the more egalitarian relationship that typified the early years of marriage. Retirement frees a couple even further from external constraints that might interfere with the process of merging their individualities into a single unit.

Types of Couples. Thus, in later life, many couples rediscover one another, to their delight and growing satisfaction. They tend to become what Cuber and Harroff call a "vital" couple:

> The vital pair can easily be overlooked.... They do the same things, publicly at least; and when talking for public consumption say the same things—they are proud of their homes, love their children, gripe about their jobs, while being proud of their career accomplishments. But when the close, intimate, confidential, empathic look is

taken, the essence of the vital relationship becomes clear; the mates are intensely bound together psychologically in important life matters. Their sharing and togetherness [are] genuine. [This relationship] provides the life essence for both man and woman (1965:55).

Cuber and Harroff (1965) describe two other types of couples that probably persist into later life: conflict-habituated and passive-congenial. The major focus of the *conflict-habituated* relationship is on controlling the ever-present potential for overt hostility. Quarreling and nagging are the major communications. It is as though the validation of each partner were provided by the existence of his or her clear opposite in the relationship. *Passive-congenial* relationships are marriages of convenience. The relationship provides little excitement or emotional support. It does get the work done in a comfortably adequate fashion, and it provides companionship. Vinick's (1979) description of late-life remarriages suggests that many such marriages are passive-congenial and that the spouses expect little more.

Functions of Couplehood.   When we look at couples in the period after child rearing, we are struck by the very wide range of functions that couplehood has for the couple. Let us discuss the functions of couplehood in terms of intimacy, interdependence, and belonging.

Intimacy.   Intimacy in the couple involves mutual affection, regard, and trust. For most couples it also involves sexual intimacy. A wife is often her husband's only confidant. Lowenthal et al. (1975) found a prevailing lack of mutuality and intimacy in relationships among men, a fact that men in midlife regret. In their review of the literature on intimacy, Lowenthal and Robinson (1976) found substantial evidence that men have difficulty establishing a close relationship with anyone but their wife. And Glick et al. (1974) found that the most common reaction to widowhood among men was a feeling of having lost a part of themselves.

Farrell and Rosenberg (1981) found that wives played a crucial role in validating middle-aged husbands' image of themselves as the beloved family patriarch. According to Farrell and Rosenberg, a major problem in most men's lives is the need to be in control at home and at the same time be loved there. In actuality, the wife more often controls the home situation and, often in collusion with the children, protects the husband by avoiding confrontations that might undermine his belief that he is in charge and has the family's support and respect. Part of the decline in marital satisfaction in middle age may be thus a by-product of the strains involved in supporting what is increasingly a myth of patriarchy. And the upturn in satisfaction after child launching may be related to the fact that when the children leave, control over them is no longer a power issue dividing the couple and interfering with intimacy.

Sexual Intimacy.   Sex is an integral part of any couple's relationship. In counseling older couples and older people in general, the sexual component of human interaction must be taken into account. Sexuality in middle and later life reflects physical capacity, emotional needs, and social norms. Unfortunately, the simultaneous influence of these various factors has seldom been studied.

Masters and Johnson (1966) found that five major factors served to limit sexual response in older females: (1) steroid starvation, which makes coitus painful, (2) lack of opportunity for a regular sexual outlet, (3) the lingering Victorian concept that women should have no innate interest in sexual activity, (4) physical infirmities of the desired partner, and (5) the fact that many older women never learned to respond to sexual desire and therefore use menopause as an excuse for total abstinence. Masters and Johnson also found, however, that with therapy to eliminate the pain associated with coitus and with the uterine contractions that often accompany orgasm, there was no time limit imposed on female sexuality by age.

Among older men, say Masters and Johnson, sexual performance does wane with age. Levels of sexual tension, ability to establish coital connection, ability to ejaculate, and frequency of masturbation and nocturnal emission all declined with age. Yet older men who established a high sexual output, by whatever means, in their middle years, showed a much less significant decline. Masters and Johnson tied the age increase in sexual inadequacy to several factors, the least significant of which was physical. The Victorian myth that older men have no sexuality was identified by Masters and Johnson as a major force leading to self-doubt and in turn to impotence among older men. Research indicates that many older men who suffer impotence as a result of psychological factors can be counseled to overcome it.

Masters and Johnson found that if an active sexual pattern is established in the middle years, it is usually physically possible to maintain it into the eighties, provided health is good. They went on to say that six factors reduced this possibility: (1) boredom with one's partner, (2) preoccupation with career or economic pursuits (this would affect only a tiny proportion of older men), (3) mental or physical fatigue, (4) overindulgence in food or drink, (5) physical and mental infirmities, and (6) fear of poor performance. Masters and Johnson further stated, "There is no way to overemphasize the importance that the factor 'fear of failure' plays in the aging male's withdrawal from sexual performance" (1966:269).

Wives sometimes lack insight into the "fear of failure" problem and are very likely to feel personally rejected by their husband's apparent disinterest in sexual activity. Thus, the older couple may face some serious sexual problems that do not usually confront younger couples. Very often the older couple is not aware of the exact nature of the problems. To solve them, the couple must understand what conditions are necessary to maintain sexual functioning and what can be done to create these conditions.

Aging can also bring some advantages in sexual expression. Starr and Weiner (1981) studied 800 people between the ages of 60 and 91 and found that 36 percent said that sex was better for them currently than when they were younger. Only 25 percent said it had gotten worse. Most felt that sex should play a large part in an older couple's life. About 80 percent were sexually active, and a majority had intercourse at least once a week. Most had experienced an increase in the spontaneity of sexual expression as a result of the empty nest and retirement. Being able to spend a long time making love whenever they wanted was seen as a major advantage to older couples. In a survey that I conducted, "being free to make love in the morning" was mentioned by several people as an advantage of retirement (Atchley, 1975c).

The prevailing myth is that older people are not interested in sex. When Starr and Weiner (1981) approached senior center staff for permission to distribute questionnaires to center participants, they encountered resistance because the staff assumed that older people would be offended by questions about sex and would be embarrassed about their lack of sexuality. In fact, however, older people responded to the questionnaire in substantially higher percentages than in other studies of sex among middle-aged adults.

Sex means much the same thing to older people as it does to others. To the question "What is a good sexual experience?" one of Starr and Weiner's older respondents replied, "To be really horny with a partner who is just as horny. To take plenty of time and when you can't stand it another minute, make it!" (1981: 5). This definition probably would find a lot of agreement from adults of any age. Starr and Weiner's respondents liked lots of things about sex: a sense of contributing to the other; feelings of desirability, zest, completion, and relaxation; feeling loved and loving; the comfort of touching and cuddling; and even transcendence. The vast majority had sex lives that were satisfying.

Fortunately, sex is one important area in

which older people generally refuse to do what society at large expects them to do. Yet undoubtedly some people withdraw from sexual activity because they feel withdrawal is expected or "normal." It is for such people that the myths and stereotypes about aging and sexuality are most harmful. But even the sexually active may feel the need to hide the fact, for fear of disapproval. This is not a healthy situation. Sex is a powerful expression of intimacy, and its continuation into later life should be celebrated.

Interdependence. Interdependence in the older couple involves instrumental sharing of housework, income, and other resources. In terms of housework, the picture is not very clear. Some studies have shown that even employed wives bear a disproportionate share of household chores (Bahr, 1973; Ballweg, 1967). Other studies have shown that with greater employment of wives, the empty nest, and retirement, couples tend to share housework (Gordon et al., 1976; Lipman, 1961, 1962; Kerckhoff, 1966a, 1966b). Changing attitudes about "men's work" versus "women's work" around the house may make it even more difficult to get a clear picture. In addition, trends may vary by type of work. Most people, especially men and better-educated women, tend to dislike routine work like housecleaning. Men may try to fall back on their traditional sex role to avoid it, while working women may lobby for hiring a maid. In both cases the idea is to avoid housework. These days, older people seem to enjoy housework more than younger people do. Whether this tendency will change over time remains to be seen.

With time, men apparently increase their involvement in more expressive or creative types of housework, such as cooking and home decorating (Gordon et al., 1976), making husbands and wives more equal in these areas in later life compared to middle age. Men seem to be expected to do heavy work and mechanical repairs throughout the life course. Husbands as well as wives tend to increase their involvement with

gardening in later life. However, apart from grocery shopping, wives show an unfortunate and persistent lack of knowledge or interest in managing finances.

Income sharing is a major dimension of interdependence for most couples. Income adequacy —what the couple have relative to what they feel they need—fluctuates across the life span. Of particular importance is the financial pinch of children. Working-class couples often recover from this by early in middle age, but for middle-class couples the financial pinch can be the worst at that stage, when their children are in college. The need to financially support older parents may arise at the same time that children need financial assistance to get launched into adulthood. The result is more than a pinch, it's a squeeze. And because partners usually share income in middle age, this can lead to conflict. Although retirement usually reduces available income, it normally does not produce a feeling of financial pressure comparable to the strains felt at midlife. Indeed, many couples find themselves more comfortable financially in retirement than at any other time in their married lives, which may also contribute to a rise in marital satisfaction later in life.

Taking care of one another in time of illness is a facet of interdependence that grows drastically important with increasing age. Shanas (1977) found that among older people who need assistance in such household matters as personal care, meal preparation, housework, or shopping, the spouse was *the* major provider of such help. Although assistance is an essential element of continuing to live in an independent household, it can be a severe strain on the spouse, particularly if he or she is also having health problems. Lopata (1973) found that 46 percent of the widows in her study had cared for their husbands at home during their final illness, and nearly 20 percent had done so for over a year. Not only do such health problems severely curtail many kinds of marital interactions, they also reduce the spouse's freedom of action.

A major problem can occur when care-giving

shifts from interdependence to dependence—when one spouse can no longer reciprocate. The more able spouse may feel resentment at the one-sided flow of attention and energy, and the reduction of equality between spouses may reduce the intimacy between them as well. Most spouses do what is needed if they can, and most could use more emotional support, aid, and counseling than they get.

Sense of Belonging.   Belonging for the older couple involves identification with the group, sharing of values and perspectives, a routine source of comfortable interaction and socializing, and a sense of safety and security. Identification with the group means that one sees oneself as a group member and that group membership says a lot about the individual. For example, traditional women are likely to answer the question "Who am I?" in terms of membership in a couple: "I am the wife of . . . and the mother of . . . and. . . ." In middle age the couple tends to be less the source of identity than in the postparental period.

A sense of belonging based on shared values or perspectives thrives on agreement. A major determinant of agreement is potential for conflict. In middle age, most couples have a high potential for conflict—over jobs, money, sex, or children. Child launching, career plateaus (and the withdrawal of personal stakes that usually goes with such plateaus), and greater financial security—all changes common to couples in late middle age—reduce the potential for conflict and increase the fund of agreement that supports a sense of belonging. The rediscovery of one's spouse can reduce sexual conflicts, and retirement can reduce disagreements over the provider function. The reduced size of the household after child launching usually means more socializing and companionship between spouses, which also increases the sense of mutual participation and belonging. Atchley et al. (1979) found that married older women interacted much less than widowed or never-married women with friends and relatives outside

the household. Finally, the availability of a spouse to provide care-giving when needed enhances most older people's sense of safety and security. Thus, care-giving supports ties of belonging as well as ties of interdependence.

It should be quite clear from the foregoing that the increase in marital satisfaction that typifies the transition from middle age to later maturity is no accident; it is the result of many forces, the vast majority of which are pulling the couple together toward a greater and greater appreciation and acceptance of one another. The empty nest and retirement increase opportunity for companionship and decrease potential for conflict, especially for those couples who remain physically healthy.

Remarriage.   As mentioned earlier, a substantial number of older couples are formed in later life. Only two studies have looked at this phenomenon in depth (McKain, 1969; Vinick, 1979). In a study of 100 older couples who married in later maturity, McKain (1969) found the desire for companionship to be by far the most frequently given reason. Previous experience with marriage also predisposed older people to remarry. Few of the couples believed in romantic love, but they were interested in companionship, lasting affection, and regard. As McKain states,

> The role of sex in the lives of these older people extended far beyond love-making and coitus; a woman's gentle touch, the perfume on her hair, a word of endearment—all these and many more reminders that he is married help to satisfy a man's urge for the opposite sex. The same is true for the older wife. (1969:30).

A few older people remarried to allay their anxiety about poor health, and some remarried to avoid having to depend on their children. Many older people tended to select mates who reminded them of a previous spouse. Also, older couples followed the same pattern of *homogamy* (the tendency for people of similar backgrounds to marry) that is found among younger couples.

Using as indicators of marriage success such unobtrusive measures as displays of affection, respect and consideration, obvious enjoyment of each other's company, lack of complaints about each other, and pride in their marriage, McKain found that successful "retirement marriage" was related to several factors. Couples who had known each other well over a period of years before marriage were likely to be successfully married. A surprisingly large number of couples McKain studied were related to each other through previous marriages. Probably the prime reason that long friendship was so strongly related to a successful marriage in later life is that intimate knowledge of the other allowed better matching of interests and favorite activities. Marriages in which interests were not alike were less successful.

Approval of the marriage by children and friends was also important for the success of marriage in later life, according to McKain's study. Apparently, considerable social pressure is exerted against marriage in later life, probably growing partly out of a misguided notion that older people do not *need* to be married and partly out of concern over what will happen to their estates. Older people are very sensitive to this pressure, and encouragement from children and from friends is important in overcoming it. Also, a marriage that alienates older people from their families or friends is not likely to be successful.

McKain also found that financial factors were related to successful marriage in later life. If both partners owned homes, success was more likely than if only one or neither did. The importance of dual homeownership was probably symbolic, indicating that each partner brought something equally concrete to the marriage. If both partners had sufficient incomes prior to marriage, they usually had a successful marriage. The arrangements for pooling property or giving it to children were important for predicting marital success because they indicated the priority one partner held in the eyes of the other. It was important for the marriage partner to have first priority on resources, if the marriage was to be successful.

Vinick (1979) found many of the same factors operating in the 24 couples she studied. She also found that the time before remarriage was easier for older women than for older men. Despite their greater financial difficulties, women had more social support than men during their time alone, especially from family. Women also found it easier than men did to ease loneliness by keeping busy. Thus, for these reasons men were much more highly motivated to remarry, and the large number of widows in later life made it a much more realistic prospect for them. Courtship did not last long, perhaps because the partners were already familiar with marriage and had a sense of what they were getting into. Family were more likely to approve of the remarriage than friends were, at least initially. After remarriage, interaction with children and friends declined as partners used one another as their primary source of interaction. Most people were quite satisfied with their remarriage.

Older People Not in Couples

The never-married, widowed, and divorced might be expected to have different patterns of family relationships than older people who are married. Indeed, Atchley et al. (1979) found that married women had much less contact with kin outside their households than women of other marital statuses.

In 1981, only 5 percent of the older people in the United States had never married. On the surface, one might expect these people to have trouble getting along as single individuals living in an independent household. M. Clark and Anderson (1967:256) found, however, that apparently because they learn very early in life to cope with aloneness and the need to look after themselves, older single people living alone have developed the autonomy and self-reliance so often required of older people. In addition, the "loners" among single people living alone are often spared the grief that comes from watching one's friends and relatives die. Thus, while it is possible to argue that people who never marry and perhaps live solitary existences are missing many of the "good" parts of life, they also apparently miss some of the "bad" parts too (Gubrium, 1975a).

Gubrium (1975a) found that never-married older people tended to be lifelong isolates who were not especially lonely in old age. He suggested that isolation is viewed by these people as normal. They resent the assumption often presented to them by researchers and service providers that relative isolation is necessarily bad and leads to loneliness. This point is a good one to bear in mind.

Most men stay unmarried because they want freedom from involvement. The bachelor appears to be motivated by an intense desire to escape the kind of involvement present in his family of orientation. The never-married older woman, on the other hand, often appears to be motivated by her desire to stay close to her family of orientation and by her choice of career* (M. Clark and Anderson, 1967).

Older people who have never married might be expected to have more contacts with extended kin than those who married. However, Atchley et al. (1979) found this contact depends a great deal on social class, at least for women. For example, never-married older women teachers interacted with extended kin significantly more than those who were married. But older telephone operators who had never married had much lower levels of interaction with extended family than did those who were married. In their total interaction patterns, teachers appeared to compensate for being single by a disproportionate involvement with relatives,

while telephone operators tended to compensate by having relatively more contacts with friends. Single older women teachers had about the same overall level of interaction as married older women teachers, but among older telephone operators, the overall interaction levels of single women were much lower than those of the married women.

Widowhood affects all family relationships. Shortly after the death of the spouse there is usually a flurry of support from family members, but this support is not very enduring. Within a few weeks, widowed persons usually find themselves on their own. Most widowed people live alone, and their major resource in coping with loneliness comes most often from friends rather than family. Widowed parents must adjust to a new relationship with their children. Widows can usually grow closer to their daughters, but not as often to their sons (Lopata, 1973). There is no clear picture of how widowed fathers' relations with their children are altered, although we can be reasonably sure that they are altered.

In 1981, about 6 percent of the older population was divorced, and about 10,000 older individuals get divorces every year in America. Yet there has been very little research on the impact of divorce on older persons or on the impact that being divorced may have on an older person's life. For example, many women who are divorced are effectively deprived of income in later life. In many cases, they are not entitled to private pension benefits. If they are not entitled to retirement benefits in their own right, they are forced into financial dependency. In addition, divorce of older parents can be expected to have an impact on relations with adult children and other kin. This topic is one of the most neglected areas of research in social gerontology.

Uhlenberg and Myers (1981) reported that recent increases in divorce rates are not restricted to young adults. Even though divorce rates among the elderly are still substantially lower than those for people in their early twenties,

---

*This latter factor is becoming less important today because there are very few careers that require one to remain unmarried. In the past, for example, women who taught school were often required to remain single.

there has been an increase in the percentage of people entering later life who are divorced. For example, in 1960, only 2 percent of those 65 to 69 were divorced compared to over 6 percent in 1980. Uhlenberg and Myers (1981:281) predict that the proportion of the elderly who are divorced will "increase quite rapidly over the next several decades."

Older Parents and Adult Children

For most older people, particularly those who are single, their most important relationships are with their adult children. There are many myths about how older people and their adult children relate in American society. It is erroneously thought that older people are abandoned by their children, that they seldom see them, that older people in nursing homes have been rejected by their families or have no family, and that older people are mainly takers rather than givers of aid. This section will give you an overview of the facts about how older people and their adult children tend to relate. It can help you identify important dimensions of these relationships and to get an idea of what is typical, so that you can put your own observations into context.

About 80 percent of the older American population has living children. About 10 percent of older Americans have adult children who are 65 or over. Most older Americans are not isolated from their children. In fact, older people and their adult children have many kinds of relationships. The relationships older people have with their adult children have been studied in terms of residential proximity, frequency of interaction, mutual aid, feelings of affection, and sense of filial duty or obligation.

Residential Proximity. Troll (1971) found more than 25 studies of residential proximity of older parents to their adult children. Older people prefer to live *near* their children, near being defined functionally in terms of travel time rather than geographic distance. Shanas (1977) found that 84 percent of older people

who had children lived less than an hour away from one of them. This proximity is probably more likely as older parents reach very advanced age.

There may be a period in the life course—when parents are middle-aged and children are beginning their own households and occupational careers—when the two generations are more geographically distant. For example, Bert Adams (1968a) found that only 33 percent of young adults live near their parents. When older parents retire, if they move, they tend to move near their children (Bultena and Wood, 1969a). There is also some evidence that people in their middle years return to the geographic areas where they grew up (Lee, 1974). In addition, some adult children migrate to be closer to an ill or disabled parent (Sussman and Burchinal, 1962a). Thus, the preliminary picture that emerges is one of residential convergence as adult children "settle down" and as older parents grow older. This possibility needs to be more carefully examined.

Interaction Frequency. Interaction frequency tends to be high among older parents and their adult children. Shanas (1977) found that 52 percent of her respondents had seen one of their children in the previous 24 hours. Harris and Associates (1975) found that 55 percent of their older sample had seen one of their children within the previous 24 hours and 85 percent within the previous week or two. These data from various sources all show that older people generally have frequent contact with their children.

However, this general trend masks variations among older people. For example, married older women interact less with their children than do those who are widowed or divorced. In urban areas, intergenerational visiting occurs more often among women than among men. But in rural areas older men may interact with their children more than older women do.

There also remains the issue of the *nature* of the contacts. Though frequent, intergenerational contacts are often brief encounters to "pass the time of day." If older parents are ill or disabled, the contacts are a way to check to see that all is well, and this sort of monitoring probably increases with the age of the parents. These frequent contacts mean that adult children are apt to learn quickly if their parents need something or have a problem.

Mutual Aid.   Mutual aid is considered the crucial intergenerational dimension by many researchers (Troll et al., 1979). Aid flows in both directions and may consist of services such as babysitting or housework, of information and advice, of moral support for various decisions, or of money or gifts. About a dozen studies have looked at this dimension.

Bracey (1966) found that less than 15 percent of the older people in his Louisiana sample got regular help with everyday household tasks from their sons or daughters. The most frequent services they received were shopping and housework, followed by cooking and advice about financial and maintenance matters. No more than 9 percent of the older people received regular financial help from a son or daughter, and an additional 4 percent said they received occasional money gifts. Atchley (1976b) found even less help; about 3 percent of retired couples reported cash gifts from family and friends. However, Bracey found no evidence of real neglect of old people by their children where there was obvious need. Thus, helping was specific, not generalized.

Riley and Foner stated:

> Contrary to the often-held theory of a one-way flow of contributions to old people, the flow of support between aged parents and their adult offspring appears to be two-directional, from parent to child or from child to parent as need and opportunity dictate. Altogether, the proportions of old people who give help to their children tends to exceed the proportions who receive help from their children (1968:551–552).

However, Reuben Hill (1965) concluded that the grandparents he studied generally gave less

often than they received for most categories of mutual aid. The differences in these results probably stem from differences in social class in the samples studied. Among the middle class, considerable aid continues to flow from older parents to middle-aged children, even into old age, but in the working class more help goes to old parents from middle-aged children. A key factor in patterns of mutual aid seems to be the financial and physical capacity of older parents to offer aid.

Seelbach (1977) found that the more vulnerable older people were, the more aid they expected and got from their adult children. Older respondents who were widowed or divorced women, who had low incomes, and who were in poor health expected and received more aid. This situation held true for both blacks and whites.

As a general rule, parents seem to give to their children one way or another for as long as they are able. A shift from this pattern may therefore coincide with a deterioration in the financial or health condition of the parents.

> In illness, from a third to two-fifths rely for help with housework, meals, and shopping upon husbands and wives and a similar proportion upon children or other relatives. . . . Between eight and nine in every ten of the bedfast at home depend primarily on members of their families for meals, housework, personal aid, and so on [Shanas et al., 1968:428–429].

Bankoff (1983) found that parents were by far the most important source of emotional support to women who became widowed in middle age, much more important than children or friends. Widows without strong parental support were more depressed, and no other source of support compensated for a lack of parental support. Bankoff attributed this to a need of widows for nurturance, which parents are best able to provide.

Whether or not older parents are satisfied with the frequency of interaction and mutual aid patterns with their adult children seems to depend on what they expect. Kerckhoff (1966b) found that older people fell into three types of orientation toward family relationships. Older parents with an extended family orientation (20 percent) expected to live near their children and enjoy considerable mutual aid and affection. Those with a nuclear family orientation (20 percent) expected neither to live near their children nor to be aided by them. And those with a modified extended family orientation (60 percent) believed in mutual aid and affection but took a middle-of-the-road position with regard to interaction frequency and extent of aid and affection. In actual experience, most of Kerckhoff's respondents had relationships that fit the modified extended family orientation. Not surprisingly, older parents with an extended family orientation tended to be disappointed, the middle-of-the-roaders were getting what they expected and were satisfied, and those with a nuclear family orientation were pleasantly surprised at the amount of interaction, aid, and affection between generations.

Affection and Regard.   Proximity, interaction frequency, and mutual aid are important indices of adult parent–child relationships. However, *qualitative* aspects such as degree of closeness or strength of feelings (affection or dislike) may be even more revealing. Investigators have only recently started to explore these more intangible aspects of kin relationships.

It is commonly assumed that closeness is synonymous with liking or loving and that distance indicates negative feelings—that we love those relatives we feel close to and hate those we feel distant from. But feelings that run high are rarely only positive or only negative. Where love can be found, so can hate. Probably most family relationships ebb and flow (Troll et al., 1979).

Most parents and children report positive feelings for each other. For example, most middle-aged parents studied by Lowenthal et al. (1975) felt good about their children. About half had only positive things to say about them,

and only about 10 percent of the middle-aged and none of those in their 60s had any strong negative comments. For older ages, Bengtson and Black (1973) found high levels of regard reported by both older parents and their middle-aged children.

Parents remain important to their children throughout the life of the children. When adults of all ages were asked to describe a person, they tended spontaneously to refer to their parents more frequently than to any other person (Troll, 1972). The oldest members of Troll's sample, in their 70s and 80s, were still using parents as reference persons.

Johnson and Bursk (1977) found that ratings of their relationship provided both by older parents and by one of their adult children were highly congruent. Occasionally, the parents rated their relationship higher than their child had. Both generations felt better about each other when the parents were in good health and able to be financially independent.

Harris and Associates (1975) found that as age increased, so did the percentage of older people who said they felt close enough to their children to talk to them about "things that really bothered them." At age 55 to 65, only 25 percent felt close enough, but at age 80 or over, 43 percent felt this way. In fact, many people cannot find substitutes for the ties they have with their children (Cumming and Henry, 1961; Rosow, 1967). Older people tend not to disengage from their children, regardless of the amount of affection present in the relationship (Brown, 1974; Ingraham, 1974).

Duty.   Feelings of obligation or a sense of duty often underlie frequent visiting and aid. Some interactions may be motivated either by shame that others would consider one delinquent in expected duties or by a more internalized guilt (Troll et al., 1979). Because dependency on the part of older parents introduces a high potential for conflict, it is surprising that nearly all adult children do carry out their responsibilities (Blenkner, 1965). There is no evidence that any but a tiny minority of adult children neglect their older parents (Troll et al., 1979). But this general finding may have socioeconomic or ethnic exceptions. For example, Brown (1960) found that about 40 percent of lower-class older black parents felt neglected by their children.

Other Factors.   The findings on various dimensions of relationships between adult children and older parents present a generally positive picture of physical nearness, frequent visiting, aid as needed, high mutual regard, and dutiful adult children. However, there are major sex, social class, and probably ethnic variations. Older women tend to have more intergenerational relationships than older men do. Some researchers contend that older women are more family oriented and thus have more contact and receive more aid, while others find little sex difference. This area needs more study.

Social class seems to have its greatest impact on the flow of mutual aid. Affluent older people tend to continue to aid middle-aged children, while blue-collar older people are more likely to be on the receiving end. However, more research is needed on class differences in family interaction patterns.

Ethnicity is a prominent influence on family life for many Americans, yet little of the research on older Americans and their families has taken this influence into account. Woehrer's (1978) excellent literature review found that nearly all the research on ethnicity and family was focused on households headed by middle-aged people. However, those studies had many implications for older family members. To begin with, compared to older whites, older blacks are much more likely to live in multigeneration households and to live with extended kin. Also, in many ethnic groups, women's roles are confined to the household, which results in strong bonds with children and perhaps a higher likelihood that older women of Italian, Puerto Rican, Mexican, or Polish descent will move in with their children if they become widowed. In addition, compared to Anglo families,

family members from Jewish, Italian, or Polish traditions tended to visit older parents more frequently and to see more ties between generations. In terms of mutual aid, the picture is less clear. It does appear that black families are involved in more mutual aid at all stages of the life course. Finally, some ethnic groups view the family as the locus of social life, and others do not. For example, people of Polish and Italian descent tend to be family centered, while those of Scandinavian descent do not. Blacks and those of Irish descent tend to be somewhere in between. Woehrer's observations provide a rich source of ideas from which further research on the impact of ethnicity could proceed.

Geographic mobility is presumed to be prevalent in American society and to lead to the breakup of extended families. Both these presumptions are ill founded. There have been a number of interesting studies of migration effects on kinship, and when the findings are pooled, disruptive effects of migration on kinship ties appear to be only temporary, at most. As Litwak (1960) suggested, kin ties in the modified extended family may even assist a nuclear unit's geographic venture for occupational advancement. Furthermore, Britton and Britton (1967) found that older people in a rural area in Pennsylvania, although they missed their distant children, reported increased morale and pride at their success. There is a tendency after a period of time for some older parents, past retirement, to move near their now-settled middle-aged children—that is, unless these offspring have not already moved back near their parents. Eventually, more kin may be available to those who have moved to the new area than to those who stayed behind.

Little is known about the extent to which middle-aged people experience being squeezed between the dependency needs of both their children and their parents. Data on typical childbearing patterns and data on the typical age of onset of physical or financial dependency lead to the conclusion that the average family should not experience such a squeeze. By the time older parents begin to need assistance, the children should be out of the middle generation's household.

Retirement of older parents frees them for more visiting with geographically distant children but it generally reduces their economic resources for doing so. Widowhood tends to increase interaction with children (Atchley et al., 1979).

We do not know how divorce or separation affects relationships between adult children and older parents. There are a good many aspects that could be studied. Do the children of divorced parents keep in touch with both parents? Is the frequency of contact affected by divorce? Are divorced parents as likely as widowed parents to receive aid from their children? Do older divorced mothers become financially dependent on their children more frequently than do widows? What effect does the timing of the divorce in the adult child's life have on the effect of divorce on parent–child relations? Does divorce affect parent–child relationships for mothers more than for fathers? Many other questions that need study could be added to this list.

The evidence indicates that most older parents understand and comply with the norms for relationships between older parents and adult children. The demands on the older parent are to recognize that the adult children have a right to lead their own lives, to not be too demanding and thereby alienate them, and above all, to not interfere with their normal pursuits. At the same time, the adult child is expected to leave behind the rebellion and emancipation of adolescence and young adulthood, and to turn again to the parent, "no longer as a child, but as a mature adult with a new role and different love, seeing him for the first time as an individual with his own rights, needs, limitations, and a life history that, to a large extent, made him the person he is long before his child existed" (Blenkner, 1965:58). This type of relationship requires that both the older parent and the adult child be mature and secure. Therefore mental, physical, and financial resources on

both sides improve the chances of developing a satisfactory relationship.

It may be worthwhile to mention that a growing number of the children of older people are themselves older people. More than one out of ten older people has a child who is over 65. In these cases, an even greater strain is usually put on both parties by the financial squeeze in which they find themselves and by the greater incidence of disabling illness among the very old.

Grandparents and Grandchildren

Seventy-five percent of older people are grandparents, and about 5 percent of households headed by older people include grandchildren. Yet the research evidence suggests that the grandparent role does not usually bring continuing interaction into the lives of the grandparents. Older people who are separated from their children for reasons of autonomy and independence are separated even farther from their grandchildren. Moreover, the strong peer orientation of adolescents in American society sometimes leaves little room in their lives for older people.

Fischer (1983) found that the meaning of grandmotherhood for her sample of middle-aged grandmothers was primarily symbolic. Grandparenthood signified continuity through generations and having a new person to love. This symbolic experience of grandparenthood was much more common than frequent interaction with grandchildren.

The satisfying period of grandparenthood is usually when grandchildren are small; but with the trend toward early marriage and early parenthood, most people become grandparents in their mid- to late forties. Few have very young grandchildren after age 65. It has been assumed that teenage grandchildren usually shy away from their grandparents, and that the grandparent role is basically an inactive one for most older people. However, Hartshorne and Manaster (1982) found that for young adults, relationships with grandparents are rated as very significant and that most see their grandparents three to four times a year. In addition, 70 percent wished they could see their grandparents more.

Grandmothers appear to have a somewhat better chance of developing a relationship with their granddaughters than grandfathers have in developing one with their grandsons, and maternal grandmothers are interacted with more than paternal grandmothers are (Hartshorne and Manaster, 1982). The key to this trend is the relative stability of the housewife role in comparison with the occupational roles of men. Grandmothers simply have more to offer their granddaughters that is pertinent to the lives they will lead. Sewing, cooking, and child rearing are but a few of the subjects that granddaughters often want to learn about. In contrast, grandfathers very often find their skills unwanted, not only by industry but by their grandsons as well. As women's roles in society change, however, grandmothers' knowledge may become less pertinent to their granddaughters' aspirations.

Visiting patterns are also important in the middle and upper classes in developing ties of affection between grandparents and grandchildren (Boyd, 1969b). Troll (1971) concluded that the "valued grandparent" is an achieved role based on the personal qualities of the grandparent and is not automatically ascribed to grandparents.

Siblings

About 80 percent of older people have living brothers and/or sisters. With the advent of old age, many older people seek to pick up old family loyalties and renew old sibling relationships. More effort is made to visit siblings, even at great distance, in old age than in middle age. The narrower the older person's social world, the more likely he or she is spontaneously to mention a sibling as a source of aid in time of trouble or need. Next to adult children, siblings

offer the best prospects for providing older people with a permanent home. Except where long-term family feuds exist, siblings offer a logical source of primary relationship, particularly for older people whose primary bonds have been reduced in number by a spouse's death or the children's marriages. Shanas and her associates (1968:166) report that siblings are especially important in the lives of older people who never married. The death of a sibling, particularly when the relationship was a close one, may shock older persons more than the death of any other kin. Such a loss apparently brings home their own mortality with greater immediacy.

Other kin, such as cousins, aunts, and nieces, also serve as a reservoir of potential relationships, but here the ties are probably more often based on individual characteristics than on the closeness of kinship. One's "favorite" niece or nephew may be a family member with whom to have a "special" relationship. Relationships with extended family are usually activated by special occasions: weddings, funerals, holidays, and reunions.

Friends and Neighbors

Friends and neighbors are important sources of relationship in later life. They also provide help and contact with the outside world, although often less importantly than children or other relatives.

Degrees of Friendship

How do older people define friendship? Quite a variety of relationships are lumped together under this label. They range from close, intense, continuous interaction marked by mutual understanding and concern, all the way to cursory contacts over the years with people whose names one happens to remember (Clark and Anderson, 1967:303–310). Probably the best way to divide such contacts is to call the former *friends* and the latter *associates*.

Clark and Anderson (1967:305) observed that older women seemed to have an abundance of friends, while older men had an abundance of associates. In comparison to men, women appeared to speak more about their friendships and to place more value on them. They also tended to depend on them more. Men were much more passive about their friendships, which Clark and Anderson attribute to the fact that many more of the men were married and thus had less need for primary friendships. Yet men seemed to feel the implied stigma that being old and friendless brings. In addition, men were apparently less willing to continue friendships via correspondence or telephone, further shutting them off from potential contacts.

Age Changes in Friendship

Friendships from middle age tend to be retained in later life, and the higher the socioeconomic status of the individual, the more pronounced this tendency is. Older people tend to pick their friends from among people with similar characteristics (including age). As a result, the longer a person lives in a given neighborhood, the more exclusive his or her ties are apt to be (Riley and Foner, 1968:561).

Most people report a decline in the number of their friendships over the years. However, a small minority of older people report they have *more* friends than ever before. Many friendships among older people are related to high socioeconomic status, good health, high density of older people in the neighborhood, long-term neighborhood residence, and residence in a small town rather than a large city (Riley and Foner, 1968:562–571).

Older people are fairly restrictive in terms of *who* they accept as friends. Age peers seem to have priority; so do those of the same sex, marital status, and socioeconomic class (Riley and Foner, 1968:571–573).

Many factors influence the age structure of friendships, including how long one has lived in the same community, the age structure of one's workplace and neighborhood, and how one's main interests relate to age. The friendships of people who live out their lives in a single community are likely to have developed in childhood and to persist into later life. Adults who settle far from where they grew up may find that they select friends from among their neighbors, their fellow employees, and fellow members of various organizations. How age integrated these various environments are obviously influences the age range of a person's friends.

But even in age-integrated environments, where one is in the life cycle has a great bearing on the age range of one's friends. People at an early age relative to their environment can have friends only their age or older. People at the middle of their environment's age range have the widest latitude on either side of their own age in selecting friends. Those who are older can have friends only about their age or younger. People with a wide age range of friends are generally less vulnerable to loss, since younger friends are less likely to die before they do. Those who select friends older than they are, are most vulnerable.

As Hess (1972) has pointed out, people's friends are selected from among those they consider social equals. The same experiences and characteristics—growing up together, living in the same neighborhood, having a similar occupation, having children the same age, having similar interests, being the same general age, and being the same sex—are all used by people at one time or another to define who is eligible for friendship. Just how age similarity compares to the other factors is unknown. Undoubtedly its influence fluctuates over historical time and depends on the age mix in the social environment. The effects of age similarity would be an excellent topic for further research.

Older people can hold on indefinitely to the role of friend. Long after the roles of worker, organization member, or even spouse have ended, the role of friend remains. The demands of friendship are flexible and can be adjusted to fit the individual's level of health and energy. Next to a spouse, a friend is the greatest source of companionship.

Most older people recognize that the loss of friends is an inevitable accompaniment to growing older. Most also believe that replacing lost friends is made very difficult by the presence of such obstacles as transportation, geographic moves, lowered economic status, and illness or disability.

Confidants are important to everyone, but especially to older people, and most older people have at least one confidant with whom they have a close, intimate relationship. Lowenthal and Havens (1968) found that presence of a confidant was an important buffer against the trauma of social losses such as widowhood.

Support Systems

Thus far we have discussed various kinds of relationships separately, but obviously this is not the way most people view them. People tend to look at their close relatives and friends as constituting a whole that serves their needs, even if each person is not in contact with every other person in that whole. The term **support system** refers to relationships that involve the giving and receiving of assistance and that are viewed by both the giver and receiver as significant in maintaining the psychological, social, and physical integrity of the receiver (Lopata, 1975a; Cantor, 1980). The assistance can be ongoing or sporadic. Cantor (1980) lists three major needs that support systems meet: socializing, carrying out the tasks of daily living, and personal assistance during crisis.

Support systems fall into two main categories: informal and formal. *Informal support* is provided by family and friends. *Formal support* is, first, occasional assistance provided by functionaries such as postal workers, building superintendents, and shopkeepers, and, second, the direct assistance of social services agencies. Finally, planning and coordinating agencies and legislative agencies establish the need for services, plan for their provision, and enact legislation to provide the necessary funds.

Shanas (1977) found that among older people who got assistance, 80 percent got it from family members, 5 percent from friends, about 20 percent from paid household staff, and only 2 to 3 percent from social services agencies. Thus, the informal support systems were crucial in maintaining older people at home. This picture has been confirmed by Weeks and Cuellar (1981), Rosel (1983), Kohen (1983), and Branch and Jette (1983).

Increasingly in industrial societies, families and social services agencies have begun to share responsibilities. Kamerman (1976) examined services to older people in eight countries and found cross-national uniformity in the assigning of responsibility for financing income and health programs for the elderly through national government programs. The picture with regard to other social services was much less consistent.

The helping professions have customarily viewed the rise of social services to the older population as a response to a weakened family system. However, this interpretation is misguided. The fact that social services organizations provide services to older people does not mean that families do not do so also. Shanas (1979) found that families were very much involved in providing help (especially in time of illness), exchanging services, and visiting with their older members. Very few older people actually lived *with* their adult children, but this situation simply reflects the preferences of both generations. Shanas (1979:169) pointed out that the emotional bond between older parents and their adult children is of prime importance. And although income and health programs for the elderly are funded by both federal and state governments, many families still provide health care and income assistance to their older members (Shanas, 1979). Shanas and Sussman have pointed out that

> The family in its everyday socializing can provide the elderly person with necessary succor, nurture, and information, and can be especially influential in decision making regarding the older person's relationships with bureaucratic organizations. It can also provide an immediate and quick response to crisis situations [involving] older persons; be a buffer for elderly persons in the latter's dealings with bureaucracies; examine the service options provided by organizations; effect entry of the elderly person into the program of bureaucratic organizations and facilitate the continuity of the relationship of the aged member with the bureaucracy (1977:216).

Bureaucratic agencies, on the other hand, are poorly equipped to handle the humanistic needs of older people. They usually lack the life history perspective needed to understand the *context* of the older person's concerns. Bureaucratic service agencies are much better equipped to deal with repetitive and relatively uniform tasks such as medical treatment, home-delivered meals, financial support, homemaker services, transportation, and home maintenance and repair. And certainly there is a need for agencies to provide recreation, education, housing, and so forth for the independent elderly.

The goal of assisting families to function effectively is more in tune with general public preferences than is the goal of having social agencies take over family functions. Service providers need to be sensitive to the client's family as part of the client's total support system. If they were, more *families* rather than individuals would be assisted by these agencies. In addition, families could benefit from education about the resources available to them through the social services network. However, at this point such notions are more idealistic than practical because the structure imposed on public social services by the legislation that created them assumes that services go to individuals directly and that families are not to be involved.

Summary

Relationships connect us to one another through our needs for interdependence, affection, and/or belonging. Relationships emerge when people interact with one another, usually in their various social roles. By personalizing role performance, long-term relationships articulate the personalities, resources, and needs of the people involved into a whole that is often greater than the sum of its parts. In this sense, the group is stronger and more capable than any individual acting alone.

Relationships based on interdependence arise from the fact that ours is a complex, technologically advanced society in which complete self-sufficiency is virtually impossible. Our need for interdependence is the foundation on which intimacy and belonging are built through communication, agreement, self-disclosure, trust, similarity, and acceptance. Relationships can be weakened by disagreement, disability, selfishness, betrayal, or withdrawal. How well relationships resist negative forces depends greatly on duration. The major long-term relationships for most adults are with spouse or partner, parent, child, relative, friend, associate, and neighbor.

Most middle-aged and older people are part of a couple. For those who have children, marital satisfaction tends to reach a low point when the children are in their teens and to improve steadily after the children leave home. Retirement also improves many marriages. One major reason for the rise in marital satisfaction in later life is probably the reduced potential for conflict over jobs and children.

There are many types of couples, and the couple relationship can serve many possible purposes for its members. Nevertheless, satisfied couples in later life tend to be egalitarian in their approach to household work, flexible in terms of traditional sex roles, deeply involved with one another psychologically, and sexually active. The availability of a spouse for care-giving if needed meets not only the need for someone to depend on but also the need to feel safe and secure. Being part of a couple is the major social resource for the vast majority of middle-aged and older adults.

Unfortunately, by age 70, half of older women are widows, and although they get social support from family and friends, they still must make major adaptations. Whether they succeed or not usually depends on their economic resources and community supports. Older men become widowed too, but most of them remarry, since they are greatly outnumbered by unmarried women of their own age and can also marry women younger than themselves. Most people remarry for companionship and affection.

Contrary to the popular myth, older people are not isolated from their adult children or neglected by them, especially when older parents need assistance. The flow of interaction, aid, and affection tends to go in both directions, with older parents giving as much as they are able. When parents are in later maturity, there is a great deal of independence among generations, with visits spaced weekly or less frequently and focused around socializing. When parents enter old age, they tend to need more assistance and support. Visits or contacts tend to be daily, particularly if the older parent has a serious chronic illness or disability, and there is much more "doing for" at this stage—housework, shopping, and transportation. The older the parents are, the more likely they are to see their adult children as confidants.

Relationships with adult children are greatly influenced by the sex of the parent, social class, and ethnicity. Older women tend to interact more with their adult children than older men do. Obviously, middle-class adult children have greater economic resources with which to aid older parents. Working-class older parents are more likely to assume responsibility for rearing their grandchildren. Black families tend to be involved in more mutual aid compared to other ethnic groups. Relationships between older parents and adult children are not generally disrupted by migration. However, we do not know how these relationships are affected by such factors as divorce.

Relationships with grandchildren, siblings, and other kin tend to be more voluntary and to have a less predictable meaning than spousal or parental relationships. The valued grandparent must earn that position, and favorite grandchildren, siblings, or cousins are selected by the same processes used to select friends. Relationships with extended kin that developed earlier in life and were then neglected for a period may be picked up again later in life. This renewal is a major resource for replacing relationships lost through death.

Friendships tend to be formed in middle adulthood and retained into later life, particularly among the middle class. Friends are selected from among people considered social equals. Most people do not have to develop new friendships because they already have a circle of friends. But aging usually means that some members of this circle die. The older the individual, the more likely this is to be true. Building new friendships is made difficult by rusty social skills and by the time and energy required. Therefore, new friends are more apt to be selected from among already existing acquaintances. Women tend to have more friends and to get more from friendship than men do. Men tend to have associates—people to do things with—but not confidants.

Support systems are the totality of family and friends that people depend on to meet their social, psychological, and physical needs. Support systems are of vital importance in helping older people adjust to changes such as widowhood and disability. Fortunately, most older people have an informal support system that complements the services available from formal service agencies.

Chapter 8

Needs and Resources

A great deal of what we experience in life is shaped by the resources available to us: How much *money* we have affects what we are able to do, the kinds of clothing we wear, where we live, whether we have cars and what kind, what foods we eat, and even whether we are able to afford medical care. The quality of our *housing* and where it is located affect not only our comfort and enjoyment but also how secure and safe we feel. Preventive and remedial *health care* affect our physical capacities and morale. Physical health in turn strongly influences the nature and amount of our activities. Transportation becomes an important necessity if we are to take advantage of the full range of activities in most communities. Finally, the kind, number, and location of community facilities and services affect our choice of activities and assistance. Because income, housing, health care, transportation, and community facilities and services enable people to participate, we call them *instrumental* factors. They are the means by which people pursue an incredible variety of goals. They also greatly affect our sense of independence.

Accordingly, to fully understand aging requires that we know how aging affects our instrumental needs as well as the resources available to meet these needs. As with physical and mental aging, instrumental needs and resources vary widely among people, and aging has neither a uniform nor predictable influence. In general, aging does not alter instrumental needs or resources enough to change life styles appreciably. However, certain categories of older people are more likely to encounter problems. In each instrumental area, we will look at: the needs and resources, the typical problems, the older people most likely to have those problems, what can currently be done about them by the individual, the family, and the community, and what changes to our social system might reduce the number of older people who have problems.

Income

Because very few of us grow all our own food, make our own clothes, construct and maintain our own homes, and so forth, it is essential that we have access to disposable income. To better understand the income issue, we need to know something about how aging influences income needs and income sources.*

Income Needs

Aging affects income needs in several ways. To begin with, retirement lowers the expenses connected with employment—for transportation, special clothing, meals away from home, and so on. And launching children into adulthood reduces day-to-day expenses for allowances, food, clothing, entertainment, vacations, and so on. At the same time, greater physical frailty increases the need to purchase services that formerly could have been done by oneself or by one's spouse. For example, people over 80 are unlikely to hang drapes, wash windows, paint the house, or work in the yard. Estimates of the average income needs of people of various ages generally assume that the elderly need slightly less income than people under 65 in order to maintain a comparable life style, a differential based entirely on the assumption that older people need less food.

Table 8-1 shows three budgets that were developed by the U.S. Bureau of Labor Statistics (BLS) for an urban retired couple. The lower budget is not a survival-only budget but represents a rather modest level of living, while the intermediate and higher budgets approach a middle-class level. These budgets were developed by estimating the costs of housing, household maintenance (e.g., utilities and repairs), household furnishings, food, clothing, transportation, medical and dental care, personal care (e.g., laundry, cleaning, and grooming sup-

plies), entertainment and recreation, insurance, taxes, and miscellaneous other expenses. The lower budget assumed almost no replacement clothing or home furnishings; very little household maintenance, recreation, entertainment, and insurance; and a subsistence level for food. The high budget allowed for such items as replacing a winter coat or television set every five years, and modest amounts for vacation travel, entertainment, eating out, insurance, and personal care. However, the biggest contrasts were in transportation and clothing, where the high budget allowed two or three times the amounts provided in the low budget.

The BLS budgets estimate income needs from data on the actual cost of various components of living expenses. However, most people judge the adequacy of their incomes in relation to what they think they need. The elderly tend to think their incomes are adequate even if well below what others think they need. For example, in an unpublished community study of older adults, I found that in 1981 only 10 percent of the men and 20 percent of the women thought their incomes were inadequate, even though many more of their incomes were lower than the BLS intermediate budget. Indeed, Liang, Kahana, and Doherty (1980) found that

TABLE 8-1 Annual budgets for a retired couple, for three levels of living: Urban United States, 1980

Component	Lower Budget	Intermediate Budget	Higher Budget
Food	$2,082	$2,772	$3,482
Housing	2,169	3,106	4,860
Transportation	487	950	1,748
Clothing	236	396	609
Personal Care	184	269	394
Medical Care	944	950	956
Other	541	992	1,874
Total	$6,644	$9,434	$13,923

Source: U.S. Bureau of Labor Statistics, 1981.

*See also the income section in Chapter 2, pp. 30–32.

actual income only indirectly affected satisfaction with one's financial resources. More important were feelings about how well off one was in relation to others at the time of the survey and to oneself in the past.

In 1980 the U.S. Census found that about 60 percent of elderly couples had incomes at the modest middle-class level or higher, while only about 25 percent of unmarried older individuals did. About 21 percent of older couples and 55 percent of older unmarried people had incomes at or below the census-defined survival-only level.* These data clearly show that most older couples have an income that can support comfortable lives, while most unmarried older people are in financial trouble.

Income Sources

Aging changes the available sources of income. Older people have access to retirement income and to financially valuable services and facilities specifically reserved for the elderly. Aging also reduces the prevalence of employment and the accompanying earnings.

Direct Income Sources.   Direct sources of income include earnings, pensions, income from assets, and public assistance. About 20 percent of men and 8 percent of women age 65 or over have earnings, and the proportion decreases for those who are older. The incomes of older people with earnings are about double the incomes of those who rely mainly on pensions. About half of those who are employed need earnings to supplement inadequate pensions.

Retirement pensions come in two basic varieties—Social Security benefits and job-related pensions. *Social Security benefits* can be *retirement benefits* paid to covered workers or *survivor benefits* paid to the surviving spouses of covered

workers. Social Security retirement benefits are available to those who have reached age 62 and have worked on covered jobs for a specified minimum period of time (usually 10 years). Social Security retirement benefits also carry a 50 percent spouse benefit, which means that retired couples receive 150 percent of the pension entitlement amount of the covered worker.

The standard retirement age under Social Security is 65. Those who retire younger receive a benefit that is reduced by an amount that roughly compensates for the greater amount of time over which benefits will be drawn. But those who retire after age 65 receive an increased benefit that only partially compensates for the shorter time that benefits must be paid; the increment for late retirement is only about half what it should be for fair compensation.

About 90 percent of older Americans draw Social Security, and over half of them draw reduced benefits as a result of having retired prior to age 65. In 1981, average Social Security retirement benefits were $4,632 per year for retired individuals and $6,969 per year for retired couples. The average Social Security benefit to surviving spouses was $4,153 annually. These rather modest average benefits replace only about 66 percent of earnings in the last year of employment for couples and only about 44 percent of earnings for single individuals. The 1981 benefits represented an increase of over 60 percent in the purchasing power of Social Security pensions since 1965, but Social Security payroll tax increases since 1977 have gone to eliminate poverty, not to provide lavish pensions (Atchley, 1982d).

In 1978, about 50 percent of older couples and 26 percent of older individuals were entitled to a job-related pension on top of Social Security (See Table 8-2). Many of these people had high preretirement earnings and were thus eligible for the highest Social Security benefits. The result has been growing disparity between the incomes of those with multiple pensions and the incomes of those entitled only to Social Security, with dual pensioners averaging incomes

---

*The census-defined "poverty level" is lower than the BLS "lower budget." See Chapter 2 for data on the numbers of older people with incomes at or below the "poverty level."

TABLE 8-2 Percentage of older households having income from selected sources, by age and household type: United States, 1978.

Income Source	Age 62–64		Age 65 and Over	
	Couples	Single Persons	Couples	Single Persons
Earnings	77%	50%	41%	15%
Social Security	46	58	91	89
Public pension	13	9	16	12
Private pension	19	13	31	14
Public assistance	2	10	5	14

Source: Social Security Administration, 1981:9.

nearly twice as high as those with Social Security alone (See Table 2-12 on p. 31).

Assets such as income-generating property, savings, and investments are often presumed to be a major source of income for the aged, but this is true only for the small proportion of very well-to-do elderly people. In fact, few people find themselves actually able to accumulate substantial amounts of savings or investments to support their later years. Friedman and Sjogren found "that as older Americans enter their retirement years, their property wealth is generally very limited and can seldom be expected to be much help in maintaining their preretirement standard of living. . . . Equity in the home is usually the most important form of asset for the elderly; liquid or income-producing assets are generally very limited in amount" (1981:16). Although about 60 percent of older couples and 30 percent of older single people own their homes free and clear, home ownership is worth only about $800 per year in savings once the expenses of home ownership are taken into account.

Supplemental Security Income (SSI) is a federal program of public assistance to the elderly. In 1984, SSI guaranteed every older American $314 per month regardless of prior work history ($472 for older couples). Here is how it worked.

Suppose an older man drew a Social Security retirement pension of $160 per month and had no other source of income. To determine his SSI income, $20 of his Social Security benefit was excluded, giving him an income for SSI purposes of $140 per month. This $140 was then subtracted from the guarantee of $314 to yield an SSI benefit of $174 per month. Over 2 million older people were drawing benefits from this program averaging about $175 per month in 1983. In addition, 27 states provided state supplements over and above SSI. All SSI applicants had to demonstrate that their incomes from other sources fell below the prescribed minimum in order to qualify for SSI. This is called a *means test*.

The number of older people drawing SSI peaked in 1975 at 2.3 million and has declined substantially since then to 1.5 million in 1983 (Social Security Administration, 1984). Drazga, Upp, and Reno (1982) reported that only about 65 to 70 percent of those eligible for SSI actually received benefits. Those who participated were most likely to live in one of the 27 states that supplement SSI benefit amounts or in states that did not have a history of attaching liens on the homes of welfare recipients. Participants were also likely to have much lower incomes than nonparticipants. Menefee, Edwards, and Scheiber (1981) found that participants were also much more likely to live alone.

Indirect Income Sources.   Indirect sources of income include many public and private programs that serve older people directly and also help indirectly by supplementing inadequate incomes. Federal programs that give indirect financial aid to older people include low-rent public housing and rent subsidy programs, Medicare, Medicaid, the Food Stamp program, and meals programs for the elderly.* Many states give property tax exemptions to people over 65. In addition, senior centers and transportation programs often provide services free or at reduced prices.

Indirect income increases the real incomes of older Americans. The U.S. Bureau of the Census (1981) collected data on receipt of means-tested noncash benefits among the noninstitutionalized population. They looked particularly at Food Stamps, government-assisted housing, and Medicaid. While the elderly represented about 11 percent of the noninstitutionalized population, they were 17 percent of those receiving Food Stamps, 34 percent of those living in government-assisted housing, and 33 percent of those living in independent households and receiving Medicaid. But although the elderly make up a large proportion of those who receive noncash benefits, ony a small proportion of all older people actually receive such benefits. For example, only 6 percent of the elderly receives Food Stamps, about 7 percent lives in government-assisted housing, and 16 percent receives Medicaid. It is probably safe to say that, as a result of their eligibility criteria, most indirect income sources help the poor rather than the middle class. Indirect income sources are also much more readily available to the urban versus the rural elderly.

Two hypothetical case histories may be useful to illustrate the variety of income sources for the elderly. Mr. B worked as an insurance actuary (someone who computes life expectancy of insurance applicants in order to determine the premiums the company must charge) for the same company for 45 years. He retired at age 65, in very sound financial shape for retirement. Having earned a high salary during his working life, and having paid the maximum Social Security taxes, he was eligible for a monthly Social Security retirement benefit of $757 for himself plus an additional $378 for his wife. In addition, Mr. B drew a private pension of $690 per month from his former employer and had an annuity income of $150 per month. His total income from all of these sources was $1,975 per month, or $23,700 per year, which represented 65.8 percent of Mr. B's income in the year preceding retirement. And only a little over $10,000 of his retirement income was taxable, compared to $36,000 of his preretirement income. Mr. and Mrs. B both reported that retirement had not affected their capacity to afford their preretirement life style.

In contrast, Mr. J had not been so fortunate in his work life. Working for various employers, mostly small business, he had done unskilled work in shipping or stocking. His last job had been as "stock boy" in a liquor store, six days a week unloading cases of liquor, wine, and beer and shelving them, earning less than minimum wage. Mr. J had been unemployed many times throughout his working life, although never for an extended period. At retirement Mr. J's Social Security benefit was only $182 per month, despite the fact that he had worked nearly 50 years. His wife received her own $122-per-month Social Security pension. Having no other income, they applied for and received $93 per month in SSI. They also moved into rent-subsidized housing for the elderly, where their monthly rent was fixed at $99 (25 percent of their monthly income), saving them $38 per month over what they had paid

---

*These programs are discussed in detail later in the chapter.

for their previous apartment and leaving them $3,576 per year for all their other expenses. Combined, their benefits replaced only 38 percent of their earnings the year before they retired. Both reported having a lot of trouble making ends meet.

Who Has Income Problems?

Retirees, widows, and the lifelong poor are most likely to have income difficulties in later life. Among retirees, those who have worked for large employers are quite likely to have private pensions in addition to ample Social Security benefits. They are most likely also to have fringe benefits such as medical and dental insurance coverage that continue into retirement. On the other hand, those who worked for small businesses are least likely to have private pensions, to have earned less for the same work, with correspondingly lower Social Security benefits, and to lack substantial fringe benefits before or after retirement.

Women are more likely than men to have worked sporadically, part time, for small businesses that lack private pensions, and in jobs not covered by union bargaining for pensions and fringe benefits. Thus, because American retirement income is so closely tied to the level of earnings over a lengthy working life, women are more likely than men to be poor in retirement.

The very old are also likely to find their retirement incomes inadequate because, although there have been cost-of-living increases in Social Security benefits, private pensions usually do not rise to match inflation, and because workers who are very old today have Social Security pension entitlement based on average wages much lower than today's, even adjusted for inflation.

Finally, retired minority group members are likely to have inadequate retirement incomes and for many of the same reasons that women's retirement incomes are too low—working for employers that provide no private pension, high rates of unemployment over the working life, lower average wages even for the same work, and so on.

Widows are more likely than married women to encounter income problems in later life. First, many women find they are too young to collect survivor benefits at the time they become widows: About 13 percent of women in their fifties are widows, yet widows do not qualify for survivor benefits under Social Security until age 60. Second, even if the widow qualifies for survivor benefits, her Social Security income will go down by one-third from before her spouse's death. Unfortunately, fixed expenses such as rent and automobile payments do not go down when household size drops from two to one. If the husband's Social Security pension was already marginal, then widowhood can bring financial disaster. Finally, some unfortunate women find out too late that in order to have a higher pension, their husbands had selected a "no-survivor-benefit" option. For example, Mrs. D was married to a man who had worked for a large office equipment manufacturer. When he retired, he was given two pension options. Under the first, he would draw $550 per month, which at his death his wife would continue to receive as a survivor benefit. Under the second option, Mr. D would receive $822 per month, with no survivor benefit to his wife. The drastic difference in pension amount with and without survivor benefits is based on an expectation of an extra seven years of pension payments because of women's longer average length of life and because Mrs. D was three years younger than her husband. Without telling Mrs. D, Mr. D had selected the "no-survivor-benefit" option in order to get the higher initial pension.

The first inkling Mrs. D had that something was wrong was when the pension check failed to arrive on time after her husband's death. She called her husband's former employer, where the poor benefits clerk had to tell Mrs. D that there would be no more pension checks. Her next shock was learning that instead of the $990-per-month Social Security pension she and Mr. D had been receiving, she would now be getting only $660. Thus the household income dropped from $1,812 per month to $660—all on top of her grief at losing her husband of over 50 years.

The lifelong poor represent a final category of people likely to have income problems in later life, because most poor people have no access to private pensions. Their low wage averages generate low Social Security benefits, even for those who remained employed nearly all of their adult lives. However, unlike Mrs. D, many poor people encounter no drastic change in their level of living. In fact, with SSI, Food Stamps, and low-rent housing for the elderly, some lifelong poor find that their situation in old age actually improves, although it is hardly a standard they would choose. In absolute terms, even Mrs. D is better off with her $660 per month.

What Can Be Done?

When older people encounter income problems, there are only a few courses of action they can take: They can get jobs, they can apply for SSI and take advantage of programs such as low-rent housing or Food Stamps (providing their incomes are low enough), or they can ask their families for financial support.

The prospects for getting a job in later life are not good, especially for those already likely to have inadequate retirement incomes. While many older people with income problems have difficulty sustaining their former middle-class life styles, their incomes are usually still high enough to disqualify them for income assistance programs. Most older people believe it is not their children's responsibility to provide them with an adequate income; they see this as a government responsibility (Harris and Associates, 1975). Older people are thus very reluctant to ask their children for money, and the end result

is that thousands of older Americans find there is virtually nothing they can do if they feel their incomes are inadequate.

What Needs to Be Done?

In 1981, the President's Commission on Pension Policy reported that

- A minimum universal pension system should be created to ensure that *all* workers are covered by job-related pensions in addition to Social Security. This system would be financed through payroll taxes on all employers and would provide minimum pensions to those who are unlikely to be covered by private pensions now.

- Postretirement survivor protection should be mandatory. (This would prevent situations such as Mrs. D's from happening.)

- Social Security benefits for divorced people should reflect a share of their former spouses' earnings.

- SSI benefits should be no lower than poverty level. (As it now stands, SSI provides benefits slightly lower than poverty level.)

If enacted, these four changes would go a long way toward preventing income problems in later life.

Housing

Housing is an important source of continuity in the lives of most middle-aged and older people. After age 35, Americans do not change residence often, partly because of home ownership, but mostly because of the feeling of comfort and ease that comes with living in a familiar environment. As we saw earlier, one way that people cope with changes in their physical and mental capacities with age is to concentrate time and attention on longstanding patterns of activity. And a large measure of this continuity comes through having lived in the same dwelling for a long time. In 1970, 66 percent of the elderly living in cities and 90 percent of those in rural areas owned their homes, which were typically more than 40 years old and more dilapidated and lower in value than the homes of younger people (Atchley and Miller, 1975). The majority of older Americans have lived in their present dwellings for more than 20 years. Montgomery, Stubbs, and Day (1980) reported that the homes the elderly owned were typically small and had numerous defects. Nevertheless, the elderly occupants subjectively felt that their houses fully met their needs; almost none wanted to move to another house.

Housing is more than a place to live. It can be a symbol of independence, a focal point for family gatherings, a source of pleasant memories, and a link to the neighborhood and surrounding community. Remaining in one's customary abode can become more important as people get older because one's home is a major symbol of one's standing in the community. Its appearance can be a source of self-esteem and also a focus of meaningful goals.

Disability Changes Housing Needs

Aging can bring a need for special modifications to housing. Disability is most common in later life. Accordingly, the elderly are more likely than the young to need ramps, widened doorways to accommodate wheelchairs, and sturdy hand-support fixtures in the bath. But as we saw earlier, the elderly usually cannot afford to renovate their homes. Disability can also bring the need for more in-home services. Almost half of the elderly who live alone need help with tasks of daily living (Better Housing League of Cincinnati, 1978). Shanas (1977) found that about 80 percent of the in-home services to the elderly were provided by family, about 15 percent, especially housework and meal preparation, by paid helpers, and only about 2 percent by social services agencies. Obviously, access to in-home services is related to the income of the

older person. The low percentage of in-home aid provided by social services agencies is a reflection of the low availability of subsidized home aid. In communities that have home aid programs, utilization is usually high. For example, Home Aid Service of Cincinnati provided regular in-home services to over 2,600 older people in 1984, with over 250 on their waiting list. Until these services are widely available, there is little way to estimate the true level of demand for them.

Disability can reach the point where some sort of specialized housing is necessary. For instance, Mrs. M was a 72-year-old widow with no children or other family living in the area. She lived alone in an older apartment building. Her neighbors had noticed that she had become increasingly disoriented. She often did not recognize her neighbors or remember their names even though she had known them for several years. The situation came to a head when Mrs. M forgot a pot on her stove, which resulted in a lot of smoke (but fortunately no fire) and which "smelled up" the building. A protective services caseworker was called to investigate the situation.*

After a thorough medical checkup, it was determined that Mrs. M was probably suffering from chronic organic brain disease and would be unable to continue to live unassisted on her income of $284 per month (a small Social Security pension plus SSI). There were several choices available to the caseworker. Adult Foster Care could monitor Mrs. M while she continued to live in her apartment, she could move to a private boarding home or nursing home, or she could move to the county home for the indigent elderly. None of these solutions was ideal. Mrs. M was too mentally impaired for Adult Foster Care. With her meager income, the private boarding and nursing homes that would take her were not appealing. And the county home had a waiting list. Eventually it was de-

---

*Protective services are discussed later in the chapter.

cided to monitor Mrs. M at home until she could get into the county home. This solution placed a heavy burden on the Adult Foster Care program, but it worked.

Housing Alternatives

Table 8-3 shows the continuum of housing alternatives for the elderly. About 5 percent of the elderly live in group housing of all types, but as age increases so does the probability of living in group housing. About 25 percent of those age 85 or over lives in group housing. Many of the elderly who live in group housing are similar to Mrs. M. They need housing that provides room and board, personal care, and supervision, but they do not need nursing care.

In 1976, there were nearly 8,000 institutions in the U.S. that housed the elderly and did not provide nursing care (U.S. Bureau of the Census, 1978b). Middle-income older people can find such housing with relative ease, but the poor have trouble because Medicaid financing is not available for group housing and SSI usually does not cover the cost of adequate care in group quarters. Congressional hearings have periodically documented unsafe and unsanitary conditions in group homes, and in 1976 Congress passed a law requiring states to set standards for admissions, safety, sanitation, and protection of civil rights for group homes where SSI recipients lived or were likely to live (Reichstein and Bergofsky, 1983). Nevertheless, because there is a lack of funding for en-

TABLE 8-3   Levels of housing, by degree of independence

Housing Type	Significant Criteria
Independent Household	
Fully independent	Household is self-contained, self-sufficient; residents do 90 percent or more of cooking and household chores.
Semi-independent	Household is self-contained but not entirely self-sufficient; may require some assistance with cooking and household chores. (E.g., an independent household augmented by Meals-on-Wheels, Homemaker Services, or Adult Foster Care.)
Group Housing	
Congregate housing	Household may still be self-contained, but is less self-sufficient; cooking and household tasks are often incorporated into the housing unit. (A common example is the retirement community.)
Personal care home	Resident unit is neither self-contained nor self-sufficient; help given in getting about, personal care, grooming, and so forth, in addition to cooking and household tasks. (A common type is the home for the aged.)
Nursing home	Resident units are neither self-contained nor self-sufficient; total care, including health, personal, and household functions. (A common example is the skilled nursing facility.)

forcement and, more important, for adequate services in group homes, the standards developed by the states have generally been loose and ineffective. Reichstein and Bergofsky (1983) recommended the development of a model set of standards that can be adopted by all states. But until an effective means is developed to pay for group-home living for the elderly poor, the situation cannot be expected to improve very much.

In older cities many older people live in residential hotels—often called *SRO's* because they consist of single-room occupancies. The stereotype SRO is a small, run-down hotel catering almost exclusively to the elderly. However, in their study of SRO's in Manhattan, Cohen and Sokolovsky (1980) found that at least a third were larger hotels (110 rooms or more) of relatively better quality. Erikson and Eckert's (1977) study in San Diego also reported a few SRO's that catered to middle-class clients. Thus, SRO's cater to a wider socioeconomic category of urban elders than has been generally assumed. Residents of SRO's have also been stereotyped as social isolates, "loners" who lack the support systems found among the elderly at large. However, Cohen and Sokolovsky (1980) found that although most SRO residents had indeed lived alone for many years and had fewer contacts with others compared to other urban elders, they were far from isolated and their contacts both within and outside the SRO were important sources of support.*

The *share-a-home* concept may offer a viable housing alternative among those who need semi-independent housing. Begun in Orlando, Florida, share-a-home puts older people in touch with others who want to establish a "family," purchase a home, and operate it together. The realities of semi-independence are built right into the concept. Each "family" hires a cook and a housekeeper, thus avoiding the problems of dividing the housekeeping

*See Chapter 15 for more details on SRO's.

among people of varying physical capacity. Though this alternative is attractive for some older people, zoning and housing restrictions in many areas are a major obstacle to starting a share-a-home. Streib and Streib (1975) point out that local bureaucratic zeal will have to be relaxed quite a bit if home sharing is to become a widespread housing alternative for older people.

Relocation Problems

Even those congregate facilities that cater to middle- and upper-income older people are not without their problems. One of the most difficult problems is developing humane procedures for dealing with residents who become disabled to the point of no longer fitting the independent or semi-independent nature of the facility. Take, for example, the York Houses in Philadelphia. They were established in the early 1960s and the initial residents were generally independent. As expected, as the residents aged, their needs for assistance increased. In addition, as the average level of functioning among the residents declined, the facilities attracted fewer fully independent older people. If they should continue in this direction, the York Houses would eventually become nursing homes, a use for which the facilities are not well-suited. To maintain their status as semi-independent housing, York Houses would have to develop "skills and sensitivity to counsel tenants for whom transfer must be sought" (Lawton, Greenbaum, and Liebowitz, 1980).

Bernstein (1982) studied the process of transferring residents from independent living in 87 federally-assisted housing projects. She found that project managers seldom had to ask tenants to leave; usually the tenant or his or her family recognized the need for a more supportive setting and took responsibility for finding alternative housing. When the tenant suffered severe illness, needed frequent medication monitoring, or was bedridden, a voluntary move was most likely. Mental decline, emotional problems, being a safety hazard to oneself or others, or having a problem with alcohol or drugs were less likely to be acknowledged by either tenants or their families and were more likely to require more active management intervention. Most facilities relaxed their retention criteria and allowed tenants more problems than would be allowed a new applicant. However, the higher the concentration of older people in the facility, the stricter the retention policy tended to be. In addition, on-site administrators, who would have to deal with complaints about inequity, tended to be stricter than absentee management staff. Right now, most facilities have only very general stated policies and have a great deal of flexibility in deciding when a tenant should be asked to leave. However, much public housing for the elderly is relatively new, and as the older population ages, tenant retention issues are going to become more problematic.

The problem is complicated by the fact that the main housing alternative for many older people is a nursing home, which older people tend to view very negatively. In 1976, there were over 11,000 nursing homes in the United States, nearly 85 percent of whose 1.2 million residents were over 65 and over half over 80. Thus, it is an accurate perception that nursing homes are primarily housing for the very old. Although many older people recognize that a nursing home may be best for people who cannot care for themselves, most fear the loss of independence and privacy that moving to one can bring and also fear that their children will desert them once they are in a "home." Despite these fears, many older people move into nursing homes.

Twenty years ago, nursing homes in America probably deserved their negative image as depressing warehouses for the afflicted. Today that image is largely inaccurate. Although problems have by no means been eliminated, the quality of care provided in most nursing homes has greatly improved. A good measure of that improvement is a result of two facts: (1) Medicaid finances most nursing care of the elderly,

and (2) facilities must conform to federal standards for care quality in order to be reimbursed. Another large measure of care-quality improvement has come from the steady rise of standards within the long-term-care industry.

But even when the image of the nursing home is not a problem, dread of relocation may be. The research on the effects of relocation has not produced consistent answers as to whether relocation increases the probability of death or worsens illness. However, it is clear that many older people are upset at the prospect of relocation. Borup (1981) suggested a few general reminders that can help ease the transition:

- Relocation stress is usually temporary.
- Unwilling movers are most likely to experience stress.
- Stress can be reduced by making the new environment predictable to the mover.
- Keeping tenants and their families informed tends to reduce stress.

Retirement Housing

Retirement can bring an opportunity for people to move away from housing or a community to which they were tied not by preference but by employment, and into housing or a community more in tune with their ideals. Some choose planned retirement communities; others move to communities not actually planned for retirement but that simply attract large numbers of retirees.*

Retirement communities tend to be homogeneous with respect to social-class, racial, and ethnic backgrounds of the residents. And although there are retirement communities for people at most points on the social spectrum, the majority draw residents from the more affluent social classes (Bultena and Wood, 1969a). Movement to retirement communities also

---

*Retired people can be referred to as *retirers* or *retirees*. Since most people retire on their own initiative, *retirer* is probably more appropriate but harder to say than *retiree*.

seems to self-select those older people who are amenable to life in age-homogeneous settings. As a result, morale in retirement communities is quite high. Conversely, there are indications that many older people who remain in age-integrated communities would not be at all happy in a retirement community (Bultena and Wood, 1969a).

The homogeneity of retirement communities fosters greater social interaction and the formation of new friendships. Because retirement communities draw heavily from former managers and professionals, their members are often quite accustomed to moving and have developed the skills needed for making new friends. For the vast majority of people in retirement communities, the move does not bring increased isolation from their children (Bultena and Wood, 1969a). Although life in a planned retirement community may not be for everyone, there is no evidence that it is detrimental for those who do choose it.

The working-class equivalent to the more affluent retirement community is the mobile home park for older adults. Basing her analysis on the situation in California in the mid-1960s, Johnson (1971) concluded that the mobile home park is a mixed blessing for retired residents. Most older people who live in mobile parks want to live in a controlled environment without having to pay a high price for it.

> Slightly authoritarian in outlook, justifiably fearful of urban violence, and anxious to maintain all the visible outward signs appropriate to "decent people," the retired working-class mobile home resident wants to live in a park that is neat, attractive, quiet, safe, all-white, and friendly (Johnson, 1971:174).

These people are willing to pay a park owner to control the neighborhood, but they complain bitterly if the controls infringe too much on *them*. All too often, the cost of living in a mobile home park also includes considerable economic exploitation by park owners (Johnson, 1971). Nevertheless, the popularity of such parks in many areas of the country attests to the felt

need for living areas that provide a safe and secure environment for a community made up largely of older adults.

Longino (1981) reported on a study of three types of retirement housing: planned, full-service retirement communities,* planned public housing for the elderly (nearly all of whom are retired), and de facto retirement communities in certain regions of the country that result from large-scale migration of retired people to small towns. Those who moved to planned, full-service retirement communities tended to be older (mean age 76), affluent individuals who were oriented around the availability of housekeeping, meals, and nursing service. Those who moved to de facto retirement communities tended to be younger (mean age 68), affluent couples who were oriented toward independence and enjoyment of nature. Movers to public housing tended to be older women (mean age 78) from the immediate area who wanted out of an unsafe neighborhood and to take advantage of the financial relief provided by subsidized housing. Longino's study supported the idea that older people select housing that meets their needs. He predicted that those who moved to planned communities probably would not move again because they had selected housing suitable to the needs of the old. However, he predicted that those who lived in de facto retirement communities would resemble people on an extended vacation who, when needs for assistance increased substantially, could be expected to return to their area of origin in order to be nearer to family.

Types of Housing Problems

Many older people cannot find housing that is both suitable and affordable. There is a short-

---

*Full-service retirement communities offer a continuum of independent and semi-independent living plus nursing home care. They also offer a wide range of programs and services, such as recreation, transportation, and education.

age of subsidized low-rent housing for the elderly, particularly outside the major metropolitan areas. The Better Housing League of Cincinnati (1978) found that the demand in Cincinnati for low-rent housing for the elderly exceeded the supply by at least 25 percent. For the middle class, the situation is not much better. For instance, John and Ethel wanted to sell their home and move into an apartment but could not find a buyer because interest rates were too high. In addition, the available apartments in their community were either too expensive or cheap and shabby, with virtually nothing in the middle. They decided to stay in their home, at least for a while, even though it has much more space than they need or want to take care of.

As mentioned earlier, to remain in independent housing, many older people need assistance in personal care (such as help in moving about, dressing, or bathing) and in housekeeping care (such as housework and meal preparation). About 12 percent of the elderly who live in independent households and are 75 or older receive such care. Although the percentage is not large, every community has some older people who need in-home services and who either do not have families that can assist them or cannot afford to pay someone. Many if not most communities lack programs that provide in-home services to the indigent elderly.

The majority of older people probably do not want to move and do not need in-home services —yet. However, they do need to maintain their homes. Because their homes tend to be older and more dilapidated than the housing of the young, more maintenance is required, a problem that translates into a need for funds to pay for maintenance and for the people to do it. In 1979, the state of Ohio began offering home maintenance and repair services to the rural elderly as part of its public Comprehensive Employment and Training Act (CETA). In the counties that instituted such programs, the demand for services was nearly four times the capacity. This statistic indicates that a main reason that older people do not maintain their homes is that they just cannot afford to. Another important factor involved sponsorship. The construction industry, especially in renovation and repair, is comprised mostly of small-scale entrepreneurs and companies that often have not been in business long. In addition, various confidence rackets involving home improvements have been widely publicized. As a result, the elderly are not sure with whom to deal and whom to trust. When government-sponsored programs came along, they were more willing to allow workers in their homes.

Who Has Housing Problems?

Older people who are most likely to have housing problems include the frail elderly, the disabled, the rural elderly, and those with low incomes. The frail elderly and the disabled are apt to find that they can get neither the in-home services they need to remain independent nor suitable group housing that can meet their needs for assistance within their capacity to pay. The low-income elderly find that there is a shortage of low-rent housing for the elderly. At the root of all three of these problems is financing; our system for financing the nonmedical care of the frail elderly and the disabled is simply inadequate. We also are not willing to divert the resources necessary to ensure that the elderly poor have adequate low-rent housing available. This latter problem is part of the larger housing shortage in the United States. The government has attempted to keep inflation under control by increasing the cost of borrowing money; the result has been high interest rates. Under these conditions, builders simply cannot build housing that can be sold or rented at affordable prices, and the elderly are the least likely to be able to afford expensive housing.

Health Care

As noted earlier, good health is a major factor enabling people to enjoy life. Aging changes the health care that people need to maintain good

health or avoid worsening health. Preventive
health care can reduce the probability of
chronic disease and disability, treatment can
often reverse the negative effects of chronic disease, and rehabilitation can help people not only
to restore lost functions but to compensate for
unrestorable functions.

Treatment

Treatment includes self-treatment with home
remedies or over-the-counter medications, visiting a doctor, going to an out-patient clinic,
short-term care in a hospital, and long-term
care of chronic diseases at home or in a nursing
home.

About 40 percent of acute conditions, such as
common colds or flu, are self-treated. Most
drugstores carry numerous preparations for the
self-treatment of colds, allergies, constipation,
indigestion, skin rashes and itching, and so on.
Indeed, many minor chronic ailments such as
eczema can be effectively treated with over-the-
counter drugs.

But as age increases, so does the severity of
both chronic and acute illnesses. As a result,
older people are more likely to go to a physician. Compared to adults under 45, older adults
make 50 percent more visits to doctors' offices.
Those elderly with incomes over $10,000 per
year are even more likely to make numerous
visits to the doctor. In 1975, over 80 percent of
the elderly saw a doctor at least once (Kovar,
1977).

In-home health care is not common. House
calls by physicians fell from 23 percent of all
doctor visits in 1959 to less than 5 percent in
1975. About 80 percent of *home health care* is
provided by family living in the household, usually the spouse. In 75 percent of the cases, home
care has lasted for one year or longer, and 30
percent of home care involves continual care.
Fortunately, only a very small proportion of the
elderly need such care—12.5 percent at age 75
or older (Wilder, 1972).

Older people are not very much more likely

than other age groups to need *short-stay hospitalization*. About 13 percent of the elderly were
hospitalized at least once in 1976, compared to
about 11 percent of the general population.
However, those elderly who have serious illnesses account for an enormous number of stays
in the hospital. As a result, the elderly have hospitalization rates three times higher than those
for people under 17, and the average duration
of stay is nearly three times as long.

At any one time, only about 4 percent of the
elderly is in **personal care homes, nursing
homes,** or **skilled nursing facilities.**[*] However,
as age goes up, so does the percentage who need
continual care. Palmore (1976) found that 25
percent of the elderly in a 20-year longitudinal
study experienced institutionalization at some
time before they died.

Types of Health Problems

The elderly are likely to find that the kind of
care they need is unavailable. The kind of care
they are offered may be inappropriate. There
may be no one willing to manage the long-term
treatment of multiple chronic conditions. They
may be plagued by problems resulting from interactions among multiple medications used to
treat multiple chronic conditions. And last but
not least, most older people find that the system
we have for financing health care is inadequate.

Mrs. C's case illustrates the problem of
needed health care being unavailable. She was
76 and lived alone. She was in good health
generally, but had come down with the flu. She
tried to manage on her own but reached the
point where she could not get out of bed to fix
meals or go to the bathroom. She called her
doctor and instead got the receptionist, who in-
sisted that Mrs. C come into the doctor's office.
When Mrs. C replied that she could not get out

---

[*]Personal care homes provide meals, housekeeping services,
and assistance with tasks such as dressing and bathing.
Nursing homes provide personal care plus minimal medical
care. People who require hospital-quality care over a long
period are cared for in skilled nursing facilities.

of bed, much less come to the office, the receptionist instructed her to call the emergency squad and go to the hospital emergency room because "that's what emergency rooms are for."

Mrs. C did as instructed, albeit more than slightly embarrassed to be carried out of her building on a stretcher "all on account of the measly flu." After a two-hour wait at the hospital, she was seen by the emergency room physician, a complete stranger who knew nothing of her medical history, which included two chronic conditions and five regular medications. He diagnosed flu and told her to go home and stay in bed. Almost in tears, she told him about being unable to care for herself at home, to which he said that there was nothing to be done about it because she was not sick enough to require hospitalization, and Medicare would not pay for it.*

Mrs. C could not afford to pay $140 per day to finance her own hospital stay, yet she needed around-the-clock care for a few days. And nursing homes usually do not admit short-term residents. In addition, the health care financing system makes no provision for personal care. In desperation, Mrs. C called her sister, over 200 miles away, who came for a few days, during which time Mrs. C recovered. What would have happened if Mrs. C had not had family?

Mrs. C's problem was partially a result of the way care is financed, but more important perhaps is the underlying philosophy about what illness is and how it should be treated that pervades our entire health care system. The **medical model** basically assumes that there are only two kinds of people to be treated, those who are seriously ill and need hospitalization and those who are up and about and can go to a doctor's office or clinic. Obviously, incapacitation is a matter of degree, and our system for treatment needs to recognize this fact.

Brody (1973) has pointed out that when

---

*Medicare, a public system for financing health care, is discussed in detail later in the chapter.

health is viewed as a positive good to be pursued rather than merely as an affliction to be eliminated, the range of services required for adequate health care expands. He argued strongly against viewing personal services such as bathing and dressing, support services such as recreational therapy, maintenance services such as housekeeping, and coordination services such as counseling or referral as "ancillary" services—as somehow not quite as essential to the maintenance of good health as direct medical care. Brody further pointed out the uneven availability of nonmedical health services. For example, Medicare and third-party medical insurance will pay for nonmedical services in a short-stay hospital or skilled nursing facility, but not in the patient's home. Although home health service is technically available under Medicare, it is seldom used because the patient must be virtually housebound but still able to make do with only intermittent care.

As noted earlier, many middle-aged and older people have more than one chronic condition requiring long-term treatment. **Long-term care** used to mean care provided by an institution, but today the term has a broader meaning and includes the long-term management of illness and disability (Koff 1982). Thus, long-term care is possible in both community and institutional settings. However, the specialization of medicine discourages the coordination required to effectively manage multiple chronic conditions in the community. As a result, an older person with several different conditions may be going to two or three doctors, often with no communication among them. Effective long-term care in the community requires **case management,** which involves looking at all of a person's needs and resources and developing a coordinated treatment plan. Unfortunately, very few communities have case management services.

Drugs are a major component in the treatment of most acute and chronic conditions common to older people. What drugs to use and in

what amounts depend on several factors: how much of the drug is *absorbed* how fast from the site of administration, how efficiently the drug is *distributed,* how quickly and completely the drug is *metabolized,* and how quickly the drug or its by-products are *eliminated* from the body (Kayne, 1976). Aging changes all these factors, "often resulting in greater concentrations of the drug at its site of activity or a longer persistence of drug activity" in older people compared to other adults (Kayne, 1976:437). For example, because kidney functioning declines sharply with age, drugs that are eliminated by the kidneys must be given in lower dosages to older people in order to avoid accumulation of the drug to the point where it produces adverse effects. Moreover, many older people have multiple chronic conditions for which they are taking several drugs.

Establishing proper dosages and avoiding adverse drug reactions or adverse interactions among drugs require initial metabolic information, history, and monitoring that is beyond the capacity of medicine as it is currently organized. In many cases, the physician does not know how age effects appropriate dosage. Sometimes such information is simply not available. As a result, establishing proper dosages is a trial-and-error process in which a great many errors are made and only sometimes detected.

About 5 percent of all hospitalizations occur as a result of adverse drug reactions, and this percentage is higher for people over 60. In addition, 10 to 30 percent of those who are hospitalized have adverse drug reactions in the hospital, and such reactions occur more often in older patients than in others (Kayne, 1976:436–437). And these data probably reflect only a small portion of the actual medical problems that result from the use of inappropriate drugs, incorrect drugs, or drug interactions. In addition, mental problems such as depression or confusion are common results of adverse drug reactions. Unfortunately, these symptoms are all too often attributed to "senility" in older patients.

Problems with Financing Medical Care

Medicare is a program of health insurance for older Americans that is administered by the Social Security Administration. It consists of two parts: hospital insurance and supplementary medical insurance. Nearly all older Americans are eligible for hospital coverage. Here is how it worked in 1984. After a $356 deductible paid by the patient, hospital insurance covered the full cost of up to 60 days of hospitalization for any illness. From 61 days to 90 days, the patient paid $89 per day. In addition, a "lifetime reserve" of 60 days could be used for illness that required hospitalization for longer than 90 days. However, the patient had to pay $176 per day during coverage under the lifetime reserve. Hospital insurance also covered up to 100 days in an approved skilled nursing facility. The first 20 days were covered in full, and after that the patient paid $44.50 per day. Hospital insurance is financed through payroll deductions and employer contributions to a Medicare trust fund, which is separate from the Social Security retirement and disability trust funds.

Supplementary medical insurance is a voluntary program administered under Medicare. It requires a monthly premium from the older person, to be matched by the federal government out of general tax revenues. In 1984, after a yearly deductible of $75, medical insurance paid 80 percent of the allowable costs of doctors' services and out-patient physical therapy. It did not pay for medical checkups, prescription drugs, eyeglasses, dentures, or hearing aids.*

Medicare has covered almost all people age 65 or over since July 1, 1966 (West, 1971). Initially, the use of in-hospital services increased,

---

*Because Medicare regulations are constantly changing, it is not feasible to include much detail about the program. This situation represents a minor headache to authors writing gerontology books and a major headache to older people, who are never quite sure what is covered or for how long.

along with the use of all supporting medical services, with the introduction of the program, and continued to increase, but at a declining rate. However, the average length of each hospital stay has actually dropped slightly. The use of ambulatory physician services has remained fairly stable throughout the period since 1966, and there has been very little use of post-hospital alternatives—skilled nursing facilities and home health services. Per capita expenditures under Medicare have more than tripled since the program began, mainly because of increases in what hospitals charged the program for covered services. A large proportion of the funds are spent on behalf of a relatively small number of people with serious illnesses. About 20 percent of the insured population uses no covered service in a given year. Another 20 percent is hospitalized. Among the 20 percent hospitalized, one-fourth are hospitalized more than once in the year, and the bulk of the physician costs arise from care for patients hospitalized for illness.

Medicaid is a comprehensive health care program designed to provide health care to the poor, regardless of age. It is administered by local welfare departments using federal and state funds and following federal guidelines and regulations. Medicaid pays for everything that Medicare does, as well as for many other services, including drugs, eyeglasses, and long-term care in licensed nursing homes.

About 55 percent of older Americans carry private health insurance to fill the major gaps in Medicare coverage. However, at present none of the available policies provide complete medical care coverage. Thus, out-of-pocket costs for medical services remain a major expense item for older Americans.

Who Has Health Care Problems?

Though virtually everyone in the United States with a serious chronic condition has some sort of problem finding appropriate and effective care or paying for it, certain subgroups of the older population are more likely than others to have problems. The very old (85 and over) are especially likely to be frail. Often the adult children who might care for these frail elderly are themselves older people with limited physical and financial resources. The very old tend to have multiple serious conditions and are much more likely to be disabled by them. Older members of certain minority groups are also more likely to have health problems, particularly blacks and Native Americans, among whom disabling chronic illness tends to occur at younger ages than among whites.

What Needs to Be Done?

In the area of health care it is literally true that an ounce of *prevention* is worth a pound of cure. Yet our approach to providing and financing care does not reflect this. At the very least we need a much greater effort to educate the public about the value of prevention, to educate health care professionals about the most effective measures, and to perform the research needed to advance our knowledge about effective prevention.

But we must also acknowledge that the major problem in prevention is not financing or lack of knowledge or lack of prevention services—it is a lack of motivation. A majority of the American population probably knows that it is unhealthy to smoke, to be overweight, to drink too much alcohol, and not to exercise. Yet cigarette sales have increased every year since the Surgeon General reported over 20 years ago that smoking was linked to lung cancer and heart disease. The average weight of the American people has gone up steadily, as has the proportion that are obese, despite widespread publicity linking overweight to heart disease. Despite the popularity of exercise right now, hundreds of thousands of adults get none.

In the area of *rehabilitation*, we should disconnect the financing of rehabilitation from the prospects for employment. Just because someone is retired is no reason to deny him or her needed rehabilitation services! We also need to do a better job of training family members to aid in the rehabilitative process, because they are the ones most likely to provide care at home.

In the area of *treatment,* we pointed earlier to the need for a continuum of services. In-home services, out-patient clinics, residential care, and long-term care are all in short supply right now. Our system is also spotty with respect to a range of mental health services. Although an estimated 15 percent of the elderly need mental health services, they represent only 2 to 4 percent of the clients of psychiatric clinics, community mental health centers, and private practitioners. These figures suggest that moving older mental patients from state-run mental hospitals out into the community may have been ill advised. Beginning in the 1960s, there was a wholesale transfer of geriatric mental patients out of mental hospitals, which has been partially responsible for the dramatic rise in nursing home residents since 1960. Such policies may look good on paper, but in actuality people are being sent out into communities that are not prepared to monitor their progress. In many cases there is no provision for continuing necessary drug therapy (Butler and Lewis, 1973).

We also need to fill in the gaps in our current systems for financing health care. For example, right now Medicare does not pay for eyeglasses, dentures, or hearing aids. It should. Medicare also does not recognize the fact that long-term care can indeed be *long*-term. As the system operates now, older people, including couples in which only one member needs long-term care, are forced to become paupers in order to qualify for the only system that provides truly long-term care—Medicaid.

Health Care Needs and Growth of the Older Population

In the 30 years from 1970 to 2000, the growth of the older population and the aging of the older population will produce significant increases in demand for all kinds of health services. At the 1980 rates of utilization, the population explosion of older Americans will increase the annual demand for space in acute care hospitals from 105 million bed-days in 1980 to 125 million in the year 2000. Demand for physician visits will increase from 117 million to 188 million annually. The number of nursing home residents will increase from 720,000 to over 1.3 million. The number of nursing home residents over 85 years of age will increase from 262,000 to 584,000.

The implications of these increases in demand are frightening. Physicians and adequate nursing homes are in short supply now. What will happen when the demand nearly doubles? The mental health needs of the older population are 85 percent unmet now. What will happen when the over-85 population more than doubles? Health insurance cannot pay for services needed now. How can it cope with both inflation and the older-adult population explosion? These are apt to be some of our most serious policy questions over the next two decades.

Transportation

Aging changes our needs and resources in the area of transportation in several ways. For some, declining sight impairs ability to drive a private automobile. Lowered income forces still others to give up their cars or to use them sparingly. The increase with age in the proportion of physically impaired people also raises the proportion who need specialized transportation.

In this country, we have been experiencing a long-term trend away from public transportation. Its use is declining in all but our largest cities. No longer a paying proposition, and usually requiring tax subsidies, public transportation is used most for travel to and from work. The needs of the elderly have not been considered in most decisions about public transportation.

Older people fall into two categories with regard to transportation: those who can use present facilities and those who cannot. Those with no transportation problems tend to be the ones who can afford to own and operate their own cars—about 46 percent of those 65 and older. For these people, public transportation is something to be used when it snows or for long trips.

Who Has Transportation Problems?

The elderly with transportation problems fall into three groups: (1) those who could use existing public transportation but cannot afford it, (2) those who for whatever reason need to be picked up from and returned directly to their homes, and (3) those who live in areas where there is no public transportation.

Cost is an important factor. In this country roughly 10 million older people are hampered by the cost of transportation, often because they cannot afford a car, because bus fares of 50¢ or higher are beyond their means, or because they cannot afford cab fares of $2.50 or more. For these people, lack of adequate, inexpensive transportation is one of the most important limitations on independence and activity.

Among older people with transportation problems, most are still able to get to the doctor, dentist, and grocery store. But many do not get out to see their friends and relatives or to go to church or for recreation. Although they manage to keep alive, they are unable to do the things that give meaning to life. And when they can get out, it must usually be at someone else's convenience. Older people's pride and dignity often prevent them from relying on friends and relatives for transportation. What they need is a dependable transportation system at prices they can afford.

What Is Needed?

The ideal transportation plan for older people would consist of four elements. First, older people need fare reductions or discounts on all public transportation, including interstate transport. Second, public subsidies are needed for adequate scheduling and routing of existing public transportation. Third, taxi fares for the disabled or infirm should be reduced. Fourth, funds should be allocated to senior centers to purchase and equip vehicles for use in transporting older people, particularly in rural areas with no public transportation.

Increasingly, the federal government has been willing to provide funds for transportation as a necessary element of service delivery in programs for older people. However, federal cutbacks now threaten the gains that were made in the 1970s.

Community Facilities and Services

The community, or subcommunity in larger areas, is an important focal point in the lives of most people. People are born, reared, educated, married, housed, fed, healed, mourned, and buried in the local community. Work, play, love, politics, fellowship, and self-discovery most often occur in the context of the local community. Thus, the picture of society people gain is substantially influenced by the extent to which the city or neighborhood in which they live is a unified community. Because older people are usually long-term community residents, they are especially likely to see the community as the locus of life's most salient moments. Thus, it is extremely important how services to the elderly are organized within communities.

The Older Americans Comprehensive Service Amendments of 1973 created a new community organization, the **Area Agency on Aging** (AAA). Along with significant increases in federal funds to local programs for older Americans, the Comprehensive Service Amendments (through the AAA) brought new priorities on coordination of services and on planning. There are currently just under 400 AAAs, each of which is charged with developing plans for a comprehensive and coordinated network of services to older people and with offering facilitating services in the areas of information and referral, escort, transportation, and outreach. The Area Agency on Aging concept emphasizes flexibility in uniting particular sets of local organizations to meet the needs of local older people, and thus it allows for local and regional variations in resources and service needs. At the same time, the AAA concept seeks to make a minimum set of services available to all older people. After the AAAs were created in 1974, services to the elderly improved dramatically in most parts of the nation.

Facilities That Serve the Elderly

Community facilities are organized service centers—stores, banks, churches, doctors' offices, hospitals, and so forth. There is usually a mixture of public and private facilities in any given community. Taietz (1975b) made an intensive study of community facilities serving the aged in 144 New York communities. He found that specialized facilities tended to be present in communities with a high degree of complexity and specialization. Only the most rudimentary facilities were available in a majority of the 144 communities surveyed, and facilities were particularly lacking in rural areas.

Because most Americans live in urban areas, it is easy to forget that the majority of communities are in rural areas. In 1974, 86 percent of the land area in the United States was rural, nonmetropolitan land. The impact of this fact on the prevalence of facilities is a topic very worthy of study.

Services

Social services consist of a broad range of often unrelated programs that revolve around a general goal of helping people get the things they need. The range includes family services, senior centers, the Foster Grandparent program, Talking Books, meals programs, employment services, and protective services. Since communities vary widely with regard to the number and range of such programs, and program titles vary as well, instead of trying to describe the typical community, we shall examine the types of programs commonly found in communities.

Services to Older People. *Meals* programs either take food to people or bring people to food. "Meals-on-Wheels" programs deliver hot meals to older people in their own homes. Congregate meals programs bring older people to a central site for meals. In recent years, the congregate meals approach has been gaining favor because it provides fellowship as well as more opportunities to tie in with other social service programs at the congregate meal sites.

Information and referral services provide a bridge between people with needs and appropriate service agencies. Area Agencies on Aging are responsible for these programs in most areas. Many areas have directories of services for older people.

Visitor programs offer contact between older shut-ins and the outside world and often serve institutionalized older people as well as older people living in their own homes. The programs are usually staffed by volunteers, and older people often serve as visitors.

Outreach services seek out older people in need of services, who often become known to the program via relatives or neighbors. Outreach workers contact the older person and refer him or her to the appropriate agency. Sometimes outreach workers make agency contacts on behalf of older people.

Telephone reassurance services give isolated older people a point of contact and a sense of continuity. In the ideal reassurance program, the people working on the phones are well trained in referral and yet also know the older person through regular telephone visits. Regular calls from the program assure older people that someone cares about them and will be checking on their welfare regularly. Volunteers are often used for telephone reassurance.

Employment services seek to connect older workers with jobs. Sometimes such services maintain a file of retired people from various occupations who are available for short-term or part-time employment.

Homemaker services provide household support services to semi-independent older people living in their own homes. In addition to the usual housekeeping chores, such as cleaning, shopping, and laundry, some programs also offer home maintenance and food preparation services. Berg et al. (1974) stress the need for a continuum of services that can be suited to the older person's level of impairment. Highly impaired people need a variety of housekeeping services on a daily basis, while others may need only occasional specialized services.

Income counseling programs help people get maximum use of their income resources by making sure they are aware of all possible sources of income and by helping them make the transition from a pre- to a post-retirement budget. Income counseling often includes such things as how to buy consumer goods at the lowest prices, how to take advantage of seasonal sales, the cost of credit buying, how to form consumer cooperatives, how to save on rent or get into low-rent public housing, ways to save on auto insurance, ways to save on building repairs, and so on. Although this type of assistance is highly valued by older people, very few communities offer it.

Most large communities have *senior centers,* which usually take the form of private nonprofit corporations, often underwritten with United Way money. There are several thousand senior centers in the United States. Often such centers constitute the sole community attempt to offer recreational and educational programs for older people. The small percentage of older people who use them (usually 1 to 5 percent) would seem to indicate that senior centers do not constitute a focal point for recreation and education

among most older people. Of course, many older people who might otherwise use a senior center's facilities are prevented from doing so by difficulties of access—poor transportation service, disability, health, and so on. Yet even in communities where a concerted effort has been made to give older people access to senior centers, only a small minority have taken advantage of them.

The average multipurpose senior center tends to adopt a flexible program—one that offers informal companionship, community services, self-government within the center, and a wide variety of other possible features. Membership in senior centers tends to be drawn from a wide area rather than from a single neighborhood. Initial membership is often related to a major life change such as retirement or widowhood, and joiners tend to be healthy and ambulatory. Members of senior centers do not seem to be different from other older people. However, Tissue (1971c) indicated that centers cannot easily accommodate members from different social classes.

Protective services take responsibility for older people who can no longer be responsible for themselves. Everyone has heard of aging, confused hermits who have outlived their families and who are starving because they have hidden their Social Security checks and cannot recall where they put them. Take, for example, the case of Mr. M, who had been complaining to a variety of agencies about Mrs. S—an 88-year-old woman whose house was adjacent to his—and finally reached the Senior Information Center. Mrs. S, a recluse, had harassed the M's by making loud noises through their bedroom window, banging her porch door, calling vile and obscene things to their children playing in the yard. Her house was run down, and weeds and bushes had overgrown the garden. Neighbors had photographed her feeding rats in her backyard. They described her as resembling a fairy-tale witch—with flowing gray hair and a long, dirty skirt, living in silent seclusion. Her only relative was a niece, who for the last several years had refused to become involved. Mrs. S's income was a mere $72 a month from Social Security.

A home call from the Senior Center caseworker confirmed the grim picture. Mrs. S, suspicious at first, refused to let the caseworker into the house, but came out on the porch to talk. She tried to hide a dirty, stained slip, and there was a strong odor of urine about her. She denied having any problems other than those caused by the "gangsters" next door, and revealed a paranoid trend in her thinking. As she talked she became almost friendly, joked about getting a miniskirt, and assured the caseworker that there was nothing to worry about. Later, a city sanitation inspector went through the house, saw one rat and evidence of rats' presence throughout the house. The odor of urine and feces was strong. The inspector also found about 50 wine bottles, which added to the frightening picture. Finally, Mr. M, angered over the continued harassment, nailed shut the back door of her house. Fortunately, another neighbor realized the danger in case of fire and removed the nails (adapted from Ross, 1968:50).

Protective services are used by the community when it becomes clear from the behavior of older people—as in the case just cited—that they are mentally incapable of caring for themselves and their interests. It is estimated that something on the order of 1 in every 20 older people needs some form of protective service, a proportion that can be expected to increase as the proportion of older people over 75 increases. The typical response to someone like Mrs. S has been to put the individual in an institution; however, this solution is coming under increased scrutiny. Many older people now in institutions could be left at home with a minimum of help in securing the support services already available to them. The most difficult problem is often to find someone who will initiate action. In many states, the law assumes the

proceedings will be initiated by a relative. In the absence of a relative, no one is willing to take responsibility. Laws need to be changed to more clearly pinpoint that responsibility.

Ultimately, protective services are outreach services rather than deskbound ones. Legal intervention is usually a last resort, to be used only when all other alternatives have been exhausted. Agencies must often seek out people who might not even want the service at all. It is obvious that while protective services must be a part of any community service program for older people, assigning responsibility for such services is a difficult task.

Summary

Availability of resources to meet instrumental needs varies widely among the elderly. Most older Americans have adequate incomes, housing, health care, transportation, and access to facilities and services. It's a good thing, too. If the nation had to finance special services to more than a very small proportion of its older citizens, the costs would be astronomical indeed. But within this generally favorable situation, there are many categories of older people that have great difficulty in meeting their instrumental needs. Compared to the general older population, financial difficulties are far more prevalent among older single women, older blacks and Hispanics, rural residents, and the very old. The fact that private pensions are least likely to be available in the lowest-paying jobs is creating an increasing gap between the haves and the have-nots with regard to retirement income. The cutbacks in both direct and indirect income support to the poor that began in October 1981 as part of the Reagan Administration's economic program have widened this gap further.

Most older people live in independent households and prefer it that way. Nevertheless, as the number of very old people increases, there will be a growing need for in-home assistance. Indications are that the need for such services is not being met now, and this situation probably will get worse. Middle-income older Americans are often frustrated by the lack of available, affordable housing. There is also a shortage of subsidized housing for the elderly poor. Retirement communities come in several varieties, and older people seem to select the variety that best meets their needs. But retirement communities are scarce in many areas of the country.

Health care problems encountered by the elderly include lack of resources for preventive health care, gaps in coverage by Medicare, lack of facilities or services to care for older people with short-term disabling acute conditions such as flu, poor availability of mental health services, and poor availability of health care facilities and services in rural areas. In addition, the growing size of the older population will place a severe strain on facilities and services, and in the future many of the elderly may not be able to meet their needs at all unless we plan now to increase the availability of health practitioners and facilities.

Dramatic increases in the over-85 population will compound the current problems of transportation. The proportion who cannot or should not drive their own automobiles is going to increase rapidly. We need to plan for this eventuality.

Older people are served by a large and complex network of public and private organizations. As federal funds earmarked for some services to the elderly disappeared into block grants to the states, the elderly who needed services were put in direct competition with other groups for resources at the local level. This competition lowered the availability and quality of services. And much energy that could have gone into delivering services has gone into political activity needed to secure funding.

More attention needs to be paid to older people as providers of services. Retired people represent a large pool of potential community resources that could be used to serve older people who need assistance.

Income problems are most likely for women, minorities, and the very old. Housing problems are most likely for middle-class elders who are not eligible for subsidized housing and for older rural people. Preventive health care is a problem for everyone. The elderly poor, who are often able to get more types of services paid for, have the most trouble finding someone to provide such services. Transportation problems are most likely among older women and the very old. No single policy can possibly meet all these various needs. We will return to the policy issue in Chapter 17, "Politics and Government," and Chapter 18, "Health and Social Services."

Chapter 9

Employment and Retirement

Employment and retirement play a big part in the adult life course. When men reach adulthood, they are expected to get a job and to remain employed until they become eligible for retirement. Men are excused from this expectation only if they become disabled. While women have the choice of being a housewife with no paid employment, about half of American women are employed and tend to remain so throughout their marriages. Age of entry into employment is governed by child labor laws and the education requirements of jobs, both of which are tied to age. Likewise, the minimum retirement age is also usually tied to chronological age.*

The labor force consists of people who are employed plus those who are unemployed but are looking for work. Labor force participation rates are the proportion of the population in each age category in the labor force. In 1980, 95 percent of men between the ages of 25 and 34 were in the labor force. The proportion in the labor force was around 95 percent through age 45. The proportions for older age groups were progressively lower (see Figure 9-1). For women, 1980 labor force participation was at a peak at ages 20 to 24. Fewer women of child-rearing age were in the labor force.** From age 35 to age 50, there was relatively little difference in women's labor force participation (see Figure 9-1).

For both men and women, there appears to be a decline in labor force participation beginning at age 50. For instance, as Table 9-1 shows, the 1970 labor force participation of men was progressively lower after age 50: The labor

---

*Years of service is sometimes the sole criterion for the minimum age of retirement; and years of service, too, is related to age. For example, if retirement is permitted after 30 years of service, the lowest possible age of retirement will still be 46, since employment prior to age 16 is unlawful.

**The proportion of women who drop out of the labor force for child rearing has been greatly exaggerated. It appears that most women who enter the labor force stay there continuously through adulthood (Jaffe and Ridley, 1976; Mallan, 1974).

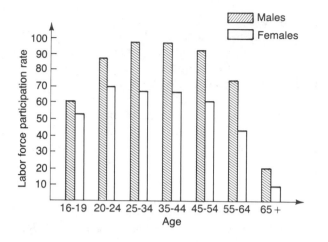

FIGURE 9-1 Labor force participation rates, by age and sex: United States, 1980. *Source:* Based on data from the U.S. Bureau of the Census, 1981c.

TABLE 9-1 Labor force participation rates, by age and sex: United States, 1970

Age	Male	Female
45	93.3%	50.3%
46	95.0	50.8
47	93.2	55.4
48	91.6	56.1
49	93.4	50.3
50	91.7	53.6
51	93.5	52.0
52	90.5	52.0
53	90.2	53.5
54	88.8	48.5
55	89.8	49.0
56	88.8	49.7
57	85.7	49.5
58	82.7	43.5
59	82.1	46.6
60	81.1	41.7
61	79.6	36.0
62	71.8	33.2
63	69.6	33.1
64	64.0	28.6
65	44.4	21.4
66	41.5	18.6
67	35.7	14.7
68	33.0	14.8
69	33.5	13.7
70	25.7	11.5

Source: Compiled from 15% public use sample of basic records, 1970 United States Census.

force participation of 61-year-old men was 13.9 percentage points lower than that for 51-year-old men. Notice also the significantly lower proportion at age 62, when men become eligible for reduced Social Security benefits, and the sharply lower proportion at age 65, the eligibility age for full Social Security retirement benefits. For women, the pattern is not so clear-cut: There was a drop of 16 percentage points from age 51 to 61, but the proportions at age 62 and age 65 are not significantly lower. This pattern may relate to a number of factors: Women who are near retirement age may retire when their husbands retire. Others may work beyond the minimum retirement age in order to increase their years of service and thereby enlarge their pensions.

The data in Table 9-1 illustrate the value of looking at labor force participation rates by single years of age. Unfortunately, published reports usually show rates only for five-year age categories. Table 9-2 shows what has happened from 1970 to 1983 in such grouped data. For men beyond age 50 there was a sharp drop in labor force participation in all age categories, al-though greatest for ages 60 to 64, indicating a trend toward retirement before age 65.

The Age Discrimination in Employment Act of 1967 was amended in 1978 to prohibit mandatory retirement before age 70 in most sectors of the economy. Many experts expected an increase in the number of workers remaining in the labor force past age 65. However, as the data in Table 9-2 show, *more* men retired before age 70 in 1983 than in 1970. Interestingly, from 1970 to 1983 there was a sharp increase in labor

TABLE 9-2 Labor force participation rates, by age and sex: United States, 1970 and 1983

	Male		Female	
Age	1970	1983	1970	1983
40–44	94.6%	95.0%	52.1%	68.3%
45–49	93.5	93.5	53.0	65.3
50–54	91.4	88.7	52.0	58.3
55–59	86.8	81.0	47.4	48.0
60–64	73.0	56.8	36.1	33.6
65–69	39.0	25.5	17.2	13.9
70+	18.2	12.3	8.1	4.5

Sources: U.S. Department of Labor, 1983; U.S. Bureau of the Census, 1973b.

force participation among women aged 40 to 54. But for women over age 60, the labor force participation dropped from 1970 to 1983, although not nearly as much as it did for men. All of this means that retirement is becoming even more common and that the trend toward earlier retirement has not abated. Withdrawal from the labor force before age 62 is mainly due to three factors: labor market problems of older workers, increasing rates of disability, and opportunities for early retirement. Withdrawal after age 62 is nearly all related to retirement, though employment problems and disability also exert pressure to retire.

Employment Problems of Older Workers

To the U.S. Department of Labor, a "mature worker" is any employee age 40 or over. Mature workers are less likely to become unemployed, but if they do, they encounter difficulty getting another job. Thus, although unemployment rates may be lower for mature workers, unemployment for them has more serious consequences: Once unemployed, mature workers are much more likely than others to remain unemployed long enough to exhaust their unemployment benefits (Sheppard, 1976).

Labor Market Problems

Several factors are responsible for employment problems among middle-aged and older workers. Changes in the labor market can result from plant closings, company reorganizations, or mass layoffs. Sheppard (1970) reported that from 1963 to 1965, over half the companies involved in a mass layoff of over 190,000 workers went out of business or relocated elsewhere. Seniority is often little protection if the job is abolished. And if experience, technical competence, and education are held constant, older workers tend to be laid off first (Sheppard, 1970; Parnes and King, 1977). Those who are laid off or otherwise lose their jobs tend to have trade or manufacturing jobs, to work for small businesses, to have no pension coverage, and to work for nonunionized firms (Parnes and King, 1977).

Displaced homemakers can also experience employment problems in middle age. These are women who chose homemaking as a full-time job and who, either through widowhood or divorce, find themselves in need of a paying job. Women who choose to be full-time homemakers generally assume that their economic support, health insurance, and retirement benefits will come as a result of their marriage to an employed man. However, women who become widowed or divorced in middle age can be thrust suddenly into the job market. They often lack marketable job skills. Because homemaking is not looked upon as employment, homemakers lack a work history and are ineligible for Social Security or SSI; yet they are old enough to encounter age discrimination in the job market (Sommers and Shields, 1979). That displaced homemakers have severe employment problems was recognized by the U.S. Congress in 1978 when displaced homemakers were categorized as "hard-to-employ" under the

Comprehensive Employment Training Act (CETA).

Age Discrimination

Once unemployed, mature workers face stiff age discrimination. The Age Discrimination in Employment Act of 1967 (ADEA) protects workers 40 or over from denial of employment strictly because of age. In 1983, over $24.6 million was awarded by courts to over 5,000 individuals as a result of violations of the ADEA. From 1979 to 1983, the number of age discrimination complaints increased over 300 percent— from 5,374 to 18,087. There is reason to believe that the cases pursued by the Equal Opportunity Commission highly underrepresent the full extent of age discrimination. Many workers are unaware of the protections offered by ADEA. Still others are reluctant to become involved in the bureaucratic legalities.

Parnes and King (1977) found that displaced middle-aged workers eventually located other employment, but at a price—both in type of employment and in earnings. Compared to others, displaced workers moved down the occupational ladder, particularly out of professional and managerial positions. As a result, from 1966 to 1971, 20 percent of displaced workers suffered a decline in earnings, while those who remained employed averaged a 25 percent increase in earnings. The longer the period of unemployment, the greater the drop in occupational level and earnings.

Stereotypes About Older Workers.   Rosen and Jerdee (1976b) wanted to know how age stereotypes influence managerial decisions. To find out, they presented a group of 42 business students in their twenties with an "in-basket" exercise involving six memos requiring action by a manager. To discover the effect of age, they referred to the focal person in the memo variously as "younger" or "older"; in addition, four cases included a personnel file with a photograph en-

closed. Since each participant received only one version of the six cases, the manipulation of the age variable was unobtrusive. The six cases were as follows:

1. A recently hired shipping room employee who seemed unresponsive to customer calls for service

2. A candidate for promotion to a marketing job that required "fresh solutions to challenging problems" and "a high degree of creative, innovative behavior"

3. A candidate for a position that required not only knowledge of the field but the capability of making "quick judgments under high risk"

4. A request to transfer a worker to a higher-paying but more physically demanding job

5. A request from a production staff employee to attend a conference on "new theories and research relevant to production systems"

6. A request for a decision whether to terminate or retrain a computer programmer whose skills had become obsolete due to changes in computer operations

These cases were based on earlier work (Rosen and Jerdee, 1976a) showing that managers stereotyped older workers as resistant to change, uncreative, cautious and slow to make judgments, lower in physical capacity, uninterested in technological change, and untrainable.

The older shipping room employee was not expected to be able to change his behavior, and most participants thought he should be replaced. The younger employee was expected to be able to change, and most felt that a reprimand would solve the problem. Only 24 percent recommended promotion if they reviewed the older candidate for the marketing job while 54 percent of those who reviewed the younger candidate recommended promotion, even though both candidates had identical qualifications. The older candidate came off worse for the risk-taking job, too. Twenty-five percent who reviewed the younger applicant recommended selection, as against only 13 percent of those who reviewed the older one. The older worker (age 56) who wanted a transfer to a more physically demanding job was significantly more likely to have his request denied. The older production staff employee was significantly more likely to get turned down on his request to attend a conference to update his knowledge. The older computer programmer was less likely to be retrained and more likely to be replaced.

Rosen and Jerdee concluded that the participants' assumptions about the physical, mental, and emotional characteristics of older workers produced managerial decisions that were obviously contrary to the well-being and career progress of older employees. Decisions about hiring, retention, correction, training, and retraining all suffered purely because of the age of the focal person. Rosen and Jerdee caution that personnel directors may not behave the way their business students did. But other evidence on employment problems of older workers indicates that they probably do.

A major controversy surrounding the employment of older workers concerns the effect of aging on employability. In Chapters 4 and 5 we saw that a majority of older people continue to function physically and psychologically at a level well above the minimum needed for most adult performance. But what has research on actual work situations shown? Doering, Rhodes, and Schuster (1983) reviewed the results of over 150 research studies related to aging and work. Some of their major conclusions were as follows:

- The attitudes and work behavior of older workers are generally congruent with effective organizational functioning.
- Job satisfaction is higher among older workers than in other age groups.
- Older workers are more loyal and less likely to leave their current work organization.

- Healthy older workers have lower rates of absenteeism compared to the young, but unhealthy older workers may have higher rates of absenteeism.
- Compared to the young, older workers are less likely to be injured on the job. However, if injured, older workers take longer to recover and are more likely to be disabled than other age groups.
- Older workers continue to learn.

In the vast majority of the studies reviewed by Doering and his associates, "older worker" was operationally defined as someone age 55 or older. They could come to no firm conclusion on the issue of whether older workers perform as well as younger ones; in some studies they did, and in others they did not. The safest assumption to make, until there is proof to the contrary, is that age makes little difference in performance. Overall, the literature provides no basis for wholesale discrimination against older workers.

All the research findings notwithstanding, it is obvious that aging does affect the ability of some people to perform a given job. What can employers do? Industrial health counseling can help minimize the problems of employing older people. In one study, an Industrial Health Counseling Service was set up in Portland, Maine. The program used a system developed by Kaye (1973) to diagnose workers' capacities in seven functional areas—general physique, upper extremities, lower extremities, hearing, eyesight, intelligence, and personality. Jobs were also rated on the same criteria. Individuals and jobs were then matched by functional profile. As a result, 51 percent of the 2,400 job applicants, half of them over age 40, were placed in jobs. Over 100 firms participated in the program. While the program was not a panacea, it was a major step toward demonstrating the feasibility of using functional criteria in hiring to replace arbitrary age criteria (Quirk and Skinner, 1973).

Cost of Fringe Benefits

Ironically, in the past, retirement pension plans represented one of the important forces operating against mature workers. Taggart (1973) reviewed the evidence on the impact of private pension plans on the labor market and concluded that the existence of retirement plans had lowered the normal retirement age and increased the number of firms using mandatory retirement ages. In addition, firms that prided themselves on providing adequate pensions were reluctant to hire workers in their fifties and sixties because they would not have long enough to work prior to the mandatory retirement age to qualify for an adequate pension. It was also more costly to provide a given benefit for a new older employee because employer contributions are spread over a shorter period. In 1978, ADEA was amended to prohibit the use of pension plans as justification for not hiring mature workers. However, Zillmer (1982) found that because of Medicare, fringe benefit costs to employ a worker 65 or over were quite similar to those for a 45-year-old, while those for a 60-year-old were nearly 60 percent higher, mainly due to higher health insurance costs. Medicare was switched to secondary provider in 1983, which increased health insurance costs for employees 65 or over. Thus, system pressure against employing workers approaching age 65 still remains high.

Disability

As age increases, so do rates of disability. For example, in 1974 only 1.4 percent of men under 45 were physically unable to work compared to 9.4 percent of those 45 to 64 (Wilder, 1977:14). Another 10.5 percent of those 45 to 64 were physically limited in the amount of work or kind of job they could do. Some proportion of this disability is a result of premature symptoms of aging, which occur most often in physically demanding jobs and in jobs with poor working conditions. However, a large proportion is the result of an accumulation of job-related injuries. For example, in 1977 there were over 11 million cases of people injured on the job seriously enough to require medical attention or more than one day of restricted activity (Howie and Drury, 1978). While older workers are less likely to be injured, there is a greater risk of disabling injury. More than half of those who apply for disability benefits under Social Security are over age 50.

Early Retirement

Retirement is discussed in considerable detail later in this chapter. For now, we will consider only some of the factors related to early retirement. The common notion is that most people who retire early do so because they want to and can afford to. And this is undoubtedly true in many cases. However, there are other factors that exert pressure for early retirement. Employment problems and poor health are the two main pressures for "involuntary" early retirement. As was pointed out earlier, unemployment is tough on mature workers, and no doubt there are many who retire early rather than brave continued unemployment and age discrimination. There are also many mature workers whose health is poor, but not poor enough to qualify them for disability benefits. Early retirement with a reduced pension is their only out. It is not known how withdrawal from the labor force in middle age is distributed among its various causes—unemployment, disability, early forced retirement, and early voluntary retirement. This would be an excellent topic for research.

Midlife Career Changes

The popular press carries frequent accounts and case studies of persons who begin new careers in middle age. However, it is difficult to find statistics on how common this phenomenon is. Troll (1975) suggested that many employed middle-aged women attend school part time in order to qualify for new careers. Military personnel often "retire" in middle age in order to take up a new career. Sarason (1977) reports widespread interest in programs designed to train middle-aged persons for new careers.

In recent years there has been an increased emphasis on the individual: Self-improvement, self-actualization, and autonomy are some of the values being emphasized in the middle class. Happiness is often tied in popular opinion to being able to change oneself and/or one's circumstances. A certain amount of romanticism is obvious in this approach, and some people subscribe to the belief that if one is unhappy with one's job, spouse, ego, car, stereo, or whatever, then the only and best way to deal with it is to ring out the old and ring in the new. No doubt a certain amount of job change is related to this more general cultural factor. Nonetheless, at this point it is difficult to say how prevalent midlife career change is, what preparations precede such changes, and what consequences they have. Numerous job changes certainly occur, but how these relate to a person's own projections about his or her occupational career is unclear. Obviously, even the idea of a career may apply to only a small portion of the labor force.

Blue-collar workers change jobs in middle age primarily as a result of poor health or being laid off (Parnes et al., 1975). For middle-class workers the situation is more complex: Midlife career change has been tied to rejection of the work ethic (Krantz, 1977), personality (Clopton, 1973), family factors (Oliver, 1971), and achievement motivation (Hiestand, 1971; Schlossberg, 1975). Interestingly, only rarely does midlife career change appear to be motivated by a desire for more money.

Thomas (1977) studied 73 middle-class men who had left managerial and professional careers between the ages of 34 and 54. He found four paths to midlife career change among these men. About 34 percent of his sample were men who had little internal motivation to change careers but were forced into it by external circumstances. Another 26 percent were faced with ex-

ternal pressures to change *and* had high internal motivation to do so. Twenty-three percent had neither high desire to change nor heavy external pressures. Only 17 percent changed purely because of their own desire to do so. External factors associated with the job career were thus the prime force in these midlife career changes. Career change was not related to rejection of the work ethic, desire for more money or job security, or family factors. There was some indication that a desire for meaningful work was important for most of these men. Thomas's study is noteworthy in that it carefully screened out those who had merely changed jobs and concentrated on those who had genuinely changed careers.

Retirement

The process of retirement involves the *transition* people experience when they move from a job role—a role performed for pay—to the role of retired person. While people can indeed give up such nonpaying positions as scoutmaster, church deacon, and volunteer worker, the term *retirement* is generally reserved for separation from a position of employment.*

An *operational definition* seeks to define an abstract concept such as retirement in terms of simple, observable procedures. At various times, "retired person" has been operationally defined as:

> any person who performs no gainful employment during a given year
>
> any person who is receiving a retirement pension benefit
>
> any person not employed full-time, year-round

Palmore (1967) found that in 1963 among men age 65 and over, 64 percent had *no* work experi-

---

*Retirement relates to *jobs* rather than *work*. In general, people never stop working; a job, however, is a position of employment, and it is from a job that an individual retires.

ence in the previous year, 80 percent received some kind of retirement benefit, and 87 percent worked less than full-time, year-round. Thus, the way "retired person" is operationally defined makes quite a difference in who is included in the category, and the definitions usually emphasize separation from the job rather than acquisition of the role of retired person.

For our purposes, an individual is retired if he or she is employed at a paying job less than full-time, year-round (whatever that may mean in a particular job) *and* if his or her income comes at least in part from a retirement pension earned through prior years of employment. Both of these conditions must be met for an individual to be retired. For example, many former military personnel draw retirement pensions but are employed full-time, year-round. Housewives often are not employed, but neither are they eligible for a retirement pension. Palmore, George, and Fillenbaum (1982:735) defined retirement as "employed less than 35 hours per week *and* receiving a retirement pension" and looked at the levels of retirement in three large longitudinal studies of men's employment. They found that 85 percent of the men had retired by age 66 to 69, and only about 40 percent before age 65.

Sometimes couples as well as individuals may be considered retired. A couple is retired if neither person is employed full-time, year-round and if most of the couple's income is from one or more retirement pensions. The extent of retirement can be measured by the number of weeks *not* employed (over and above usual vacation periods) for individuals who are drawing retirement pensions (Palmore, 1971a). These definitions are arbitrary to some extent, but they illustrate some important dimensions of retirement: namely, that retirement is an *earned* reward and that its main effects concern separation from a job and a shift in the source, and usually the amount, of individual or family income.

There is increasing recognition that housewives make an enormous contribution to society through maintaining households and rearing children. Perhaps one day this recognition will be appropriately translated into the right to a general public retirement pension, but this probably will not happen in the near future.

The Link Between People and Jobs

Retirement marks the end of what is generally thought to be a close relationship between the kind of job an individual holds and the kind of life style and livelihood he or she enjoys. This relationship results, of course, from the fact that for most people in American society, employment is the only fully acceptable way of getting money. Americans tend to identify a job with a style of life, and this way of assessing a person's status is usually correct, for job usually determines income and income sets limits on life style.

Another factor in the relationship between people and their jobs is the idea that a career can be pursued as an end in itself, purely for the satisfaction of doing a fine job. A related notion is that job careers can give people their greatest opportunities for creation, and in this way can become their entire life. Mills incorporates these ideas into his concept of craftsmanship:

Craftsmanship as a fully idealized model of work gratification involves six major features: There is no ulterior motive in work other than the product being made and the processes of its creation. The details of daily work are meaningful because they are not detached in the worker's mind from the product of the work. The worker is free to control his own working action. The craftsman is thus able to learn from his work; and to use and develop his capacities and skills in its prosecution. There is no split of work and play, or work and culture. The craftsman's way of livelihood determines and infuses his entire mode of living (1956: 220).

Mills also says,

Work may be a mere source of livelihood, or the most significant part of one's inner life; it may be experienced as expiation or as exuberant expression of self; as bounded duty, or as the development of man's universal nature. Neither love nor hatred of work is inherent in man, or inherent in any given line of work. For work has no intrinsic meaning (1956:215).

Understanding retirement thus involves understanding the nature of the links between people and their jobs. It can be said with some certainty that this relationship has changed over the years. In the peasant economy, there was no concept of occupational position or employment. In the days of medieval guilds, the idea of a vocation as a way of life was generally accepted. Not many people lived to become old in those days, but those who did continued to be employed until they grew too feeble or died. Since there were no provisions for gaining income in any other way, people worked as long as possible. The industrial revolution, assembly line production, and automation have made some important changes in this picture.

To begin with, our system has become increasingly productive; today, fewer and fewer people are needed to produce the nation's greater and greater output. This increase in productivity was made possible largely by the switch from low-energy power converters such as animals, wind, and water to high-energy converters such as steam and electricity (Cottrell, 1955). Also, the demographic revolution reduced death rates, particularly in infancy, and prolonged life. Birth rates also declined. The eventual result meant a smaller proportion of young dependents to support, and this decline meant that it was possible to defer income in order to support retirement.

The rise of industrial production systems increased the need for planning and coordination within the economic system. Mechanisms such as the corporation and the bureaucracy were introduced into the economic system and gradually spread throughout society. Government bureaucracy grew to become the political counterpart of the economic corporation. Once the state became a large-scale organization, it was capable of pooling the nation's resources and allowing a segment of society to be supported in

retirement. It was thus no accident that the first retirement program, inaugurated in 1810, consisted of pensions for civil service workers in England. America's failure to introduce civil service pensions until 1920 can be partly explained by the slow development of our national government.

The rise of industrialization brought with it urbanization and extensive residential mobility. These two factors combined to change the traditional ties to family and local community that had been the source of a great many different kinds of services. These trends resulted in a redefinition of the relationship between the individual and the government. At the same time, the wage system was putting an end to the traditional economic functions of the family. All of these trends combined to give individualism more weight in the relationship between the person and society.

The Evolution and Institutionalization of Retirement

Accordingly, the link between people and jobs came to be separated from political and family life. One important result was to reduce the amount of cohesion that people could gain in their lives through their jobs. Another result was that the new relation between the individual and the state set the stage for establishing an institutionalized right to financial support in one's old age, partly as a reward for past contributions to the economic system and partly as a result of deferring income during one's years of employment. Thus, Social Security was established, and with its introduction the institution of retirement came of age in the United States.

As the concept of retirement has continued to mature, it has come to embody the idea that, by virtue of a long-term contribution to the growth and prosperity of society, its individual members earn the right to a share of the nation's prosperity in their later years without having to hold a job. For example, Ash (1966) found that between 1951 and 1960, steelworkers shifted substantially in terms of how they justified retirement. In 1951, the majority said that retirement was justified only if the individual was physically unable to continue. By 1960, the majority of steelworkers felt that retirement was justified by years of prior service on the job. The idea that the right must be earned is related to the fact that retirement is reserved only for those who have served the required minimum time on one or more jobs.*

Industrialization and the rise of the corporation led to the development of the concept of *job*, as opposed to *craft*, and generated a large economic surplus that could be used to support adults who were not jobholders. The rise of strong national government created the political machinery that could then divert part of the economic surplus to support retired people. The Depression provided strong incentive to cut down on the number of older workers competing for scarce jobs. Because industrial jobs are often boring and meaningless to the people who do them, the promise of retirement also served as an incentive for people to endure a growing number of repetitive industrial jobs. And gradually the average jobholder has come to accept the idea that people can legitimately live in dignity as adults without holding jobs, provided they have earned the right to do so. All of these conditions helped to pave the way for the development of retirement as an institution in American society.

Retirement's main function for the society was and is to keep down the number of persons holding or looking for jobs. Providing a reward for service or supporting persons too old or disabled for employment were important but secondary considerations. But retirement was initially sold to the public primarily as a means of supporting people who were physically unable to hold jobs. This linkage was expedient at the time but had the long-run disadvantage of inappropriately connecting the concept of retire-

ment with the concept of functional old age and incapacity for employment. Thus, when 65 was set as the "normal" retirement age, the public made the incorrect logical inference that 65 also meant old age and functional incapacity, and this incorrect notion was in turn used as a fundamental justification for the development of mandatory retirement provisions. It is important to recognize that while retirement was historically linked with old age, this linkage has never had substantial basis in fact. And as the "normal" retirement age has crept downward and the health of the older population has improved, the association of retirement with old age and disability has become even less applicable.

Among industrial nations, only Japan has a high proportion of its older population in the labor force—55 percent in 1965. Palmore (1975a) found that almost twice as many aged men continue employment in Japan as compared to other industrial countries. The reasons for this divergence include a national system of retirement pensions that only very recently allowed people to develop entitlement to a pension that would provide enough to live on; higher-than-average proportions of people employed in small business and farming (areas of the economy in which partial retirement is common in the United States as well as Japan); and chronic labor shortages, which, combined with low pension levels, created incentives to use older workers as a labor reserve. But this unusual situation does not necessarily mean that the lot of older Japanese is easier or that they enjoy higher status as compared to older workers in other countries. Japanese typically retire at age 55, and at that point they may receive a meager pension. They lose their seniority, and most must leave the jobs they held prior to retirement. They become part of what the Japanese government euphemistically calls "the mobile labor reserve," which means in reality that older employees are temporary employees who get shuffled from one job to another.

Thus, retirement does not automatically

---

*For more detail on the development of retirement as a social institution, see Atchley (1982d).

emerge as a result of industrialization. In order for it to do so, there must be a mechanism to generate retirement income; there must be incentives to allow older people to leave the labor force; and older people must be able to accept life in retirement as good and proper.

The Retirement Process

Retirement is a process that involves withdrawing from a job and taking up the role of retired person. In studying individual retirement,* we are interested in the preparations people make both for withdrawing from the job and for taking up the retirement role, the decision to retire, the retirement event, and the dimensions of retirement as a social role. We are also interested in the consequences of retirement both for the individual and for the society, and in how individuals adjust to the changes retirement brings. Retirement is a complex social institution that is intertwined with the economy, the family, and the life course of individuals. Therefore, several different approaches are required for a balanced understanding of how retirement operates in society and in the lives of individuals.

Attitudes Toward Retirement

The retirement process begins when individuals recognize that some day they will retire. How younger people view the prospect of retirement has a bearing on how they assess their retired friends and, more importantly, perhaps, on how they themselves fare when retirement comes. In general, people's ideas about retirement seem to be favorable. In a study of adults ranging in age from 45 on up, Atchley (1974a) found that the concept of retirement had four separate dimensions—activity, physical potency, emotional evaluation, and moral evaluation. On all four dimensions, the concept of retirement was very

positive, regardless of the age or sex of the respondent. The only variation from this very positive view of retirement occurred among retired people who would have liked to have continued on the job. These people felt that retirement was unfair and bad. Most adults expect to retire (less than 10 percent do not), and most of them expect to retire before age 65 (Harris, 1965a; Goudy, 1981; Prentis, 1980). Only a very few say they dread retirement (Katona, 1965). Generally, the individual's attitude toward retirement is closely allied to his or her financial situation. The higher the expected retirement income, the more favorable the attitude. About two-thirds of employed adults envision no financial troubles in retirement, although most expect retirement to reduce their incomes by up to 50 percent from preretirement levels.

The relationship between social status (usually measured by income, education, and occupation) and attitudes toward retirement is complex. People with high incomes realistically expect to be financially secure in retirement, although they tend to estimate their income requirements at a level substantially below their present incomes. People with a college education are more likely than others to plan an early retirement (Morgan, 1962). Workers at the higher occupation and education levels not only have higher earnings and favorable attitudes toward retirement, but they also find their jobs more interesting and in actual practice are less prone to retire (Riley and Foner, 1968:445). People who feel they have achieved what they wanted in life are very likely to favor retirement, but people who still feel committed to their work seldom seek retirement, although they may not be antagonistic toward it (Atchley, 1971c).

People at lower occupational levels have less income and anticipate more financial insecurity in retirement. These people favor retirement, but dread poverty. Here the question is money. Apparently, few people at the lower occupational levels continue to work because they love

---

*The role of retirement as a social institution in the economic system will be considered more fully in Chapter 16. See also Chapter 3.

their jobs. At the middle occupational level, positive orientation toward retirement is at its peak. These people anticipate sufficient retirement income and at the same time have no overriding commitment toward the job.

At the upper occupational level, the picture is mixed. Income is less problematic. The primary factor that produces attitudes against retirement appears to be commitment to the job. In terms of proportions, the evidence indicates that more than half of the people who occupy upper-level occupations have a high work commitment, but also look forward to retirement (Atchley, 1971b).

Age does not appear to be related to attitudes toward retirement. Early studies found that the older a person, the more likely he or she was to dread retirement (Katona, 1965). However, more recent cohorts are more accepting of retirement. Ash's (1966) data, coupled with those of Streib and Schneider (1971), suggest that retirement is becoming more accepted over time within various age cohorts and that younger cohorts are more accepting of retirement than are older cohorts. Finances are important in the relationship between age and attitude toward retirement. This is illustrated by the fact that if adequate income could be assured, the proportion who would retire increases steadily with age from 21 to 64 years of age (Riley and Foner, 1968:445). Atchley and Robinson (1982) found no correlation between age and attitude toward retirement in a study of over 1,000 adults age 52 and older.

Retirement Preparation

Since almost everyone expects to retire, it is useful to examine the planning and preparation that precede retirement. A minority of people make concrete plans for retirement, and very few are exposed to retirement preparation programs (Kroeger, 1982; Szinovacz, 1982b). Yet most people manage to adjust quite well to retirement even though they have had little formal preparation for it. The main psychological

effect of retirement preparation programs is to reinforce pre-existing positive orientations toward retirement (Green et al., 1969; Atchley et al., 1978).

As we shall see later on in this chapter, the retirement role requires that retired persons be financially independent, physically able-bodied, and able to make decisions about how to structure their own lives.

The most important facet of any retirement preparation program is a very early exposure to the facts of life concerning retirement income. This is the only area where a majority of employees see a need for information (Atchley et al., 1978; Szinovacz, 1982b). Some employers or unions will be able to point with pride to programs providing a retirement income high enough to meet the individual's needs. Others will have to spell out the shortcomings of their programs and the steps individual employees can take to guarantee their own financial security in retirement. Professional associations can also make it a point to provide realistic retirement information to their members, particularly to those just entering the profession.

It is imperative for employees to know as soon as possible precisely where they stand with regard to retirement income. For example, some employees will receive only Social Security on retirement. They do not know specifically what benefits they will receive; they only feel vaguely that Social Security will somehow take care of them or not. A direct comparison between the average salary of a mature employee in a given occupation and the Social Security benefits he or she would receive is probably the quickest way to illustrate the need for additional individual financial planning. And this information should be offered before it is too late for the individual to do anything about planning. The retirement income picture has improved in recent years, but at present the most important element of retirement preparation still is teaching people how to assure their own financial security, if indeed it is possible to do so. In addition to the usual ways of trying to provide increased income, programs can also point out ways to minimize expenditures.

Retaining good health, keeping active, and finding part-time employment are other topics that interest people facing retirement (Atchley et al., 1978). In addition, retirement preparation programs often include topics such as retirement communities or legal affairs that are not spontaneously mentioned by employees.

Gradually increasing the time spent in roles other than the job and gradually decreasing the time spent on the job can be particularly useful. This tapering off has been accomplished by gradually increasing the length of the annual vacation, but perhaps a method more in tune with the physical decline in energy is gradually reducing the length of the work day. This proposal would only apply if the transition were to begin after age 60. Before that, the declines in energy are probably not great enough to matter. Right now, most people retire suddenly. There is seldom an opportunity to "rehearse" retirement by gradually reducing the amount of employment. Quinn (1981) found that among men who retired between age 58 and 63, about a third of wage and salary workers were partially retired, whereas among the self-employed, where opportunities for partial retirement are greater, 60 percent were partially retired.

Education, above all, determines the need for retirement preparation. Generally, the higher the level of formal education, the less retirement preparation is needed. However, the high correlation among income, education, and occupation means that those people who need retirement preparation most are at income and occupational levels at which they are least likely to get it (Atchley, 1978).

Retirement preparation programs are on the increase. Almost all are offered by companies whose workers are covered by a private pension and by government agencies. These retirement preparation programs fall into two categories. The limited programs do little more than explain the pension plan, the retirement timing options, and the level of benefits under various options. The comprehensive programs attempt to go beyond financial planning and deal with such topics as physical and mental health, housing, leisure activities, and legal aspects of retirement. About 30 percent of the programs surveyed by Green and his associates (1969) were comprehensive.

However, retirement preparation programs cover only a minority of the labor force (Schulz, 1973). In addition, most programs should begin sooner, especially if they are to succeed in encouraging the development of activities and interests and adequate financial planning. Thus far, the need for retirement preparation is not being met for the vast majority of people. In addition, more adequate evaluation of retirement preparation programs needs to be done. Kasschau (1974) concluded that group information programs were more in line with the retirement preparation needs of most jobholders than were individual counseling programs.

The Decision to Retire

As a process, a rational decision to retire involves three elements: (1) how individuals come to consider retirement; (2) the factors that influence the consideration of the retirement option; and (3) factors that influence the timing of retirement. Figure 9-2 is a schematic that shows how these elements interact in the decision process. It assumes that the individual is eligible to retire and is not retiring from one full-time job in order to take another.

Considering Retirement. People mainly come to consider retirement because it is a desired goal. But people can also come to consider retirement through unemployment, having reached a mandatory retirement age, experiencing illness or disability that makes the current job difficult or impossible to perform, peer pressure to retire, or employer pressure to retire. In all of these cases, the individual may or may not consider retirement, depending on his or her felt need to continue employment. If

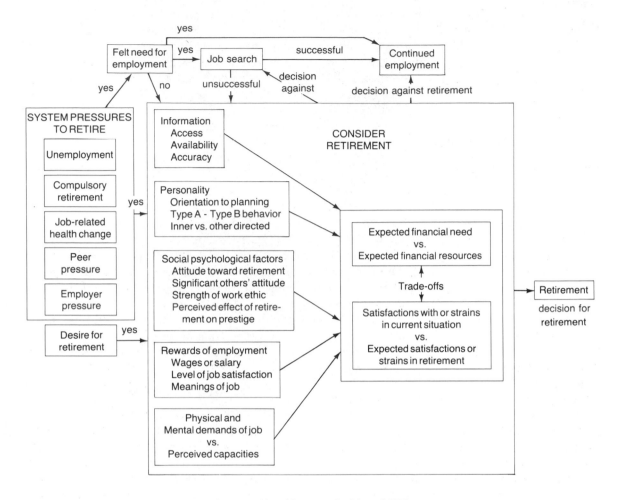

FIGURE 9-2   Factors in the decision to retire. *Source:* Atchley, 1979.

a job separation is involved and the person feels a need to continue employment, then a job search can be expected, and, if successful, retirement will not be considered. However, if there is no felt need to continue employment or if the job search is unsuccessful, retirement will be considered. In these cases, retirement is considered as a result of external pressures.

In the process of considering retirement, two comparisons are crucial. The first is a comparison of expected financial needs in retirement with expected financial resources. The second is a comparison of satisfaction with, or strains in, the current social situation with expected satis-

factions or strains associated with retirement. Some trade-offs can be expected to occur between these two comparisons. For example, if the satisfactions of retirement are expected to be very great, then the person may be willing to settle for a lower degree of income adequacy. These two basic comparisons and the trade-offs between them can be influenced by numerous additional factors. Access to information, availability of information, and accuracy of information have an impact on both comparisons, as do various personality factors. For example, whether the individual is active or passive in relation to his or her social environment has an influence on the degree to which that person is oriented toward planning, which in turn has a bearing on whether retirement will be considered rationally.

Others factors influence only the comparative satisfactions. Both the economic and noneconomic rewards of employment will have a bearing on the comparison of current satisfaction with expected satisfaction. Particularly relevant here is the meaning the person attributes to employment. Other social psychological factors such as attitude toward retirement, perceived attitudes of others toward retirement, strength of the "work ethic," and perceived effect of retirement on prestige can also influence this comparison. Finally, this comparison is also affected by the individual's perception of his or her capacity to meet the physical and/or mental demands of employment. If retirement compares favorably to continued employment or job search, then the individual will be motivated to retire. The timing of retirement is particularly sensitive to the income comparison. If retirement does not compare favorably, then the person can be expected to continue employment or engage in a job search.

Of course, the decision to retire and the timing of retirement may not be the result of a rational process. For example, many workers accept the idea that retirement at 65 is "normal" and nothing happens in their working life that requires them to actively think about retirement. These people retire when they are "supposed to," without considering that there might be an alternative.

Pressures to Retire. These ideas about the retirement decision are rather general. Now let us look at more specific influences. Both attitudes toward retirement and planning or preparation for it have an impact on the decision to retire. Other important factors include the hiring and retirement policies of employers and the health of the individual.

Employment Problems. First, an individual may decide to retire because he or she cannot find a job. Hiring policies, particularly in manufacturing, tend to discriminate against older workers. Almost the only jobs that are not harder to find as one grows older are those that pay badly or those for which there is a chronic labor shortage. This pattern has been found in the United States, West Germany, and Japan and probably applies to most industrialized nations (Atchley, 1976b; Fulgraff, 1978; Palmore, 1975a). When asked to defend their hiring policies, employers usually say that older people cannot meet the physical or skill requirements of the jobs. There is apparently no foundation for these allegations; nevertheless, they are acted on as if they were true.

A case illustration may make clear just how this kind of hiring discrimination can influence decisions to retire. In December of 1956, a large printing company that published several widely circulated magazines ceased operations and closed down its nine-story plant. Over 2,500 workers were left jobless. Among those affected was John Hilary, age 59, who was a master printer with 42 years of experience. Hilary was put in a real bind by the shutdown. He could have secured employment elsewhere, but it would have meant a move of over 1,000 miles for himself and his family. Hilary was reluctant to leave his home town. He had been born there and many of his relatives and all of his friends were there. He was active in his church and in local politics. In short, his ties to the community were too strong to make it worth his while to uproot himself completely in order to continue his chosen trade.

Instead, Hilary tried to find employment outside his profession. His age prevented him from being hired by any of the many local manufacturing concerns, even though his skills were easily adaptable to any situation requiring skill in running or repairing machinery. Even though he was willing to work for less than he had made as a printer, he was unable to get a job. He decided to retire from the labor force when he reached age 62. At 73, Hilary supplemented his union and Social Security retirement incomes by doing carpentry work for relatives and neighbors. He said bluntly that he was not really sorry he'd been forced to retire, but that if he could have found a job he would have continued to work for another five or ten years. He was bitter that in order to get any kind of job that would allow him to maintain his self-respect, he would have had to leave everything else that had any meaning to him. Hilary's decision to retire clearly was precipitated prematurely by the fact that employer hiring policies prevented him from gaining employment.

Employer Policies.   On the other side of the coin are employer policies that allow employees to generate entitlement to early retirement. Early retirement plans usually allow employees to retire before they become eligible for a Social Security retirement pension by providing supplemental pension payments to keep pensions at an adequate level until the retired person becomes eligible to collect Social Security. For example, in 1970 the United Auto Workers negotiated a contract with General Motors that allowed employees with 30 years of service to retire at age 56 on a pension of $500 per month. At age 65, the private pension would drop to cover the difference between the employee's Social Security retirement pension and $500 per month.

Early retirement is being promoted by dissatisfied factory workers who want to retire as soon as it is economically feasible (Barfield and Morgan, 1969, 1978a) and by employers who see early retirement as an effective way to deal with technological change, mergers, plant closings, and production cutbacks.

Mandatory Retirement.   A third factor involved in the retirement decision is *mandatory retirement*, that is, compulsory retirement at a specific chronological age. Reno (1972) found that 36 percent of the men and 23 percent of the women who retired in the last half of 1969 reported a compulsory retirement age on their most recent job. The most common was age 65

(68 percent of the cases) followed by age 70 (20 percent of the cases). The existence of compulsory retirement fluctuated a great deal by occupation. For example, 56 percent of men with professional and technical jobs were subject to mandatory retirement compared to only 23 percent among service workers. Schulz (1974) estimated that in a cohort of retired male workers only about 7 percent were retired unwillingly at a mandatory retirement age and were unable to find new employment. Parnes and Nestel (1981) put the figure at only 4 percent. Women were even less likely to be affected by mandatory retirement (Reno, 1971, 1972). In addition, mandatory retirement usually occurred in conjunction with private pensions. Thus, numerically, mandatory retirement affected a small minority of workers who tended to be relatively advantaged in terms of retirement income.

Nevertheless, mandatory retirement has not been popular. Harris and Associates (1975) found that 86 percent of both the older population and the general public felt that people should not be forced to retire purely because of age if they wanted to continue and were still able to do the job. Accordingly, in 1978, Congress amended the Age Discrimination in Employment Act to abolish mandatory retirement in the federal civil service and generally to raise the mandatory retirement age to 70. Several states had earlier abolished mandatory retirement for state civil servants. Because there is a relatively small proportion of people affected adversely by mandatory retirement (estimated to be around 4 to 7 percent), the overall impact of this change has been minimal.

Mandatory retirement is most often rationalized by contending that it is simple and easy to administer; that retirement "for cause" would require complicated measures; that mandatory retirement eliminates bias or discrimination in the phase-out process; and that it opens channels of promotion for younger workers (Palmore, 1972). None of these arguments is very persuasive. Since most people retire before the mandatory retirement age, especially in more recent years, an unpredictable point of retirement is obviously quite possible to administer. If incompetence is neither obvious nor easy to measure, then how serious a problem could it be? Employers consistently exercise bias in the face of mandatory retirement policies by keeping people on after the mandatory retirement age if it suits their purposes and if labor unions allow it. Thus, mandatory retirement policies are not a foolproof way to eliminate discrimination.

No one today can seriously argue that at age 65 or 70, people in general are so decrepit that they should be automatically excluded from the labor force. Mandatory retirement policies by definition discriminate against an age category, and thus violate the principle of equal employment opportunity. Since chronological age alone is a poor predictor of ability to perform on the job, it is seen by many older workers as an inappropriate criterion for use in implementing a mandatory retirement policy. Mandatory retirement policies also waste talent and productive potential (Palmore, 1972).

Unfortunately, the debate over abolishing mandatory retirement or raising the age for mandatory retirement has obscured a more important policy issue, the gradual decline of the minimum retirement age. All evidence indicates that most workers retire as soon as it is financially feasible (Barfield and Morgan, 1969; Bixby, 1976). Thus, policies governing the minimum age for retirement have a much more direct effect on the level of retirement (proportion retired in the population) than mandatory retirement policies do. This is amply illustrated by the fact that as soon as Social Security retirement benefits became available to men at age 62 rather than 65, the "typical" age of retirement under Social Security quickly went from 65 to 63, even though early retirement means reduced benefits.

Other Pressures. Much—maybe most—of the pressure for early retirement comes from workers who want retirement simply in order to en-joy life more (Pollman, 1971a), but some of it comes from workers who find employment increasingly more difficult. Most men who retire early under Social Security cite their health as the most important reason for retirement (Reno, 1971).

Most jobs in American society are full-time. There is no mechanism for adjusting conditions of work to fit the capacities of older workers. This problem is no doubt related to the fact that applications for disability benefits under Social Security increase dramatically with age. Well over half of the men and women who apply for disability benefits are over 50. In addition, the proportion of applicants who are awarded disability benefits increases from 32 percent under age 30 to 68 percent at ages 60 to 64 (Lando, 1976).

The issue of health pressures toward early retirement is cloudy. On the one hand, both disability data and survey data on reasons for retirement indicate that there is a substantial health component to the decision to retire (Lando, 1976; Reno, 1971). However, among those who retire before age 60, health seems to be declining in importance (Pollman, 1971a). In addition, people sometimes cite health as the reason they retired because they see it as more socially acceptable than is the simple desire for retirement (Schulz, 1976a). No doubt variations in working conditions over the life course are important determinants of the extent to which poor health is an actual factor in early retirement. Research is needed on this topic.

Undoubtedly an individual's decision to retire is also influenced by the informal norms of the work situation. For example, most professionals are probably discouraged from retiring by the attitudes of their colleagues. Since retirement tends to be viewed negatively among professionals, to retire is to buck the system. On the other hand, assembly line workers are generally favorable toward retirement and indeed show a growing tendency to retire early (Barfield and Morgan, 1969). It would be absurd to assume that two individuals anxious to retire face the same decision in these two quite distinct occupational areas.

Attitudes of friends and family also probably play an important role in the retirement decision. One man's children may want him to retire, another's may not. One woman's husband may want her to retire, another's may not. One man lives in a neighborhood where retirement is sneered at, another lives in a leisure community where retirement is the rule rather than the exception. If we retire, then the characteristics our friends and family impute to retired people will be imputed to us. All of these factors may encourage or discourage retirement (Atchley, 1976b).

Employers sometimes exert pressure on employees to retire. This may be done by suggestion or by job transfers or job reclassifications that substantially alter the employee's working conditions. There are countless ways that employers can apply pressure to retire, but as yet we have no basis for estimating what proportion of older workers experience such pressures, although three-fourths of the complaints of age discrimination in employment concern conditions of employment other than hiring or firing (U.S. Department of Labor, 1979).

Rosen and Jerdee (1982) studied how flexible versus inflexible company retirement policies affected decisions concerning retention of employees past age 65. Interestingly, they found that when flexible options such as reassignment or redesign were available, a majority of managers asked to make termination decisions chose not to terminate but to reassign, redesign, or retain the worker for another year. In another study, Rosen, Jerdee, and Lunn (1980) found that managers were less likely to recommend termination for workers of retirement age if the worker's retirement income would be low or if the prognosis was for a poor social adjustment to retirement. These studies indicate that problems may result more from rigid company policies than from rigid or discriminatory managers.

Most people want to retire and to do it while they are still physically able to enjoy life in retirement. The small proportion that does not want to retire can expect to find it increasingly easier to stay on as long as they can still do the job.

The decision to retire is more a question of when to retire rather than whether or not to retire. The timing of retirement appears to be influenced primarily by the minimum age of eligibility for socially adequate retirement income. Desire for retirement and poor health combine to produce a situation in which most retirements occur shortly after the minimum age. Desire for retirement is overshadowing poor health as a reason for retirement among more recent retirees. Mandatory retirement ages are involved in the timing of retirement for only a small minority of employees.

This general analysis of decisions to retire is based primarily on research from the United States. Shanas and her associates (1968) found that Americans were more likely to retire voluntarily than either Danes or Britons. However, Phillipson (1977) found that retirement has become increasingly attractive in Britain, even though pensions tend to be low. Olsen and Hansen (1977) found that older Danes tend to retire at the minimum age of pension eligibility. Fulgraff (1978) reported that when the minimum retirement age went down in West Germany, so did the average retirement age. Thus, the relation between chosen age of retirement and government minimum-retirement-age policies seems to prevail throughout the industrialized world. Health pressures to retire understandably vary cross-nationally with minimum retirement age: The higher the minimum retirement age, the greater the health pressures to retire. Other cross-national variations relate to the cultural acceptability of retirement. Retirement is viewed very positively in the United States (Atchley, 1974a; Atchley and Robinson, 1982), and, at the other extreme, as "social death" in France (Guillemard, 1972).

Retirement as an Event

When retirement occurs abruptly, it may become an occasion for ceremony, that is, rites of passage to mark the end of employment and the beginning of retirement, or the passage from one role to another. Unfortunately, we don't know very much about retirement ceremonies or the part they play in the transition from employment to retirement. Certainly, the stereotype "gold watch" ceremony has never been part of the retirement experience of most workers, and as retirement has become more and more desired and commonplace, the austerity and mock honor of the stereotype seem even further out of place.

The most notable characteristic of retirement events is their complete lack of standardization (as compared to ritualistic events such as graduations or weddings). Retirement ceremonies range from highly personalized, informal affairs involving current coworkers only to all-day tributes and speeches involving colleagues from around the country. Sometimes the occasion is a dinner party for family members as well as coworkers. Others are late afternoon events at the workplace. Most are arranged by the employer but some are planned by friends at work. Some are mass ceremonies honoring several people approaching retirement; others are for a particular individual. People whose job performance was highly respected tend to be singled out, whereas ordinary performers tend to be honored as part of a group. When speeches are made, they tend to focus on acknowledgment for past contributions, with much less emphasis on the transition or on the "new career" as a retired person. However, informal conversations usually display plentiful expressions of envy and good wishes. The atmosphere is seldom negative.

We do not know how common retirement ceremonies are, but it is probably safe to say that they are most likely for those whose upcoming retirement is known well in advance.

Those who retire unexpectedly or gradually or because of ill health or unemployment would seem less likely to experience a ceremony.

Retirement as a Role

After the retirement event, be it formal or not, the individual is expected to assume the role of "retired person." Gerontologists have had a lengthy debate over the nature of the retirement role, and, in fact, over whether such a role even exists. Most people agree that there is a "retired person" position that individuals enter when they retire. The disagreement comes when specifying the role associated with that position. The term *role* can refer either to the culturally transmitted norms governing the rights and duties associated with a position in society or to a relationship between holders of complementary positions.

The *rights* of a retired person include the right to economic support without holding a job (but at the same time without the stigma of being regarded as dependent on society, as in the case of the unemployed); the right to autonomy in managing time and other resources; and often more specific rights associated with the former job, such as library privileges or access to employer health facilities.

The retirement role also involves *duties*— things that are expected of a retired person. The foremost duty is to avoid full-time employment. This expectation is backed up by the provision in Social Security of a benefit deduction for retired persons with annual earnings from employment that exceed the allowable amount. Retired persons are also expected to carry over into retirement their skills, experience, knowledge, and identity with the jobs or positions they had. They are sometimes expected to provide free services to community projects or organizations. In addition, retired people are expected to assume responsibility for managing their own lives. For a great many people, retirement adds a lot of decision-making responsibility, which added to the continuing responsibilities of parenthood, friendship, and so forth means that not all of the time formerly spent on a job is available for new pursuits.

Retired people also have the duty to live within their incomes. Although some people fail to live up to this expectation—usually through no fault of their own—the expectation is there, nevertheless. Retired people are expected to avoid becoming dependent either on their families or on the community (Atchley, 1976b).

As a relationship, the retirement role connects retired people to those who are still employed, either in a particular trade, craft, or profession or in a particular organization. The crux of the relationship is that both the retired person and the person still on the job identify themselves in terms of the same occupation or work organization. In this sense the position of retired person is similar to the position of alumnus or alumna. The role of retired person is usually defined in terms that are flexible and qualitative rather than concrete and instrumental.* It was probably the absence of the instrumental element in job roles that led many investigators to view retirement as a "roleless role" and therefore as an inevitable problem for the retired person. In this view, retirement creates a gap that only a new instrumental or "functional" role could fill. Much of the retirement literature still contains discussions of possible functional alternatives to work (Miller, 1965). However, other work (Schneider, 1964; Streib and Schneider, 1971) indicates that instrumental norms may never have to develop around retirement. Schneider makes the point well:

> A clearly defined role facilitates activity and gives a sense of security to a person involved in a network of impersonal universalistically oriented judgments and evaluations. This may not be the kind of world in which many older people live. In

the later years of life, the important persons in one's life—friends and relatives—know who the older person is and, therefore, he moves in a world that is familiar to him, and with which he is familiar. He may not need a sharply defined extrafamilial "role" to give him an identity or to facilitate his own activity in his everyday world. We suggest, therefore, that so far as the older person himself is concerned, his willingness to leave the work force and perhaps his satisfaction with other aspects of life are not dependent upon whether he has a clearly defined alternative role or not (Schneider, 1964:56).

Following this rationale, the retirement role, by its very vagueness, allows the individual a certain amount of flexibility in adjusting to his or her less consistent physical capabilities.

Phases of Retirement

It is useful to consider the various phases through which the retirement role is approached, taken on, and relinquished.*

Preretirement.   The preretirement period includes a *remote* phase, in which retirement is vaguely seen as something positive that will happen someday, and a *near* phase, in which individuals orient themselves toward a specific retirement date. Two important things often happen during the near phase of preretirement. First, people begin to gear themselves for separation from their jobs and the social situations in which they carried them out. They may adopt a "short-timer's attitude." They may begin to notice subtle differences in how they are viewed by others. Second, people often develop fairly detailed fantasies of what they think their retirement will be like. These fantasies may turn out to be quite accurate pictures of the future or they may be totally unrealistic. If realistic, they can serve as a "dry run" that smooths the transition into retirement by identifying is-

---

*Jobs also have important qualitative aspects, but these are seldom emphasized in "job descriptions" or in discussions about jobs. This is perhaps a major oversight.

*These phases of retirement were identified through a series of empirical studies of retirement (Atchley, 1967; Cottrell and Atchley, 1969; Atchley, 1974a; Atchley, 1982b).

sues that require advanced decision making. But if the fantasies are unrealistic, they may thwart a smooth transition by setting up detailed but unrealistic expectations. Worries about retirement revolve around income and health with little concern about missing the job (Atchley et al., 1978).

Honeymoon.   The retirement event is sometimes followed by a rather euphoric period in which the individual tries to "do all of the things I never had time for before." A retired person going through this honeymoon phase typically says, "What do I do with my time? Why, I've never been so busy!" Extended travel is common in the honeymoon phase.

Some people do not go through a honeymoon phase. For one thing, a honeymoon requires a positive orientation. It also requires money, a scarce commodity for some older people. Most people cannot keep up the hectic pace of the honeymoon indefinitely, and they soon settle into a retirement routine.

Retirement Routine.   The nature of the retirement routine is important. If the individual is able to settle into a routine that provides a satisfying life, then that routine will probably stabilize. People whose off-the-job lives were full prior to retirement are often able to settle into a retirement routine fairly easily. These people have already made their choices among activities and groups earlier in life; all that remains is to realign time in relation to those choices.

Rest and Relaxation.   Following retirement, many people go through a period of low activity that is in marked contrast to the very active honeymoon phase. Atchley (1982b) called this the "R and R" phase to emphasize the temporary nature of the decline in activity. In a cohort of 168 persons Atchley followed for four years, activity levels went down following retirement, but returned to preretirement levels after three years of retirement. After a long period of having been employed, many people apparently

welcome a period of "taking it easy." But after sufficient rest and relaxation, they begin to get restless and at that point resume a normal round of activities.*

Disenchantment.   Some people do not find it so easy to adjust to retirement. For a small number of people, once the honeymoon is over and life begins to slow down, or if retirement has not turned out as expected, there is a period of letdown, disenchantment, or even depression. During the honeymoon period the retired person lives out the preretirement fantasy. The more unrealistic the preretirement fantasy turns out to have been, the more likely the individual is to experience a feeling of emptiness and disenchantment. The failure of the fantasy actually represents the collapse of a structure of choices, and what is depressing the individual is that she or he must start to restructure life over again in retirement. Disenchantment can also result when the situation one expects in retirement is disrupted, death of a spouse being the most common such difficulty. What proportion of persons become disenchanted is not known. However, cross-sectional surveys have found less than 10 percent at any one point in time who were disenchanted with retirement (Atchley, 1976b:110). In Atchley's (1982b) longitudinal study, no one became disenchanted, which suggests that disenchantment may in fact be rare.

Reorientation.   A period of reorientation often occurs among the few retired people who are disenchanted with retirement. During reorientation, depressed individuals "take stock" and "pull themselves together." This process involves using their retirement experiences to develop a more realistic view of alternatives within their particular set of resources. Reorientation also involves exploring new avenues of involvement. Very few people elect to become a hermit

---

*Activities will be considered in more detail in Chapter 10.

in retirement; most want to remain involved with the world around them.

Groups in the community sometimes help people reorient themselves toward retirement. For example, many people become involved in senior center activities for the first time during this phase. But for the most part, people are on their own during the reorientation phase, seeking help most often from family and close friends. The goal of this reorientation process is a set of realistic choices that establish a structure and a routine for living in retirement that provides at least a modicum of satisfaction.

Routine.   People develop a set of criteria for dealing routinely with change. People with stable retirement life styles have well-developed criteria for making choices, which allows them to deal with life in a reasonably comfortable, predictable fashion. Life may be busy, and certainly it may have exciting moments, but for the most part it is stable and satisfying. Many people pass into this phase directly from the honeymoon phase; others reach it only after a painful reassessment of personal goals; others never reach it. People with a satisfying retirement routine have mastered the retirement role. They know what is expected of them and they know what they have to work with—what their capabilities and limitations are. They are self-sufficient adults, going their own way, managing their own affairs.

Termination.   Some people reach a point at which the retirement role becomes irrelevant to their lives. Some return to a job, but most often the retirement role is canceled by illness and disability. When an individual is no longer capable of engaging in major activities such as housework, self-care, and the like, the retirement role is displaced by the sick and disabled role as the primary organizing factor in the individual's life. This change is based on the loss of able-bodied status and the loss of independence, both of which are necessary to adequately play the retirement role.

The increasing dependence of old age usually comes so gradually that the retirement role can be given up in stages. Only with institutionalization does independent choice become so limited that the dignity of the retirement role is diminished.

Timing of Phases.   Because there is no universal point of retirement, there is no way to tie the phases of retirement to a chronological age or to a period of time. Rather, the phases are a group of processes involved in approaching, playing, and giving up the retirement role. They represent a device for making it easier to view retirement as a process, *not* as an inevitable sequence that everyone must go through.

Effects of Retirement on the Individual

In addition to affecting the individual's other roles, retirement and the loss of a job have various effects on the individual and his or her situation. Retirement is widely thought to have an adverse effect on health. Everyone seems to know people who carefully planned for retirement only to get sick and die shortly after leaving their jobs. However, the crucial question is whether people retire because they are sick or whether they are sick because they retire. If people retire because they are sick, then it is not surprising that some of them die.

The decisive test of the impact of retirement on health is to compare the states of health following retirement and just preceding retirement. Using their data from a large longitudinal study of people both before and after retirement, Streib and Schneider (1971) concluded that health declines are associated with age but not with retirement. That is, retired people are no more likely to be sick than people of the same age who are still on the job. In fact, unskilled workers showed a slight improvement in health following retirement. Haynes et al. (1978) studied nearly 4,000 rubber-tire workers before and after retirement and found that preretirement health status was the only significant predictor of mortality within the five years after retirement. More recently, Ekerdt, Baden, Bossé, and Dibbs (1983) used longitudinal data from the Veterans Administration Normative Aging Study to examine the relation between retirement and health. After excluding men who retired because of illness or disability, they found no difference in health change between those who retired and those who did not. This study is noteworthy because it used physical examinations to corroborate earlier studies of self-reports of health.

Ekerdt, Bossé, and LoCastro (1983) went even further. They examined the possibility that retirement might actually *improve* health among those who retire because of ill health. They found that retirement did not improve the level of preretirement self-reported health, but did reduce perceived health-connected *role strains*. This led the investigators to suggest that retirement can improve functional health without improving health level by reducing the level of demands placed on the individual.

Although a good deal of research has been devoted to the impact of retirement on mental disorders, no definite impact has yet been found (Nadelson, 1969). Lowenthal (1964b) found that mental illness tended to cause social isolation, not the reverse. Likewise, it is quite probable that mental illness causes retirement, rather than the other way around. It is true that several studies point to a higher incidence of mental impairment among retired people (Nadelson, 1969:10). However, Lowenthal and Berkman (1967:76) found that the association between retirement and mental illness was mainly a function of poor health, low social activity, and unsatisfactory living arrangements rather than a consequence of retirement itself.

Much of the research on the personal consequences of retirement concerns the impact of retirement on social adjustment. The broad category of social adjustment includes such factors as acceptance of retirement, life satisfaction, morale, self-esteem, age identification, and job deprivation. It has been generally assumed that retirement has a negative impact on social adjustment, but research disproves this assumption.

Morale and life satisfaction are two concepts that have been used to assess overall emotional reaction to one's life at a given point in time. For example, Simpson et al. (1966c) found that morale was generally unconnected to work or retirement. They concluded that morale is influenced more by health, family situations, and other personal factors than by work and retirement. Using the same data, Kerckhoff (1966a:192) found that high morale was associated with independence between generations in the family and with a functional, home-based pattern of activities within the older couple. The only work-related factor associated with morale was the tendency for those with orderly work histories to have high morale in retirement (Simpson et al., 1966c:67). Streib and Schneider (1971) found that retirement produced no significant change in life satisfaction. Nearly half of their respondents did not expect retirement to reduce life satisfaction, but even so a sizeable proportion overestimated the adverse effect of retirement on life satisfaction. George and Maddox (1977) found a great degree of longitudinal consistency in morale during the retirement transition.

Cottrell and Atchley (1969) found that depression was uncommon among retired teachers and telephone company employees of both sexes. No sex-job category showed as much as 10 percent with a high degree of depression. However, women were significantly less likely to show a low degree of depression (72 percent), as compared to men (80 percent), particularly among the teachers. In all four sex-job categories, however, over 70 percent showed a low degree of depression.

From the foregoing it appears that retirement makes little difference according to any of our measures of subjective reaction to retirement. The proportion highly satisfied depends more on factors such as family situation, job history, and other personal factors such as health than on retirement itself.

Another important effect of retirement concerns the self. Back and Guptill (1966) used a semantic differential to study the self-concept among preretirees and retirees. They identified three dimensions—involvement, optimism, and autonomy—and found that the involvement scores for retired people were considerably lower than for people in preretirement, regardless of socioeconomic characteristics. However, retirement had very little effect on the optimism or autonomy dimensions. Back and Guptill concluded that the decline in perception of self as involved resulted almost entirely from loss of job. Their findings indicated that an individual who was healthy, had a middle- or upper-class occupation, and had a high number of personal interests, would feel a minimal loss involvement brought on by retirement. But they also concluded that even these people did not successfully fill the gap left by the loss of job. However, Atchley's (1982b) more recent longitudinal findings suggested that this reduction in involvement may be only temporary.

Cottrell and Atchley (1969) studied the impact of retirement on the self-esteem of older adults. Using Rosenberg's (1964) scale, they found that self-esteem in retirement tended to be quite high, much higher than among the high school students studied by Rosenberg. They also found that retirement produced no differences in self-esteem scores. This finding was replicated by Atchley (1982b).

The construct of *job deprivation* refers to the extent to which an individual misses his or her job. Simpson et al. (1966a) found that low job deprivation in retirement was related to (1) having looked forward to retirement,* (2) having achieved most of one's job-related ambitions, and (3) having an adequate retirement income. From these findings, it appears that job

deprivation in retirement depends on how retirement compares with life on the job. If retirement is anticipated as a negative thing; if the individual feels that job goals remain unmet; if retirement income is inadequate; and if health is poor in retirement—then it should not be too surprising if the retired individual misses the "good old days" on the job. Fortunately, most people confront none of these conditions.

Another area in which retirement is widely thought to have a negative effect is *social participation*. Social participation is assumed to be tied to support from a job role; loss of the job role presumably hinders participation. Only in a relatively small minority of cases does retirement produce a drop in participation and consequent loneliness and isolation. And if the effects of widowhood are controlled, the proportion in this category is substantially reduced. Rosenberg's (1970) data suggest, however, that retirement is more likely to produce social isolation among the working class.

Bengtson (1969) examined the level of role activity among retired teachers and factory workers in six national samples (Austria, West Germany, the Netherlands, Italy, Poland, and the United States). He found three basic patterns of activity in relation to roles in the family, organizational or formal settings, and informal settings. The most prevalent pattern—present among the Polish and Italian samples, and among factory workers in the United States, West Germany, and Austria—consisted of a high level of family activity, intermediate activity in informal settings, and low activity in organizational settings. The pattern for teachers in the United States and West Germany involved moderate to high activity in each of the three areas. Finally, the Dutch showed a pattern of very high family activity, considerably lower activity in formal settings, and the lowest activity in informal settings. However, within the Dutch sample, the teachers showed much higher levels of activity in nonfamily settings than did the factory workers. Bengtson's data

---

*This finding matches those of Thompson (1958) and Streib and Schneider (1971).

indicate that there were definite national differences in the kinds of activities that occupied people in retirement. The Dutch retirees, especially, showed a unique lack of involvement with friends and neighbors. Yet certain trends reflected occupational rather than national differences. For example, a low degree of involvement in organized settings was typical of retired factory workers in all six national samples.

Simpson et al. (1966a) found that many patterns of involvement supported by jobs persisted into retirement. They found that having a higher-status occupation and an orderly work career were as crucial for involvement during retirement as at earlier ages. They also found that if social involvement did not develop prior to retirement, it was unlikely to be initiated after retirement. Finally, they found that retirement itself was not responsible for lack of involvement among semiskilled retired people and some middle-status workers; instead it was their *work histories* that had not allowed these people to become integrated into society. Simpson and her coworkers stressed particularly the role of financial security in providing support for participation in society.

Most people in retirement continue to do the same *kinds* of things they did when they were working. About a third increase their level of nonjob-related role activity in order to fill the gap left by retirement. About a fifth of the retired population experiences a decrease in amount of activity. However, gains or losses in activity level are a relative matter. For someone uninvolved prior to retirement, leaving the job can result in an increase in the number of activities and still leave gaps of unfilled, unsatisfying time. On the other hand, for an overinvolved professional, retirement may reduce the net amount of activity, but at the same time bring it down to a level more suitable to the person's capabilities and desires.

A great deal of attention has been paid to the impact of retirement on *leisure participation*. According to one school of thought, leisure cannot legitimately be engaged in full-time by adults in Western nations without bringing on an identity crisis for the individual and a social stigma of implied inability to perform (Miller, 1965). At one time, and in some cultures more than others, this set of assumptions may have been widely applicable. In fact, much of the retirement research done in the United States in the early 1950s supports such a view. However, there is growing evidence that in recent years the relatively greater freedom of retirement is viewed both by retired people and by society at large as an earned privilege and opportunity (Atchley, 1971c; Thompson, 1973). The "embarrassment" that has been cited as an obstacle to leisure participation among retired people is probably more a function of the low income retirement sometimes brings than a function of embarrassment and feelings of worthlessness consequent to leaving the job.*

Another source of embarrassment stems from the social context in which older adults must learn activity skills. If they can be learned in an environment structured around the needs and abilities of older people, then embarrassment can be minimized. However, all too often older adults must learn in an environment developed for children—an embarrassing situation. Of course, the first few, inept steps toward learning a new skill are always embarrassing, regardless of age or social position.

Situational Consequences

Much of the preceding discussion focused on individual responses to retirement in general. We will now discuss three specific situational changes associated with retirement: income changes, changes in residence, and changing family structure.

Chapter 8 dealt with income *sources and strategies* in detail. In the present context, our concern is the *social impact* of the income changes that accompany retirement. Income in retire-

---

*For a more thorough discussion of this issue, see Atchley (1971a).

ment is usually about half what it was prior to retirement. And not only is income reduced, but *feelings* of economic deprivation increase (Riley and Foner, 1968:455). However, the prevalence of such feelings tends to decrease as the number of years retired increase. Clark and Anderson (1967) found that reduced income has a significant impact on self-image, especially for people at the bottom of the socioeconomic scale. However, they concluded that lifelong poverty has more impact on self-esteem than does a deteriorating standard of living. McConnel and Deljavan (1983) found that even with the drop in income at retirement, the typical retired household did not feel economically strapped; it was no more likely than the employed household to spend more income on necessities or to supplement regular income with savings.

Change of residence is closely associated with retirement in the minds of not only laymen but professionals as well.* For example, Rose (1965a) considered the movement of older people to retirement communities as a major impetus for the development of an old age subculture. However, because of their very high densities of older people, retirement communities such as Sun City, Arizona, and St. Petersburg, Florida, have perhaps commanded more attention than they deserve, given that only a tiny proportion of the older population moves to such communities.

The fact is that while older people do move, migration rates actually decline substantially from age 25 on, with only a slight rise at retirement (Wiseman, 1978). From 1965 to 1970, 3.8 percent of the elderly moved to another state and 1.7 percent moved to another country. Most elderly migrants were in their sixties. Half of them came from just five states—New York, Pennsylvania, Ohio, Illinois, and Michigan, most moved to Florida (see Figure 2-11 on p. 41).

Movers are not randomly distributed in the older population, but instead are concentrated among the widowed, disabled, retired, well educated, and those living in households other than their own. When the effects of retirement alone are examined, it becomes clear that retirement has little impact on migration: The percentage who move is slightly higher among retired people age 65 and over, as compared to those still on the job at that age, but the difference is significant only for men who move across county lines. Retirement has little impact on people who move within the same county (Riley and Foner, 1968).

The overwhelming majority of those who retire do not relocate. The most significant impact of retirement is the economic incentive to find less expensive housing; even then, such moves are usually made within the same general locality. The common notion that retirement inevitably brings on migration is a myth. However, in the future, as younger, better-educated cohorts become old, the trend to move at retirement may increase somewhat, although it probably will never become prevalent.

Retirement can also be expected to affect *family structure*. Most retired people are married, and retirement sometimes affects marital relationships. Kerckhoff (1966b) found that retiring husbands look forward to retirement more than their wives, experience more satisfaction in retirement, and are more involved in the retirement process.* Compared to couples with a higher-level occupational background, couples in which the husband was retiring or had retired from a semiskilled, unskilled, or service job were more passive in their anticipation of retirement. They also regarded retirement as an unpleasant experience and tended to view retirement much more negatively.

Kerckhoff attributed this difference to the impact on the couple of the husband's greater involvement in household tasks following retirement. Across all occupational levels, retired

---

*Retirement housing is discussed in Chapter 8.

*Kerckhoff did not ascertain whether or not the wives themselves were also retired from jobs of their own.

men took greater part in household tasks after retirement; the difference was in how the wives viewed this increase. In the middle and upper strata, the increase was welcomed by the wives and seen as desirable by both husbands and wives. The picture was different in the lower stratum. Working-class marriages were less companionate and more authoritarian. In addition, working-class wives expected more exclusive control over the household. Thus, after retirement in the working class, husbands and wives both tended to see increased involvement of the husband as undesirable. But the husbands increased their involvement despite themselves, which led to conflict based on the guilt of the husbands and on the irritation of the wives at having had their exclusive domains invaded.

Heyman and Jeffers (1968) also studied the impact of retirement on couples. They found that more than half of the wives were sorry that their husbands had retired. These wives tended to be working class, had husbands in poor health, and had unhappy marriages before retirement.

Personal Adjustment

As public acceptance of retirement has grown and as the systems that provide retirement income have matured, adjustment to retirement has become easier. Cottrell and Atchley (1969) found that as many as 30 percent of retirees in the 1960s reported they would never adjust to retirement. By the 1970s this proportion had dropped to less than 10 percent (Parnes and Nestel, 1982).

Some people avoid the problems of adjustment to retirement by going back to a paying job. In their longitudinal study of retirement, Streib and Schneider (1971:145–158) observed a number of people (about 10 percent) who returned to jobs after having retired. Those who returned characteristically had had a negative attitude toward retirement, attached a positive value to the satisfactions of work, had been forced to retire, and had a high degree of *felt* economic deprivation. Of these factors, low income provided the greatest incentive to reject retirement and seek a job. Factors that *allow* people to return to a job are good health and an upper-status occupation. Motley (1978) surveyed a sample of workers who retired in 1969 and found that no more than 12 percent would both want to return to employment and be physically able to do so.

Heidbreder (1972a) examined differences between white-collar and blue-collar adjustment to early retirement. While she found that an overwhelming majority were satisfied with retirement, she also found that adjustment problems were concentrated among former blue-collar workers who had low incomes, poor health, and little education.

About a third of those who were retired in 1965 encountered difficulty adjusting to it, broken down as follows: 13 percent had income difficulties, 13 percent had difficulties with factors not directly related to retirement, such as declining health and death of a spouse, and 7 percent missed their jobs (Harris, 1965a). Barfield and Morgan (1978b) found poor health to be the main factor for the 22 percent of their 1976 sample who were dissatisfied with retirement life. Similar results were obtained by Parnes and Nestel (1982).

Adjustment to retirement is greatly enhanced by sufficient income, the ability to give up one's job gracefully, and good health. In addition, adjustment seems to be smoothest when situational changes other than loss of job are at a minimum. In other words, assuming that people's notions about the retirement role are based on reality, factors that upset the ability of retired people to live out their retirement ambitions hinder their ability to adjust smoothly to retirement.

Atchley (1975a) developed an approach to explaining retirement adjustment that is based on the impact of retirement on the individual's hierarchy of personal goals. If a job is high in that goal hierarchy and yet is unachieved, then the individual can be expected to seek another job. If a substitute job cannot be found, then the hierarchy of personal goals must be reorganized. If the individual is engaged in a wide variety of roles, then reorganization can take place by simple consolidation. If the individual has few roles other than a job, then he or she must seek an alternative role. If an alternative is not available, the individual must disengage. Of course, if the job is not high on the individual's list of priorities to begin with, then no serious change in personal goals is occasioned by retirement.

Any type of role behavior is at least partly the result of negotiations between the role player and the other role players to whom his or her behavior relates. Thus, retirement also changes the set of people with whom one negotiates. At work one negotiates one's work role behavior with one's peers, superiors, subordinates, and audiences. One's family and friends are involved only on the periphery of work role negotiations. In retirement, the people associated with one's former work drop out of the picture almost entirely (except for friends who also were work associates) and one negotiates primarily with family and friends in order to translate the general demands of retirement into particular behavior. Most people seem able to make these transitions reasonably smoothly. A major influence on this transition is the commonly held stereotype of the retired person. The fact that both the retired person and the people with whom he or she interacts share at least to some extent a common idea of the nature of the retirement role gives everyone a place to begin the interaction. Very quickly, however, the individual retired person learns how to personalize this interaction. Thus, the vagueness of both the retirement role and the stereotype allows retired individuals to negotiate definitions of the retirement role that fit their particular situations and that are consistent with their own personal goals.

The Future of Retirement

The future of retirement as an institution seems assured. Increasingly larger proportions of our labor force can be expected to retire and to do so at a relatively early age. The strength of commitment to a vocation as an end in itself will probably continue to decline. There is no indication at present that the nature of jobs in American society will change enough to reverse this trend.

Compulsory retirement will continue to decline in importance. However, as the older population increases in size relative to the employed population, the realities of financing Social Security and other retirement benefits may bring a reversal of the trend toward lower minimum retirement ages. Retirement age under Social Security probably will not drop below its current minimum of 62, and minimum ages for retirement under private pensions may increase.

The retirement income picture may improve somewhat, but it is unlikely that Social Security benefits will rise above their current levels of earnings replacement in the near future. The prospects for individual planning to fill the gap left by Social Security and private pension levels are poor because information programs tend to be too little and too late, and because the people who need self-planning the most are the ones least likely to grasp its importance on their own. Thus, during the next two decades income is likely to remain the major problem associated with retirement.

Summary

Participation in the labor force tends to be high until age 50, when it begins to decline. About 10 percent of both men and women workers leave the labor force in their fifties. For men, there is a sharp drop at age 62 and again at 65. For women, the decline is more gradual, with drops at 62 and 65 not much greater than those at other ages over 60. Withdrawal from the labor force before age 62 results from prolonged unemployment, disability, and early retirement. Most withdrawals after age 62 are retirements. Age discrimination in hiring and retention plays an important part in early withdrawal from the labor force. Job changes among mature blue-collar workers occur primarily as a result of health or layoffs. Midlife career changes tend to be responses to external pressures rather than an acting out of individual desires.

The term *retirement* refers to a situation in which an individual is employed less than full-time and year-round *and* in which he or she receives a retirement pension. A household is considered retired if retirement pensions represent its major source of income.

Economic and social change have altered the linkage between people and jobs. In industrial societies today, jobs are not necessarily the prime determinant in the structure of people's lives. Many jobs are boring and meaningless to the people doing them. The right to economic support in retirement is widely considered an incentive for people to put up with less desirable jobs. A mature retirement system in society requires an economic system productive enough to support people who have no jobs, a political system strong enough to divert some of that surplus to support people in retirement, and acceptance by the public that retirement is a legitimate adult role.

Retirement can be viewed as a process in which the retirement role is approached, taken up, and eventually (if the person lives long enough) given up. The process begins with people's attitudes toward retirement, which are generally favorable. Acceptance of retirement is closely related to having achieved one's job-related goals.

In preparing people for retirement, society should alert them to the financial, physical, and social prerequisites of retirement, and should do so early enough to be effective. Retirement preparation involves informing people about decisions they need to make as well as helping them to get the information and to learn the skills necessary to making wise decisions. Information is usually more effective than counseling as an approach to retirement preparation.

Individuals often have a period within which they *can* retire and a final date at which they *must* retire. Most people retire before the date they must retire, and even among those who wait for the mandatory date there is a sizable proportion who look on that date as permission to retire and who eagerly await it. Thus, most people are not negatively affected by mandatory retirement rules. However, for a small proportion of older workers, mandatory retirement means denial of their right to hold a job. The use of age as the sole criterion for mandatory retirement cannot be defended on rational grounds. The minimum age of eligibility for retirement is the most important factor in the decision to retire; next is health. Decisions about the if and when of retirement are also influenced by occupational norms and by family and friends.

The retirement event is a rite of passage, one that is only now beginning to deal with the opportunities and obligations of the retirement role. Yet retirement is a definable role offering people freedom of time and space and requiring physical, social, and financial independence. The retirement role also demands a certain amount of continuity in areas of life not related to the job. As a relationship, the role of retired person is similar to that of alumnus or alumna. However, the freedom given to the retired person also makes the retired person responsible for defining his or her own life style. As such, the retirement role is flexible. Some gerontologists have argued that such a role has negative consequences for self-esteem, but the research results do not support this argument. It appears that poverty, not the vagueness of the retirement role, is primarily responsible for problems of self-esteem in later life.

The retirement process can have several phases. In the preretirement period, attitudes toward retirement tend to be positive. Some people develop fantasies about what their lives in retirement will be like and begin to make some decisions in advance. When retirement actually occurs, three possible patterns can be observed: a highly active honeymoon period, an inactive rest and relaxation period, and movement straight into a period of retirement routine. The successful retirement routine is characterized by a firm set of criteria for making day-to-day decisions and for structuring time.

If the person's expectations of retirement are unrealistic, then he or she may become disenchanted with retirement and be forced to go through a reorientation in order to develop a more realistic approach to life in retirement. Finally, if a retired person loses physical or financial independence, the retirement role is replaced by the role of sick person, the role of dependent person, or perhaps the role of institutional resident, as important organizing forces in life.

Despite the popular myth, there is no evidence that retirement has a significant impact on either the physical health or mental health of the vast majority of people who retire. Health declines can be traced to aging but not to retirement. In terms of social adjustment, retirement has been found to have no effect on morale, life satisfaction, depression, or self-esteem. Activity patterns tend to be carried over into retirement.

Only a small proportion of people change residence as a result of retirement, and those who do often do so to be nearer their children. Retirement tends to be good for middle-class marriages and to put a strain on working-class marriages.

About 10 percent of those who retire at age 65 eventually get another job, primarily because they need the money. However, most people get used to retirement within three months or less. Adjustment to retirement requires sufficient income, willingness to gracefully give up one's job, and good health. Smooth adjustment to loss of job at retirement depends largely on whether job-related goals have been achieved and on whether the individual has developed interests and skills apart from those centered on the job. Sometimes retirement requires negotiating a new social identity.

In the future, retirement will probably become an even more well-entrenched institution. However, a relative shortage of labor caused by present declines in the birth rate may result in more flexible retirement policies, including more options for those who prefer partial retirement. Retirement incomes should rise as more retired people are covered by better private and public pensions over and above their Social Security benefits. However, income will probably remain the primary retirement problem for the foreseeable future.

Chapter 10

Activities

People like rhythm in their lives, and the ebb and flow of activity provide it. Each of us has a familiar routine for approaching the day. Our routines can also vary on holidays, on weekends, in the summer months, and on special occasions. These routines give a comfortable predictability to life, especially if they are satisfying ones. Our routines can be highly structured or not, but they are constructed of expected and/or preferred activities.

Aging changes activities in many ways. Role changes in later life, such as retirement or launching one's children into adulthood, change the amount of time that must be given to the job and to child rearing. Changes in physical functioning can impose limits on what we are able to do physically and may eventually become serious enough to restrict our activities to an institutional environment. Age discrimination can also limit the quality and quantity of activities available to us. Thus, age-related role changes may free us to concentrate our efforts on activities of our own choosing, while declining physical capacity or financial resources and age discrimination may constrict our choices. The balance between freedom and constriction that an individual experiences is greatly influenced by his or her position in the social hierarchy. People who are well-to-do and powerful are not likely to find their activities seriously limited, because they are likely to remain in good health and to have the economic resources necessary to enjoy the freedom of retirement. However, for those at the lower end of the social ladder, inadequate incomes and serious health limitations are more likely, and so is age discrimination.

When aging becomes obvious, the gradual attrition of activities can be quite distressing. The case of Mrs. A is not necessarily typical in its particulars, but it illustrates the process. Mrs. A was first interviewed at age 70. At that time she lived alone in a comfortable apartment. Her daily round of activities was not a complex one. She spent a good deal of time keeping her apartment and herself comfortably neat and clean.

She took frequent walks to nearby stores to pass the time of day as well as to make purchases. She spent an hour or more per day just talking with friends. On Thursdays, she usually drove to a nearby city to attend the program at a senior center. Afterward she would often visit with friends. Her major pastimes were reading, watching television, talking with friends, and housekeeping.

However, Mrs. A's most meaningful activities involved visiting and talking with her daughter and her grandchildren. Although these contacts were not always smooth ones, because of generational differences in values, the level of mutual affection and respect was an absolutely essential element of Mrs. A's life. Although Mrs. A had several close friends, they were not able to provide for her a feeling of belonging. Whatever her pattern of activities, Mrs. A needed enough interaction with her family to maintain this sense of belonging.

At age 74, Mrs. A's situation had changed remarkably. She had increasingly found the stairs to her apartment difficult to negotiate, especially with packages, laundry, or groceries. As a result, she had moved to a first-floor apartment in another neighborhood. This move relieved the problem of the stairs, but it cost Mrs. A her contacts with neighbors and shopkeepers in the area she had left. These contacts were no longer a convenient by-product of everyday living. To see these people became a special project. About this same time she had begun to have difficulty driving at night and had to give up her visits to the senior center and to her friends in the nearby city. She still talked frequently with friends, but such contact was more likely to be by phone rather than face to face. Mrs. A had had to curtail her reading because of eye trouble. She could still read, but not as much. Her eye specialist said nothing could be done about the problem. She seemed to feel that she was watching about all the television she could stand. To add to her distress, Mrs. A was finding it more difficult to care for herself and her apartment. She resented the fact that

she could not vacuum under her furniture without being "out of commission" for two days afterward. She seemed particularly angry at having had to give up tub baths in favor of showers because she could no longer easily get up and down in the tub. Thus, Mrs. A had not only had to relinquish activities, but had had to substitute less preferred options for several of those she retained.

The big gap in Mrs. A's activity pattern was contact with people and with the outside world. She lost the contacts in her old neighborhood, at the senior center, and in the nearby city. She compensated somewhat by talking to old friends on the phone and by making new friends in her new neighborhood. But her decreased physical capacity made it difficult for her to get out into the community. She turned to her daughter for more interaction and for assistance in getting out and about, especially when Mrs. A was feeling bad. So far these increased demands have been met, but Mrs. A is fearful lest she jeopardize the most meaningful relationships in her life.

As Mrs. A's case illustrates, changes in activity patterns as a result of aging are not simply a matter of dropping activities and sometimes substituting others. Lifelong preferences, emotional reactions, and social relationships are usually involved. This area is not an easy one to research, especially if the research is to adequately follow people through time. Nevertheless, such research is essential if we are to have an authentic understanding of the dynamics of aging.

In this chapter, we look first at some general factors that influence the mix of activities going into middle age and later life. Then we look at some changes often connected with aging and at how they influence activities. Finally, we look at some of the age-related factors that influence activities in particular environments such as the workplace, the home, and the community. The goal is to provide an overview of the forces that influence activities and the context in which activities are performed. This understanding is vital if you are to be able to understand how older people relate to their activities.

Activities in Middle Adulthood

The range of activities that occupy human time and attention is practically infinite. Nevertheless, we can predict with some assurance that most middle-aged adults will have jobs, will spend time at home, will be involved in community activities to some extent, and will do things with their families. Within these general areas or spheres of participation, the factors that influence the choice of *particular* activities include the meanings attached to activities and how these meanings relate to the personal goals of the individual, to the person's sense of competence for various activities, and to sex, social class, and ethnic norms about the desirability of various activities.

The Meaning of Activity

The same activity can mean quite different things to different people. The following is an incomplete list of some of the meanings activities can have.

- A source of personal identity—I am what I do
- A way to make money
- A way to be with people
- A way to get the "vital juices" flowing
- A source of personal development
- A way to focus creativity
- A source of sensory experience
- A source of prestige or status
- A source of new experience
- A way to be of service to others
- A way of passing time
- Something to look forward to
- A way to exercise competence
- A source of peace and quiet
- A means of escape
- A source of joy and fun
- A source of feelings of accomplishment

Any activity can be rated as to how much these various meanings are attached to that activity for a given individual. For example, writing a book could be a source of personal development, a way to focus creativity, a source of prestige or status, a way to be of service to others, a way to exercise competence, a source of feelings of accomplishment, and a way to make money —not necessarily in that order. The point is that any activity can have many meanings for an individual. In order to understand how an activity fits into an individual's life, we must know the meaning of that activity for that person *and* how that activity (given its meaning) fits into the person's life goals. We cannot assume that we know the meaning of an activity for a particular person—we have to find it out.

Activity Competence

Although there are plentiful opportunities to enjoy a wide variety of activities in adulthood, people need *skills* and *knowledge* to take advantage of them. For example, older people—particularly the less educated—are reluctant to engage in activities such as art, music, handiwork, or writing. And this reluctance is at least partly caused by the older person's feelings of incompetence in such activities.

Critics of education have attacked this apparent deficiency in our orientation toward education. Contemporary education, it is said, devotes anywhere from 80 to 90 percent of the students' time for 12 to 19 years to teaching them how to fill jobs, but makes little effort to prepare them for life outside the job. As the noted publisher Norman Cousins (1968:20) put it, "I contend that science tends to lengthen life, and education tends to shorten it; that science has the effect of freeing man for leisure, and that education has the effect of deflecting him from the enjoyment of living." The point is that to open up the full range of possible activities requires some training.

Research on exposure to "high culture" in American society has shown that college-educated people are no more likely to enjoy a wide range of activities than are semiskilled workers (Wilensky, 1964; Marquis Academic Media, 1978). Television, which often requires little competence, is the major leisure activity in American society. One could conclude that our education and communication systems do little to develop the potential for the creative use of free time.

There is some evidence that the learning necessary to take advantage of available opportunities must begin early. The decline in learning speed that occurs with age, the reluctance most older people show toward attempting anything entirely new, and the extreme stability that activity patterns show lead to the conclusion that activity competence created early in life can be maintained into later life. Oliver (1971) found little change with age in the types of activities among his healthy, financially solvent respondents. But if activity competence is not learned by middle age, it may never be. Lambing (1972a) found, for example, that lack of skills and literacy seriously limited the leisure activities available to older lower-class blacks in Florida, a situation that Lambing's respondents recognized and wished to correct. The individual should probably begin to develop activity competence as soon as possible. An active and creative use of free time in one's youth is the surest way to guarantee a similar pattern in old age, because older people tend to retain patterns and preferences developed in the past.

Sex, Social-Class, and Ethnic Differences

Although many choices of activities are based purely on individual preferences, many others are constrained by what is considered "normal" for a person of a given sex, social class, or ethnic group.

Sex roles have received increased attention over the past decade. Many activity differences between men and women are not the result of "natural" differences in preferences but instead are the result of differences in the cultural conditioning that boys and girls receive. Thus, right now middle-aged men are much more likely than women to be involved in vigorous sports, crafts such as woodworking or metal work, or repair work involving machinery. Women, on the other hand, are much more likely than men to be involved in needlework, cooking, or child care.

Substantial social class differences also exist in preferences for activities. For example, while upper-middle-class people may watch television about as much as others do, they tend to watch different programs. A large portion of the audience of the Public Broadcasting System (PBS) is made up of the upper middle class, while the audience for all-sports networks tends to be mainly working class. Havighurst (1973a) found that voluntary associations, sports, reading, and gardening were much more common among the upper middle class; that the middle-middle class was more inclined toward crafts and television; and that members of the working class were more likely to spend their time visiting with neighbors and kin. Social class also has obvious economic effects on the range of possible activities. Traveling, entertaining, going to concerts or plays, playing golf or tennis, and dining out require much more money than watching television, talking with neighbors, or puttering around the yard. Thus, some social-class differences in activities are the result of differences in what people are taught to prefer, and part is due to differences in financial capacity.

We do not know very much about ethnic differences in activity patterns, but certainly they exist. For example, blacks participate in church activities more than whites do. People of Italian or Mexican descent are more likely to spend time with their families compared to people of English or Scandinavian descent.

Thus, meanings, skills, and values all influence the activity patterns that adults develop. And age changes in activities occur in the context of these various influences. We now turn to some of the changes that commonly occur with age and how they influence activities.

Aging and Changes in Activities

The life course exerts significant pressure to make choices about jobs and family. Most remaining choices of activities result from preferences that have been learned by trying the alternatives in vogue at the time of one's early adulthood. Once adult activity patterns are established, they tend to persist. Yet aging and changes associated with it cause activity patterns to change—if not in the type of activity, at least in the amount of it. The common factors that could potentially affect activities include the completion of child rearing, retirement, physical aging, a move to congregate housing, and institutionalization.

Completion of Child Rearing

Life after having launched the children does not seem to require a large emotional adjustment for most people. However, it probably does mean some adjustments in the use of time. In the middle class, lost interaction with children tends to be replaced by increased interaction with one's spouse. Reduced demand for service work in the household is offset by employment for many women. Social circles that brought parents together as a by-product of having to do things for their children, such as parent-teacher organizations and car pools, are likely to disappear. Leisure activities probably do not change very much after the empty nest. This area is much in need of research.

Retirement

Retirement is usually total, and most retired people go from full-time employment to no em-ployment quite abruptly. Yet for most people, this anticipated change produces little feeling of discontinuity. Cottrell and Atchley (1969) found that 80 percent of their retired respondents saw their friends either as often or more often than they did before retirement. Three-fourths of the respondents reported the same or more involvement in organizations following retirement. Their findings generally showed that social participation was not adversely affected by retirement.

Simpson et al. (1966a) found that many activity patterns that were supported by the job persist into retirement. Factors such as having a higher-status job and an orderly work career were as important in predicting a high level of activity with friends, organizations, and interests after retirement as they were before retirement. These researchers found that if social participation was not developed prior to retirement, it was not likely to be. They also concluded that having had irregular work histories was responsible for the low levels of social participation among retired semiskilled workers and that retirement was not a factor.

When people retire, they increase the amount of time spent at both obligatory and leisure activities. Many find that properly taking care of financial and social affairs occupies much more time than they were able or willing to devote to such activities prior to retirement (Atchley, 1976b). As one woman put it, "Now that I'm retired, I feel guilty if I put off answering letters. I sometimes spend a whole morning on one letter!" About 25 percent of those who retire experience an overall decrease in activity. But this decrease is sometimes welcome. For some, it is a relief not to have to keep up the pace of the preretirement period. This is particularly true for people who retire for health reasons.

Apart from the impact of retirement on activity *level*, there is the question of retirement's effect on the *meaning* of activity. According to one school, leisure activities cannot be done full-time by adults in Western societies without provoking an identity crisis. The thesis is that the job identity mediates all other activities and that without it other activities cannot provide the person with an identity (Miller, 1965). This view was very prevalent in the 1950s, and it received modest support from research being done at that time. However, more recent research shows that job identity carries over into retirement (Cottrell and Atchley, 1969) and that an increase in the amount of leisure activity in retirement is viewed by society as an earned privilege and opportunity (Atchley, 1971a; Thompson, 1973). The fact that only a small proportion of people take up entirely new activities following retirement does not appear to be the result of an identity crisis.

Retirement also tends to diminish financial resources, which in turn tends to reduce activity level. Simpson et al. (1966a) stress the role of financial security in providing support for participation in various activities. Atchley (1976b) points out that poverty creates a barrier to getting involved in new activities in the general community, especially for those who formerly had middle-class incomes.

Physical Aging

Physical change has two types of influences on activities. The first is a series of changes that move individuals from more active pursuits to more sedentary ones. The second is the constraining effects of serious illness and disability. Gradually, as the human body ages, it becomes less capable of high rates of physical output, and recovery from strenuous activity takes longer. This decline probably accounts for some movement away from strenuous activities in middle age. However, people who have remained in peak physical condition can probably continue these activities into later maturity. Perhaps more important influences on strenuous activity come from life-course factors and age norms. Middle-aged people who are highly involved in job, family, and community responsibilities may find it difficult to allot time to stay

at a level of physical conditioning that allows strenuous activity without discomfort. In addition, there is a general expectation (age norm) that after about age 35, people should be exempt from pressures to involve themselves in strenuous activities. It will be interesting to see what effect the current exercise craze has on attitudes about strenuous activity in middle age and later maturity.

The relatively sedentary activity patterns of most middle-aged Americans are well within the physical capabilities of later maturity. Only when symptoms of disabling illness or old age appear must there be a change in activity patterns. How disability and aging change activities is a highly individualized matter. It depends on the mix of activities prior to physical change, the specific physical changes that occur, and the individual's capacity to adapt to them. Generally, the narrower the range of activities in middle age, the more vulnerable the individual is to physical change.

A Move to Congregate Housing

A move to congregate housing generally increases the opportunity for activity, and activity levels usually increase for the mover. This increase is not simply a short-term flurry of activity in response to a new environment, but instead is a genuine change that is maintained over time. In a well-done longitudinal study of this subject, Carp (1978–1979) found that compared to older people who did not choose to move to an activity-rich congregate housing environment, people who did move reported increased activity levels. Increases in activity took place both in "regular responsibility" activities, such as lobby receptionist, senior center responsibilities, and church work, and in pastimes such as club meetings, table games, and visiting. Over the eight-year period of the study, movers maintained their increased activity levels even though they averaged 72 years of age when the study began. On the other hand, comparison respondents in the community showed a decline in activity over this same period. People who move to congregate housing with extensive activity programs are self-selected, and certainly it would be incorrect to assume that a high level of activity is good for everyone. Perhaps more important is the degree of fit between the person's desire for activity and the opportunities present in that person's living environment. Carp's findings show that, for people who want a high activity level, congregate housing that offers plentiful opportunities for activity can successfully meet this need.

Institutionalization

Institutionalization by its very nature could be expected to reduce activity. It cuts people off from their daily contacts in the community. And it is usually the result of disability that curtails activity. Yet little research has been done on before-and-after changes in activity resulting from institutionalization. We don't know for a comparable disability if the activity reductions due to disability occur more frequently in institutions than in the community. We don't know how institutionalization influences the person's desire for activity or how discontinuity between wants and possibilities for activity in the institution influences adjustment to the institution. Whether the disability that led to institutionalization is mental or physical undoubtedly influences activity. All these topics deserve further research.

Spheres of Activity

All the common life changes that accompany aging can potentially influence activity patterns. In addition, age discrimination and societal disengagement do not operate with the same force in all areas of life. Accordingly, we now examine how aging influences activity within various domains: on the job, in community organizations, and at home.

The Job

Aging affects employment from several standpoints. Aging can cause job-related disabilities, it can cause people to be denied the opportunity to work even when they are able-bodied, and it can increase the motivation to leave the workforce in favor of the freedom of retirement.* Whether people continue to hold a job into later life depends on several factors. First, there must be an opportunity to continue. Second, the person must want to continue, for instance, to supplement insufficient retirement income, or for satisfactions that only can be gained on the job, or for associations with others that would be lost if the person retired. Third, the person must be physically able to continue. Unless the person can continue in the same job past the normal retirement age, employment is tough to come by in later life. As we saw in Chapter 9, age discrimination in employment is common. In addition, most people who reach retirement age feel they have served their time and deserve to be allowed to retire. The end result is that jobs are a major activity for only a small minority of the elderly.

We should not confuse retirement with stopping work. Work is the expenditure of energy toward a goal. Able-bodied adults never stop work; they simply stop working toward economically motivated goals in a position of employment. They become "self-employed" in that they are free to decide for themselves what goals to pursue. Indeed, life satisfaction in retirement is very much tied to having numerous personal goals (Atchley, 1982b).

Community Organizations

Community organizations are groups that develop around a collective desire to achieve some purpose or pursue some interest. Most communities have churches, political parties, labor unions, veterans' groups, fraternal organiza-

---

*See also Chapter 9.

tions, community service groups such as Kiwanis and Rotary, professional associations, and parent-teacher organizations. Most communities also have hobby and garden groups, groups related to sports, and other special-purpose groups. In this section we look first at how aging affects participation in community organizations in general, and then at participation in churches, political groups, and volunteer work.

Participation in General. Cutler (1976a) reported that if the effects of socioeconomic status were controlled, then age produced little or no change in organizational participation from middle age into later life. He found that young adults tended to have low levels of participa-

tion, middle-aged people had higher levels, and the participation levels for older adults were at the middle-age level or higher.

Cutler and Hughes (1982) also examined age and sex patterns in membership in various types of organizations (see Table 10-1). For both men and women, affiliation with church-related groups was by far the most common, with women being slightly more involved than men. This pattern persisted across the entire age range. For men, involvement with sports-related, labor, and professional organizations peaked in middle age and was lower for older age categories. Involvement with fraternal, veterans', and service groups was generally consistent across the age categories. For women, involvement in sports-related groups diminished

TABLE 10-1   Percent of people belonging to various types of associations, by age and sex: United States, 1978–1980

Type of Association	Age (years)				
	35–44	45–54	55–64	65–74	75+
Men					
Church-related	29%	32%	33%	34%	42%
Sports-related	29	18	18	10	11
Fraternal	15	16	25	24	27
Labor unions	26	25	24	17	21
Veterans' groups	7	18	29	10	18
Professional	19	19	18	7	7
Service	14	16	10	9	12
Hobby or garden	10	7	6	7	3
Women					
Church-related	43%	47%	38%	43%	51%
Sports-related	18	17	9	3	2
Fraternal	7	9	9	13	11
Labor unions	11	6	7	6	1
Veterans' groups	1	6	5	6	5
Professional	14	12	9	5	6
Service	10	13	8	10	4
Hobby or garden	11	9	9	11	14

Source: Adapted from Cutler and Hughes, 1982.

across the age categories, while involvement with professional, hobby or garden, and discussion or study groups remained relatively stable. Note that although women were less involved than men in professional groups in middle age, after age 55 their involvement paralleled that of men. This goes contrary to the stereotype and indicates a greater interest in career among women. Except for church-related groups, participation in voluntary associations was less common among women than among men.

Participation in Later Life. Changes such as residential mobility, retirement, and widowhood have no predictable, consistent impact on participation in community organizations. For example, depending on the situation, retirement has been found to either increase, decrease, or produce no change in participation (Cottrell and Atchley, 1969). In a longitudinal study, Cutler (1977) found that people with either increased or stable participation far outnumbered those whose participation declined. However, poor health or dwindling financial resources—factors that are particularly prevalent among the working class—have a predictable dampening effect on participation. The impact of declining health is direct and obvious. Eroded financial resources have a subtler impact. Because community groups are almost always nonprofit, they must be subsidized, usually by members' contributions. Older people on tight budgets can be forced out of participation by the embarrassment of being unable to contribute.

For those who do continue to participate, community organizations take up a great deal of time. Yet many experience a decline with age in the satisfaction they report from participation as they see groups "letting in a different sort of people" or "having changed so much." Others are self-conscious of their age and would rather "leave it to the youngsters." Still others have done every job in the organization two or three times and see little opportunity for continued growth in further participation. Thus, older

members are often subtly "squeezed out."

Transportation problems can limit participation, particularly in small towns and rural areas that lack public transportation. Cutler (1974) found that older people who did not drive or have a car had much lower levels of participation than did those with access to a car. He also found that this effect increased with distance between residence and meeting site, particularly with respect to frequency of attendance at meetings.

Thus, we see that aging in and of itself has no predictable effect on overall participation in community organizations. Changes that do occur are most likely to be declines in participation associated with poor health, inadequate income, and transportation problems. We will now look at some specific types of organizations, beginning with churches.

Churches. Churches are the most common type of community organization membership for older people. Membership in churches also tends to be higher at the older ages, especially after 75. Leadership positions in churches also tend to be concentrated among older people, and participation in religious organizations declines among older people at a much slower rate than does participation in other types of organizations (Riley and Foner, 1968).

About half of the general population attends church regularly (twice a month or more). Catholics are much more likely to attend regularly than Protestants or Jews, although this tendency is diminishing. A higher proportion of women than men attend frequently. Also, church attendance is positively related to income, education, and length of residence in the community. Age is thus only one of many factors that influence church attendance. If we look at age patterns in church attendance at a given point in time, there is a steady increase from the late teens until attendance peaks in the late fifties to early sixties at about 60 percent. After that, the curve shows a consistent but very slight decline, almost certainly the result of the increasing prevalence of ill health, disability, and transportation difficulties. Among older people, there is also an increase in percentage never attending.

What about older people's place in the church? Most ministers, priests, and rabbis assume that worship services are as available to older people as they are to others. It is usually through contacts with shut-ins, hospitalized older people, and older people in nursing homes that local congregation pastors first confront the problem of older members of the congregation. Only gradually do they come to recognize that many of their ambulatory older members also have problems. Longino and Kitson (1976) found that although there was some ageism among American Baptist clergy in the form of preference for working with youth, the majority did not have an aversion to ministering to the elderly.

Older people can come to feel neglected by churches in a number of ways. Moberg (1972) notes that many churches tend to emphasize programs for adolescents and young families, lack outreach programs for older people, and tend to push older people out of positions of responsibility within the church. These tendencies are important mechanisms that encourage older adults to disengage from organized religion. In research on church attendance, for example, it would be useful to relate feelings of neglect by organized religion to church attendance by age. What many consider to be personal disengagement might turn out to be socially induced.

Some churches set up senior centers or clubs for older people; others allow their facilities to be used by such groups. The churches are also becoming interested in housing programs, particularly retirement homes for middle-income older people. They are beginning to see housing programs as a legitimate service, and not merely as an act of charity. Because the proportion of older people in the average congregation is about the same as the proportion in the total population, it is not too surprising that

churches have begun to feel some pressure from their older members concerning housing problems. At this point, however, church programs for older people are few and far between. Although 80 percent of the Presbyterian churches, for example, report special social groups for older people (including age-segregated Sunday school classes), only two-thirds report any type of educational program specifically for older people, and very few have employment, homemaker, or health services. Thus while it appears that most churches are quite willing to *passively accept* the participation of older people in church affairs, few are willing or able to *actively solicit* the participation of ill, handicapped, or isolated older people.

Political Participation.   There is a significant increase with age in political activity, such as working for the party in a local vote, signing petitions, and belonging to political groups. Older people represent the same percentage in party organizations that they do in the general population. In addition, older party members have more power at nominating conventions compared to their younger counterparts (Kapnick et al., 1968), which gives them a great deal of influence over the selection of party-supported candidates for political office.

One reason why older members of political parties are influential is the weight that tenure carries in politics compared to other types of groups. In politics, the older person can play the role of sage. In fact, the word *politic* means "wise" or "shrewd." Political prowess is still something one learns mainly from experience rather than from a book or a professional school.

Glenn and Grimes (1968) suggested that as people grow older, politics becomes more a source of personal fulfillment and less a means to a concrete end. This notion is supported by studies showing that as they grow older, people maintain and perhaps even increase their involvement in politics, while simultaneously feeling that their individual political action neither does nor can have an impact on the political process (Schmidhauser, 1968). In short, older people enjoy political participation, but at the same time are cynical about its results.

Volunteer Work.   Older people participate in a variety of volunteer work. The Older Americans Act has increased opportunities for this by providing administrative support and transportation services.

The *Retired Senior Volunteer Program (RSVP)* offers people over age 60 the opportunity of doing volunteer service to meet community needs. RSVP agencies place volunteers in schools, hospitals, libraries, courts, day care centers, nursing homes, and a host of other organizations. RSVP programs provide transportation to and from the place of service.

The *Service Corps of Retired Executives (SCORE)* offers retired businessmen and businesswomen an opportunity to help owners of small businesses and managers of community organizations who are having management problems. Since 1965, over 175,000 businesses have received help from SCORE. Volunteers receive no pay but are reimbursed for out-of-pocket expenses.

The *Senior Companion Program,* modeled after Foster Grandparents, offers a small stipend to older people who help adults with special needs, such as the handicapped and the disabled.

A program called *Green Thumb,* sponsored by the National Farmers Union in 24 states, provides part-time employment in conservation, beautification, and community improvement in rural areas and existing community service agencies.

The U.S. Department of Labor has three programs that offer older people part-time employment as aides in a variety of community agencies, including child care centers, vocational training programs, building security, clerical service, and homemaker services. The *Senior Aides* program is administered by the National Council of Senior Citizens; *Senior Community*

Service Aides is sponsored by the National Council on the Aging; and *Senior Community Aides* is sponsored by the American Association of Retired Persons (AARP).

The success of these programs illustrates that older people can be quite effective in both volunteer positions and paid positions. For the time being, however, we can expect volunteer opportunities to outnumber opportunities for part-time employment. A major obstacle to the effective use of older volunteers has been an unwillingness to assign them to responsible, meaningful positions on an ongoing basis. The result is a vicious circle. Because volunteers are assigned to menial tasks, they get bored or frustrated and quit. Because they quit, administrators are reluctant to put volunteers in anything other than nonessential jobs.

Studies have shown that older volunteers can be counted on to perform well on an ongoing basis (Babic, 1972; Sainer and Zander, 1971), particularly if the agency placing volunteers adheres to the following guidelines. First, agencies must be flexible in matching the volunteer's background to assigned tasks. If the agency takes a broad perspective, useful work can be found for almost anyone. Second, volunteers must be trained. All too often agency personnel place unprepared volunteers in an unfamiliar setting. Then the volunteer's difficulty confirms the myth that you cannot expect good work from volunteers. Third, a variety of placement options should be offered to the volunteer. Some volunteers prefer to do familiar things; others want to do anything but familiar things. Fourth, training of volunteers should not make them feel that they are being tested. This point is particularly important among working-class volunteers. Fifth, volunteers should get personal attention from the placement agency. There should be people (perhaps volunteers) who follow up on absences and who are willing to listen to the compliments, complaints, and experiences of the volunteers. Public recognition from the community is an important reward for voluntary service. Finally, transportation to and from the placement should be provided (Sainer and Zander, 1971).

The Home

The tendency to view activities in terms of roles has led to an artificial separation of the study of activities. Work, home, community, and other environments are viewed separately and studied by different researchers with different concepts and research agendas. Even those who look at activities at home tend to study specific types of activities rather than the entire array of at-home activities.

Table 10-2 shows a classification of at-home activities with examples. The examples are not exclusive, in the sense that a particular activity could fit into different categories, depending on its meaning to the individual. For example, if a person gardens mainly to supplement the family food budget and does not enjoy it very much, then gardening would be mainly a household chore rather than an appreciation of or contact with nature. Cooking can be either a chore or a creative act. The examples have been placed in

the categories that fit the meaning of the activity to most middle-aged or older adults most of the time.

The amount of activity centered on the home depends on the amount of time spent there, which even before retirement tends to increase with age past age 50. Part of this increase is due to a loss of roles in environments outside the household and part is due to a growing preference for in-home activities. Physical limits restrict activities to the home for only a small proportion of adults, including those over 75.

The distribution of in-home activities was reported by one sample of older people as follows: sleep, 37.5 percent; work (meals, housework, personal care, shopping, care for others), 27.9 percent; diversion (television watching, reading), 14.5 percent; socializing, 8.8 percent; crafts and gardening, 5 percent; other, 6.3 percent (Riley and Foner, 1968:513). Thus, what people mostly do at home is sleep and perform various tasks. Leisure or "free-time" activities account for only about a third of the time spent at home.

Moss and Lawton (1982) studied time bud-

TABLE 10-2   Types of at-home activity

Type of Activity	Examples
Work	Housework, home maintenance, household chores
Relaxation	Resting, sleeping, meditating
Diversion	Television watching, listening to music, reading
Personal development	Studying, learning, practicing, inquiring, personal care, worshiping
Creativity and problem solving	Crafts, cooking, planning, handiwork, arts
Sensory gratification	Sexual activity, eating, drinking, smoking
Socializing	Discussing, arguing, entertaining, gossiping
Appreciation of nature	Walking, gardening, bird watching

Source: Adapted and modified from Gordon et al., 1976.

gets in a sample of older people living independently in the community. The average age of the sample was 76; 57 percent of the sample was female. They found that the respondents occupied their days with a diversity of activities. (see Table 10-3). Obligatory activities, such as shopping and housework, took up 22.7 percent of the day; discretionary activities, such as socializing and watching television, occupied 39.2 percent of the day; and sleep accounted for 32 percent. Although watching TV was the most common discretionary activity, it occupied only a little over three hours per day, no more than is average for all adults.

What Activities Are Desirable for Older People?

Middle-class professionals often judge the activities of all older adults in terms of their appropriateness for middle-aged, middle-class people. Thus, the literature often implies that work is better than other kinds of activity and that group-centered activities are "better" for people than solitary activities. From the viewpoints of older people, this evaluation may not be justified. Because activity patterns established in early adulthood tend to persist and because what is fashionable in the way of activities varies from time to time and between social groups, it seems safe to assume that no single standard can be used to determine the "adequacy" of activity patterns among mature adults.

The tendency to assume that only leisure activities or employment can give meaning to life has caused many researchers to overlook the potential importance of mundane activities such as personal care, housekeeping, cooking, shopping, tinkering, and puttering (Lawton, 1978). In later life, these activities reflect the continued ability to be independent in the face of age, whereas earlier the ability to do them is taken for granted. Likewise, there is a common conception that inactivity is detrimental. In massive doses, inactivity is undoubtedly harm-

TABLE 10-3 Percent of time spent by independent older people on various activities

Type of Activity	Percent of Time Spent
Obligatory	22.7
Personal/sick care	3.4
Eating	5.3
Shopping	1.3
Housework	5.8
Cooking	5.1
Helping others	0.6
Discretionary	39.2
Family interaction	4.0
Friend interaction	3.1
Religious activity	0.8
Reading	4.3
Listening to radio	2.1
Watching TV	14.3
Recreation	2.8
Rest and relaxation	7.7
Unaccounted time	1.7
Travel	2.6
Sleep	32.0
TOTAL	98.2

Source: Adapted from Moss and Lawton, 1982.

ful, but the general statement overlooks the benefits of contemplation. It is important to find out what is happening inside a person during physically inactive but wakeful time rather than simply to assume the result is negative.

Summary

Activities structure our lives and, for many people, satisfaction with life depends on having a satisfying and meaningful round of activities.

Activities can be categorized in a vast number of ways. Some important dimensions of an activity are its intensity, the frequency with which it recurs in a person's life, the number of different environments in which the activity occurs, the skills and the knowledge required to do the activity, the extent to which the activity is obligatory, the capacity of the activity to provide a sense of leisure, the meaning(s) of the activity for a particular individual and for people in general, whether the activity can be solitary or requires others, and how costly the activity is.

The knowledge and skills needed for a varied set of activities are generally developed in early or middle adulthood and are maintained into later life. If people want to develop new activities in later life, they can sometimes get assistance from organizations such as senior centers, continuing education institutions, and voluntary organizations. But most older people find they are on their own if they want to take up new activities.

It is important not to impose our own notions of which activities "ought to be" satisfying to older people. For example, mundane activities around the house are meaningful to many older people—much more than many people who work with the elderly would expect.

Activities generally show a great deal of stability in later life, even with the substantial environmental changes that can occur as a result of child launching and retirement. People tend to cope with lost activities by becoming increasingly involved in the activities that remain. Most people have a wide variety of activities that can absorb even important losses. However, some people have a limited set of alternatives or place a very high value on a lost activity and so are distressed by changes in activities.

As a prevalent activity, employment begins to fade in importance in the early fifties, although much of the decline prior to age 65 is related to problems such as ill health or unemployment rather than personal choice. By age 65 and later, the overwhelming majority of retirements are voluntary.

Participation in community organizations tends to be high in middle and later life. Transportation problems, poor health, and lack of money are the major factors hampering participation for older people. Religious groups are the most common voluntary associations with which middle-aged or older people are involved. Churches generally welcome the participation of older people but do little to actively promote it. Apart from churches, no other type of voluntary organization involves participation by as much as a third of the middle-aged or older population. Older people who have been involved in local politics for many years usually find that their skills and experience give them a good deal of political influence. Volunteer work by older people has expanded dramatically in the past decade, although its exact prevalence is as yet unknown.

Activity patterns are highly individualized and highly stable across the life course. Nevertheless, options are sometimes limited in later life by physical, financial, or transportation factors. Personality, family, and social class values can narrow the range of options even further. It is probably fortunate that as they age, people tend to gravitate from obligatory activities to discretionary activities, from activities outside the home to at-home activities, and from social activities to solitary activities. This general movement can create flexibility and freedom for the individual, provided it is what he or she wants; in most cases it is.

Chapter 11

Dying, Death, Bereavement, and Widowhood

In the 19th century, death was a common occurrence at all stages of the life course. For example, Uhlenberg (1969) studied deaths of native-born Massachusetts women born in 1830. He found that 36 percent died before they reached age 20 and another 12 percent died while giving birth. Nine percent were widows before they were 55, and only 20 percent survived to age 55 as a member of a married couple. But by 1920, mortality was concentrated much more in the late stages of life. Uhlenberg (1969) found that of Massachusetts women born in 1920, only 10 percent died before reaching age 20, while only 4 percent died giving birth. There was no change in the proportion who were widowed by age 55 (9 percent), but the proportion who survived to age 55 as part of a couple had increased to 57 percent, compared to only 20 percent for the cohort born in 1830.*

In addition to the increasing concentration of death among the old since the 19th century, there has also been a sizable change in *where* people die. In 1900, a majority of older Americans died at home, but in 1970, two-thirds died in hospitals, another 13 percent died in nursing homes, and only 16 percent died in private homes (Kastenbaum and Candy, 1973).

These trends are important for our understanding of how people view death. In earlier times, death was a more "normal" part of everyday life at all life stages. People died in everyday environments, and physical death was something that most people had witnessed directly by the time they reached adulthood. Today, most deaths occur among old people and in institutional environments, where family and friends are often prevented from actually seeing the death or from seeing the dead body until it has been restored to a lifelike appearance by a mortician. Given these circumstances it should not be surprising that death has little reality for the young. Nor should it be surprising that older people are concerned about where

---

*See Chapter 2 for more detail on the demography of death.

they will die, since institutional environments are designed more to prevent death than as good places to die.

In this chapter we will examine various definitions needed to understand dying and death, what death means to most people and to older people in particular, the process of dying, care for dying persons, the consequences of death for the survivors, and life as a widow or as a widower.

Defining Death

Death can be defined as a process of transition that starts with *dying* and ends with being dead (Kalish, 1976).* For practical purposes, a *dying person* is a person with a bodily condition from which no recovery can be expected. *Dying* is thus the period during which the organism loses its viability. The term **dying trajectory** refers to the speed with which a person dies, that is, the rate of decline in functioning. In addition, the word *death* can be defined as the point at which a person becomes physically dead. Ordinarily when we say that someone died yesterday we are referring not to the entire dying process but instead to its final product. It was once considered an easy practical issue to establish the moment in time when a person becomes dead. Recently, however, it has become possible to artificially stimulate both breathing and heartbeat. As a result, there is currently a huge legal tangle over the issue of when a person is actually dead physically.

Death can also be a social process (Kastenbaum, 1969). A person is *socially dead* when that person is no longer treated as a person but as an unthinking, unfeeling object. Social death can be said to have occurred when people talk *about* the dying person rather than *to* the dying

person, even when the dying person is capable of hearing and understanding what is being said. Thus, social death sometimes occurs *before* actual physical death.

Thinking About Death

How people approach their own deaths and the deaths of others depends to some extent on what death means to them—and death can have many meanings. Back (1971a) examined the meaning of death, through ratings of various metaphors about death. He found little age variation in the meaning of death among respondents over age 45. Kalish (1976) suggested that death is more salient for older adults than younger ones because older adults see themselves as having less time remaining in their life spans and because their own physical condition and the deaths of others in their age group serve as constant reminders of the nearness of death.

Back (1971a) found a significant sex difference in the meaning of death: Women tended to be accepting of death, to see it as a peaceful thing, and to see it as most like a compassionate mother and an understanding doctor. Men tended to see death as an antagonist, as a grinning butcher or a hangman with bloody hands.

Fear of death is common among young people (Marshall, 1980:72). Whether fear of death is inevitable or a learned response is an unresolved issue. But whatever the cause, death fears exist. Older people appear not to be extremely afraid of death, and they are much less likely to have death fears than are younger people (Kastenbaum, 1969; Kalish, 1976). There also appears to be no tendency for death fears to increase among older people with a terminal condition (Kastenbaum, 1969). Among the young, however, terminal illness increases the prevalence of death fears (Feifel and Jones, 1968). Kalish (1976) attributes the lower prevalence of death fears in the face of a higher prevalence of death to several factors: (1) older

---

*I owe a tremendous debt to Richard Kalish for allowing me to draw from an advance copy of his (1976) synthesis of the literature on death and dying.

people see their lives as having fewer prospects for the future and less value; (2) older people who live longer than they expected have a sense of living on "borrowed time"; and (3) dealing with the deaths of friends can help socialize older people toward acceptance of their own death. Fear of death also depends to some extent on religiosity. Kalish's (1976) most consistent finding was that people who are strongly religious or are confirmed atheists have few death fears. Uncertain and sporadically religious people show the most death fears. Garfield (1974) reported that people who use psychedelic drugs or practice meditation have lower death anxiety than others. Kalish (1976) suggested that because "altered mind states" tend to blur ego boundaries, death of the self is less threatening to people familiar with such mental states. Peck (1968) found that the blurring of ego boundaries in old age served as a mechanism for transcending pain, and Kalish feels that this blurring may account for the lower prevalence of death fears among older people.

To *deny* death is to believe that people continue to be able to *experience* something after their physical death. Physical death is undeniable; only mental death is deniable. Belief in an afterlife, in the existence of ghosts, spirits, angels, or demons, and in reincarnation are all ways of denying that the ability to experience actually dies. Denial can also mean repressing the knowledge that one's physical death is imminent. Kalish (1976) reports that physicians often tell patients directly and clearly that they are going to die only to find out later that the message was not heard.

Death is accepted by older people presumably because they have more experience with death, regard it as fair, and are less integrated into society. However, it seems reasonable to assume that certain categories of older persons would not react to death in this way, for instance, the older person with dependent children or with a disabled spouse or with career goals still unachieved, or holding a socially crucial position. We know, for example, that legislators are often old. How does the prevalence of death fears among older legislators compare with that of the general older population? This and other similar questions need to be researched.

Planning in connection with death is much more common among older people than among the young. Kalish and Reynolds (1976) found that over 40 percent of respondents over age 60 had already arranged for a cemetery plot, made a will, and arranged for someone to handle their affairs, compared to only about 10 percent of adults under 40. Thus, not only does old age make death more salient but it results in concrete planning for death among a significant minority of the elderly.

Dealing with Dying

Dying is quick for some people; for others, it is slow. When a person is diagnosed as terminal, that person is assigned the social role of *dying person*. The exact content of the role depends on the *age* of the dying person and his or her *dying trajectory*. Regardless of age, people with a short dying trajectory spend only a brief time in the role of dying person. However, age heavily determines whether or not a person is defined as terminal. Sudnow (1967) found older people to be more likely than the young to be routinely defined as dead in hospital emergency rooms, with no attempt made to revive them. Among those with a long trajectory, however, age is an important element in determining what is expected of the dying person. Young persons are expected to fight death, to try to finish up business, to cram as much experience as possible into the lifetime remaining. In short, young people are expected to be active and antagonistic about dying. Older persons who are dying are expected to be more passively accepting. The older dying person is less likely than the young one to see a need to change life style or day-to-day goals (Kalish, 1976). Older people are also less apt to be concerned about caring for dependents or about causing grief to others

(Kalish, 1976). Older people are more apt than the young to find that the role of dying person also means having less control over their own lives. Many dying people, particularly the old, find that family members and medical personnel take away their freedom of choice, usually with good intentions. Finally, while all people in the role of dying person are expected to cope with their impending death, older people are allowed less leeway than the young in expressing anger and frustration about it.

A great deal has been written about the stages people pass through in the process of dying. Kubler-Ross (1969) proposed a five-stage process: (1) denial, (2) anger, (3) bargaining (such as asking God to postpone death in exchange for good behavior), (4) depression and sense of loss, and (5) acceptance. The universality of the Kubler-Ross model has not been determined. Kalish (1976) suggested that while denial is probably more common in the early stages of dying and acceptance more common later on, there is considerable movement back and forth. People may also simultaneously show the characteristics of several stages. It is doubtful that Kubler-Ross's stages represent a regular progression. Kalish (1976) reports that many people have mistakenly treated Kubler-Ross's stages of dying as an inevitable progression. As a result, people have been chided for not moving through their own dying on schedule, and dying persons have felt guilty for not having accomplished various tasks.

Certainly, accepting death is not the same as wanting to die. Weisman (1972) has called attention to the fact that acceptance of death as an outcome does not necessarily translate into capitulation during the dying process. For people approaching death, the where and when of death can also be important (Kalish, 1976). Most people die in a health care institution, but most people *prefer* to die at home. Death at home imposes a heavier burden on the family, but most family members are glad when death at home is possible (Cartwright et al., 1971).

Awareness that one's death may not be far off

can substantially affect the choices one makes. Sill (1980) found that as the perceived length of time before death decreased, activity decreased. In fact, perceived length of time remaining was a much more powerful predictor of activity level than either age or physical incapacity.

No doubt a good bit of the anxiety about death results not so much from the idea of death itself but from uncertainty about how we will die. We usually don't know what the cause of death or the circumstances will be, or when or where death will occur. Although it is impossible to predict the cause or circumstances in individual cases, age tells us what one is liable to die from and under what circumstances. For instance, beyond age 45, getting older dramatically increases the probability of dying from heart disease over other causes and decreases the probability of dying from cancer.

As for when death occurs, the prime issue is when a person should be permitted to die. There is no clear consensus among older people about whether "heroic" measures should be used to keep them alive or whether death should be speeded in hopeless cases involving great pain. However, many older people are aware of the financial burden their medical care may place on their families and may prefer to die rather than continue the expense of keeping them alive a little longer.

Kalish (1976) reported that "living wills" are one means used to give patients' wishes more weight. A Living will specifies the conditions under which a person prefers not to be subjected to extraordinary measures to keep him or her alive. Kalish (1976) pointed out that although living wills are not now legally binding, some states are drafting laws to make them so. He went on to say:

> One drawback, of course, is that the person facing imminent death may feel quite differently about his desires for heroic methods than he had anticipated when his death appeared much further removed in time, yet his condition may well preclude any opportunity to alter his living will (Kalish, 1976:496).

Care of the Dying

In caring for the dying, it is important to remember that most dying persons fear being abandoned, humiliated, and lonely at the end of their lives (Weisman, 1972). Thus, encouraging the maintenance of intimate personal relationships with others is an important aspect of the social care of the dying. Deciding who should be told about a terminal diagnosis has a significant impact on intimate relationships. Kalish (1976) concludes that it is difficult for the patient to maintain such relationships unless the topic of death can be openly discussed. Thus, when dying people are kept in the dark about the nature of their condition, they are denied an opportunity to resolve the question of death in the company of those they love, for by the time the prognosis becomes obvious their condition may prevent any meaningful discussion. In evaluating the question of who should know, Weisman suggests that "to be informed about a diagnosis, especially a serious diagnosis, is to be fortified, not undermined" (1972:17). Yet some people do not want to be told that they are dying (Kalish, 1976). In addition, some dying people keep their own prognosis secret.

A lengthy dying trajectory not only allows the dying person to resolve the issue of dying but also allows the survivors to resolve many grief reactions in advance. In some cases, the dying process is slow enough that the final event brings more relief than grief (Kalish, 1976). This does not mean that the survivors are calloused people who have no regard for the person who has died. It merely means that it is possible to grieve *in advance*. To assess a person's grief reaction to another's death requires knowledge of the reaction during the entire dying process, not just at the funeral.

Hospices represent an innovative way to organize the efforts of health service providers and families around the goals of eliminating pain associated with terminal illness and allowing terminally ill people to die with dignity. The multidisciplinary hospice staff seeks to care not only for dying people but for their families as well.

The first well-known hospice, St. Christopher's, was started in London. The primary goal at St. Christopher's is to make the patient free of pain and of any memory or fear of pain. Besides providing freedom from pain, the staff at St. Christopher's provides comfort and companionship to their patients. Families, including children, are free to visit any time (except Mondays, when families are given a day off and do not have to feel guilty for not visiting). Families are also encouraged to help with the patient's care. Patients often go back and forth between hospice and home. The median length of stay at St. Christopher's is two to three weeks; about half of the patients return home to die, with dignity and without pain, after a ten-day session with the hospice staff (Saunders, 1976).

Interest in the hospice movement has grown rapidly in the United States. In 1977 there were about 50 hospices in various stages of development, in 1980 about 400, and by 1983 the number had risen to 1,200. The hospice movement was given a big boost in 1982, when the U.S. Congress made hospice benefits available to all persons eligible for Medicare Part A and having a life expectancy of six months or less. These benefits cover routine home care, continuous home care, in-patient respite care, and general in-patient care and include nursing services, medical social services, physician's services, counseling, physical therapy, home health services, homemaker services, and medical supplies. In 1983, there was a limit on benefits: $6,500 per person per year (Aging Services News, 1983:1).

Bereavement

Bereavement is getting over another person's death, a process that may be finished quickly or that may never be finished. In Lopata's (1973) study of widows, 48 percent said they were over their husband's death within a year, while 20 percent said they had never gotten over it and did not expect to. Individual bereavement takes three forms: physical, emotional, and intellectual. Some common physical reactions to grief include shortness of breath, frequent sighing, tightness in the chest, feelings of emptiness in the abdomen, loss of energy, lack of muscular strength, and stomach upset (Kalish, 1976). These reactions are particularly common in the period immediately following a death; they generally diminish with time. The mortality rates of widowed people are slightly higher than those of the married.

Emotional reactions to bereavement include anger, depression, anxiety, and preoccupation with thoughts of the deceased (Parkes, 1972). Such responses also diminish with time. A longitudinal study of widows and widowers found that those who reacted to bereavement by becoming depressed were more likely than others to report a disproportionately higher level of poor health a year later (Bornstein et al., 1973).

The intellectual side of bereavement consists of what Lopata (1973) called the "purification" of the memory of the deceased. In this process, the negative characteristics of the person who died are stripped away, leaving only a positive, idealized memory. Somehow we think it wrong to speak ill of the dead. Lopata (1973) reported that even women who hated their husbands thought the statement "My husband was an unusually good man" was true. The content of obituaries and memorial services also attests to the results of this process. The idealization of the dead has positive value in that it satisfies the survivors' need to believe that the dead person's life had meaning. But it can have serious negative consequences for the future of the bereaved widow or widower because it can interfere with the formation of new intimate relationships (Lopata, 1973).

Glick et al. (1974) found that men and women reacted somewhat differently to bereavement. Men more often responded to loss of a loved one in terms of having lost part of themselves, while women responded in terms of having been deserted, abandoned, and left to fend for themselves. Men found it more difficult and less desirable to express grief, and they accepted the reality of death somewhat more quickly than women did. On the other hand, men found it more difficult to work during bereavement than women did.

People usually do not have to go through bereavement alone. There are various ways in which others help the individual through bereavement. At the beginning, bereaved people become exempt from certain responsibilities: They are not expected to go to their jobs; family and friends help with cooking and caring for dependents; older women often find decisions being made for them by their adult children. But social supports to the bereaved person are temporary. People are expected to re-engage the social world within a few weeks at most.

Death of a Spouse

Widowhood is often thought to be something that happens primarily to women, yet in 1970 about a third of the male population over 75 was widowed. It is reasonable to assume that losing a spouse has different effects on women than on men; therefore, we will first examine the role of widow and then look at the role of widower. We will then discuss the controversy over whether losing a spouse is harder for women or for men.

Being a Widow

The role of widow in American society is a long-term role primarily for older women. Young widows can play the widow role for only a short time and then they are considered single rather than widowed (Lopata, 1973). Younger widows feel stigmatized by widowhood because they are so much in the minority, but older widows see widowhood as more normal because even as young as 65, 36 percent of women are widows. The prevalence of widowhood in later life combines with low rates of remarriage to produce for women a more definite social position for the older widow.

Yet the role of older widow is a vague one. Ties with the husband's family are usually drastically reduced by widowhood. The position of older widow serves primarily to label a woman as a member of a social category with its own salient characteristics. For instance, older widows are supposed to be interested in keeping the memory of their husbands alive. They are not supposed to be interested in men and are expected to do things with other widows or with their children. Thus, being an older widow says more about the appropriate social environment for activity rather than the activity itself.

Being a widow changes the basis of self-identity for many women. For traditionally oriented women, the role of wife is central to their lives. It structures their lives not only in their households but also on the job. In answering the question "Who am I?" these women often put "wife of" at the top of their list. In addition to loss of a central role, widowhood often also causes the loss of the person best able to support the woman's concept of herself in terms of her personal qualities. If a woman's husband knows her better than anyone else and is her best friend and confidant, his opinions may be very important in supporting her view of herself as a good person. I have encountered older widows who after more than ten years of widowhood still "consulted" their dead husbands about whether they were "doing the right thing" by referring to the husband's values. How these women cope with the identity crisis that widowhood brings depends to a large extent on whether they base their identity on roles, on personal qualities, or on possessions. Role-oriented women often take a job or increase their investment in a job they already have. They may also become more involved in various organizations. Those who need confirmation of their personal qualities may become more involved with friends and family. Those who are primarily acquirers base their identity

on things rather than on people. For such women, an adjustment in self-concept is required only if widowhood brings a substantial change in acquisition power. Unfortunately, many widows find that their level of living changes markedly. Of course, all of these orientations may exist in the same person.

Widowhood obviously carries great potential for an identity crisis. However, that potential remains unrealized far more than might be imagined. The ability of older women to maintain their conceptions of self as "Mrs. John Doe" means that their memories can preserve a continued identity. Having other widows around helps legitimize this continuity. Children are also important reinforcers of a continued identity.

However, women vary a great deal in the extent to which the role of wife is central to their identity. For many women, the role of mother supersedes the role of wife, and after the children grow up and leave, the role of wife becomes an empty prospect. Other women have resented the traditional role of wife because of its subordinate status. Others have never developed a close, intimate relationship with their husbands. For any or all of these reasons, some widows do not wish to preserve the wife identity. These widows must then negotiate with family and friends to gain acceptance in their own right rather than as a wife. This renegotiation of social identity is a particularly necessary prelude to remarriage. Thus, for some widows, the identity problems brought on by widowhood are more external and social than they are internal and psychological.

Loneliness is generally thought to be a particularly prevalent problem among widows. Widows most often miss their husbands as persons and as partners in activities (Lopata, 1973). While no doubt much of the loneliness stems from the absence of a long-standing and important relationship, some of it results from economic factors. Widowhood means poverty for most working-class women, which translates into lower social participation outside the home

(Atchley, 1975b). The influence of economic factors on loneliness in widowhood deserves more research attention than it has received thus far. But not all studies show loneliness to be such a problem in widowhood. Kunkel (1979) reported that only a quarter of her small-town sample of widows felt lonely a lot, which suggests that there may be important differences in reactions to widowhood between those who live in large urban areas and those who live in small towns. Lopata (1973) and Blau (1961) found high levels of loneliness among urban widows, while Atchley (1975b) and Kunkel (1979) found low levels of loneliness in medium-sized cities and small towns. Both Atchley (1975b) and Morgan (1976) suggested that there is an economic component to loneliness in widowhood, and Kunkel (1979) pointed out that economic conditions for widows have greatly improved in recent years. This may also play a part in the lower prevalence of loneliness in more recent studies.

However, it would be a mistake to equate aloneness with loneliness. Many widows quickly grow accustomed to living alone, and more than half continue to live alone. And as they become more involved with friendship groups of older widows, they tend to miss a partner in activities less. In residential areas with a high concentration of older widows, loneliness is much less prevalent.

The social disruption caused by widowhood depends largely on the number of role relationships affected by the spouse's death. Middle-class widows are particularly likely to have seen themselves as part of a team and to see their involvement in a wide variety of roles as having been impaired by widowhood. Such feelings are particularly common in cases where the couple operated a family-owned farm or business.

Widowhood has the most immediate impact on family roles. When older women become widows, they usually lose their contacts with in-laws, especially if their children are grown. Contacts with children usually increase for a time, but those widows who move in with their

children do so as a last resort (Lopata, 1973). There are two basic reasons why widows seem to prefer "intimacy at a distance." First, they do not wish to become embroiled in conflict over managing the flow of household activity, and after being in charge it is hard for widows to accept a subordinate position in another woman's house, especially a daughter-in-law's. Second, they do not want to be involved in the dilemmas of rearing children. They feel they have done their work, raised their children, and deserve the rest (Lopata, 1973).

Patterns of mutual aid between children and parents are altered by widowhood. Older widows often grow closer to their daughters through patterns of mutual assistance (Adams, 1968a). Widows sometimes grow more distant from their sons. Because adult sons often feel responsible for their mothers' welfare and because older widows often want to be responsible for themselves, there is great potential for conflict and guilt in the older widow–son relationship.

Relationships with extended family (brothers, sisters, aunts, uncles, cousins, and so on) increase immediately following the spouse's death. But within a short time, widows generally retain only sparse contact with extended kin (Lopata, 1973). This decrease is partly caused by the fact that married women tend to focus on wife and mother roles and spend little time maintaining close relationships with other kin.

The impact of widowhood on friendship largely depends on the proportion of the widow's friends who are also widows. If she is one of the first in her group of friends to become widowed, she may find that her friends feel awkward talking about death and grief, not wanting to face what in all likelihood is their own future. If friendship groups had consisted mainly of couples, then the widow may be included for a time, but she will probably feel out of place. The widow may also encounter jealousy on the part of still-married friends. On the other hand, if the widow is one of the last to become widowed in a group of friends, then she may find great comfort among friends who identify very well with the problems of grief and widowhood. As a group of women friends grows older, those who are still married sometimes feel somewhat "left out" because their widowed friends do many things as a group that they do not feel free to leave their husbands in order to do. For these people, widowhood brings the compensation of being among old friends again.

Churches and voluntary associations offer avenues for increased contact with people. Church groups often present opportunities for increased involvement that do not hinge on having a spouse. The same is true of voluntary associations oriented around interests (as opposed to purely social clubs). However, in heterosexual groups, widows are apt to encounter the stigma of the lone woman. It is no accident that many widows are drawn more to women's groups than to heterosexual groups. Again, the age at which widowhood begins is important in determining its impact on community involvement.

Throughout the discussion of the impact of widowhood, the importance of age has cropped up again and again. The younger the widow, the more problems she faces; the older the widow, the more "normal" widowhood is considered to be and the more supports are available from family, friends, and the community at large to help women cope with widowhood. Older widows appear to adjust better than younger widows (Blau, 1961).

The impact of widowhood also varies considerably, depending on the social class of the widow. Middle-class women tend to have balanced their roles between being a wife and companion to their husbands and being mothers. The loss of comradeship triggers considerable trauma at the spouse's death. As a result, middle-class women tend to have difficulty dealing with grief. However, middle-class women also tend to be broadly engaged. They have a number of friends and belong to various organizations. They have many personal resources for

dealing with life as widows. They usually have a secure income, are well educated, and often have job skills and careers. In contrast, working-class women tend to emphasize the mother role more than the wife role. Consequently, they may experience less trauma associated with grief. But working-class women have fewer friends, fewer associations, less money, and fewer of the personal resources that make for an adequate long-term adjustment to widowhood. Working-class widows are thus much more likely to be isolated and lonely than are middle-class widows.

Class differences are particularly pronounced among blacks. Working-class black women tend to become widowed at much earlier ages than working-class whites. Overt hostility between the sexes is more prevalent among blacks, so widows sanctify the husband's memory less. As a result, widowhood results in even less emotional trauma among working-class blacks than among working-class whites (Lopata, 1973).

There are also considerable ethnic differences in the impact of widowhood. Foreign-born widows are much more likely than others to have had a traditional marriage, which, as we saw earlier, can entail greater identity problems for widows. In addition, widowhood brings more potential for family conflict among the foreign-born. Many foreign-born older women were reared in cultural traditions that offer widows a great degree of involvement with extended kin. To the extent that extended kin do not share this orientation, there is room for a greater gap between what the older foreign-born widow expects from her family and what she gets. A similar pattern prevails among older widows reared in the Appalachian tradition.

Being a Widower

The impact of widowhood on older men has received little attention. The literature on this subject is long on speculation and short on systematic research. Nevertheless, as a stimulus for further research, it is important to outline both what little we know and what we need to know about being a widower.

The role of widower is probably even more vaguely defined than that of widow. Because there are relatively few widowers in any community until after age 75, the status of widower does not solidify groups of older men as that of widow does groups of older women. But older widowers are expected to preserve the memories of their wives, and not to show an interest in women. Indications are that many widowers adhere to the former expectation but ignore the latter.

Because the male role traditionally emphasizes other roles in addition to the role of husband, widowers are probably not as apt as widows to encounter an identity crisis caused by loss of the spouse *role*. But men are more likely than women to see their spouse as an important part of themselves (Glick et al., 1974). In addition, older men are less likely than women to have a confidant other than their spouse (Powers et al., 1975). Thus, both widows and widowers are likely to have problems because the spouse was a significant other.

How older men cope with widowhood's impact on their identity also probably depends, as older women's reactions do, on how the lost relationships fit into personal goal structures. Despite current stereotypes concerning men's overinvolvement with their jobs, there is little evidence that widowhood is any less devastating for men than for women. In fact, widowhood is very likely to wreck a man's concept of life in retirement. Likewise, there is little basis for assuming that marriage is less important to older men than it is to older women.

There is no apparent difference in the extent to which older widows and widowers experience loneliness (Atchley, 1975b). However, this finding may be an artifact of the higher average age of widowers. Were age to be controlled in research, older widowers might turn out to be less lonely than older widows.

Thus far there has been little study of the impact of widowhood on men's roles outside the household. Widowers have more difficulty with work during the grief period (Glick et al., 1974). It also appears that widowers are more cut off from their families than widows are (Troll, 1971). Widowhood tends to increase contacts with friends among middle-class widowers and to decrease them among lower-class widowers (Atchley, 1975d). It is quite likely that the large surplus of widows inhibits widowers in developing new roles in terms of community participation. Particularly at senior centers, widowers tend to be embarrassed by the competition among the widows for their attention. They also feel pressured by widows who constantly try to "do" for them.

Very little has been written about age, social class, racial, or ethnic variations in the impact of widowhood on older men. However, some of the variations noted for widows no doubt apply to men as well. This area is greatly in need of research.

Comparisons Between Widows and Widowers

There is currently some disagreement over whether widowhood is more difficult for older women or more difficult for older men. Age is an important compounding factor in comparing the experience of being a widow with that of being a widower. Widowhood occurs in old age for most men, while it occurs in middle age or later maturity for most women. It is important therefore to compare widowers with widows *of a similar age* in order to cancel out the impact of age. Much of the research that has been done to date has not controlled for age.

Berardo (1968, 1970) has contended that older men find widowhood more difficult than older women do. He suggested that men are ill-prepared to fend for themselves—to cook their own meals, keep house, and so on—and therefore end up having to give up their independent

households. Berardo also felt that men have more difficulty finding a substitute source of intimacy. He said that courtship opportunities are limited for widowers and that friends and children see them as being too old for "that sort of thing." Widowers also find it more difficult to move into their children's homes and find a useful place there. In addition, widowhood combines with retirement to give the widower a severe identity problem. The retired widower has no job that can serve as an alternate source of identity and behavioral norms. On the other hand, Berardo felt widows have the advantage of the continuation of the role of housewife, a meaningful activity that provides continuing standards for behavior. He saw widows as much more able to maintain an independent residence and at the same time more able to gain acceptance in the households of their children should the need arise.

On the other side, Robert Bell (1971:509) concluded that widowhood is harder on older women than on older men because: (1) being a wife is a more important role for women than being a husband is for men; (2) widows are given less encouragement to remarry; (3) widows face a bleaker financial future with fewer financial skills; (4) widows are more isolated (because women are expected not to be socially aggressive); and (5) the lack of prospects makes remarriage difficult for all but a few older widows.

Atchley (1975b) compared various dimensions of widowhood among 72 widowers and 233 widows, all 70 to 79 years old. The widows were significantly more likely than the widowers to suffer high anxiety, although even then only 15 percent of the widows had experienced high anxiety. The widowers were more likely to have a high level of anomie, but even the widowers had only 20 percent with a high level of anomie. The widowers were more likely to increase participation in organizations and to increase contacts with friends than were widows. Sex differences in response to widowhood were

greater among working-class respondents. Here the widows were more likely than the widowers to be isolated and to have inadequate incomes. Atchley concluded that the working-class widows were considerably worse off than the middle-class widows and widowers in both social classes. The key seemed to be their inadequate incomes. Income inadequacy in turn produced lowered social participation and loneliness.

Kunkel (1979) studied widows and widowers over age 50 in a small town. She found that the vast majority of both men and women adjusted well to widowhood. High morale, good health, adequate incomes, high levels of self-confidence, and positive attitudes toward retirement typified both widows and widowers. Age had no effect on adjustment to widowhood. Length of time widowed generally had little affect on adjustment. Widows were slightly more likely to have physical symptoms of stress, but these symptoms did not affect either physical health or morale. Widowers had lower levels of interaction with family and friends *and* were more satisfied with their level of interaction, compared to widows. It appears that widows *expect* a high level of interaction, usually get it, and want still more, especially among those widowed longer than one year. Widowers expect little, get more than they expect, and are satisfied.

These separate and diverse accounts raise a number of important issues in comparing widowers with widows. We shall, therefore, now examine in more detail the following: living alone, living with children, problems with retirement, alternate sources of intimacy, financial resources and skills, and isolation and loneliness.

Ability to Live Alone.   Many widowers have to learn to care for themselves. There is little evidence that they cannot do so. Berardo's (1968) research is inconclusive in this respect because his study sample consisted primarily of very old, rural widowers—a population in which

health and disability cloud the issue of ability to care for oneself. Table 11-1 indicates that in 1970, from age 65 to 74, slightly more widowers than widows lived in group quarters rather than independent households, and that after age 75 there was little difference. Table 11-2 shows that in 1970, among those living in households, slightly *more* widowers than widows lived alone. Thus, those men who remained widowers were not significantly less likely than widows to live alone.

Living with Children.   Table 11-3 shows that in 1970, fewer widowers than widows were living with children, although the differences were not large. Interestingly, about equal proportions of widows and widowers were parents-in-law of the household head as were parents of the head. Only among widows over age 75 was there a significantly greater proportion who were a parent rather than a parent-in-law of the household head. When widowers lived in multi-person households, they were much more likely than widows to be considered the household head rather than a subordinate member of the household.

Problems with Retirement.   Berardo (1968) made the usual assumptions that jobs are more important to men than to women and that

TABLE 11-1   Living arrangements of widowed men and women, by age: United States, 1970

	Widowers	Widows
Age 65 to 74 (N)	(594,514)	(2,946,251)
Total	100.0%	100.0%
In households	94.0	96.8
In group quarters	6.0	3.2
Age 75 and Over (N)	(847,435)	(3,141,386)
Total	100.0%	100.0%
In households	86.5	86.8
In group quarters	13.5	13.2

Source: U.S. Bureau of the Census, 1973c.

TABLE 11-2   Living arrangements of widowed men and women living in households, by age: United States, 1970

	Widowers	Widows
Age 65 to 74		
In families	32.0%	35.8
Living alone	63.5	62.4
Living with nonrelatives	4.5	1.8
Age 75 and over		
In families	42.6%	46.0%
Living alone	54.0	52.2
Living with nonrelatives	3.4	1.8

Source: U.S. Bureau of the Census, 1973c.

retirement poses an identity crisis primarily for men. He saw widowhood as a cumulative loss only for men. Atchley (1976b) presented a somewhat different analysis. Since he found little evidence that leaving the job at retirement represented an identity crisis for a large proportion of either men or women, he concluded that job loss is not a significant source of distress even in widowhood. He suggested that widowhood interacts with retirement to the extent that widowhood wrecks plans for a retirement life style built around being a member of a couple. And this type of interaction between retirement and widowhood is probably as applicable to widows as to widowers.

But what about the housewife role? Berardo (1968) felt that the continuity of the housewife role is advantageous for widows. However, what is retained is the role of house*keeper*, not house*wife*. The widow loses the housewife role because widowhood and the empty nest take away her clients (Lopata, 1973). The satisfaction of doing for oneself is often much less than the satisfaction of doing for others.

In sum, then, an effective case can be made for the idea that retirement and widowhood interact just as much for older women as for older men. However, more research is needed on this topic.

TABLE 11-3   Family position of widowed men and women living in families, by age: United States, 1970

	Widowers	Widows
Age 65 to 74		
Head	53.0%	49.9%
Parent of head	16.3	22.7
Parent-in-law of head	16.8	20.9
Sibling of head	5.9	6.1
Sibling-in-law of head	2.7	1.9
Other relative of head	5.3	3.5
Age 75 and over		
Head	36.5%	28.7%
Parent of head	27.5	33.1
Parent-in-law of head	26.8	28.5
Sibling of head	3.0	4.2
Sibling-in-law of head	1.3	1.0
Other relative of head	4.9	4.5

Source: U.S. Bureau of the Census, 1973c.

Alternate Sources of Intimacy. Berardo (1968) felt that widowers have more difficulty than widows with finding alternate sources of intimacy because of social norms against courtship and remarriage for older men. However, the statistics of the matter indicate that if such norms exist, older widowers do not need them. Every year nearly 30,000 older widowers remarry, compared to about 15,000 older widows who remarry. Moreover, older widows outnumber older widowers four to one. Not only do older widows have to fight the scarcity of older widowers, but *half* of those older widowers who do remarry choose wives that are under age 65. Thus, older widowers have a much greater chance than older widows of finding new intimacy through remarriage.

Widowers are much less likely than widows to have had a confidant other than their wives. Therefore, widowers *need* remarriage more than widows do, in order to find a new confidant. As far as the social discouragement of remarriage, McKain (1969) reports no sex differences in the extent to which children oppose remarriage. However, he does report that children's opposition to remarriage is a significant obstacle to remarriage.

Financial Resources and Skills. There can be little doubt that widows are far worse off financially than widowers, especially among the working class. In traditional marriages, the wife is usually ignorant of the family finances and has no training in managing money (Lopata, 1973). In addition, the incomes of widows average considerably less than the incomes of widowers. And Atchley's (1975b) research suggests that this poverty is a critical factor for working-class widows. Kunkel (1979) found that widows are more likely to be of low socioeconomic status (measured in terms of her or her husband's occupation, and education) compared to married women age 50 and over.

Isolation and Loneliness. Atchley (1975b) found that widowed older people were significantly more often lonely than married older people, and that working-class widowed older people were more often lonely than those in the midde class. Atchley found no significant sex differences in the prevalence of loneliness among the widowed. However, widowers were much more likely than widows to increase their participation in organizations and their contact with friends.

Thus, as these foregoing comparisons show, no aspect of widowhood appears demonstrably more difficult for older widowers than for older widows, although widows are worse off than widowers in terms of finances and prospects for remarriage.

Summary

Death touches the lives of older people more often than it touches people of other age categories. The process of dying, the meaning of death, bereavement, and widowhood are all more salient to older people than to younger people, at least in industrialized societies. Death is both an end state and a physical and social process. In a given year, about 6 percent of the older population will die. Yet more and more people are not only surviving *to* old age but *in* old age as well. Due to variations in death rates women vastly outnumber men; fewer blacks than nonblacks survive to old age; married people have higher rates of survival compared to others; and poor people die at higher rates than others.

Men tend to see death as an antagonist while women tend to see death as merciful. In general, older people fear death less than do other age categories. However, more research is needed on acceptance of death among specific categories of older people who are still highly integrated into society.

For older adults, the role of dying person demands passive acceptance of death. Older people are less apt than the young to change their life style when they learn that they are dying. Older people are also apt to find that being a dying person means having less independent control over one's life.

People go through various stages in dying, but there is no set sequence or necessary progression. Denial, anger, bargaining, depression and sense of loss, and acceptance are all common reactions to dying—and dying persons often experience more than one of these at the same time. Acceptance of death does not mean a wish to die; it is merely an ackowledgement of an inevitability. Where and when a person dies is a matter of values. Most people prefer to die at home. However, at what point in the process of dying a person should be allowed to die is still a subject of controversy.

Two crucial aspects of care for the dying are maintaining personal relationships and reassuring the dying person that he or she will not be abandoned or humiliated. A lengthy dying trajectory *allows* survivors to grieve in advance and often softens the final blow.

Bereavement is the process of dealing with someone's death. It usually encompasses symp-

toms of physical, psychological, and emotional stress. In addition, bereavement usually results in a sanctification of the memory of the person who died. People usually receive social support during bereavement, but only for a short time.

Being a widow is a long-term role primarily for older women. The prevalence of widowhood in later life combines with low prospects for re-marriage to create a "community of widows." For women with traditional marriages, widowhood creates identity problems. It removes a valued role that is hard to regain, and it takes away the person who was most able to confirm the older woman's conception of herself. Some of the potential for crisis is softened by the fact that society allows older widows to maintain an identity based on being someone's wife in the past. However, not all women have a high investment in the role of wife. For these people, the impact of widowhood on identity may be minimal.

Loneliness was and perhaps still is prevalent among urban widows, but recent studies of widows in middle-sized cities and small towns have found less loneliness. Widows tend to miss having someone around the house and someone to go places with. However, aloneness does not necessarily mean loneliness. Many widows adjust very quickly to living alone.

The impact of widowhood on family relations is ambiguous. Children respond to the widow's needs in times of illness, but the widow enters the household of a married child only as a last resort. "Intimacy at a distance" is the preferred pattern. Extended kin are not usually important sources of interaction for widows.

If a woman is one of the first of a group of friends to become widowed, she tends to be cut off from friends; but if she is one of the last, widowed friends can be an important source of support and interaction. Generally, the younger the widow, the more problems she faces, and the older the widow, the more "normal" widowhood is considered to be.

Widowhood's impact seems to differ according to social class. On the average, working-class widows adjust better during bereavement but later have economic problems that make widowhood difficult. On the other hand, middle-class widows encounter more problems with bereavement, but because of their greater personal and economic resources they make a better long-term adjustment to widowhood. Class differences are especially great among widows who are black. Owing to their traditional values, foreign-born widows also have more difficulty.

Widowers have many of the same problems that widows face—vague role definition, identity problems, and loneliness. Widowers seem to be able to take care of a household. They are only slightly less likely than widows to live with children.

Both widows and widowers are likely to see their retirement plans wrecked by widowhood, a problem that is perhaps worse for some older women than for the average older man. The housewife role is lost without clients to serve. Widowers are more likely than widows to remarry, but widowers are less likely to have a confidant other than their wife. Both may have trouble replacing the intimacy lost through widowhood. Widows are far worse off than widowers economically, including both income and personal finance skills. Widowhood can be a difficult role for persons of either sex. In the last analysis, however, widowers have better economic resources and a better chance for remarriage.

PART IV

Personal Adaptation to Aging

Part IV deals with how individuals cope with the hundreds of changes detailed in Parts II and III. To understand many of the strategies that older people adopt requires background knowledge of the physical, psychological, social, and situational changes that often accompany aging. Adaptation is more than simply another psycho-logical process; it is a creative synthesis of the various components of a person and his or her physical and social environment. That is why adaptation is not just added to the chapter on psychological aging, but is given a separate place in the book.

Chapter 12

Personal Adaptation to Aging

As shown in previous chapters, aging brings many types of changes. This chapter discusses how people adapt to these changes and achieve the generally positive adjustment that typifies most older people. It begins with a definition of adaptation and a discussion of some general means and goals of adaptation. Then the chapter considers some specific ways that individuals adapt to specific changes associated with aging. Finally, the chapter focuses on ways people try to avoid adapting, and finishes with a discussion of successful aging.

What Is Adaptation?

Adaptation is the process of adjusting ourselves to fit a situation or environment. It is actually several processes we use to deal with constant changes that we encounter in our everyday lives. Changes that require adaptation can occur either in ourselves or in our situations or environments. Early in our lives we develop basic routine approaches to dealing with change. For each of us there is a certain amount of change that can be taken in nearly automatically, without special effort. However, some changes surpass our capacity for such routine, perhaps unconscious, adjustment and require that we take unusual, nonroutine steps to deal with them. We adjust to changes associated with aging in both ways. As we saw earlier, many age changes occur gradually and so can be dealt with routinely. Gradual declines in athletic ability are an example. Other changes are both sudden and serious and require conscious attention and social support. Widowhood is an example.

Just as the changes that require adaptation can be internal or external, so can the means for adapting. **Assimilation** is an internal process of adaptation in which new experience is modified in the process of perception so as to fit in with already existing ideas. It adjusts the outer "reality" to fit the inner. Thus, an older person insulted by a youngster may simply alter his or her perception of the younger person's behavior so as to deny the insult. **Accommodation** is a process of altering one's behavior to more nearly conform to external demands. An example might be an older mother who stops visiting with her friends at a local tavern because her daughter told her she is too old for that activity. Both assimilation and accommodation can be conscious or unconscious.

Three General Ways to Adapt

Habituation, continuity, and conflict management are three general means of adaptation. When we are exposed to the same experience over and over, we gradually pay less and less attention to it. This process is called **habituation.*** It is learning *not* to pay attention. Habituation is vital in early childhood because it allows us to ignore most environmental stimuli and to concentrate our attention, and thus is an important prerequisite for learning. The speed with which individuals habituate varies considerably; once learned, habituation tends to be a widely applied skill. Habituation is a way of ignoring millions of small changes that occur in both self and environment. Kastenbaum (1980–1981) has suggested that psychological symptoms of aging may in fact be the result of overhabituation. That is, the person has become so habituated that he or she is aware of vey little new information and so may seem psychologically stagnant. To the extent that people live in familiar environments and experience only very gradual changes in themselves, habituation may cause them to perceive very little need to adapt. Optimal habituation is somewhere between being so overhabituated that no adjustment seems needed and being so underhabituated that every small change seems to require attention. Habituation generally lowers the perceived need for attention and adjustment, and may increase

---

*For a more detailed discussion of habituation, see Kastenbaum (1980–1981).

with age. This latter possibility needs to be studied.

Like adaptation in general, *continuity* can be both internal and external. The term **internal continuity** refers to the persistence of a personal structure of ideas based on memory. The term **external continuity** refers to living in familiar environments and interacting with familiar people. Continuity does not mean that nothing changes. Rather, it means that new life experiences occur against a solid backdrop of familiar and relatively persistent attributes and processes for both the self and the environment. One of the most frequent findings in gerontology is that continuity overshadows change for most people in midlife and after. This finding is true for internal aspects such as personality and self as well as for external aspects such as relationships, housing, community residence, activities, and life styles. *Continuity is an adaptive response to both internal and external pressures.*

Internal pressures toward continuity come from our basic need for stable viewpoints concerning ourselves and the world we live in that we can use as a basis for anticipating what will happen and for deciding how to respond to what does happen. Epstein (1980) has pointed out that these constructs are often preconscious and that the individual may not be aware of them as viewpoints or be able to describe them. Once developed, these viewpoints exert pressure toward continuity because of the nature of assimilation. Assimilation requires that new information be reconciled with the old; therefore, the more experience that is contained in memory, the less effect new information can be expected to have. This is why new information does not have the same weight for older people as for youngsters and also why it reinforces the appearance of conservatism in the aged. The greater the weight of previous evidence, the greater the pressure toward continuity. Thus, the more experienced the person (and usually the older), the higher the likelihood that new information will be interpreted as continuity and thus as not requiring adaptation. The focus of internal continuity is a unique past history; therefore, what seems to be continuity to one person may not to another.

We defend our personal viewpoints, once they are developed, because to us they seem necessary for our security and survival. And *the more vulnerable the person sees him- or herself to be, the stronger the internal motivation for continuity.* This is one reason why older people in institutions so often think and talk about the past. Their present offers them little opportunity to reinforce their images of themselves as capable and self-reliant, so they concentrate their attention so as to maintain ties to the past. Older people who are involved in current activities in the community are not nearly so likely to focus on the past.

External pressures for continuity come from environmental reinforcement and from the demands of the roles we occupy. Environments condition us to fit them, and to the extent that environmental demands remain relatively constant, there is pressure for continuity in our responses. To the extent that older people live in familiar environments, conditioning exerts pressure for continuity.

The people we interact with in the roles we play expect us to remain the same from one time to another. They want us to be predictable, which of course involves maintaining continuity in our actions, appearance, mannerisms, and thoughts. But lest we think that this expectation overly constrains our freedom, remember that we also have internal motives for wanting the same thing. In addition, the constraints of continuity provide us with useful guidelines for deciding how to adapt to change. Obviously, *the more relationships a person is involved in, the greater the potential for external pressures for continuity.*

Conflict management involves placing experiences in a context that changes our perceptions of the conflict from negative to positive or at least neutral. We can use various mechanisms to accomplish this shift. Vaillant (1977) found that some mechanisms were more effec-

tive than others, the most effective being altruism, humor, sublimation, anticipation, and suppression (Vaillant, 1977:80). *Altruism* is a type of unselfishness that allows people to see their own needs in a context that includes the needs of others. *Humor* allows people to defuse the anger associated with conflict by focusing on its comical elements. *Sublimation* directs the energies produced by conflict into constructive and socially acceptable channels. *Anticipation* is the capacity to perceive future conflicts clearly, and as a result to minimize their effects. *Suppression* is the ability to cope with conflict by putting it out of one's consciousness temporarily. All these very effective strategies are skills or habits of mind. They all involve learning how to adapt to life without persistently denying or severely distorting one's own nature or the situation within which one is trying to adapt.

People can also react to conflict in less adaptive ways. People who in their youth wanted sexual freedom but were afraid to go for it might become staunch puritans with regard to their children's sexuality. People may permanently repress their internal conflicts over care of an aged parent, only to have them resurface later as the seemingly irrational fear that they themselves will not be cared for when the need arises. People who experience conflict in their relationships with others may respond by adopting overly rigid approaches to people. People who make mountains out of molehills are often trying to shift their emotional attention away from what to them are real mountains (Vaillant, 1977:139). Some people cope with conflict by becoming "too sick" to deal with it. People sometimes turn anger on themselves in an attempt to preserve important social relationships that nevertheless are in conflict.

The habitual pattern of coping with conflict that people learned in the process of growing up and the amount of conflict both affect the selection of mechanisms of conflict reduction. Through a combination of disposition, guidance, and luck, most people develop the ability to adapt effectively when conflict is at its "normal," or usual, level. However, *as the amount of conflict increases above its usual level, the probability increases that a less effective mechanism may be activated.* The usual level of conflict fluctuates widely from person to person. Some people thrive on large amounts of conflict (Lieberman, 1975), and others try to avoid conflict at all costs. Most people operate somewhere in between.

Goals of Adaptation

As shown earlier, aging brings new opportunities for freedom and autonomy. But it also can bring physical and social constraints on what people are able or allowed to do. It often brings losses of relationships and activities. And it changes instrumental needs and resources.

In adapting to these changes, individuals seek first to preserve continuity, for the reasons given earlier. But this motivation for continuity is also in part based on the perception that continuity is the best way to achieve certain ends. First, continuity of life style and residence is seen as a way of preserving one's ability to meet instrumental needs for food, clothing, shelter, and transportation. Second, continuity of roles and activities is seen as an effective way to maintain one's capacity to meet socioemotional needs for interaction and support. Third, continuity of independence and personal effectiveness is seen as the best way to maintain one's self-esteem.

A second major focus of adaptation in later life is to allow a gradual shift in life purpose. As people grow older, many find that achievement, social position, and acquisition of wealth or property are no longer their most important life goals. Instead they want to concentrate their attention on personal qualities such as dependability, reliability, self-reliance, or having good relationships with their families.

Specific Adaptations

In this section we look at how older people typically adapt to specific changes. We consider how people adjust to reduced financial resources, increased physical dependency, lost roles and activities, declining independence and personal effectiveness, and new life goals.

Adapting to Less Income

The major way that older people adapt to reduced financial resources is learning to make do with less. Certainly a large part of the adjustment to reduced income in retirement is made easier by the fact that employment expenses such as transportation or special clothing are no longer required. However, economizing is still necessary for most retired couples to make ends meet, which the vast majority do. Single retired people often face a very difficult financial situation, since retirement income for single individuals averages only about 40 percent of preretirement income (see Chapter 8).

Relatively little research has been done on how people cope specifically with reduced incomes. Douglass (1982) studied the impact of the rapid rise in fuel costs for home heating on the elderly living in Michigan. He found that 40 percent cut down on their expenditures for food and another 16 percent did without needed medical care in order to pay their fuel bills. The elderly often have no frills in their budgets that can be cut out in order to deal with unanticipated expenses, so they must dip into the more flexible items in their budget—food and medical care.

Many of us live well above what we actually need in order to enjoy satisfying lives. In this respect, retired people can offer the rest of us an example of how to get by on less without sacrificing the enjoyment of living. We need more research on the *processes* people go through in making this adaptation.

Adapting to Increased Dependency

Coping with increased physical infirmity and disability cannot be an easy matter for adults who have not only been responsible for themselves but for others as well. A major task is to learn how to accept assistance from others without losing one's self-respect. We know that many older people learn to do so, but very little study has been made of *how* they learn. Lieberman (1975) suggested that people who are able to adjust well to increased dependency need two things. They need sufficient physical and mental resources to mobilize the energy used to adapt, and they need to be tough-minded and stubborn about their own worth. For example, the "nice" older people who moved into institutions did not fare nearly so well as those who were aggressive, irritating, narcissistic, and demanding (Lieberman, 1975). In other words, it may take a big ego to accept assistance effectively. Certainly it must take a sturdy one. Fortunately, as noted earlier, most older people have high self-esteem.

Adapting to Lost Roles or Activities

Gerontologists have paid more attention to the problem of adapting to the loss of roles and activities than they have to the preceding topics. When people lose activities or roles, they can react in three possible ways. They can replace the losses with new roles or activities, they can concentrate their energies on the roles and activities that remain, or they can withdraw. These approaches are called **substitution, consolidation,** and **disengagement,** respectively.

Substitution

When people lose certain roles or the capacity to perform certain activities, an obvious way to adapt is to find a substitute (Friedmann and Havighurst, 1954; Havighurst, 1963).* How feasible this avenue is depends on a number of factors. First, substitutes must be available. Second, the person must have the physical and mental capacity to perform a substitute role or

---

*This approach is often called "activity theory" because it implies that older people want to maintain high levels of activity.

activity effectively. Finally, the person must *want* a substitute.

Substitutes are often not readily available. Retired people often cannot easily find new jobs; widows cannot easily find new mates. If roles or activities are lost through income decline or physical decline, then substitution is not a readily available strategy. And to the extent that the person has been too active, he or she may not want to look for a replacement for lost activity. Thus, although substitution may be a feasible and attractive way to cope with loss early in life, with age it becomes increasingly more difficult to put into practice. Nevertheless, activity levels of the elderly remain quite high as long as they are not disabled.

Consolidation

Consolidation of commitments and redistribution of available energy is another way to cope with lost roles, activities, or capacities. People who are involved in several roles and a variety of activities may not need to find a substitute for lost roles. They may find it easier simply to redistribute their time and energies among their remaining roles and activities. The general level of activity that results from this redistribution may be on a par with the preloss level, or may be somewhat reduced. For example, retirement commonly involves role loss that for most people can be compensated for through consolidation. When Mr. A retired, the time he spent on the job became available for other activities. He now sleeps about an hour longer than he did when he was employed and he spends more time reading the morning paper. In good weather, the rest of his morning is spent puttering around the yard. He fixes lunch—usually a sandwich and a beer, and then straightens up the house. Around 3 P.M. he walks to a nearby cafe, has coffee, and talks with friends, some retired and some not. Around 4:30, Mr. A goes home and starts supper. He has always like cooking, and since he retired he has more or less taken over the job of preparing evening meals for himself and his wife, who still works.

Nothing in Mr. A's day is new to him. What has changed is how he distributes the time and energy he devotes to activities he has done most of his adult life. As a result, Mr. A's home is in the best condition ever, Mrs. A is delighted to have less housework to do, and Mr. A is proud of the good adjustment he has made to retirement.

The consolidation approach is available to most people. However, some people have so few roles or activities that when they lose some of them, there are not enough remaining to absorb the energies freed by the loss. Unless they can find a substitute, these people are forced to disengage. Consolidation also may not be a satisfactory solution if the lost activity was extremely important to the person and if the remaining activities, though perhaps plentiful, are not meaningful.

Disengagement

Disengagement occurs when people withdraw from roles or activities and reduce their activity level or sense of involvement. Based on their work in Kansas City in the 1950s, Cumming and Henry (1961) theorized that the turning inward typical of aging people produces a natural and normal withdrawal from social roles and activities, an increasing preoccupation with self, and decreasing involvement with others. Individual disengagement was conceived as primarily a psychological process involving withdrawal of interest and commitment. Social withdrawal was a consequence of individual disengagement, coupled with society's withdrawal of opportunities and interest in older people's contributions (societal disengagement).

Disengagement theory caused a flurry of research because, in positing the "normality" of withdrawal, it challenged the conventional wisdom that keeping active was the best way to deal with aging. Now, after 20 years of research, it is clear that disengagement is neither natural nor inevitable and that most cases of disengagement result from a lack of opportunities for continued involvement (Atchley,

1971b; Roman and Taietz, 1967; Carp, 1968b).

Streib and Schneider (1971) suggested that **differential disengagement** was more likely than total disengagement. That is, people may withdraw from some activities but increase or maintain their involvement in others. Differential disengagement is similar to the consolidation approach mentioned earlier. Troll (1971) supported this notion when she talked of disengagement *into* the family, meaning that older people cope with lost roles by increasing their involvement with their families.

Disengagement theory went astray at many points (Hochschild, 1975). Because it was based on observations of older people in the 1950s, it dealt with people who typically were trying to adapt to a much more adverse situation than that since 1965, particularly in terms of retirement income and public attitudes toward the aged. Perhaps more people did disengage in those days, but it is certain that they do not do so now. However, the results that Cumming and Henry (1961) attributed to a voluntary process of psychological disengagement could have been the unconscious results of habituation and continuity. Remember, someone that is habituated pays relatively little attention. This inattentiveness could resemble disengagement. Also, when people are threatened, their motivation for continuity increases, which in turn means that they restrict their activities to those areas where habituation is likely to be the highest. The fact that relatively few people appear to be disengaged today as compared to the 1950s may thus be the result of improved living conditions and attitudes toward the elderly, which in turn may have reduced the threat perceived by the elderly. If this hypothesis is true, then whenever living conditions for the elderly worsen, we would expect a larger percentage of them to appear withdrawn and stagnant.

Implications

None of the preceding approaches to coping with lost roles and activities is by itself a successful model. People can be found who fit each approach. The real question is "What proportion of people fit which model?" Right now the consolidation approach seems to be the most inclusive, partly because it allows the greatest flexibility. The balance among the three outcomes that role or activity loss can have depends partly on social conditions. Opportunities to replace lost roles and activities determine the availability of substitution. Norms about what is acceptable or proper for older people affect what friends and relatives advise in coping with role loss. Consolidation may be the most common outcome because it preserves continuity both for the individual and for those around him or her. Clark and Anderson (1967) refer to it as the "path of least resistance." The extent of disengagement may depend very much on how threatened by their environment older people feel. Finally, the balance among consolidation, substitution, and disengagement depends very heavily on health. Good health is a prerequisite for the consolidation and substitution approaches to coping with role and activity losses. People in poor health are much more likely to be forced into disengagement.

Coping with Threats to Self-Concept and Self-Esteem

Declining independence and increasing vulnerability threaten older people's self-concepts. The major ways that they can cope with these threats are to use defense mechanisms (covered in Chapter 5), to develop an acceptance of themselves as aging people, and to emphasize their maintained competence.

Older people can use the past to sustain an image of themselves as worthwhile. This is easier to do in a group of friends or in a community of long-time residents because the people the older person interacts with tend to share the older person's view of the past and may well have participated in the older person's life history. When we interact with older people we do not know, we must keep in mind that their talking about their past is their way of telling us the basis for their self-esteem.

People who are becoming less independent are most likely to use the past in this way, and they are also most likely to have to deal with service providers who are essentially strangers. This fact no doubt has added to the stereotype that "older people live in the past." For example, the superintendent of one country home for the aged included this statement in the brochure for the home. His experience with older people coming into an institution for older people who were financially but not physically dependent had convinced him that the stereotype was true of all older people.

By comparing themselves with other older people who are worse off, people can minimize the importance of their dependencies. Selective interaction and selective perception allow people to concentrate their attention on people and messages that support their own view of themselves and to avoid those that do not. But these defenses gradually lose their power as the person becomes more and more dependent. At the point where the person becomes bedfast either at home or in an institution, he or she loses the control necessary for defenses such as selective interaction. And the shift in power that accompanies severe dependency means that the older person can no longer influence people to accept relative appreciation or past accomplishments as valid bases for his or her self-concept. This shift explains why the behavior of older people in institutions often appears strange. They are among strangers and in a situation in which their self-concepts are severely threatened, while they have few resources for defending them. As a result they may be combative, apprehensive, untrusting, and anxious.

Many young people do not understand why some older people get angry when younger people try to help them. They are angry because they believe their image of self-sufficiency is being threatened. Older people revere self-reliance. As a result, they try to do things for themselves as long as possible and to resist letting anyone know that sometimes they just cannot. This is why many older people gradually and knowingly let their homes deteriorate.

They do not want people coming in and realizing how helpless they are at times.

It is most important for older people to have some way to maintain a sense of competence. We need to work with them to see how *they* would like to accomplish this goal, and we should be as flexible as possible in accommodating their preferences. It's okay if their views are somewhat unrealistic as long as behavior that endangers themselves or others is not the result. Nevertheless, learning to accept a definition of competence appropriate to their age is also useful. At some point it is adaptive for the older person to acknowledge that certain activities can no longer be done as successfully as when he or she was younger. This recognition is an important prerequisite for the person's conservation of energy. It is also important for the elderly to recognize that social norms impose very real limits on what one is allowed to do as an older person. One need not *like* these limits, only accept their reality. Clark and Anderson (1967) found that people tended to try denying aging and its effects in two ways. The first is by trying to avoid looking old through the use of cosmetics, hair dyes, figure control devices, and so on. Second, people sought to deny aging by attributing their limitations to sickness rather than aging.

Some people seek to deny aging by refusing to go along with rules that exclude them from participation and by fighting the system. In itself, this strategy is not bad if the person is indeed still capable. However, it is maladaptive when the individual's level of functioning means that continuation is not a real possibility. For example, Mr. G had played in the Thursday afternoon men's golf league for over 20 years, and at age 68 he was very proud that he was still capable of playing. But by age 70 Mr. G was no longer able to keep up with the other players. When the league secretary asked him to drop out and allow a substitute to play for him, Mr. G. refused. He spoke heatedly with individual league members about the unfairness of the request but got little support, since most of the players agreed with the league secretary. By

refusing to withdraw, Mr. G forced the league to exclude him formally. In the process, Mr. G probably became more depressed than if he had made the decision himself.

In addition to accepting changes in their concept of activities and roles that are appropriate to the self, it is also useful for older people to accept changes in the criteria used to evaluate the self and that serve as the basis for self-esteem. Regardless of older people's capacities to continue in positions of leadership and to further their achievements, societal disengagement and age discrimination combine to make continuation an unrealistic goal for many older people. Moving toward less emphasis on position and achievement as personal goals is typical of older people, and thus most people seem to accomplish this adaptive change.

But there is probably no easy way to help those older people who resist being realistic about either their capacities or their opportunities. A certain amount of realism is necessary for adaptation, and almost the only thing one can do is to tell the truth in as kind a way as possible. It is also essential to be sure that the limits one is trying to get an older person to accept are indeed genuine and not based on one's own age biases.

Most people can adapt to changes without losing their self-esteem because most have never become so disabled that they lose their sense of continuity. Even among people in institutions a sizable proportion are able to maintain a sense of continuity with their pasts. But people—both in the community and in institutions—who perceive that changes in themselves or in their social situations have produced a negative discontinuity are likely to feel bad about themselves and to be depressed. Some try to escape their situation through isolation, alcohol, drugs or even suicide.

Escape Rather than Adaptation

Why do some people confront and resolve the conflicts posed by aging while others choose various forms of escape? Based on bits and pieces of information on various forms of escape, a picture begins to emerge: People who encounter many losses are prone to seek escape. Although social supports from the community, family and friends often can lead the person out of escapism, some people perceive their losses as too great to be coped with. Others see the available "solutions" as intolerable compromise. For these people, escape is a preferred alternative.

We should not assume that escape is always an irrational choice. For some people, it is the most viable alternative given their values. Some people are able to satisfy their need for escape through withdrawal, alcohol, tranquilizers, or some combination of the three. For others, the pain is too great, and they eventually choose suicide.

Isolation

Bennett (1980) reviewed 20 years of research on social isolation in the elderly and found that isolation in later life was connected to the past. Many aged isolates had been isolates their entire adult lives. Others had been outgoing earlier and had only become isolates in later life. Some were voluntary isolates, and others became isolates as a result of changing circumstances, such as widowhood.

Those who use isolation as an adaptive strategy tend to have the freedom to withdraw from interactions and roles they define as unsatisfactory. Retirement, widowhood, and divorce are examples of changes that can free people to choose isolation. Lowenthal and Berkman (1967) found that mental illness tended to lead to social isolation, leading us to expect that people who have difficulty in getting along with others (one symptom of mental illness) would be more likely to withdraw in later life, particularly in reaction to conflicts over their own self-concepts.

Bennett (1980) found that social isolation prior to moving to an institution was associated with difficulty in adjusting to the institution.

She concluded that this difficulty was the result of "desocialization," in which the individuals forgot what they had learned earlier in life about conformity to norms and how to get on with others. However, another possible interpretation is that those people chose isolation because they were already having difficulty conforming and getting along with others. In the Scripps Foundation longitudinal study of adaptation, Atchley (1982b) found that less than 1 percent of older respondents were voluntary isolates who had chosen low levels of social activity. This finding suggests that isolation is a seldom-used adaptive strategy.

Alcohol

Zimberg (1974) reviewed the literature on alcohol use in later life and concluded that about 15 percent of the elderly have serious alcohol problems with a proportion as high as 40 percent in some urban neighborhoods. Mishara and Kastenbaum (1980) put the figure somewhat lower, 8 percent for older men and only about 1 percent for older women. The elderly are less likely to have alcohol problems than are younger age categories. For example, the incidence of problem drinking is twice as high among men age 21 to 39 as among those 60 and over.

Zimberg (1974) found that there were two types of older alcoholics—long-term alcoholics who had grown older and people who had become alcoholics in later life. As yet no reliable estimates exist of what proportion of older people have turned to alcohol in later life, although we know that some do. People who become problem drinkers in later life are usually responding to depression and boredom, which are often associated with life changes such as widowhood or physical decline (Butler and Lewis, 1973).

Drugs

Anxiety sometimes accompanies the changes that aging brings, physicians often prescribe tranquilizers to alleviate these anxieties. In one study, tranquilizers accounted for 35 to 40 percent of the medication prescribed for older Medicaid patients in Illinois, Ohio, and New Jersey (Butler and Lewis, 1973:249). Of the top 20 drugs commonly prescribed for older adults, 12 are tranquilizers. Tranquilizers such as Librium can be addictive, that is, emotional dependence develops and physical withdrawal symptoms can occur if the drug is withheld.

Suicide

Suicide is a disturbing and fascinating subject for most of us. We have a deep-seated drive to learn why suicides occur, why some people purposefully reject what most of us value highest—life itself. Suicide is related to age for men, but not for women.* Suicide rates increase steadily from age 15 to age 85 for men, with around 60 suicides per 100,000 men at age 85 and over (Atchley, 1980). Most of the literature on the subject starts by assuming that suicide is more common among the elderly and then proceeds to speculate about why age is related to suicide. Bereavement, social isolation, failing health, depression, sexual frustrations, and retirement have all been suggested as causes of suicide in the elderly. However, these factors are usually more common among women than among men, so we cannot use them to explain suicides, since male suicide rates at the older ages are seven times higher than those for women. Many of the proposed explanations look good on the surface but do not stand up under close examination. For example, it is widely held that suicide is related to retirement. However, if we look at the suicide data we find that from age 55 to 70—the prime years for retirement to occur—there is relatively little change in the

suicide rate and that after age 70 the suicide rate increases sharply. Although some people no doubt commit suicide as a result of retirement, if retirement-related suicide were a systematic trend, such a trend would appear in the suicide data.

Menninger (1938) proposed a classification of suicide motives into the wish to kill, the wish to be killed, and the wish to die. Analysis of suicide notes indicates that the elderly are much more likely than other age groups to see suicide as a release. Their motive is simply to be dead. The individual reasons for this choice are many, and no single or simple explanation can encompass the wide variety of situations that lead to suicide. Nevertheless, certain groups of the elderly are at high risk. For example, very old men who have recently been widowed, who have recently been given a terminal diagnosis by a physician, or who have experienced rapid physical deterioration are all at high risk. Older people in institutions are high risks for suicide, especially if they receive no visitors. Older people who are severely depressed are at a higher risk. Miller (1978) reported that in many cases older people gave clear signals that they were intending to kill themselves, but they were ignored. Generally, when older people suggest that they might kill themselves, they mean it. And when older people attempt suicide, they usually succeed. To stop elderly suicides, we have to prevent the attempt.

In addition to active suicide, some older people die because they have given up. Failing to continue treatment for illnesses such as heart disease or diabetes, engaging in detrimental or dangerous activities, or neglecting one's health are all indirect ways to kill oneself. No one knows how many older people die as a result of such actions.

Successful Adaptation

How do we know that a person has successfully coped with aging? Whereas earlier we were concerned with the various means of adapting, here

---

*While age is correlated with suicide for men in all countries for which the cause of death statistics are reliable, for women the picture is mixed. For example, in German-speaking countries, women's suicide rates tend to be highly correlated with age, but in English-speaking countries they are not (Atchley, 1980).

we are concerned with the *outcome* of the adaptive process. The internal adaptive process is successful if the person has a high degree of life satisfaction and if the person is able to remain relatively autonomous at least psychologically and able to maintain his or her sense of continuity. External adaptation is successful if the individual continues to receive rewards for participation.

If older people are satisfied with their present and past lives, they have adapted to aging. Havighurst et al. (1963) identified five components of *life satisfaction:*

1. *Zest*—showing vitality in several areas of life, being enthusiastic

2. *Resolution and fortitude*—not giving up, taking the good with the bad and making the most of it, accepting responsibility for one's own personal life

3. *Completion*—a feeling of having accomplished what one wanted to

4. *Self-esteem*—thinking of oneself as a person of worth

5. *Outlook*—being optimistic, having hope

The scale they developed to measure these components of life satisfaction has been used in hundreds of studies. The results indicate that a majority of the elderly have high life satisfaction; that is, on this very general criterion a majority has successfully adapted to aging. Harris and Associates (1975:161) found that when income was controlled, life satisfaction of the elderly was equal to or greater than that of younger age categories.

Autonomy is the perception that one is responsible for one's own life satisfaction. *Continuity* is the persistence of one's views of self and environment. These topics have been researched less than has life satisfaction. Williams and Wirths (1965) reported that 65 percent of their sample had successfully adapted to aging. In the Scripps Foundation longitudinal study of adaptation, Atchley (1982b) found that about 55 percent of the elderly saw themselves as highly autonomous, and nearly 90 percent saw their lives

as extensions of their pasts. These were relatively healthy older people who lived in a community setting. Lieberman (1975) reported that failure to preserve a sense of continuity occurred in about half of their subjects who moved to institutions. Thus, those who remain in community settings are much more likely to adapt successfully, compared to those who enter institutions.

External adaptation involves adjusting to aging so as to maintain participation in social life and to continue to receive the rewards it brings. Most older people adapt well in terms of maintaining informal social ties, but are generally unsuccessful in retaining formal ties, as as result of age discrimination. Thus, given sufficient instrumental resources, the vast majority of the elderly cope well with aging both internally and in their informal relationships. At this point, let us look at a case of successful adaptation to aging.

A Case of Successful Adaptation

Clark and Anderson (1967) cite the following interesting case history of a person who had aged successfully.

We first saw Mr. Ed Hart when he was 90 years old. He was born in 1870, the only child of middle-aged parents. He started working and contributing significantly to the household budget at a very early age; while still in his teens, he turned over his considerable savings to his parents, enabling them to purchase a home. Still in his youth, he assumed a "parental" role toward his parents, being obliged to do so because much of his father's time was spent taking care of the then invalid mother. Mr. Hart attended school, learned cabinet making from his father, and devoted himself to caring for this parents.

Mr. Hart idolized his father throughout his life. Cabinet work was always dear to him because it had been taught him by his father. He regarded his father's guidance as invaluable; it was he who kept his own son away from the alcohol which he dearly loved, and it was also from his father that he acquired a sincere love for people. The relationship was a very harmonious one, each gladly accommodating himself to the wishes of the other. Although Mr. Hart married at the age of 24, he and his wife continued to live with his parents until their death in 1912. Mr. Hart was closely attached to his wife, but his father had always remained the most important figure in his life.

He was content with cabinet work until the age of 35, at which time he bought a ranch, deciding to become a financial success for the sake of his children. He describes himself during this period as overambitious and given to excessive chronic worry. His preoccupation with making a fortune from this ranching endeavor led to a nervous breakdown and confinement in a sanitarium for two months. This experience, when he was about 40, proved to be the turning point of his life. He emerged with a highly integrated personality and a satisfying personal philosophy. He had formerly been a zealous member of the Methodist Church, but following his hospitalization, he eschewed all organized religions, feeling he needed no one to dictate to him how he should serve God. Nonetheless, Mr. Hart expresses a profound belief in divinity, a love of his fellow man, a full acceptance of everything life has to offer, and an adamant refusal to be unhappy.

Following this hospitalization, Mr. Hart sold his ranch and worked as a vocational teacher for the following six years. Again, he found deep satisfaction in his work and was loved by students and fellow teachers alike. He showed great understanding and evidently displayed remarkable skill in nurturing the talents of his students, adapting his teaching to the individual child's potential. His dislike for the regimentation practiced in the school led him to resign and to return to his former vocation of cabinet making, work he pursued up to the age of 55. An injury to his arm, however, finally made him give up this successful occupation (some of his work had been exhibited at the 1939 San Francisco International Exposition). For the next 20 years, he was employed in the hotel business, work that he found congenial because of his interest in people. Retirement did not find him idle. Up to the age of 90, he did cabinet work as a hobby, manufacturing various items to present to his numerous friends.

Mr. Hart looks back on 64 years of harmonious and contented married life. His first wife died suddenly after 25 years of marriage when he was 49 years old. After living alone with his children for two years, he remarried at the age of 51. Thirty years later, he lost his second wife, and it was upon her "last request" that he again married. His third wife had been a widowed friend they had both known for almost 30 years. This final marriage lasted for nine years. During the last two years of her life, the third wife was severely ill, and Mr. Hart nursed her through to the end. She died in 1960. Even during his last wife's terminal illness, Mr. Hart showed the same serenity and the same positive acceptance of life he expressed in all of our interviews with him. He does not differentiate among his wives: he describes them all as "dear, loyal women."

Mr. Hart finds it somewhat "humiliating" that he has outlived three wives and both of his sons. He took pains to raise his children as best he could and was anxious to let them develop their own individual ways. Rather than seeing himself as the provider of an estate, a role he had once thought so important, he finally perceived his parental role as that of the provider of good example and wise guidance. His close relationship with his sons changed when they married, and Mr. Hart believes that it is only right that this should be so: "With marriage the offspring form independent units of their own, and parents should release their hold upon them." Mr. Hart was never possessive in his life. The persons closest to him at present are his daughter and stepdaughter, who are equally dear. He mentions with pride that both have invited him to come and live with them, but he will not take this step until it is absolutely necessary. He does not wish to inconvenience them, but unlike many other of our subjects, he does not harp on the prospect of "becoming a burden" to somebody else.

From his middle years onward, Mr. Hart suffered a number of major illnesses: in 1926 he was operated on for a bilateral hernia; and in 1949, for a perforated ulcer; finally, a prostatectomy and colostomy in 1953 (he was 83 years old at the time) resulted in a complete loss of control over his bladder, requiring him to wear a urinal 24 hours a day. When he was 90, his physical condition no longer permitted him to indulge in his hobby of woodworking, and, at 93 his failing eyesight ruled out television and limited his reading to one hour a day. Yet he takes his declining physical functions in stride, not finding it irksome to make necessary adjustments. His mental facilities have remained remarkably intact. He is keenly aware that few men his age are as mentally alert as he is, or have aged as gracefully. He is proud of this fact and attributes it to the philosophical orientation he has worked out for himself and incorporated into his life.

Although Mr. Hart has been obliged to curtail many of his social activities, he still corresponds with numerous friends and receives almost daily visits from solicitous neighbors. He gives much of himself and is warmly appreciated by others; he appears to bring out the best in others, which may be one of the reasons he claims he has never been disappointed by a friend. Mr. Hart has led a full, creative, and serene existence. It is perhaps because his life has been one of fulfillment that he is ready to surrender it at any moment; he still finds life quite enjoyable, but he is as willing to die as he is to continue living.

This man has made a profound impression on all our interviewers. They found him alert, intelligent, serene, and wise. His self-acceptance is complete. He found it difficult to answer our self-image questions or to describe himself in terms of the list of various personality traits we submitted to him; he simply stated, more appropriately, "I'm Ed Hart and I dont want to be anyone else— I will be the same ten years from now, if I'm alive."

According to American middle-class standards, Mr. Hart has not been a particularly successful man. Looking at his life in one way, he has no particular reason not to be disappointed with his past and depressed with his present. He failed in his one great effort to become wealthy. After a nervous breakdown, he gave up on this venture altogether. He quit a second time when he dropped out of the teaching profession because he disagreed with established policy. One might expect him to be bitter about this, or terribly lonely, since he has outlived nearly all his friends and relatives—but he is neither. Crippled with disease, forced to wear a urinal at all times, and nearly blind, Mr. Hart gave one of our interviewers his philosophy of life: "I have an original motto which I follow: 'All things respond to the call of rejoicing; all things gather where life is a song.' "

It is clear that Mr. Hart has adapted to aging. He has admitted to and accepted physical limitations, first giving up the demanding manual labor of cabinet making, and later retiring without regret from hotel work.

Mr. Hart has no problems in controlling his life space—he does not overextend himself: "As long as I don't strain myself, I'm okay. I take it easy. The other day I declined an invitation to go on board a ship, since I knew there would be stairs there."

All his life, Mr. Hart has successfully practiced substitution, so this adaptation has been natural for him. He enjoyed married life and never remained a widower for long. He was capable of substituting one vocation for another, as necessity required, developing a deep interest and satisfaction in each. Even after his retirement from hotel work, his last job, he continued to be interested and active in union affairs. "That's my pork chop, so to speak," he says.

In personal philosophy, Mr. Hart has no problems at all. His standards for self-evaluation are not predicated on mutable factors such as productivity, wealth, or social status. He is first, last, and always himself: "I'm Ed Hart and I don't want to be anyone else." This is a standard not likely to totter with age.

However, his discovery of adaptive values and life goals was hard-won: at 40, he early found himself unable to cope with the instrumental and achievement-oriented values of his society. He suffered a severe emotional upheaval at that time, was hospitalized for a period, and emerged with a warm humanistic philosophy which has carried him not only through middle age, but through old age as well. (Clark and Anderson, 1967:415–419, reprinted by permission).

Summary

Adaptation is both an internal and external process. Internally, it involves the assimilation of new information about changes in the self and in the environment. Externally, it involves the modification of behavior to accommodate changing demands of the social world. The internal and external aspects of adaptation interact.

Habituation, continuity, and conflict management are three general means of adaptation. Habituation involves learning not to pay attention to nonessential aspects of the environment. Optimum habituation occurs when the individual has the skill to ignore trivial changes but to pay attention to changes that require conscious action in order to adapt. The lack of attention to the environment that is found in some older people may be overhabituation rather than disengagement.

Maintaining continuity of personal viewpoints and familiar associations and environments is an adaptive response to both internal and external pressures. Internal pressures for continuity come from the need to make new information consistent with the old. The older the individual, the greater the backlog of information with which new information must be reconciled, and the greater the likelihood of continuity. Individuals who feel threatened by change feel more pressure to stick with tried and true ways of doing things than others do. External pressures for continuity are exerted by the conditioning we receive from our environments and by the demands of the roles we play. The more consistent the individual's environments and the greater the number and familiarity of the person's relationships with others, the greater the external pressures for continuity. Aging can bring a greater perception of threat, usually brings a large backlog of experience, and increases the duration of residence in a given environment and participation in a given set of relationships. Therefore aging very greatly increases the pressure for continuity as an adaptive strategy. Continuity is also a means for maintaining the capacity to meet instrumental needs, needs for interaction and support, and needs for sources of self-esteem.

Conflict management involves transforming negative energy associated with conflict into a more positive form. Altruism, humor, sublimation, anticipation, and suppression are adaptive mechanisms that can be used to manage conflict. Less effective means include repression, rigidity, overreaction, and self-hatred. People usually develop a habitual pattern of coping with what for them is a normal amount of conflict. Aging can increase the amount of conflict. As the amount of conflict increases above the "normal" level for the individual, the probability also increases that less effective means will be used to handle it.

Specific adaptations to aging include learning to live on a lower income, learning to accept help from others without losing one's self-respect, coping with lost roles and activities, and coping with threats to self-esteem. We don't know very much about how people adjust to lowered incomes. As long as the reduction is less than 50 percent, most people seem to be able to adjust somehow. But when the reduction is greater, financial dependency is likely to result. Older people cope with unexpected demands on their incomes by cutting down on food and needed medical care.

Physical energy and solid self-concepts help people adjust to needing assistance from others. Most older people have both. Nevertheless, because of the high value most people place on self-reliance, there is great potential for both internal and external conflict for older people who must rely on others for financial or physical assistance.

Most older people cope with role losses by redirecting their time and attention within the roles and activities that remain. Those who are younger, healthier, and more financially secure are more likely to be able to substitute for lost roles and activities. Disengagement, which is not very common, is usually imposed by age discrimination or ill health rather than being a voluntary choice.

Threats to self-esteem are dealt with through selective interaction, selective perception, use of the past, and relative appreciation. Sometimes they are dealt with by increasing isolation. To maintain a sense of competence in later life, it is also useful for the aging person to develop a self-concept that incorporates real changes in both capacities and opportunities. By revising the ideal self, people can maintain self-esteem.

Most older people are able to maintain a sense of continuity and meaning throughout later life. But a few experience changes so great that, rather than try to adapt, they try to escape through isolation, drugs, alcohol, or suicide. Less than 1 percent of the elderly apparently become isolates in an attempt to escape from the realities of their situation. Many more turn to alcohol. As much as 10 percent of the elderly have drinking problems, although we do not know what percentage have turned to alcohol only in later life and how many for whom alcohol abuse represents the continuation of a lifelong pattern. Perhaps 10 percent of the elderly are also taking tranquilizers routinely and are essentially addicted to them. Many of these people also have problems with alcohol abuse.

Suicide is not very common, but men over age 70 are much more likely to commit suicide than any other age-sex category in the United States. Factors that expose older people to high suicide risk include severe depression, recent bereavement, terminal diagnosis for a physical ailment, rapid physical deterioration, and living in an institution and having no visitors. Other factors such as retirement are occasionally associated with suicide, but not often enough to represent a trend.

Family and community supports are often successful in helping older people to abandon escapism. But in the case of signals of an impending suicide, it is important to act quickly. When older people mention suicide, they are often serious, and if they attempt suicide they usually succeed on the first try.

Success of adaptation to aging can be measured through self-ratings of life satisfaction and a sense of autonomy and continuity. Well over half of the elderly (about 60 percent) have adapted to aging quite well by these criteria, and perhaps another 25 percent could be said to have adapted adequately. The overall adaptation of the elderly is not much lower than the level for people under 55. Older people also adapt well in terms of maintaining their participation in social life. Only age discrimination and disability seem to thwart the adaptive attempts of a majority of those who experience them. Given sufficient health and instrumental resources, the elderly are quite able to adapt to aging. The "problems" they encounter are more often social in origin than due simply to personal aging.

PART V

Aging and Society

In contrast to Parts II through IV, Part V focuses on society at large and its institutions rather than on aging individuals. It begins with general social ideas about aging and how they become translated into age discrimination and societal disengagement. It then considers various ways that social inequalities affect aging and the aged. Next, it discusses deviance among the elderly and how society seeks to control it, followed by a discussion of older people as the ob-

ject of crime, exploitation, and neglect and abuse. Then it looks at the economy as it affects and is affected by the elderly, followed by a consideration of how the aged fit into politics and are treated by government. Part V concludes with a chapter on health and human services. As we shall see, most of the problems of the elderly stem not from the effects of individual aging but from inadequacies in our social institutions.

Chapter 13

General Social Responses to Aging

Culture is the way of life of a people that is handed down from generation to generation. Culture influences people's language and thought, their habitual ways of meeting their needs, and their physical and social environments. Culture provides the *context* within which life at a particular time and place is led. In this chapter we will be looking at the cultural context as it affects aging in the United States. We will look first at ideas about aging and the aged: values, beliefs, and attitudes. We will then consider how aging and the aged are portrayed by education and by the media. Finally, we will examine the extent to which these cultural forces are translated into two negative social forces: age discrimination *toward* older people and disengagement *from* older people.

Ideas About Aging

Culture consists mainly of *ideas* and their manifestations. These cultural ideas include values, beliefs, norms, and stereotypes. *Values* tell us the relative desirability of various goals, *beliefs* tell us the nature of the reality in which these values are pursued, and *norms* tell us what we can or cannot do in the process. *Stereotypes* are generalizations about the characteristics of a group or category of people. Stereotypes try to tell us what kind of people we are dealing with in situations where we must interact with strangers.

Values

One key cultural issue concerns how aging fits into the general values of a society. Rokeach (1973) has done what is perhaps the most comprehensive work on personal values in American society. Rokeach's approach recognizes that values concern not only the desirability of various outcomes or goals, but the means for achieving them as well. Accordingly, he developed two scales, one that asked people to rank various *outcomes* and another that asked people to rank various personal *instrumental qualities* in terms of their importance as guiding principles in their lives. Tables 13-1 and 13-2 show the results from a probability sample of 665 men and 744 women age 21 or over in 1968. Despite the common notion that men and women are socialized to have different values, there is a great deal of overlap between men and women both at the top and at the bottom of the value hierarchies for both outcome values and instrumental quality values. For both men and women, peace, family security, freedom, happiness, and self-respect were the most desired outcomes, and social recognition, pleasure, and an exciting life the least desired. In pursuing these outcomes, honesty, ambition, responsibility, broad-mindedness, courage, and forgivingness were the most desirable personal qualities, while being logical, intellectual, obedient, and imaginative were valued least.

Does aging pose a threat to any of these personal values? Maybe. Individuals who value family security, freedom of choice, and contentment may believe these outcomes to be threatened by their own aging, the aging of family members, or the aging of society in general. Their own aging may threaten family security, freedom, and happiness by reducing their economic resources or by reducing their level of physical self-sufficiency. These values also may be threatened if elderly family members are forced to become dependent. And to the extent that taxes go up as a result of demands for increased services to the elderly, the reduced income that results may be seen as a threat to family security, freedom, and happiness. The fact that aging can potentially affect highly desired values in several different ways no doubt contributes to a general sense of uneasiness about aging. Even if we acknowledge that most people never become poor or highly dependent, that most families do not have to handle severe dependency of older members, and that American tax burdens are still quite low compared to

TABLE 13-1   Rank order of outcome values, by sex: United States, 1968

Rank	Men	Women
1	World at peace (free of war and conflict)	
2	Family security (taking care of loved ones)	
3	Freedom (independence, free choice)	
4	Comfortable life (prosperous life)	Salvation
5	Happiness (contentedness)	
6	Self-respect (self-esteem)	
7	Accomplishment (lasting contribution)	Wisdom
8	Wisdom (a mature understanding of life)	Equality
9	Equality (equal opportunity for all)	True friendship
10	National security (protection from attack)	Accomplishment
11	True friendship (close companionship)	National security
12	Salvation (saved, eternal life)	Inner harmony
13	Inner harmony (freedom from inner conflict)	Comfortable life
14	Mature love (sexual and spiritual intimacy)	
15	World of beauty (beauty of nature and of the arts)	
16	Social recognition (respect, admiration)	Pleasure
17	Pleasure (an enjoyable, leisurely life)	Social recognition
18	Exciting life (a stimulating, active life)	

Source: Adapted from Rokeach, 1973.

TABLE 13-2   Rank order for personal instrumental quality values, by sex: United States, 1968

Rank	Men	Women
1	Honest (sincere, truthful)	
2	Ambitious (hard-working, aspiring)	Forgiving
3	Responsible (dependable, reliable)	
4	Broad-minded (open-minded)	Ambitious
5	Courageous (standing up for your beliefs)	Broad-minded
6	Forgiving (willing to pardon others)	Courageous
7	Helpful (working for others' welfare)	
8	Capable (competent, effective)	Clean
9	Clean (neat, tidy)	Loving
10	Self-controlled (restrained, self-disciplined)	Cheerful
11	Independent (self-reliant, self-sufficient)	Self-controlled
12	Cheerful (light-hearted, joyful)	Capable
13	Polite (courteous, well-mannered)	
14	Loving (affectionate, tender)	Independent
15	Intellectual (intelligent, reflective)	Obedient
16	Logical (consistent, rational)	Intellectual
17	Obedient (dutiful, respectful)	Logical
18	Imaginative (daring, creative)	

Source: Adapted from Rokeach, 1973.

other industrial societies, the possibility of *negative* outcomes is bound to have an effect on how aging and the aged are viewed, and this effect is likely to be negative.

In addition to the values that individuals use as guiding principles, there are values that guide the operation of organizations. Growth of production and profits, efficiency, and conformity are examples. Aging is sometimes seen as a threat to these values as well. If aging reduces people's capacities for productivity and efficiency (which, by the way, it usually does not), then growth of production and profits (and in turn wages and benefits) would be jeopardized by an aging workforce.

Aging also seems to affect personal values. In his cross-sectional sample, Rokeach (1973) found that a comfortable life, true friendship, and being forgiving and cheerful were more important to older cohorts compared to younger ones (see Table 13-3). Accomplishment, wisdom, responsibility, happiness, and being loving were less important for older cohorts than for young cohorts. There were few age differences in the value of family security, self-respect, social recognition, honesty, ambition, and helpfulness. Equality of opportunity was more important to those in their twenties and those in their seventies than to those in between these two ages, perhaps because age discrimination operates at both ends of the adult age continuum. Likewise, independence is more salient to the young and old than to those in between because for those people it is more problematic.

If these age differences reflect the effects of social maturation and are not simply cohort differences in socialization, then aging brings shifts in values that are adaptive for older people. There is indeed some movement toward what Clark and Anderson (1967) call "secondary values," such as friendship and being forgiving, and away from values more amenable to

TABLE 13-3   Rank order of selected values, by age: United States, 1968

	Age				
	30–39	40–49	50–59	60–69	70 or Over
Outcome Values					
Family security	1	2	2	2	2
Comfortable life	12	8	11	6	6
Happiness	6	4	6	7	9
Self-respect	4	5	5	5	5
Wisdom	5	6	7	8	11
Accomplishment	8	9	9	11	12
Equality	7	10	12	13	7
True friendship	10	12	8	9	8
Social recognition	17	16	16	14	16
Pleasure	18	17	17	17	15
Instrumental Values					
Honest	1	1	1	1	1
Responsible	2	3	4	6	8
Ambitious	3	2	3	2	3
Helpful	7	7	7	7	5
Cheerful	13	12	9	8	9
Forgiving	5	4	5	3	2
Independent	11	13	14	13	11
Loving	9	11	11	14	14
Intellectual	15	15	15	16	16
Imaginative	18	18	18	18	18

Source: Adapted from Rokeach, 1973.

the market place, such as accomplishment and responsibility. However, what is striking is not the differences in values across age categories, but the similarities. The only values (out of Rokeach's 36) that showed large age differences were a comfortable life and wisdom (in the opposite direction from what one might expect). The others showed either modest age differences or none at all.

Beliefs and Stereotypes

Beliefs are assertions about what is true that are accepted as true. To believe that retirement causes illness means to accept this idea as being

true and to *act as if* it were true. *Stereotypes* are usually composites of several beliefs about a category of people such as middle-aged persons, widows, or the disabled. Some beliefs and stereotypes are essentially accurate descriptions of reality and others are not.* For example, the belief that aging adversely affects sight is correct, but the belief that aging adversely affects worker performance is not. *Whether or not beliefs or stereotypes are widely held has nothing to do with whether or not they are actually*

---

*Some writers use *stereotype* to refer only to inaccurate and disparaging composites of characteristics (Theodorson and Theodorson, 1969).

true. A main aim of this book has been to test widely held beliefs. More often than not our cultural beliefs about the causes and consequences of aging have turned out to be either substantially incorrect or so incorrect that they are misleading. For example, it is often said that suicide rates go up after age 65. This is true, but misleading. As we saw in Chapter 12, suicide rates start going up in young adulthood and the rate of increase actually slows down slightly from age 65 to age 75. Beliefs are used to make inferences or draw conclusions. To the extent that our beliefs are faulty, so too will be our conclusions. Thus, if we accept the implication that suicide rates do not begin to go up until age 65, then we may come to the faulty conclusion that retirement (which often occurs at age 65) may be the cause.

Harris and his associates (1975) compared what the general public *believed* were the most serious problems of older people with what older people actually experienced. Table 13-4 shows that the general public substantially overestimated the prevalence of problems such as poor health, inadequate income, loneliness, keeping busy, or poor housing. This perception of "most people over 65" as beset with numerous problems is a double-edged sword. On the one hand, it garners political support for programs serving older Americans, but on the other hand, it perpetuates the stereotype of later life as an unattractive life stage.

Tuckman and his associates developed a questionnaire that asked respondents to agree with various beliefs about old people (Tuckman and Lorge, 1958a, 1958b, 1956, 1953a, 1953b, 1953c; Tuckman and Lovell, 1957). Table 13-5 shows the beliefs that were agreed with by 60 percent or more of Tuckman and Lorge's respondents. These same results were found in several later studies. Note the variety of the items.

One reason beliefs are difficult to study is that beliefs tend to be *specific,* whereas values are often quite general. Also, some beliefs about older people are accurate, some are inaccurate, and some cannot be judged as accurate or inaccurate because research has not been done in these areas. Table 13-5 shows that the view of older people in the 1950s in the United States was as often positive as negative. And those beliefs that were negative were mostly inaccurate. Accurate negative beliefs tended to reflect the facts about physical aging.

TABLE 13-4   Beliefs about older people's problems versus their actual experiences

Problem	Percent of Older People Actually Experiencing the Problem	Percent of General Public that Attributed the Problem to "Most People Over 65"
Fear of crime	23	50
Poor health	21	51
Inadequate income	15	62
Loneliness	12	60
Not feeling needed	7	54
Keeping busy	6	37
Sparse job opportunities	5	45
Poor housing	4	35

Source: Adapted from Harris et al., 1975:31.

TABLE 13-5   Beliefs about older people

Accurate Beliefs
Older People:

are able to learn new things
have poor coordination
walk slowly
need glasses to read
are *not* unproductive
are useful to themselves and to others
do *not* become less intelligent
are able to concentrate
are set in their ways
do not die soon after retirement
are not bedridden much of the time
worry about their health

are *not* helpless
are *not* in their second childhood
have to be careful about their diet
are more interested in religion
are likely to have friends
can manage their own affairs
get love and affection from their children
do *not* feel neglected by their children
are interested in the opposite sex
are *not* a nuisance
worry about finances

Inaccurate Beliefs
Older People:

are conservative
like to doze in a rocking chair
are lonely
repeat themselves in conversation

are forgetful
usually live with their children
are frequently at loose ends

Other Beliefs (that may or may not be accurate)
Older People:

like to give advice
like to gossip
are very sensitive to noise
avoid going out in bad weather
are good to children
spoil their grandchildren
love life
would like to be young again
are *not* bossy
are *not* selfish

are *not* grouchy
are kind
respect tradition
like to be waited on
are *not* suspicious
do *not* meddle in other people's affairs
feel that young parents do not know how
   to bring up children properly
do *not* prefer to live alone

Source: Adapted from Tuckman and Lorge, 1953a.

Axelrod and Eisdorfer (1961) used the Tuckman and Lorge questionnaire to see if results varied when specific ages were used rather than simply relating the belief statements to "old people." Table 13-6 shows some of their results. Generally the level of agreement with beliefs about older people increased with the age of the person being rated. It is noteworthy that spoiling grandchildren is seen as more prevalent at 55 or 65 than at 75, and that financial worries are seen as much more prevalent around retirement age than either before or after.

Thus, the conventional wisdom about older people is probably correct at least as often as it is incorrect, but those beliefs that are incorrect or doubtful provide justification for those who would discriminate against older persons.

Beliefs about the capacities of older workers

TABLE 13-6   Percentage of agreement with beliefs about people of various ages

Belief Statement	Age		
	55	65	75
They are set in their ways	83	86	89
They are conservative	85	86	91
They like to think about the good old days	57	81	95
They worry about financial security	55	73	54
They walk slowly	35	86	96
They have poor coordination	28	42	71
They spoil their grandchildren	72	83	64
They worry about unimportant things	29	51	63
They are lonely	16	46	63
They repeat themselves in conversation	33	61	66

Source: Adapted from Axelrod and Eisdorfer, 1961.

compared to their younger counterparts are particularly relevant to the situation of older people in the labor force. Rosen and Jerdee (1976a) found that prospective business managers rated older workers (age 60) lower than younger workers (age 30) on productivity, efficiency, motivation, ability to work under pressure, and creativity. Older workers were also seen as more accident-prone and as having less potential. Not only were they seen as not being as eager, but they also were seen as unreceptive to new ideas, less capable of learning, less adaptable, and less versatile. Older workers were also seen as more rigid and dogmatic. On the plus side, older workers were seen as more reliable, dependable, and trustworthy, and as less likely to miss work for personal reasons. No age differences were seen in the area of interpersonal skills.

Obviously, the stereotype as applied to older workers operates to their disadvantage. And it is mostly inaccurate. Older workers are *not* consistently less productive or efficient. Older workers are less accident-prone (McCormick and Tiffin, 1974). Generally, the research shows little age difference on job-relevant factors.

In a Canadian sample of college students and older people, Bassili and Reil (1981) found that older people were stereotyped by young and old alike as conservative, traditional, and present oriented. But they also found that older men described as "former engineers" were stereotyped almost identically with younger men who were currently engineers. In addition, Levin and Levin (1981) found that upper socioeconomic status offset the negative image of old age. Thus, age is but one of many characteristics used for stereotyping. Note: Negative stereotypes can also sometimes have positive consequences. For example, Kearl (1982) cited the negative stereotype as a reference point many elderly people use to perceive themselves as relatively advantaged.

Finally, Schonfield (1982) has pointed out that the proportion believing a given stereotype to be true does not necessarily reveal all we might want to know. He went further and asked what proportion of older people fit each of several stereotypes. Surprisingly, Schonfield found that although most of his respondents believed several stereotypes about the elderly were true, it was common for them to believe also that there were numerous exceptions to the stereotypes. When he coupled belief that a stereotype was true with belief that no more than 20 percent of older people were exceptions, in order to isolate those who "stereotyped" the elderly, Schonfield found that at most, 20 percent could be classified as stereotyping the elderly and that rarely did the same individual qualify as a stereotyper for more than three of the ten stereotypes presented.

Attitudes

Attitudes are likes and dislikes. They may develop out of purely personal preferences, but often they are logical extensions of beliefs and values. It is commonly assumed that Americans in general have negative attitudes about aging and older people. However, upon reviewing the literature, McTavish (1971) concluded that only 20 to 30 percent are negatively disposed toward the elderly. Yet there is evidence that the later stages of life are not preferred and that older people are not preferable companions. Harris and his associates (1975) found that a large majority of their respondents saw the twenties to the forties as the preferred age to be. Those who did choose later stages of life tended to do so because to them later life represented a period of reduced responsibility and pressure and of increased enjoyment. Poor health, disability, and financial worries were the main reasons people did not choose the sixties or seventies as ages to be.

Seefeldt et al. (1977) used drawings to determine children's preferences to be with men of different ages. These preschool to sixth-grade children's attitudes may reflect general likes and dislikes stripped of social checks and balances. Nearly 60 percent chose to be with the youngest man, and only 20 percent chose the oldest. These preferences were related to perceptions (beliefs) about aging and the aged. The children felt that aging was a time of poor health. They saw the oldest man as not doing much for them, and when they were asked to describe what they would do with the oldest man they tended to describe helping behavior such as "get his glasses" or "help him clean" or "carry things

for him." Thus, the predisposition to dislike aging and the oldest man relative to the others seems to have been related to how the children would fare in exchange relations. They saw themselves as giving more and getting less from the oldest man.

The findings of Seefeldt and his colleagues are consistent with other studies (Hickey et al., 1968; Hickey and Kalish, 1968). However, Thomas and Yamamoto (1975) did a similar study using photographs with children in grades 6 to 12 and found less negativity with regard to attitudes toward the elderly. They found that as adult age increased, the children perceived the adults as less pleasant, happy, or exciting. However, these older children saw goodness and wisdom as increasing with age. In addition, they wrote stories that presented the oldest man as a "loving grandfather type who had time for grandchildren" (p.127). Unfortunately, this type of research has seldom been done with adults.

A common measure of attitudes toward aging and the aged has been the *semantic differential,* which taps the degree of positiveness or negativeness more in terms of *evaluation* than in terms of liking or disliking. It does this by presenting a series of polar adjectives, such as happy-sad, relaxed-tense, active-passive, or healthy-sick, and asking respondents to locate themselves on a seven-point continuum between the two opposites. The standard semantic differential presents 20 adjective pairs. Eisdorfer and Altrocchi (1961) found that compared to the "average adult," both old men and old women were negatively evaluated. Collette-Pratt (1976) also found that older adults were negatively evaluated by young, middle-aged, and older respondents alike. This negative evaluation was most strongly related to ideas about the negative effects of age on productivity, achievement, independence, and in particular health.

Putting these bits and pieces together is difficult. The effects of aging on health, activity level, and dependency seem to predispose people to dislike both the process of aging and the people who experience it. Yet this negativism is offset to some extent by the perceptions that older people are free to pay more attention to their families, experience greater freedom and happiness, and become kinder and wiser. As Kastenbaum and Durkee (1964b) have pointed out, attitude structure is a complex of specific likes and dislikes that so far has defied easy generalizations. Certainly we need more research in this area.

Aging as Portrayed in Children's Books

General orientations toward aging and the aged can also be studied by looking at how these topics are treated in the educational system. After all, schools are the primary mechanism society uses to exert social pressure on young people to adopt the attitudes, values, beliefs, and norms that make up their culture. This pressure is more often subtle and indirect rather than heavy-handed. For example, children's books seldom say "do this" or "don't do that" or "think this, but not that." Instead they most often present the child with an attractive young character—a role model—and simply describe how heroes and heroines ideally deal with various types of situations.

Several studies have analyzed the content of children's books. Old characters are common in children's books, but tend to be undeveloped and peripheral (Peterson and Eden, 1977; Peterson and Karnes, 1976). The older characters in children's books are portrayed in a consistently positive way (Robin, 1977), and illustrations tend to present attractive, healthy older people (Storck and Cutler, 1977). Seltzer and Atchley (1971a) surveyed children's books from the past 100 years and concluded that there was little change over time in the evaluation of old people and that if there is a negative attitude or evaluation of the elderly, it is not to be found in children's books. Ansello (1977b) found few hostile or negative characterizations of older characters. However, Ansello argued that older characters ultimately come off negatively not in content but by virtue of their blandness; older characters were poorly developed and old age seemed boring.

Writers try to write for an audience. Fiction writers in particular try to develop central characters with whom readers can identify and then place the characters in conflict situations that readers can understand. Given these constraints, it is hardly surprising that few older characters are central figures in children's literature. The main characters in children's literature tend to be children, and their interactions with adults are governed by role relationships that do not depend on having an in-depth understanding of adult characters. Thus, the characters of school principal, camp counselor, grandparent, and so forth often can be sketchy. What seems more relevant is that to the extent that children's books specify *ideal* ways of perceiving older people, the ideal presented tends to be a positive one.

Aging as Portrayed in the Media

People also learn what to think about aging through media portrayals.

Television.   Television is the most important mass medium of communication in American society. Americans watch television more than three hours a day on the average, and television watching is the leading pastime of middle-aged and older Americans (Pfeiffer and Davis, 1971; Moss and Lawton, 1982). How television treats the topic of aging varies by the type of message, and in a medium as varied and complex as American television it is difficult to generalize how aging is portrayed. In our discussion we will consider separately how aging is treated in prime-time series, in news and documentary programs, and in commercials.

Researchers who have studied the treatment of aging in nighttime television series have concentrated on the proportion of older characters and on how these older characters are portrayed. Estimates of the proportion of elderly characters range from 1.5 to 13 percent. Jeffreys-Fox (1977) found that 75 percent of older characters were men. The weight of the evidence seems to indicate that about 10 percent of characters are older—which is close to their prevalence in the population. Of course, the main reason for such varied estimates is that raters have to guess TV characters' ages, and this is apparently a haphazard method of assessing age (Petersen, 1973; Aronoff, 1974; Harris and Feinberg, 1977). There is also wide variation in the findings about how older characters are portrayed. Petersen (1973) found that 60 percent of older characters were presented in a favorable light. On the other hand, Aronoff (1974) found that older characters were portrayed as "bad guys," prone to failure, and generally unhappy. Jeffreys-Fox (1977) found that older characters were rated as less attractive, sociable, warm, and intelligent compared to younger characters. He found no age difference in rated happiness. These findings are also quite sensitive to the cues raters use to select "elderly" characters and to the raters' own biases about older people.

Research into television viewing has generally used *content analysis,* a technique in which *samples* of program content are rated by judges *according to a set of pre-existing categories.* If the researcher is not prepared to find positive outcomes, this is often reflected in the categories and in the research results. In addition, sampling program content often does not capture the context within which characterization occurs.

I took a somewhat different approach in looking at how aging was treated in television series. In March of 1979, there were 45 continuing series appearing on three networks. For each of these series, the *continuing characters* were rated as to whether they were teenagers or younger, young adults (age 20 to 35), middle-aged (35 to 55), mature adults (55 to 70), or older adults (70 or over). Series were also rated as to whether intergenerational themes were emphasized, and

if so, whether the intergenerational themes involved older people. About 12 percent of the continuing characters in series were judged as being over 55. Of the 45 series, 24 portrayed intergenerational themes, and 8 of these involved mature or older adults. There appears to be a trend in television drama toward recognition of adult child–older parent relationships as a dramatic issue viewers can identify with. In addition, adults of widely varied ages are being shown working together in a wide variety of occupational settings (radio and television, law enforcement, small business, the military, the press, and education). In addition, when mature adults are shown working with young and middle-aged adults, the mature adults usually supply the experience and leadership while the young adults supply the enthusiasm, eagerness, and physical prowess. Mature and even older adults are shown as capable of running if necessary, as interested in romance, and as capable human beings. Intergenerational relations in families are portrayed as conflict-ridden situations in which love and family ties generally prevail.

What emerges with respect to contemporary television series is a picture of a medium responding to changing times. In dramatic series, intergenerational cooperation and conflict resolution are presented as ideals. In comedy series, the humor in intergenerational situations is exposed, presumably with some cathartic effects. And these portrayals are not unrealistic. Older and younger people can and do work well together, and families do love each other and manage to transcend their conflicts.

In general, television seems to be moving toward more representative and accurate portrayals of mature adults in continuing series. This is noteworthy because continuing characters can be developed in real depth. What may start out as a relatively stereotyped older character can eventually become a realistic one—a person who can be charming one time and cranky another, depending on the situation or circumstances.

Television's treatment of aging in news and

documentary programming is another matter. Network, local news, and documentaries thrive on sensationalism. There is nothing sensational about individuals and families who are successfully coping with the trivial conflicts of everyday life. As a result, the typical middle-aged or older person is ignored by news programming along with most other typical people. Those older people who are given attention in the news are those who have "a problem" that can be a springboard for human interest or commentary. The two main games in human interest are "Can you believe this?" and "Ain't it awful!" Usually the object is some disaster. Needless to say, the portrayal of older people in this system is seldom positive.

On the other hand, public affairs and talk shows generally present aging in a favorable light (Harris and Feinberg, 1977). Older people on public affairs and talk shows tend to be influential business leaders or politicians, or respected actors or creative artists. Interestingly, the late 1970s saw the development of two successful information and talk shows specifically aimed at mature adults, *Over Easy* and *Prime Time*.

Commercials also present a mixed picture of aging. Francher (1973) found that the majority of commercials present young, attractive people, and that over half of television commercials were "action-oriented." Harris and Feinberg (1977) found that the proportion of older characters presented in commercials generally matched the proportion of older people in the population. Older characters in commercials were less likely to be physically active and more likely to have health problems, but none were portrayed as physically disabled or incapacitated. However, older characters were substantially overrepresented in commercials for health aids and totally absent from commercials for clothing, appliances, cars, and cleaning products.

Print Media. Less attention has been paid to the treatment of aging in the press and in popular magazines. Some of the comments made

about television news probably apply to newspapers, but research is needed to establish how the newspapers differ from television news. Buckholz and Bynum (1982) examined 1,703 newspaper articles from 1978 and found that 56 percent presented a neutral picture of the aged, 30 percent a positive picture, and only 14 percent a negative picture. Schuerman et al. (1977) examined fiction in nine women's magazines and found that older characters were more likely to be portrayed positively than negatively.

Sohngen (1977) analyzed the *experience* of old age as depicted in 87 contemporary novels. She felt it significant that so many novels dealt with the actual experience of growing old (compared with simply presenting well-developed older characters). The demographic emphasis was upon middle-class WASP characters. Nearly half of these novels employed life reviews as a technique for examining the experience of aging. Otherwise, the content was quite varied but tended to center on gerontological issues such as institutionalization, retirement, isolation, segregated living, or intergenerational relations. Sohngen was impressed with these books. In general, she found that they used language freshly, avoided soap-opera clichés, and presented vivid characters in an entertaining, readable, and sometimes moving way. Laughman (1980) found similar positive portrayals.

Much research is needed before we will have a solid picture of how aging is treated by the media. Some researchers see a very negative emphasis, others do not. However, it seems that media portrayals of aging are moving in a positive direction; we hope this is simply an accurate response to the changing age structure of American society.

Harris and his associates (1975) studied how older people *perceived* the treatment of aging in the media. Just under two-thirds thought that television, newspapers, magazines, and books give a fair picture of what older people are like. Older people felt that television treats older people with respect, makes them look like important members of their families, wise, and successful. They did not feel that television portrays older people as narrow-minded or old-fashioned, meddlesome, sick or incapacitated, useless, or unattractive.

Age Prejudice and Discrimination

Prejudice is an unfavorable attitude toward a category of persons based on negative traits assumed to apply uniformly to all members of the category. *Age prejudice,* or *ageism,* is a dislike of aging and older people based on the belief that aging makes people unattractive, unintelligent, asexual, unemployable, and senile (Comfort, 1976). It may be that only a quarter or less of the general public endorses this extreme and inaccurate view (McTavish, 1971), but most Americans probably subscribe to some erroneous beliefs about aging and have at least a mild degree of prejudice against aging and the aged. This notion is borne out by the bits and pieces of research reviewed so far.

If people kept their prejudices to themselves, no harm would come from them. But people act on their prejudices. Discrimination is some sort of negative treatment that is unjustly applied to members of a category of people. *Age discrimination* is treating people in some unjustly negative manner because of their chronological age and for no other reason. Age discrimination occurs when human beings are avoided or excluded in everyday activities because they are "the wrong age." Older people sometimes must intrude into various spheres of daily life in order to make people aware that they have something to offer. Most older people are not willing to fight for this recognition, and as a result, there is a great deal of age segregation in activities and interactions. Only in the family do older people usually escape this sort of informal age discrimination.

Equally important is the impact of age discrimination on opportunities for beginning or continuing participation in various organiza-

tions. As we saw in Chapter 9, job discrimination makes it more difficult for older workers to continue in the labor force or to find jobs if unemployed. The stigma of implied inability and the resulting discrimination sometimes extends past paying jobs and into volunteer jobs and other types of participation as well. Organizations especially for older adults offer an alternative to those who have been rejected by organizations in the "mainstream," but at the cost of age segregation. While many older adults prefer associating mainly with their age peers, those who do not often find themselves without choices. Research on age discrimination in non-job organizational settings is greatly needed.

Age discrimination can also take the form of unequal treatment by public agencies. In a report from the U.S. Commission on Civil Rights (1977) it was found that age discrimination was present in numerous federally funded programs —community mental health centers, legal services, vocational rehabilitation, social services to low-income individuals and families, employment and training services, the Food Stamp program, Medicaid, and vocational education. And this problem existed in all regions of the country. The higher the age of older people, the more likely they were to experience discrimination from public agencies. In addition, age discrimination was often compounded by discrimination on the basis of race, sex, national origin, or handicap status. The Commission on Civil Rights concluded that much of this discrimination stems from a narrow interpretation of the goals of legislation. For example, community health centers generally interpret "preventive health care" as applying only to children and adolescents. Directors of employment programs see their most appropriate clients to be males aged 22 to 44. Even age 22 is too old as far as some job-training programs are concerned. The commission also found that state legislatures sometimes convert federal programs designed to serve all Americans into categorical programs aimed at specific age groups. For example, the state of Missouri passed a strong child abuse and neglect law—a worthy goal. But the state provided no funds to carry it out. Instead, federal funds for social services to everyone were earmarked to support the child abuse program, and as a result most cities in the state discontinued their adult protective services programs. In many cases where states or local governments are responsible for defining the population eligible for federal programs, age discrimination results. For example, several states excluded older people from vocational rehabilitation programs because they were not of "employable age." Age discrimination sometimes occurs when services are provided under contract with agencies that limit the ages of people they will serve. For example, a general social services contract with a child welfare agency is unlikely to result in social services to older adults. The commission also found that outreach efforts are often aimed at specific age groups, which lessens the probability that other age groups will find out about programs for which they are eligible. The commission also concluded that general age discrimination in the public and private job market was an important underlying factor in age discrimination in employment, training, and vocational rehabilitation programs. As long as older people are denied jobs, agencies see little value in preparing them for jobs.

Societal Disengagement

Social institutions outlive the people who comprise them, and thus most social institutions are constantly phasing young people in and older people out. However, this pattern is most common in *occupational* positions associated with various institutions such as the economy, education, politics, government, religion, health, and the arts. This sort of analysis is less applicable to more private institutions, such as the family, marriage, or friendship. The process whereby society withdraws from or no longer seeks the individual's effort or involvement is called **societal disengagement.**

As part of an overall theory of disengagement, Newell (1961) suggested that societal disengagement is half of the "inevitable" withdrawal of older people and society from each other. Societal disengagement is characterized by a "thinning out of the number of members in the social structure surrounding the individual, a diminishing of interactions with these members, and a restructuring of the goals of the system" (Newell, 1961:37). From the societal point of view, older people may no longer be sought out for leadership in organizations, their labor may no longer be desired by their employers, their unions may no longer be interested in their financial problems, and their government may no longer be responsive to their needs. Sometimes societal disengagement is unintended and sometimes even unrecognized by society, but it remains an important reality for older adults.

Role Loss

To measure societal disengagement, Newell and his associates first took a *role count*, an inventory of the number of separate *active* relationships the individual had. Then they used an *interaction index* to measure the amount of daily interaction with others. Newell found that role count "is quite stable between the ages of 50 and 64; about 60 percent of this younger group act in six or more roles, but by age 65 only 39 percent do, and the proportion decreases steadily until at age 75 and over, only 8 percent act in more than five roles" (1961:39). Fewer work and family roles account for most of the age difference for both older men and older women. Thus, in older cohorts the variety of roles people play is lower than in younger cohorts.

The interaction index was concerned with the density of interaction, and again Newell found a decrease with age. However, here there are marked declines after age 65. Table 13-7 shows that interaction declines steadily from age 50 onward, the average decline between five-year age groups being just over 11 percent.

TABLE 13-7   Rates of interaction, by age

Age	Percent with High Daily Interaction
50–54	72.2
55–59	58.8
60–64	58.8
65–69	45.2
70–74	34.0
75 +	15.4

Source: Adapted from Cumming and Henry, 1961:40.

Atrophy of Opportunity

For those who use society as a point of departure, the major criticism of disengagement theory is that it does not give enough weight to the role of the socially determined situation in the genesis or processes of disengagement (Roman and Taietz, 1967). The crux of the matter is whether the pattern observed by Newell and others* is the result of individual disengagement or societal disengagement or both.

One important aspect of the problem has been dealt with by Carp (1968b), who set out to study the effect of moving from "substandard housing and socially isolating or interpersonally stressful situations to a new apartment house" having within it a senior center. Prior to the move, the 204 respondents were assessed in terms of their engagement in three separate roles: paid work, volunteer work, and leisure pastimes. Opportunities for all three were very limited in the premove situations of the study sample. "Special effort was necessary in order to participate in any of the three. Expenditure of this effort was assumed to express a strong need for involvement." (Carp, 1968b:185).

*For example, Havighurst et al., 1963; Williams and Wirths, 1965.

Following the move, opportunities for volunteer work and leisure pastimes were expanded, but opportunities for paid work remained about the same. Carp predicted that those who had expended the effort on leisure or volunteer work in the antagonistic premove setting would be happier and better adjusted in an environment that facilitated continued engagement. She also predicted that those who had worked for pay in the premove setting would be no different in terms of satisfaction or adjustment after the move. Her results fully supported her predictions. People who had been involved in leisure pursuits or volunteer work prior to entering the apartment building tended to be happier, more popular, and better adjusted than the other tenants. On the other hand, those who had worked were not significantly different from the other tenants. Carp interpreted her findings as supporting the idea that the greater the congruence between the person's desires for continued engagement and the opportunities for such engagement offered by the situation, the higher the degree of adjustment and satisfaction. She concluded:

> The results suggest that involvement is reactive to person-situation congruence, and that engagement-disengagement is not a general trait but one which is specific to various domains of involvement. . . . They suggest also that services for the elderly might profit from prior awareness of prospective clients' engagement in various behavioral domains (Carp, 1968b:187).

Implicit in these conclusions is the idea that many people want to remain engaged, and that one of the main obstacles preventing them from doing so is societal disengagement, which creates a situation in which continued engagement is difficult.

In order to assess the impact of societal disengagement directly, Roman and Taietz (1967) undertook the study of an occupational role in which continued engagement after retirement is allowed—the role of the "emeritus professor." Unlike most organizations, American colleges and universities, instead of removing retired faculty from the organization, make available a formalized, postretirement position with a flexible role, whose definition is a function of the individual's preretirement position, as well as of his or her own choice of postretirement activity. The important point here is that this system allows the *opportunity* for role continuity between full-time employment and retirement.

In Roman and Taietz's study, the amount of continuity possible varied. The research professors had the most, since they could generally continue to get research grants through the university. Those involved in teaching, public service, or administration still had opportunities for involvement, but their emeritus role was quite different from their preretirement role. They often ended up writing books, consulting, or becoming administrators. In no case, however, was the continuity complete. The emeritus professor always gave up a measure of involvement (Roman and Taietz, 1967). This situation was perfect for studying individual disengagement, since societal disengagement exerts less pressure.

Disengagement theory would lead us to believe that since the individual naturally wants to disengage, he or she would do so in the situation of the emeritus professor. Roman and Taietz assumed that disengagement was the product of *particular* social systems, not of systems in general, and that opportunity structures would greatly influence the individual's readiness to disengage. Cumming and Henry (1961) had viewed readiness to disengage as being a result of aging, regardless of the social system. Given their own assumptions about opportunity structures, Roman and Taietz predicted "that a significant proportion of emeritus professors would remain engaged, and that those allowed role continuity would exhibit a higher degree of continued engagement than those required to adopt new roles" (1967:149). They found that 41 percent of the emeritus professors were still engaged within the same university, 13 percent had taken employment in their profession elsewhere, 24 percent were in bad health, and 22

percent were disengaged from both the university and their profession. If these percentages are recomputed leaving out the group in bad health, for whom no determination of voluntary disengagement is possible, and combining both categories of those still engaged, the pattern shows 71 percent still engaged and 29 percent disengaged. In addition, they found that those emeritus professors who had had a research role were still engaged significantly more often than the others. Thus, all of Roman and Taietz's predictions were supported by their findings. These data suggest that the frequency of disengagement is very much a product of the opportunity for continued engagement. The fact that the organization provided a continuing role after retirement allowed 71 percent of the healthy people to remain engaged, whereas in many occupations the percent allowed to remain engaged would have been near zero. This finding is all the more revealing given that almost half of Roman and Taietz's sample was over 75 years old.

Tallmer and Kutner (1969) attempted to assess the impact of "stress-inducing environmental and circumstantial disturbances" in producing consequences similar to those generally attributed to disengagement. The stress factors they used included illness, widowhood, retirement, receiving welfare, and living alone. One of the fundamental tenets of the Cumming and Henry disengagement theory is that growing old causes, or is at least associated with, disengagement. Tallmer and Kutner found that *practically all of the relationship between age and engagement was accounted for by the relationship between age and the various stress situations.* They concluded:

> There appears to be substantial evidence for our hypothesis that disengagement among the aged can be predicted to occur as a concomitant of physical or social stresses which profoundly affect the manner in which the life pattern of the person is redirected. Because they have ignored the apparently definitive effect of such factors on disengagement, Cumming and Henry were led to the

conclusion that advancing age was a sufficient explanation of the facts obtained in their study. It is not age which produces disengagement in our investigation but the impact of physical and social stress which may be expected to increase with age. It is tempting to hypothesize that as one enters into later decades, disengagement is bound to grow, and indeed it does. The real difficulty lies in the fact that it is the correlates of old age, i.e., failing health, loss of peers, death of relatives, and the general shrinking of the social world due to factors related to aging, that appear to produce the social withdrawal known as disengagement (Tallmer and Kutner, 1969:74).

The point is that the external aspects of aging and the socially structured situation can have a far greater influence than personal desires on the social withdrawal of older people. A recurrent theme throughout our examination of how older people fit into a modern industrial society will be that the difficulties many older people face are brought on less by withdrawal on their own part than by decisions, often consciously made, on the part of others to exclude them from the mainstream of society. Illness, loss of peers and relatives through death, and the shrinking pool of alternatives the older person faces are often unnecessarily stressful simply because, in a social system built around production, rationality, and efficiency, it is often more expedient to write off older people than to expend the energy required to create a "citizen emeritus" role. Disengagement theory is comforting in a way, particularly for the young, because it seems to justify the way older people are treated; after all, being cut off from everything is just what they want. Nevertheless, the research evidence shows that disengagement is *not* what most older people want. It is, however, what many older people get.

Summary

General social responses to aging exist in the ideas of a culture, in the media and educational materials through which people learn these ideas, and in the attitudes and actions that result. America appears to be genuinely ambivalent about aging. While most people seem to want to think well of older people, aging poses both real and imagined threats to important social values. Family security, freedom of choice, and general happiness are all vulnerable to the ups and downs of one's own aging, the aging of family members for whom one may be responsible, and the aging of society in general. In addition, what is generally *believed* to be true about physical and mental aging makes it *appear to be* a threat to societal values such as productivity and efficiency. Yet our general beliefs and stereotypes about aging are not predictably negative or inaccurate; sometimes they are and sometimes they aren't. More important perhaps is the set of negative and inaccurate beliefs about older people as jobholders that serves to underpin widespread age discrimination in employment.

People seem to dislike both the idea of aging and the people who experience it. This is true throughout the life cycle. And this dislike seems to result from the public's association of aging with unpleasant outcomes such as illness, unattractiveness, and inability. On the other hand, people also seem to like the idea that wisdom, warmth, and goodness increase with age. Such is the nature of ambivalence.

Contemporary children's books and adult novels seek generally to portray aging in a positive and humanistic light. Children are presented with the idea that older people are to be treated with respect. Adults are presented with older characters who represent a full range of human qualities. There is also evidence that contemporary television drama is moving toward a recognition of multigenerational relationships as a natural and interesting part of life. Older characters in continuing series are often well-developed, successful people who can serve as models for either being or interacting with older adults, particularly in family or job situations. However, television's treatment of older people in news programming tends to present the inaccurate view of later life as a life stage beset with serious problems, and this tends to reinforce the prevalent view of later life as an undesirable life stage.

Our ambivalent beliefs and attitudes about aging and the perception of aging as a threat to important values are translated into age prejudice, or ageism, which in turn feeds age discrimination. Age discrimination imposes negative outcomes on older people just because they are older. Some of it is subtle, as when older people are ignored or avoided in interaction or social planning. It is more direct where people are denied participation because of their age. Direct age discrimination is especially prevalent in the occupational sphere but also appears to operate in volunteer work and other areas, too. Age discrimination also occurs when public agencies fail to orient public programs meant for the general population as much toward older people as they do toward younger people.

Societal disengagement is the withdrawal of interest in the contributions or involvement of older people. It is *not* a mutually satisfying process but instead one that is imposed on older people by the withdrawal of opportunities to participate and by circumstances such as ill health. Like age discrimination, the more general process of societal disengagement rests not so much on the functional needs of society but rather on its prejudices.

Chapter 14

Social Inequality

All known societies afford differential treatment to various categories of people, usually based on the values of the dominant culture. And as with other elements of culture, those social inequalities are passed on from one generation to the next. In the previous chapter we considered inequalities people encounter as a result of growing older. To a great extent, the experience of aging is also mediated by other sources of inequality—social class, race, ethnicity, and sex. This chapter focuses on these sources of inequality and their impact on aging.

Social Class

"I don't go to senior citizens (meetings) because the others who go there are not my class of people. We have no interests in common." This quote from a retired woman manager reflects the essence of social class. A *social class* is a body of persons considered to have certain social, economic, educational, occupational, or cultural characteristics in common. Furthermore, social classes are arranged in a *hierarchy* of relative social desirability. Social classes are not organized. Instead they are categories of people who recognize one another as overall social peers and who are recognized as such by others.

The study of social class in American society is made difficult because there are a number of factors that affect social class. To begin with, ours is an open class system in which persons may move up or down. Although most people live their entire lives in the social class into which they were born, there is enough upward and downward mobility to complicate the study of social class in life course or intergenerational perspectives. Second, the criteria used to categorize people into social classes vary between social classes. For example, family history may confer little status in the working class, whereas among the rich it may be of crucial importance in defining the individual's peers. Social class criteria also vary by size of community: In large urban areas, "objective" characteristics such as occupation, education, income, and residence generally carry a great deal of weight. "Appearances" is another important factor influencing secondary social relationships with service personnel, bureaucrats, shopkeepers, and the like. This reliance on attributes is an obvious outgrowth of the relative anonymity of large cities. In medium-sized cities or smaller communities, criteria for class assignment tend to focus on behavior as well as attributes. Thus, in longstanding neighborhoods and small communities, a person's or family's past history of performance is usually an important dimension of social class assignment by the community at large. There are also regional differences in class criteria. Finally, there are class criteria specific to certain life course stages. For example, there is a class of retired persons in American society in which peers are defined by their affirmation of leisure as the focus of their life style and by having the financial resources to lead such a life style.

Class Differences in Aging

There are no clearly defined points that separate various social classes in American society. The terms *upper class*, *middle class*, and *lower class* refer to stereotyped composites of life styles, educational backgrounds, family values, occupations, housing, and so forth. In fact, the attributes and behavior used to rank others in relation to an individual form a continuous distribution over which a very large number of distinctions can be made. Yet, it is still possible to discuss general categories if we keep in mind that in every case the boundaries of the categories are fuzzy.

The upper class is typified by wealth, and distinctions within the upper class center on family history and values. Upper-class children are educated in private schools with other upper-class children. They attend the "best" private universities. Their occupational careers prepare them for their "proper" place as leaders of the nation's corporate, military, financial, political, and legal institutions. Upper-class people lead very private lives in circles largely unknown to the general public.

Upper-class people have access to wealth and power. Our tax structure allows Americans to amass great fortunes and to pass them on from generation to generation (Streib, 1976). The fortunes of upper-class people do not depend on their having jobs, and upper-class people carry their fortunes into later life. In fact, most of the *very* rich (centimillionaires) are over 65 (Louis, 1968). As a result, older upper-class family members have wealth and the power that comes with wealth. This privileged position means continuity of power within the family, generally better health and vigor, and much less likelihood of facing dependency in old age. Nevertheless, no amount of money can forestall aging; it can only delay it. Eventually even upper-class people experience a decline in physical functioning and erosion of the social environment as their friends and associates die. Because the upper class tends to insulate itself rather severely from others, developing new relationships in old age may be more difficult. In addition, physical aging in the upper class may produce much greater change in life style than in the middle class. These topics deserve much more research.

The middle class in America is a large and heterogeneous category. Jobs and educational attainment are the measures most often used for sorting out various subcategories of the middle class. At the top are college-educated people with professional and managerial jobs. The middle area consists of well-educated white-collar workers who push the nation's paper and market its goods. The lower reaches of the middle class consist of skilled blue-collar and service workers who may or may not be well-educated, whose jobs involve "dirty" work, but whose incomes are often more than sufficient to allow them a middle-class life style. Middle-class life styles emphasize both "getting ahead" in the educational and occupational sphere and diverse activity patterns that often revolve around the family. Middle-class jobs and values usually result in good health and adequate financial resources in retirement. And family values in the middle class usually insure prompt response to dependency needs of older family members.

The working class is made up of people whose livelihood is or was generated by semiskilled and unskilled blue-collar and service jobs. Working-class people often do not finish high school and their jobs are more physically demanding and precarious than those of the middle class. Working-class life styles emphasize avoiding slipping downward more than getting ahead, and activity patterns tend to separate men and women. Working-class jobs carry more health and disability hazards, and are less likely to produce adequate retirement benefits compared to middle-class jobs. Family values of the working class support the idea of caring for older family members, although the financial capabilities to do so are limited. Working-class people often find it necessary to rely on public assistance to supplement inadequate retirement income.

The poor are those who live on incomes from the least desirable types of jobs—dishwasher, busboy, presser in a cleaning shop, farm laborer, private household worker. Many poor people never have much success at getting or holding a good job. They have neither the education nor the family upbringing necessary to get steady jobs. Life styles emphasize survival, and older family members' old age benefits are sometimes a crucial source of family income. In fact, the availability of SSI and all sorts of indirect income assistance can mean a substantial *improvement* in level of living for those poor people who survive to become eligible for them. Yet even though aging may improve their financial situation, the aged poor are apt to find themselves physically less able to take advantage of these opportunities compared to their working-class counterparts.

Social class has often been used as a variable in gerontological research. Studies of retirement, widowhood, adaptation to aging, and numerous other topics have found that social class makes a difference. For example, compared to the working class and the poor, the middle class enters later life with better health, more financial resources, more activities, better housing, and fewer worries.* Accordingly, middle-class people seem to cope better with just about every life course change in later life, particularly in the long run. Comparatively, middle-class people have good marriages that tend to get better as a result of child launching and retirement. This is less often true for the working class and poor. Middle-class people generally adjust better and more quickly to widowhood compared to working-class people. Loss of independence and institutionalization are both less likely for middle-class people compared to the working class and the poor. Thus, to a great extent the optimistic picture of aging presented in earlier chapters is a result of the fact that most Americans are middle class. But for those who are not, the picture is much less rosy. A lifetime of poverty translates into poor health and poor living conditions in later life. Poor working conditions earlier in life translate into greater rates of disability in later life. Semiskilled and unskilled jobs provide meager financial resources not only during working life but in retirement as well. To the extent that adequate income and good health are prerequisites for a satisfying life in the later years, the working class and the poor are at a distinct disadvantage. Their jobs are unlikely to entitle them to adequate retirement income and expose them to a greater risk of premature physical aging and disability.

From a research perspective, the foregoing general view is well-supported. We need to know more about precisely where in the occu-

---

*Source references for the social class findings can be found in the other chapters of this book. Their inclusion here would not only be repetitious, but would also needlessly interrupt the flow of the text.

pational structure the high risk begins. Jobs that produce adequate salaries and wages are not necessarily jobs that produce adequate retirement income, although there is considerable overlap. For example, a television repair specialist may earn a salary sufficient to support a middle-class life style, but may work for a small business with no pension plan. The result could be a retirement income that does not support a middle-class life style. We also need to know more about illness and disability histories in various occupations. For example, people who work in construction jobs are much more likely to enter later life with disability than people who work at clerical jobs.

Because social class position tends to persist across generations, not only are the lower-class older person's physical, financial, and social resources for coping with life more limited than those of their middle-class agemates, but the adult children of lower-class older persons are also substantially less likely to have financial resources sufficient to aid their older parents.

Social class position is central to later life because it is central to life in general. The social class into which one is born or adopted determines the family context of early socialization. One's values, attitudes, beliefs, life style, and opportunities early in life depend largely on the social class position of one's parents. Social class also has a great influence on role models. Imitation is an important social process. Children try to be like their parents (although they often do not like to admit it). They also look to people around them for ideas about what their options are with regard to jobs, marriage, and other aspects of life style. Middle-class children have access to a different set of role models than lower-class children do. Those people who manage to rise out of lower-class beginnings are predominantly those whose families had middle-class values and made sacrifices to create opportunities opportunities for their children (Billingsley, 1968). There is a great deal of intergenerational inertia in the social class system, particularly in the pool of jobs and life styles

available to family members. Educational, occupational, and marital decisions made early in the life course are heavily influenced by the perceptions and social pressures that grow out of the social position of one's family. For the children of the working class and of the poor, the working people around them are laborers, waitresses, dry cleaning employees, equipment operators, truck drivers, and the like. Early in life they learn that employment for the people around them is hard and unpredictable. These children may want to be astronauts but they expect to have to settle for considerably less. And when they settle for job and family responsibilities before or soon after high school graduation, they have made decisions that are hard to reverse and that greatly influence the physical and financial resources with which they approach middle age and later life. Not only that, but less education also usually means fewer skills for enjoying life off the job.

Race

In 1980, over 92 percent of the older population of the United States was white. Another 7 percent was black, and the remaining 1 percent was made up of Asian Americans* (0.8 percent), American Indians (0.3 percent), and a smattering of other races. Perhaps because the United States is so predominantly white, white Americans tend to view persons of other races unfavorably.

Racism is a complex of attitudes and discriminatory behavior patterns based on the notion that one racial category is inherently superior to another. In American society the dominant white majority behaves in general as if it were superior to several other racial categories, but particularly to black Americans, Asian Americans, and American Indians.

---

*Asian Americans are those of Japanese, Chinese, Filipino, Korean, or Hawaiian descent.

Black Americans

In 1980, the 1.7 million older black Americans represented 6.6 percent of the older population and were by far the largest racial minority. The visibility of the black population is heightened by its concentration in central cities as a result of residential segregation.

Racial discrimination has also produced a situation in which the black population is concentrated in the less desirable jobs within the blue-collar category (see Tables 14-1 and 14-2). For example, among employed black men age 55 to 59 in 1980, 57.5 percent were working as laborers, nonprecision equipment operators, janitors, helpers, and other menial jobs, compared to 25.8 percent in the same types of jobs among white men of the same age. Among black women age 55 to 59 in 1980, 63.7 percent were working as maids, food service helpers, nurse aides, and other menial jobs, compared to 29.4 percent of white women of the same age. In addition, unemployment rates of blacks are much higher than those for whites. And while the occupational situation for blacks has improved substantially since 1964, this is of little benefit to middle-aged or older blacks who are much less likely to have benefitted from expanded occupational opportunities. For example, in Table 14-3 (for 1980), if we compare black workers age 30 to 34 ("settled" adults) with those age 60 to 64 (on the eve of retirement), the occupational differences are striking. A greater proportion of young black males had middle-class jobs compared to older black males (32 percent compared to 19.9 percent), and 60.5 percent of young black women compared to 28.8 percent of older black women had middle-class jobs. A much greater proportion of younger blacks were working as teachers, social

TABLE 14-1   Occupational distribution of employed males age 55 to 59, by race and ethnicity: United States, 1980

	Total	White	Black	Asian	Spanish Origin
Number Employed	4,250,807	3,837,338	301,803	50,562	158,336
Occupation					
Managerial and professional	25.8%	27.2%	10.4%	26.7%	13.0%
Technical, sales, and administrative support	19.1	19.8	11.4	18.7	12.5
Service	8.2	7.0	19.2	18.5	15.6
Farming, forestry, and fishing	5.0	4.8	4.4	8.0	8.2
Precision production, craft, and repair	21.8	22.3	16.2	14.3	20.9
Operator, fabricators, and laborers	20.3	18.8	38.3	13.8	29.6
Total	100.2*	99.9	99.9	100.0	99.8

*Due to rounding error, columns may add to more or less than 100 percent.

Source: Compiled from unpublished data from the U.S. Bureau of the Census.

TABLE 14-2 Occupational distribution of employed females age 55 to 59, by race and ethnicity: United States, 1980

	Total	White	Black	Asian	Spanish Origin
Number Employed	**2,846,785**	**2,501,746**	**271,458**	**39,032**	**92,388**
Occupation					
Managerial and professional	19.7%	20.4%	15.0%	16.5%	11.4%
Technical, sales, and administrative support	43.3	46.4	18.5	35.2	25.3
Service	19.4	15.9	50.4	21.3	29.1
Farming, forestry, and fishing	1.2	1.1	0.7	2.4	1.9
Precision production, craft, and repair	2.7	2.7	2.1	5.0	5.0
Operators, fabricators, and laborers	13.6	13.4	13.3	19.6	27.2
Total	99.9*	99.9	100.1	100.0	99.9

*Due to rounding error, columns may add to more or less than 100 percent.

Source: Compiled from unpublished data from the U.S. Bureau of the Census.

workers, engineers, nurses, retail managers, secretaries, policemen, or skilled factory workers compared to blacks on the eve of retirement. Older blacks, on the other hand, were much more likely to be janitors, laborers, or maids. This cohort difference in the occupational distribution is the result of job discrimination many years ago, but older blacks are still paying for it, particularly in terms of their ability to generate adequate retirement income.

A main effect of racism toward blacks has been to restrict the number able to get jobs that would support a middle-class life style. For example, in the 1920s college-educated blacks had to settle for jobs as porters on the nation's trains (Drake and Cayton, 1962). Yet many black families adapted in ways that allowed them to retain middle-class values. It is common to assume that stifling of opportunities gradually erodes values, but this certainly has not been the case for blacks. Even in the face of job discrimination and low incomes, many black families raised their children to value education in itself and to live by the middle-class values of thrift, hard work, sacrifice, and getting ahead. Liebow (1967) found these values to be alive and well even among the black working poor. While a smaller proportion of blacks are middle class compared to whites, there has been a black middle class for many decades (DuBois, 1915), and many black Americans were well-prepared to take advantage of new opportunities that grew out of the Civil Rights Act of 1965 (Kronus, 1971). As a result, future cohorts of older blacks will be more like older whites not only in terms of values but also in terms of education, health, and financial resources.

Sterne et al. (1974) studied the aged poor in

TABLE 14-3 Occupational distribution of employed black workers of selected ages, by sex: United States, 1980

	Age 30–34		Age 60–64	
	Male	Female	Male	Female
Number Employed	652,457	680,805	195,630	171,567
Occupation				
Managerial and professional	15.1%	20.3%	9.5%	13.3%
Technical, sales, and administrative support	16.9	40.2	10.4	15.5
Service	12.0	19.0	22.4	57.0
Farming, forestry, and fishing	2.3	0.4	6.1	0.8
Precision production, craft, and repair	17.1	2.6	14.5	1.8
Operators, fabricators, and laborers	36.7	17.3	37.0	11.5
Total	100.1*	99.8	99.9	99.9

*Due to rounding error, columns may add to more or less than 100 percent.

Source: Compiled from unpublished data from the U.S. Bureau of the Census.

Model Cities areas of Rochester, New York. They found that older blacks were disadvantaged *even in relation to the white elderly poor.* The white elderly poor had had better jobs, had higher incomes, and were better educated. Older blacks in poverty were poorer and had little education. These differences reinforced the already negative view that the elderly white poor had about blacks. As a result, the white elderly poor resisted the idea of integrated clubs, employment, or advocacy. These findings may or may not be typical of racial differences and relations among the urban elderly, but these conditions are probably common enough to present a problem for the elderly black poor. Older whites deal with differences they see, not with the causes of what they see. Older whites have little awareness of, much less compassion for, the effects of racial segregation in the South on the educational level, life styles, speech, and

values of those blacks who moved to the cities. And residential segregation and job discrimination have often perpetuated these differences in the nation's cities. These differences are largely a creation of the racism built into America's social institutions, yet many Americans, particularly older Americans, continue to see these differences as the result of skin color.

Older black Americans also suffer the effects of numerous inaccurate stereotypes. It is commonly assumed that all blacks are lower class, that most black families are headed by women, that older blacks die substantially earlier than older whites, and that older blacks are mostly dependent on welfare. However, as Table 14-3 shows, a substantial portion of older blacks in 1980 were indeed middle class. "The black experience" in American society is definitely mediated by social class, and so is the experience of black aging. In 1977, 69 percent of black households with older heads were headed by men, and only about 3 percent of black households with younger heads included older members (Hill, 1978).

Because life expectancy at birth is about five years higher for whites than for blacks, it is commonly assumed that older blacks die much sooner than older whites do, on the average. However, most of this differential is due to mortality differences early in life. Table 14-4 shows that in 1973 at age 65 and over there was little racial difference in average life expectancy. In fact, there appears to have been a crossover at age 75, with black life expectancy having been *greater* after that age. However, this crossover has been questioned on the grounds that age data on blacks over 75 are suspect (Jackson, 1975). In any case, there is no support for the notion that older blacks suffer higher mortality rates than older whites do. But older blacks do have a higher incidence of illness and disability. For example, Jackson (1978) reports that older blacks were more likely than whites to suffer from hypertension but were like whites with respect to prevalence of heart disease, cancer, and strokes—the main causes of death among older people. However, about 25 percent of older blacks had serious physical limitations of mobil-

ity or activity, compared to about 14 percent of older whites.

In terms of income, older blacks had incomes in 1976 that averaged about 70 percent of those for older whites (Hill, 1978). This represented a substantial improvement over the situation in the mid-1960s and was mainly the result of the advent of SSI as a supplement to Social Security. The poor occupational histories of older blacks due to racial job discrimination was reflected in the fact that much smaller proportions got private pensions compared to older whites. Hill (1978) reported that Social Security, earnings, and SSI were the major income sources for older blacks, and that for older whites the major sources were Social Security, pensions (not SSI), and earnings. Since 90 percent of older blacks draw Social Security retirement benefits and only 25 percent draw SSI, the stereotype of older blacks as mainly dependent on welfare is degradingly inaccurate.

Racial segregation in housing has resulted in a much higher percentage of older blacks than of older whites in substandard housing. In 1977, 70 percent of all black families headed by an older person lived in an owned home, while nearly 60 percent of older blacks living alone were in rented housing. About a third of elderly blacks lived alone (Hill, 1978). This pattern was similar to that for whites. However, the housing of older blacks tends to be older and of lower value than that of whites. Housing of older blacks is especially poor in rural areas of the South. Atchley and Miller (1975) found that more than half of older blacks living in rural areas of the South were living in housing that lacked one or more basic features, such as plumbing, kitchen facilities, central heating, or sewage disposal, compared to the national average in rural areas of only 13 percent.

In summary, the racial discrimination that has typified the treatment of black Americans for many decades has concentrated older blacks in low-paying jobs and in substandard housing. These conditions continue into later life in the form of lower Social Security benefits, fewer

TABLE 14-4   Life expectancy, by age, sex, and color: United States, 1973

Age	White		Black	
	Males	Females	Males	Females
50–54	23.6	29.5	21.5	26.4
55–59	19.7	25.2	18.3	22.7
60–64	16.2	21.1	15.6	19.3
65–69	13.2	17.3	13.1	16.2
70–74	10.4	13.7	10.7	13.2
75–79	8.1	10.4	9.2	11.3
80–84	6.3	7.9	7.9	9.4
85 +	4.7	5.7	6.3	7.3

Source: National Center for Health Statistics, 1977.

private pensions, and more prevalent health problems. There is evidence that the situation of black Americans is improving, which should mean less disadvantage for upcoming cohorts when they reach later life. However, parity with older whites is still nowhere in sight.

Asian Americans

In 1980, there were over 190,000 older Americans of Asian races—primarily Japanese, Chinese, and Filipino. Although the white majority tends to see these various categories of Asian Americans as similar, they differ substantially in language, customs, background of involvement in American life, and social class structure. For example, older Japanese Americans are quite similar to older whites in terms of the occupations they held. A bigger proportion of older Chinese Americans held jobs as professionals or managers, compared to older whites. But at the other end of the occupational range, a bigger proportion of older Filipino and Chinese Americans had held menial jobs compared to whites. As Table 14-5 (for 1969) shows, older Japanese Americans had a median income near that of older whites, and all Asian races were

TABLE 14-5 Median income of persons 65 and over, by sex, race, and ethnicity: United States, 1969

Race	Males	Females
White	$2,892	$1,525
Black	1,711	1,098
Spanish surname	1,946	1,231
Japanese	2,482	1,312
Chinese	1,943	1,188
Filipino	2,528*	1,130
American Indian	1,383	785

*This value reflects a much higher than average proportion of older Filipinos still in the labor force.

Source: U.S. Bureau of the Census, 1973c; 1973f; 1973g; 1973h.

better off than older blacks. Yet the wide variations within the older Asian category mean that a substantial proportion was financially comfortable and a substantial proportion was financially poor.

The situation of the older Asian American poor was highlighted by a special concerns session at the 1971 White House Conference on Aging. Older Asian Americans have unique language, dietary, and cultural problems that make the current mix of services for the elderly more difficult for them to use. Older Asian Americans have much higher proportions of men than the general population does because immigration laws that allowed men to enter as laborers did not allow entry of women and children. In addition, the ebb and flow of "yellow peril" fears in America has resulted in a reluctance of older Asian Americans to utilize public programs and services.

American Indians

The situation of Native Americans, or American Indians, in the United States is clouded by numerous issues, not the least of which is difficulty in gathering information about those who do not live on reservations. According to the Bureau of the Census, there were about 75,-000 older American Indians in the United States in 1980, of which about 30 percent lived on reservations. About 53 percent of Native Americans lived in rural areas compared to 25 percent of the white population. In 1970, at age 55 to 59 only 69 percent of American Indian men and 37 percent of women were in the labor force, compared to 88 percent and 47 percent of white men and women. And those Native Americans who were employed at age 55 to 59 were much less likely than whites to have upper-level jobs. Incomes of older American Indians were the worst for any minority (see Table 14-5).

Older Native Americans on reservations face conditions that are substantially different from the older population in general. They lead an agricultural life style that has changed much more slowly than has society as a whole. The federal government views American Indians not as independent citizens but as poor unfortunates to be protected. Accordingly, many services to older American Indians on reservations are overly paternalistic compared to services to older Americans in general. In addition, Native Americans share in the general unavailability of Federal programs for the elderly in rural areas. Housing and sanitation on Indian reservations are the most substandard in America. Tuberculosis, cirrhosis of the liver, diabetes, and alcoholism are all more common among Native Americans than in the general population (Benedict, 1972). In cities, the older Native American poor suffer disadvantages similar to those experienced by poor blacks. They have had poor jobs, little education, and little preparation for life in urban America. And like Asian Americans, they often have language problems.

The problems of older Native Americans are likely to persist. Younger generations of American Indians are not making the same strides as other minorities. Only if American society is opened to full participation by the continent's first settlers can elderly Indians solve their problems in the same ways other older Americans do.

Ethnicity

The cultural and ethnic differences that are certainly present among the various racial minorities in American society influence the patterns discussed in the previous section. In this section we will deal with Hispanic Americans.

Hispanic Americans

In 1980, about 2.5 percent of America's older population was of Spanish heritage—mainly Mexican, Puerto Rican, and Cuban. While black Americans have experienced discrimination based on their skin color, Hispanic Americans have experienced discrimination because of their language. Succeeding generations can adopt the language of the dominant white majority, but adopting skin color is another matter. As a result, older Hispanic Americans are substantially better off than older blacks (see Tables 14-1, 14-2, and 14-5). Their occupational histories and incomes are generally better than those of blacks. Yet Hispanic Americans still have a substantial distance to go before they will be on a par with whites.

Unemployment just before retirement is particularly prevalent among Hispanic Americans. In addition, like older Asian Americans, the Hispanic elderly make up a diverse category. The Hispanic elderly poor share with other minority poor the problems of little education, high illiteracy, high incidence of disability, language barriers to participation in society, and cynicism with regard to the effectiveness of government programs. However, there are substantial numbers of Hispanic American older people who have the resources to live middle-class life styles in retirement. In addition, Mexican-Americans in the southwest, Puerto Ricans in the northeast, and Cubans in Florida are quite different in terms of culture of origin and the economic and social situation in their area of settlement in the United States. Generally, Cuban Americans are more advantaged than Mexican Americans and Mexican Americans are more advantaged than Puerto Ricans.

There are thousands of Mexicans who live in the United States illegally. Yet very little information is available on aging among illegal aliens, and given the difficulties of doing research on this population, we are not likely to learn very much.

Gender

Only recently has America become aware that women constitute one of its most oppressed minorities. *Sexism*—the belief that women are generally less capable than men and fit only for certain jobs—has resulted in a unique position for women in relation to jobs. To many, a woman's place is in the home. As we saw in Chapter 9, substantial proportions of older women have been nonemployed housewives, and while the percentage of employed women may be increasing, there are still substantial proportions who will be nonemployed housewives throughout their adult lives. These women are completely dependent on their husbands' lifetime earnings and the retirement income those earnings can generate, and they are *quite* vulnerable to the effects of divorce and widowhood. If they become divorced after age 35, they will find it difficult to work long enough to get adequate Social Security pensions on their own. The system is stacked against persons not employed throughout adulthood, since Social Security benefits are tied to average earnings over as many as 35 years. For example, let's say a person is in a category in which earnings are averaged over 35 years, and that person has worked only 25 years with average earnings

of $10,000 a year. The Social Security Administration would divide the total earnings of $250,-000 by 35, yielding a pension tied to average earnings of $7,143 rather than the actual $10,-000 average over the 25 years worked.

In addition, women who become divorced in middle age often find themselves with no marketable job skills and as a result either have to go back to school or settle for a low-paying job with little or no chance for advancement and little likelihood of generating an adequate retirement pension.

Widows who have been nonemployed housewives over their adult lives are less likely to find themselves out in the cold economically, but it can happen. For example, some husbands select pension options that do not provide a survivor benefit and some pension systems do not provide a survivor benefit. In such cases, widows are often surprised to find that they have lost not only their husbands but a large chunk of their incomes as well. Many women like caring for house, husband, and children rather than participating in the job market. But by selecting

TABLE 14-6   Most common jobs among employed women of selected ages: United States, 1980

Age 30–34		Age 55–59	
Job	Number Employed (in thousands)	Job	Number Employed (in thousands)
Office clerk	1,056	Office clerk	570
Secretary/typist	606	Secretary/typist	287
Manager/administrator	469	Manager/administrator	233
Teacher	458	Sales worker	226
Machine operator	290	Machine operator	203
Sales worker	268	Food service worker	185
Food service worker	225	Janitor/maid	179
Hairdresser/cosmetologist	220	Teacher	128
Registered nurse	189	Nurse aide	85
Nurse aide	160	Registered nurse	78
Percent of all employed: 74%		Percent of all employed: 76%	

Source: Compiled from unpublished data from the U.S. Bureau of the Census.

this option they take a sizable gamble that the marriage will stay intact long enough to give them financial security in their later years. Women who do seek employment find themselves channeled into "women's work." Table 14-6 shows for 1980 the ten most common jobs held by women at ages 30 to 34 and 55 to 59. These jobs are precisely the ones that fit the stereotype of "women's work." Note also that these ten stereotyped women's jobs account for the *majority* of women's employment. The situation in 1980 was little different from that in 1940 (Baxandall et al., 1976). Even if a move toward sexual equality should take place in the job market, it is unlikely to affect the position of middle-aged and mature women for some time to come. It appears that the position of minority women may be improving (see Table 14-3), but the end result would be parity with white women and that is not necessarily an enviable parity.

Of the top ten women's jobs, only teachers and nurses have a high probability of getting a private pension in addition to Social Security. In addition, women's earnings average only about 60 percent as high as men's earnings at the same occupational and educational levels (see Table 14-7). These various factors mean

TABLE 14-7 Median earnings of persons age 55 to 64 employed full-time, by occupation and education, for white, black, and Spanish-surname persons: United States, 1969

Occupation	Males			Females		
	White	Black	Spanish Surname	White	Black	Spanish Surname
Professional and technical	$14,049	$8,099	$11,640	$8,060	$6,937	$8,297
Managers and administrators						
High school	11,389	7,652	9,133	6,209	5,485	4,729
College	18,990	9,800	12,190	8,171	—	—
Craftspersons						
Less than high school	8,876	7,107	8,191	5,273	4,299	—
High school	9,384	7,456	8,697	5,764	5,790	—
College	11,881	9,121	—	6,876	—	—
Clerical workers						
Less than high school	8,223	7,018	7,103	5,307	5,126	5,424
High school	8,558	7,555	7,209	5,608	5,658	5,758
College	10,598	8,638	—	6,069	7,357	—
Operatives						
Less than high school	8,060	6,789	6,992	4,476	4,141	4,087
High school	8,257	7,433	7,658	4,600	4,446	4,013
Sales workers						
Less than high school	7,346	4,967	5,665	3,735	3,386	3,861
High school	7,999	—	7,537	3,901	4,207	3,708
Laborers	6,798	6,077	6,875	4,258	—	—
Service workers						
Less than high school	6,400	5,122	5,529	3,659	—	—
High school	6,836	5,808	5,374	3,932	—	—
Private household workers	3,671	2,326	—	1,922	1,778	2,196

Source: U.S. Bureau of the Census, 1973i.

that retirement incomes of women average only about 55 percent as high as those enjoyed by men. And for minority women the situation is especially dismal (see Table 14-5).

Multiple Jeopardy

Thus far we have been concerned primarily with how various types of social inequality, taken separately, affect aging. But many older Americans are simultaneously members of several disadvantaged groups. For example, compare an upper-class white older man and a lower-class black older woman, and imagine their lives as they grow older. Beyond such obvious extremes, however, it is difficult to get an idea of just how various minority characteristics interact.

One way to examine the issue is to look at how education (social class related), race and ethnicity, and sex simultaneously affect earnings *within* various occupations. Table 14-7 allows us to do this. In 1969, earnings rose with occupational status. Within most occupational categories, lower education and being black were decided disadvantages. However, *the great disadvantage was being a woman.* Among poorly educated women in menial jobs, minority status was of little consequence, while among men there were substantial racial and ethnic differences across the occupational and educational range.

Palmore and Manton (1973) examined inequality on a number of dimensions. They addressed themselves to three important questions: How do ageism, racism, and sexism compare in terms of observable inequality? Are their effects cumulative? How have these various types of inequality changed in recent years? In terms of the relative power of the various types of inequality, they found substantial inequalities, of all three types, in income, occupational distribution, and education. Income and occupational inequalities were greatest with

regard to sex, and educational inequality was greatest with regard to age. Palmore and Manton also reported that age inequality is highest in terms of number of weeks worked. No one form of inequality was consistently greatest on all dimensions.

Age inequality in income was much greater among men than among women and was somewhat greater among nonwhites than among whites. It is particularly noteworthy that there was almost no overlap between the income distribution of younger white men and that of older black women. This is the reality of triple jeopardy! They found that from 1950 to 1970, racial inequality decreased, sexual inequality stayed about the same, and *age inequality increased* substantially.

Palmore and Manton concluded that most of the age inequality in education and occupation was a result of cohort differences. The aged have simply been left behind as the educational and occupational levels of younger cohorts have risen. On the other hand, income inequality was a function of a combination of cohort differences and age discrimination in employment.

These concrete data result from actions taken on the basis of people's social class, race, ethnicity, and sex. And based on the preceding chapter we must add age to the list. Inequality becomes injustice when the basis for the inequality has no validity. A large proportion of the social inequality in the United States rests on categorical assumptions—ageism, racism, and sexism—that are at least as much a *result* of our system for linking people with jobs as they are a justification for it.

The quality of life in the later years is heavily dependent on health and financial resources. In our society both are closely tied to jobs. For this reason we must conclude that while they may have a bearing on the availability of housing and services, *the primary impact of social class, race, ethnicity, and sex on aging is their impact on jobs* and on the opportunities those jobs allow or the limitations they impose.

Summary

Social class influences aging by influencing the attitudes, beliefs, and values people use to make life-course choices and by influencing life-course opportunities, particularly in terms of education and jobs. People whose social class backgrounds lead to middle-class jobs or higher approach aging with much greater resources—knowledge, good health, adequate retirement income—compared to the working class and the poor. The positive picture of individual aging presented earlier is primarily middle class because most older Americans are middle class. On the other hand, many of the problematic aspects of aging are concentrated among the working class and the poor.

Racial discrimination has concentrated black Americans disproportionately in low-paying jobs and in substandard housing, and this applies more to older blacks than to blacks in general. Compared to older whites, older blacks have lower Social Security benefits, lower prevalence of private pensions, and greater incidence of illness and disability.

Older Native Americans face an even worse situation than older blacks do. Excluded from participation in American society and heavily concentrated in rural areas and on Indian reservations, older American Indians are much less likely than other older people to have access to services. Compared to older whites, older Native Americans are much less likely to have had middle-class jobs and much more likely to have inadequate incomes and poor health.

The picture for older Asian Americans is mixed, although all groups show some negative effects of racism. Japanese American older people have had jobs that closely parallel those of whites and as a result have retirement incomes closer to those of whites than any other racial category. There is great diversity among older Chinese Americans in terms of jobs and retirement income. Filipino American older people are more likely to have had low-paying jobs and thus low retirement incomes. Despite their lower incomes, older Asian Americans tend to be in better health than older whites.

The Hispanic population is quite diverse also. Older Hispanic Americans tend to be better off than older blacks but not as well off as older whites or older Asian Americans in terms of health and retirement income. Very little is known about aging among Mexicans living illegally in the United States.

Of the categories of people who experience discrimination in American society, women experience the greatest injustice. Women who opt to be housewives are quite vulnerable economically to the breakup of their marriages via divorce or widowhood. Those who are employed are concentrated in "women's work," which tends to be low-paying and not covered by private pensions. As a result, retirement incomes of women are only about 55 percent as high as those for men.

Multiple jeopardy increases the probability of having poor health and inadequate income. Being a woman is the greatest disadvantage, followed by having less than high school education (being working-class), and by being black.

Social inequality has a great influence on aging through its effect on jobs and lifetime earnings and through their consequent impact on health and retirement income in later life.

Chapter 15

Deviance and Social Control

All societies use general standards to judge the appropriateness of a given behavior, human condition, or situation. If a departure from conventional custom or practice is seen as merely unusual, we call it "eccentricity." But if the departure is so great that the behavior or condition would be condemned, then we call it *deviance*. Deviance is always defined from the point of view of a particular normative structure. In large societies such as ours there are many subgroups and conflicting standards of behavior. The same act can be defined as deviant by one group, as eccentric by another, and as "normal" by yet another. For example, what is seen as deviant in a suburban neighborhood is quite different from what is seen as deviant on skid row.

Norms are by definition ideas about how human behavior ought to be, and it is no surprise that societies set up mechanisms to prevent and control both the incidence and degree of deviance. Social roles, socialization, and the internalization of norms are all important processes in the prevention of deviance. Formal social controls that seek to limit and discourage deviance include laws, rules, regulations, and authority systems. Informal social controls include customs such as ridicule, disapproval, and ostracism.

This chapter examines how aging interacts with deviance and social control. First we will look at deviance among older people. We will consider crime, alcoholism, disability, sexual deviance, homosexuality, mental disorder, and skid-row residence as examples. We will then look at how being elderly influences definitions of deviance and the selection of social controls. We will then shift to an examination of the elderly as victims of deviance. We will consider crime against the elderly, and neglect, abuse and economic exploitation of the elderly.

Elderly Deviants

The common conception of the elderly as moralistic and conforming often leads people to assume that deviance is relatively rare among the elderly. This view is reflected in the fact that there has been little systematic study of deviance among elderly people, especially in comparison with the volume of research on deviance in other age groups. In this section, an attempt is made to gather and synthesize the bits and pieces of data that do exist. However, at this point the research base is so sparse that there are bound to be large gaps. We begin with crimes committed by the elderly and we then look at mental disorder, disability, alcoholism, sexuality, homosexuality, and skid-row life styles as examples of deviant behavior among the elderly.

Crime by the Elderly

Crime is behavior that is prohibited by law or the omission of behavior required by law. As such, crime is a very broad category indeed, ranging from violation of laws against littering to mass murder. For practicality we will look only at crimes for which incarceration is a possible punishment. Even here there is considerable variation in the seriousness of the punishments, ranging from an overnight stay in jail to a lifetime in prison.*

Crime is difficult to study for several reasons. First, many crimes go unreported. People may not realize that they have been robbed. Undetected shoplifting is seldom reported, for example. Victims of rape may not report the incident because they fear the treatment they may receive from law enforcement agencies, or they fear retaliation from the offender. Second, even when crimes are reported, the age of the offender is often unknown unless he or she is apprehended. Third, even when the offender is

known, there may not be an arrest. For example, the person may be allowed to restore stolen goods in order to avoid arrest and prosecution. Fourth, even when there is an arrest and ample evidence that a crime has been committed, charges may be dropped for a variety of reasons. For example, first offenders who commit petty crimes and who are middle-class are likely to have charges dismissed. Thus, it is not at all clear where a researcher should look to examine crimes. Should they be crimes admitted to by social survey respondents, crimes known to the police, crimes for which there has been an arrest, crimes for which there has been a conviction, crimes for which there has actually been a jail sentence, or yet some other category? We will look at two types of data on crime by the elderly—crimes for which arrests have been made and crimes for which older men have been imprisoned.

Arrests.   In looking at age data on arrests, we should bear in mind that although age most surely affects the probability of arrest, we do not know precisely how. For example, there is evidence that middle-aged, well-dressed men are much less likely to be arrested for drunkenness than either younger men or older men (Wiseman, 1970). On the other hand, there is evidence that behavior treated as criminal in younger people may be viewed as less serious when committed by older people. For example, Stephens (1976) reports a case of indecent exposure by an elderly woman that was ignored by the residents of the hotel where she lived. Systematic research is much needed on this topic.

Table 15-1 shows the number of arrests in 1982, by age and type of offense charged. Arrests are concentrated mostly among the young: Sixty-nine percent of the 10 million arrests made in 1982 were of persons under age 30 (29 percent teenagers or younger, 23.9 percent age 20–24, and 16.1 percent age 25–29). The elderly represented under 1 percent of the arrests, and the total arrest rate at age 65 and over is a tiny fraction of the rates for other age categories.

---

*Capital punishment is technically possible for certain crimes but it is rarely applied to elderly offenders.

TABLE 15-1   Arrests by type of offense charged and total arrest rates, by age: United States, 1982

Total Offenses	Age 25–29		Age 40–44		Age 65+	
	Number	Percent	Number	Percent	Number	Percent
	1,623,271	16.1	447,450	4.4	92,580	0.9
Offense Charged						
Violent crime[a]	78,578	4.8	18,117	4.0	3,021	3.3
Property crime[b]	211,968	13.1	44,306	9.9	14,673	15.8
Alcohol-related	471,546	29.0	186,618	41.7	43,418	46.9
Driving under the influence	271,547	57.5	100,479	53.8	19,219	44.3
Liquor law violation	26,378	5.6	7,661	4.1	1,979	4.6
Drunkenness	173,621	36.8	78,478	42.1	22,148	51.0
Total Arrest Rate[c]	167		78		4	

[a]murder, forcible rape, robbery, or aggravated assault
[b]burglary, larceny-theft, motor vehicle theft, or arson
[c]Arrests per 1,000 population per year
Source: U.S. Department of Justice, 1983.

In looking at age differences in types of offenses committed, probably the most useful comparison is between young adults (25–29), the early middle-aged (40–44), and the elderly (65 and over). As Table 15-1 shows, arrests for violent crimes such as murder and robbery are a small percentage of all adult arrests. There is a small decline in prevalence of arrests for violent crime as age increases. Property crime arrests are less prevalent in the middle-aged, compared to young adults and the elderly. Larceny-theft accounts for 95 percent of the property crime arrests among the elderly, compared to 68 percent for young adults. The elderly are much less likely to be arrested for burglary or car theft. Alcohol-related arrests as a percentage of all arrests increase from young adulthood (29 percent) to early middle age (41.7 percent) to later life (46.7 percent). But keep in mind that young adults are over 12 times more likely to be arrested than the elderly. Young adults are most likely to be arrested for driving under the influence of alcohol, whereas the elderly are more likely to be arrested for drunkenness.

Thus, it appears to be true that crime, as indicated by arrest rates, decreases in prevalence with age. In this sense deviance declines with age, although it does not disappear. In 1982, older people committed over 250 murders, over 2,500 aggravated assaults (a serious form of assault usually involving some sort of deadly weapon), and nearly 3,000 less serious assaults. Thus, the idea that older people do not become violent is inaccurate.

Imprisonment.   Older people are even less likely to be in prison than they are to be arrested. Rubenstein (1982) reported that less than one-half of 1 percent of prison inmates are over 65. Indeed, in most studies of older inmates, "older" begins at age 45 or 50 (Rubenstein, 1982; Hamill, 1982). Hamill (1982) studied 90 inmates of a state prison who were age 50 or over and found that most (57 percent) were not "lifers" who had been in prison since young adulthood, but were men who had been sent to prison in middle age or later. Murder was the most common crime for which these men had been imprisoned, accounting for 43 percent; 37 percent were in for sexual offenses such as rape, corruption of a minor, and gross sexual imposition; 13 percent were in for robbery and assault; and 7 percent had committed other crimes. There was a substantial racial difference in type of crime. Seventy percent of "older" black inmates were in for murder, compared to 30 percent of whites; while 51 percent of whites were in for sexual offenses, compared to 10 percent of blacks. Hamill's sample divided about evenly among inmates who had no prior convictions, those with one or two priors, and those with three or more. Men in these categories were quite different in terms of the crimes for which they were in prison: Over two-thirds of "older" inmates with no prior convictions were in for murder; just over half of those with one or two priors were in for sexual offenses; the most common offense among those with 3 or more prior convictions was robbery. These results are consistent with the literature reviewed by Rubenstein (1982) who found that older first offenders most often commit crimes of passion—killing wives, neighbors, or relatives. Just why older white men are more likely to be incarcerated for sexual offenses than are the young is unclear and would be an excellent topic for research.

Because prison is largely a world of violent young men, older men in prison face potential difficulties. Wiltz (1979) found that older inmates were more likely to conform to prison rules, to be given special privileges by correctional officials, and to feel a stake in maintaining order within the prison as a way of controlling the violence of younger prisoners. Older chronic offenders were usually well-integrated into the prison system, but elderly first offenders often had difficulty adjusting and were sometimes put in sections of the prison relatively isolated from the younger prisoners (Rubenstein, 1982). Whether older prisoners should be in separate facilities from the young is an unresolved debate and is another good topic for research.

White Collar Crime.   Crime that is committed by a person of respectability and high social status in the course of his or her occupation is called white-collar crime (Sutherland, 1949). Such crimes include price fixing, misrepresentation in advertising, fee-splitting, bribery, and adulteration of food or drugs. White-collar crimes cost the public a great deal of money but are much less likely to result in arrest or jail as compared to offenses committed by working-class people. Although little study has been made of the relation between age and white-collar crime, we can suggest some ideas that could be used to guide research. White-collar crime is probably most common in middle age or later but at the same time is uncommon among the elderly. The reasoning here has to do with access. In order to commit white-collar crimes, people have to be in positions of authority, which are related to age and seniority. On the other hand, retired persons probably have little access because they have no occupational arena in which to operate. Interestingly, arrests for fraud and embezzlement are most common in the 20 to 29 age group, although these data may simply indicate an age difference in the disposition of such cases; that is, younger offenders may be prosecuted to set an example, while older offenders, who often have higher positions and could cause more embarrassment to the organization, may be more likely to be allowed to make restitution.

Thus, the available data suggest that the elderly are less likely than other adults to commit crimes or to be arrested, convicted, and imprisoned. Part of the explanation for this is undoubtedly that young adults prone to crime and violence are less likely to live to become old. Part is probably due to greater conformity by the elderly. Another part is probably due to the common conception that aging makes people less responsible for their actions—that aging leads to deterioration of mental faculties. For example, Frankfather (1977) found that the police would ignore all sorts of strange behavior by the elderly because they perceived it as harmless and felt that older people tended to be mentally incompetent. In the words of one officer, "One old man gave me the finger so I stopped him. He said, 'I was just saying hi.' I let him go." (Frankfather, 1977:91). This leads to our next topic: senile dementia as deviance.

Senile Dementia as Deviance

As we learned in Chapter 5, about 5 percent of the elderly and about 20 percent of those 85 and over have symptoms of organic brain disorder. Both the causes and consequences of senile dementia are unclear, mostly because the disorder tends to be highly individualized in both etiology and mental functions affected. Symptoms include such diverse patterns as incoherent or nonresponsive speech, wandering, nonfunctional repetitive actions such as screaming or banging, disorientation in time and place, incontinence, bizarre behavior such as removing clothing at inappropriate times, trying to eat from someone else's plate, or directing traffic in pajamas, and sometimes violence such as punching, kicking, or biting. Such symptoms defy easy diagnosis, but people who work with the older population on a regular basis usually develop a strategy for identifying "senile" older people and treat them differently from the "normal" elderly. Although it is easy to condemn this as discriminatory, there are often very real considerations that make it necessary. For example, "normal" older people often refuse to associate with mentally impaired older people in meals programs, senior centers, and the like. When older people behave inappropriately, they are likely to be labelled as "senile" and to receive a different type of treatment or to be simply excluded.

In the 1960s, there was a concerted effort to move people out of mental hospitals and into "the community." It was argued that many of the patients of state mental hospitals were not dangerous to the public and were not mentally disturbed so severely as to warrant hospitaliza-

tion. In addition, new drugs made it possible to "manage" mental problems enough to allow the person to at least approximate "normal" behavior. Finally, it was argued, taking care of these people in "the community" was much less expensive for the state. Unfortunately, "the community" was not prepared for the influx of people with mental problems. In addition, the growing number of elders meant more people with senile dementia, since rates of senile dementia are much higher in the older population.

The experiences of all those who encounter senile dementia in community settings probably have one thing in common—frustration. When we interact with people, we expect them to be able to pay attention and to take part of the responsibility for the interaction. When people are trying to run programs for a large number of people, they expect the people not to require constant monitoring. Unfortunately, people with senile dementia do not fit such expectations. On top of that, there are very few specialists serving those with senile dementia. The result is that in most communities the confused and mentally fragile elderly have nowhere to go. No one wants them. They are disruptive at senior centers, unresponsive to the therapy provided by mental health centers, not disturbed enough to qualify for hospitalization, unwanted by public housing officials who may rightly consider them dangerous, rejected by family who are tired of their antics, and so forth.

Frankfather (1977) found that mentally impaired older people tended to be shuffled from one place to another in a "loop" of agencies, making temporary stops at various institutions —usually nursing homes or hospitals, institutions that operate on a "medical model" and where the usual response to problems in "managing" the demented older person is to prescribe tranquilizers. Hospitals, especially emergency rooms, often experience an increase in "difficult" cases on weekends and holidays, inconvenient times when families and nursing homes "dump" their most demanding cases. Hospital discharge planners find it most frustrating to place these people in appropriate facilities. As one said, "Her problem is that nobody wants a screamer. The previous social worker tried three times to place her" (Frankfather, 1977:150). Older people who wander, or are incontinent, unable to feed themselves, or not ambulatory are especially difficult to place because most nursing homes do not have sufficient staff to care for them.

Senile dementia is frightening to most people. They do not want to end up in such a state and are unable to do anything that will guarantee that they will not. In addition, some of the behavior of demented people is so outside the realm of social acceptability that it is disgusting to be around. For both of these reasons, most people shun the mentally impaired elderly. But even though we do not want to be around the mentally impaired, neither are we willing to pay for adequate caretakers. This will certainly be one of the greatest challenges facing our society over the next several decades, as our older population ages and the number of elders with senile dementia dramatically increases. Unlike most other shunned categories, the mentally impaired elderly have few resources with which to care for themselves.

Disability as Deviance

A *disability* is a long-term functional incapacity (Nagi, 1965). Although 46 percent of the elderly are somewhat limited, and only about 14 percent of all elderly have severe functional limitations, at age 85 or over, 31 percent have serious limitations. Among those 75 or over, 16 percent use canes and 5 percent use walkers. Among those 85 or older, nearly 20 percent need some assistance in dressing and bathing. About 5 percent of the elderly in independent households cannot go outdoors unassisted (Miller, 1982).

Whereas the *behavior* of people with senile dementia stigmatizes them as deviant, the stigma for the disabled more often comes from their *physical appearance*. The existence of a handicap signifies that the person is different in a way that most people judge as undesirable. The handicapped or disabled deviate from the expectation that "normal" adults should be of "sound" body. And as with mental impairment, the typical social reaction is to isolate the "problem" so that "normal" people do not have to cope with the handicapped in everyday situations. Of course this means that the handicapped are liked best when they keep (or are kept) out of sight.

The traveler to Africa or Asia is very quickly struck by the large number of handicapped people on the streets. People with birth defects, amputees, people with cerebral palsy, and those with a host of other afflictions can be seen on every busy street of large cities. In many cases, these individuals are proprietors of small street stalls. Such people were once common on the streets of America, but "progress" has led us to eliminate the unsightly—not only buildings, but people as well. In most cases, no alternative arena for participation has arisen, leaving the handicapped isolated or segregated in programs designed to deal with "their own kind."

The Vietnam War resulted in a large number of relatively young handicapped people. Their numbers plus perhaps our national guilt about having sent them to a questionable war have led to an increased awareness of the problems of the handicapped and an expansion of facilities and services. Disabled people can participate in American society only with a great deal of help. Special transportation, motorized wheelchairs, ramps, sidewalk cuts, paid assistance at home, and physical rehabilitation services are just some of things disabled people need if they are to move about the community with some semblance of the freedom and opportunity enjoyed by the nondisabled. In recent years, we have made significant strides toward making these items available to young and middle-aged disabled people, yet they are still relatively unavailable to the elderly. The problem is that rehabilitation services such as physical therapy tend to be tied to employment prospects. Most disabled older Americans, being retired, are judged ineligible for most such services. We cannot even be sure of the numbers who are not being served, since Social Security Administration research on disability stops at age 64. Because of ageism in services to the handicapped, elderly handicapped people have even less access to American society than do handicapped people in general. So far very little has been done even to draw attention to this problem, much less solve it.

Alcoholism as Deviance

Just about every textbook on deviance contains a section on *alcoholism*. Addiction to alcohol has probably been recognized as disruptive to society's functioning for thousands of years. Alcohol abuse as a form of escapism was dealt with in Chapter 12. In this section we will look at alcoholism as it contributes to the image of the elderly as deviant.

Mishara and Kastenbaum (1980) reviewed much of the literature on aging and alcoholism and found wide variation in the estimated extent of alcoholism among the elderly, largely due to differences in research methodology. They concluded that somewhere under 10 percent of the elderly are "problem drinkers"—defined as persons who have either physical symptoms of alcoholism or social difficulties arising from alcohol use, such as problems with family, neighbors, employers, or the police. A great many studies have documented that heavy drinking is an important background variable for a large minority of the elderly being treated in mental health programs (Mishara and Kastenbaum, 1980). In many cases, elderly alcoholics were also suffering from symptoms of senile dementia. Part of the inconsistency in the estimates of alcoholism rates probably results from some alcoholism's being reported as senile dementia and vice versa.

The fact that alcoholism is related to deviance is dramatically illustrated by the finding that 53 percent of men and 30 percent of women over 60 admitted to a Texas psychiatric screening agency were diagnosed as suffering from alcoholism. And among the elderly alcoholics, 60 percent were also suffering from some degree of organic brain disease. Only 11 percent of the elderly alcoholics had begun heavy drinking in later life (Gaitz and Baer, 1971). Most of the studies of the elderly in health care institutions show a larger percentage of alcoholics than do studies of the general older population. This suggests that alcoholism is an important factor in poor health in later life and that it plays an important role in precipitating deviant behavior. As noted earlier, more than half of the arrests of older people are alcohol related.

In its most extreme form, alcoholism reduces people to derelicts living hand to mouth on the skid rows of America. Bogue (1963) reported that of the 12,000 men living in Chicago's skid row in 1958 about 3,000 (25 percent) were age 60 or over. Of these men, 661 (23 percent) were borderline alcoholics, and 328 (11 percent) were chronic alcoholics. Thus, elderly men were overrepresented among the residents of skid row, and elderly men with alcoholism were a sizable minority.

Aged alcoholics on skid row are seldom treated unless they are severely physically ill. The police tend to ignore them unless they pass out on the street or create a disturbance. The same sort of "loop" of agencies that we discussed earlier in connection with dealing with people with senile dementia is used to manage alcoholics, including the elderly. Only, in this case the agencies include the city jail, the jail clinic, the state mental hospital, the county home for the aged, the city hospital, and the city hospital emergency room (Wiseman, 1970). Wiseman (1970) concluded that the main focus of public action toward the elderly alcoholics on skid row was on keeping them from offending members of the public who passed through skid row on their way to work or shopping. This is consistent with the "out of sight–out of mind" approach to the issue of where deviants fit into society.

Sexual Deviance in the Elderly

That the elderly engage in any form of sexual behavior is considered deviance by many. For example, Harris and Associates (1975) found that only 5 percent of the public thought the elderly were very active sexually. Indeed, sexual inactivity is so deeply ingrained in our expectations of the elderly that we tend to be scandalized when we find that older people continue to enjoy sex.

In the movie *Rose By Any Other Name,* an adult daughter is called in by a nursing home administrator because her elderly mother has been "caught sneaking into" the room of a male resident of the nursing home at night. The administrator, offended by what he sees as clearly deviant behavior, tells the daughter that if the mother doesn't stop, she will be evicted from the home. The daughter, also appalled, chides her mother. However, the mother sticks up for her need for and right to a sex life, even in a nursing home, and she uses examples from various stages of the daughter's life to persuade the daughter that we are never without the need for physical intimacy and that some of us feel very lonely without it. Convincing the home's staff is another matter. The movie ends with the issue unresolved.

In their study of sex and sexuality among older people, Starr and Weiner (1981) encountered marked resistance from the gate-keeping professionals (whose permission they needed) on the grounds that the elderly were not interested in sex and would find a study of sex embarrassing and offensive. As it turned out, the elderly were quite willing to participate in the study and offered many examples of sexuality among the elderly.

These examples illustrate that merely linking the concept of sex with the concept of later life is in itself considered suspect. Most people now accept as appropriate the tasteful discussion of sexual behavior in novels, as indicated by the brisk sales of "romance" novels. However, almost never are elderly characters depicted as sexually interested, much less aroused. And when older men are depicted as interested in sex it is often just to illustrate how unbalanced or perverse the character is. Normal sexual urges and behavior simply become redefined as deviant when the actors are older people.

Active sexuality has been linked to life satisfaction among older men, and failing sexuality among them has been associated with depression and suicide. Thus, it appears that sexual urges are still important to men in later life. However, when older men with organic brain disorder or alcoholism experience these urges, they may be less likely to deal with them appropriately. This may partly account for the earlier-mentioned tendency for older men to be imprisoned for sex offenses. This would be a good topic for more research.

The 'dirty old man"—one who is willing to go to great lengths for sexual stimulation and who is preoccupied with sex—is certainly a well-entrenched social type in American lore. Older men are depicted in cartoons and jokes as being the prime consumers of sexually oriented entertainment. But if we look at arrest data, we find that the 1982 arrest rate for sex offenses was only 43 per 100,000 for men age 65 and over, compared to 1,081 per 100,000 at age 25 to 29 and 482 per 100,000 at age 45 to 49. At this level at least, the stereotype seems to have little validity. More research is needed on this topic, too.

Prostitution is usually thought to be an activity reserved for the young, but Stephens (1976) reported that several older women who lived in the skid-row hotel she studied would engage in prostitution in order to get money to pay their rent. Thus, even this form of sexual deviance is carried into later life by some older people.

Homosexuality Among the Elderly

Homosexuality is either a feeling of sexual desire for persons of one's own sex or sexual relations with a member of one's own sex, or both (Thio, 1983:220). Most people have some experience that fits this definition, but only a minority act on their homosexuality. Because people do not fit into neat categories of heterosexual or homosexual, defining who is homosexual is difficult. Researchers who have studied homosexuality have been impressed by the wide range of individual differences in both preferences and behavior among homosexuals (Kinsey, Pomeroy, and Martin, 1948; Kinsey and Gebhard, 1953; Bell and Weinberg, 1978; Berger, 1982). Thus, homosexuals fit no stereotype. Bell and Weinberg (1978) concluded that knowledge that a person is homosexual implies no more than knowledge that a person is heterosexual.

Estimates of the proportion of the population that is homosexual are difficult to make, for obvious reasons. When a particular sexual preference and life style is stigmatized and punishable by law, survey results can only indicate what proportion of the population is willing to admit to being homosexual. Kinsey and his colleagues (1948, 1953) found that 37 percent of white males and 13 percent of white females had engaged in homosexual behavior at some time between adolescence and old age. However, only 4 percent of the men and 1 percent of the women were exclusively homosexual. These findings were replicated in a later study by Athanasiou et al. (1970). If these proportions hold for the older population, then in 1980 there were about 400,000 older men and 150,000 older women who were exclusively homosexual.

Bell and Weinberg (1978) found that about 20 percent of men who identified themselves as gay and 30 percent of women who identified themselves as lesbian had married, and that about half of those who had married had children. Thus, contrary to the stereotype, many older homosexual men and women can be expected to have adult children and grandchildren.

Life as a homosexual in the United States is difficult. Although at least some forms of homosexual behavior are considered "normal" in many cultures, ours is not one of them. A majority of Americans define homosexuality as "harmful" to society and find it personally disgusting (Clinard, 1974). In most states, homosexual behavior is illegal, even when it occurs in private between consenting adults. Homosexuality is widely disapproved of and can result in loss of employment, rejection by family, difficulty finding a place to live, and exclusion from community participation. In recent years, attitudes toward homosexuality have become more accepting, particularly in certain communities: The American Psychiatric Association has removed homosexuality from its list of psychiatric disorders; there have been organized efforts to repeal statutes punishing homosexual behavior; and corporations have openly announced a willingness to hire homosexuals (Thio, 1983:242). However, there is still a great deal of prejudice and discrimination against homosexuals in most situations. Given the difficulty of being homosexual in America, we might expect older homosexuals to be bitter and to have low self-esteem. However, researchers have found that morale of older homosexuals (variously defined and ranging from age 45 up) is not significantly different from other groups (Weinberg and Williams, 1975; Minnigerode and Adelman, 1976).

Part of the expectation that older homosexual men will have greater problems with aging compared to heterosexual men is based on an assumption that among gay men, physical attractiveness is the most important determinant of a satisfactory life style, especially sex life. West described the "problem" as follows:

> Many aging homosexuals, having organized their lives and interests around sexual adventures, to an extent almost unimaginable to staid married people, find eventually that they are left without family, roots or purpose. Some of them can be seen wearily trailing their old haunts, trying to bribe themselves back into the company of young men. . . . Others retire to a grimly isolated existence. The dread of growing old is a noticeable feature of male homosexuals (1967:58).

However, research on older homosexuals has shown that this view is inaccurate. Weinberg and Williams (1975) found that compared to younger gay men, older gay men had more positive and more stable self-concepts. Minnigerode (1976) found that gay men did not see themselves as "old" any sooner than did heterosexual men. Berger (1982:187) found that his older gay respondents had not easily accepted their homosexual identities and that acceptance of themselves as homosexual was the result of having successfully resolved many years of ambivalence and anxiety.

Kelly (1977) and Berger (1982) both found that older gay men were generally well-adjusted. Their life satisfaction was high, they had satisfying life styles, including satisfying sex lives, and they were not isolated. Older gay men did tend to participate less in impersonal sex via gay bars or bathhouses. Berger (1982:193) pointed out that in some ways being homosexual actually prepares men for old age by forcing them to become more independent than heterosexual men usually are. Thus, aging seems to have the same capacity to increase self-acceptance and life satisfaction among homosexuals that we earlier found it to have for the general population. Aging per se does not seem to have a greater effect on homosexuals than on other subgroups.

The problems that older homosexuals face are those that are common to other older people, such as ill health or financial difficulties, or common to other homosexuals, such as difficulty in gaining legal and social recognition for homosexual couples. Kelly (1977) cites a particularly poignant case of an older lesbian dying in a hospital who was allowed visits by her immediate family only; her partner of over 20 years was excluded.

The generally positive picture of aging among older homosexuals despite society's hostility toward them needs to be tempered with caution. The research on older homosexuals is biased toward the experiences of middle-class survivors. Shapiro (1971) noted that the lesbian

couples and triangles living in New York City's run-down hotels were viewed as low-class tenants even by the other residents. Sigrang (1982) estimated that as much as 30 percent of the gay population is alcoholic, which certainly has a bearing on survival. And many skid-row men's homosexual experiences occur in jails (Spradley, 1970). Thus, just as heterosexual life styles have their seamy varieties, so also do homosexual life styles.

Right now we know more about aging among gay men than about aging among lesbians. And much more research is needed on both groups.

Living in Single Room Occupancy Hotels

Most older people live in their own detached houses or in apartments that include independent cooking and bathroom facilities. However, there is a class of older people, mostly poor, who live in run-down hotels in the core areas of American cities. These buildings have been termed SRO's, since in most cases the housing consists of a single sleeping room, often without bath or cooking facilities. In most cases only some of the rooms in the building are occupied by the elderly, with the remaining rooms being rented to the transient poor of various types. These hotels are usually in slum neighborhoods in which violent crime and other forms of deviance such as prostitution, drug trafficking, and public alcoholism are prominent. Street crime such as brawls, muggings, robberies, and even killings are commonplace and as a result the elderly residents of these areas often live in constant fear.

Research on SRO's indicates that many of the elderly who live in them are themselves deviant —mentally impaired, petty hustlers, alcoholics, drug users, or the like. Thus, despite the climate of fear, many of these people find that their behavior and life styles cause them fewer problems in these neighborhoods than might be the case elsewhere. Most cities have "rough" areas in which police attitudes are aimed at containment of only the most serious deviance, and less serious forms of deviance are largely ignored. Most SRO's are in these rough areas. But it would be a mistake to assume that SRO's are all basically alike. Research studies have shown great variability in the economic level of the residents, the types of elderly people who live in SRO's, the degree of cooperation among residents, the proportion of elderly in the building, and the character of the surrounding neighborhood (Stephens, 1976; Shapiro, 1971; Sokolovsky and Cohen, 1981a; Cantor, 1975; Tissue, 1971a; Lawton, Kleban and Singer, 1971; Erickson and Ekert, 1977). We will briefly look at three of these studies.

Shapiro (1971) estimated that in 1970 there were over 400 SRO's in Manhattan, housing about 30,000 people. She reported that although about two-thirds of these buildings were well-managed, provided adequate housing for their residents, and were socially accepted by the neighborhood, the remaining third were characterized by "physical deterioration and conspicuous antisocial behavior" (pp. 16–17). Unlike the run-down SRO's in most cities, those in Manhattan were not located in or adjacent to skid row but in "better" neighborhoods and were therefore seen by the other neighborhood residents as pockets of blight. If they had been alongside other blighted residences there might not have been as much attention to the "SRO problem." Few of the residents of the nine buildings that Shapiro studied in detail were under age 40. A sizable proportion was black or Hispanic. Men outnumbered women by two to one. More than half were on welfare. Rents averaged about $60 per month. At least 75 percent of the occupants had major health problems such as tuberculosis, heart disease, diabetes, and cirrhosis of the liver. On top of the health problems, deviance was common. In some buildings, more than half of the residents were alcoholics. Others were drug addicts or obviously mentally ill. Residents with similar afflictions tended to be grouped together on the same floor by the building managers.

Shapiro found considerable mutual aid in the SRO's she studied. There were matriarchal quasi-"families" consisting of an older woman and several alcoholic middle-aged or older men, the "bottle-gang" of middle-aged alcoholics who spent time together drinking in a member's room, or the addict-prostitute and one or two male addicts she supported. Shapiro found that some residents looked after and cared for other residents for no other reason than the status they felt it gave them. For example, one elderly woman cared for several bedridden residents. She cleaned and cooked for them regularly without compensation.

"Check day" was an important event in all of the SRO's. There was a flurry of activity as residents gathered in the lobbies to get their checks, cash them at the office (with rent and loans withheld), and scurry off to pay minor debts and catch up on shopping. Diets of the residents were visibly lacking in meat, milk, and fresh fruits and vegetables, and emphasized cereal, bread, pasta, rice, peanut butter and jelly, and cold cuts.

Most of the building managers were elderly immigrants who had very ambivalent attitudes toward their jobs. On the one hand, they tended to recognize that their tenants were damaged people who needed compassion and protection. On the other hand, they viewed the residents as an unruly lot that must be handled with a firm hand. As Shapiro put it, "They consider themselves real estate businessmen, but they are in reality untrained directors of staffless institutions" (1971:40). Shapiro concluded that the SRO's she studied represented private poorhouses supported by public funds but without public accountability. They served the city by providing housing for people unable to function more autonomously, but they offered no protection for these very vulnerable citizens other than the highly unpredictable good will of the managers or the other residents.

Sokolovsky and Cohen (1981a) studied 11 Manhattan SRO's catering primarily to whites and not defined by the neighborhood a part of the "SRO problem." The proportion of elderly in these buildings ranged from 15 to 25 percent. These buildings housed people with relatively high education and incomes sufficient to pay rents up to $200 per month. In contrast to Shapiro's observations of rampant deviance and neighborhood ostracism, Sokolovsky and Cohen found that many residents had frequent interaction and mutual aid relationships with family and friends outside the SRO. Many of the elderly residents had never married and had lived in the hotel an average of ten years. Friendship networks within the SRO were common and so was mutual aid, especially for those over age 70 and in poor health. Reports of victimization within the SRO, and of alcoholic, mentally impaired, or other deviant residents are conspicuously absent from Sokolovsky and Cohen's account. Clearly, these were not SRO's for elderly deviants. Thus, SRO residence in itself does not indicate deviance. Rather, the character of the residents of the particular SRO and of the surrounding neighborhood indicates the relevance of a deviance perspective.

Stephens (1976) studied the elderly residents of a single SRO characterized by one of the residents as "one of your better low-class hotels" and located in the skid row area of a large midwestern city. About a third of the 371 tenants of the SRO were elderly. The average rent was about $80 per month. Most residents were white, and older males outnumbered older females by about ten to one. The average length of residence was nine years. Half of the elderly males had never married, whereas most of the women were widowed. Like Shapiro, Stephens found that health problems were widespread as were alcoholism, disability (especially blindness, deafness, and paralysis), and mental illness. The manager tended to locate those with physical disabilities on the lower floors, "nuts and mentals" on the top floor. However, the residents of this particular hotel were functioning better than similarly afflicted residents in adjacent hotels, some of whom had once lived in the hotel that Stephens studied but who had

"slipped." The tenants knew their environment was not ideal, but they viewed it as vastly superior to nursing homes, about which the tenants were uniformly hostile and suspicious.

The elderly residents consisted of alcoholics, street peddlers (who referred to one another as "carnies"), pensioners, and "mentals." All of these residents were viewed by the manager as disreputable, in that they were loners and misfits—people who in one way or another did not fit into the larger society. As in Shapiro's study, the manager was ambivalent about the residents and likewise the residents about the manager. There was evident conflict between managing deviants and making money on the one hand and care and concern for fellow humans on the other.

Unlike Shapiro, Stephens found little in the way of relationships among the residents. Each one seemed to feel that singularity was necessary as protection in an environment where most everyone had a money-making "hustle" that usually involved exploiting someone else. Because the hotel catered to people with a little more money than those in the surrounding area, the residents were also targets of exploitation from outside. For example, at the first of every month—"check day"—prostitutes from the area would descend on the hotel to "skim the top off" the male residents' incomes. Elderly women residents of the hotel also sometimes sold their sexual services to elderly male residents if they were short of rent money. Stephens felt the residents knew they could not control deviance directed at them, but knew they could avoid it by minimizing their relationships with others. Deviance by fellow residents was tolerated as long as it involved no danger to the other residents. Stephens cited this tolerance as a major means by which many residents were able to function outside institutions.

Earlier in this chapter, we discussed problems faced by alcoholic and mentally impaired older people who try to live "in the community." From the above examples, it should be clear that in some cases, SRO's are surrogate institutions helping to achieve society's goal of managing deviants and keeping them out of sight.

Tramps and Shopping Bag Ladies

There are older Americans who cannot afford even the cheapest SRO's. Tramps and shopping bag ladies are two obvious examples. *Tramps*—homeless men who are often alcoholic wanderers working sporadically, if at all—do not qualify for public assistance because of their lack of residence. Spradley (1970) has provided a stark description of life on Seattle's skid row. He found a great deal of resourcefulness among the tramps on skid row. They knew numerous ways to survive without living quarters. They slept in boxes, under piles of newspapers, in vacant buildings, and in a host of other places. Most knew the advantages and liabilities of each type of "flop" (place to sleep). All had some way of getting money: Some panhandled, some worked odd jobs, some stole. All agreed that their appearance and their associates enabled the police to define them as deviants needing to be controlled. Most of the tramps Spradley studied had been in jail for vagrancy or drunkenness over 50 times. These men were familiar with the courts and the penal system, and often moved from one community to another in order to minimize the amount of time spent in jail. Despite the high degree of mobility among tramps, Spradley found a tramp culture consisting of common language and customs and allowing tramps to enter the scene in a new town quickly and easily. He also found a great deal of interaction and friendship among these men, who were usually relative strangers to one another. They often helped each other out of jams.

Bogue (1963) reported that 25 percent of the men on Chicago's skid row were age 60 or over. Most cited access to cheap food and lodging as the main feature drawing them to skid row. Despite the familiar skid row culture and the presence of other homeless men with whom they could interact, 75 percent of the men Bogue studied disliked living on skid row, disliked living in the cheap hotels there, had very few close friends there, and disliked the type of men who lived there. Most of all, they disliked living around people who were heavy drinkers (even though they were usually heavy drinkers themselves). As Spradley (1970) pointed out, men who do not want to settle down to home and job do not have a place in American society. Besides skid row, where else can they go? Bogue (1963) cited as the leading reasons for living on skid row, cheap lodging and food, tolerance of deviant and unusual persons, rejection by family and local community, withdrawal from society, companionship and association with others of the same group, ready access to welfare activities of missions and other agencies, opportunities for unlimited and cheap drinking, secondary importance of dress and physical appearance, and tolerance of homosexuals.

Society's reaction to skid row is one of containment. Every morning, before the journey to work begins for the general population, the police may make a sweep of the skid row area and pick up drunks passed out on the street or men sleeping in alleys or doorways, load them into a police van, haul them to jail, and put them in the "drunk tank," usually a large empty cell with one toilet and wash basin. As many as 50 men at a time may go before the judge of "drunk court." Most of them are repeat offenders and receive jail sentences for drunkenness. Spradley (1970) found that it was not at all unusual for skid row men to spend most of the year in jail. Life in drunk tanks and jails is difficult. As one man put it, "If you're a young fellow, you can take it. It's miserable, but you can take it. . . . I've been in there when there is standing room only, in one of those concrete cells, for two or three days" (Spradley, 1970:161).

Certainly, there is no easy answer to the question of why some men become tramps or bums and others with similar origins and experiences do not. However, as Spradley (1970) pointed out, the degrading treatment that these people receive from the police and the courts actually perpetuates their behavior rather than discouraging it. Most men who are tramps in their old age have been living that life for some time. They often have serious chronic illnesses that are unlikely to be treated. They may also be mentally impaired to some degree. As a group they are very much in need, yet many people who work with them believe they are truly beyond help.

Shopping bag ladies are homeless vagrants living in urban public places and carrying their households around with them in shopping bags (Hand, 1983). Hand (1983) estimated that there were 400 to 500 shopping bag ladies living in Manhattan, most of them in their fifties and early sixties, who at one time were integrated into society's institutions but who found themselves cut off from family, income, and a place to live. Hand (1983) reported that many were former mental patients. Their lives revolved around places and things rather than people. They needed places to sleep that were safe, warm, and dry. They needed food, places to be, and something to do. They slept in bus stations, public restrooms, apartment lobbies, subways, and a host of other public places. They welcomed pedestrian traffic for the safety it brought but wanted nothing to do with people. Shopping bag ladies felt that in order to protect themselves—in order to avoid "being locked up and put away"—they had to avoid people. Unlike the homeless men on skid row, shopping bag women did not talk to one another or help one another (Hand, 1983:160).

Shopping bag ladies found places to be in locations open to the public—libraries, churches, waiting rooms of clinics, doctors, lawyers, and so on. They existed there by blending into the surroundings. They tried to look like they belonged. They tried to avoid drawing attention to themselves. They ate "other people's leftovers found in garbage cans or still on the plates of self-service cafeterias" (Hand, 1983). Scavenging was a major form of recreation for shopping

bag women. They sorted through the plentiful trash on the streets of Manhattan and collected familiar articles that to them became their own belongings and to them signified status. Obviously, shopping bag ladies are even further outside the "system" than are the tramps on skid row. They are unknown to social agencies and do not want to be known by them. They lack reliable access not only to shelter, food, and clothing, but to health care as well.

Alcoholism does not seem to play a part in the lives of shopping bag ladies and their strategy of avoiding people and remaining unobtrusive makes them less likely to be rousted by the police. Nevertheless, they are deviant in that they make their homes—washing up, changing clothes, sleeping, and existing—in public places. The driving forces that push women into this life style are poverty and the absence of a network of family or friends that might otherwise help them solve the dilemma of finding a place to live.

Varieties of Deviance

Elderly deviants come in many varieties, as we have seen. For some, the underlying causes of their deviance are not different from those of younger deviants. Poverty and alcohol influence crime, alcoholism, SRO residence, and skid row residence for young and old alike. For others, age-related factors such as organic brain disease and disability push them into deviance in later life. In addition, accumulated loss of roles and social supports may lead to alcoholism and homelessness. Despite an antagonistic culture, homosexuals seem to benefit from aging in most of the same ways that heterosexuals do—more stable self-concept, greater self-acceptance, and greater life satisfaction.

A common thread running through our discussion has been the repressive nature of society's approach to deviants, including elderly deviants. As a society, we do not tolerate deviants well, and we have created various social patterns to keep them out of sight. Although we give lip service to rehabilitating the criminal, the mental patient, or the alcoholic, in practice we are not very good at it. Even if more resources are invested in rehabilitating such deviants, there is no guarantee that we would get what we want—conformity. Perhaps deviants, including elderly deviants, are inevitable in complex societies, and perhaps the best way to deal with this inevitability is to set up institutions that control deviants as humanely as possible.

The elderly are probably more often the targets of deviant behavior than they are the perpetrators of it. We will discuss deviant behavior that is directed at the elderly—a much more common theme in gerontology.

Deviance Directed at Older People

In the gerontology literature in recent years there has been a growing interest in the vulnerability of older people to crime, neglect and abuse, and economic exploitation through fraud and quackery.

Economic Exploitation

Older people are particularly vulnerable to fraud, deception, and quackery. To begin with, older people on fixed incomes and with barely enough to live on are very susceptible to any "sure-fire" scheme to get more money or a supplementary income. Also, loneliness and isolation sometimes make older people susceptible to deception by a friendly, outgoing person who takes an apparent interest in them. Finally, hopeless illness is more frequent among older people, and many unscrupulous people have exploited the desperation that such illness can evoke. Harris (1978) reported that more than 90 percent of confidence scheme victims in two large metropolitan areas were older people. A few examples should illustrate the point.

Perhaps the most vicious of the "get-more-money-for-your-money" swindles was the Maryland savings and loan scandal of 1961. From 1958 to 1961, many state-chartered savings and loan associations operating in Maryland were not federally insured. These companies advertised nationally that savings invested with them would yield as high as 8 percent interest, twice the rate at most legitimate, federally insured institutions. The appeal of increased yields was particularly attractive to older people trying to live on a fixed amount of savings. For people in this situation, such a promise was like saying, "Double your income in one easy step." Hundreds of older people from all over the country transferred their life savings into these companies. At best these companies were ill conceived. They were able to pay the high rates of interest only by investing heavily in second, third, and even fourth mortgages—a lucrative but risky business. Following a wide-scale investigation, many of these companies' officers were indicted on charges of fraud and embezzlement. Most of the companies went bankrupt, and hundreds of people lost their entire life savings.

Another example of economic exploitation of the elderly is the "investment property" business, in which promoters bought large tracts of cheap land—often swampy land in Florida or desert in Arizona—and carved the property up into the smallest parcels allowable. Beautiful brochures and advertisements in newspapers, magazines, and so on promoted the land as an investment for resale later at a profit, or as a place for a retirement home. In the words of a Florida realtor:

Lots are usually sold on installment contracts, and no deed is recorded until the contract is paid off. Most contracts stipulate that the property reverts to the seller if the buyer misses one or two payments, and the seller is not required to notify the buyer that he is delinquent.

Many, but not all, contracts carried interest on the unpaid balance, usually 5 or 6 percent. Many of these lots were sold over and over again, year after year, as buyers stop their monthly payments for any number of reasons—they die, come upon hard times, come down and see the land, et cetera.

Several years ago I spent almost two days, using a slow plane and a four-wheel drive, radio-equipped jeep, trying to locate a certain parcel (a Florida development) located approximately ten miles west of Daytona Beach in a dismal swamp.

After two days of some of the roughest riding, we had to give up, as it was impossible to penetrate deep enough into the swamp to the point we had spotted from the air.

Incidentally, this parcel was sold to a woman from Syracuse, N.Y., who had intended to use it as a homesite for a trailer home (U.S. Senate Special Committee on Aging, 1965:34).

Many other examples could be given of "make-money" or "save-money" schemes that have bilked older people out of what little they have. Other Confidence people as well have preyed on older people. One of the more frequent con games has been the "bank-examiner" gambit. A person posing as a bank examiner calls on the intended victim and explains that one of the bank employees is suspected of embezzlement, but that unfortunately the bank officials have been unable to catch the employee in the act. The "examiner" requests that the victim go to the bank and withdraw all of his or her savings, to thereby force the suspect in the bank to alter account books so the bank would then "have the goods" on the employee. If the intended victim takes the bait and withdraws the savings, the "examiner" telephones, says they have caught the suspect, thanks the victim, and then offers to send a "bank messenger" to pick up the money—"to save you the trouble of having to come all the way down here, since you have been so kind as to cooperate with us." The "messenger" then appears, takes the money, and gives the victim an official-looking deposit slip. That is usually the last the victim ever sees of his or her money. Unfortunately a large number of older people have fallen for this ruse.

Many practices in the "preneed" funeral business have also been fraudulent. People have been sold "complete burial service" for $1,000 or more, and all the survivors received (if they were lucky) was a cheap casket. People have been sold crypts in nonexistent mausoleums. One ad read, "Do you qualify for these U.S. Government death benefits? U.S. Social Security, maximum $255, United Memorial's answer to the ever-increasing cost of funeral services, the United Plan. The preneed plan that costs $10." For $10, the customers got a "guarantee" from United Memorial that their burial service would be performed by whatever mortuary they chose. When the customer died, however, the relatives found that most mortuaries "endorsed" by United Memorial had no contract with them and refused to perform the service for anything even approaching a Social Security benefit price. It has been estimated that in Colorado alone the annual sales of preneed burial services totaled $8 to $10 million (U.S. Senate Special Committee on Aging, 1965). This business thrived on the deep-seated desire of many older people to take care of burial arrangements ahead of time in order to "avoid being a burden" on their relatives. It may be unethical for reputable businesspeople to take money from older people for prearranged funerals, since businesspeople fully realize the problems of prearranging funeral services in a society where people travel as much as they do in ours. If the person dies far away from the city in which the prearrangements were made, the relatives either lose the money spent for the prearranged funeral or must pay to have the remains shipped back for burial. By encouraging prepayment, the funeral director is merely relieving the older person of his or her savings, often without paying interest on the money held.

The most frequent hazard to older people is medical swindles and quackery. Arthritis is a good case in point. The U.S. Senate Special Committee on Aging found that:

Arthritis offers special opportunities to the unscrupulous. Twelve million Americans have some form of arthritis; and, as one witness testified: "If we fall for the phoney, and sooner or later most of us do, it is because the pains of arthritis are something that you just can't describe because nobody knows why it comes or how or when it goes." . . . Mrs. Bramer also made a comment often expressed by arthritis victims: "There must be an exchange list of arthritic victims because if you get on one list you receive material advertising all manner of devices, items such as vibrators, whirlpool baths, salves, uranium mitts, and things of that sort" (1965:7).

The committee commented on various aspects of fraud:

Worthless devices

These devices are often used by phoney practitioners to impress victims with "up-to-date" methods of "secret" treatments. One highly mobile pitchman, using and selling a machine that did little more than give colonic enemas to victims of major diseases, made an estimated $2.5 million before conviction on a mail fraud charge (1965:3).

Misleading claims

People will buy almost anything that purports to cure whatever real or imaginary ailments they have. The enforcement of fraud laws is a constant word game between those who are trying to protect the public and those who are trying to swindle it. Thus, "cures" is replaced by "aids in curing" is replaced by "is thought to aid in curing" (1965:8).

The victims

The actual extent of frauds is unknown because many victims either never suspect that they have been taken, or more likely, they are afraid to report it for fear of appearing the fool (1965:8).

Complex technology

This gives the quack the capability of sowing the seed of doubt about the validity of accepted medical methods because most people are not able to evaluate his claims (1965:8).

The cost of quackery in 1965 alone was estimated as follows: vitamin and health food quackery, $500 million; arthritis quackery, $250 million; ineffective drugs and devices for reducing, $100 million (U.S. Senate Special Committee on Aging, 1965). And this review probably only scratches the surface. The true cost of fraud and quackery was summed up well by the chairman of the U.S. Senate Special Committee on Aging:

> It seems to me that there are losses that go far beyond the original purchase price for the phoney treatment, the useless gadget, the inappropriate drug or pill. How can you measure the cost in terms of suffering, disappointment, and final despair? (1965:10)

One of the heaviest of these costs is surely the attitudes such practices create among older people. They become suspicious and reluctant to get involved with strangers.

Violent Crime

Older people fear crime much more than the general population does, even though they are less likely than the general public to be actually victimized by crime. Antunes et al. (1977), reporting on a study of both reported and unreported crime against the public, including the elderly, found that the main crime against the elderly was robbery on the street by unarmed black youths who were strangers acting alone. Thus, for older people living in high-crime areas, any strange black youth on the street represents a potential threat. In addition, although older people were less likely than the general public to be victims of violent crimes such as assault or rape, when they were, it was most likely to occur *in their homes*. Little wonder, then, that older people in inner cities are afraid to let strangers into their homes. Older people in high-crime areas see and hear about crime all around them and see themselves defenseless against it.

Lawton et al. (1976) found that while the elderly were less likely to be victimized when all types of crimes were considered, they were as likely or more likely than the young to be victims of robbery with injury or larceny with personal contact. Thus, property crimes directed at the elderly tend to involve direct contact between the elderly person and the offender. Sundeen and Mathieu (1976a) found residents of core areas of the city to be much more fearful of crime than were suburb residents, and retirement community residents to feel safest of all. Longino (1980) found personal security to be a major reason behind inner city residents' moving to public housing for the elderly. Thus, it appears that age segregation in housing does reduce fear of crime among the elderly.

As victims, the elderly are often damaged more by crime than are similarly victimized young people. For example, the older woman who has her purse snatched may be losing all her cash. Where is she then to get money to buy food? How are the elderly poor to replace the items they lose in burglaries? These problems have led to the development of victim assistance programs, which thus far have been mainly experimental and which most communities still lack.

Abuse and Neglect

Although *not* common, abuse and neglect of the elderly by family members tend to be seen as such by many older people and by service providers. Hickey and Douglass (1981) classified neglect and abuse by order of prevalence and seriousness as perceived by a sample of service providers. They found that *passive neglect*— leaving the older person alone, isolated, and forgotten—was seen as the most common and least serious form. Passive neglect most often occurs when families are too preoccupied to pay attention to older members. *Verbal or emotional abuse* —situations in which older people are humiliated, frightened, insulted, threatened, or treated as children or in a demeaning or overprotective way—was seen as the next most common form. *Active neglect*—forced confinement, isolation, and withholding of food or medication—

was seen as not very common. Actual *physical abuse*—hitting, slapping, or physical restraint— was seen as the least common type of mistreatment. Thus, it appears, abuse and neglect are not widespread, and what clues we have indicate that the more serious types of abuse and neglect are relatively rare. Nevertheless, for its victims, such abuse is undoubtedly traumatic, a failure in what most people see as the safest possible environment—the family. Hickey and Douglass (1981) reported that the most common problem seen as leading to abuse and neglect was a poor initial relationship among family members compounded by sudden and severe dependency of the older person.

Cases of abuse and neglect of the elderly are highly dramatized by the media because they offend values central to Americans—respect and consideration for elders. They arouse the fears of the elderly because there is no way to guarantee it will not happen to them.

Summary

Deviance consists of substantial departures from conventional custom or practice that are condemned by the public and constrained by systems of social control. Although ideas as to what specific behaviors constitute deviance vary from group to group, within American society there is widespread disapproval and punishment of crime, alcoholism, vagrancy, and homosexuality. Senile dementia and disability are less clear-cut forms of deviance. Although we are less likely to attribute moral degeneracy to the mentally impaired or physically disabled, we nevertheless prefer these types of people to be out of sight. SRO residence and the life styles of tramps and shopping bag ladies are in themselves deviant and at the same time strategies for coping with being deviant. They represent realms where deviance is more accepted. Society makes fewer attempts to control deviance in these environments.

As we have contended throughout this book,

the elderly come in amazing variety. It should come as no surprise that most of the types of deviance found among the general population can be found among the elderly, too. Nevertheless, there has been relatively little research on the elderly as deviants, and our conclusions in this area must be more cautiously drawn than in many other areas of gerontology.

The elderly constitute 11 percent of the population but account for only 1 percent of the arrests and only 0.5 percent of those in prison. In addition, when the elderly are arrested it is more often for alcohol-related offenses than for crimes against property or persons. Nevertheless, older people do commit violent crimes—usually assault or murder of spouse, family, or neighbors. Older people in prisons usually are quite compliant, as a way of protecting themselves against the violence of younger prisoners.

Organic brain disease, or senile dementia, causes symptoms such as nonpurposeful wandering, nonpurposeful repetitive actions (e.g., yelling or banging), bizarre behavior, incontinence, and even violence. Such symptoms are considered deviant and usually result in the person's being segregated from "normal" people. However, because effective care for the mentally impaired is not high on our list of funding priorities and because such care is difficult to provide, many mentally impaired elders find themselves being shuffled through a loop of agencies, none of which is prepared or able to care for them. Effective care for older people with senile dementia is not available now and developing a strategy for providing it can be expected to be one of our greatest challenges over the coming years.

Physical disability creates many obstacles to participation in society's institutions. Families, employers, and government agencies all find it difficult to accommodate physically disabled people. As a society, we tend to segregate the handicapped from others so that "normal" people do not have to cope with their difficulties in doing even the simplest things. We also

tend to tie the availability of rehabilitative services to the disabled to the prospect of employment, which obviously puts the elderly at a disadvantage. In fact, we do not even know the proportion of the elderly who need rehabilitation services. Yet a large percentage of the disabled in later life became so in later life.

As behavior, the drinking of alcoholic beverages is not in itself deviant. Overindulgence is what is deviant. The evidence suggests that a smaller proportion of the elderly have drinking problems compared to other adult age categories. However, drinking has been found to be an important background factor in mental illness, physical illness, and suicide among the elderly. In addition, much of the deviant behavior of the elderly that is noticed by agents of social control is related to alcohol use. The elderly are overrepresented among the alcoholic derelicts on skid row and among the deviants living in inner-city SRO's and among the loop of agencies that deal with alcoholics.

Normal sexuality carried into old age is often defined as deviant. Yet older people themselves do not consider it as such and lead healthy sex lives. Older men do not fit the stereotype of the dirty old man. In that homosexuality is widely regarded as deviant, aging homosexuals are aging deviants. However, contrary to the stereotype of the aging homosexual as a pathetic figure, the research—mainly on men—indicates that older homosexuals have a high degree of self-acceptance and have satisfying lives.

Run-down hotels in the nation's cities often become SRO's (single room occupancy) that cater to deviants of all sorts—alcoholics, drug addicts, petty criminals, the mentally impaired. A large proportion of elderly residents of SRO's at the lower end of the economic scale is alcoholic. The SRO managers exploit, and are exploited by, the residents. Victimization of elderly residents by other residents is common. Health problems are rampant. In short, life in the SRO is largely one of misery and fear. While the low-income SRO's serve the function for society of housing its poor and damaged people, the people housed there receive little of society's protection.

Tramps are homeless wanderers who are unconnected or only sporadically connected to family or employment. Many have never married or held steady jobs. Most are alcoholics. They survive by means of a skid row culture that provides a source of interaction, strategies for getting food and shelter, and an environment that not only tolerates drinking but in some ways encourages it. About a fourth of the men on skid row are elderly. Skid row men spend most of their time in jail.

Shopping bag ladies are homeless vagrant women who live in public places in our large cities and who carry their households with them in shopping bags. Unlike homeless men, the shopping bag ladies are a solitary lot, seldom speaking to one another. They solve the problem of shelter by unobtrusively blending into public places and by taking over public facilities intended for other uses. They eat other people's leftovers and are usually hungry. They are the poorest of the poor. Their main pastime is scavenging through trash in search of articles to keep rather than as a way to get money. Most are in their fifties and many are former mental patients "returned to the community." They get no assistance from the community and avoid contact with police and social agencies.

Elderly deviants are sometimes treated as if their age makes them less responsible for their actions compared to younger people, but in the end they are segregated from the general population just as younger deviants are.

The elderly are probably more often targets of deviants than they themselves are deviant. Although they are less likely to be victims of crime in general, they are as likely as any other age category to experience robbery with injury and larceny with contact. Thus, when the elderly do experience crime, they usually come in direct contact with the criminal, often on a public street. As a result, fear of crime is high among the elderly. One of the major motives for living in age-segregated housing for the elderly is safety and security.

Because the elderly are often trying to live on limited budgets, they are likely targets for get-rich-quick frauds, such as home-improvement and real-estate frauds. They also are the targets of medical quackery. Problems such as ill health and inadequate income apparently make the elderly more vulnerable than the general population to such fraud and quackery.

Abuse and neglect of the elderly occur, but we do not know to what extent. Indications are that actual physical abuse of older people is relatively rare and usually connected with severe impairment of the older person. Psychological abuse and neglect are perhaps more common, but they are also very difficult to define and study.

Chapter 16

The Economy

The complex system we call "the economy" is a hodgepodge of organizations and activities that extract raw materials and food from the physical environment, transform them into consumer goods, convert people's knowledge and energies into services, and distribute these goods and services to the American people. The amount of goods and services the economy produces provides subsistance for the general population plus an economic surplus—the value of goods and services over and above what is required to sustain those who do the producing. In American society, the economic surplus is distributed among various groups: owners get profits; workers get salaries, wages, and fringe benefits; retirees get earned pensions; governments get taxes on wages, salaries, profits, and pensions; the poor, the disabled, and the unemployed get financial support from governments; and the public gets facilities and services from governments (roads, fire and police protection, national parks, public health programs, national defense, and so on).

Economic Ideology

How an economy responds to an aging population is to some extent shaped by the fundamental organization and underlying values of the economy. All economies produce goods and services; they differ mainly in how the benefits of that production are distributed. The American economy is basically a capitalist economy, which means that one of its primary goals is private accumulation of wealth (capital), which can then be invested in ownership of the organizations that produce and distribute goods and services. Additional goals include a drive for constant growth and "progress," limitation of government's share of profits by limiting taxation, and individual wealth as a "measure" of the person.

Underlying our capitalist system is a free-market ideology that assumes that all people have equal access to the means of gaining wealth, that the free market is the fairest way to distribute goods and services, that poverty or need is the result of individual weakness, that the family and the private sector are the "proper" agents to respond to need, and that in order to minimize demand on public services to the disadvantaged, these services must be punitive and stigmatizing.

The free-market economic ideology sees the major functions of government as supporting the private sector by keeping economic growth a prime goal, minimizing restrictions on production and distribution, providing incentives such as tax breaks for those who accumulate capital, minimizing the amount of goods and services produced by nonprofit organizations, including governments, and financially underwriting production costs through such mechanisms as tax breaks, military research and development, and government loan guarantees. Regardless of how one feels about the appropriateness of this ideology, it is a fundamental basis for our economic system and its supporting political structure.

However, as we saw in Chapter 3, the Great Depression of the 1930s was seen by many as a failure of the capitalist free market to provide adequately for the needs of the public as a whole. The "Roosevelt revolution" marked the entrance of government into major areas of the economy: public works, public health, education, occupational health and safety, environmental conservation, and social services.

Americans also espouse a humanitarian ideology in which the alleviation of human suffering is a major goal. Thus, government involvement in promoting the well-being of the people and the humanitarian principles of service to humankind both offer ideological tools to those who oppose the free-market ideology. This opposition has produced a countervailing ideology that assumes that, left unchecked, the free market leads to exploitation of the powerless and disregard for the public good. To provide the needed checks, government must regulate economic activity to prevent exploitation such as child labor or unsafe working conditions and government must tax the profits from economic activity in order to provide public benefits such as public health, highways, national defense, unemployment insurance, and public education. The dialectic between these two opposing viewpoints has led to a complex web of laws and regulations that constrains the economic system but cannot be said to actually control it.

Economic Structure

In the 1980s, the American economy can be divided into three major sectors: a core private sector, a peripheral private sector, and a government sector. The *core private sector* is made up of the largest corporations and financial institutions, organizations that use technology, economies of scale, and noncompetitive pricing to achieve high output per worker and relatively high profits. People who work for core private sector organizations tend to be unionized, to have relatively high wages and fringe benefits, and to be covered by both private pensions and Social Security. The *peripheral private sector* is made up of relatively small organizations that tend to be labor intensive, to have relatively low output per worker, and to have lower profit margins. Workers in the peripheral private sector tend to have relatively low wages and fringe benefits, and to lack private pensions. Although these workers generate income entitling them to Social Security pensions, the level of benefits reflects their generally lower career earnings. In addition, workers in the peripheral sector who are covered by private pensions are less likely to get those pensions because labor turnover is high in the peripheral sector and because workers usually must work at least ten years for the same employer to qualify for a pension. In 1981, 75 million Americans, representing 83 percent of the labor force, worked in the private sector—about 25 million in the core segment and 50 million in the peripheral segment (U.S. Bureau of the Census, 1982a:396).

In 1981, the government sector was made up of 16 million persons working for federal, state, and local governments, and comprising 17 percent of the labor force (U.S. Bureau of the Census, 1982). The nearly 3 million federal employees had relatively stable employment and received salaries, benefits, and pensions similar to those in the core private sector. Until recently, most federal employees did not participate in the Social Security system, but as of 1983, new federal employees contribute and are covered. The 13 million state and local government employees in 1981 were a more variable lot. Some had relatively high wages and fringe benefits, pension and Social Security coverage, and stable employment. Others had relatively low wages, government pension coverage but no Social Security, and insecure employment. About 30 percent of government workers then were unionized and they tended to have done better in recent years at securing better wages and pensions. Many local government pensions are unfunded, which means they must be paid for out of current revenues. And this in turn means that in the future, these may not be very secure.

Thus, how well a worker fares in the American economy in terms of wages, fringe benefits, and retirement income depends to a very important degree on the sector of the economy in which he or she works. Incidentally, work in the three sectors of the economy is not evenly distributed across all segments of the population. For example, workers in the core private sector are predominantly white males.

We are interested both in how the nature of the American economy affects its ability to deliver income, goods, and services to the aged and in how retirement and aging affect the operation of the economy. We will consider first how effective the economy is at providing income for older people. We will then look at its ability to deliver goods and services. Then we will examine the role that retirement plays in the economy through such means as controlling unemployment and encouraging capital accumulation. Finally, we will look at the emergence of the aging as a new consumer group.

The Economics of Retirement Income

The elderly are commonly thought to comprise an economically dependent category, and it is often held that the aging of the population constitutes an economic "problem" because the older population is growing faster than the younger population, who presumably must "support" the elderly. But if we examine the sources of income for the aged, we see a different picture.

Sources of Retirement Income

Although we tend to think of the older population as being retired, a significant minority is employed. In 1981, at ages 65 to 69, 28 percent of men and 15 percent of women were employed, and at age 70 and over, 13 percent of men and 5 percent of women were employed (U.S. Bureau of the Census, 1983). Earnings accounted for about 25 percent of the aggregate income of the elderly. For almost all of these people, earnings from employment supplemented retirement income. Many of these older people worked part time. Thus, the elderly continued to make important contributions through their labor in the economy, and the money they received from employment certainly could not be labeled "economic dependency."

Private and public pensions earned in connection with previous employment accounted for 13 percent of the aggregate income of the elderly in 1981. In most cases, employee contributions were deducted over the working life of the individual and employer contributions were made in lieu of salary or other benefits. Thus, private pension income could hardly be called economic dependency, either. Income from property, in the form of rent, dividends, and interest, constituted 23 percent of the aggregate income of the elderly. Income from this source is concentrated amongst the most well-to-do older people and so could not be classified as economic dependency.

Social Security benefits represented 37 percent of the aggregate income of the elderly in 1981. Since this income was financed with revenues from current payroll taxes, it might appear that it represents economic dependency. However, there is another way to look at this issue. Anyone eligible for Social Security retirement benefits has helped to support the system financially during his or her working years. No cash fund accumulated for the individual to be used later to pay a pension mainly because business interests did not want the government controlling a large fund of investment capital. Instead, the transaction was in the form of a social contract between the U.S. government and the Social Security taxpayer: In return for taxes paid at the going rate, based on current earnings, the individual became *entitled to a pension* based on the level of earnings subject to Social Security taxes over the total number of years of employment. The entire society incurred an obligation to pay these pensions.

However, payroll taxes are not the only way to meet Social Security pension obligations; they simply represent the current *concept* of how best to meet them. When someone pays off a debt, we do not call the agent they pay "economically dependent." Likewise, it is misleading to refer to paying off our national obligations to retirees as "economic dependency." These pensions are IOU's being called in under the terms of an agreement.

This kind of confusion has led to frequent reference in the media to the "fact" that 26 percent of the federal budget is going to "support" the elderly. However, if we examine the budget more closely, we can see how misleading this statement is. Table 16-1 shows a breakdown of the federal budget for fiscal year 1981. Money set aside to cover our IOU's to the elderly and

their survivors or dependents consisted of Social Security and other federal pensions ($109.7 billion), veterans' benefits ($3.4 billion), and Medicare ($33.7 billion), and totaled $146.8 billion. If we subtract these obligations from the total "expenditures for the elderly," we get a grand total of $16 billion being spent on "dependent" older people, an amount representing *only 2.6 percent of the federal budget! In 1981, less than 5 percent of the aggregate income of the elderly came from "unearned" sources such as Supplemental Security Income, Medicaid, or Food Stamps.*

Retirement Income Problems

As a result, we must conclude that the incomes of today's elderly are incomes they or their spouses earned by generating entitlement over their working lives, which is not to say that these incomes are adequate. As pointed out on Chapter 8, single individuals, women, and minorities among the elderly are very likely to have incomes at or below the poverty level. This situation arises because the income inequalities of the workplace tend to carry over and to affect income in retirement. The minority of workers in the core private sector tend to get a disproportionate share of personal income not only during their working years but in retirement as well. They are more likely to have substantial private pensions, profit-sharing plans, near-maximum Social Security benefits, and continuation into retirement of their health insurance. In addition, workers in the core private sector are most likely to have had incomes that would allow substantial accumulation of assets. Workers in the government sector tend to do well in terms of public pensions, although these pensions often do not increase with inflation, and those workers not also covered by Social Security can see the purchasing power of their benefits decrease quite rapidly. In addition, those with unfunded local or state pensions have less pension security. Workers in the peripheral private sector have the least chance

TABLE 16-1   U.S. federal expenditures affecting the elderly: fiscal year 1981

	Amount (in $ billions)	Percent of Federal Budget
Earned Entitlements		
Social Security and federal pensions	109.7	
Veterans' benefits	3.4	
Medicare	33.7	
Subtotal	146.8	23.8
Public Assistance		
Supplemental Security Income	2.0	
Medicaid	7.6	
Food Stamps	0.8	
Subsidized public housing	2.6	
Housing loans	0.7	
Other	1.2	
Subtotal	14.9	2.4
Social Services		
Older Americans Act programs	0.7	
Older-volunteer programs	0.1	
Senior employment	0.3	
Subtotal	1.1	0.2
Total Federal Budget	616.0	100.0

Source: Federal Council on Aging, 1981.

of securing adequate retirement incomes. Their wages were lower during their working years, which discouraged the accumulation of savings. They are unlikely to have private pensions or health benefits from their former employers. They tend to have below average Social Security pensions because of their low earnings.

Many of the problems identified thus far stem from the fact that ours is not a single retirement income "system" but rather a large number of systems overlapping and supplementing one another for a minority of workers and ignoring a majority of workers. Proposals by the President's Commission of Pension Policy (1981) included the establishment of a Minimum Universal Pension System covering all workers and funded by employer contributions. The commission felt such a system was necessary in order to give everyone access to pensions to supplement Social Security. However, the commission's recommendations were rejected. The conclusion we are left with is that the retirement income systems we now have continue and even increase the income gap between the haves and the have-nots. This gap is further widened by our tax system.

The Tax System

Government expenditures can be divided into two categories: direct expenditures and tax expenditures. Direct expenditures are easy to understand because they involve payments. Tax expenditures are more difficult to understand because they represent *potential* revenues intentionally not collected from a specific category of taxpayer. We refer to them colloquially as "tax breaks." In 1982, the following tax breaks were available to middle-aged and older people: exclusion of Social Security, Railroad Retirement and veterans' benefits from taxable income, an additional tax exemption for each person age 65 or older, a tax credit for people with taxable retirement income, and the exclusion of capital gains on sales of homes of people age 55 or older. In addition, the tax structure supports private pensions by allowing both employees and employers to deduct their pension contributions from their taxable income. As we have seen, private pensions are not available to most workers in the peripheral private sector. Table 16-2 shows the dollar breakdown of tax expenditures for the elderly in 1982.

If a large majority of older people actually lived on low incomes, then these tax expenditures might seem justified, for they would allow the elderly poor to stretch their incomes farther. However, Gary Nelson (1983) analyzed tax expenditures by income class and found that only 2 percent of 1982 tax expenditures went to older individuals with incomes of less than $5,000 per year, while 50 percent went to those with incomes over $20,000 per year. In other words, the federal government did without $98 in taxes from each older person with $5,000 in taxable income and did without $697 in taxes from those with incomes of $20,000. Thus, not only do the systems that generate retirement income enlarge the gap between the well-off and the poor, but so does the tax system.

Retirement Income in the Future

Figure 16-1 illustrates some of the factors involved in financing retirement. The level of retirement (the proportion of the population retired) appears to be influenced primarily by two factors: the *minimum age of eligibility* for Social Security or other retirement benefits, and the *financial adequacy* of retirement benefits. Opportunities for continued employment affect the level of retirement only slightly. Thus, as the minimum retirement age goes down and the adequacy of retirement benefits goes up, the level of retirement increases. This is what has been happening in the United States. Recent changes in mandatory retirement policies will have little effect on this picture. However, as the funds required to pay pensions for retired

TABLE 16-2   Estimated tax expenditures affecting older adults: United States, 1982

	Amount (in $ millions)
Exclusion of capital gains on home sales for people age 55 and over	510
Exclusion of Social Security benefits	11,895
Exclusion of Railroad Retirement benefits	380
Exclusion of contributions to pension plans	28,325
Additional tax exemption for those 65 and over	2,335
Tax credit for those elderly with taxable income	135
Exclusion of Veterans' pensions	85

Source: Adapted from Gary Nelson, 1983.

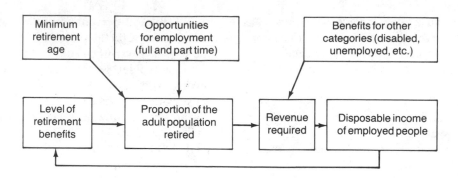

FIGURE 16-1   Factors in the economic support of retirement benefits.

people increase, so do demands for contributions from the working population. For example, the recent increases in Social Security benefits required sharp increases in Social Security taxes over several years. The increased taxes lowered the disposable incomes of employed persons unless benefits to other categories such as the handicapped or the unemployed were cut. For example, cutting out Social Security survivor benefits to college students has partially offset the increased costs of retirement benefits.

As the disposable incomes of employed people go down (or at least lose ground to inflation), popular support for adequate retirement benefits goes down. If this lowered support for retirement benefits means these benefits become less adequate, then the level of retirement may go down as people delay retirement in order to boost their expected benefits.

Since 1965, American economic policy has consistently favored lowered retirement ages and more adequate retirement benefits. Sheppard and Rix (1977) speculated that changes in the American economy will not permit this policy to continue. Aging of the population will increase the tax burden on the employed population by increasing the number of persons collecting their Social Security IOU's. Any increases in longevity will increase the tax burden even further. At the same time, reduced fertility since 1957 means fewer employed people. Add to this the prospect that the decline in nonhu-

man energy resources may curtail the economy's capacity to produce an economic surplus as large as we are accustomed to. Sheppard and Rix concluded that this combination of factors will almost certainly drive up the minimum retirement age and perhaps drive down the adequacy of retirement benefits as well. Their prediction came true in 1982 when the Social Security Act was amended to gradually increase retirement age around the turn of the century and to cut benefits immediately by delaying cost-of-living adjustments.

Sheppard and Rix (1977) contended that since sooner or later we will have to abandon the policy of encouraging "early" retirement, doing it sooner will be less traumatic economically. It is difficult to envision what form the debate on this issue will take, but it is sure to be spirited. Both employers and employees have come to view early retirement as economically beneficial, a view that is unlikely to change quickly. On the other hand, the realities of financing retirement may hasten the awareness that we may be unwilling to pay for early retirement.

At the federal level, both military retirement and civil service early retirement programs are coming under increasingly heavy criticism. From 1960 to 1976, military retirement benefits, which are funded from current general tax revenues, rose from 6 percent to 25 percent of the U.S. defense budget (Sheppard and Rix, 1977:121). With average "retirement" ages in the early forties, military retirement programs represent a sizable commitment of future federal funds. These programs are criticized partly because most military "retirees" go on to other full-time jobs. However, the number who fully retire after 30 years' service appears to be increasing. In addition, the Federal Civil Service retirement system is amassing future liabilities at a rapid rate because inflation-eroded employee contributions will not generate enough revenue to meet future obligations. As a result, future taxpayers will have to foot much of the bill for Civil Service pensions being promised today (Sheppard and Rix, 1977:126).

While the strains on the federal budget are obvious, they are still at tolerable levels. Not so with some state and local systems. Many state and municipal governments have pension systems funded completely or largely from current revenue, which has led to severe economic problems for many government systems. For example, some cities have bargained with municipal unions to keep down current salaries and wages by liberalizing retirement ages and benefits. But eventually these pension IOU's come due. And when they do, governments often have difficulty finding the necessary revenue. Part of this problem is no doubt related to the fact that the political regime creating the liability will probably not be the one that has to satisfy it.

Private pension systems are less likely to encounter these funding problems because their prepayment schedules are relatively sound. However, the ability of even the most well-designed pension program to meet its liabilities depends on a healthy economy. When economic times are hard, income generated by the assets of pension funds goes down, and with it the reserves of the pension plan.

Thus, there are numerous indications that the policy of promoting early retirement may be too expensive and that some other alternative may have to be found. Sheppard and Rix (1977) performed a valuable service in raising consciousness about the magnitude of the issues involved.

In addition to the early retirement issue, policy makers may well have to deal with a large increase in retired population (even if the minimum retirement age goes up slightly), accompanied by a relative decrease in the number of employed persons available to help meet retirement pension obligations.

Inflation can influence retirement income in several ways. To the extent that retirement income comes from assets that do not increase in value with inflation, such as savings, then the value of savings and savings income may be reduced. Likewise, income from fixed pensions and annuities is quickly eroded by inflation, and few private pensions are adjusted for inflation. Even if income sources such as Social Security or private pensions are adjusted for inflation, the adjustments usually lag behind and thus real income is still reduced. Whenever income does not increase as fast as inflation, then real income (purchasing power) is reduced. Increases in earnings often lag behind inflation, too.

Increases in Social Security benefits, the introduction of SSI and Medicare, and increases in in-kind benefits such as low-rent housing for the elderly have tended to improve the economic position of older Americans over the past decade. However, these improvements will be only temporary if inflation continues to erode the value of supplements to Social Security. Certainly the explosion of benefits and programs for the elderly that occurred from 1965 to 1979 is very unlikely to occur again. Indeed, what is more likely is that these benefits, like Medicare, will be eroded by pressures on the federal budget.

Interestingly, retirement also probably adds to inflation. For example, that people can sometimes work at a full-time job *and* draw full retirement benefits artificially increases the supply of money with no corresponding increase in production. In addition, large pension funds are among the nation's largest investors. They have an obligation to deliver a certain level of income; and in periods of economic slowdown, these large investors are forced into rather conservative investment strategies that are not conducive to increased production. Very little systematic analysis has been made of the impact of retirement on inflation. This background work is needed to reevaluate retirement policies.

Private Enterprise and Service Delivery

Many of the needs of the elderly can be readily met in the marketplace. Most older people can purchase food, clothing, housing, and so on from local businesses. But there is a substantial minority of the elderly who are not served adequately by the private marketplace. Let us look at a few examples.

Many older people cannot find housing that is both suitable and affordable. There is a severe shortage of low-rent housing for the elderly, particularly in rural areas, and even middle-income older people have difficulty finding affordable apartments. This is because private developers and lending institutions concentrate their resources where the most money can be made, and there is much less money to be made in constructing or remodeling housing for low- or even middle-income older people (Olson, 1982). Given a shortage of mortgage money and the profit motive, the response of the housing industry is predictable; but this is little comfort to older people who cannot find a place to live.

When the government intervenes in this housing shortage, it is primarily through the construction of subsidized housing for the low-income elderly. For example, suppose that a private developer builds and manages a low-rent housing project for the elderly, and that the builder has agreed to do so because the government guaranteed to subsidize the rents of the low-income elderly tenants. Let us say that the residents are required to contribute 25 percent of their monthly incomes towards the rent, the difference between that figure and the actual

rental price being paid by the federal government. So far, so good. But let us also say that the rental rate structure of this privately built low-rent housing for the elderly has been set substantially higher than that of similar housing in the open market. Thus, for instance, Mrs. A. lives in a one-bedroom apartment for which she pays $71.25 per month—one-fourth of her monthly income. The rental rate used to compute the government subsidy is $260 per month—which means that the government is paying $188.75 per month for Mrs. A's apartment. But quite adequate one-bedroom apartments are available in Mrs. A's community for $180 per month! This is a good example of government operating for the benefit of private business at public expense. It is too easy to blame this situation on bad government. The fact is that it arose from a long-standing practice in the private sector of only doing business with the government at high rates of profit. And when government tries to change the rules they encounter stiff political resistance from the private sector.

Health care is another example of how the private sector inadequately serves the elderly. Virtually every older person with a serious chronic condition has some problem finding appropriate and effective health care or paying for it. Why are costs of health care soaring out of control? Why are major categories of care such as in-home services so difficult to find? The answers to these questions are found at least partly in the economic structure of health care organizations.

Health care is planned, directed, and controlled by a set of identifiable groups: hospital associations, medical associations, drug companies, nursing home associations, and so on. The major goal of most of these organizations is making money. Even "nonprofit" hospitals and nursing homes seek to increase their revenues and lower their costs (or pass the costs on to the public) in order to expand their sphere of operation, because money is needed for growth and growth is seen as the basis of power and prestige. Thus, the "bottom line" even in care for the sick and the dying is often economic. This is certainly not to say that people in health care do not care about their clients. It is simply to say that the priority that decision makers give to these concerns often is lower than that given to financial considerations.

These examples certainly do not exhaust the list of inadequate private services to the elderly. Many of the difficulties cited in Chapter 8, such as inadequate services to the handicapped, lack of home health care, transportation problems, and the like, have resulted from the fact that the private sector has not responded, and cannot be expected to respond, to many of the needs of the elderly because there is not enough economic profit to be made. When we look at government programs (the next chapter), we will need to keep these limits of the private sector in mind.

The Economic Functions of Retirement

People commonly assume that retirement and the pension systems that support it were created to provide for the welfare of the aged. But although income security for the aged played a part in the development of Social Security, the major functions of retirement for the American economy have mainly revolved around controlling the labor force. Private pensions were initially developed to tie workers to particular employers and to cut down on labor mobility. Social Security was fostered by a need to control unemployment as much as by a desire to improve the lot of the elderly poor. Retirement still performs these functions today. Private pensions are most prevalent in the core private sector, where workers are highly skilled and where labor mobility is less desirable. Social Security has tended to become more liberal during

times of high unemployment. When unemployment is high or when organizations must make cutbacks in personnel, then encouraging workers near retirement to get out of the labor force is often one of the first actions taken.

As pointed out in Chapter 3, our high-energy economy simply does not need every able-bodied adult to be employed in order to produce all of the goods and services we need. And our economic surplus is more than sufficient to generate retirement incomes. Retirement benefits the entire society by keeping the number of people in the labor force closer to the number of jobs available. Without retirement, the unemployment rate would be much higher than it is today.

Retirement also serves as an incentive for workers to put up with less than satisfying jobs, by setting a limit on how long a bad job situation has to be endured. It is also seen by employers as a way to phase out less effective workers and by unions as a way to create new jobs and opportunities for promotion. Thus, for workers, unions, and employers, retirement serves different but generally positive functions.

Retirement as a life stage and the corresponding need to create resources to finance it have played a major role in capital formation in the American economy since World War II. By 1980, retirement trusts, usually managed by banks or insurance companies, had over $650 billion invested in common stocks, which represented more than 20 percent of the value of all common stocks listed on the New York and American stock exchanges (Olson, 1982). Drucker (1976) has called this trend "pension fund socialism," since a great deal of the ownership of American business is in the hands of workers in the form of pension entitlements. However appealing this concept may be, the fact is that these huge pension funds are not being managed to maximize pension income but rather to fulfill what the financial decision makers see as the need for capital investment. Olson (1982) found that compared to other large investors, such as mutual funds, pension funds' performance was extremely poor. In fact, between 1962 and 1978, 87 percent of over 100 pension funds studied showed well-below-average returns compared to the performance of the stock market as a whole (Olson, 1982:111). Apparently because pension funds do not have to increase benefits to keep up with inflation, managers do not put a high priority on the funds' getting their share of the capital growth available through the stock market. This issue is further complicated by the fact that employers' choices of pension fund trustees are sometimes not based on pension fund performance at all. Olson (1982) pointed out that a corporation may select a bank to manage its pension fund in return for prime rate loans and other benefits. Thus, the contributions of workers to pension funds have been a very important source of capital for the American economy, but these assets have not always been managed with the workers' best interests in mind.

Older People as Consumers

People in later maturity have traditionally been treated as an unimportant market by those in charge of developing and marketing goods and services. This view was based mainly on the notion that the elderly had relatively low incomes and relatively low consumption and expenditure patterns (Clark et al., 1978). However, most of the "facts" that supported this view came from an era when retirement income systems were in their infancy and many older Americans were indeed poor. As the incomes of the elderly have improved, they have become a force to be reckoned with in the marketplace.

A great deal of the growth of the American consumer economy since World War II has been tied to a rapidly increasing population with a high proportion of young people. But since the 1960s, lower birth rates have meant fewer young people entering the population. The fastest growing segment of the U.S. population is now older people, particularly the old-old. There are signs that the consumer economy is beginning to recognize the true consumer potential of the elderly. Allen (1981) reported that sporting goods companies are beginning to market products such as lightweight rifles and special golf clubs specifically designed to meet the needs of older consumers. Travel agents and major carriers have begun aiming travel packages specifically at the older market. Allen (1981) also reported that households with heads age 55 or over accounted for 80 percent of the deposits in savings and loan institutions and spent 28 percent of all discretionary money—money not spent on necessities—in the marketplace. This figure was nearly double the amount spent by households with heads age 34 and under. The much-sought-after under-25 youth market accounted for only 1 percent.

Although it is commonly thought that older people are unwilling to spend money even if they have it, Allen (1981) found this notion inaccurate: The 55 to 64 age group was *the* most important consumer market in the country, leading other categories in sales for a wide variety of purchases ranging from vacation travel and restaurant meals to garden supplies and luxury automobiles. The 65 and over population was also above the national averages for categories such as vacation travel, women's clothing, mobile homes, and magazine and newspaper subscriptions. High-income older households are the most conspicuous consumers of luxury goods and services such as furs and jewelry, expensive clothing, and cruises.

In the coming years we can expect an expanding interest in developing and marketing new products for the elderly. Already, products are being developed that use available technology to help the elderly compensate for physical decrements. Home-delivered services such as meals, housekeeping, personal care, and health care aimed at older people able to pay will come when the concentration of people wanting such services increases to the payoff point. We can also expect to see personal care items that take into account age changes in the skin, such as makeup, hair care products, soaps and deodorants. And advertising campaigns for such products can be expected to make greater use of older models, who will in turn provide images of physical attractiveness appropriate to older people. The list of interesting possibilities seems endless.

Summary

The economy is a very complex social institution, one that affects middle-aged and older people by governing their access to jobs, by providing the economic surplus needed to finance retirement income, and by its approach to aging people as consumers. The American economy is influenced by a long-standing free-market ideology that seeks to increase the wealth of private individuals and sees the operation of this accumulated wealth in the private market as the most appropriate way to meet people's needs.

However, access to wealth is not equal in American society. There is a core private sector of the economy comprised of the largest business and financial corporations in which there are relatively plentiful opportunities to earn high incomes, amass substantial investments, and generate entitlement to high retirement incomes. Workers in this sector are predominantly white males; and at the upper echelons, where opportunities are greatest, they tend to be from the most well-to-do families. The peripheral private sector is made up of smaller, more competitive businesses that operate on lower profit margins and in which wages tend to be low and fringe benefits and private pension coverage tend to be inadequate or nonexistent. Most American workers are employed in the peripheral private sector. The government sector of the economy employs about 17 percent of the labor force and offers a high range of wages, fringe benefits, and pension adequacy. Some government workers fare

nearly as well as those in the core private sector, but most are somewhere between the core and peripheral private sectors. Thus, access to fully adequate retirement income is not available to all Americans, only those in about the top 30 percent of jobs. The incomes that support the elderly are overwhelmingly *earned* income from wages, accumulated assets, and pension credits. Less than 5 percent of the incomes of the elderly come from "unearned" sources such as Supplemental Security Income or Medicaid.

The income inequalities among people increase as they move into later maturity, a result of inequities in access to retirement pensions and assets and also of a tax structure that concentrates tax breaks for the elderly among the most well-to-do. There is a large minority of older people for whom the American economy does not deliver adequate retirement income.

Future trends will probably increase the difficulties of providing adequate retirement income. Unless we find an alternative to the payroll tax for meeting our Social Security and Medicare obligations, there will continue to be pressure to increase retirement ages and cut benefits, particularly if inflation in medical care costs continues at its present very high rate. These difficulties can be expected to increase the problems of the low-income elderly more than those of the middle class.

For many older people, the private economy is effective in delivering food, clothing, housing, transportation, recreation, and the like. But there are also many needs of the elderly, particularly in housing, health care, and transportation, where the economy has not responded simply because meeting those needs was not profitable enough. Attempts at government intervention are sometimes ineffective and overly costly because government must work through private businesses committed to making high profits from work done for government.

Retirement is not only a life stage that must be financed, it is an important tool of employment policy. It helps society to keep unemployment within acceptable bounds, it helps to reduce labor mobility in highly skilled jobs, it gives workers incentive to endure undesirable or overly demanding jobs by limiting their duration, it provides a graceful means of phasing out ineffective workers, and it creates opportunities for younger workers. Accordingly, retirement benefits the entire society, not just currently retired individuals.

The need to provide retirement income has played an important role in capital formation since World War II. Pension funds now own substantial interests in the corporations of America. However, thus far these large pension funds have not been managed with the goal of maximizing pensions but instead to provide capital for low-growth corporations, freeing other investors to seek the high-yield, high-growth investments.

Older people have customarily been treated as a trivial market for consumer goods. However, with the declining numbers of young people, the slowing of population growth, and the improvement of retirement incomes for the middle class, business is beginning to show an interest in older markets. Indeed, the over-55 population is currently spending more discretionary money than any other age category in the population, particularly on luxury goods and services. In the future we can look for businesses to develop more products and services aimed directly at the older population.

Chapter 17

Politics and Government

Power, the ability to realize goals even against opposition, is the central core of politics; and people engage in politics as a way of securing power. Practically all large-scale institutions have their power aspects and their political aspects, but we generally reserve the label *politics* for the relationships surrounding the struggle for power over the machinery of government. In examining the relationship between aging and politics, we will concentrate on three fundamental issues: the political *participation* of older people, the political *power* of older people and their advocates, and finally the political *response* to older people as evidenced through governmental programs and policies.

Political Participation

Political participation takes many forms in American society: expressing political opinions, voting, participating in voluntary associations revolving around politics, or holding political office.

Political Opinions

Forming political opinions requires the least involvement on the part of the individual. Several researchers have found that the proportion of people who answer "no opinion" to political poll questions increases with age, and have taken this finding as an indication of the relatively disengaged status of older people in American society (Turk et al., 1966; Gergen and Back, 1966). However, Glenn (1969) found that when the effect of *education* was accounted for, there was no evidence that older people became less interested in political affairs or less likely to form political opinions. In fact, he found, when education was precisely controlled for, older people were slightly *more* likely to hold opinions than were younger people. Also, Turk and his coworkers (1966) found that people committed to the community and anchored to the community through social ties tended to increase in opinionation with age. Although the tendency to form political opinions, by itself, may possibly decline with age, education and involvement in the community were strong forces that more than counteracted this trend for many people.

People are commonly thought to become more politically conservative as they grow older. However, the available evidence does not support this notion. Glenn (1974) concluded that in recent years people who have passed middle age have become *more* liberal in many respects. But political liberalism has grown more slowly in older cohorts than in younger, which means that older cohorts have become *relatively* more conservative while they have grown more liberal *absolutely*. Thus, though there is evidence to suggest that attitudes become somewhat less susceptible to change as people age, there is no evidence that their attitudes become more conservative (Glenn, 1974; Foner, 1974; Lipsett and Ladd, 1972; Agnello, 1973; S. Cutler and Kaufman, 1975; N. Cutler, 1981; J. Davis, 1981).

In an ambitious cohort analysis of political opinion data from 1940 to 1970, Douglass et al. (1974) assessed the separate effects of *time, cohort,* and *age.** They found, in general, that political opinions were more sensitive to time effects than to age or cohort effects. That is, the time period when the opinion was asked was more important than the age of the respondents or the era in which the respondents were reared. Age was usually a secondary effect and then only if the opinion concerned family issues. They also found that which effect (time, cohort, or age) was significant varied with the specific political attitude. For example, *none* of the effects was significant in determining which respondents saw economic issues as the foremost national problem. On the other hand, *time* was the only significant factor in

determining who saw foreign policy as the prime national problem.

Similarly, Cutler and Bengtson (1974) found that political alienation was more closely related to the historical time of measurement than to either age or cohort effects. In their analysis, the impact of educational differences between cohorts was controlled for. However, a somewhat different pattern emerged when Martin, Bengtson, and Acock (1974) examined various dimensions of alienation. Although the elderly scored lowest of all age categories on "alienation from self" and on "social isolation," they scored highest on "powerlessness." Indeed, Miller, Gurin, and Gurin (1980) found that age consciousness did not lead to political action precisely because the elderly felt they lacked influence. Thus, it would appear that the elderly remain interested in politics but skeptical about their ability to influence the process.

Opinion formation is no doubt related to information seeking, and research results indicate that older people try hard to remain informed about political affairs. In comparison with the young, older people give greater attention to political campaigns and are more likely to follow public affairs in the news (Riley and Foner, 1968:468). In addition, older people are more apt to seek practical knowledge, such as the name of their own congressional representative, than academic knowledge, such as the makeup of the electoral college (Erskine, 1963). Glenn and Grimes (1968) found that those showing the highest interest in politics were consistently those aged 60 or over.

Voting

Voting behavior ranks just above opinion formation as a relatively mild form of involvement in politics. Voting behavior shows a pattern of change with age that is as complex as it is interesting. In general, it appears that voting participation is lowest at age 18; it builds to a plateau in the fifties, and then begins a gradual decline after age 65. People in their eighties still vote

*See Chapter 1 for a more detailed discussion of time, cohort, and age effects.

more than people in their early twenties. Men and women show approximately the same curve of voter participation, although the overall participation of women is lower for all ages. Hence, a substantial part of the apparent decline in voter participation among older people results from sex differences in voter participation coupled with the higher mortality rates among older men.

Table 17-1 shows that voters' educational level had a significant impact on the age pattern of voting in the November 1980 election. Among men, age made much more difference in percent voting for those with only elementary or some high school education than for those who graduated from college (read down the columns

in Table 17-1). Among women, age made less difference, but the effect of education on the age pattern was about the same. Among those with some college, the difference between men and women in terms of percent voting was quite small, whereas it was greatest among older men and women who had not completed elementary school. Thus, the higher the level of education, the less the relationship of both age and sex to voting.

In an interesting analysis of aging, voting, and political interest, Glenn and Grimes (1968) found scarcely any change in voting turnout when the same age cohort was examined over the course of six presidential elections (20 years), which suggests that people develop a

TABLE 17-1   Voter participation (percent voting), by age, sex, and education: United States, November 1980

Age	Highest School Year Completed								Effect of high vs. low Education
	Elementary School			High School		College			
	0–4	5–7	8	1–3	4	1–3	4	5+	
Males									
22–24	—	6.8	3.5	14.6	39.6	52.8	70.2	73.7	—
25–34	9.8	12.8	21.5	23.1	46.0	57.7	72.4	78.7	+68.9
35–54	24.8	33.7	44.6	50.1	65.0	74.5	81.3	82.9	+58.1
55–64	35.1	51.3	61.1	69.2	78.7	81.5	86.6	86.7	+51.6
65+	46.0	57.0	67.1	76.3	75.7	83.0	85.6	87.0	+41.0
Effect of Age (old vs. young)	—	+50.2	+63.6	+61.7	+36.1	+30.2	+15.4	+13.3	—
Females									
22–24	—	14.0	11.8	18.2	40.8	57.2	72.6	68.6	—
25–34	6.6	14.1	16.8	28.2	51.4	66.3	76.1	78.8	+72.2
35–54	17.7	29.4	42.0	56.3	70.2	80.5	82.8	85.8	+68.1
55–64	35.8	43.6	53.7	62.6	77.3	82.1	87.7	87.7	+51.9
65+	27.5	44.7	53.2	62.9	72.2	78.7	80.5	84.0	+56.5
Effect of Age (old vs. young)	—	+30.7	+41.4	+44.7	+31.4	+21.5	+7.9	+15.4	—

Source: U.S. Bureau of the Census (1982b: 51–53).

style of participation as a result of their own unique political socialization and then stick to it. Hout and Knoke (1975) reported similar results. The importance of this finding is its implication that as the average level of education in our population increases, we should expect the age pattern of voter participation to rise faster, peak higher, remain at the high plateau longer, and decline even more slowly than the cross-sectional data given in Table 17-1 indicate. It also implies a generational change in the direction of greater voter participation on the part of older people. For example, between 1964 and 1980, there was a general decline in the percent voting. This decline was the smallest at age 65 and over (U.S. Bureau of the Census, 1982b:5).

In fact, Glenn and Grimes carried their analysis even further to hypothesize that "only widespread disability and lack of transportation keep the voter turnout of the elderly down near that of the middle-aged person with the same amount of education" (1968:570). Otherwise, older people would vote in *higher* proportions than middle-aged persons of the same sex and with the same education. In support of this idea, Turk and his associates (1966) found an increase with age in the proportion voting among people who were involved in the community. In addition, Gubrium (1972a) found that widowhood and divorce tended to reduce the proportion of older people who voted.

Party Affiliation

Party affiliation is another significant political variable. Nie et al. (1976) found that the proportion who identified strongly with a political party increased gradually with age; but unlike voting behavior, party identification did not decline in the later years. The strength of a person's party attachment appeared to be a function less of age than of the duration of that particular bond. Age provided the opportunity for the long-term identification that appears to

be necessary for a strong bond, although among those with the same duration of affiliation, age was *negatively* associated with the strength of the bond. The end result, however, was that people in their twenties were only half as likely as people over 65 to identify themselves with a major party. However, as cross-sectional data, Nie's findings should be approached with caution. Glenn and Hefner (1972) found that between 1945 and 1969 younger cohorts had become less likely to identify with a political party. They interpreted the age differences as cohort differences:

> The older cohorts, as aggregates, always had stronger party identification than the younger cohorts, probably because their early political socialization occurred when the two major parties were more salient in American life (1972:43–44).

Thus, as younger, more independent cohorts age, we can expect a decline in party identification among the elderly (N. Cutler, 1981).

Among older people, there are about equal proportions of Republicans and Democrats, which implies a substantial change with age, since at younger ages there are many more Democrats than Republicans. Here again, however, we run into the difficulty of trying to infer changes through time from data collected at one point in time. A closer examination of the longitudinal data suggests that when those reared during and after the New Deal become a majority among older people (about the year 2005), a preponderance of Democrats may emerge (Glenn and Hefner, 1972). There is no evidence that people are more likely to become Republican as they grow older.

Older people seem to be amply represented in party organizations. What evidence there is indicates that older people represent about the same percentage of party organizations as they represent of the total population. In addition, one study has shown that older people have a disproportionately greater influence at nominating conventions (Kapnick et al., 1968) Thus, it appears that older members of party organizations have a great deal of influence over the selection of party candidates for political office.

Holding Political Office

Indeed, older people are also overrepresented in various political offices. Leadership in all areas related to public affairs seems to be amply accessible to older political leaders. Presidents, cabinet ministers, and ambassadors usually acquire their positions in their late fifties, and often retain them well beyond age 60. Supreme Court justices are also most likely to be appointed in their late fifties, and most continue to serve well beyond age 65, since retirement usually depends on their personal desire. In the 97th Congress (1980), 66 representatives (15 percent) and 20 senators (20 percent) were 60 or over. Thirteen representatives and 6 senators were 70 or over. However, there has been a steady trend toward a younger Congress since 1971, when there were 108 representatives and 40 senators 60 or over (U.S. Bureau of the Census, 1982a). Proportions of older people in state and local offices (whether elected or appointed) are substantially higher than among the rank and file of other occupations.

One reason why older members of political organizations are influential is the weight that tenure alone carries in politics. In politics, perhaps more than in any other institution, the older person is still able to play the role of sage (in fact, the word *politic* means "wise" or "shrewd"), probably partly because political processes have felt the impact of industrialization and rationalization less than has the economy or even the family. The professionalization of politics is much less complete than that of education or the economy. As a result, political prowess is still felt to be largely learned from experience rather than out of a book or in a professional school. There seems to be public appreciation of this factor. Turner and Kahn (1974) found age of a candidate to be an insig-

nificant issue among voters of all ages. However, experience does seem to be a salient factor. Schlesinger and Schlesinger concluded that "American politics has not been especially cordial to the older political neophyte" (1981:235).

Thus, older people do not seem to be at any great disadvantage in terms of access to political roles. Yet what does this accessibility mean to the older person? Glenn and Grimes (1968) felt that people turn increasingly *toward* political activity as they age. They further suggested that as one grows older, politics tends to be viewed more as a means of personal fulfillment and less as a means to some instrumental end. Their rationale gains support from studies showing that as people grow older they maintain and perhaps even increase their interest in politics, while simultaneously feeling that their individual political action neither has nor can have an impact on the political process (Schmidhauser, 1968). In short, older people appear to enjoy political participation, but at the same time are somewhat cynical about its concrete effects.

Political Power

There are many approaches to the study of older people's political power. Some say that older people serve primarily as a pressure group that attempts to coerce politicians into either enacting legislation beneficial to them or opposing legislation harmful to them. Others see the problems of aging as the central focus for the formation of a social movement involving not only older people but people of all ages in an attempt to solve these problems. Still others view older people as a category that, because of the discriminatory and categorical treatment it receives at the hands of society at large, is rapidly developing a subculture of its own. All of these approaches contain some truth and none is sufficient in itself to explain the treatment of the elderly in politics.

Older People as a Pressure Group

Political success for political groups formed around older people's interests has been more often a hope than a reality. As Carlie concluded:

> We have indicated [previously] that the old age political organization left a great deal to be desired as pertains to such matters [as] organization (a failure to develop strong secondary leadership), pressure (if there were not too few members then they were regionally segregated), votes (the aspiring representatives of old age political programs failed to secure enough votes to place them in pivotal political positions), and money. . . .
>
> It seems as though one of the necessary conditions for the formulation and maintenance of interest groups is a homogeneity of characteristics among the membership. An effective interest group, then, should have more in common than just age. Other important shared characteristics may be ethnicity, nativity, educational background, occupational status, race, and rural-urban residency. Lacking similarity beyond age (and perhaps the state of retirement), the old age political movements were handicapped from their very inception (1969:259–263).

Effective political pressure groups often purport to be able to deliver votes in a bloc. But there has never been an instance in the history of the United States in which the leadership of an old-age interest group could deliver what would even approach "the old folks' vote." Thus, the view that older people comprise a unified interest group that can mobilize political pressure by bloc voting is an illusion, and is quite likely to remain so (Binstock, 1972).

Arnold Rose (1965a) was perhaps the strongest proponent of the idea that patterns of aging in American society would produce a subculture of the aged. According to Rose, a subculture would develop when people in a given category interacted with each other more than they interacted with people in other categories. The subculture would grow as a result of the positive affinity that drew like people together and the discrimination that excluded these same people from interacting with other groups. Rose cited the growing numbers of older people with common problems—usually related to health—living out their retirement in self-segregated retirement communities where a relatively high standard of living made possible the development of a unique life style. And he contended that older people were rapidly shifting from the status of a category to that of a group. He further stated that, in addition to pure self-interest, there was an interactional basis for the development of an age-conscious group. This interaction resulted from our society's policy of phasing older people out of almost every other kind of group, thus forcing them to seek out each other. Rose felt that this trend cut across the subcultures based on occupation, sex, religion, and ethnic identification that typify the middle-aged population. Old-age group identification, rather than any specific organization of older people, led Rose to conclude that "the elderly seem to be on their way to becoming a voting bloc with a leadership that acts as a political pressure group" (1965a:14).

This type of analysis is intuitively attractive to many because it postulates the existence of the old-age pressure group without necessarily requiring that this group manifest itself in an overt form of organization. The "leaders" speak for a kind of silent group—a group that recognizes itself and is capable of the bloc voting required to achieve political influence. But there are major problems with this approach. To begin with, most older people interact *across* generational lines as well as within them, simply because a frequent source of interaction is their adult children and grandchildren. Second, the stereotype that older people are flocking in masses to retirement communities is largely a myth. The data on migration show that only a small minority of older people move. In fact, most older people have lived in the same residence for more than 20 years. As a result, older people tend to be interspersed among the general population. Third, while there may be a rising number of older people who can afford a unique leisure life style, life styles vary widely among older people. Thus, several of the key conditions on which Rose based his case for the subculture approach turn out to be questionable. In fact, Longino et al. (1980) found that although older people in retirement communities tended to develop a subculture that enhances their self-esteem, the political attitudes of this subculture were *retreatist* and thus lead to little likelihood of concerted political action.

Advocacy for the Aged

The view that political action favoring older people stems from a social movement involving not only the aged but others as well is the view that has most often been expressed by political scientists (Cottrell, 1960a). According to this approach, older people have a great deal of *potential* power by virtue of the fact that in the more rural areas they constitute a larger proportion of the population, and that these rural areas are overrepresented in both the state legislatures and the U.S. Senate. The presumed reason that this potential has never been realized, however, is that the older population is divided among a great many interest groups, most of which do not make the welfare of the aged their primary goal. But if this reasoning is valid, we may ask, how did legislation in behalf of older people manage to get passed?

The answer seems to be that old-age political organizations, while not effective as pressure groups, have been effective in making the older population's plight politically visible. As a result, the "cause" of the elderly has been picked up by groups not based on age, such as unions and political parties. The readiness of various groups interested in the general welfare to commit themselves to programs for the aged was caused largely by the existence, at almost every level of organization, of large numbers of middle-class adult children who were anxious to shift financial support for older people off themselves and onto the government. It is for this reason, as well as the votes the elderly themselves command, that no major political

party, trade union, or other large-scale organization dares oppose the income provisions of Social Security. This view of older people's power fits the facts better than any other so far. It describes relatively accurately the political processes that brought passage of Social Security and Medicare, the two most sweeping legislative proposals affecting older people.

In addition to persistently keeping problems of the aged in the public eye, organizations such as the National Council of Senior Citizens (NCSC—3 million members) and the American Association of Retired Persons (AARP—13 million members up from 6 million in 1974) have been reasonably effective in gaining a larger share for older people from existing federal programs (Binstock, 1972; Pratt, 1974). In a very lucid article, Pratt (1974) attributed the increased effectiveness of current voluntary associations for older people, compared with the old-age interest groups of the 1930s, to three factors: (1) sources of funds in addition to member dues, (2) reliance on bureaucratic performance rather than charisma as a criterion for selecting leaders, and (3) a sympathetic political climate for lobbying activities. The NCSC derived nearly half its financial support from the large labor unions while AARP got most of its income from insurance programs and other services it offered to its membership (Pratt, 1974). While both organizations were headed by persons over 65, in both cases they were people of proven administrative capability. Political sensitivity to the concerns of old-age interest groups was readily apparent in the concessions extracted from the Nixon Administration through a threatened boycott of the 1971 White House Conference on Aging.

In addition to the organizations discussed above, several other organizations promote political attention on behalf of older people. The National Council on the Aging (NCoA) is a federation of over a thousand agencies that deal with older people. The National Caucus on the Black Aged is a group of professionals seeking to emphasize the unique problems of black older people. The Gray Panthers, in 1984 under the leadership of Maggie Kuhn, is a coalition of young and old persons that publicizes and promotes alternative life styles for older people. Estes (1979) has pointed out that the "aging network"—a loosely connected array of personnel from government and nongovernment agencies serving the elderly—depends for survival on a strong federal commitment to programs for the elderly, especially those related to health and social services. These people can be expected to operate through various professional organizations to oppose cutbacks in programs for the elderly and to advocate expansion in many cases. Thus, while interest groups of older people have not been, and are not likely to be, very effective in bringing about a drastic move toward equality for older people, they have been effective in improving results of current programs for older people.

Political Legitimacy and Utility

We emerge from this survey of organizations of and for the elderly with the view that older people themselves have relatively little power *as older people*. Some powerful people are old, but they are not powerful *because* they are old. Most of the political power behind programs for older people is generated by others on behalf of older people rather than by older people themselves. Hudson (1978) identified two reasons why this has been so: the *legitimacy* of the aged as a target for governmental efforts, and the *utility* of the aged as potential voters. Legislators can only legislate in areas that the voting public considers to be a legitimate concern of government. And no other constituency on the domestic scene has been seen as a more appropriate concern of government than the elderly. Hudson argued that this legitimacy has rested on widespread public acceptance of the belief that the aged represented the most undeservedly disadvantaged category of people in American society in terms of income, health, and vulnerability. There are other factors, too. Age discrimination

in the economy means that older people cannot do anything about their situation through the job market. They do not participate in general increases in wages and salaries. No other category of people is so systematically excluded from this means of coping with economic change. Support for the legitimacy of programs for the elderly also comes from families who fully realize that adequate financial assistance to retired family members is beyond their capability. Finally, the legitimacy of programs for the elderly comes also from the fact that everyone eventually gets old, so creating adequate social supports for the elderly is a form of self-protection.

The effectiveness of older people as a political force is a sometime thing. When the issues concern the elderly directly (Social Security, Medicare, etc.), the elderly and their advocates can indeed represent a sizable political force. In other areas, such as aging research or direct services to the elderly, the political effectiveness of the elderly is less clear-cut.

Hudson (1978) cited several factors that may threaten the political legitimacy of the elderly. Cost pressures, especially for Medicare and long-term care under Medicaid, are making it increasingly difficult to meet the needs of the aged with the resources Congress has been willing to appropriate for these programs. In addition, recent improvements in the economic circumstances of older people have altered their public image as a disadvantaged group. This could have especially dire consequences for older minorities and women, among whom large proportions are still quite disadvantaged. These pressures have led to a reexamination of our policy of providing support for all older Americans regardless of their personal resources.

The role older people themselves are left to play in politics is generally confined to the local community, unless they have been involved in politics steadily throughout their lives. At the local level, older people may indeed be influential, particularly in close elections on nonpartisan issues; but nationwide politics offers older people as such very little in terms of either power or participation. Therefore, while politics is relatively unique in not *demanding* disengagement from its older participants, it does not very often offer older people the opportunity to *increase* their active participation, even though they might like to do so. Older people can form strong opinions in political affairs, and they can increase their involvement in voting; but unless they have "paid their dues" in the form of earlier participation in politics, they are unlikely to gain access to positions within party organizations or government itself.

Government Response to the Aged

As we begin this discussion of government response to the elderly, it is essential to have a common understanding of the term *welfare state*. Webster's Unabridged Dictionary (1981:2594) defines *welfare state* as "a social system based on the assumption by a political state of primary responsibility for the individual and social welfare (health, happiness, and prosperity) of its citizens usually by enacting specific public policies (such as health or unemployment insurance, minimum wages, or subsidies to housing or transportation) and their implementation directly by government agencies." Thus, the government in the welfare state takes responsibility in a wide variety of areas for creating conditions that promote the general well-being of its population. For Americans, the use of the term *welfare* in this concept has often had the unfortunate effect of confusing the broad-based notion of a responsible state with the more circumscribed social welfare institution, which in the main is devoted to preventing or alleviating social problems such as poverty, delinquency, or mental illness.

Thus, when we speak of the welfare state in the United States, we are referring to more than programs for the disadvantaged, such as SSI or Medicaid; we are also referring to governmental

efforts to improve public health through control of disease, to safeguard the environment from unhealthy levels of pollution, to enhance the productivity of the population by providing high-quality education, to promote safety by requiring that what we know about safety be applied to new products, to improve commerce by maintaining an interstate network of roads, to protect workers from exploitation by establishing a minimum wage consistent with our national level of living, and a host of other efforts.

The United States has lagged behind most of western Europe in its development of a responsible state. As we saw in Chapter 3, Social Security was very late in coming to America compared with European countries. In addition, the United States has been highly inconsistent in pursuing its responsibilities. For example, we have funded a national network of highways from taxes but insist that rail transport be privately financed. As a result, we have the best highways in the world and some of the worst railroads. We have enacted minimum wage legislation that has countless loopholes and that effectively omits millions of American workers. We have a well-funded Public Health Service that has led the world in prevention of infectious diseases, yet we have no national system guaranteeing health care to all of the public.

These inconsistencies can be traced largely to our preference for private, individual solutions rather than public, collective solutions. We also prefer to distribute goods and services based on wealth more than need. The individualistic ethic held by many Americans assumes that people in need have brought misery on themselves. In order to prevent abuses of public charity, the assumption has most often been that such programs must be degrading and punitive, an assumption that completely ignores the reality of job discrimination, which is such a widespread problem in America for women, minorities, and the aged. And because we have been ambivalent about providing public programs of health care and income security even for the elderly, those programs that have been developed have not been very effective. In the previous chapter we saw that much of our expenditure for "the elderly" goes to support the middle class and that despite a large expenditure, there are still millions of older Americans who still lack income security or access to adequate health care, particularly long-term care.

With the presidential election of 1980, the United States moved even further from the principles of a responsible state. Although the American public placed a high priority on public expenditures for health, education, and the environment and very little priority on spending for arms (Davis, 1981), the Reagan Administration moved very quickly to reduce federal involvement in protecting the public interest in areas such as natural resources, the environment, and education. At the same time, the Reagan Administration cut taxes to high-income Americans and increased spending for defense, resulting in a large federal budget deficit, which was then used to defend massive cuts in "social programs"—loosely defined as federal expenditures in any area either where private enterprise could conceivably operate or directed toward assisting disadvantaged people. All Americans were presumably being asked to make sacrifices in the name of "economic recovery," but the bulk of the sacrifices were actually made by the disadvantaged. From fiscal years 1982 to 1985, given changes enacted at the behest of the Reagan economic recovery plan, expenditures for Social Security were reduced by $24.1 billion, the largest single reduction of any federal human services program. The third largest cut—$13.2 billion—was in Medicare. The Congressional Budget Office (1983) concluded that these changes mainly affected households with less than $10,000 annual income. These cuts meant that many disabled persons were removed from the Social Security disability rolls without adequate case review. The proportion of medical care for the elderly covered by Medicare dipped to less than 40 percent.

The Reagan Administration was convinced that the Great Society programs of the 1960s and 1970s had led to massive abuse by thieves and freeloaders, and that the best way to cope with this problem was to drastically reduce the number of people eligible for public programs. Thus, it was decided that large numbers of people would be indiscriminately removed from federal benefit programs. Those who were "truly needy" would be those who succeeded in getting back on the federal benefit rolls. This approach had tragic results in which completely helpless, disabled Americans were deprived of any source of financial support. Local public welfare offices were besieged with desperate people with nowhere to turn. And since federal welfare funds had been cut, there was little the welfare departments could do, particularly to provide immediate food, shelter, or health care.

The Reagan Administration defended its actions by defining assistance to the disadvantaged as inappropriate for federal attention. Instead, state and local governments and private philanthropy were exhorted to assume the costs of providing such assistance. Families were also to be expected to "do their duty" to their disadvantaged members.

As ideology, these assumptions may or may not be valid. However, the traditional American approach to solving problems has a strong pragmatic thread running through it that demands that policies be based as much as possible on an accurate assessment of the facts. And the assumptions of fact made by the Reagan Administration were seriously inaccurate in many cases. The administration position was that the elderly had been provided for by earlier legislation, that 25 percent of the federal budget was going to support them, and that families, communities, and private philanthropy could assume most of the costs of caring for those in need. In fact, as we saw earlier, in 1980 we still had 15 percent of the elderly with incomes at or below the poverty level and another 15 percent near that level. Of the 26 percent of the federal budget earmarked for programs for the elderly, only 2.4 percent was allocated to public assistance for the elderly. The remainder was going to programs that benefited primarily the middle- and upper-income elderly. To help put this in perspective, Americans spent more money on jewelry and watches in 1981 than was allocated to public assistance for the elderly (U.S. Bureau of the Census, 1982a).

Although state, local, and philanthropic involvement and commitment are very important in an overall effort to meet the needs of the elderly, it was a grave mistake for the government to assume that we could do without a strong and persistent leadership and financing at the national level. There are two important reasons for this. First, experience in delivering services to the elderly is not evenly divided throughout the states. Some states have a great deal of experience and others have very little. The existence of a national network of agencies greatly facilitates communication among communities and states. The "Aging Network"—made up of local Area Agencies on Aging, local service providers, State Units on Aging, Administration on Aging regional offices, and the federal Administration on Aging—has been a very vital part of the improvement in services to the elderly since 1970. In addition, the national commitment has important symbolic value. It indicates through action our national value of caring for elderly people. Second, the federal government has vastly greater power and resources than state or local governments. For example, in 1980 the federal government had revenues of $564 billion, state governments collected only $213 billion, and local government revenues were only $156 billion. United Way programs throughout the country raised $1.7 billion, and private philanthropic organizations—churches, foundations, corporations, and so on—raised $53.6 billion, most of it earmarked for church programs. Only $5.3 billion of private philanthropic money was earmarked for public assistance programs (U.S. Bureau of the Census, 1982a). Thus, it should be clear that state and local governments and "the private sector" have relatively few resources compared to the national government. In addition, state and local govern-

ments must support activities that the federal government plays little or no role in financing, such as education, transportation, fire and police protection, and local courts.

The assumption that families can do more than they are currently doing was also quite misinformed. Shanas (1977) reported that 80 percent of the in-home care being provided the elderly was already coming from family, 15 percent from helpers paid by the older person or his or her family, and only 2 percent from social agencies. In terms of financial aid, those older people whose families can afford to support them financially are the most unlikely to need such support, while those most in need are quite likely either to be without family or to have families who are also poor.

Thus, many of the assumptions used by the Reagan Administration to justify program cutbacks were erroneous, and as a result the policies enacted were also misguided and brought about a substantial decline in the access of older Americans to adequate housing, health care, and income. To make matters worse, cutbacks in funds allotted to publish federal statistics on the performance of various programs made it increasingly difficult for individuals and organizations outside government to document the results of the cutbacks in programs like Social Security disability, Medicaid, and Medicare.

These problems illustrate the dangers of basing policies on ideological rather than factual assumptions. Fortunately, the federal administration is not the only agent of social policy, as we shall see in the next section. For the future, it is worth noting that the population explosion of older people has not actually peaked yet and that coping with it will require a national commitment.

Making Policy

It is well known that the United States government operates Social Security and Medicare primarily for older people. The goals of these programs are to shift the financial responsibility for income and health maintenance for older people onto the federal government. Older people have other needs, however, that many people feel could best be served by government. Consider the following list:

Vocational rehabilitation

Housing

Transportation

Taxes

Recreation

Mental health

Consumer protection

Suicide prevention

Referral services

Independence

Poverty

Activity

Long-term care

Nutrition

Nursing-home financing

Design (buildings,
    furniture, clothing, etc.)

Inflation

Homemaker services

Retirement

Protective services

Alcoholism

Blindness and deafness

Education

Dental care

How likely is the government to respond to these needs? To satisfy them requires, first, a commitment to spend government money on the aged and, second, some consensus on priorities. The first requirement brings us to perhaps the most fundamental problem that politicians face—choosing the things that are possible from among the many things that people want, given that government can almost never command enough resources to satisfy everybody. As Cottrell has pointed out:

> They [the politicians] know that to gain anything people must sacrifice something else they might have had. They try to judge the worth of an objective in terms of what the voter is willing to sacrifice to achieve it. If they judge correctly, they can continue to make policy; but if they err too greatly, policy will be made by others who have organized a more effective coalition in support of [other] policies (1966:96).

To build the power necessary to design, develop, and implement governmental programs for older people, the politician must find out the areas in which older people's interests coincide enough with those of other groups to form an effective voting coalition—since, as we have already seen, older people do not by themselves have the necessary power. The politician must also stay out of areas, however strong the need, that most people consider none of the government's business.

There are some sizable obstacles to governmental programs intended only for the aged. The first obstacle is *conflict of interest*. Meeting the needs of older people often conflicts with meeting the needs of the young, such as choosing between aid to schools and aid to nursing homes. *Vested interests* also play their part. The opposition of the American Medical Association (AMA) to Medicare is a good example. Physicians did not oppose better medical care for older people; they opposed the idea of government involvement in programs traditionally dominated by physicians. It was to protect this vested interest that the AMA opposed Medicare. Its intent is quite evident from the fact that over 80 percent of doctors expressed approval within the first six weeks after Medicare was put into operation, by which time it had become obvious to most of them that the government had no intention of becoming involved in their everyday decisions. The fact that the AMA's fears for its vested interest were unfounded is unimportant; merely *feeling* threatened was enough to block the passage of Medicare for quite some time. (Ironically, the future of Medicare is now threatened by the fact that health care providers have benefitted *too much* from the program.)

Another thing that inhibits programs for older people is the inertia of bureaucratic organizations. For instance, when first proposed, Social Security legislation was up against the lack of any recognized bureaucratic structure in the government around which those interested in supporting income programs for the aged could rally. At the time, both the Townsend Movement and Eliminate Poverty in California (under Upton Sinclair) were going strong, but there was no Washington office through which their support could be funneled. At the time Medicare was being considered, there was an Office of Aging under the Department of Health, Education, and Welfare (HEW) and the Special Committee on Aging in the U.S. Senate, which made gaining support for programs for older people easier in the sense that there was an office staff paid by the government to keep tabs on the interests of the aged.

The Senate Special Committee on Aging, created in 1961 as a temporary study group (as opposed to a committee with the authority to report legislation to the full Senate), has repeatedly survived its one-year mandate and become a de facto, 21-member standing committee of the Senate. In an analysis of the committee's role, Vinyard (1972) concluded that it served several important functions: (1) as a watchdog, seeing that the interests of older Americans do not get lost or ignored in broad-ranging government programs; (2) as a legislative catalyst, supporting legislation and lobbying for the aged within Congress; (3) as a rallying point for senators wishing to demonstrate to the public their interest and support; (4) as a frequent legislative ally of old-age interest groups; and (5) as a symbol of Congress' concern for the interests of older Americans.

Many political scientists are convinced that, Social Security's and Medicare's having both been enacted, there will never again be an issue relating primarily to older people that will mobilize the support of the young. Accordingly, they say, the only hope for older people seeking government action on their problems is to attach their requirements to broader legislative proposals. Over the past several years, the track record of lobbyists using this strategy has been encouraging. From 1967 to 1985, the share of all federal money that went to people over 65 will have risen from less than 15 percent to 28 percent (U.S. Senate Special Committee on Aging, 1984).

This train of argument brings us to the political role of the "expert." Trained or experienced gerontologists potentially have great impact on the formulating of policy toward older people. They have access to more information about older people; and, as a society, we are accustomed to letting the experts handle our problems. Government experts on gerontology can influence programs being developed in various agencies. The only difficulty here is that gerontology "experts" are in fact much less expert than, let us say, agricultural experts. There is simply not enough evidence yet for gerontologists to make policy recommendations with full confidence that they know what is best or what most older people want. This uncertainty arises largely because we do not know enough yet about age changes in people's values.

Fortunately, the Senate Special Committee on Aging and the House Select Committee on Aging serve a very useful function here by allowing input from interested citizens concerning older people's problems. In hearings throughout the country, these two committees attempt to give as many older people as want it a chance to be heard. Of course, a great many older people are never heard from; but access is there should they need it.

Aside from the issue of how programs for older people can win political support, there is the equally important issue of how the programs should be organized and coordinated. The federal government can do a reasonable job of providing direct support to older people through agencies such as Social Security. However, solutions to a great many of the problems older people face must be based on personal considerations and the *local* situation. In cases where personalized service is necessary, only the local governmental agency is capable of doing the job.

Cottrell has outlined several important questions concerning the nature of governmental programs:

> What should be the function of a central agency on aging and what are the relationships between it and other departments and agencies within the federal government?

> What should be the functions of official state agencies on aging? Where should they be located, and what should be their relationships with other units of state government?

> What type of agency is needed at the community level to serve as a focal point for broad action in aging? What should its functions be? From whence should it derive its authority and financial support?

> What is the most desirable method of integrating or interrelating the activities of overall agencies in aging at federal, state, and community levels?

> How can government at each level best maintain working relationships with voluntary organizations and with the private sector of the economy?

> What should be the division of responsibility among public and private agencies and organizations?

> Should government take initiative in stimulating roles in aging on the part of organizations? If so, what types of organizations? (1971a:1–2)

Another policy issue concerns the variety of different chronological ages used in the law to differentiate older people from the general public. Cain (1974) reports that legal definitions of "old" begin as early as 45 and as late as 72. This sort of nonuniformity creates problems of confused eligibility for government services for the elderly.

The existing intergovernmental division of labor with respect to programs for older people has resulted from variations in the ability of various agencies to muster the political power needed to enact legislation. The record at the national level is familiar: Social Security, Medicare, and agencies on aging in various federal departments attest to a small but sometimes effective political power base. At the state and local levels, however, the picture has changed greatly since 1973. Prior to that time, most state programs for older people were very limited, and the average state agency for aging had a staff of three people. Various governors' conferences on aging, forums, and so on brought home to state politicians that the aging represent an interest group to be served. However, state involvement in programs for older people was hindered, primarily by the fact that the four major programs—Social Security, Medicare, Old Age Assistance, and Federal Housing—all bypassed state government on their way to the people. At the local level, the only governmental agency serving older people was usually the county welfare department. Given the negative connotations attached to welfare programs by the public and by older people themselves, this situation was highly unsatisfactory. Only in very large cities had the concentration of older people been great enough to produce a separate local office for their needs. Multipurpose senior centers were also sometimes an effective community agency translating public programs for older people into action.

Since 1972, the situation has changed considerably. Based on 1971 White House Conference on Aging recommendations, the 1973 Comprehensive Service Amendments to the Older Americans Act required each state to set up a network of Area Agencies on Aging in order to receive federal funds. The nutrition program funneled large amounts of federal funds through state agencies. In addition, a great deal of the responsibility for planning and for administering training and demonstration programs was delegated to the states. This reorganization had sweeping effects. For the first time, state agencies on aging had administrative control over a sizable budget. Accordingly, state agencies have grown considerably in size and power since 1973. Also, the need for Area Agencies on Aging required that local areas designate a single agency to serve as local coordinator for both state and federal programs, thus improving coordination at the local level. This reorganization has created effective advocates for older people in many areas of the country where previously there had been none. In the next chapter we will look at some of the services that resulted from this system.

Summary

Politics is the route to political power, and political power means control over the machinery of government. We know that older people are concerned with politics and government because they participate in politics through voting, working in political organizations, and holding office. Older people are also the object of governmental programs.

Older people seek to remain informed about and interested in politics, particularly if they are well educated or involved in local affairs. Older people vote in about the same proportions as when they were middle aged. Each age cohort apparently develops its own level of participation, which stays relatively stable throughout the life course. But differential mortality and the tendency for women to vote less both reduce the actual proportion voting.

Older people have stronger party identification than the young only if they have been associated with a party over many years. It is number of years of affiliation, not age itself, that produces a strong party identification. Older people are evenly split between the Republican and Democratic parties. Since they are overrepresented among people who have served long apprenticeships in politics, older people are also overrepresented at nominating conventions and public offices. However, there is no evidence that this overrepresentation is the result of deference to age. In politics, youth apparently still bows to experience, and experience rather than age is the crucial variable. Older people have equal opportunity in politics, but only if they have been lifelong participants. There is little room for the retired grocer who suddenly decides to get into politics.

In terms of political power, pressure groups of older people have suffered from lack of leadership, regional segregation, heterogeneity of interests among older people, and lack of funds. These same factors have prevented older people from developing into a subculture or a genuine minority group. Action in behalf of older people has almost always depended on the political support of organizations not based on age, such as unions or political parties. The role of old-age interest groups is to make the need for action highly visible and to lobby for the interests of older people within existing programs. In recent years, older Americans have gradually increased their share of benefits from general government programs.

In 1980, the Reagan Administration began a federal pullback from a national commitment to insuring health, happiness, and prosperity for all American citizens. Based on inaccurate assumptions about the actual situation of the elderly, severe cuts were made in Social Security, Medicare, and Medicaid. The tragic results of these cuts illustrate the need to base policy on facts rather than ideological assumptions.

Governmental programs for older people assign responsibility for meeting some of their needs to various levels of government. The federal government operates programs in income and health maintenance. But many other needs require involvement on the part of state and local governments. The 1973 reorganization of the Older Americans Act, which gave states and local areas authority, funds, and responsibility, was a large step toward creating local advocates for older Americans.

The biggest problems in creating governmental programs for older people are convincing the public at large that older people deserve a higher priority than other needy groups, setting priorities among older people themselves, and deciding how these programs should be organized and coordinated, particularly in terms of intergovernmental relations. Older people have benefited a great deal from the fact that they were the first target for large-scale social programs in the United States. It is unlikely that SSI, Medicare, or many of the other supports to older Americans would be there if such supports had to be provided to everyone. American politics is still very sensitive to "government intervention" on too large a scale.

In terms of organization, the best system for governmental programs seems to be a strong federal agency capable of gathering support for national fund-raising legislation, and strong state agencies on aging to administer federally funded programs through local agencies.

Chapter 18

Health and Social Services

The health status of the elderly, their use of specific health services, and common problems in securing services were covered in Chapter 8, which also dealt with specific social services to the elderly. The availability and operation of health and social services to the elderly largely depends on how these services function as societal institutions—how they are organized, funded, and regulated. Accordingly, the present chapter deals with concepts used to structure health and social services delivery, the types of organizations that provide such services, organizations that attempt to influence service policies, and the means for financing and regulating health care and social services.

Health Care Services

The health care institution in the United States is a very loosely organized conglomeration of individual and organizational service providers, suppliers, professional and trade associations, and government agencies. The people involved range from nurses' aides to surgeons, from government bureaucrats to private entrepreneurs, from local to national officials. The facilities range from storefront clinics to huge medical centers, from small proprietary nursing homes to long-term care corporations controlling thousands of long-term care beds. Financing comes from a wide variety of sources. Any attempt to discuss such a complex system is bound to be difficult. Nevertheless, it is important that students of gerontology have some grasp of the basic societal issues that influence health services to the elderly.

Models of Health Service

There are three basic models used to develop and operate health care services: the medical model, the social model, and the holistic model. Right now, the medical model is dominant, at least in part because it is favored by governmental and private insurance payment systems for health services. The **medical model** is oriented around the treatment of disease and injury, and services are controlled by physicians. The settings in which services dominated by the medical model are most often provided are physicians' offices, out-patient clinics, acute-care hospitals, mental hospitals, community mental health centers, Veterans Administration hospitals, and many nursing homes. The dominant medical view of treatment favors surgical repair, chemical treatment through drugs or diet, and rehabilitation through exercise, physical therapy, or prostheses. Although many physicians are quite humanistic in their orientation toward patients, they are trained primarily in medical intervention, with little attention to the social components of care, such as counseling, education, activity therapy, and long-term case management.

The **social model** of care assumes that medical services are only part of the total array of services needed to promote good health or deal adequately with disease or injury. *In addition to* medical interventions, patients and their families may need: education in order to comply with the prescribed medical treatment, counseling that can help minimize the deleterious effects of anxiety on the prognosis for recovery or adaptation, monitoring for changes that may require a new approach to treatment, or other services that might help prevent further deterioration of the individual's condition, such as housekeeping. In the social model, physicians are only one among an array of other professionals, such as social workers, nurses, physical therapists, and case managers. Ideally, a variety of professionals would be involved in developing a treatment plan. The social model is favored in many long-term care facilities, personal care homes for the aged, and community-based long-term care systems. However, its usefulness has been severely hampered by the fact that many nonmedical services, even if ordered by a physician, are not covered by Medicare, Medicaid, and most private health insurance plans. Consequently, the social model functions most

often in nonprofit long-term care facilities and in facilities that serve private-pay* residents.

The **holistic model** of health care emphasizes education and responsibility for self and is aimed at *high-level wellness*—a positive state of well-being, not merely the absence of disease. Prevention of disease and injury is a major thrust of the holistic approach. Prepaid group health systems—often called *health maintenance organizations (HMO's)*—have built-in incentives for prevention because the system receives the same amount of money from each participant regardless of the type of service provided, and prevention is generally much cheaper than treatment. Accordingly, other than a few HMO's that have been active in promoting prevention through education and self-responsibility, there have been few organizational advocates of the holistic approach; and virtually no governmental or private insurance reimbursement is available for holistic health either in the form of education or prevention.

Patient and Client Flow

The operation of the health care "system" is best seen through the way patients—persons under medical treatment—and clients—persons to whom professional services are being rendered—are categorized and steered through the maze of organizations providing health care. There is no single, readily identifiable point of entry. People enter the system through physicians' offices, out-patient clinics, hospital emergency rooms, and nursing homes. Of course, they may be referred there by a variety of sources: family, minister, social worker, landlord, and so forth. If the person is able to manage treatment on his or her own at home, then out-patient services are most likely to be used. If the person requires admission to an acute-

---

*Residents who pay for all of their own health care are called *private-pay* residents to distinguish them from residents who receive *third-party* benefits such as Medicare, Medicaid, or Blue Cross/Blue Shield.

care hospital—a facility oriented around high-technology medicine and relatively rapid recovery, then a hospital tends to be selected on the basis of the patient's ability to pay. Private hospitals tend to serve mainly private-pay patients and those who have third-party medical care insurance such as Blue Cross/Blue Shield. Public hospitals tend to receive the poor, whose care is most often financed by Medicaid. If the person requires long-term care—one or more services, provided on a sustained basis, enabling individuals with chronically impaired functional capacities to be maintained at maximum levels of health and well-being (Elaine Brody, 1977), then the person may be routed to an agency that provides in-home services, if such services are available and the client has a way to pay for them. If in-home long-term care services are not available or are inappropriate, then placement in a long-term care facility may be sought.

Very often the job of identifying possible institutional placements is taken on by hospital discharge planners, who are responsible for seeing that the needed post-hospital care is arranged for. Sometimes family members are involved in placement decisions, but often they are not made aware that they might have more than one choice. Private-pay clients are relatively easy to place because they can afford the more expensive long-term care facilities. But those who must rely on Medicaid to finance their care, especially those requiring extensive care, are often difficult to place, since private-sector nursing homes often limit their proportion of Medicaid patients because Medicaid reimbursement does not fully cover the costs of care. In addition, public nursing homes often have a waiting list.

There is a great difference between the philosophy of care that typifies acute-care settings and that typical of long-term care programs. In acute-care settings, the medical model is dominant, with the idea being to treat the immediate condition and discharge the patient as soon as possible. In long-term care settings, the goal is to manage one or more chronic conditions over

an extended period. In long-term care, several specialists may be involved in managing a variety of chronic conditions, and acute episodes connected with them, perhaps over a period of years. While much long-term care is controlled by physicians using a medical model, there are programs that employ "case managers" to monitor the condition of the client and to coordinate the activities of a variety of health and social service professionals, and there are still other programs in which decisions about care are made mainly by long-term care administrators and directors of nursing. These variations do not exhaust the possibilities, but they do suggest the variety of ways in which long-term care is organized and delivered.

Funding sources exert a major influence on the ways that care can be organized and delivered. Rules and regulations of funding agencies have had a major impact on the kinds of care available, the quality of care provided, and the kinds of professionals who provide services. The emphasis has been on services provided by acute-care hospitals, services using the medical model, and services provided by physicians and nurses, all of which have tended to raise the financial cost of providing care.

Financing Health Care Services

The funds for health care services to the elderly are provided by the elderly and their families, Medicare, Medicaid, third-party health insurance plans, and private philanthropy. Since each of these sources tends to operate a separate accounting system, it is difficult to pin down precisely the relatively importance of the various sources of funding for health care. For example, many church-related homes for the aged use church funds to underwrite costs of care for needy residents that exceed what Medicaid will pay. However, such expenditures do not usually become part of our national statistics on the costs of long-term care. Likewise, contributions to the financing of health care of the elderly by their families are difficult to estimate because data on these contributions are not collected. In addition, funding sources vary considerably by type of care. For example, nursing homes received only 1.5 percent of the funds spent by Medicare for the elderly in 1979, but 35 percent of Medicaid funds went to nursing homes (Eustis, Greenberg, and Patten, 1984).

Although it is widely thought that Medicare covers most of the costs of health care for the elderly, the fact is that no single source of funding bears a majority of the responsibility. For example, in 1981, personal health care expenditures for the elderly amounted to $83.2 billion. Of this amount, 30 percent was provided by the elderly and their families, 45.3 percent by Medicare, 13.7 percent by Medicaid, 5.1 percent by private insurance, 4.9 percent by state and local supplements to Medicaid, and 1 percent by private philanthropy (U.S. Senate Special Committee on Aging, 1982). Nevertheless, Medicare and Medicaid between them provide well over half the funds used to provide health care for the elderly. In addition, because Medicare and Medicaid reimburse health care providers only for specifically defined categories of people and specifically defined services, Medicare and Medicaid policies have had an enormous effect on the structure and operation of health care delivery to the elderly. To understand this impact, let us examine each of these programs in detail.

Medicare

Medicare* is a federal program of health insurance for the elderly and the disabled. First enacted in 1965, Medicare now covers people 65 and over who have the required number of quarters of coverage in Social Security–covered employment plus those not covered by Social Security but who "buy in" by paying a monthly premium. Medicare consists of two parts: Part A, called *hospital insurance*, and Part B, called *supplementary medical insurance*. Part A is automatically provided to covered persons at age 65. Part B is optional and requires a monthly premium paid by the covered individual.

Medicare *hospital insurance (Part A)* is geared to hospital episodes, called "benefit periods." The benefit period begins when an insured elderly person enters a hospital and ends when that person has not been in a hospital or skilled nursing facility for 60 consecutive days. During a benefit period, Medicare will reimburse up to 90 days of hospital care and 100 days of skilled nursing care. To be eligible for reimbursement, skilled nursing care must immediately follow at least 3 days of hospital care. Each covered individual has a "lifetime reserve" of 60 extra days' care reimbursement, which can be used if more than 90 days of hospitalization are required.

Medicare *Part B*, which covers physicians' services, medical therapy, diagnostic tests, surgical dressings, prostheses, ambulance service, home health care, and rural health clinic services, can be used to cover hospital costs not covered by Part A, but excludes eyeglasses, hearing aids, dental services, physical examinations, immunizations, and out-patient psychiatric care exceeding $250 in cost. It also excludes prescription drugs except when administered in-hospital.

Part A is financed through Social Security payroll deductions and copayments from those receiving benefits. A *copayment* is the share of the cost of care that must be assumed by the covered individual. For example, in 1983 the individual was responsible for the first $304 of hospital care for each benefit period. This is called a *deductible*. In addition, if hospitalization continued beyond 60 days, the individual was liable for a copayment of $76 per day. If days of lifetime reserve were needed, the individual copayment was $152 per day. If skilled nursing care followed at least three days in-hospital, then the first 20 days required no copayment,

---

*These sections on Medicare and Medicaid financing and regulation are adapted from the excellent discussion in Eustis, Greenberg, and Patten, 1984.

but after 20 days there was a copayment of $38 per day. In 1983, in the extreme case in which all benefits were used to the maximum, the elderly patient's copayment liability would have amounted to $14,744 for hospital and skilled nursing services for less than six-months' care.

In 1983, the monthly premium for Part B was $12.20. In addition, the individual was responsible for a deductible of $75 and all costs exceeding 80 percent of "reasonable charges" for services covered. The copayment for services covered by Part B often exceeds 20 percent because nearly half of physicians charge more than Medicare defines as "reasonable" (U.S. Senate Special Committee on Aging, 1982).

Medicare spent $268 per covered person in 1968, and by 1978 the figure had increased to $858. This dramatic increase has been blamed on "overutilization" of health services by the elderly. However, over 90 percent of this increase can be traced to inflation in hospital costs alone. Thus, it was runaway inflation in hospital costs that produced impending problems in Medicare financing, not irresponsible use of services by the elderly.

Although Medicare ostensibly covers long-term care, in fact very little long-term care of the elderly is funded by Medicare. Only 4 percent of the $24.4 billion spent by Medicare on care for the elderly in 1979 went to provide long-term care in skilled nursing facilities or at home. Part of the reason for this is a logical contradiction in the regulations: Many individuals requiring long-term care are not sick enough to qualify for three days of hospital care, yet if they do not qualify for hospital care, they cannot qualify for nursing care. Another reason is the "episode" assumption built into Medicare reimbursement, that is, the assumption that illness occurs in episodes. But long-term care is continuous, not episodic. Medicare provides less than six months' long-term care coverage, even for those who manage to qualify for Medicare long-term care reimbursement. Thus, our national health insurance program for the elderly provides virtually no protection for the vast majority of middle-class older Americans in the event they need long-term care.

Medicaid

Medicaid is a federal and state program that uses general revenues to fund health care for the poor. Eligibility for Medicaid is tied closely to low income and wealth. To be eligible, an individual must have not only a low income but also few assets that can be converted into income. There are two major categories of eligibility for Medicaid: the categorically needy and the medically needy. *Categorically needy* older people are those who receive SSI or who would be eligible for SSI if they applied for it, plus certain others who qualify by virtue of their status at the time the SSI legislation was passed in 1972. States have the option of adopting an eligibility standard for Medicaid that is lower than the income and assets standards for SSI. In such states, SSI-related individuals must be allowed to "spend down" to the more restrictive asset or income level in order to qualify for Medicaid. The *medically needy* are people who ordinarily would not qualify for SSI but who have incurred medical expenses Medicaid would normally cover and whose incomes are below eligibility level, usually lower than the eligibility criteria for SSI. Not all states offer Medicaid to the medically needy, and those that do use complicated formulas to define spending-down and eligibility criteria. Eustis, Greenberg, and Patten reported that "the considerable choice in program eligibility has led to wide variations in coverage across the states. Some states have chosen the federal SSI definition for eligibility. Others have liberalized cash assistance benefits and extended Medicaid eligibility to more individuals. Finally, some 25 states have more restrictive requirements. . . . These states are generally more concerned with client assets than with income" (1984:122). The 1982 Tax Equity and Fiscal Responsibility Act allowed states to place liens on the property of Medicaid recipients, although not if the home was occupied by a spouse, a disabled or dependent child, or a sibling who had lived in the home over a year and had equity in the home.

Medicaid is not a program directed primarily to the elderly, but rather to the poor. In 1979, only 18.8 percent of the 21.5 million recipients of Medicaid were 65 or over. However, 37.4 percent of the payments for Medicaid were used to pay for services to the elderly. This reflects the fact that a large proportion (over 80 percent) of the Medicaid expenditures for long-term care goes to provide care for the elderly, most of it in nursing homes. Less than 5 percent of long-term care payments went to provide home care, and more than 75 percent of that was paid out in one state, New York (Eustis, Greenberg, and Patten, 1984).

Thus, both Medicare and Medicaid stress payment for care in institutions and provide very little support to noninstitutional alternatives. Indeed, both have regulations that greatly restrict the use of home care, adult foster care, and group homes. Part of the reason for this is the fear of legislators and government officials that the financial costs of more liberalized noninstitutional care would be too high. Another factor may be the fact that mechanisms for policing the adequacy, financial accountability, and safety of hospital and nursing home care are already in place, while the means to police other alternatives would in many cases have to be created, also tending to increase their cost. And while it is often assumed that noninstitutional care is less expensive than institutional care, recent studies have shown this may not be true (U.S. General Accounting Office, 1982). Finally, the providers of institutional care are well-organized to protect their interest in funding for institutional care, whereas those who might provide alternative care are not.

Private Medical Insurance

Private insurance is a minor source of funding for hospital care for the elderly. Nearly all of the 5.1 percent of personal health expenditures of the elderly funded by private insurance goes for hospital care. Eustis, Greenberg, and Patten (1984) reported that "the private market for long-term care insurance is virtually nonexistent." There have been several arguments advanced to account for this, but none of them is especially persuasive. For example, it is held that the costs of long-term care are uncertain, which means that calculation of premiums is difficult. However, it is not obvious why long-term care costs are more difficult to predict than ordinary medical insurance costs, given inflation. In addition, insurers could simply limit their liability for coverage. It is held that the premiums would be too high, yet only a small percentage of people would ever use their coverage for long-term care. More research is needed into the obstacles to private insurance for long-term care and the means to overcome them. It is ridiculous that the average middle-class American must become a pauper just to qualify for *any* program that will finance long-term care.

Gaps in Financing for Health Care

By now it should be obvious that there are substantial gaps in our systems for financing health care for the elderly. For one, there are many aspects of care not covered by Medicare; dental care, eye care, and hearing aids are particularly important exclusions. In addition, overly restrictive criteria keep Medicare support for long-term care very low. Although Medicaid ostensibly covers many of the areas not covered by Medicare, Medicaid is not available to most older Americans. And even for those who are eligible for Medicaid, there are restrictions on availability of important services. For example, the oral health of many Medicaid patients in nursing homes is atrocious. Yet although older people get over 80 percent of the Medicaid support for nursing care, they receive only 6 percent of the Medicaid payments for dental services, and not because of lower need for service—the elderly in general need more dental care than younger age groups do. Yet most states have adopted Medicaid rules that exclude reimbursement to the elderly for all but the most severe dental problems, exclusions that do *not* apply to younger Medicaid recipients. Finally, as we have seen, neither Medicare nor private insurance provide much protection against the need to finance long-term care; and although Medicaid does, it is unavailable to most middle-class people and it provides little funding for noninstitutional alternatives.

The Structure of Advocacy

As we have seen, the health care "system" is structured in favor of reimbursement for services provided in hospitals and nursing homes, a major reason for which is the institutional bias in the laws and regulations that provide federal funding. To understand why this bias exists and persists, we must consider what groups are involved in developing and maintaining health policy and which ones have the most power. The groups involved include federal and state governmental agencies, state and national professional and trade associations, and organizations in the "aging network."

Although federal and state governmental bodies must develop and administer legislation that provides structure and funding for health care, they do not perform these functions in a vacuum. Health policies and regulations are subjected to a review process, during which the advocates of various interest groups have an opportunity to become informed about legislative and administrative proposals and to address their concerns about them. In the area of health policies toward the elderly, one might expect reactions from professional associations such as the American Medical Association; from trade associations such as the American Association of Homes for the Aging (an organization representing the interests of nonprofit homes), the American Health Care Association (representing the interests of for-profit nursing homes) or the American Hospital Association; from third-

party insurers such as Blue Cross/Blue Shield; and from advocates for the interests of the elderly such as the National Council on the Aging (representing agencies serving the elderly) or AARP (a large membership organization of older people). While not exhaustive, these examples indicate the diversity of organized efforts to influence the development and implementation of health care policies toward the elderly.

A detailed analysis of how these various interest groups have influenced specific legislation or regulations is far beyond the scope of this book. Nevertheless, it is obvious from the results that, more than other advocates, physician-directed advocates such as the AMA, the American Hospital Association, and Blue Cross/Blue Shield seem to have been more influential in creating the system, largely due to the resources available to these organizations, whose members can afford to pay for first-class lobbying efforts in their behalf. By contrast, organizations such as NCoA have only very limited funds they can use for this purpose.

The general American tendency to consider physicians *the* authority on health care has also tended to give physicians a greater voice in these matters than other equally well-informed professions such as nursing, social work, long-term care administration, and gerontology. There are many groups with useful contributions to make to the development of health care for the elderly, and some practitioners in nursing, social work, occupational therapy, gerontology, and other professions have training and experience in health aspects of aging that far exceed the average physician's. Physicians tend to favor institutional forms of health care because that is what they learn in medical school. Physicians tend to do their internships and residencies in hospitals, not in home health agencies or nursing homes. Thus, the medical model has tended to dominate the thinking of physicians about how health care for the elderly should be provided. In addition, physicians tend to affiliate with hospitals and not with nursing homes, home health agencies, or homes for the aged, which increases their willingness to advocate for hospitals but not for other types of health care organizations and which goes a long way toward explaining Medicare bias toward hospital care. The medical-model bias in Medicaid arose mainly from the use of Medicare as a model for organizing Medicaid (Eustis, Greenberg, and Patten, 1984).

There is nothing immoral about physicians' organizing to pursue their own interests. The potential for harm comes from the fact that those who oppose the physicians' positions are seen as having less credibility. If the situation is to become more balanced, then governmental officials, legislators, and the general public must learn that no single group's perspectives can suffice in planning and developing programs to serve a population as diverse as the elderly in a field of service as diverse as health care.

Dunlop reported that the physician-directed organizations mentioned above were very instrumental in the 1950s in redefining the hospital's primary concern as acute care and in defining the medically-dominated nursing home as "*the* specialized setting for the delivery of long-term care for the elderly in this country. Virtually no one questioned the medical model employed for their development both by Congress and the Public Health Service. That model is easily discernible, first in the standards applied to facilities [built with federal assistance] as early as 1954, and then in those applied to all Medicare and Medicaid certified homes" (1979:101). A leading textbook for long-term care administrators follows the medical model strictly. All decisions about care are to be made by physicians, and the description of the Medical Director position is practically identical to that of Hospital Chief of Staff (Miller and Barry, 1979). This model is unrealistic for a majority of nursing homes because it is difficult to get physicians to even visit such facilities, much less find one to serve half-time or more as Medical Director. As a result, administrators and nursing staff are faced with regulations reflect-

ing a medical model and with physicians who in general are reluctant to get involved in long-term care.

Regulation of Health Care

The quality and cost of health care are regulated in several ways: licensing of people to provide care, licensing of facilities in which care is provided, certification and accreditation of facilities, and periodic review of facilities for compliance with standards of quality and cost of care (Eustis, Greenberg, and Patten, 1984).

Regulating the Quality of Care

All states require physicians, registered nurses, practical nurses, hospital administrators, nursing home administrators, dentists, physical therapists, and the like to be *licensed*. This means that in order to perform professional services in the state, an individual practitioner must pass a licensure examination and have the appropriate training. In addition, there are state laws governing licensure of hospitals and nursing homes that specify the conditions facilities must meet in order to qualify for licensure; without licensure, facilities cannot operate as hospitals or nursing homes. Licensure laws set standards in areas such as staff qualifications, the number and type of staff required in relation to the number of residents, medical supervision, use of restraints, required equipment and supplies, dispensing of medications, food and nutrition, space requirements, fire protection, and physical plant features such as dining rooms, plumbing, water supply, sanitation procedures, and building maintenance.

Certification ensures that an agency or facility is eligible for reimbursement from Medicare or Medicaid. When Medicare was initiated in 1965, standards and conditions of participation were developed for hospitals and hospital-like nursing homes called "extended-care facilities." Medicaid standards were developed for a less intensive form of nursing care in facilities called "skilled nursing facilities." In 1971, Medicaid standards were expanded to include care in nursing homes called "intermediate-care facilities." In 1972, Medicare extended-care facilities and Medicaid skilled nursing facilities were combined under the single label of "skilled nursing facility." The major difference between skilled and intermediate care is in the seriousness of the resident's condition and the type of personnel needed to provide care. Skilled nursing care is practiced predominantly by registered nurses, and intermediate nursing care is provided mainly by licensed practical nurses.

Setting federal standards is the responsibility of the Health Care Financing Administration, but responsibility for administering the process rests with the states, which must do all of the fieldwork and inspections, as well as the paperwork. In many states the certification process is identical to state licensure (Eustis, Greenberg, and Patten, 1984).

Accreditation is generally handled by organizations sponsored by professional or trade associations, not by governmental agencies. For example, hospitals are accredited by the Joint Commission on Accreditation of Hospitals (JCAH). JCAH accreditation indicates that a hospital exceeds state licensure standards and is automatically certified for Medicaid and Medicare. JCAH also has accreditation standards for long-term care facilities, although such accreditation does not bring automatic certification for Medicare and Medicaid.

Responsibility for enforcement of standards of licensure and certification generally falls to the states. State inspectors periodically check hospitals and nursing homes for compliance with state licensure laws. Compliance with Medicare and Medicaid conditions of participation is checked through periodic review by Professional Standards Review Organizations (PSRO's), which are local or regional nonprofit organizations headed by physicians and authorized by federal law to review the quality of and need for services reimbursed by Medicare and Medicaid. PSRO's have concentrated mainly on review of hospital care, but in 1978 federal guidelines were issued to specify the role of PSRO's in review of long-term care.

Thus, state licensure laws and federal conditions of participation coupled with state inspection and PSRO review would seem to be adequate to ensure that standards for quality of care are being met. However, Butler (1980) has pointed out that many nursing homes are cited over and over for the same violations, and certification or licensure are revoked only under the most extreme circumstances. There are several factors that interfere with the enforcement of quality of care standards. First, little Medicare or Medicaid funding is available for enforcement. Second, governmental agencies are sensitive to charges of heavy-handed "overregulation" of private business. Finally, the legal constraints on enforcement have rendered enforcement very difficult. In most states, the only action that can be taken against facilities that violate the law is to revoke their operating licenses. In a few states, fines are also possible. However, both measures require lengthy court proceedings, so as a result states have been reluctant to use them. In addition, in many locales there is a shortage of nursing home spaces, and closing down one home would merely increase pressure on those remaining. As a consequence, enforcement officials are often reduced to relying on harassment through frequent inspections and citation of deficiencies as their only usable enforcement tool.

Regulating the Cost of Care

From 1979 to 1981, the average Medicaid reimbursement for hospital care increased from $164 per day to $230, skilled nursing care reimbursement increased from $26 to $32 per day, and intermediate-care reimbursement increased from $19 to $24 per day (Newcomer and Harrington, 1983). Medicaid hospital reimbursement also increased substantially during this two-year period. The rates of increase were very much higher than the general level of inflation and are indicative of a long-standing trend toward excessive inflation in health care costs. In response, federal and state governments have attempted to regulate the rate of growth in Medicare and Medicaid costs through changing the eligibility standards, the definitions of services covered, and the reimbursement methods.

States have seldom lowered the actual dollar values of the income and assets criteria used to establish eligibility for Medicaid. But by not increasing these ceilings to account for inflation, most states have actually increased substantially the number of poor who do not qualify for Medicaid. Newcomer and Harrington (1983) reported that since 1977, Medicaid population growth has not kept pace with the growth in the population in poverty and that by 1981 about half the population with incomes below the federal poverty level were ineligible for Medicaid.

Under federal legislation, states are allowed to establish "utilization controls" on services that must be provided under Medicaid. For example, half of the states limit the number of days of hospitalization and the number of physician visits that Medicaid will reimburse in a given year. More than two-thirds of the states require approval by the state prior to admission to a skilled nursing facility if Medicaid reimbursement is involved. Although such measures may have resulted in some savings, they have tended to create as many problems as they have solved. For example, arbitrary limits on number of hospital days obviously have no relationship to needed lengths of care. Likewise, prior authorization is a moot point for nursing home residents who have been Medicare or private-pay patients prior to qualifying for Medicaid.

Reimbursement formulas represent another way that states can attempt to control costs. These formulas fall into two general classes: those that incorporate some recognition of differences in costs among facilities and those that attempt to establish standard rates for service independent of variations in costs to the facility. *Cost-based reimbursement* provides little incentive for efficiency. The institution's allowable costs are simply passed on to Medicaid. Indeed,

these systems provide incentives to inflate cost figures and, therefore, require careful cost monitoring to prevent abuse. On the plus side, cost-based reimbursement provides no incentives to limit the quality of care. *Standardized reimbursement* is easier to administer and provides incentives for providers to be cost conscious. However, standardized rates tend not to cover the costs of high-quality care and thus tend to lead to lower-quality care (Eustis, Greenberg, and Patten, 1984).

Kennedy (1984) has rightly pointed out that whatever means we take to contain the costs of health care must address the costs to all categories of care recipients. For example, if Medicaid constrains reimbursement, providers may simply pass the unreimbursed cost of care on to private-pay patients or clients. It is safe to say that the methods employed thus far have been relatively ineffective and that health care cost containment will remain a major issue in the coming years. And although we have seen that there is need for expansion of services covered by our health care financing systems, such expansion is most unlikely so long as costs keep escalating at such a high rate.

Health Planning

We know that the older population is growing older, and that the need for health services is going to increase dramatically as a result. In order to cope with the increase in demand, we need planning to ensure that adequate facilities, personnel, and financing are available. Unfortunately, the history of health planning in the United States over the past decade gives little cause to be optimistic that the needed planning will get done. Instead, we will probably continue our piecemeal and uncoordinated approach to the development and delivery of health care services.

The infusion of federal funding for the construction of health facilities in underserved areas took place in 1946 under the Hill-Burton

Act. Included in the act was provision for a planning process. In 1974, the National Health Planning and Resources Development Act provided funds to establish state and local planning agencies charged with assessing area health needs, setting priorities, identifying populations or geographic areas most in need, and controlling health costs. Unfortunately, these agencies were established at a time of high inflation in health costs, and controlling health costs soon overshadowed planning as their primary function.

Local planning agencies' control over health costs was exercised indirectly by limiting the construction of new facilities. In most states, in order to build new hospital or nursing home facilities that would be eligible to receive Medicare or Medicaid reimbursement, organizations were required to obtain "certificates of need" (CON's) certifying a need for the facility. The major goal of certificate-of-need review was to prevent the use of federal funds to finance "excess capacity, unnecessary duplication of services, . . . and maldistributed health services" (Benjamin and Lindeman, 1983:213). Although such reviews were developed mainly in reaction to growing costs for hospital care, CON review was also applied to the construction of long-term care facilities in many states. The result was a restriction of competition in the long-term care field that defeated many efforts to enforce quality of care standards.

Since 1981, federal funding for health planning has been severely cut, and in many states local health planning agencies have been abolished. Benjamin and Lindeman concluded: "Any analysis of health planning in the 1980s is likely to have an unhappy ending. What began as a grand experiment in state and local planning has fallen victim to excessive expectations, inadequate authority, the intractability of medical care costs, and finally to a substantial decline in federal funding" (1983:222). Thus, we are in great need of health planning in order to cope with an aging society, and what planning organizations we have had have been curtailed or eliminated.

Overview

As a result of our piecemeal approach to the provision of health care, numerous important gaps exist in our ability to deliver needed care to older Americans. Many of these gaps have been caused by our concepts about how to organize and pay for care. The domination of health care financing by organizations employing the medical model has led to unnecessarily costly care in institutions and a virtual absence of alternatives to institutional care for older people. And the high costs of this care have worked against those who favor broadening the coverage of Medicare, Medicaid, and private insurance. Attempts to regulate the quality of care have improved the general level of care, but the results have not been as effective as they might have been because enforcement efforts are limited. Cost containment regulations have succeeded in reducing the number of people being served and increasing the portion of care that the elderly themselves must pay for, but they have had little effect on the inflation in care costs.

Despite all of these difficulties, many older people are able to satisfy their needs for health care within the existing system. But those who are poor or who need long-term care are particularly likely to find that what they need is not available. The result in human misery is a scene largely hidden from public view but all too familiar to those who work in the aging network. Next we turn to those programs that provide social services to the elderly.

Social Services

Social services assist people to improve their level of functioning or to reduce their difficulties in securing adequate income, health care, housing, transportation, or social participation. Such assistance can take many forms: financial aid, information and referral, counseling, education, physical assistance, chore services, in-kind assistance such as rent subsidy or free meals, and a host of others.

Like health care, social services are provided by a wide variety of types of personnel and types of organizations, with funds from a variety of sources. At the national level, various federal departments include social services among their responsibilities. However, federal funds for social services to the elderly are provided mainly through the programs of the Older Americans Act and through Social Services Block Grants to state and local governments.

State Units on Aging and State Departments of Welfare administer both state and federal social services funds at the state level, and local Area Agencies on Aging and Welfare Departments administer them at the local level. Local United Way organizations also provide local funding for social services, as do many local philanthropic foundations. In addition, many social services agencies do independent local fund-raising. As a result, it is impossible to identify the precise amounts of funding for social services to the elderly at all levels. However, given that federal programs provided at least $26 billion and state programs another $16 billion for social services in 1979 compared to $1.7 billion from all United Way programs and $5 billion from private philanthropy (mostly from churches), it seems safe to conclude that social services to the elderly are greatly influenced by the structure of our national programs. Accordingly, we will look at the Older Americans Act and Social Services Block Grants in detail.

The Older Americans Act

The Older Americans Act of 1965* identified a series of broad objectives aimed at improving the lives of older Americans, facilitated the agencies responsible for funding, planning, coordinating, and monitoring social services to the elderly, and provided funding for specific social services such as multipurpose senior centers and community service employment. In 1972, the Act was amended to create a national nutrition program for the elderly and to authorize grants to public and nonprofit agencies for the development of congregate meal services for the elderly. In 1973, the Act was amended to create a network of Area Agencies on Aging (AAA's), which were given the major responsibility for planning, coordinating, and advocating local programs that would benefit older people. In 1973, amendments created a special authorization for home-delivered meals for the elderly and required states to establish state-wide nursing home ombudsman** programs. During its first decade, the Older Americans Act was supported repeatedly by Congress, and it gradually developed into a major social services resource for agencies providing social services to the elderly.

As amended in 1981, the Older Americans Act has six sections, called *titles*. Separate appropriations are usually made for each title and sometimes for separate components within titles.

Title I outlines ten broad objectives for older Americans—those age 60 and over—including (1) adequate income, (2) physical and mental health, (3) suitable housing, (4) full restorative services for those needing institutional care, (5) employment without age discrimination, (6) retirement in health, honor, and dignity, (7) participation in civic, cultural, and recreational activities, (8) efficient community services, (9) benefits from research designed to sustain and improve health and happiness, and (10) freedom to plan and manage their lives. These very general goals are for the entire society, and they are addressed through many efforts at the federal, state, and local levels. However, the Older

---

*Material in this section is drawn from the U.S. Senate Special Committee on Aging, 1983.

**An *ombudsman* is an agency official responsible for investigating citizen complaints, especially against government-funded programs.

Americans Act clearly states that a policy of responsibility for the well-being of the elderly is a high-priority national goal.

Title II established the Administration on Aging (AoA) as the principal agency for carrying out the purposes of the Older Americans Act and for administering the various programs authorized by it. Located within the Office of Human Development Services, AoA is directed by the U.S. Commissioner on Aging, who is appointed by the President and confirmed by the Senate. AoA was intended to have high visibility in the executive branch of government and to serve as an effective advocate on all matters related to the field of aging.

Title II also authorized the Federal Council on Aging, a 15-member body whose members are appointed by the President. Members of the Council cannot be federal employees, and at least five of them must be older individuals. The Council was intended to serve as an advisory and advocacy body to the President and the Commissioner on Aging, to inform the public about matters related to aging, and to provide a forum for discussion of problems and needs of the aging.

Title III authorized grants to state agencies on aging for the development of a comprehensive and coordinated delivery system of supportive social services and senior centers, congregate nutrition services, and home-delivered nutrition services. To qualify for funds, the state agency was required to divide the state into separate geographic areas, called Planning and Service Areas (PSA's), and establish Area Agencies on Aging (AAA's) charged with developing generally comparable delivery systems within each PSA. AAA's were responsible for coordinating existing services and fostering the expansion and development of community services for the elderly. This organizational structure was intended to form an "aging network" made up of AoA, State Units on Aging, AAA's, other public and private agencies, and local service providers, and to provide a continuum of services to older people.

Title III required AAA's to allocate "an adequate proportion" of their funds to three categories of social services: access services such as transportation, outreach, and information and referral; in-home services such as homemaker, home-health, telephone reassurance, and friendly visiting; and legal services. In addition, AAA's were allowed to contract for ombudsman services, counseling, case management, health screening, employment services, crime prevention, victim assistance, and volunteer service opportunity programs. Funds for these services were authorized under Title III-B.

Title III also authorized grants to establish and/or operate congregate and home-delivered meals programs for persons age 60 or over and their spouses of any age. Grants could go only to public and nonprofit organizations. Participants could be asked to pay what they felt they could afford, with the proceeds used to increase the number of meals served. Funds for meals programs came from Title III-C.

Title IV authorized support for training, education, research, demonstration, and evaluation projects that would add knowledge that could be used to improve the effectiveness and efficiency of Older Americans Act–sponsored programs. Part A provided funds to recruit and train personnel for the field of aging. Part B provided research and demonstration funds for projects in a variety of areas, such as long-term care, rural transportation, and mental health. Title IV-B provided most of the applied research funding for gerontology.

Title V established the Senior Community Service Employment Program within the Department of Labor, which created part-time public service employment positions at the minimum wage for people 55 and older who had incomes no higher than 125 percent of the poverty level. Positions created under Title V included aides in schools, libraries, hospitals, and social service agencies. This program is managed by State Units on Aging and eight national contractors, including the National Council on Aging, the National Council of Senior Citizens, and AARP.

Title VI promotes the development and delivery of services to older Indians (Native Americans) through grants to tribal organizations.

In 1981, more than $913 billion was appropriated for Older Americans Act programs. There were 57 State and Territorial Units on Aging, 682 Area Agencies on Aging, 6,674 multipurpose senior centers designated as community focal points, and over 13,000 congregate meals sites. Over 9 million older Americans were served by Older Americans Act programs —3 million on nutrition sites—and most of those served were in the greatest economic need (U.S. Senate Special Committee on Aging, 1983:448). Table 18-1 shows appropriations for Older Americans Act programs from fiscal years 1973–1983. Funding has generally increased, but the total Older Americans Act budget is still a minuscule part of the total federal budget. In addition, each year the Older Americans Act appropriations must be defended against budget cutting, which has had a high Congressional priority at least since 1978.

Social Services Block Grants

Before 1981, federal funds for social services to the poor were provided by Title XX to the Social Security Act, which targeted specific populations to be served, such as those on SSI or Medicaid. In 1981, Congress created less restrictive "block grants" for social services, but at the same time reduced the federal appropriations for social services by 20 percent. A total of $2.45 billion was authorized for fiscal year 1983. Social Services Block Grant funds are funneled to local agencies through state and local welfare departments. Because the states had great latitude in determining on whom to spend their federal social services dollars, the proportion going to services to the elderly in 1982 ranged from 4.5 percent to 40 percent. Area Agencies on Aging reported that Social Services

Block Grant funds averaged about 7 percent of the total aging-services budgets for their areas. Nevertheless, in some areas block grants are an important but unpredictable source of funds for social services to the elderly.

The Older Americans Act, Social Services Block Grants, United Way, private philanthropy, and local foundations together may have provided as much as $2 billion for social services to the elderly in 1982 (an educated guess). In addition, about $1.5 billion from Medicare and Medicaid went for social services. Thus, a total of perhaps $3.5 billion was available from all sources, amounting to about $135 per older person per year. Contrast this with the $52 billion for Medicare and $7.6 billion to the elderly from Medicaid—a total of about $2,290 per older person per year. From this it should be obvious that although many of the needs of the elderly in 1982 involved in-home services of a nonnursing nature, such as homemaker or meals services, 98 percent of the federal dollars were going to health care. Given that health and social services support one another, our health efforts would probably be more effective if the social services activities were not so severely underfunded. Ironically, social services to the elderly tend to be much better coordinated than health services are. Perhaps coordination is improved when it is required and when the amount of money to be made is insufficient to attract competing, large organizations.

The Reagan Administration justified its recommendations for cuts in social services on grounds that social services were the responsibility of family and community, not of government, despite the fact, as we saw earlier, that most social services to the elderly are already being provided by family. Yet the demand for services to the elderly and to the families who care for them drastically exceeds the capacity of the system, given current levels of funding.

The demand for services, the cuts in funding for social services, and the projected growth in the older population are all fueling a debate over whether social services to the elderly

TABLE 18-1 Older Americans Act appropriations, 1973–1983 (in thousands of dollars)

Fiscal Year	1973	1974	1975	1976	1977	1978	1979	1980	1981	1982	1983
Title II:[a]											
National Information and Resource Clearinghouse	none	none	none	none	none	2,000	2,000	2,000	1,800	1,721	none
Federal Council on the Aging	none	none	0.575	0.0575	0.575	.450	.450	.450	.481	.191	0.175
Title III:											
Area planning[c] and social services	68,000	68,000	82,000	93,000	122,000	193,000	196,970	246,970	251,473	240,869	240,869
State agency activities[c]	12,000	12,000	15,000	17,035	17,000	19,000	22,500	22,500	22,675	21,673	21,673
Multipurpose senior centers	none	none	none	none	20,000[d]	40,000[d]	[e]	[e]	[e]	[e]	[e]
Nutrition program	100,000	104,800	125,000	125,000[f]	203,525[f]	250,000	277,046	320,000	350,000	344,099	381,099
Title IV:											
Training	8,000	10,000	8,000	10,000	14,200	17,000	17,000	17,000			
Research	9,000	7,000	7,000	8,000	8,500	8,500	8,500	8,500			
Model projects, special projects	16,000	16,000	8,000	13,800	12,000	15,000	15,000	25,000	40,500[i]	22,175[i]	22,175[i]
Multidisciplinary centers of gerontology	none	none	none	1,000	3,800	3,800	3,800	3,800			
Title V:											
Community service employment for older Americans[g]	none	10,000	42,000	55,900	90,600	200,900	200,900	266,900	277,100	277,100	281,950
Title VI:											
Grants for Indian tribes,	[b]	[b]	[b]	[b]	[b]	[b]	none	6,000	6,000	5,735	5,735
Foster Grandparent Program	25,000	[h]	[h]	[h]	[h]	[h]	[h]	[h]	[h]	[h]	[h]
Retired Senior Volunteer Program	15,000	[h]	[h]	[h]	[h]	[h]	[h]	[h]	[h]	[h]	[h]
Total	253,000	227,800	287,575	324,310	492,200	749,650	744,166	919,120	950,029	913,563	953,676

[a] Title numbers are based on the 1981 amendments.

[b] Not authorized

[c] Between 1965 and 1970, Title III funds were allocated to states for social services. There was no appropriation for state or area planning activities. Beginning in 1970 funds were appropriated for statewide planning. In 1973 funds were appropriated for area planning and social services.

[d] Funds were appropriated for grants, mortgage insurance, and annual interest subsidies, but were allocated only for grants.

[e] Multipurpose senior centers are funded under the Title III area planning and social services appropriation.

[f] Congressionally mandated operating levels made possible through forward funding were $150 million for fiscal year 1975 and $187 million for fiscal year 1976. Program operating level for fiscal year 1977 was $225 million.

[g] Funding is available on an annual basis beginning July 1 and ending the following June 30.

[h] From 1967–1968 the Foster Grandparent Program was funded under a general poverty program through the Economic Opportunity Act. This program was given a statutory basis under the Older Americans Act of 1969. In addition, the Retired Senior Volunteer Program was created under the 1979 amendments. Legislative authority under the Older Americans Act was repealed in 1973 and both these programs were reauthorized under the Domestic Volunteer Service Act of 1973 (Public Law 93-113).

[i] Includes funding for training, research, discretionary programs, and multidisciplinary centers for gerontology.

Source: U.S. Senate Special Committee on Aging, 1983.

should continue to be made available to all older people, as they are now in most cases, or whether we should go further toward means-tested programs, as is now the case for those receiving SSI and Medicaid-related social services. This debate will surely intensify in the coming years and should be a fertile field for research.

Summary

Health care and social services to the elderly have increased dramatically in scope and amount since the early 1960s, just as the older population has increased in size. As a result, there are substantial gaps in our national programs to finance health care and social services that continued inflation, especially in health care costs, has prevented from being closed.

When individuals have difficulty in getting adequate services, they may think theirs is an isolated case and ask, "Why me?" But in the case of health care and social services to the elderly, the problems are greatly influenced by the haphazard nature of the social structures we have created to provide these services. In health care, although all models of care delivery have their appropriate applications, the medical model has tended to dominate definitions of who could get services, what services they could get, and from whom they could get them. In addition, our national programs for financing health care for the elderly have emphasized funding for institutionally provided medical services and have discouraged less expensive institutional services such as personal care and noninstitutional services such as home health care. The dominance of the medical model is due to an imbalance of resources and credibility between physician-directed advocates and advocates for the social and holistic models of care, which call for a greater variety of care alternatives and involvement of a wider variety of types of care-givers.

Medicare, a major financer of hospital care for the elderly, is much less effective in its coverage of physicians' fees, home health care, and long-term care. It completely ignores the needs for eyeglasses, hearing aids, dental care, and immunizations.

Medicaid is a major source of funding for long-term care, but to qualify for it, older people must deplete their resources until they become eligible for welfare. Medicaid is not available to most middle-class older Americans. Elderly Medicaid recipients are discriminated against in that they have less access to dental care compared to younger Medicaid recipients.

Inflation in health care costs has been substantially higher than in other areas of the economy over the past several years. This has created severe problems in financing, not only for Medicare and Medicaid but for private health insurance as well. A good bit of the federally supported effort originally intended to fund the enforcement of care quality and to accomplish planning has instead gone into trying to contain increasing costs. There has been a resulting reduction in the number of people being served and an increase in that part of the financial burden falling on the older individual, but there has been little effect on the rate of inflation in health care costs.

Governments attempt to regulate the quality of care by licensing both people and organizations as care-providers. They also use certification requirements to ensure care quality standards from those who seek reimbursement from Medicare and Medicaid. However, enforcement is not as effective as it could be, mainly because the only sanctions that governments can apply tend to be too severe.

Social services are provided to the elderly through a network of federal, state, and local agencies created by the Older Americans Act and funded through the Older Americans Act, Social Services Block Grants, local United Way agencies, local foundations, and a variety of other minor sources.

The Older Americans Act has encouraged the development of an array of services that is similar in most communities, including information and referral, transportation, outreach, both congregate and home-delivered meals, homemaker and home health services, telephone reassurance, and legal services. However, funding levels for these services have been at spartan levels, especially in comparison with the sums spent on health care.

As a result of the increased numbers of older people and the increasing costs of health and social services, a debate has emerged over whether age or need is the more appropriate criterion to use in establishing eligibility for services. This debate is likely to remain spirited.

PART VI

Aging and the Future

This book began with an examination of the demographic and historic forces that have produced our aging society and our responses to that aging society. It then considered physical, psychological, and social aging; situational aspects of aging such as social relationships, instrumental needs and resources, employment and retirement, and activities. We have examined the factors involved in individual adaptation to aging, and we have looked at how society has responded to having aging members. Now it is time to turn our attention to how aging may alter the future and how the future may alter aging. Part VI will first consider the interaction of aging and social change and then look into the future of social gerontology as a field of study and practice.

Chapter 19

Aging and the Future

Just as today's adaptation to aging occurs within a framework of physical, psychological, and social realities, the adaptations of tomorrow's older people will be shaped by changes in the older population, in the nature of physical and psychological aging, in the social rules shaping the aspirations and opportunities of older people, and in the social institutions that serve the elderly. And to retain its viability as a field of knowledge and practice, social gerontology will have to change as well.

Aging and Social Change

Planning involves anticipating the future and identifying and developing ways to meet emerging needs. Given the huge number of factors that can influence the future, it should be obvious that predictions are difficult to make and rarely foolproof. In addition, there are so many individual aspects of aging that will affect the future or be affected by it that a complete inventory is far beyond what we can do here. Instead, we will simply offer a few illustrations of the kinds of analyses that can help us visualize the future.

Demographic Clues to the Future

Demographic indicators usually change slowly, both in magnitude and direction. For instance, birth rates seldom double overnight, and death rates usually drop slowly. In addition, the population that will become old over the next 50 years has already been born. We know the current size of our population and we can predict relatively well how many will survive to each age. Demographic projections can thus give us some of our best clues to the future.

As we saw in Chapter 2, population aging has only just begun in the United States. Over the next several decades, the size of the older population will increase dramatically. By the year 2050, there will probably be around 67 million Americans age 65 and older, compared with

25.5 million in 1980. The proportion of older people in the population will increase from 11.3 percent in 1980 to 21.7 percent in 2050 (U.S. Bureau of the Census, 1983). More than 50 percent of the population growth in the U.S. over the next 70 years is expected to occur in the older population as more and more people survive to fill the oldest age categories, and the proportional increases will be greatest in the 85-and-over age categories.

Demographic analysis is useful in projecting needs and resources of the elderly in a number of areas, including health care, housing, and availability of kin. For example, in the area of health care, the need for long-term care can be expected to increase dramatically. In 1980, there were about 440,000 people age 85 and over living in long-term care facilities. At the 1980 rates of utilization—which may go up as a result of the aging of even the old-old population—we can expect at least a million people age 85 and over to need long-term care spaces by the year 2000, and that number by 2020 to be 1.5 million, and by 2050, to be over 3 million! Thus, we will have to have about six times as many long-term care spaces for people 85 and over in 2050 as we had in 1980.

In this case the 85-and-over population is a better illustration than the 65-and-over population. Changes in the availability of in-home services could dramatically change the proportion of young-old people (under age 85) needing long-term care space, since they are much more likely to need only minimal assistance. At age 85 and over, however, care needs increase dramatically and are not as likely to be amenable to in-home services. Projections of health care needs not only involve projecting population sizes but utilization rates and availability of alternative forms of health care.

Projecting the housing needs of the elderly also is quite complex and also begins with demographic projections. Soldo (1981) used current trends in housing for the elderly to anticipate their future needs. She concluded that "the demand for independent types of living arrangements will increase in the near future. Even if the same age-specific patterns of living arrangements are maintained, by the turn of the century, there will be 8 million older persons . . . living alone—a net increase of 3 million since 1970" (1981:505). Soldo went on to say that increased aging of the older population might tend to reduce the proportion living alone, but that this would probably be offset by improvements in the financial status of the elderly as a result of the maturation of private pension and individual retirement plans, especially among women. However, Soldo cautioned, this projected increase in housing units headed by older people living alone would occur only if there were a sufficient supply of moderately priced living units suitable for the elderly. This is another good example of how demographic information must be related to social trends in order to be useful in planning.

Since, as we have seen, aid from family members is currently a major source of in-home services for the elderly, the availability of kin in the future is an important issue. Hammel, Wachter, and McDaniel (1981) used population simulations to look at the future availability to the elderly of spouses, children, grandchildren, and siblings. They found that compared to 1950, the elderly of the year 2000 will be more likely to have living kin: spouses, siblings, and larger numbers of children and grandchildren. But after the year 2000, the availability of kin to the elderly can be expected to decline as a result of the lowered fertility that began in the 1960s. After the year 2000, siblings will be more prevalent among the elderly, while children and grandchildren will become less prevalent. This could have important ramifications for the capacity of families to care for their very old members. Note how, in this example, several cohorts were used to make demographic projections of kin availability.

The Future of Physical Aging

Although physical aging has existed among humans for as long as they have been on earth, the typical rate of aging has changed and so has the array of diseases associated with later life. Extrapolating from mortality data, Fries (1980) hypothesized that in the future the onset of physical decline will occur later on the average than it does now and that the rate of disintegration of physical functioning will be more rapid than it is now. Fries predicted that the vast majority of people would be physically able until their eighth decade and also that most deaths would occur within the eighth decade of life. Fries' predictions have stirred controversy, but they illustrate how current trends can be extrapolated to provide educated guesses about what the future will bring and thereby serve to focus debate and guide research.

Cobb and Fulton (1981) used trends in health behavior, such as reductions in per-capita consumption of cigarettes and in the proportion of red meat in the average diet, to project changes in the prevalence of various diseases in later life. Specifically, they predicted lower prevalence of cancer, emphysema, and arteriosclerosis. They also predicted greater early detection and treatment of hypertension. However, they also predicted that as the older population itself ages, the incidence of diseases of bones and joints and of senile dementia would increase. All these changes have implications for health planning. For example, increases in the incidence of senile dementia will increase the demand for space in long-term care facilities, and increases in incidence of diseases of the bones and joints may spark more health research and medical specialization in these areas.

The Future of Psychological Aging

There are numerous ways in which the experience of aging may change. For example, in the future the proportion of older people in the population will be much greater than it is now, which could mean that reaching old age will be experienced less as an achievement than it is now. On the one hand, the greater proportion of older people might lead older people to feel a greater sense of potential for collective power. But on the other hand, the greater numbers of

older people could lead to greater divisions within the older population and even less tendency for the individual elder to identify with "older people" than is true now. The point is that the concentration of aging people in the population may have an effect on the subjective experience of growing older, and we will need to be observant to find out just what that effect is. Thus, imagining how trends might influence the future can help us identify areas for research.

Social change might also have an impact on the process of human development. For example, in the future, more people can be expected to have to grapple with a conflict between their retirement plans and their responsibilities for caring for frail aged parents. Resolution of this conflict may involve new types of developmental tasks or might lead to a new life stage.

The Future of Social Aging

The development of new stages in later life would obviously alter our conception of the life course. In addition, we can already see how improvements in health and financial resources in later life are leading us to question the appropriateness of some of our age norms. For example, the use of 65 as the normative retirement age has been called into question. Most people are beginning to recognize that there is no physical or psychological basis for it—it has been merely a social convenience. In the future, retirement ages may be dictated more by financial factors than by our ideas about age-appropriate behavior. And as we become more aware of the tremendous variety of situations and capacities among the elderly, we could see a decline in the use of age norms in favor of more person-specific norms. This is another area where researchers would do well to be on the alert.

Society's Future Response to the Elderly

As we have seen, ageism and societal disengagement are pervasive forces in American society now. Will they increase or decrease in the future? To the extent that there is an increase in the concentration of mentally and/or physically impaired older people living in the community, there may be an increase in both ageism and societal disengagement. On the other hand, an increase in the proportion of healthy, financially secure, and well-educated older people could lead to a decrease in ageism and societal disengagement.

Kiesler (1981) hypothesized that the increasing concentration of older people in the population, coupled with improvements in health, educational levels, and financial security among the elderly, would bring more Americans into contact with capable older people and would lead to improvements in attitudes toward the elderly. However, one could also argue that an increased number of older people with mental and physical disabilities will merely reinforce existing stereotypes, causing attitudes toward the elderly to become even more negative. But having some notion of which way attitudes might go, and why, is an important prerequisite for doing sound and relevant research in the future.

Neal Cutler (1981) looked at how social and demographic changes could be expected to alter the politics of aging in the future. He noted that there would be a larger proportion of the elderly and a drastic reduction in the educational differences between generations of voters. These trends would presumably give the elderly as a category relatively more political resources than they enjoy now. In addition, the trend toward lower levels of identification with the major political parties might lead to a focusing of political energies around other interests, such as age. But for age-consciousness to become a more important focus for political action, people would have to identify with the category "older people" more than they do now. The existence of organizations such as AARP may lead to greater age-identification, at least for purposes of political action. On the other hand, the fact that most people will probably still find their greatest satisfactions in their families may retard any tendency toward collective age-consciousness and political action. Again, we know something about what to look at in the future, but not precisely what we will find.

This very incomplete survey of the issues of the future should convince you that one of the major benefits of having conceptual frameworks and information about trends is that they create the capability for planning. They help us identify potential needs of older people, potential problems, and areas needing research. The future of aging will also be influenced by the future of social gerontology.

The Future of Social Gerontology

Obviously, lots of work is needed in social gerontology. But where do we go from here? What are the implications of the facts, figures, and perspectives given in this book for the field of aging?

Research

There is no single area of social gerontology that does not need more answers to crucial questions. In fact, the past decade of work in social gerontology has only enabled us just to begin asking the right questions. Yet there are some areas where the need for research is particularly pressing. For example: We know very little about America's older minority group people. We still do not fully understand the retirement process. Very little is known about religion as it relates to older people. We still do not understand why some people are devastated by old age and others are not. We do not fully understand the dynamics of age differentiation. The vast amount of research on aging in the United States needs to be complemented by research in other areas of the world.

In addition to the many stones as yet unturned, there is a crying need for *replication*. Knowledge is built piece by piece, and it takes many repeated studies to establish a scientific proposition. Social gerontology is loaded with conflicting research evidence, and only more high-quality research can give us the tools to sort it out. Thankfully, since the earlier editions of this book, the quality of research reports in the field of aging has risen steadily, as has the number of replications.

Because social gerontologists focus on only a portion of the total social reality, there are many opportunities for genuinely interdisciplinary research. The Kansas City Study of Adult Life and the Langley Porter Institute Studies in Aging were both noteworthy because their study designs brought together psychologists, social psychologists, sociologists, and social anthropologists to do simultaneous longitudinal studies on the same samples of older people. In fact, the interplay of various traditions in social gerontology could be viewed as a step in the direction of needed theoretical integration in the social sciences in general. The literature of social gerontology is full of cases where supposedly general social theories failed the test when applied to older people, and of cases where insights gained from theories of personality or developmental psychology have helped to refine sociological theories that were otherwise found wanting and vice versa.

In particular, detailed research on community systems holds great promise for understanding how the various social institutions interact with aging. Often, institutions and organizations pick up each other's slack, and needs not being met by one will be met by another. This kind of give-and-take is most observable at the local level. It is also at the local level that the individual most often comes into direct contact with the economy, politics, religion, health and welfare institutions, and his or her family, friends, and neighbors. The impact of any given institution or organization thus occurs in the context of a locally based *system* of institutions and organizations. We are just beginning to sort out the various types of community systems.

To date, there have been very few attempts to study the *interdependent situational context* in which the individual experiences later life. To my mind, more interdisciplinary, community-based research like the Kansas City Study of Adult Life and the Langley Porter Institute Studies in Aging is needed. Much was learned from those studies that could be used to do new and better community studies. The work of Clark and Anderson (1967) in particular shows that both the individual's personal system and his or her interaction with the social system can be studied successfully in a community context. More studies of this kind are needed, especially to partially offset the tunnel vision often found in large-scale survey research studies on specific topics, such as retirement, widowhood, or voting behavior, done by scholars within a single discipline. But large-scale studies are also necessary in order to get a view of a phenomenon, such as retirement or income, that is *representative* of an entire nation or set of nations and not just of a particular community. Earlier large-scale studies tended to suffer greatly from sampling problems, although in the last decade we have seen more well-designed national surveys.

An important key to the quality of research in social gerontology is the amount of research money available in the United States. When the Older Americans Act was passed in 1965, it established the U.S. Administration on Aging and included funds for research in social gerontology. For a while there was a flurry of research activity, but slowly the funds for research into aging were diverted to other purposes, so that by 1983 there was only a trickle of research money available. There are signs that the level of research funding from the National Institute on Aging may be increasing somewhat, but the important question is whether or not this will be *sustained* support. Gerontology research centers cannot be established and maintained with only sporadic funding. A lasting commitment is needed. The funding of research has always been a complicated matter, but with the rising cost of social research and the growing inability of state and local governments to increase public revenue, the federal government becomes the primary source of research funds. And until there is greater federal support of research in social gerontology, closing the research gaps we have listed will be a slow process.

The National Institute on Aging (NIA), which was established in the late 1970s as an arm of the National Institutes of Health, has provided research leadership and financial support at the national level. Part of Congress's rationale in creating NIA was a recognition that the level of support for research into aging has not come anywhere near matching the significance of the effects of aging on the lives of the general population. In beginning its efforts, NIA commissioned three separate panels to develop research priorities in (1) biomedical sciences, (2) behavioral and social sciences, and (3) services for older people. The following list of topics is representative of the kinds of research NIA has supported.

Psychological research that differentiates age decrements caused by environmental and disease factors from those caused by aging, and to identify decrements that will yield to intervention

Demographic projections and simulations aimed at constant reevaluation of retirement and income-maintenance policies

Research on personality, social, and environmental factors affecting social competence and life satisfaction, particularly sex and ethnic differences

Research on the family as a support system for older people

Research on the relationships among psychological, social, and physical health

Research to evaluate "natural" social experiments such as gradual retirement, service networks, or specially designed housing

Congressional support for research on aging has been encouraging.

The primary reponsibilities for funding federally sponsored research on aging have been given to the Administration on Aging, the National Institute on Aging, and the Center on Aging of the National Institute of Mental Health. Although the Reagan Administration sought to reduce research funding drastically, Congress has resisted cutting budgets for aging research. I hope this indicates Congress' recognition of the vital role research must play in developing the information base needed by teachers, program planners, and policy makers.

Education and Training

Education about aging is important at a number of levels of training. First, there is a growing need for continuing education programs for people employed full-time in agencies that serve older Americans. A solid information base in gerontology is also needed by students being trained at vocational schools for service jobs in health care and other areas related to aging, students enrolled in undergraduate programs in the helping professions, and graduate students in a wide variety of areas.

Ideally, education in gerontology imparts several kinds of knowledge. *General knowledge* is useful for establishing a broad context within which specific problems or issues are imbedded. For example, knowing that most older people do not find retirement difficult implies that we do not need to reform all of society in order to handle the problems of those who do find it difficult. *Theoretical perspectives* provide important diagnostic tools for figuring out what is going on—what is causing what. *Substantive knowledge* provides in-depth understanding of specific areas—cognition, widowhood, methodology, aging in literature, and the like. Knowledge of *issues* focuses on the boundaries and core of debate about *what to do* in specific areas of public policy regarding aging or the aged. Most educational programs in aging comprise all of these varieties of knowledge, although emphasis may vary.

If there is to be an increased research effort in social gerontology, obviously, people must be trained to do it. There has been an encouraging increase in the number of institutions offering research training in social gerontology at both the graduate and undergraduate levels, much of it financed through federal programs. Not only does the actual research depend on a continuing federal commitment to research in social gerontology, but so does the existence of trained researchers. In addition, more training in social gerontology is needed for professionals working in fields serving older people. In turn, there must be organizations to provide this training. Experience in recent years has shown that gerontology is attractive to students and that courses in aging can more than pull their weight in student demand. Such courses are essential for students in the human services professions.

Unfortunately, federal support for education in gerontology has all but disappeared. As a result, many financially troubled universities have found it difficult to sustain their relatively new gerontology programs when resources are scarce and the existence of even traditional disciplines seems threatened.

Policy and Planning

The theme of the 1971 White House Conference on Aging was "Toward a National Policy on Aging." A dozen years later, many of the policy objectives identified by the conference are still relevant. It is impossible to present all of the issues or recommendations that came out of the conference, but here are a few that are particularly pertinent.*

---

*There were White House Conferences on Aging in 1961, 1971, and 1981. The 1971 conference recommendations are reported here because the 1981 conference recommendations that related to aging were mixed in with economic and social initiatives of the Reagan Administration, which tended not to match the views of a majority of the conference delegates. Thus, the 1971 recommendations are a clearer reflection of the issues as seen by the conference delegates.

Education

1. Adult education should be expanded to include more of the specific concerns of the elderly.
2. Federal funds should be earmarked specifically for library services to older people.
3. Knowledge relative to aging should be part of educational curricula from preschool through higher education.
4. Preretirement education should be available to *everyone*, and well in advance of retirement.

Employment and Retirement

1. Employment and retirement policy should create a climate of free choice, whether to continue in employment as long as one wishes and is able, or retire on adequate income with opportunities for meaningful activities.
2. More rigorous efforts are needed to eliminate age discrimination in employment.
3. Retirement ages should be more flexible.
4. More effort should be made to use the talents of older people in public service jobs.

Physical and Mental Health

1. Present health care delivery systems should be expanded to include preventive medicine, long-term health care, special needs—such as eyeglasses and dental services—and rehabilitation services.
2. Adequate, appropriate alternatives to institutional care should be developed.

Housing

1. Housing programs should give special attention to the housing needs of older people who are poor, who live in rural areas, who are members of minority groups, who are disabled, or who are isolated.

2. The range of housing choice for older people should include long-term care facilities; facilities with limited medical, food, and homemaker services; congregate housing with food and personal services; and housing for independent living with recreational and activity programs.

3. Housing for older people should adopt architectural guidelines based on the needs of the elderly and the disabled.

Income

1. Older people (individuals as well as couples) should have a total cash income in accordance with the "American standard of living."

2. More earnings should be allowed without penalty under Social Security.

3. Private pension plans should be solvent and should provide for early vesting, portability, survivor benefits, and complete disclosure of provisions to those covered.

Spiritual Well-Being

1. Institutions for the aged should include chaplain services.

2. More religious programs should be available to older people in their own homes.

3. Religious bodies and the government should affirm the right to, and reverence for, life and recognize the individual's right to die with dignity.

Transportation

1. Increased transportation services should be provided to both rural and urban older people. System subsidies and payments to elderly individuals should both be available, depending on the accessibility and usability of public and private transportation.

2. Individualized, flexible transportation should be part of social service programs.

3. Insurance companies should be prevented from raising premiums on, or canceling, auto insurance on the basis of age alone.

4. Special attention should be given to the transportation needs of the rural elderly.

Facilities, Programs, and Services

1. All older persons should have real choices as to how they spend their later years.

2. Older people should be enabled to maintain their independence and their usefulness at the highest possible levels.

3. Older people should have the opportunity for continued growth, development, and self-fulfillment and for expanded contributions to a variety of community activities.

4. An effective network of facilities, programs, and services should be readily available and accessible to permit older people to exercise a wide range of options, regardless of their individual circumstances or where they live.

5. Specific agencies at the local, state, and federal levels should be assigned the responsibility for planning and coordinating services to older people.

6. Consumer protection of the elderly should be emphasized.

7. Protective services should be developed for those older persons in the community who are unable to manage their affairs because their mental and/or physical functioning is seriously impaired.

Government and Nongovernment Organizations

1. Planning and programming for the aged should coordinate the efforts of both private and public agencies at the local, state, and federal levels.

2. Government action on issues pertaining to older people must include a local-state-federal partnership.

3. Agencies responsible for programs in aging should be strong advocates for older people's interests.

4. Responsibility for planning and coordinating programs for older people should be consolidated under a single high-level office of government, and this pattern of pinpointing responsibility should apply at all levels of government.

Planning

1. Comprehensive planning in aging should be done on both a statewide basis and a local basis.

Research and Demonstration

1. Research aimed at understanding the basic processes of aging and alleviating the suffering of those who encounter difficulty in adapting to this phase of life should be accelerated.

2. Research on racial and ethnic minority groups should assume a proportional share of the total research effort.

3. A major increase in research and research training funds in aging should be appropriated and allocated.

Training

1. Additional federal funds should be provided for the training of professionals in both colleges and universities and on an in-service basis.

2. All service programs for older people should contain funds earmarked for the training of personnel.

This incomplete list of the concerns of the 1971 White House Conference on Aging includes many of the problems highlighted in this book and shows that they have received the at-
tention of politicians and planners. However, implementing these policy recommendations has been a political problem. If these recommendations are to receive high priority, older people and their advocates must pressure politicians to not ignore their needs. Many of the listed recommendations have received favorable attention in the years since the 1971 White House Conference. Yet, the agenda for the future is sure to contain many of these same topics because they have become issues of continuing policy concern.

Jobs

Since 1973 there has been an explosion of employment in the field of aging, most of it related to the establishment of the Area Agencies on Aging, the strengthening of State Units on Aging, and dramatic increases in the number and size of local programs for the elderly financed by Older Americans Act funds. Many of these jobs, if not most, went to people with no training in gerontology (Klegon, 1977). As a result, AAA's across the country have mounted substantial efforts toward in-service training. Colleges and universities are offering night courses for people already employed in the field. In addition, gerontology training programs are turning out graduates well suited to entry-level jobs in the aging service networks, and the number of jobs in these networks is still on the increase.

There are many other gerontological areas that will be experiencing dramatic increases in number of jobs in the coming years. For example, the U.S. Senate Special Committee on Aging (1973) estimated that between 1970 and 1980 there would be a need for nearly 20,000 additional managers of retirement housing, 25,000 additional licensed practical nurses and 8,000 additional registered nurses to handle the increased demand for nursing home care, 17,000 additional recreation-program specialists to serve older people, and several thousand additional positions in other types of employment.

And all of this is prior to the dramatic increase in the size of the over-75 population that will occur sometime well after 1995.*

Summary

Future growth of the older population is going to be explosive. With the older population growing so fast, there is little chance that interest in aging will lessen. In fact, during the coming decades, services to older people may well represent one of the fastest-growing areas of employment in the Western world. And the demand for knowledge in the field of social gerontology can be expected to grow accordingly. All of this implies a rosy future for social gerontology—and it's about time.

There are plentiful career opportunities in social gerontology. We are just beginning to grapple with the problems in many areas of research and practice. The "establishment" in the field is relatively small, and interest in research results and innovative programs is high. Funding for gerontology research and demonstration projects is available, and gerontology centers have been established in many universities. This situation offers people ready to embark on a new career an opportunity to "get in on the ground floor." I hope this book motivates some of its readers to join me in this fascinating field.

Yet, one does not have to become a gerontologist to benefit from a general education in gerontology. Although many people in academia have considered gerontology a vocational field, our society is aging, and to the extent that liberal education is designed to provide perspectives and information that can help to creatively solve our common human problems, gerontology can be expected to become a more important part of the liberal arts over the coming decades.

---

*For a sampling of places to look for jobs in the field of aging as well as some sound hints on how to land them, see Fecko, 1979.

Glossary

accommodation   Altering one's behavior to more nearly conform to the demands of an external situation.

acculturation   The process of learning a culture.

acute condition   An illness or injury expected to be temporary.

adaptation   The process of adjusting oneself to fit a situation or environment.

age changes   For an individual, differences, from one age to another, that result from internal physical or psychological change.

age differences   Differences between people of different ages; may be due to age changes, cohort differences, period effects, or some combination of the three.

age discrimination   The overt denial of opportunity based on age.

age norms   Norms tied to the life course that tell people of a given age what is allowed or not allowed for someone of that age.

aged   People age 65 or older.

ageism   Prejudice based on age.

aging (adj.)   In the process of becoming old. Does not imply that the person *is* old.

aging (n.)   The physical, psychological, and social processes that over time cause changes in a person's functional capacities and that influence social definitions.

Alzheimer's disease   Chronic organic brain disease caused by deteriorative loss of brain cells (as opposed to loss through injury or arteriosclerosis). (See also *dementia.*)

anticipation   Identifying in advance the rights, obligations, prerequisites, resources, and outlook of a position one will occupy in the future.

Area Agency on Aging (AAA)   Local agencies charged with planning and coordinating services to older people and with providing information and referral. Older Americans Act funds flow to local community agencies through the AAA's.

assimilation   An internal process in which new experience is absorbed and modified in the process of perception so as to fit better with already-existing ideas.

case management   Looking at the totality of a person's needs and resources and developing an integrated treatment plan. (See also *long-term care*.)

chronic condition   An illness or injury expected to be long-term or permanent.

chronological age   The number of years a person has lived.

cohort   An aggregation of people having a common characteristic, usually the time period in which they were born.

compensation   The processes whereby aging people or others around them offset detrimental effects of aging.

conflict management   A mental process that changes our perception of conflicts from negative to positive by altering the context in which the conflict is viewed. Includes techniques such as altruism, humor, sublimation, anticipation, and suppression.

consolidation   Adapting to role or activity loss by redistributing time and energy to roles and activities that remain.

continuity, external   Living in familiar environments and interacting with familiar people.

continuity, internal   The persistence of a personal structure of ideas based on memory.

decision demand   A type of norm that requires people to choose a course of action *within* a specified time period and *from* an age-linked field of possibilities.

dementia   An organic brain disease characterized by mental confusion, poor memory, incoherent speech, and poor orientation to the environment.

dependency   The condition of receiving assistance from others for the necessities of life.

dependency ratio, aged   The number of people age 65 and over divided by the number of people age 15–64, and the result multiplied by 100.

dependency ratio, total   The number of people age 0–14 plus the number of people age 65 and over, divided by the number of people age 15–64, and the result multiplied by 100.

dependency ratio, youth   The number of people age 0–14 divided by the number of people age 15–64, and the result multiplied by 100.

disability, major   A condition that causes restriction in a major area of life such as employment, child care, or housework.

disability, minor   A condition that causes restriction of activities, but not in major areas such as employment, child care, or housework.

disengagement   Adapting to role or activity loss by withdrawal.

disengagement, differential   Adapting to loss by withdrawal in selected areas of life. (See also *consolidation*.)

disengagement, societal   A process whereby people who reach an arbitrary age are no longer encouraged to seek positions for which they are qualified or are not encouraged to remain in positions in which they are functioning well.

dying trajectory   The speed with which a person dies; the rate of decline in functioning.

elderly   People age 65 or older.

functional age definition   The use of attributes such as appearance, mobility, strength, and mental capacity to assign people to broad age categories such as middle age and old age.

gerontology, social   See *social gerontology*.

habituation   The process of learning not to pay attention to stimuli we encounter over and over.

holistic model   A health care model stressing self responsibility, prevention, and wellness.

hospice   An organization that delivers services to dying persons and their families.

human development   The evolution of the human mind, including its patterns of thought, emotion, perception, memory, and temperament, but constituted as an interactive whole.

independence   The capacity to rely on oneself.

later maturity   A life-cycle stage socially defined or typified by energy decline; awareness of sensory loss; onset of chronic health problems, difficulty in remaining future oriented; recognition that one's time is growing short; loss of social contacts through retirement, widowhood, and movement of children; and freedom from responsibilities such as work and child rearing.

life course   An ideal sequence of events people are expected to experience and positions they are expected to occupy as they mature and move through life.

life expectancy   The *average* length of time a group of individuals of the same age will live, given current mortality rates. Life expectancy can be computed for any age, life expectancy from birth is the most common statistic.

life span   The length of life that is biologically possible for a given species.

life stages   Broad age categories loosely based on ideas about effects of aging. Examples include middle age, later maturity, and old age.

life table   A demographic model used to project the average number of years of life remaining at various ages, given current age-sex mortality rates.

long-term care   Long-term management of illness or disability.

maturation   The process of development. Can be physical, psychological, or social.

maturity   A quality of being fully grown. Physical maturity usually occurs much earlier than psychological and/or social maturity. Indeed, many contend that psychological development is never complete in the sense that physical development is.

Medicaid   A comprehensive health care program for the poor. Finances both acute and long-term care.

medical model   A health care model revolving around medical treatment, hospital-like environments, and care provided by physicians and nurses.

Medicare   A program of national health insurance for persons covered by Social Security and age 65 and over. Finances primarily acute care.

menopause   The period of natural cessation of menstruation, usually occuring between ages 45 and 50.

mental disorders, chronic organic   mental dysfunctions caused by chronic physical conditions from which no recovery can be expected.

mental disorders, functional   mental dysfunctions, having no apparent physical cause, such as schizophrenia and paranoia.

mental disorder, reversible organic   Mental dysfunction caused by physical conditions that can be treated and from which recovery can be expected, such as stroke and alcoholism.

middle age   A stage of the life cycle socially defined or typified by: energy decline, shifting from physical to mental activities, feeling of having reached a goal or plateau in one's career, awareness that life is finite, shrinking of family as children leave home, entry of women into the labor force, employment troubles, and feelings of restlessness or of not getting anywhere. (See also *later maturity; old age.*)

midlife   Middle age.

modernization theory   The theory that industrialization caused older people to lose status in society.

norms   Socially agreed-upon standards used to define behavior as acceptable or unacceptable.

nursing home   A facility that provides personal care plus health care such as administering medication.

old age   A stage of the life cycle socially defined or typified by: increasing frailty and disability, much introspection and concern over the meaning of life, distinct awareness of approaching death, financial and physical dependency, isolation, boredom, and loneliness. (See also *middle age; later maturity.*)

Older Americans Act   Legislation that created a national network of services and programs for older people. It also provides funds for research, training, and demonstration projects.

older people   People age 65 or older.

older person   Conceptually, an individual in later maturity or old age. Socially, an individual chronologically 65 or older. Legally, an individual of any of several chronological ages, beginning as early as 45. (See also *later maturity; old age.*)

pension   A periodic payment to a person or his or her family, given as a result of previous on-the-job service.

pension, job-related   Retirement pension available only through a specific position of employment and administered by a work organization, union, or private insurance company.

pension, retirement   Income received by a retired person by virtue of having been employed at least a minimum number of years on a job covered by a pension system. (See also *pension, job-related.*)

period effects   Differences resulting from measures having been taken at different time periods.

personal care home   A facility that provides meals, housekeeping services, and assistance with tasks such as dressing and bathing, but that does not provide nursing or medical care.

personal effectiveness   The capacity to influence the conditions of one's life.

personality   The unique pattern of attitudes, values, beliefs, habits, mannerisms, and preferences that allows one to think of oneself and others as individuals.

population pyramid   A graph showing the distribution, in either numbers or proportions, of population by age and sex.

proportion of older people in the population   The number of people age 65 and over divided by the number in the total population.

relationships   Reciprocal bonds of interdependence, affection, or belonging.

relative appreciation   A favorable attitude toward oneself or one's situation based on a comparison with others whose characteristics or situations are less fortunate.

reliability   The extent to which a measuring instrument produces consistent results.

rest home   See *personal care home*.

retirement   The period following a career of job holding, in which job responsibilities and often opportunities are minimized and in which economic support comes by virtue of having held a job for a minimum length of time in the past.

retirement community   A community most of whose residents are retired.

retirement community, de facto   A retirement community that results from large-scale migration of retired households to small towns in certain regions of the country.

retirement community, full-service   A retirement community that offers its residents a continuum of services and levels of care.

role relationship   The ground rules that define what the players of reciprocal social roles can expect from one another.

selective appreciation   A recognition that people offer more in some situations than in others and an emphasis on areas where their potential contribution is the highest.

self   A person's awareness of his or her own nature and characteristics. The person as an object of his or her own awareness.

senility   An out-dated term formerly used as a general term for mental infirmities thought to be the result of aging.

sex ratio   The number of males per 100 females in a population.

skilled nursing facility   A facility that provides hospital-quality nursing care around the clock.

social gerontology   A subfield of gerontology dealing with the developmental and group behavior of adults, and with the causes and consequences of having older people in the population.

social model   A health care model involving a wide range of types of care-givers in making decisions about health care and provision of health care.

social roles   The expected or typical behavior associated with positions in the organization of a group.

Social Security   Colloquially, the general public retirement pension administered by the federal government. Technically, Social Security also provides a number of other types of benefits to survivors and disabled people. It also administers Medicare.

social situation   The total structure of social forces influencing an individual's behavior or experience at a particular time. Social situations vary over time and from place to place.

socialization   The processes through which a group recreates in its members the distinctive way of life of the group.

SSI   Supplemental Security Income, a federal program of public assistance to indigent older people.

stereotype   A composite of beliefs about a category of people. May be either accurate or inaccurate.

substitution   Adapting to loss by substituting a new role or activity for the one lost.

support system   The total of a person's relationships that involve the receiving of assistance and that are viewed by both the giver and receiver as playing a significant part in maintaining the psychological, social, and physical integrity of the receiver.

theory   A set of interrelated principles and definitions used conceptually to organize observations, information, or communication about a particular aspect of reality.

typology A set of two or more mutually exclusive categories. Typologies specify relevant characteristics of each category and are used to identify differences and to make comparisons.

validity The correspondence between what a measuring instrument is supposed to measure and what it actually measures.

vulnerability The actual or perceived probability that one may experience loss or harm.

Bibliography

5*   Aaronson, Bernard S.
        1966   Personality stereotypes of aging. Journal of Gerontology 21:458–62.
8, 12   Abdo, E., J. Dills, H. Schectman, and M. Yanish
        1973   Elderly women in institutions versus those in public housing; comparison of personal and social adjustments. Journal of American Geriatrics Society 21:81–87.
        Achenbaum, W. Andrew
3   1978   Old Age in the New Land. Baltimore: Johns Hopkins University Press.
3   1983   Shades of Gray: Old Age, American Values, and Federal Policies Since 1920. Boston: Little, Brown.
3   Achenbaum, W. Andrew, and Peggy Ann Kusnerz
        1978   Images of Old Age in America, 1790 to the Present. Ann Arbor: University of Michigan/Wayne State University, Institute of Gerontology.
        Adams, Bert N.
7   1964   Structural factors affecting parental aid to kin. Journal of Marriage and the Family 26: 327–31.
7   1968a   Kinship in an Urban Setting. Chicago: Markham.
7   1968b   The middle-class adult and his widowed or still-married mother. Social Problems 16:51 –59.
12   Adams, David L.
        1971   Correlates of satisfaction among the elderly. The Gerontologist 11 (4, part 2):64–68.
2   Aday, Ron H., and Laurie A. Miles
        1982   Long-term impacts of rural migration of the elderly: implications for research. The Gerontologist 22:331–36.
18   Adelson, R., A. Nasti, J. N. Sprafkin, R. Marinelli, L. H. Primavera, and B. S. Gorman
        1982   Behavioral ratings of health professionals' interactions with the geriatric patient. The Gerontologist 22:277–81.
9   Agan, D.
        1966   The employment problems of people over forty. Journal of Employment Counseling 3:10–15.
5   Ager, Charlene Lee, Louise Wendt White, Wanda L. Mayberry, Patricia A. Crist, and Mary Elizabeth Conrad
        1981   Creative aging. International Journal of Aging and Human Development 14:67–76.
11   Aging Services News
        1983   Aging Services News, No. 146, Sept. 15.
17   Agnello, Thomas J., Jr.
        1973   Aging and the sense of political powerlessness. Public Opinion Quarterly 37:251–59.
5   Ahammer, I. M.
        1973   Social-learning theory as a framework for the study of adult personality development. Pp. 283–84 in Paul B. Baltes and K. Warner Schaie (eds.), Life-Span Developmental Psychology: Personality and Socialization. New York: Academic Press.
8   Ailor, James W.
        1969   The church provides for the elderly. Pp. 191–206 in Rosamonde R. Boyd and Charles G. Oakes (eds.), Foundations of Practical Gerontology. Columbia: University of South Carolina Press.
7   Albrecht, Ruth
        1969   The family and aging seen cross-culturally. Pp. 27–34 in Rosamonde R. Boyd and Charles G. Oakes (eds.), Foundations of Practical Gerontology. Columbia: University of South Carolina Press.

*Relevant text chapters are listed in this column.

Aldous, Joan

7   1965   The consequences of inter-generational continuity. Journal of Marriage and the Family 27:462–68.

7   1978   Family Careers: Developmental Change in Families. New York: Wiley.

7   1981   From dual-earner to dual-career families and back again. Journal of Family Issues 2:115–25.

8   Alford, Harold J.

     1968   Continuing Education in Action: Residential Centers for Lifelong Learning. New York: Wiley.

16   Allen, Carole B.

     1981   Measuring mature markets. American Demographics 3(3):17.

16   Almeder, Robert F.

     1983   Materialism and the future of aging in America. International Journal of Aging and Human Development 16:161–65.

     Alpaugh, Patricia K., and James E. Birren

5   1975   Are there sex differences in creativity across the adult life span? Human Development 18:461–65.

5   1977   Variables affecting creative contributions across the adult life span. Human Development 20:240–48.

12   Alpaugh, Patricia K., and Margaret Haney

     1978   Counseling the Older Adult. A Training Manual for Paraprofessionals and Beginning Counselors. Los Angeles: University of Southern California Press.

12   Alston, J. P., and C. J. Dudley

     1973   Age, occupation, and life satisfaction. The Gerontologist 13:58–61.

8, 18   American Association of Homes for the Aging

     1979   Long-Term Care of the Aging: A Socially Responsible Approach. Washington, D.C.: The Association.

5, 12   Amster, L. E., and H. H. Krauss

     1974   The relationship between life crises and mental deterioration in old age. International Journal of Aging and Human Development 5:51–55.

11   Anderson, Barbara G.

     1965   Bereavement as a subject of cross-cultural inquiry: an American sample. Anthropological Quarterly 38:181–200.

     Anderson, Nancy N.

5, 8   1965   Institutionalization, interaction, and self-conception in aging. Pp. 245–57 in Arnold M. Rose and Warren A. Peterson (eds.), Older People and Their Social World. Philadelphia: F. A. Davis.

5   1967a   Effects of institutionalization on self-esteem, Journal of Gerontology 22:313–17.

6   1967b   The significance of age categories for older persons. The Gerontologist 7:164–67.

8, 18   Anderson, Peggye D.

     1978   Support services and aged blacks. Black Aging 3:53–59.

17   Anderson, William A., and Norma D. Anderson

     1978   The politics of age exclusion: the adults-only movement in Arizona. The Gerontologist 18:6–12.

5, 12   Andrew, J. M.

     1973   Coping style and declining verbal abilities. Journal of Gerontology 28:179–83.

     Andrews, R. B.

8   1963a   Housing for the elderly: aspects of its central problems. The Gerontologist 3:110–16.

8   1963b   Housing for the elderly: state and city-county–based market analysis, an outline of method and administration. The Gerontologist 3:148–51.

9   Andrisani, Paul J.
    1977   Effects of health problems on the work experience of middle-aged men. Industrial Gerontology 4:97–112.

Ansello, Edward F.

13   1977a   Age and ageism in children's first literature. Educational Gerontology 2:255–74.

13   1977b   Old age and literature: an overview. Educational Gerontology 2:211–18.

12   Antonucci, T.
    1974   On the relationship between values and adjustment in old men. International Journal of Aging and Human Development 5:57–59.

15   Antunes, George E., Fay L. Cook, Thomas D. Cook, and Wesley G. Skogan
    1977   Patterns of personal crime against the elderly: findings from a national survey. The Gerontologist 17:321–27.

15   Apfeldorf, M., P. J. Hunley, and G. D. Cooper
    1972   Disciplinary problems in a home for older veterans: some psychological aspects in relation to drinking behavior. The Gerontologist 12:143–47.

7   Apple, Dorrian
    1956   The social structure of grandparenthood. American Anthropologist 58:656–63.

Arenberg, David

5   1968   Concept problem solving in young and old adults. Journal of Gerontology 23:279–82.

5   1974   A longitudinal study of problem solving in adults. Journal of Gerontology 29:650–58.

5   Arenberg, David, and Elizabeth A. Robertson-Tchabo
    1980   Age differences and age changes in cognitive performance: new "old" perspectives. Pp. 139–57 in R. L. Sprott (ed.), Age, Learning Ability, and Intelligence. New York: Van Nostrand Reinhold.

7, 11   Arens, Diana Antos
    1982   Widowhood and well-being: an examination of sex differences within a causal model. International Journal of Aging and Human Development 15:27–40.

Arling, Greg

7, 11   1976a   The elderly widow and her family, neighbors and friends. Journal of Marriage and the Family 38(4):757–68.

7, 11   1976b   Resistance to isolation among elderly widows. International Journal of Aging and Human Development 7:67–86.

13   Aronoff, Craig
    1974   Old age in prime time. Journal of Communication 24:86–87.

Arth, Malcolm

    1968   An interdisciplinary view of the aged in Ibo culture. Journal of Geriatric Psychiatry 2:33–39.

    1972   Aging: a cross-cultural perspective. Pp. 352–64 in D. P. Kent, R. Kastenbaum, and S. Sherwood (eds.), Research Planning and Action for the Elderly: The Power and Potential of Social Science. New York: Behavioral Publications.

9   Ash, Phillip
    1966   Pre-retirement counseling. The Gerontologist 6:97–99, 127–28.

8   Ashford, N., and F. M. Holloway
    1972   Transportation patterns of older people in six urban centers. The Gerontologist 12:43–47.

Atchley, Robert C.

5, 9, 12   1967   Retired women: a study of self and role. Unpublished doctoral dissertation. Ann Arbor, Michigan: University Microfilms.

5   1969   Respondents vs. refusers in an interview study of retired women. Journal of Gerontology 24:42–47.

10   1971a Retirement and leisure participation: continuity or crisis? The Gerontologist 11(1, part 1):13–17.

13   1971b Disengagement among professors. Journal of Gerontology 26:476–80.

9   1971c Retirement and work orientation. The Gerontologist 11(1, part 1):29–32.

        1972   The Social Forces in Later Life, first edition. Belmont, Calif: Wadsworth.

9   1974a The meaning of retirement. Journal of Communications 24:97–101.

13   1974b Social problems of the aged. Pp. 391–415 in Rodney Stark (ed.), Social Problems. New York: CRM Books/Random House.

9, 12   1975a Adjustment to loss of job at retirement. International Journal of Aging and Human Development 6:17–27.

11, 12 1975b Dimensions of widowhood in later life. The Gerontologist 15:176–78.

6   1975c The life course, age grading, and age-linked demands for decision making. Pp. 261–78 in Nancy Datan and Leon H. Ginsberg (eds.), Life-Span Developmental Psychology: Normative Life Crises. New York: Academic Press.

5, 8, 10   1975d Sex differences among middle-class retired people. Pp. 22–31 in Robert C. Atchley, Research Studies in Social Gerontology. Oxford, Ohio: Scripps Foundation.

9   1976a Orientation toward the job and retirement adjustment among women. In Jaber F. Gubrium (ed.), Time, Self, and Aging. New York: Behavior Publications.

9   1976b The Sociology of Retirement. Cambridge, Mass.: Schenkman.

12   1977   Predictors of morale in later life. Paper presented at the annual meeting of The Gerontological Society, San Francisco, Calif.

9   1978   Retirement preparation for women. Pp. 126–139 in Ann F. Cahn (ed.), Women in Midlife—Security and Fulfillment. Washington, D.C.: House Select Committee on Aging.

9   1979   Issues in retirement research. The Gerontologist 19:44–54.

12   1980   Age and suicide: reflection on the quality of life? Pp. 141–62 in S. G. Haynes and M. Feinleib (eds.), The Epidemiology of Aging. Bethesda, Maryland: National Institutes of Health.

        1980   The Social Forces in Later Life, third edition. Belmont, Calif.: Wadsworth.

5   1982a The aging self. Psychotherapy: Theory, Research, and Practice 19:388–96.

9   1982b The process of retirement: comparing women and men. Pp. 153–68 in M. Szinovacz (ed.), Women's Retirement. Beverly Hills, Calif.: Sage.

9   1982c Retirement: Leaving the world of work. Annals of the American Academy of Political and Social Sciences 464:120–31.

3, 9   1982d Retirement as a social institution. Annual Review of Sociology 8:263–87.

6   Atchley, Robert C., and Linda K. George
        1973   Symptomatic measurement of age. The Gerontologist 13:136–41.

        Atchley, Robert C., and Sheila J. Miller

8   1975   Housing of the rural aged. Pp. 95–143 in Robert C. Atchley (ed.), Environments and the Rural Aged. Washington, D.C.: The Gerontological Society.

7   1980   Older people and their families. Annual Review of Gerontology and Geriatrics 1:337–369.

9   Atchley, Robert C., Suzanne R. Kunkel, and Carl Adlon
        1978   An evaluation of preretirement programs: results from an experimental study. Oxford, Ohio: Scripps Foundation Gerontology Center.

7   Atchley, Robert C., Linda Pignatiello, and Ellen Shaw
        1979   Interactions with family and friends: marital status and occupational differences among older women. Research on Aging 1:83–94.

9   Atchley, Robert C., and Judith L. Robinson
        1982   Attitudes toward retirement and distance from the event. Research on Aging 4:299–313.

5   Atchley, Robert C., and Judith A. Seltzer
        1975   Prediction of age identification. Pp. 32–44 in Robert C. Atchley, Research Studies in
                Social Gerontology. Oxford, Ohio: Scripps Foundation.
        Atchley, Robert C., and Mildred M. Seltzer
        1976   The Sociology of Aging: Selected Readings. Belmont, Calif.: Wadsworth.
15   Athanasiou, Robert, Phillip Shaver, and Carol Tavris
        1970   Sex. Psychology Today. July:50.
18   Atlas, L., and M. M. Morris
        1971   Resident government: an instrument for the change in a public institution for indigent
                elderly. The Gerontologist 11:209–12.
12, 15 Attkisson, C. C.
        1970   Suicide in San Francisco's skid row. Archives of General Psychiatry 23:149–57.
9, 16   August, R. L.
        1974   Age discrimination in employment: correcting a constitutionally infirm legislative judg-
                ment. Southern California Law Review 47:1311–52.
18   Avant, W. Ray, and Paula L. Dressel
        1980   Perceiving needs by staff and elderly clients: the impact of training and client contact.
                The Gerontologist 20:71–77.
11   Averill, J. R.
        1968   Grief: its nature and significance. Psychological Bulletin 6:721–48.
13   Axelrod, S., and C. Eisdorfer
        1961   Attitudes toward old people: an empirical analysis of the stimulus-group validity of the
                Tuckman-Lorge questionnaire. Journal of Gerontology 16:75–80.
7, 12   Axelson, Leland L.
        1960   Personal adjustments in the postparental period. Marriage and Family Living 22:66–70.
10   Babic, Anna L.
        1972   The older volunteer: expectations and satisfactions. The Gerontologist 12:87–89.
7   Bachrach, C. A.
        1980   Childlessness and social isolation among the elderly. Journal of Marriage and the
                Family 42:627–37.
        Back, Kurt W.
9   1969   The ambiguity of retirement. Pp. 93–114 in Ewalde W. Busse and Eric Pfeiffer (eds.),
                Behavior and Adaptation in Late Life. Boston: Little, Brown.
5, 11   1971a   Metaphors as a test of personal philosophy of aging. Sociological Focus 5:1–8.
5   1971b   Transition to aging and the self-image. Aging and Human Development 2:296–304.
5   1976   Personal characteristics and social behavior: theory and method. Pp. 403–31 in Robert
                H. Binstock and Ethel Shanas (eds.), Handbook of Aging and the Social Sciences. New
                York: Van Nostrand Reinhold.
        Back, Kurt W., and Kenneth J. Gergen
5   1966a   Cognitive and motivational factors in aging and disengagement. Pp. 289–95 in Ida H.
                Simpson and John C. McKinney (eds.), Social Aspects of Aging. Durham, No. Caro-
                lina: Duke University Press.
5, 12   1966b   Personal orientation and morale of the aged. Pp. 296–305 in Ida H. Simpson and John
                C. McKinney (eds.), Social Aspects of Aging. Durham, No. Carolina: Duke University
                Press.
5, 9   Back, Kurt W., and Carleton S. Guptill
        1966   Retirement and self-ratings. Pp. 120–29 in Ida H. Simpson and John C. McKinney
                (eds.), Social Aspects of Aging. Durham, No. Carolina: Duke University Press.
10   Bahr, H. M.
        1970   Aging and religious disaffiliation. Social Forces 49:59–71.

15   Bahr, H. M., and G. R. Garrett
     1976   Homeless Women: The Disafilliation of Urban Females. Lexington, Mass.: D.C.
            Heath and Co.
7   Bahr, S. J.
     1973   Effects of power and division of labor on the family. Pp. 167–85 in Lois W. Hoffman
            and Ivan F. Nye (eds.), Working Mothers. San Francisco: Jossey-Bass.
4   Bakerman, Seymour (ed.)
     1969   Aging Life Processes. Springfield, Ill.: Charles C. Thomas.
11   Balkwell, C.
     1981   Transition to widowhood: a review of literature. Family Relations 30:117–27.
7   Ballweg, John A.
     1967   Resolution of conjugal role adjustment after retirement. Journal of Marriage and the
            Family 29:277–81.
     Baltes, Paul B.
1   1968   Longitudinal and cross-sectional sequences in the study of age and generation effects.
            Human Development 11:145–71.
1   1973   Prototypical paradigms and questions in life-span research on development and aging.
            The Gerontologist 13:458–67.
5   Baltes, Paul B., and Gisela V. Labouvie
     1973   Adult development of intellectual performance: description, explanation, and modifica-
            tion. Pp. 157–219 in C. Eisdorfer and M. P. Lawton (eds.), The Psychology of Adult
            Development and Aging. Washington, D.C.: American Psychological Association.
     Baltes, Paul B., and K. Warner Schaie
5   1973a (eds.) Life-Span Developmental Psychology: Personality and Socialization. New York:
            Academic Press.
1   1973b On life-span developmental research paradigms: retrospects and prospects. Pp. 365–95
            in Paul B. Baltes and K. Warner Schaie (eds.), Life-Span Developmental Psychology:
            Personality and Socialization. New York: Academic Press.
5   1974   Aging and I.Q.: the myth of the twilight years. Psychology Today 7(10):35–38, 40.
5   1976   On the plasticity of intelligence in adulthood and old age: where Horn and Donaldson
            fail. American Psychologist 31:720–25.
1   Baltes, Paul B., Hayne W. Reese, and John R. Nesselroade
     1977   Life Span Developmental Psychology: Introduction to Research Methods. Monterey,
            Calif.: Brooks/Cole.
7   Bankoff, Elizabeth A.
     1983   Aged parents and their widowed daughters: a support relationship. The Gerontologist
            38:226–30.
13   Banziger, George, and Jean Drevenstedt
     1982   Achievement attributions by young and old judges as a function of perceived age of
            stimulus person. Journal of Gerontology 37:468–74.
9   Barfield, Richard E.
     1970   The Automobile Worker and Retirement. Ann Arbor, Michigan: University of Michi-
            gan, Institute of Social Research.
     Barfield, Richard E., and James N. Morgan
9   1969   Early Retirement: The Decision and the Experience. Ann Arbor, Michigan: University
            of Michigan, Institute of Social Research.
9   1978a Trends in planned early retirement. The Gerontologist 18:13–18.
9   1978b Trends in satisfaction with retirement. The Gerontologist 18:19–23.
9   Barresi, C. M.
     1974   The meaning of work: a case study of elderly poor. Industrial Gerontology 1:24–34.

9   Barresi, C. M., and H. F. Coyle, Jr.
        1972   Elderly services and industries: a pilot program of part-time employment for elderly
                poor. The Gerontologist 12:371–74.
9   Barron, Charles I.
        1975   Medical considerations in planning for retirement. Industrial Gerontology 2:189–99.
13   Barron, Milton L.
        1953   Minority group characteristics of the aged in American society. Journal of Gerontology
                8:477–82.
5   Barton, Elizabeth M., Judy K. Plemons, Sherry L. Willis, and Paul B. Baltes
        1975   Recent findings on adult and gerontological intelligence: changing a stereotype of de-
                cline. American Behavioral Scientist 19:224–36.
11   Bascue, L. O., and R. E. Lawrence
        1977   A study of subjective time and death anxiety in the elderly. Omega 8:81–90.
13   Bassili, John N., and Jane Reil
        1981   On the dominance of the old-age stereotype. Journal of Gerontology 36:682–88.
9   Bauder, Ward W., and Jon A. Doerflinger
        1967   Work roles among the rural aged. Pp. 22–43 in E. Grant Youmans (ed.), Older Rural
                Americans. Lexington, Kentucky: University of Kentucky Press.
4, 8 Bauer, Mary Lou
        1972   Health characteristics of low-income persons. Vital and Health Statistics, Series 10, No.74.
9, 14 Baxandall, Rosalyn, Linda Gordon, and Susan Reverby
        1976   America's Working Woman. New York: Random House.
5   Bayley, Nancy
        1968   Cognition and aging. Pp. 97–119 in K. Warner Schaie (ed.), Theory and Methods of
                Research on Aging. Morgantown, W. Virginia: West Virginia University.
5   Bayley, Nancy, and Melita Oden
        1955   The maintenance of intellectual ability in gifted adults. Journal of Gerontology 10:91–
                107.
8   Bayne, J. R. D.
        1971   Environmental modification for the older person. The Gerontologist 11:314–17.
2   Bayo, F. R., H. W. Shiman, and B. R. Sobus
        1977   Actuarial Study No. 76. Washington, D.C.: Social Security Administration.
2   Beale, Calvin L.
        1964   Rural depopulation in the United States: some demographic consequences of agricultur-
                al adjustments. Demography 1:264–72.
18   Beattie, Walter M., Jr.
        1976   Aging and the social services. Pp. 619–42 in Robert H. Binstock and Ethel Shanas
                (eds.), Handbook of Aging and the Social Sciences. New York: Van Nostrand Rein-
                hold.
     de Beauvoir, Simone
        1972   The Coming of Age. New York: G. P. Putnam's Sons.
9   Beck, Scott H.
        1982   Adjustments to and satisfaction with retirement. Journal of Gerontology 37:616–24.
18   Becker, Babette
        1982   The nursing home scoring system: a policy analysis. The Gerontologist 22:39–44.
18   Becker, Gaylene, and Gay Nadler
        1980   The aged deaf: integration of a disabled group into an agency serving elderly people.
                The Gerontologist 20:214–21.
5   Becker, Howard S., and Anselm Strauss
        1968   Careers, personality, and adult socialization. Pp. 311–20 in Bernice L. Neugarten (ed.),
                Middle Age and Aging. Chicago: University of Chicago Press.

7, 12   Beckman, Linda J., and Betsy Bosack Hauser
         1982   The consequences of childlessness on the social-psychological well-being of older women. Journal of Gerontology 37:243–50.

13   Bekker, L. de Moyne, and Charles Taylor
         1966   Attitudes toward aging in a multigenerational sample. Journal of Gerontology 21:115–18.

9   Belbin, E., and R. Meredith Belbin
         1969   Selecting and training adults for new work. Pp. 66–81 in A. T. Welford (ed.), Decision Making and Age. New York: S. Karger.

9   Belbin, R. M., and S. Clarke
         1971   International trends in employment among men over 65. Industrial Gerontology 9:18–23.

7   Belcher, John C.
         1967   A consequence of the isolated nuclear family. Journal of Marriage and the Family 29:534–40.

15   Bell, A. P., and M. S. Weinberg
         1978   Homosexualities: A Study of Diversity Among Men and Women. New York: Simon & Schuster.

    Bell, Bill D.
12   1974   Cognitive dissonance and the life satisfaction of older adults. Journal of Gerontology 29:564–71.

5, 12   1975   The limitations of crisis theory as an explanatory mechanism in social gerontology. International Journal of Aging and Human Development 6:153–68.

8   1976   The impact of housing relocation on the elderly: an alternative methodological approach. International Journal of Aging and Human Development 7:27–38.

    Bell, Bill D., and G. G. Stanfield
5   1973a   Chronological age in relation to attitudinal judgments: an experimental analysis. Journal of Gerontology 28:491–96.

13   1973b   The aging stereotype in experimental perspective. The Gerontologist 13:341–44.

9   Bell, D. R.
         1975   Prevalence of private retirement plans. Monthly Labor Review 98(10):17–20.

7, 11   Bell, Robert
         1971   Marriage and Family Interaction. Homewood, Ill.: Dorsey Press.

12   Bell, Tony
         1967   The relationship between social involvement and feeling old among residents in homes for the aged. Journal of Gerontology 22:17–22.

8   Bell, W. G., and W. T. Olsen
         1974   An overview of public transportation and the elderly: new directions and social policy. The Gerontologist 14:324–30.

17   Bell, William G., Winsor Schmidt, and Kent Miller
         1981   Public guardianship and the elderly: findings from a national study. The Gerontologist 21:194–202.

14   Benedict, Robert.
         1972   A profile of the Indian aged. Pp. 51–57 in Minority Aged in America. Occasional Papers in Gerontology, Number 10. Ann Arbor, Michigan: University of Michigan-Wayne State University Institute of Gerontology.

    Bengtson, Vern L.
9, 10   1969   Differences between subsamples in level of present role activity. Pp. 35–49 in Robert J. Havighurst, J. M. Munnichs, B. Neugarten, and H. Thomae (eds.), Adjustment to Retirement: A Cross-National Study. New York: Humanities Press.

7   1971   Inter-age perceptions and the generation gap. The Gerontologist 11(4, part 2):85–89.

8   1973   Self-determination: a social-psychologic perspective on helping the aged. Geriatrics 28: 118–30.

5, 7   1975   Generation and family effects in value socialization. American Sociological Review 40: 358–71.

5   1983   The Self Concept. Unpublished Manuscript.

7   Bengtson, Vern L., and Dean Black
         1973   Intergenerational relations and continuities in socialization. Pp. 208–34 in P. B. Baltes and K. W. Schaie (eds.), Life-Span Developmental Psychology: Personality and Socialization. New York: Academic Press.

6, 7   Bengtson, Vern L., and Neal E. Cutler
         1976   Generations and intergenerational relations: perspectives on age groups and social change. Pp. 130–59 in Robert H. Binstock and Ethel Shanas (eds.), Handbook of Aging and the Social Sciences. New York: Van Nostrand Reinhold.

5, 7   Bengtson, Vern L., and Joseph Kuypers
         1971   Generational difference and the developmental stake. Aging and Human Development 2:249–60.

5   Bengtson, Vern L., and M. C. Lovejoy
         1973   Values, personality and social structure: an intergenerational analysis. American Behavioral Scientist 16:880–912.

11   Bengtson, Vern L., Jose B. Cuellar, and Pauline K. Ragan
         1977   Stratum constrasts and similarities in attitudes toward death. Journal of Gerontology 32(1):76–88.

5, 7   Bengtson, Vern L., M. J. Furlong, and R. S. Laufer
         1974   Time, aging, and the continuity of social structure: themes and issues in generational analysis. Journal of Social Issues 30:1–30.

6, 13   Bengtson, Vern L., Patricia L. Kasschau, and Pauline K. Ragan
         1977   The impact of social structure on aging individuals. Pp. 327–53 in James E. Birren and K. Warner Schaie (eds.), Handbook of the Psychology of Aging. New York: Van Nostrand Reinhold.

2   Bengtson, Vern L., James J. Dowd, David H. Smith, and Alex Inkeles
         1975   Modernization, modernity, and perceptions of aging: a cross-cultural study. Journal of Gerontology 30:688–95.

7, 17   Benjamin, A. E., Carroll L. Estes, James H. Swan, and Robert J. Newcomer
         1980   Elders and children: patterns of public policy in the fifty states. Journal of Gerontology 35:928–34.

18   Benjamin, A. E., and David A. Lindeman
         1983   Health planning and long-term care. Pp. 207–226 in Carroll L. Estes and R. J. Newcomer (eds.), Fiscal Austerity and Aging: Shifting Government Responsibility for the Elderly. Beverly Hills, Calif.: Sage.

         Bennett, Ruth G.
8   1963   The meaning of institutional life. The Gerontologist 3(3, part 3):117–25.

6   1970   Social context—a neglected variable in research on aging. Aging and Human Development 1:97–116.

8   1973   Living conditions and everyday needs of the elderly with particular reference to social isolation. International Journal of Aging and Human Development 4:179–98.

12   1980   Aging, Isolation and Resocialization. New York: Van Nostrand Reinhold.

5, 13   Bennett, Ruth G., and J. Eckman
         1973   Attitudes toward aging: a critical examination of recent literature and implications for future research. Pp. 575–97 in C. Eisdorfer and M. P. Lawton (eds.), The Psychology

of Adult Development and Aging. Washington D.C.: American Psychological Association.

Bennett, Ruth G., and Lucille Nahemow

8, 12   1965   Institutional totality and criteria of social adjustment in residences for the aged. Journal of Social Issues 21:44–76.

8, 12   1972   Socialization and social adjustment in five residential settings for the aged. Pp. 514–24 in D. P. Kent, R. Kastenbaum, and S. Sherwood (eds.), Research Planning and Action for the Elderly: The Power and Potential of Social Science. New York: Behavioral Publications.

12   Benson, R. A., and D. C. Brodie

        1975   Suicide by overdoses of medicine among the aged. Journal of American Geriatric Society 23:304–08.

Berardo, Felix M.

7, 11   1968   Widowhood status in the U.S.: perspectives on a neglected aspect of the family life cycle. The Family Coordinator 17:191–203.

7, 11   1970   Survivorship and social isolation: the case of the aged widower. The Family Coordinator 19:11–15.

5   Beres, Cathryn A., and Alan Baron

        1981   Improved digit symbol substitution by older women as a result of external practice. Journal of Gerontology 36:591–97.

8   Beresford, John C., and Alice M. Rivlin

        1966   Privacy, poverty, and old age. Demography 3:247–58.

Berezin, Martin A.

5   1969   Sex and old age: a review of the literature. Journal of Geriatric Psychiatry 2:131–49.

5   1976   Normal psychology of the aging process revisited. I. Sex and old age: a further review of the literature. Journal of Geriatric Psychiatry 9:189–209.

12   Berg, Stig, Dan Mellstrom, Goran Persson, and Alvar Swanborg

        1981   Loneliness in the Swedish aged. Journal of Gerontology 36:342–49.

8   Berg, W. B., L. Atlas, and J. Zeiger

        1974   Integrated homemaking services for the aged in urban neighborhoods. The Gerontologist 14:388–93.

15   Berger, Raymond M.

        1982   Gay and Gray: The Older Homosexual Man. Chicago: University of Illinois Press.

8   Bergman, Simon, and Ilene Ora Cibulski

        1981   Environment, culture, and adaptation in congregate facilities: perspectives from Israel. The Gerontologist 21:240–46.

8, 18   Berkman, Barbara, and Helen Rehr

        1975   Elderly patients and their families; factors related to satisfaction with hospital social services. The Gerontologist 15:524–28.

Berkowitz, Sandra

        1978   Informed consent, research and the elderly. The Gerontologist 18:237–43.

8   Bernstein, Judith

        1982   Who leaves—who stays: residency policy in housing for the elderly. The Gerontologist 22:305–13.

8   Bernstein, M. C.

        1974   Forecast of women's retirement income: cloudy and colder, 25 percent chance of poverty. Industrial Gerontology 1(2):1–13.

8   Better Housing League of Cincinnati

        1978   Housing for Older Americans in Hamilton County, Ohio. Cincinnati, Ohio: Better Housing League.

8   Beyer, Glenn H.
        1963   Economic Aspects of Housing for the Aged. Ithaca, New York: Cornell University
                Center for Housing and Environmental Studies.
8   Beyer, Glenn, and F. H. J. Nierstrasz
        1967   Housing the Aged in Western Countries: Programs, Dwellings, Homes and Geriatric
                Facilities. New York: Elsevier.
12   Bigot, Arthur
        1974   The relevance of American Life Satisfaction Indices for research on British subjects be-
                fore and after retirement. Age and Aging 3:113–21.
14   Billingsley, Andrew
        1968   Black Families in White America. Englewood Cliffs, N.J.: Prentice-Hall.
        Binstock, Robert H.
17   1972   Interest-group liberalism and the politics of aging. The Gerontologist 12:265–80.
17   1974   Aging and the future of American politics. Pp. 199–212 in Frederick R. Eisele (ed.),
                Political Consequences of Aging. Philadelphia: American Academy of Political and So-
                cial Sciences.
19   1975a   Planning for tomorrow's urban aged: a policy analyst's reaction. The Gerontologist 15:
                42.
19   1975b   Social goals in contemporary society. Pp. 32–41 in Carter C. Osterbind (ed.), Social
                Goals, Social Programs and the Aging. Gainesville, Fla.: University of Florida Press.
17   1983   The aged as scapegoat. The Gerontologist 23:136–43.
17   Binstock, Robert H., and Martin A. Levin
        1976   The political dilemmas of intervention policies. Pp. 511–35 in Robert H. Binstock and
                Ethel Shanas (eds.), Handbook of Aging and the Social Sciences. New York: Van Nos-
                trand Reinhold.
        Birren, James E.
5   1959   (ed.), Handbook of Aging and the Individual. Chicago: University of Chicago Press.
5   1964   The Psychology of Aging. Englewood Cliffs, N.J.: Prentice-Hall.
5   1973   A summary: prospects and problems of research on the longitudinal developments of
                man's intellectual capacities throughout life. Pp. 149–54 in L. F. Jarvik, C. Eisdorfer,
                and J. E. Blum (eds.), Intellectual Functioning in Adults: Psychological and Biological
                Influences. New York: Springer.
5   Birren, James E., Walter R. Cunningham, and Koichi Yamamoto
        1983   Psychology of adult development and aging. Annual Review of Psychology 34:543–75.
5   Birren, James E., and K. Warner Schaie (eds.)
        1977   Handbook of the Psychology of Aging. New York: Van Nostrand Reinhold.
5   Birren, James E., and R. B. Sloane (eds.)
        1980   Handbook of Mental Health and Aging. Englewood Cliffs, N.J.: Prentice-Hall.
5   Birren, James E., and D. S. Woodruff
        1973   Human development over the life span through education. Pp. 305–37 in Paul B.
                Baltes and K. Warner Schaie (eds.), Life-Span Developmental Psychology: Personality
                and Socialization. New York: Academic Press.
        Bixby, Lenore E.
8   1970   Income of people aged 65 and over: an overview from the 1968 survey of the aged.
                Social Security Bulletin 33(4):3–34.
9   1976   Retirement patterns in the United States: research and policy interaction. Social Secu-
                rity Bulletin 39(8):3–19.
9   Bixby, Lenore E., and E. Eleanor Rings
        1969   Work experience of men claiming retirement benefits, 1966. Social Security Bulletin
                32(8):3–14.

2, 8   Bixby, Lenore E., Wayne Finegar, Susan Grad, Walter Kolodrubetz, Patience Lauriat, and Janet Murray
   1975   Demographic and Economic Characteristics of the Aged: 1968 Social Security Survey. Washington, D.C.: U.S. Government Printing Office.

16   Blackburn, John O.
   1963   Pensions, the national income, and the national wealth. Pp. 178–98 in Juanita M. Kreps (ed.), Employment, Income, and Retirement Problems of the Aged. Durham, No. Carolina. Duke University Press.

7   Blau, Zena S.
   1961   Structural constraints on friendship in old age. American Sociological Review 26:429–39.
   1981   Aging in a Changing Society, second edition. New York: Franklin Watts.

11   Blauner, Robert
   1968   Death and social structure. Psychiatry 29:378–94.

10   Blazer, Dan, and Erdman Palmore
   1976   Religion and aging in a longitudinal panel. The Gerontologist 16:82–85.

8, 18   Bleiweiss, L., and S. Simson
   1976   Building a comprehensive geriatric health care system: a case study. Journal of Community Health 2:141–52.

7, 8   Blenkner, Margaret
   1965   Social work and family relationships in later life with some thoughts on filial maturity. Pp. 46–59 in Ethel Shanas and Gordon F. Streib (eds.), Social Structure and the Family. Englewood Cliffs, N.J.: Prentice-Hall.

8   Blenkner, Margaret, Edna Wasser, and Martin Bloom
   1967   Protective Services for Older People: Progress Report for 1966–67. Cleveland, Ohio: The Benjamin Rose Institute.

10   Bley, N., M. Goodman, D. Dye, and B. Harel
   1972   Characteristics of aged participants and non-participants in age-segregated leisure program. The Gerontologist 12:368–70.

5   Block, Jack
   1975   Change and sameness in personality development; unwarranted conclusions. International Journal of Aging and Human Development 6:277–81.

9   Block, Marilyn
   1982   Professional women: work pattern as a correlate of retirement satisfaction. Pp. 183–94 in M. Szinovacz (ed.), Women's Retirement. Beverly Hills, Calif.: Sage.

8   Blonsky, Lawrence E.
   1974   Problems in development of a community action program for the elderly. The Gerontologist 14:394–401.

5   Bloom, Kenneth L.
   1961   Age and self-concept. American Journal of Psychiatry 118:534–38.

5   Bloom, Martin
   1964   Life-span analysis: a theoretical framework for behavioral science research. Journal of Human Relations 12:538–54.

8   Bloom, Martin, and M. Nielsen
   1971   The older person in need of protective services. Social Casework 52:500–09.

4   Blumenthal, H. T., and Aline W. Berns
   1964   Autoimmunity and aging. Pp. 289–342 in Bernard L. Strehler (ed.), Advances in Gerontological Research. Volume 1. New York: Academic Press.

12   Bock, E. Wilbur
   1972   Aging and suicide: the significance of marital, kinship, and alternative relations. Family Coordinator 21:71–80.

15   Bogue, Donald J.
        1963   Skid Row in American Cities. Chicago: University of Chicago Community and Family Studies Center.

15   Bohannan, Paul
        1981   Food of old people in center-city hotels. Pp. 185–200 in Christine L. Fry (ed.), Dimensions: Aging, Culture, and Health. New York: Praeger.

11   Bok, S.
        1973   Euthanasia and the care of the dying. Bioscience 23:461–66.

12   Borgatta, Edgar F., Rhonda J. V. Montgomery, and Marie L. Borgatta
        1982   Alcohol use and abuse, life crisis events, and the elderly. Research on Aging 4:378–408.

13   Borges, Marilyn A., and Linda J. Dutton
        1976   Attitudes toward aging: increasing optimism found with age. The Gerontologist 16:220–24.

7   Borland, Delores C.
        1982   A cohort analysis approach to the empty-nest syndrome among three ethnic groups of women: a theoretical position. Journal of Marriage and the Family 44:117–29.

11   Bornstein, P. E., and others
        1973   The depression of widowhood after thirteen months. British Journal of Psychiatry 122:561–66.

1   Bornstein, Robert, and Mark T. Smircina
        1982   The status of the empirical support for the hypothesis of increased variability in aging populations. The Gerontologist 22:258–60.

8, 18   Borup, Jerry H.
        1981   Relocation: attitudes, information network and problems encountered. The Gerontologist 21:501–11.

8, 18   Borup, Jerry H., Daniel T. Gallego, and Pamela G. Heffernam
        1980   Relocation: its effect on health, functioning and mortality. The Gerontologist 20:468–79.

16   Borzilleri, Thomas C.
        1978   The need for a separate Consumer Price Index for older persons. A review and new evidence. The Gerontologist 18:230–36.

9, 10   Bossé, Raymond, and David J. Ekerdt
        1981   Change in self-perception of leisure activities with retirement. The Gerontologist 21:650–54.

     Botwinick, Jack
5   1959   Drives, expectancies, and emotions. Pp. 739–68 in James E. Birren (ed.), Handbook of Aging and the Individual. Chicago: University of Chicago Press.

5   1967   Cognitive Processes in Maturity and Old Age. New York: Springer.

5   1977   Intellectual abilities. Pp. 580–605 in James E. Birren and K. Warner Schaie (eds.), Handbook of the Psychology of Aging. New York: Van Nostrand Reinhold.

5   1978   Aging and Behavior, second edition. New York: Springer.

     Botwinick, Jack, and M. Storandt
8   Bourestom, Norman, and Sandra Tars
        1974   Alterations in life patterns following nursing home relocation. The Gerontologist 14:506–10.

5   1974a   Cardiovascular status, depressive affect, and other factors in reaction time. Journal of Gerontology 29:543–48.

5   1974b   Memory, Related Functions and Age. Springfield, Ill.: Charles C. Thomas.

6   Bourque, Linda Brookover, and Kurt W. Back
    1977   Life graphs and life events. Journal of Gerontology 32:669–74.
2   Bouvier, Leon F.
    1974   The demography of aging. Pp. 37–46 in W. C. Bier (ed.), Aging: Its Challenge to the Individual and to Society. New York: Fordham University Press.
5   Bowles, Nancy L., and Leonard W. Poon
    1982   An analysis of the effect of aging on recognition memory. Journal of Gerontology 37: 212–19.
    Boyd, Rosamonde R.
7   1969a   Emerging roles of the four-generation family. Pp. 35–50 in Rosamonde R. Boyd and Charles G. Oakes (eds.), Foundations of Practical Gerontology. Columbia, So. Carolina: University of South Carolina Press.
7   1969b   The valued grandparent: a changing social role. Pp. 90–102 in Wilma Donahue (ed.), Living in the Multigenerational Family. Ann Arbor, Michigan: University of Michigan/Wayne State University Institute of Gerontology.
9   Bracey, H. E.
    1966   In Retirement. Baton Rouge: Louisiana State University Press.
5   Bradley, Robert H., and Roger Webb
    1976   Age-related differences in locus of control orientation in three behavior domains. Human Development 19:49–55.
8   Brady, Dorothy S.
    1965   Age and Income Distribution. Washington, D.C.: U.S. Government Printing Office.
7   Branch, Laurence G., and Alan M. Jette
    1983   Elders' use of informal long-term care assistance. The Gerontologist 23:51–56.
8, 12   Brand, Frederick N., and Richard T. Smith
    1974   Life adjustment and relocation of the elderly. Journal of Gerontology 29:336–40.
9   Breen, Leonard Z.
    1963   Retirement—norms, behavior, and functional aspects of normative behavior. Pp. 381–88 in Richard H. Williams, Clark Tibbits, and Wilma Donahue (eds.), Processes of Aging. Volume 2. New York: Atherton Press.
16   Brennan, Michael J., Philip Taft, and Mark Schupack
    1967   The Economics of Age. New York: Norton
8   Breslau, Naomi, and Marie R. Haug
    1972   The elderly aid the elderly: the Senior Friends Program. Social Security Bulletin 35(11):9–15.
7   Brickel, Clark M.
    1981   A review of the roles of pet animals in psychotherapy and with the elderly. International Journal of Aging and Human Development 12:119–28.
5   Brim, Orville
    1968   Adult socialization. Pp. 182–226 in John Clausen (ed.), Socialization in Society. Boston: Little, Brown.
5   Brim, Orville, and Stanton Wheeler
    1966   Socialization After Childhood. New York: Wiley.
16   Brinker, Paul A.
    1968   Economic Insecurity and Social Security. New York: Appleton-Century-Crofts.
5   Brinley, G. F.
    1965   Cognitive sets and accuracy of performance in the elderly. Pp. 114–49 in Alan T. Welford and James E. Birren (eds.), Behavior, Aging and the Nervous System. Springfield, Ill.: Charles C. Thomas.

5   Britton, Joseph H.
        1972   Personality Changes in Aging. New York: Springer.
7   Britton, Joseph H., and Jean O. Britton
        1967   The middle-aged and older rural person and his family. Pp. 44–74 in E. Grant You-
                mans (ed.), Older Rural Americans. Lexington, Kentucky. University of Kentucky.
10   Britton, Joseph H., William G. Mather, and Alice Lansing
        1962   Expectations for older persons in a rural community: community participation. Rural
                Sociology 27:387–95.
        Brody, Elaine M.
8, 18   1971   Long-term care for the elderly: optimums, options and opportunities. Journal of
                American Geriatrics Society 19:482–94.
8, 18   1977   Long-Term Care of Older People: A Practical Guide. New York: Human Sciences
                Press.
7   1981   Women in the middle and family help to older people. The Gerontologist 21:471–80.
8   Brody, Elaine M., and C. Cole
        1971   Deferred status applicants to a voluntary home for aged. The Gerontologist 11:219–25.
7, 8   Brody, Elaine M., and Geraldine M. Spark
        1966   Institutionalization of the aged; a family crisis. Family Process 5:76–90.
4   Brody, Harold, and N. Vijayashankar
        1977   Anatomical changes in the nervous system. Pp. 241–61 in Caleb E. Finch and Leonard
                Hayflick (eds.), Handbook of the Biology of Aging. New York: Van Nostrand Rein-
                hold.
8, 18   Brody, Stanley J.
        1973   Comprehensive health care for the elderly: an analysis. The continuum of medical,
                health, and social services for the aged. The Gerontologist 13:412–18.
5   Bromley, D. B.
        1974   The Psychology of Human Ageing, second edition. Baltimore: Penquin Books.
8   Bronson, E. P.
        1972   An experiment in intermediate housing facilities for the elderly. The Gerontologist 12:
                22–26.
7   Brown, A. S.
        1974   Satisfying relationships for the elderly and their patterns of disengagement. The Geron-
                tologist 14:258–62.
16   Brown, J. D.
        1972   An American Philosophy of Social Security: Evolution and Issues. Princeton, N.J.:
                Princeton University Press.
12   Brown, Julia S., Bette S. Perman, and Jeri L. Dobbs
        1981   The will-to-live: dependence on a prosthesis for survival. Research on Aging 3:182–201.
7   Brown, Robert G.
        1960   Family structure and social isolation of older persons. Journal of Gerontology 15:170–
                74.
9   Brubaker, Timothy H., and Charles B. Hennon
        1982   Responsibility for household tasks: comparing dual-earner and dual-retired marriages.
                Pp. 205–20 in M. Szinovacz (ed.), Women's Retirement. Beverly Hills, Calif.: Sage.
13   Brubaker, Timothy H., and Edward A. Powers
        1976   The stereotype of old: a review and alternative approach. Journal of Gerontology
                31:441–47.
5   Bruce, Patricia R., Andrew C. Cayne, and Jack Botwinick
        1982   Adult age differences in metamemory. Journal of Gerontology 37:354–57.

1, 8   Bruhn, J. G.
      1971   An ecological perspective of aging. The Gerontologist 11:318–21.

13   Buchholz, Michael, and Jack Bynum
      1982   Newspaper presentation of America's aged: a content analyses of image and role. The Gerontologist 22:83–88.

6   Buhler, Charlotte, and D. Massarik (eds.)
      1968   The Course of Human Life. New York: Springer.

10, 12   Bull, C. N., and J. B. Aucoin
      1975   Voluntary association participation and life satisfaction: a replication note. Journal of Gerontology 30:73–76.

Bultena, Gordon L.
8, 9   1969a Health patterns of aged migrant retirees. Journal of the American Geriatrics Society 17:1127–31.

12   1969b Life continuity and morale in old age. The Gerontologist 4(4, part 1):251–53.

7   1969c The relationship of occupational status to friendship ties in three planned retirement communities. Journal of Gerontology 24:461–64.

7   1969d Rural-urban differences in family interaction of the aged. Rural Sociology 34:5–15.

12   1974 Structural effects on the morale of the aged: a comparison of age-segregated and age-integrated communities. Pp. 18–31 in Jaber F. Gubrium (ed.), Late Life. Communities and Environmental Policy. Springfield, Ill.: Charles C. Thomas.

12   Bultena, Gordon L., and R. Oyler
      1971   Effects of health on disengagement and morale. Aging and Human Development 2:142–48.

Bultena, Gordon L., and Vivian Wood
8   1969a The American retirement community: bane or blessing? Journal of Gerontology 24:209–17.

13   1969b Normative attitudes toward the aged role among migrant and nonmigrant retirees. The Gerontologist 9(3, part 1):204–08.

11, 12   Bunch, J.
      1972   Recent bereavement in relation to suicide. Journal of Psychosomatic Research 16:361–66.

3   Burgess, Ernest W. (ed.)
      1960   Aging in Western Societies. Chicago: University of Chicago Press.

13   Burke, Judith Lee
      1981   Young children's attitudes and perceptions of older adults. International Journal of Aging and Human Development 14:205–22.

8   Burnham, Clinton E.
      1974   Edentulous persons: United States—1971. Vital and Health Statistics, Series 10, No. 89.

Burnside, Irene M.
8, 18   1971 Long-term group work with hospitalized aged. The Gerontologist 11:213–18.

5, 7   1975 (ed.) Sexuality and Aging. Los Angeles, Calif.: Ethel Percy Andrus Gerontology Center, University of Southern California.

4, 8, 18   1981 Nursing and the Aged, second edition. New York: McGraw-Hill.

7   Burr, Wesley
      1970   Satisfaction with various aspects of marriage over the life cycle: a random middle-class sample. Journal of Marriage and the Family 32:29–37.

7   Burr, Wesley, R. Hill, I. F. Nye, and I. L. Reiss
       1979   Contemporary Theories About the Family, Volumes 1 and 2. New York: Free Press.

5   Busse, Ewald W., and Dan G. Blazer (eds.)
       1980   Handbook of Geriatric Psychiatry. New York: Van Nostrand Reinhold.

5   Busse, Ewald W., and Eric Pfeiffer (eds.)
       1969   Behavior and Adaptation in Late Life. Boston: Little, Brown.

18   Butler, P. A.
       1980   Nursing Home Quality of Care Enforcement. Washington, D.C.: Legal Services Corporation.

      Butler, Robert N.

5, 12 1963   The life review: an interpretation of reminiscence in the aged. Psychiatry 26:65–76.

5   1968   Patterns of psychological health and psychiatric illness in retirement. Pp. 27–41 in Frances M. Carp (ed.), The Retirement Process. Washington, D.C.: U.S. Government Printing Office.

13   1969   Age-ism: another form of bigotry. The Gerontologist 9:243–46.

8, 17 1973   Public interest report No. 9. How to grow old and poor in an affluent society. International Journal of Aging and Human Development 4:277–79.

12   1974   Successful aging and the role of the life review. Journal of American Geriatric Society 22:529–35.

13   1975   Why Survive? Being Old in America. New York: Harper and Row.

19   1980   Kent Lecture, 1979: the alliance of advocacy with science. The Gerontologist 20:154–62.

      Butler, Robert N., and Myrna I. Lewis

5, 7   1976   Sex After Sixty: A Guide for Men and Women for Their Later Years. New York: Harper and Row.

5, 12 1977   Aging and Mental Health, second edition. St. Louis, Missouri: C. V. Mosby.

13   Butsch, Richard, and Ava Baron
       1980   Reviewing the reviews: a note—the portrayal of elderly in films and reviews. The Gerontologist 20:602–03.

8   Byerts, T., J. Gertman, A. M. Gillemard, M. P. Lawton, M. Leeds, R. Rajie, and F. M. Carp
       1972   Transportation. The Gerontologist 12(2, part 2):11–16.

      Cain, Leonard D., Jr.

6   1964   Life course and social structure. Pp. 272–309 in Robert E. L. Faris (ed.), Handbook of Modern Sociology. Chicago: Rand McNally.

2, 6   1967   Age status and generational phenomena: the new old people in contemporary America. The Gerontologist 7:83–92.

3   1968   Aging and the character of our times. The Gerontologist 8:250–58.

17   1974   The growing importance of legal age in determining the status of the elderly. The Gerontologist 14:167–74.

17   1975   The young and the old: coalition or conflict ahead. American Behavioral Scientist 19:166–75.

9   1976a   Mandatory retirement: the Murgia decision and its likely consequences. Industrial Gerontology 3:233–50.

17   1976b   Aging and the law. Pp. 342–68 in Robert H. Binstock and Ethel Shanas (eds.), Handbook of Aging and the Social Sciences. New York: Van Nostrand Reinhold.

8   Callison, James C.
       1974   Early experience under the supplemental security income program. Social Security Bulletin 37(6):3–11.

18   Calsyn, Robert J., Esther O. Fergus, and Jonathan L. York

1977   Interrupted time series analysis: a research technique for evaluating social programs for the elderly. Journal of Gerontology 32:89–96.

Cameron, Paul

12   1967   Ego strength and happiness of the aged. Journal of Gerontology 22:199–202.

18   1972a   Pre-Medicare beliefs about the generations regarding medicine and health. Journal of Gerontology 27:536–39.

12   1972b   Stereotypes about generational fun and happiness versus self-appraised fun and happiness. The Gerontologist 12:120–23, 190.

5, 13   1973   Which generation is believed to be intellectually superior and which generation believes itself to be intellectually superior? International Journal of Aging and Human Development 4:257–70.

12   1975   Mood as an indicant of happiness: age, sex, social class, and situational differences. Journal of Gerontology 30:216–24.

5, 13   1976   Masculinity/femininity of the generations: as self-reported and as stereotypically appraised. International Journal of Aging and Human Development 7:143–51.

5, 7   Cameron, Paul, and H. Biber

1973   Sexual thought throughout the life-span. The Gerontologist 13:144–47.

11   Cameron, Paul, L. Stewart, and H. Biber

1973   Consciousness of death across the life-span. Journal of Gerontology 28:92–95.

5   Cameron, Paul, L. Stewart, L. Craig, and L. J. Eppelamn

1973   Thing versus self versus other mental orientation across the life-span: a note. British Journal of Psychology 64:283–86.

17   Campbell, Angus

1971   Politics through the life cycle. The Gerontologist 11(2, part 1):112–17.

5   Campbell, Byron A., and Vahram Haroutunian

1981   Effects of age on long-term memory: retention of fixed interval responding. Journal of Gerontology 36:388–41.

17   Campbell, John Creighton, and John Strate

1981   Are old people conservative? The Gerontologist 21:580–91.

8, 18   Campbell, M. E.

1971   Study of the attitudes of nursing personnel toward the geriatric patient. Nursing Research 20:147–51.

1   Campbell, Richard T., and Elizabeth Mutran

1982   Analyzing panel data in studies of aging: applications of the LISREL model. Research on Aging 4:3–42.

8, 16   Campbell, Rita R.

1977   Social Security; Promise and Reality. Stanford, Calif.: Hoover Institute Press.

8   Cantelli, Edmund J., and June L. Shmelzer (eds.)

1970   Transportation and Aging: Selected Issues. Washington, D.C.: U.S. Government Printing Office.

Cantor, Marjorie H.

7   1975   Life space and the social support system of the inner city elderly of New York. The Gerontologist 15:23–27.

7   1979   Neighbors and friends: an overlooked resource in the informal support system. Research on Aging 1:434–63.

7   1980   The informal support system: its relevance in the lives of the elderly. Pp. 131–46 in N. G. McClusky and E. F. Borgatta (eds.), Aging and Society: Current Research and Policy Perspectives. Beverly Hills, Calif.: Sage.

8 Cantor, Marjorie H., and Mary Mayer
  1976 Health and the inner city elderly. The Gerontologist 16:17–24.

9, 16 Cantrell, R. Stephen, and Robert L. Clark
  1980 Retirement policy and promotional prospects. The Gerontologist 20:575–80.

17 Carlie, Michael K.
  1969 The politics of age: interest group or social movement? The Gerontologist 9(4, part 1):259–63.

Carp, Frances M.

8 1966a A Future for the Aged: Victoria Plaza and Its Residents. Austin: University of Texas Press.

8 1966b Effects of improved housing on the lives of older people. Pp. 147–67 in Frances M. Carp and W. M. Burnett (eds.), Patterns of Living and Housing of Middle-Aged and Older People. Washington, D.C.: U.S. Public Health Service.

5, 13 1967 Attitudes of old persons toward themselves and toward others. Journal of Gerontology 22:308–12.

8, 14 1968a Factors in the Utilization of Services by the Mexican-American Elderly. Palo Alto, Calif.: American Institutes for Research.

12 1968b Some components of disengagement. Journal of Gerontology 23:382–86.

9 1968c The Retirement Process. Washington, D.C.: U.S. Department of Health, Education and Welfare.

9, 10 1968d Differences among older workers, volunteers, and persons who are neither. Journal of Gerontology 23:497–501.

10, 12 1968e Person-situation congruence in engagement. The Gerontologist 8:184–88.

5 1969a The psychology of aging. Pp. 100–16 in Rosamonde R. Boyd and C. G. Oakes (eds.), Foundations of Practical Gerontology, second edition. Columbia, So. Carolina: University of South Carolina Press.

8 1969b Use of community services and social integration of the aged. Pp. 169–76 in Frances C. Jeffers (ed.), Duke University Council on Aging and Human Development: Proceedings of Seminars 1965–69. Durham, No. Carolina: Duke University Center for the Study of Aging and Human Development.

1 1969c Compound criteria in gerontological research. Journal of Gerontology 24:341–47.

8 1969d Housing and minority-group elderly. The Gerontologist 9:20–24.

2 1970 The mobility of retired people. Pp. 23–41 in Edmund J. Cantelli and June L. Shmelzer (eds.), Transportation and Aging: Selected Issues. Washington, D.C.: U.S. Government Printing Office.

19 1971a Research goals and priorities in gerontology. The Gerontologist 11(1, part 1):67.

9 1971b (ed.) Retirement. New York: Behavioral Publications.

8 1972a Retired people as automobile passengers. The Gerontologist 12:66–72.

8 1972b The mobility of older slum-dwellers. The Gerontologist 12:57–65.

8 1972c Mobility among members of an established retirement community. The Gerontologist 12:48–56.

5 1974 Reactions to gifts as indicators of personality-behavior traits in the elderly. International Journal of Aging and Human Development 5:265–80.

8 1975a Long-range satisfaction with housing. The Gerontologist 15:68–72.

8 1975b Life-style and location within the city. The Gerontologist 15:27–34.

8, 12 1975c Impact of improved housing on morale life satisfaction. The Gerontologist 15:511–15.

5 1975d Ego-defense or cognitive consistency effects on environmental evaluations. Journal of Gerontology 30:707–11.

8 1976a Housing and living environments of older people. Pp. 244–71 in Robert H. Binstock

and Ethel Shanas (eds.), Handbook of Aging and the Social Sciences. New York: Van Nostrand Reinhold.

8   1976b User evaluation of housing for the elderly. The Gerontologist 16:102–11.

10   1978–79 Effects of the living environment on activity and use of time. International Journal of Aging and Human Development 9:75–91.

Carp, Frances M., and Abraham Carp

5, 12   1981   Age, deprivation, and personal competence: effects on satisfaction. Research on Aging 3:279–98.

8   1982a The ideal residential area. Research on Aging 4:411–39.

12   1982b Test of a model of domain satisfactions and well-being: equity considerations. Research on Aging 4:503–22.

12   Carp, Frances M., Abraham Carp, and Roger Millsap

1982   Equity and satisfaction among the elderly. International Journal of Aging and Human Development 15:151–66.

8   Carp, Frances M., and Eunice Kataoka

1976   Health care problems of the elderly of San Francisco's Chinatown. The Gerontologist 16:30–38.

11   Cartwright, A., L. Hockey, and J. L. Anderson

1971   Life Before Death. London: Routledge and Kegan Paul.

8   Casey, G. M.

1971   Public library service to the aging. American Libraries 2:999–1004.

11   Cassell, E. J.

1973   Permission to die. Bioscience 23:475–78.

12   Cath, Stanley H.

1975   The orchestration of disengagement. International Journal of Aging and Human Development 6:199–213.

7   Cavan, Ruth S.

1956   Family tensions between the old and the middle-aged. Marriage and Family Living 18: 323–27.

12   Cavan, Ruth S., E. W. Burgess, Robert J. Havighurst, and H. Goldhamer

1949   Personal Adjustment in Old Age. Chicago: Science Research Associates.

7   Chappell, Neena L.

1983   Informal support networks among the elderly. Research on Aging 5:77–100.

7   Chappell, Neena L., and Laurel A. Strain

1982   Confidants: do they make a difference in quality of life? Research on Aging 4:479–502.

Charles, Don C.

9   1971   Effect of participation in a preretirement program. The Gerontologist 11(1, part 1):24–28.

5   1973   Explaining intelligence in adulthood: the role of life history. The Gerontologist 13:483–88.

5   Charness, Neil

1981   Visual short-term memory and aging in chess players. Journal of Gerontology 36:615–19.

12   Chatfield, Walter

1977   Economic and sociological factors influencing life satisfaction of the aged. Journal of Gerontology 32:593–99.

12   Chellam, Grace

1977–78 Awareness of death and self-engagement in later life: the engagement continuum. International Journal of Aging and Human Development 8:111–27.

Chen, Yung-Ping

8   1966a Economic poverty: the special case of the aged. The Gerontologist 6:39–45.

8   1966b Low income, early retirement and tax policy. The Gerontologist 6:35–38.

Cherlin, Andrew

7   1977   The effect of children on marital dissolution. Demography 14:265–72.

7   1978   Remarriage as an incomplete institution. American Journal of Sociology 84: 634–50.

2, 7   1983   Changing family and household: contemporary lessons from historical research. Annual Review of Sociology 9:51:66.

7, 11   Chevan, A., and J. H. Korson

1972   The widowed who live alone: an examination of social and demographic factors. Social Forces 51:45–53.

8   Chinn, A. B. (ed.)

1971   Working with Older People: A Guide to Practice. Volume 4. Clinical Aspects of Aging. PHS Publication No. 1459. Washington, D.C.: U.S. Government Printing Office.

Chiriboga, David A.

6, 12   1982a An examination of life events as possible antecedents to change. Journal of Gerontology 37:595–601.

7   1982b Adaptation to marital separation in later and earlier life. Journal of Gerontology 37:109 –14.

5   Chiriboga, David, and Majda Thurnher

1975   Concept of self. Pp. 62–83 in Marjorie F. Lowenthal, Majda Thurnher, David Chiriboga, and Associates (eds.). The Four Stages of Life. San Francisco: Jossey-Bass.

Chown, Sheila M.

5   1961   Age and the rigidities. Journal of Gerontology 16:353–62.

9   1972   The effect of flexibility-rigidity and age on adaptability in job performance. Industrial Gerontology 13:105–21.

5   Chown, Sheila M., and Klaus F. Reigel (eds.)

1968   Psychological Functioning in the Normal Aging and Senile Aged. New York: S. Karger.

10   Christ, Edwin A.

1965   The "retired" stamp collector: economic and other functions of a systematized leisure activity. Pp. 93–112 in Arnold M. Rose and Warren A. Peterson (eds.), Older People and Their Social World. Philadelphia: F. A. Davis.

5, 7   Christenson, Cornelia V., and John H. Gagnon

1965   Sexual behavior in a group of older women. Journal of Gerontology 20:351–56.

5, 7   Christenson, Cornelia V., and A. B. Johnson

1973   Sexual patterns in a group of older never-married women. Journal of Geriatric Psychiatry 6:80–98.

5   Christenson, James A.

1977   Generational value differences. The Gerontologist 17:367–74.

6, 7   Chudacoff, H. P., and Tamara K. Haraven

1979   From the empty nest to family dissolution: life course transitions into old age. Journal of Family History 4:69–83.

5   Cicirelli, Victor G.

1980   Relationship of family background variables to locus of control in the elderly. The Gerontologist 35:108–14.

5   Cijfer, E.

1966   An experiment on some differences in logical thinking between Dutch medical people, over and under the age of 35. Acta Psychologica 25:159–71.

18   Ciliberto, David J., Jack Levin, and Arnold Arluke
      1981   Nurses' diagnostic stereotyping of the elderly: the case of organic brain syndrome. Research on Aging 3:299–310.

9, 10   Clague, Evan
      1971   Work and leisure for older workers. The Gerontologist 11(1, part 2):9–20.

9, 16   Clague, Evan, B. Palli, and L. Kramer
      1971   The Aging Worker and the Union: Employment and Retirement of Middle-Aged and Older Workers. New York: Praeger.

19   Clark, Margaret
      1967   The anthropology of aging, a new area for studies of culture and personality. The Gerontologist 7:55–64.

8, 11   Clark, Margaret, and Barbara Anderson
      1967   Culture and Aging. Springfield, Ill.: Charles C. Thomas.

13   Clark, Martha
      1980   The poetry of aging: views of old age in contemporary American poetry. The Gerontologist 20:188–91.

16   Clark, Robert, Juanita Kreps, and Joseph Spengler
      1978   Economics of aging: a survey. Journal of Economic Literature 16:919–62.

17, 19   Clark, Robert, and John A. Menefee
      1981   Federal expenditures for the elderly: past and future. The Gerontologist 21:132–37.

2, 16,
19   Clark, Robert, and Joseph Spengler
      1978   Population aging in the twenty-first century. Aging 6–13,279–80.

      Clausen, John
6   1968   (ed.) Socialization in Society. Boston: Little, Brown.
6   1976   Glimpses into the social world of middle age. International Journal of Aging and Human Development 7:99–106.

      Clayton, P. J.
11   1973   The clinical morbidity of the first year of bereavement: a review. Comparative Psychiatry 14:151–57.
11   1974   Mortality and morbidity in the first year of widowhood. Archives of General Psychiatry 30:747–50.
11   1975   The effect of living alone on bereavement symptoms. American Journal of Psychiatry 132:133–37.

5   Clayton, Vivian
      1982   Wisdom and intelligence: the nature and function of knowledge in the later years. International Journal of Aging and Human Development 15:315–21.

9, 16   Clelland, P. G.
      1973   Age discrimination law: rights and responsibilities of employers and individuals. Industrial Gerontology 18:53–64.

      Clemente, Frank
9   1973   Age and academic mobility. The Gerontologist 13:453–56.
17   1975   Age and the perception of national priorities. The Gerontologist 15:61–63.

5   Clemente, Frank, and Jon Hendricks
      1973   A further look at the relationship between age and productivity. The Gerontologist 13:106–10.

8, 15   Clemente, Frank, and Michael B. Kleiman
      1976   Fear of crime among the aged. The Gerontologist 16:207–10.

12   Clemente, Frank, and W. J. Sauer
        1974   Race and morale of the urban aged. The Gerontologist 13:342–44.

2, 3   Clemente, Frank, and G. F. Summers
        1973   Industrial development and the elderly: a longitudinal analysis. Journal of Gerontology 28:479–83.

10   Clemente, Frank, Patricia A. Rexroad, and Carl Hirsch
        1975   The participation of the black aged in voluntary associations. Journal of Gerontology 30:469–72.

7, 11   Cleveland, William P., and Daniel T. Gianturco
        1976   Remarriage probability after widowhood: a retrospective method. Journal of Gerontology 31:99–103.

5   Clifford, M. E.
        1972   Learning ability and age: a bibliography for training programs. Industrial Gerontology 12:50–68.

15   Clinard, Marshall B.
        1974   Sociology of Deviant Behavior. New York: Holt, Rinehart and Winston.

5, 9   Clopton, Will
        1973   Personality and career change. Industrial Gerontology 17:9–17.

7, 12   Cobb, Sydney
        1976   Social support as a moderator of life stress. Psychosomatic Medicine 38:300–14.

8, 19   Cobb, Sidney, and John Fulton
        1981   An epidemiologic gaze into the crystal ball of the elderly. Pp.75–90 in Sara B. Kiesler et al. (eds.), Aging: Social Change. New York: Academic Press.

5   Coe, Rodney M.
        1965   Self-conception and institutionalization. Pp. 225–43 in Arnold M. Rose and Warren A. Peterson (eds.); Older People and Their Social World. Philadelphia: F. A. Davis.

8, 10   Coe, Rodney M., and Elizabeth Barnhill
        1965   Social participation and health of the aged. Pp. 21–23 in Arnold M. Rose and Warren A. Peterson (eds.), Older People and Their Social World. Philadelphia: F. A. Davis.

8   Coet, L., and R. C. Tindall
        1974   Definition of "handicap" as a function of age and sex. Psychological Reports 34:1197–98.

8, 18   Coffman, Thomas L.
        1981   Relocation and survival of institutionalized aged: a re-examination of the evidence. The Gerontologist 21:483–500.

2   Cohen, Burton H.
        1964   Family patterns of mortality and life span. Quarterly Review of Biology 39:130–81.

Cohen, Carl I., and Jay Sokolovsky
15   1979   Health-seeking behavior and social network of the aged living in single-room occupancy hotels. Journal of the American Geriatrics Society 27:270–78.
8, 15   1980   Social engagement versus isolation: the case of the aged in SRO hotels. The Gerontologist 20:36–44.

7   Cohen, Carl I., and Henry Rajkowski
        1982   What's in a friend? Substantive and theoretical issues. The Gerontologist 22:261–66.

Cohen, Elias S.
19   1974   Legal research issues on aging. The Gerontologist 14:263–67.
8, 18   1981   Legal issues in "transfer trauma" and their impact. The Gerontologist 21:520–22.

16   Cohen, Wilbur J.
        1970   Social Security—the first thirty-five years. Pp. 1–32 in Occasional Papers in Gerontolo-

gy, Number 7. Ann Arbor, Michigan: University of Michigan-Wayne State University
Institute of Gerontology.

13 Collette-Pratt, Clara
    1976   Attitudinal predictors of devaluation of old age in a multigenerational sample. Journal
          of Gerontology 31:193–97.

  Comfort, Alex
4   1964a Ageing: The Biology of Senescence. New York: Holt, Rinehart and Winston.
4   1964b The Process of Aging. New York: New American Library.
13   1976   Age prejudice in America. Social Policy 7(3):3–8.

17 Congressional Budget Office
    1983   Major Legislative Changes in Human Resources Programs Since January, 1981: Staff
          Memorandum.

12 Conner, Karen A., and Edward A. Powers
    1975   Structural effects and life satisfaction among the aged. International Journal of Aging
          and Human Development 6:321–27.

9 Connor, Catherine L., R. Patricia Walsh, Debra K. Litzelman, and Maria G. Alvarez
    1978   Evaluation of job applicants; the effects of age versus success. Journal of Gerontology
          33:246–52.

8, 15 Cook, Fay L., and Thomas D. Cook
    1976   Evaluating the rhetoric of crisis: a case study of criminal victimization of the elderly.
          Social Service Review 50:632–46.

8, 15 Cook, Fay L., Wesley G. Skogan, Thomas D. Cook, and George Antunes
    1978   Criminal victimization of the elderly: the physical and economic consequences. The
          Gerontologist 18:338–49.

8, 10 Cook, T. C., Jr. (ed.)
    1976   The Religious Sector Explores Its Mission in Aging. Athens, Georgia: National Inter-
          faith Coalition on Aging.
8, 10   983   Religion and aging. Generations, Fall, 1983.

18 Cooper, Barbara S., and Mary F. McGee
    1971   Medical care outlays for three age groups: young, intermediate, and aged. Social Secu-
          rity Bulletin 34(5):3–14.

18 Cooper, Barbara S., and Paula A. Piro
    1974   Age differences in medical care spending, fiscal year 1973. Social Security Bulletin 37:3
          –14.

18 Corbin, Mildred, and Aaron Krute
    1975   Some aspects of Medicare experience with group-practice prepayment plans. Social Se-
          curity Bulletin 38(3):3–11.

5 Corso, John F.
    1977   Auditory perception and communication. Pp. 535–53 in James E. Birren and K. War-
          ner Schaie (eds.), Handbook of the Psychology of Aging. New York: Van Nostrand
          Reinhold.

8 Costa, Frank J., and Marnie Sweet
    1976   Barrier-free environments for older Americans. The Gerontologist 16:404–09.

  Costa, Paul T., Jr., and Robert R. McCrae
5   1977–78 Age differences in personality structure revisited; studies in validity, stability, and
          change. International Journal of Aging and Human Development 8:261–75.
5   1978   Objective personality assessment. Pp. 119–43 in Martha Storandt, I. C. Seigler, and M.
          F. Elias (eds.), The Clinical Psychology of Aging. New York: Plenum.

12 Costa, Paul T., Robert R. McCrae, and Arthur H. Norris
    1981   Personal adjustment to aging: longitudinal prediction from neuroticism and extrover-
          sion. Journal of Gerontology 36:78–85.

5, 6   Costello, Mary T., and John A. Menacham
    1981   Sex differences in perceptions of aging. International Journal of Aging and Human Development 12:283–90.

Cottrell, Fred
2   1955   Energy and Society. New York: McGraw-Hill.
17   1960a   Governmental functions and the politics of age. Pp. 624–65 in Clark Tibbitts (ed.), Handbook of Social Gerontology. Chicago: University of Chicago Press.
2   1960b   The technological and societal basis of aging. Pp. 92–119 in Clark Tibbitts (ed.), Handbook of Social Gerontology. Chicago: University of Chicago Press.
17   1966   Aging and the political system. Pp. 77–113 in John C. McKinney and Frank T. de Vyver (eds.), Aging and Social Policy. New York: Appleton-Century-Crofts.
17   1968   Political deprivation and the aged. In Perspectives on Human Deprivation. Washington, D.C.: National Institute of Mental Health.
17, 19   1971a   Government and Non-Government Organizations. Washington, D.C.: White House Conference on Aging.
8   1971b   Transportation of older people in a rural community. Sociological Focus 5:29–40.

5, 9   Cottrell, Fred, and Robert C. Atchley
    1969   Women in Retirement: A Preliminary Report. Oxford, Ohio: Scripps Foundation.

10   Cousins, Norman
    1968   Art, adrenalin, and the enjoyment of living. Saturday Review, April 20, pp. 20–24.

12   Covey, Herbert C.
    1981   A reconceptualization of continuity theory: some preliminary thoughts. The Gerontologist 21:628–33.

Cowgill, Donald O.
3   1972   A theory of aging in cross-cultural perspective. Pp. 1–14 in Donald O. Cowgill and Lowell Holmes (eds.), Aging and Modernization. New York: Appleton-Century-Crofts.
2   1974a   The aging of populations and societies. Pp. 1–18 in Frederick R. Eisele (ed.), Political Consequences of Aging. Philadelphia: American Academy of Political and Social Sciences.
3   1974b   Aging and modernization: a revision on the theory. Pp. 123–46 in Jaber F. Gubrium (ed.), Late Life: Communities and Environmental Policy. Springfield, Ill.: Charles C. Thomas.
12   1976   A previous incarnation of disengagement theory: an historical note. The Gerontologist 16:377–78.

10   Cowgill, Donald O., and Norma Baulch
    1962   The use of leisure time by older people. The Gerontologist 2:47–50.

2   Cowgill, Donald O., and Lowell Holmes
    1972   Aging and Modernization. New York: Appleton-Century-Crofts.

11   Cox, Peter R., and J. R. Ford
    1964   The mortality of widows shortly after widowhood. Lancet 1:163–64.

Cribier, F.
2, 9   1970a   Les migrations de retraite en France: materiaux pour une geographie du troisieme age. Bulletin, Association de Geographes Francais 381:1–4.
2, 9   1970b   La migration de retraite des fonctionnaires Parisiens. Bulletin, Association Geographes Francais 381:16–24.

Crittenden, John
17   1962   Aging and party affiliation. Public Opinion Quarterly 26:648–57.
17   1963   Aging and political participation. Western Political Quarterly 16:323–31.

16   Crockett, Jean A.
    1963   Older people as consumers. Pp. 127–46 in Harold L. Orbach and Clark Tibbitts (eds.), Aging and the Economy. Ann Arbor, Michigan: The University of Michigan Press.

7   Crossman, Linda, Celilia London, and Clemmie Barry
       1981   Older women caring for disabled spouses: a model for supportive services. The Geron-
              tologist 21:464–70.

14   Crouch, B. M.
       1972   Age and institutional support: perceptions of older Mexican-Americans. Journal of
              Gerontology 27:524–29.

12   Crumbaugh, J. C.
       1972   Aging and adjustment: the applicability of logotherapy and the Purpose-in-Life Test.
              The Gerontologist 12:418–20.

       Cryns, A. G., and A. Monk
5   1972   Attitudes of the aged toward the young: a multivariate study of intergenerational per-
              ception. Journal of Gerontology 27:107–12.

5   1973   Attitudes toward youth as a function of adult age: a multivariate study of intergenera-
              tional dynamics. International Journal of Aging and Human Development 4:23–33.

7   Cuber, John F., and Peggy Harroff
       1965   The Significant Americans. New York: Appleton-Century-Crofts.

       Cumming, Elaine
12   1964   New thoughts on the theory of disengagement. Pp. 3–18 in Robert Kastenbaum (ed.),
              New Thoughts on Old Age. New York: Springer.

12   1975   Engagement with an old theory. International Journal of Aging and Human Develop-
              ment 6:187–91.

12, 13 Cumming, Elaine, and William E. Henry
       1961   Growing Old: The Process of Disengagement. New York: Basic Books.

12   Cumming, Elaine, Lois R. Dean, David S. Newell, and Isabell McCaffrey
       1960   Disengagement—a tentative theory of aging. Sociometry 23:23–35.

16   Cummings, Frank
       1974   Reforming private pensions. Pp. 80–94 in Frederick R. Eisele (ed.), Political Conse-
              quences of Aging. Philadelphia: American Academy of Political and Social Sciences.

10   Cunningham, David A., Henry J. Montoye, Helen L. Metzner, and Jacob B. Keller
       1968   Active leisure time activities as related to age among males in a total population. Jour-
              nal of Gerontology 23:551–56.

5   Cunningham, W. R., V. Clayton, and W. Overton
       1975   Fluid and crystallized intelligence in young adulthood and old age. Journal of Geron-
              tology 30:53–55.

4   Curtis, Howard J.
       1966   Biological Mechanisms of Aging. Springfield, Ill. Charles C. Thomas.

8, 10 Curtis, Joseph E., and Dulcy B. Miller
       1967   Community sponsored recreation in an extended care facility. The Gerontologist 7:196–
              99.

       Cutler, Neal E.
17   1969   Generation, maturation, and party affiliation: a cohort analysis. Public Opinion Quar-
              terly 33:583–88.

17, 19 1981   Political characteristics of elderly cohorts in the twenty-first century. Pp. 127–57 in
              Sara B. Kiesler et al. (eds.), Aging: Social Change. New York: Academic Press.

5, 17 Cutler, Neal E., and Vern L. Bengtson
       1974   Age and political alienation. Pp. 160–75 in Frederick R. Eisele (ed.), Political Conse-
              quences of Aging. Philadelphia: American Academy of Political and Social Sciences.

       Cutler, Stephen J.
13   1972a An approach to the measurement of prestige loss among the aged. Aging and Human
              Development 3:285–92.

8, 12	1972b	The availability of personal transportation, residential location, and life satisfaction among the aged. Journal of Gerontology 27:383–89.

8, 12   1972b   The availability of personal transportation, residential location, and life satisfaction among the aged. Journal of Gerontology 27:383–89.

17   1973a   Perceived prestige loss and political attitudes among the aged. The Gerontologist 13:69–75.

10, 12   1973b   Voluntary association membership and life satisfaction: a cautionary research note. Journal of Gerontology 28:96–100.

8, 10   1974   The effects of transportation and distance on voluntary association participation among the aged. International Journal of Aging and Human Development 5:81–94.

8, 12   1975   Transportation and changes in life satisfaction. The Gerontologist 15:155–59.

10   1976a   Age differences in voluntary association memberships. Social Forces 55:43–58.

10   1976b   Age profiles of membership in sixteen types of voluntary associations. Journal of Gerontology 31:462–70.

10, 12   1976c   Membership in different types of voluntary associations and psychological well-being. The Gerontologist 16:335–39.

10   1977   Aging and voluntary association participation. Journal of Gerontology 32:470–79.

5   1982   Social issues among the elderly: long-term antecedents of current attitudes. Research on Aging 4:441–56.

5   1983   Aging and changes in attitudes about the women's liberation movement. International Journal of Aging and Human Development 16:43–51.

10   Cutler, Stephen J., and J. J. Hughes
   1982   The age structure of voluntary association memberships: some recent evidence. Paper presented at the annual meeting of the Gerontological Society of America, Boston, November 21.

5, 17   Cutler, Stephen J., and R. L. Kaufman
   1975   Cohort changes in political attitudes: tolerance of ideological nonconformity. Public Opinion Quarterly 39:69–81.

5, 17   Cutler, Stephen J., Sally Ann Lentz, Michael J. Muha, and Robert N. Riter
   1980   Aging and conservatism: cohort changes in attitudes about legalized abortion. Journal of Gerontology 35:115–23.

3, 7   Dahlin, Michel
   1980   Perspectives on the family life of the elderly in 1900. The Gerontologist 20:99–107.

14   Dancy, Joseph, Jr.
   1977   The Black Elderly: A Guide for Practitioners. Ann Arbor, Michigan: University of Michigan-Wayne State University, Institute of Gerontology.

6   Datan, Nancy
   1980   Transitions of Aging. New York: Academic Press.

16   David, Z. M.
   1960   Old-age, survivors, and disability insurance: twenty-five years of progress. Industrial and Labor Relations Review 14:10–23.

9   Davidson, Wayne R., and Karl R. Kunze
   1965   Psychological, social and economic meanings of work in modern society: their effects on the worker facing retirement. The Gerontologist 5:129–33.

8, 18   Davis, Bleddyn, and David Challis
   1980   Experimenting with new roles in domiciliary service: Kent community care project. The Gerontologist 20:288–99.

9, 16   Davis, H. E.
   1973   Pension provisions affecting the employment of older workers. Monthly Labor Review 96(4):41–45.

13, 17   Davis, James A.
   1981   Conservative weather in a liberalizing climate: changes in selected NORC General So-

cial Survey items, 1972–1978. Pp. 93–126 in Sara B. Kiesler et al. (eds.), Aging: Social Change. New York: Academic Press.

18   Davis, K.
     1973   Hospital costs and the Medicare program. Social Security Bulletin 36(8):18–36.

   Davis, R. H. (ed.)

8, 14   1972   Community Services and the Black Elderly. Los Angeles: Ethel Percy Andrus Gerontological Center, University of Southern California.

11   1973a Dealing with Death. Los Angeles: Ethel Percy Andrus Gerontological Center, University of Southern California.

8   1973b Health Services and the Mexican-American Elderly. Los Angeles: Ethel Percy Andrus Gerontological Center, University of Southern California.

8, 18   Davis, R. H., and W. K. Smith (eds.)
     1973   Non-Profit Homes for the Aging: Planning, Development, and Programming. Los Angeles: Ethel Percy Andrus Gerontological Center, University of Southern California.

8   Davis, R. H., M. Audet, and L. Baird (eds.)
     1973   Housing for the Elderly. Los Angeles: Ethel Percy Andrus Gerontological Center, University of Southern California.

   Davis, Robert W.

5   1963   The relationship of social preferability to self-concept in an aged population. Journal of Gerontology 18:431–36.

5   1967   Social influences on the aspiration tendency of older people. Journal of Gerontology 22:510–16.

9   Davis, Stanley M.
     1979   No connection between executive age and corporate performance. Harvard Business Review 57:1–3.

   Davis-Friedmann, Deborah
     1983   Long Lives: Chinese Elderly and the Communist Revolution. Cambridge, Mass.: Harvard University Press.

10, 12 Dawson, A. M., and W. R. Baller
     1972   Relationship between creative activity and the health of elderly persons. Journal of Psychology 82:49–58.

7   Dean, A., and N. Lin
     1977   The stress-buffering role of social support. Journal of Nervous and Mental Disorders 165:403–17.

1   Dean, Laura L., Jeanne A. Teresi, and David E. Wilder
     1977–78 The human element in survey research. International Journal of Aging and Human Development 8:83–92.

5   Dean, Lois R.
     1962   Aging and the decline of affect. Journal of Gerontology 17:440–46.

10, 12 DeCarlo, T. J.
     1974   Recreation participation patterns and successful aging. Journal of Gerontology 29:416–22.

3   deCharms, R., and G. H. Moeller
     1962   Values expressed in children's readers: 1800–1950. Journal of Abnormal and Social Psychology 64:136–42.

8   De Crow, Roger
     1975   New Learning for Older Americans: An Overview of National Effort. Washington, D.C.: Adult Education Association.

8   De Friese, Gordon H., and Alison Woomert
     1983   Self care among U.S. elderly: recent developments. Research on Aging 5:3–24.

18   Deimling, Gary T.
        1982   Macro- and microlevel aging service planning and the 1980 census. The Gerontologist 22:151–52.

9, 15   DeLury, Bernard E.
        1976   The Age Discrimination in Employment Act: background and highlights from recent cases. Industrial Gerontology 3:37–40.

3, 6   Demos, J., and S. S. Boocock (eds.)
        1978   Turning Points. Chicago: University of Chicago Press.

13   Demos, Vasilikie, and Ann Jache
        1981   When you care enough: an analysis of attitudes toward aging in humorous birthday cards. The Gerontologist 21:209–15.

5   Denney, D. R., and N. W. Denney
        1973   The use of classification for problem solving: a comparison of middle and old age. Developmental Psychology 9:275–78.

8   Denney, Duane, Delbert M. Kole, and Ruth G. Matarazzo
        1965   The relationship between age and the number of symptoms reported by patients. Journal of Gerontology 20:50–53.

5   Denney, Nancy Wadsworth
        1980   Task demands and problem-solving strategies in middle-aged and older adults. Journal of Gerontology 35:559–64.

5   Denney, N. W., and M. L. Lennon
        1972   Classification: a comparison of middle and old age. Developmental Psychology 7:210–13.

        Dennis, Wayne
5   1960   Long-term constancy of behavior. Journal of Gerontology 15:195–96.
5   1966   Creative productivity between the ages of 20 and 80 years. Journal of Gerontology 21:1–8.

7, 9   Depner, Charlene, and Berit Ingersoll
        1982   Employment status and social support: the experience of mature women. Pp. 61–76 in M. Szinovacz (ed.), Women's Retirement. Beverly Hills, Calif.: Sage.

7   Deutscher, Irwin
        1968   The quality of postparental life. Pp. 263–68 in Bernice L. Neugarten (ed.), Middle Age and Aging. Chicago: University of Chicago Press.

18   Devitt, Mary, and Barry Checkoway
        1982   Participation in nursing home resident councils: promise and practice. The Gerontologist 22:49–53.

8   Dick, Harry R.
        1964   Residential patterns of aged persons prior to institutionalization. Journal of Marriage and the Family 26:96–98.

11   Dickstein, L. S.
        1972   Death concern: measurement and correlates. Psychological Reports 30:563–71.

18   Diech, Margret
        1980   Residential and community provisions for the frail elderly in Germany—current classes and their history (West Germany). The Gerontologist 20:260–72.

8   Dillingham, Alan E.
        1981   Age and workplace injuries. Aging and Work 4:1–10.

13   Dillon, Kathleen M., and Barbara Spiess Jones
        1981   Attitudes toward aging portrayed by birthday cards. International Journal of Aging and Human Development 13:79–84.

8   Dingfelder, Adele G.
    1969   Chronic conditions causing activity limitation: United States, July 1963 to June 1965. Vital and Health Statistics, Series 10, No. 51.

5, 9   Distefano, M. K.
    1969   Changes in work related attitudes with age. Journal of Genetic Psychology 114:127–34.

9   Doering, Mildred, Susan R. Rhodes, and Michael Schuster
    1983   The Aging Worker: Research and Recommendations. Beverly Hills, Calif.: Sage.

    Donahue, Wilma
8   1963   Rehabilitation of long-term aged paients. Pp. 541–65 in Richard H. Williams, Clark Tibbitts, and Wilma Donahue (eds.), Processes of Aging. Volume 1. New York: Atherton Press.

8   1966   Impact of living arrangements on ego development in the elderly. Pp. 1–9 in Frances M. Carp and W. M. Burnett (eds.), Patterns of Living and Housing of Middle-Aged and Older People. Washington, D.C.: U.S. Public Health Service.

7   1969   Living in the Multigenerational Family. Ann Arbor, Michigan: University of Michigan, Institute of Gerontology.

17   Donahue, Wilma, and Clark Tibbitts (eds.)
    1962   Politics of Age. Ann Arbor, Michigan: University of Michigan Press.

9   Donahue, Wilma, Harold Orback, and Otto Pollak
    1960   Retirement: the emerging social pattern. Pp. 330–406 in Clark Tibbitts (ed.), Handbook of Social Gerontology. Chicago: University of Chicago Press.

17   Douglass, Elizabeth B., William P. Cleveland, and George L. Maddox
    1974   Political attitudes, age, and aging: a cohort analysis of archival data. Journal of Gerontology 29:666–75.

8, 12   Douglass, Richard L.
    1982   Heating or eating? The crisis of home heating, energy costs and well-being of the elderly in Michigan. Ann Arbor: University of Michigan Institute of Gerontology.

    Dowd, James J.
6   1975   Aging as exchange: a preface to theory. Journal of Gerontology 30:584–94.

13   1980   Exchange rates and old people. Journal of Gerontology 35:596–602.

14   Dowd, James J., and Vern L. Bengtson
    1978   Aging in minority populations: an examination of the double jeopardy hypothesis. Journal of Gerontology 33:427–36.

15   Dowd, James J., Rose P. Gisson, and Dennis M. Kern
    1981   Socialization to violence among the aged. Journal of Gerontology 36:350–61.

14   Drake, St. Clair, and Horace Cayton
    1962   Black Metropolis. New York: Harper and Row.

9   Draper, J. E., E. F. Lundgren, and G. B. Strother
    1967   Work attitudes and retirement adjustment. Madison, Wisconsin: University of Wisconsin Bureau of Business Research Services.

8   Drazga, Linda, Melinda Upp, and Virginia Reno
    1982   Low-income aged: eligibility and participation in SSI. Social Security Bulletin 45(5):28–31.

7, 12   Dressler, D. M.
    1973   Life adjustment of retired couples. International Journal of Aging and Human Development 4:335–49.

    Drevenstedt, Jean
5   1975   Scale-checking styles on the semantic differential among older people. Journal of Gerontology 30:170–73.

6   1976   Perceptions of onsets of young adulthood, middle age, and old age. Journal of Geron-
               tology 31:53–57.

5   1981   Age bias in the evaluation of achievement: what determines? Journal of Gerontology
               36:453–54.

10   Drickhamer, J.
       1971   Rhode Island project: book reviews by older citizens. Library Journal 96:2737–43.

16   Drucker, Peter F.
       1976   The Unseen Revolution: How Pension Fund Socialism Came to America. New York:
               Harper and Row.

14   DuBois, W. E. B.
       1915   The Negro. New York: Holt, Rinehart and Winston.

10   Dumazedier, Joffre, and A. Ripert
       1963   Retirement and leisure. International Social Science Journal 15:438–47.

18   Dunlop, Burton D.
       1979   The Growth of Nursing Home Care. Lexington, Mass.: D. C. Heath.

9   Dunning, B. B., and A. D. Biderman
       1973   The case of military "retirement." Industrial Gerontology 17:18–37.

5   Durand, Richard M., Lucinda Lee Roff, and David L. Klemmack
       1981   Cognitive differentiation and the perception of older persons: a test of the Vigilance
               Hypothesis. Research on Aging 3:333–34.

5, 10 Durkee, Stephen
       1964   Artistic expression in later life. Pp. 305–15 in Robert Kastenbaum (ed.), New
               Thoughts on Old Age. New York: Springer.

10   Dye, D., M. Goodman, R. Roth, N. Bley, and K. Jensen
       1973   The older adult volunteer compared to the nonvolunteer. The Gerontologist 13:215–18.

12   Edwards, John N., and David L. Klemmack
       1973   Correlates of life satisfaction: a reexamination. Journal of Gerontology 28:497–502.

       Ehrlich, Ira F.
8   1972   Life-styles among persons 70 years and older in age-segregated housing. The Gerontolo-
               gist 12:27–31.

14   1973   Toward a social profile of the aged black population in the United States: an explorato-
               ry study. International Journal of Aging and Human Development 4:271–76.

19   Ehrlich, Ira F., and Phyllis D. Ehrlich
       1976   A four-part framework to meet the responsibilities of higher education to gerontology.
               Educational Gerontology 1:251–60.

       Eisdorfer, Carl
19   1968   Patterns of federal funding for research in aging. The Gerontologist 8:3–6.

9   1972   Adaptation to loss of work. Pp. 245–66 in Frances M. Carp (ed.), Retirement. New
               York: Behavioral Publications.

5, 8   1975   Observations on the psychopharmacology of the aged. Journal of the American Geria-
               trics Society 23(2):53–57.

19   1976   Issues in health planning for the aged. The Gerontologist 16:12–16.

5   Eisdorfer, Carl, and J. Altrocchi
       1961   A comparison of attitudes toward old age and mental illness. Journal of Gerontology
               16:940–43.

5   Eisdorfer, Carl, and M. Powell Lawton (eds.)
       1973   The Psychology of Adult Development and Aging. Washington, D.C.: American Psy-
               chological Association.

6   Eisenstadt, S. N.
        1956   From Generation to Generation: Age Groups and Social Structure. Glencoe, Ill.: Free Press.

9   Ekerdt, David J., and Raymond Bossé
        1982   Change in self-reported health with retirement. International Journal of Aging and Human Development 15:213–23.

9   Ekerdt, David J., Lynn Baden, Raymond Bossé, and Elaine Dibbs
        1983   The effect of retirement on physical health. American Journal of Public Health 73:779–83.

9   Ekerdt, David J., Raymond Bossé, and Sue Levkoff
        1984   An empirical test for phases of retirement: Findings from the normative aging study. Journal of Gerontology (forthcoming).

9   Ekerdt, David J., Raymond Bossé, and Joseph S. LoCastro
        1983   Claims that retirement improves health. Journal of Gerontology 38:231–36.

9   Ekerdt, David J., Raymond Bossé, and John Mogey
        1980   Concurrent change in planned and preferred age for retirement. Journal of Gerontology 35:232–40.

    Elder, Glen H., Jr.
3   1974   Children of the Great Depression—Social Change and Life Experiences. Chicago: University of Chicago Press.
6   1975   Age differentiation and the life course. Annual Review of Sociology 1:165–90.
7   1977   Family history and the life course. Journal of Family History 2:279–304.
7   1978   Family history and the life course. Pp. 21–57 in T. Haraven (ed.), Transitions: The Family and the Life Course in Historical Perspective. New York: Academic Press.

5   Elias, Merrill F., and Penelope Elias
        1977   Motivation and activity. Pp. 357–83 in James E. Birren and K. Warner Schaie (eds.), Handbook of the Psychology of Aging. New York: Van Nostrand Reinhold.

5   Elias, Merrill F., P. K. Elias, and J. W. Elias
        1977   Basic Processes in Adult Developmental Psychology. St. Louis: C. V. Mosby.

9   Ellison, David L.
        1968   Work, retirement, and the sick role. The Gerontologist 8:189–92.

12   Ellison, Jerome
        1978   Life's Second Half: The Pleasures of Aging. Old Greenwich, Conn.: Devin-Adair.

5   Elsayed, Mohamed, A. H. Ismail, and John R. Young
        1980   Intellectual differences of adult men related to age and physical fitness before and after exercise program. Journal of Gerontology 35:383–87.

12   Elwell, F., and Alice D. Maltbie-Crannell
        1981   The impact of role loss upon coping resources and life satisfaction of the elderly. Journal of Gerontology 36:223–32.

3   Emerson, Ralph Waldo
        1867   Progress of culture. Address to the Phi Beta Kappa Society, July 18.

5.   Engen, Trygg
        1977   Taste and smell. Pp. 554–61 in James E. Birren and K. Warner Schaie (eds.), Handbook of the Psychology of Aging. New York: Van Nostrand Reinhold.

15   English, Clifford, and Joyce Stephens
        1975   On being excluded: an analysis of elderly and adolescent street hustlers. Urban Life 4:201–12.

9   Epstein, Lenore A.
        1966   Early retirement and work-life experience. Social Security Bulletin 29(3):3–10.

9   Epstein, Lenore A., and Janet H. Murray
       1968   Employment and retirement. Pp. 354–56 in Bernice L. Neugarten (ed.), Middle Age
               and Aging. Chicago: University of Chicago Press.
5, 12 Epstein, Seymour
       1980   The self-concept: A review and the proposal of an integrated theory of personality. Pp.
               82–132 in E. Staub (ed.), Personality: Basic Issues and Current Research. Englewood
               Cliffs, N.J.: Prentice-Hall.
9   Eran, Mordechai, and Dan Jacobson
       1976   Expectancy theory prediction of the preference to remain employed or to retire. Journal
               of Gerontology 31:605–10.
5   Erber, Joan T.
       1982   Memory and age. Pp. 569–85 in T. M. Field et al. (eds.), Review of Human Develop-
               ment. New York: Wiley.
5   Erikson, Erik H.
       1963   Childhood and Society. New York: Macmillan.
15   Erikson, R., and K. Eckert
       1977   The elderly poor in downtown San Diego hotels. The Gerontologist 17:440–46.
17   Erskine, Hazel G.
       1963   The polls. Public Opinion Quarterly 27:137–39.
       Estes, Carroll L.
19   1973   Barriers to effective community planning for the elderly. The Gerontologist 13:178–83.
19   1974   Community planning for the elderly: a study of goal displacement. Journal of Geron-
               tology 20:684–91.
19   1976   Revenue sharing: implications for policy and research in aging. The Gerontologist 16:
               141–47.
17, 18 1979   The Aging Interprise. San Francisco: Jossey-Bass.
17, 18 Estes, Carroll L., and Robert J. Newcomer (eds.)
       1983   Fiscal Austerity and Aging: Shifting Government Responsibility for the Elderly. Bever-
               ly Hills, Calif.: Sage.
2   Eteng, W. I. A., and D. G. Marshall
       1970   Retirement and Migration in the North Central States: A Comparative Analysis in Wis-
               consin, Florida and Arizona. Population Services No. 20. Madison, Wisconsin: Univer-
               sity of Wisconsin, Department of Rural Sociology.
17   Etzioni, Amitai
       1976   Old people and public policy. Social Policy 7(3):21–29.
8   Euster, G. L.
       1971   A system of groups in institutions for the aged. Social Casework 52:523–29.
18   Eustis, Nancy, Jay Greenberg, and Sharon Patten
       1984   Long-Term Care for Older Persons: A Policy Perspective. Belmont, Calif.: Wadsworth.
8, 18 Evans, Ron L., and Beth M. Juarequy
       1982   Phone therapy outreach for blind elderly. The Gerontologist 22:32–35.
8, 18 Eve, Susan Brown
       1982   Older Americans' use of health maintenance organizations. Research on Aging 4:179–
               204.
5   Eysenck, M. W.
       1974   Age differences in incidental learning. Developmental Psychology 10:936–41.
12   Faberow, Norman I., and Sharon Y. Moriwaki
       1975   Self-destructive crises in the older person. The Gerontologist 15:333–37.

Faletti, Martin V.
8   1982   Human factors analysis of functional ability in daily living. Paper presented at the annual meeting of the Gerontological Society of America, Boston.
8   1984   Human factors research and functional environments for the aged. In I. Altman, J.
Wohlwill, and M. P. Lawton (eds.), The Elderly and the Environment. (forthcoming)
6   Fallo-Mitchell, Linda, and Carol D. Ryff
1982   Preferred timing of female life events: cohort differences. Research on Aging 4:249–68.
7, 8   Fandetti, Donald V., and Donald E. Gelfand
1976   Care of the aged; attitudes of white ethnic families. The Gerontologist 16:544–49.
7   Farrell, Michael P., and S. D. Rosenberg
1981   Men at Midlife. Boston: Auburn House.
8, 10 Faulkner, Audrey Olsen
1975   The black aged as good neighbors; an experiment in volunteer service. The Gerontologist 15:544–59.
19   Fecko, Leonard J.
1979   Job Newsletter. Oxford, Ohio: Scripps Foundation Gerontology Center.
Federal Council on the Aging
16   1975   The Impact of the Tax Structure on the Elderly. Washington, D.C.: U.S. Government
Printing Office.
18   1981   Toward a More Effective Implementaton of the Older Americans Act. Washington,
D.C.: Federal Council on Aging.
5   Feier, Claudette D., and Louis J. Gerstman
1980   Sentence comprehension abilities throughout adult life span. Journal of Gerontology
35:722–28.
17, 18 Feingold, Eugene
1966   Medicare, Policy and Politics. San Francisco: Chandler.
9   Feingold, H.
1971   The effects of the meaning of work on retirement attitudes among civil servants. Industrial Gerontology 9:46.
9, 16 Feldman, L.
1974   Employment problems of older workers: a review by the International Labor Organization Advisory Committee. Industrial Gerontology 2:69–71.
11, 12 Feldman, M. J., P. J. Handal, and H. S. Barahal
1974   Fears Related to Death and Suicide. New York: Manuscripts Information Corporation.
11   Fell, J.
1977   Grief reactions in the elderly following death of a spouse: the role of crisis intervention
and nursing. Journal of Gerontological Nursing 3:17–20.
8   Felton, B., and E. Kahana
1974   Adjustment and situationally bound locus of control among institutionalized aged. Journal of Gerontology 29:295–301.
7, 9   Fengler, Alfred P.
1975   Attitudinal orientations of wives toward their husbands' retirement. International Journal of Aging and Human Development 6:139–52.
8, 11 Fengler, Alfred P., and Nicholas L. Danigelis
1982   Residence, the elderly widow, and life satisfaction. Research on Aging 4:113–35.
9   Fengler, Alfred P., and Nancy Goodrich
1980   Money isn't everything: opportunities for elderly handicapped men in a sheltered work-
shop. The Gerontologist 20:636–41.

12   Fengler, Alfred P., and Leif Jensen
        1981   Perceived and objective conditions as predictors of the life satisfaction of urban and
                non-urban elderly. Journal of Gerontology 36:750–52.

12   Fengler, Alfred P., Virginia C. Little, and Nicholas L. Danigelis
        1983   Correlates of diversions of happiness in urban and nonurban settings. International
                Journal of Aging and Human Development 16:53–65.

5   Fengler, Alfred P., and Vivian Wood
        1972   The generation gap: an analysis of attitudes on contemporary issues. The Gerontologist
                12:124–28.

8   Fennell, Valerie I.
        1977   Age relations and rapid change in a small town. The Gerontologist 17:405–11.

9   Ferman, Louis, A., and Michael Aiken
        1967   Mobility and situational factors in the adjustment of older workers to job displacement.
                Human Organization 26:235–41.

8   Ferraro, Kenneth F.
        1981   Relocation desires and outcomes among the elderly: a longitudinal analysis. Research
                on Aging 3:166–81.

11   Ferraro, Kenneth F., and Charles M. Barresi
        1982   The impact of widowhood on the social relations of older persons. Research on Aging
                4:227–48.

5   Ferris, Steven H., Thomas Crook, Elisabeth Clark, Martin McCarthy, and Donald Rae
        1980   Facial recognition memory deficits in normal aging and senile dementia. Journal of
                Gerontology 35:707–14.

1   Fienberg, S. E., and W. M. Mason
        1979   Identification and estimation of age-period-cohort models in the analysis of discrete ar-
                chival data. Sociological Methodology 10(1):1–67.

5   Filer, Richard N., and Desmond O. O'Connell
        1964   Motivation of aging persons. The Gerontologist 19:15–22.

        Fillenbaum, Gerda G.
9   1971a   A consideration of some factors related to work after retirement. The Gerontologist 11:
                18–23.
9   1971b   On the relation between attitude to work and attitude to retirement. Journal of Geron-
                tology 26:244–48.
9   1971c   Retirement planning programs—at what age, and for whom? The Gerontologist 11:33–36.
9   1971d   The working retired. Journal of Gerontology 26:82–89.

9   Fillenbaum, Gerda G., and G. L. Maddox
        1974   Work after retirement: an investigation into some psychological relevant variables. The
                Gerontologist 14:418–24.

8, 9   Fillenbaum, Gerda G., and Elizabeth Willis
        1976   Effects of a training program: older persons caring for the elderly. Industrial Geron-
                tology 3:213–21.

4   Finch, Caleb E.
        1977   Neuroendocrine and autonomic aspects of aging. Pp. 262–80 in Caleb E. Finch and
                Leonard Hayflick (eds.), Handbook of the Biology of Aging. New York: Van Nostrand
                Reinhold.

4   Finch, Caleb E., and Leonard Hayflick (eds.)
        1977   Handbook of the Biology of Aging. New York: Van Nostrand Reinhold.

5   Finkle, A. L.
        1973   Emotional quality and physical quantity of sexual activity in aging males. Journal of
                Geriatric Psychiatry 6:70–79.

9   Finley, Gordon E.
      1983   American retirement abroad. Pp. 276–291 in D. Landis and R. W. Brislin (eds.), Handbook of Intercultural Training, Volume III. New York: Pergamon.

10   Finney, John M., and Gary R. Lee
      1977   Age differences on five dimensions of religious involvement. Review of Religious Research. 18(2):173–79.

3   Fischer, David H.
      1978   Growing Old in America. expanded edition. New York: Oxford University Press.

11   Fischer, H. K., and B. M. Dlin
      1971   Man's determination of his time of illness or death. Anniversary reactions and emotional deadlines. Geriatrics 36:88–94.

7   Fischer, Lucy Rose
      1983   Transition to grandmotherhood. International Journal of Aging and Human Development 16:67–78.

5   Fisher, Jerome
      1973   Competence, effectiveness, intellectual functioning and aging. The Gerontologist 13:62–68.

5   Fisher, Jerome, and Robert C. Pierce
      1967   Dimensions of intellectual functioning in the aged. Journal of Gerontology 22:166–73.

8   Fisher, L. D., and J. R. Solomon
      1974   Guardianship: a protective service program for the aged. Social Casework 55:618–21.

      Fisher, Paul
16   1973   Major social security issues: Japan, 1972. Social Security Bulletin 36(3):26–38.
9, 16   1975   Labor force participation of the aged and the social security system in nine countries. Industrial Gerontology 2:1–13.

5   Fiske, D. W.
      1974   The limits for the conventional science of personality. Journal of Personality 42:1–11.

5   Fitzgerald, Joseph M.
      1978   Actual and perceived sex and generational differences in interpersonal style: structural and quantitative issues. Journal of Gerontology 33:394–401.

5   Fitzgerald, Joseph M., and Cal Vander Plate
      1976   Personality factors and perceived peer personality as predictors of social role variables in the aged. Human Development 19:40–48.

11   Flannery, R. B., Jr.
      1974   Behavior modification of geriatric grief: a transactional perspective. International Journal of Aging and Human Development 5:197–203.

18   Flynn, Marilyn L.
      1980   Coordination of social and health care for the elderly: the British and Irish examples (United Kingdom). The Gerontologist 20:300–07.

17   Foner, Anne
      1974   Age stratification and age conflict in political life. American Sociological Review 39:187–96.

12   Fontana, Andrea
      1977   The Last Frontier. The Social Meaning of Growing Old. Beverly Hills, Calif.: Sage Publications.

18   Fottler, Myron D., Howard L. Smith, and William L. James
      1981   Profits and patient care quality in nursing homes: are they compatible? The Gerontologist 21:532–38.

      Fox, Alan
8, 16   1974   Earnings Replacement from Social Security and Private Pensions: Newly Entitled Beneficiaries, 1970. Washington, D.C.: Social Security Administration.

8   1976   Work status and income change, 1968–1972: retirement history study preview. Social
                 Security Bulletin 39(12):15–31.

         Fox, Judith Huff
9, 12   1977   Effects of retirement and former work life on women's adaptation in old age. Journal
                 of Gerontology 32:196–202.

12   1981–82 Perspectives on the continuity perspective. International Journal of Aging and Hu-
                 man Development 14:97–115.

17   Fox, Richard G.
         1981   The welfare state and the political mobilization of the elderly. Pp. 159–82 in Sara B.
                 Kiesler et al. (eds.), Aging: Social Change. New York: Academic Press.

5   Fozard, James L., and Gordon D. Carr
         1972   Age differences and psychological estimates of abilities and skill. Industrial Gerontology
                 13:75–96.

13   Francher, J. Scott
         1973   It's the Pepsi generation . . .: accelerated aging and the TV commercial. International
                 Journal of Aging and Human Development 4:245–55.

9, 16   Franke, Walter H.
         1963   Labor market experience of unemployed older workers. Monthly Labor Review 86:282
                 –84.

15   Frankfather, Dwight
         1977   The Aged in the Community. New York: Praeger.

8, 11   Franklin, Paula A.
         1975   The disabled widow. Social Security Bulletin 38(1):20–27.

7   Freed, Anne O.
         1975   The family agency and the kinship system of the elderly. Social Casework 56:579–86.

8   Freeman, J. T.
         1972   Elderly drivers: growing numbers and growing problems. Geriatrics 27(7):45–56.

8, 10   Freund, J. W.
         1971   The meaning of volunteer services in schools—to the educator and to the older adult.
                 The Gerontologist 11:205–08.

8   Fried, Marc
         1968   Grieving for a lost home. Pp. 151–71 in Leonard Duhl (ed.), The Urban Condition.
                 New York: Basic Books.

5   Friedman, Alfred S., and Samuel Granick
         1963   A note on anger and aggression in old age. Journal of Gerontology 18:283–85.

8   Friedman, Joseph, and Jane Sjogren
         1981   Assets of the elderly as they retire. Social Security Bulletin 44(1):16–31.

9   Friedmann, Eugene A., and Robert J. Havighurst (eds.)
         1954   The Meaning of Work and Retirement. Chicago: University of Chicago Press.

9   Friedmann, Eugene A., and Harold L. Orbach
         1974   Adjustment to retirement. Pp. 609–45 in Silvano Arieti (ed.), American Handbook of
                 Psychiatry. New York: Basic Books.

1   Friedrich, Douglas
         1972   A Primer for Developmental Methodology. Minneapolis: Burgess.

10   Friedsam, H. J., and C. A. Martin
         1973   Travel by older people as a use of leisure. The Gerontologist 13:204–07.

2   Fries, James F.
         1980   Aging, natural death, and the compression of morbidity. New England Journal of
                 Medicine 300:130–35.

17   Fries, Victoria, and Robert N. Butler
       1971   The congressional seniority system: the myth of gerontocracy in Congress. International
               Journal of Aging and Human Development 2:341–48.
14   Fujii, Sharon
       1976   Older Asian Americans: victims of multiple jeopardy. Civil Rights Digest 9:22–29.
10   Fukuyama, Yoshio
       1961   The major dimensions of church membership. Review of Religious Research 2:154–61.
 1   Fulgraff, Barbara
       1978   Social gerontology in West Germany: a review of recent and current research. The
               Gerontologist 18:42–58.
       Funk & Wagnalls
       1963   Standard College Dictionary, Text Edition. New York: Harcourt, Brace & World.
18   Furchtgott, Ernest, and Jerome R. Busemeyer
       1981   Age preferences for professional helpers. Journal of Gerontology 36:90–92.
 3   Furnas, J. C.
       1969   The Americans: A Social History of the United States 1587–1914. New York: G. P.
               Putnam's Sons.
18   Gadow, Sally
       1980   Medicine, ethics, and the elderly. The Gerontologist 20:680–85.
12   Gage, F. B.
       1971   Suicide in the aged. American Journal of Nursing 71:2153–55.
8, 18 Gagnon, Raymond O.
       1974   Selected characteristics of nursing homes for the aged and chronically ill: United States,
               June–August 1969. Vital and Health Statistics, Series 12, No. 23.
15   Gaitz, C. M., and P. E. Baer
       1971   Characteristics of elderly patients with alcoholism. Archives of General Psychiatry 24:
               372–378.
13   Gaitz, Charles M., and J. Scott
       1975   Analysis of letters to "Dear Abby" concerning old age. The Gerontologist 15:47–50.
8, 18 Gaitz, Charles M., M. Powell Lawton, and Raymond Harris
       1968   Goals of Comprehensive Health Care in Advanced Old Age. Ann Arbor, Michigan:
               University of Michigan-Wayne State University Institute of Gerontology.
 3   Galbraith, J. Kenneth
       1958   The Affluent Society. Boston: Houghton Mifflin.
11   Gallagher, Dolores E., Larry W. Thompson, and James A. Peterson
       1981–82 Psychosocial factors affecting adaptation to bereavement in the elderly. International
               Journal of Aging and Human Development 14:79–95.
 9   Gallaway, Lowell E.
       1965   The Retirement Decision: An Exploratory Essay. Social Security Administration Re-
               search Report No. 9. Washington, D.C.: U.S. Government Printing Office.
11   Garfield, C. A.
       1974   Psychothanatological concomitants of altered state experience. Unpublished doctoral
               dissertation, University of California at Berkeley (as cited in Kalish, 1976).
15   Geis, Gilbert
       1976   Defrauding the elderly. Pp. 7–19 in Jack Goldsmith and S. S. Goldsmith (eds.), Crime
               and the Elderly. Lexington, Mass.: Lexington Books.
 8   Gelfand, Donald E.
       1968   Visiting patterns and social adjustment in an old age home. The Gerontologist 8:272–
               75.

8   Gelfand, Donald E., and Donald V. Fandetti
       1980   Suburban and urban white ethnics: attitudes toward care of the aged. The Gerontolo-
               gist 20:588–94.
18   Gelfand, Donald E., and Jody K. Olsen
       1983   The Aging Network, second edition. New York: Springer.
8   Geltner, Luzer
       1969   Somatic illness: prevention and rehabilitation. Pp. 76–87 in Marjorie F. Lowenthal and
               Ariv Zilli (eds.), Colloquium on Health and Aging of the Population. New York: S.
               Karger.
9   George, Linda K., and George L. Maddox
       1977   Subjective adaptation to loss of the work role: a longitudinal study. Journal of Geron-
               tology 32:456–62.
1   George, Linda K., Ilene E. Siegler, and Morris A. Okun
       1981   Separating age, cohort, and time of measurement: analysis of variance of multiple
               regression. Experimental Aging Research 7:297–314.
11   Gerber, I., R. Rusalem, N. Hannon, D. Battin, and A. Arkin
       1975   Anticipatory grief and aged widows and widowers. Journal of Gerontology 30:225–29.
5   Gergen, Kenneth J., and Kurt W. Back
       1966   Cognitive constriction in aging and attitudes toward international issues. Pp. 322–34 in
               Ida H. Simpson and John C. McKinney (eds.), Social Aspects of Aging. Durham, No.
               Carolina: Duke University Press.
9   Germant, L.
       1972   What 814 retired professors say about retirement. The Gerontologist 13:349–53.
       Gerontological Society
19   1971   Research designs and proposals in applied social gerontology: third report, 1971. The
               Gerontologist 11(4, part II).
19   1971   Research proposals in applied social gerontology. The Gerontologist 11(1, part 2):2–4.
8   Ghez, Gilbert R., and G. S. Becker
       1975   The Allocation of Time and Goods Over the Life Cycle. New York: Columbia Univer-
               sity Press.
       Giambra, Leonard M.
5   1974   Daydreaming across the life span: late adolescent to senior citizen. International Journal
               of Aging and Human Development 5:115–40.
5   1977a   Daydreaming about the past: the time setting of spontaneous thought intrusion. The
               Gerontologist 17:35–38.
5   1977b   A factor-analytic study of daydreaming, imaginal process, and temperament: a replica-
               tion on an adult male life-span sample. Journal of Gerontology 32:675–80.
7   Gibson, Geoffrey
       1972   Kin family network: overheralded structure of past conceptualizations of family func-
               tioning. Journal of Marriage and the Family 34:13–28.
5   Gibson, J. G.
       1973   Thirty-five year follow-up study of intellectual functioning. Journal of Gerontology 28:
               68–72.
18   Gilbert, Neil, and Harry Specht
       1982   A "fair share" for the aged: Title XX allocation patterns, 1976–1980. Research on Ag-
               ing 4:71–86.
7   Gilford, R., and V. Bengtson
       1979   Measuring marital satisfaction in three generations: positive and negative dimensions.
               Journal of Marriage and the Family 41:387–98.

5   Gilmore, A. J. J.
       1972   Personality in the elderly: problems in methodology. Age and Aging 1:227–32.
8   Giordano, Enrico A., and D. F. Seaman
       1968   Continuing education for the aging—evidence for a positive outlook. The Gerontologist
               8(1, part 1):63–64.
       Glamser, Francis D.
9   1976   Determinants of a positive attitude toward retirement. Journal of Gerontology 31:104–07.
9   1981a   The impact of preretirement programs on the retirement experience. Journal of Geron-
               tology 36:244–50.
9   1981b   Predictors of retirement attitudes. Aging and Work 4:23–29.
9   Glamser, Francis D., and Godon F. DeJong
       1975   The efficacy of preretirement preparation programs for industrial workers. Journal of
               Gerontology 30:595–600.
11   Glaser, B. G.
       1966   The social loss of aged dying patients. The Gerontologist 6:77–80.
       Glaser, B. G., and A. L. Strauss
11   1965   Awareness of Dying. Chicago: Aldine.
11   1968   Time for Dying. Chicago: Aldine.
       Glenn, Norval D.
5, 17 1969   Aging, disengagement, and opinionation. Public Opinion Quarterly 33:17–33.
5, 17 1974   Age and conservatism. Pp. 176–86 in Frederick R. Eisele (ed.), Political Consequences
               of Aging. Philadelphia: American Academy of Political and Social Sciences.
12   1981   Age, birth cohorts, and drinking: an illustration of the hazards of inferring effects from
               cohort data. Journal of Gerontology 36:362–69.
17   Glenn, Norval D., and Michael Grimes
       1968   Aging, voting, and political interest. American Sociological Review 33:563–75.
17   Glenn, Norval D., and Ted Hefner
       1972   Further evidence on aging and party identification. Public Opinion Quarterly 36:31–47.
9   Glenn, Norval D., P. A. Taylor, and C. N. Weaver
       1977   Age and job satisfaction among males and females; a multivariate, multisurvey study.
               Journal of Applied Psysiology 62:189–93.
5, 12 Glenwick, David S., and Susan K. Whitbourne
       1977–78 Beyond despair and disengagement: a transactional model of personality development
               in later life. International Journal of Aging and Human Development 8:261–67.
11   Glick, Ira O., Robert S. Weiss, and C. Murray Parkes
       1974   The First Year of Bereavement. New York: Wiley.
7   Glick, Paul C.
       1977   Updating the life cycle of the family. Journal of Marriage and Family. 39:5–13.
7   Glick, Paul C., and Robert Parke, Jr.
       1965   New approaches in studying the life cycle of the family. Demography 2:187–202.
8   Goff, Phoebe H.
       1971   Disabled beneficiary population, 1957–66. Social Security Bulletin 34(7):32–43.
17   Gold, Byron D.
       1974   The role of the federal government in the provision of social services to older persons.
               Pp. 55–69 in Frederick R. Eisele (ed.), Political Consequences of Aging. Philadelphia:
               American Academy of Political and Social Sciences.
       Golden, Herbert M.
12   1973   The dysfunctional effects of modern technology on the adaptability of aging. The
               Gerontologist 13:136–43.

12, 14   1976–77 Life satisfaction among black elderly in the inner city. Black Aging 2(2,3):21–41.

14   Golden, Herbert M., and C. S. Weinstock

1975–76 The myth of homogeneity among black elderly. Black Aging 1(2,3):1–11.

7   Goldfarb, Alvin I.

1965   Psychodynamics and the three-generational family. Pp. 10–45 in Ethel Shanas and Gordon F. Streib (eds.), Social Structure and the Family: Generational Relations. Englewood Cliffs, N.J.: Prentice-Hall.

12   Goldsamt, Milton R.

1967   Life satisfaction and the older disabled worker. Journal of the American Geriatrics Society 15:394–99.

Goldscheider, Calvin

2   1966   Differential residential mobility of the older population. Journal of Gerontology 21:103–08.

2   1971   Population, Modernization and Social Structure. Boston: Little, Brown.

8, 15   Goldsmith, Jack, and Sharon Goldsmith

1976   Crime and the Elderly. Lexington, Mass.: D. D. Heath & Co.

Goldstein, Sidney

16   1960   Consumption Patterns of the Aged. Philadelphia: University of Pennsylvania Press.

8, 16   1965   Changing income and consumption patterns of the aged, 1950–1960. Journal of Gerontology 20:453–61.

16   1966   Urban and rural differentials in consumer patterns of the aged. Rural Sociology 31:333–45.

16   1968   Home tenure and expenditure patterns of the aged, 1960–1961. The Gerontologist 8:17–24.

14, 16   1971   Negro-white differentials in consumer patterns of the aged, 1960–1961. The Gerontologist 11:242–49.

8   Gombeski, William Robert, Jr., and Michael H. Smolensky

1980   Non-emergency health transportation needs of the rural Texas elderly. The Gerontologist 20:452–56.

9, 13   Goodman, Eugene

1983   All the Justice I Could Afford. New York: Harcourt Brace Jovanovitch.

10, 12   Goodman, M., N. Bley, and D. Dye

1974   The adjustment of aged users of leisure programs. American Journal of Orthopsychiatry 44:142–49.

8, 18   Goodsell, Charles T.

1981–82 The contented older client of bureaucracy. International Journal of Aging and Human Development 14:1–9.

16   Goodwin, Leonard, and Joseph Tu

16, 17   1975   The social psychological basis for public acceptance of the Social Security System. The American Psychologist 30:875–83.

2   Goody, Jack

1976   Aging in nonindustrial societies. Pp. 117–29 in Robert H. Binstock and Ethel Shanas (eds.), Handbook of Aging and the Social Sciences. New York: Van Nostrand Reinhold.

10   Gordon, Chad, Charles M. Gaitz, and Judith Scott

1976   Leisure and lives: personal expressivity across the life span. Pp. 310–41 in Robert H. Binstock and Ethel Shanas (eds.), Handbook of Aging and the Social Sciences. New York: Van Nostrand Reinhold.

8   Gordon, Gerald

1966   Role Theory and Illness. New Haven, Conn.: College and University Press Services.

Gordon, Margaret S.

8   1960   Aging and income security. Pp. 208–60 in Clark Tibbitts (ed.), Handbook of Social Gerontology. Chicago: University of Chicago Press.

9   1961   Work and patterns of retirement. Pp. 15–53 in Robert W. Kleemeier (ed.), Aging and Leisure. New York: Oxford University Press.

8, 9   1963   Income security programs and the propensity to retire. Pp. 436–58 in Richard H. Williams, Clark Tibbitts, and Wilma Donahue (eds.), Processes of Aging, Volume 2. New York: Atherton Press.

5   Gordon, S. K.

       1973   The phenomenon of depression in old age. The Gerontologist 13:100–05.

8   Gordon, Tavia

       1964   Blood pressure of adults by age and sex. Vital and Health Statistics, Series 11, Number 4. Washington, D.C.: U.S. Government Printing Office.

11   Gorer, Geoffrey

       1965   Death, Grief and Mourning. Garden City, New York: Doubleday.

       Gottesman, Leonard E.

19   1970   Long-range priorities for the aged. Aging and Human Development 1:393–400.

8   1973   Milieu treatment of the aged in institutions. The Gerontologist 13:23–26.

8,18   Gottesman, Leonard E., Barbara Ishizaki, and Stacey Mong McBride

       1979   Service management—plan and concept in Pennsylvania. The Gerontologist 19:379–85.

5   Gottsdanker, Robert

       1982   Age and simple reaction time. Journal of Gerontology 37:342–48.

       Goudy, Willis J.

9   1981   Changing work expectations: findings from the Retirement History Study. The Gerontologist 21:644–49.

9   1982   Antecedent factors related to changing work expectations: evidence from the Retirement History Study. Research on Aging 4:139–58.

9   Goudy, Willis J., E. A. Powers, and Patricia M. Keith

       1975   Work and retirement: a test of attitudinal relationships. Journal of Gerontology 30:193–98.

9   Goudy, Willis J., Edward A. Powers, Patricia M. Keith, and Richard A. Reger

       1980   Changes in attitudes toward retirement: evidence from a panel study of older males. Journal of Gerontology 35:942–48.

5   Gozali, J.

       1971   The relationship between age and attitude toward disabled persons. The Gerontologist 11:289–91.

8   Grabowsky, S., and W. D. Mason

       1974   Learning for Aging. Washington, D.C.: Adult Educational Association.

       Grad, Susan

8   1973   Relative importance of income sources of the aged. Social Security Bulletin 36(8):37–45.

9   1977   New retirees and the stability of the retirement decision. Social Security Bulletin 40(3):3–12.

3, 9   Graebner, William

       1980   A History of Retirement: The Meaning and Function of an American Institution, 1885–1978. New Haven: Yale University Press.

10   Graney, Marshall J.

       1975   Happiness and social participation in aging. Journal of Gerontology 30:701–06.

9   Graney, Marshall J., and Doris M. Cottam

       1981   Labor force nonparticipation of older people: United States, 1890–1970. The Gerontologist 21:138–41.

	Graney, Marshall J., and Edith E. Graney
12	1973 Scaling adjustment in older people. International Journal of Aging and Human Development 4:351–59.
12	1974 Communications activity substitutions in aging. Journal of Communication 24(4):88–96.
8	Graney, Marshall J., and Renee M. Zimmerman
	1980–81 Causes and consequences of health self-report variations among older people. International Journal of Aging and Human Development 12:291–300.
1	Granick, S., and R. D. Patterson (eds.)
	1972 Human Aging II. An Eleven-Year Follow-Up Biomedical and Behavioral Study. Washington, D.C.: U.S. Government Printing Office.
9	Gratton, Brian, and Marie Haug
	1983 Decision and adaptation: research on female retirement. Research on Aging 5:59–76.
8	Grauer, H.
	1971 Institutions for the aged—therapeutic communities? Journal of American Geriatric Society 19:687–92.
10	Gray, Robert M., and David O. Moberg
	1962 The Church and the Older Person. Grand Rapids, Michigan: W. B. Eerdsman.
9	Gray, Susan, and Dean Morse
	1980 Retirement and re-engagement: changing work options for older workers. Aging and Work 3:103–12.
9	Green, Mark., H. C. Pyron, O. V. Manion, and H. Winkelvoss
	1969 Pre-Retirement Counseling, Retirement, Adjustment and the Older Employee. Eugene, Oregon: University of Oregon Graduate School of Management.
13, 19	Green, Susan K.
	1981 Attitudes and perceptions about the elderly: current and future perspectives. International Journal of Aging and Human Development 13:99–119.
8	Greenleigh Associates
	1966 An Evaluation of the Foster Grandparent Program. New York: The Greenleigh Associates.
5	Greenwald, Anthony
	1980 The totalitarian ego: fabrication and revision of personal history. The American Psychologist 35:603–18.
14	Griffiths, K. A., O. W. Farley, W. P. Dean, and L. L. Boon
	1971 Socio-economic class and the disadvantaged senior citizen. Aging and Human Development 2:288–95.
5	Griffitt, W., J. Nelson, and G. Littlepage
	1972 Old age and response to agreement-disagreement. Journal of Gerontology 27:269–74.
11	Gruman, G. J.
	1973 An historical introduction to ideas about voluntary euthanasia, with a bibliography survey and guide for interdisciplinary studies. Omega 4(2):87–138.
8, 18	Grunow, Dieter
	1980 Sozialstationen: a new model for home delivery care and service (West Germany). The Gerontologist 20:308–17.
	Gubrium, Jaber F.
8, 12	1970 Environmental effects on morale in old age and the resources of health and solvency. The Gerontologist 10:294–97.
17	1972a Continuity in social support, political interest and voting in old age. The Gerontologist 12:421–23.
6	1972b Toward a socio-environmental theory of aging. The Gerontologist 12:281–84.

5, 12	1973a	Apprehensions of coping incompetence and responses to fear in old age. International Journal of Aging and Human Development 4:111–25.
6	1973b	The Myth of the Golden Years: A Socio-Environmental Theory of Aging. Springfield, Ill.: Charles C. Thomas.
11	1974a	Marital desolation and the evaluation of everyday life in old age. Journal of Marriage and the Family 36:107–13.
8	1974b	Late Life: Communities and Environmental Policy. Springfield, Ill.: Charles C. Thomas.
7, 8	1975a	Being single in old age. International Journal of Aging and Human Development 6:29–41.
8	1975b	Living and Dying and Murray Manor. New York: St. Martin's Press.
11	1976	Death worlds in a nursing home. Pp. 83–104 in L. H. Lofland (ed.), Toward a Sociology of Death and Dying. Beverly Hills, Calif.: Sage Publications, Inc., Sage Issues 28.
5	1978	Notes on the social organization of senility. Urban Life 7:23–44.

9 Guillemard, A. M.

	1972	Le Retraite. Une Morte Sociale. Paris-La Haye: Mouton.

5 Gurin, Gerald, Joseph Veroff, and Sheila Feld

	1960	Americans View Their Mental Health: A National Interview Study. New York: Basic Books.

5 Gurland, Barry J., Laura Lee Dean, John Copeland, Roni Gurland, and Robert Golden

	1982	Criteria for the diagnosis of dementia in the community elderly. The Gerontologist 22:180–86.

Gutmann, David L.

5	1969	The Country of Old Men: Cultural Studies in the Psychology of Later Life. Ann Arbor, Michigan: University of Michigan-Wayne State University, Institute of Gerontology.
10	1973	Leisure-time activity interests of Jewish aged. The Gerontologist 13:219–23.
12	1976	Individual adaptation in the middle years. Developmental issues in the masculine mid-life crisis. Journal of Geriatric Psychiatry 9:41–59.
1, 5	1977	The cross-cultural perspective: notes toward a comparative psychology of aging. Pp. 302–26 in James E. Birren and K. Warner Schaie (eds.), Handbook of the Psychology of Aging. New York: Van Nostrand Reinhold.

8 Gutmann, David, Frances L. Eyster, and Garland Lewis

	1975	Improving the care of the aged through interdisciplinary efforts. The Gerontologist 15:387–92.

5 Gutmann, David, Leonard Gottesman, and Sydney Tessler

	1973	A comparative study of ego functioning in geriatric patients. The Gerontologist 13:419–23.

10, 12 Guy, Rebecca Faith

	1982	Religion, physical disabilities and life satisfaction in older age cohorts. International Journal of Aging and Human Development 15:225–32.

5 Haan, Norma

	1976	Personality organizations of well-functioning younger people and older adults. International Journal of Aging and Human Development 7:117–27.
12	1977	Coping and Defending: Processes of Self-Environment Organization. New York: Academic Press.

5 Haan, Norma, and David Day

	1974	A longitudinal study of change and sameness in personality development: adolescence to later adulthood. International Journal of Aging and Human Development 5:11–9.

8, 16 Haanes-Olsen, Leif
    1978 Earnings replacement rate of old-age benefits, 1965–75, selected countries. Social Security Bulletin 41(1):3–14.

3 Haber, Carole
    1978 Mandatory retirement in nineteenth-century America: the conceptual basis for a new work cycle. Journal of Social History 12:77–96.

3   1983 Beyond Sixty-Five. Cambridge, Mass.: Cambridge University Press.

9 Hall, Arden, and Terry R. Johnson
    1980 The determinants of planned retirement age. Industrial and Labor Relations Review. 33:241–54.

5 Hall, E. H., R. D. Savage, N. Bolton, D. M. Pidwell, and G. Blessed
    1972 Intellect, mental illness, and survival in the aged: a longitudinal investigation. Journal of Gerontology 27:237–44.

8 Hall, Gertrude H.
    1966 The Law and the Impaired Older Person. New York: National Council on Aging.

    Hall, Gertrude H., and Geneva Mathiasen (eds.)

8   1968 Overcoming Barriers to Protective Services for the Aged. New York: National Council for the Aging.

8   1973 Guide to Development of Protective Services for Older People. Springfield, Ill.: Charles C. Thomas.

8 Hameister, Dennis R.
    1976 Conceptual model for the library's service to the elderly. Educational Gerontology 1:279–84.

15 Hamill, Lynn L.
    1982 Life in Prison: An Exploratory Study of the Elderly Inmate. Unpublished MGS Thesis. Oxford, Ohio: Miami University

7, 19 Hammel, E. A., K. W. Wachter, and C. K. McDaniel
    1981 The kin of the aged in A.D. 2000. Pp. 11–39 in Sara B. Keisler et al. (eds.), Aging: Social Change. New York: Academic Press.

8 Hamovitch, Maurice B., and J. E. Peterson
    1969 Housing needs and satisfactions of the elderly. The Gerontologist 9:30–32.

8, 15 Hampe, Gary D., and Audie L. Blevins, Jr.
    1975 Primary group interaction of residents in a retirement hotel. International Journal of Aging and Human Development 6:309–20.

15 Hand, Jennifer
    1983 Shopping-bag women: aging deviants in the city. Pp. 155–77 in E. W. Markson (ed.), Older Women: Issues and Prospects. Lexington, Mass.: Lexington Books.

11 Handal, P. J.
    1969 The relationship between subjective life expectancy, death anxiety, and general anxiety. Journal of Clinical Psychology. 25:39–42.

1 Hansen, P. From (ed.)
    1964 Age with a Future. Copenhagen: Munksgaard.

9, 16 Hanson, P. M.
    1972 Age and physical capacity to work. Industrial Gerontology 12:20–28.

10 Hanssen, Anne M., Nicholas J. Meima, Linda M. Buckspan, Barbara E. Henderson, Thea L. Helbig, and Steven H. Zarit
    1978 Correlates of senior center participation. The Gerontologist 18:193–99.

8, 9 Hardcastle, D. A.
    1981 Getting along after retirement: an economic inquiry. Pp. 151–68 in F. J. Berghorn et al. (eds.), The Dynamics of Aging. Boulder, Colo.: Westview Press.

Hardy, Melissa A.

9   1982a Job characteristics and health: differential impact on benefit entitlement. Research on
               Aging 4:457–78.

9   1982b Social policy and determinants of retirement: a longitudinal analysis of older white
               males, 1969–75. Social Forces 60:1103–22.

8, 18   Harel, Zev
        1981   Quality of care, congruence and well-being among institutionalized aged. The Geron-
               tologist 21:523–31.

8, 18   Harel, Zev, and Linda Noelker
        1982   Social integration, health, and choice: their impact on the well-being of institutionalized
               aged. Research on Aging 4:97–112.

2, 19   Harootyan, Robert A.
        1982   Aging population research: suggestions for a model data system for service planning.
               The Gerontologist 22:164–69.

16, 17 Harrington, Charlene
        1983   Social Security and Medicare: policy shifts in the 1980s. Pp. 83–111 in Carroll L. Estes
               and R. J. Newcomer (eds.), Fiscal Austerity and Aging: Shifting Government Respon-
               sibility for the Elderly. Beverly Hills, Calif.: Sage.

13   Harris, Adella J., and Jonathan F. Feinberg
        1977   Television and aging; is what you see what you get? The Gerontologist 17:464–67.

2, 8,
9, 15   Harris, Charles S.
        1978   Fact Book on Aging: A Profile of America's Older Population. Washington, D.C.: Na-
               tional Council on the Aging.

        Harris, Louis
9   1965a Pleasant retirement expected. Washington Post, November 28.
5   1965b Thoughts of loneliness haunt elderly Americans. Washington Post, November 29.

8, 9,
12,
13, 18 Harris, Louis, and Associates
        1975   The Myth and Reality of Aging in America. Washington, D.C.: National Council on
               Aging.

5   Hartley, Alan A.
        1981   Adult age differences in deductive reasoning processes. Journal of Gerontology 36:700–06.

7   Hartshorne, Timothy A., and Guy J. Manaster
        1982   The relationship with grandparents: contact, importance, role conception. International
               Journal of Aging and Human Development 15:233–45.

11   Harvey, Carol D., and Howard M. Bahr
        1974   Widowhood, morale, and affiliation. Journal of Marriage and the Family 36:97–106.

        Haug, Marie
8, 11   1978   Aging and the right to terminate medical treatment. Journal of Gerontology 33:586–91.
8, 18   1981   Age and medical care utilization patterns. Journal of Gerontology 36:103–11.

10, 12 Havens, Betty J.
        1968   An investigation of activity patterns and adjustment in an aging population. The Geron-
               tologist 8:201–06.

        Havighurst, Robert J.
10   1960   Life beyond the family and work. Pp. 299–353 in E. W. Burgess (ed.), Aging in West-
               ern Societies. Chicago: University of Chicago Press.

12   1963   Successful aging. Pp. 299–320 in Richard H. Williams, Clark Tibbitts, and Wilma
               Donahue (eds.), Processes of Aging. Volume 1. New York: Atherton Press.

14   1971   Social class perspectives on the life cycle. Human Development 4:110–24.

10   1972   Life style and leisure patterns: their evolution through the life cycle. Pp. 35–48 in Leisure in the Third Age. Paris: International Center for Social Gerontology.

6, 9,
10   1973a   Social roles, work, leisure, and education. Pp. 598–618 in C. Eisdorfer and M. P. Lawton (eds.), The Psychology of Adult Development and Aging. Washington, D.C.: American Psychological Association.

5   1973b   History of developmental psychology: socialization and personality development through the life span. Pp. 3–24 in Paul B. Baltes and K. Warner Schaie (eds.), Life-Span Developmental Psychology: Personality and Socialization. New York: Academic Press.

10   Havighurst, Robert J., and Kenneth Feigenbaum
       1968   Leisure and life-style. Pp. 347–53 in Bernice L. Neugarten (ed.), Middle Age and Aging. Chicago: University of Chicago Press.

5   Havighurst, Robert J., and R. Glasser
       1972   An exploratory study of reminiscence. Journal of Gerontology 27:245–53.

9   Havighurst, Robert J., Bernice L. Neugarten, and Vern L. Bengtson
       1966   A cross-national study of adjustment to retirement. The Gerontologist 6:137–38.

     Havighurst, Robert J., Bernice L. Neugarten, and Sheldon S. Tobin
5, 12   1963   Disengagement, personality, and life satisfaction. Pp. 319–24 in P. From Hansen (ed.), Age with a Future. Copenhagen: Munksgaard.

12   1968   Disengagement and patterns of aging. Pp. 161–72 in Bernice L. Neugarten (ed.), Middle Age and Aging. Chicago: University of Chicago Press.

9   Havighurst, Robert J., Joseph M. A. Minnichs, Bernice L. Neugarten, and Hans Thomae
       1969   Adjustment to Retirement: A Cross-National Study. New York: Humanities Press.

     Hayflick, Leonard
4   1968   Human cells and aging. Scientific American 218(3):32–37.
4   1975   Cell biology of aging. Bioscience 25:629–37.

9   Haynes, Suzanne G., Anthony J. McMichael, and Herman A. Tyroler
       1978   Survival after early and normal retirement. Journal of Gerontology 33:269–78.

5   Hayslip, Bert, Jr., and Kevin J. Kennelly
       1982   Short-term memory and crystallized-fluid intelligence in adulthood. Research on Aging 4:314–32.

9, 10,
14   Hearn, H. L.
       1971   Career and leisure patterns of middle-aged urban blacks. The Gerontologist 11(4, part 2):21–26.

5   Heath, Douglas H.
       1977   Maturity and Competence; A Transcultural View. New York: Gardner.

8   Hedden, L. J.
       1974   Intergenerational living: university dormitories. The Gerontologist 14:283–85.

8, 16   Heflin, Thomas L.
       1976   Social security: individual or social equity? The Gerontologist 16:455–57.

     Heidbreder, Elizabeth M.
9   1972a   Factors in retirement adjustment: white-collar/blue-collar experience. Industrial Gerontology 12:69–79.

9   1972b   Pensions and the single woman. Industrial Gerontology 15:52–62.

6   Heilbrun, Alfred B., Jr., and Charles V. Lais
       1964   Decreased role consistency in the aged. Journal of Gerontology 19:325–29.

Hellebrandt, Frances A.

5   1978   The senile dement in our midst: a look at the other side of the coin. The Gerontologist 18:67–70.

14   1980   Aging among the advantaged: a new look at the stereotype of the elderly. The Gerontologist 20:404–17.

8   Helling, J. F., and B. M. Bauer
       1972   Seniors on campus. Adult Leadership 21(December):203–05.

7, 8   Heltsley, Mary E., and Ronald C. Powers
       1975   Social interaction and perceived adequacy of interaction of the rural aged. The Gerontologist 15:533–36.

16   Hendricks, Gary L., and James R. Storey
       1982   Economics of retirement. Pp. 136–90 in M. Morrison (ed.), The Economics of Aging: The Future of Retirement. New York: Van Nostrand Reinhold.

3   Hendricks, Jon A., and C. Davis Hendricks
       1977–78 The age-old question of old age: was it really so much better back when? Interna-

12   1964   Disengagement, personality and life satisfaction in the later years. Pp. 419–25 in P. From Hansen (ed.), Age with a Future. Copenhagen: Munksgaard.
       tional Journal of Aging and Human Development 8:139–54.

8   Hendrickson, A. (ed.)
       1973   A Manual on Planning Educational Programs for Older Adults. Tallahassee: Florida State University, Department of Adult Education.

       Heneman, H. G.

16   1972   The relationship between age and motivation to perform on the job. Industrial Gerontology 16:30–36.

13, 16 1974   Age discrimination and employment testing. Industrial Gerontology 1:65–71.

8, 17 Henig, Jeffrey R.
       1981   Gentrification and displacement of the elderly: an empirical analysis. The Gerontologist 21:67–75.

8   Henle, Peter
       1972   Recent trends in retirement benefits related to earnings. Monthly Labor Review 95:12–20.

8, 14 Henretta, John C., and Richard T. Campbell
       1976   Status attainment and status maintenance: a study of stratification in old age. American Sociological Review 41:981–92.

1   Henretta, John C., Richard T. Campbell, and Gloria Gardocki
       1976   Survey research in aging; an evaluation of the Harris Survey. The Gerontologist 17:160–66.

8   Henri, Judy
       1980   An alternative to institutionalization. The Gerontologist 20:418–20.

8   Henry, Jules
       1963   Culture Against Man. New York: Knopf.

       Henry, William E.

12   1964   The theory of intrinsic disengagement. Pp. 415–18 in P. From Hansen (ed.), Age with a Future. Copenhagen, Munksgaard.

6   1971   The role of work in structuring the life cycle. Human Development 14:125–31.

4, 5   Heron, Alastair, and Sheila Chown
       1967   Age with Function. Boston: Little, Brown.

8, 18 Herz, Kurt G.
       1968   New patterns of social services for the aging and the aged. Journal of Jewish Community Services 44:236–45.

Herzog, A. Regula, and Willard L. Rodgers

12   1981   Age and satisfaction: data from several large surveys. Research on Aging 3:142–65.

12   1981   The structure of subjective well-being in different age groups. Journal of Gerontology 36:472–79.

Hess, Beth

7   1972   Friendship. Pp. 357–93 in Matilda White Riley et al. (eds.), Aging and Society. Volume Three: A Sociology of Age Stratification. New York: Russell Sage.

13   1974   Stereotypes of the aged. Journal of Communications 24(4):76–85.

8   1976a   Self-help among the aged. Social Policy 7(3):55–62.

11   Heyman, Dorothy K., and D. T. Gianturco

        1973   Long-term adaptation by the elderly to bereavement. Journal of Gerontology 28:359–62.

Heyman, Dorothy K., and Frances C. Jeffers

14   1964   Study of the relative influence of race and socio-economic status upon the activities and attitudes of a southern aged population. Journal of Gerontology 19:225–29.

7, 9   1968   Wives and retirement: a pilot study. Journal of Gerontology 23:488–96.

Hickey, Tom

10   1972   Catholic religious orders and the aging process: research, training and service programs. The Gerontologist 12:16.

19   1974   In-service training in gerontology: toward the design of an effective educational process. The Gerontologist 14:57–64.

15   Hickey, Tom, and Richard L. Douglass

        1981   Neglect and abuse of older family members: professional's perspectives and case experiences. The Gerontologist 21:171–76.

19   Hickey, Tom, and J. W. Hodgson

        1974   Contextual and developmental issues in the evaluation of adult learning: training and applied gerontology as an example. Pp. 235–55 in Jaber F. Gubrium (ed.), Late Life: Communities and Environmental Policy. Springfield, Ill.: Charles C. Thomas.

13   Hickey, Tom, and Richard A. Kalish

        1968   Young people's perceptions of adults. Journal of Gerontology 23:215–19.

13   Hickey, Tom, Louise A. Hickey, and Richard A. Kalish

        1968   Children's perceptions of the elderly. Journal of Genetic Psychology 112:227–35.

13   Hicks, Dale A., C. Jean Rogers, and Kenneth Shemberg

        1976   Attitudes toward the elderly: a comparison of measures. Experimental Aging Research 2:119–24.

Hiemstra, R. P.

8   1972   Continuing education for the aged: a survey of needs and interests of older people. Adult Education 22:100–09.

8   1973   Educational planning for older adults: a survey of "expressive" versus "instrumental" preferences. International Journal of Aging and Human Development 4:147–56.

9   Hiestand, D. L.

        1971   Changing Careers After Thirty-Five. New York: Columbia University Press.

7   Hill, Reuben

        1965   Decision making and the family life cycle. Pp. 113–39 in Ethel Shanas and Gordon F. Streib (eds.), Social Structure and the Family. Englewood Cliffs, N.J.: Prentice-Hall.

7   Hill, Reuben, and R. H. Rodgers

        1964   The developmental approach. Pp. 171–211 in Harold T. Christensen (ed.), Handbook of Marriage and the Family. Chicago: Rand McNally.

14   Hill, Robert

        1978   A demographic profile of the black elderly. Aging 287–88:2–9.

11   Hinton, J.
        1972   Dying, second edition. Baltimore: Penguin Books.
8, 14   Hirsch, C., D. P. Kent, and S. L. Silverman
        1972   Homogeneity and heterogeneity among low-income negro and white aged. Pp. 484–500
                in D. P. Kent, R. Kastenbaum, and S. Sherwood (eds.), Research Planning and Action
                for the Elderly: The Power and Potential of Social Science. New York: Behavioral
                Publications.
1, 19   Hirschfield, Ira S., and David A. Peterson
        1982   The professionalization of gerontology. The Gerontologist 22:215–19.
10   Hoar, Jere
        1961   Study of free-time activities of 200 aged persons. Sociology and Social Research 45:157–
                63.
10   Hobart, Charles W.
        1975   Active sports participation among the young, the middle-aged and the elderly. Interna-
                tional Review of Sport Sociology 10(3–4):27–44.
        Hochschild, Arlie Russell
8   1973   The Unexpected Community. Englewood Cliffs, N.J.: Prentice-Hall.
5, 12   1975   Disengagement theory: a critique and proposal. American Sociological Review 40:553–69.
15   Hoffman, H., and P. C. Nelson
        1971   Personality characteristics of alcoholics in relation to age and intelligence. Psychological
                Reports 29:143–46.
9, 12   Holahan, Carole Kavalic
        1981   Lifetime achievement patterns, retirement, and life satisfaction of gifted aged women.
                Journal of Gerontology 36:741–49.
5   Holcomb, Walter L.
        1975   Spiritual crises among the aging. Pp. 235–78 in M. G. Spencer and C. J. Dorr (eds.),
                Understanding Aging: A Multidisciplinary Approach. New York: Appleton-Century-
                Crofts.
9   Holden, Karen C.
        1978   Comparability of the measured labor force of older women in Japan and the United
                States. Journal of Gerontology 33:422–26.
16   Hollister, Robinson
        1974   Social mythology and reform: income maintenance for the aged. Pp. 19–40 in Frederick
                R. Eisele (ed.), Political Consequences of Aging. Philadelphia: American Academy of
                Political and Social Sciences.
6, 12   Holmes, Thomas H., and M. Masuda
        1974   Life change and illness susceptibility. Pp. 45–72 in Barbara S. Dohrenwend and Bruce
                P. Dohrenwend (eds.), Stressful Life Events: Their Nature and Effects. New York:
                Wiley.
        Holtzman, Abraham
17   1954   Analysis of old age politics in the United States. Journal of Gerontology 9:56–66.
17   1963   The Townsend Movement: A Political Study. New York: Bookman Associates.
14   Holzberg, Carol S.
        1982   Ethnicity and aging: anthropological perspectives on more than just the minority elder-
                ly. The Gerontologist 22:249–57.
12   Horan, Patrick M., and John C. Belcher
        1982   Lifestyle and morale in the southern rural aged. Research on Aging 4:523–49.
8, 16   Horlick, Max
        1973   Supplemental security income for the aged: foreign experience. Social Security Bulletin
                36(12):3–12, 24.

5   Horn, John L.
       1966   Integration of structural and developmental concepts of the theory of fluid and crystal-
               lized intelligence. Pp. 162–81 in R. B. Cattell (ed.), Handbook of Multivariate Experi-
               mental Psychology. Chicago: Rand McNally.
     Horn, John L., and Gary Donaldson
5   1976   On the myth of intellectual decline in adulthood. American Psychologist 31:701–19.
5   1977   Faith is not enough. A response to the Baltes-Schaie claim that intelligence does not
               wane. American Psychologist 32:369–73.
5   Horn, John L., Gary Donaldson, and Robert Engstrom
       1981   Apprehension, memory, and fluid intelligence decline in adulthood. Research on Aging
               3:33–84.
12   Horrocks, J. E., and M. C. Mussman
       1970   Middle-scence: age-related stress periods during adult years. Genetic Psychology mono-
               graphs 82:119.
17   Hout, Michael, and David Knoke
       1975   Change in voting turnout, 1952–1972. The Public Opinion Quarterly 39:52–68.
8, 11 Howard, E.
       1974   The effect of work experience in a nursing home on the attitudes toward death held by
               nurse aides. The Gerontologist 14:54–56.
8   Howie, Lonnie J., and Thomas F. Drury
       1978   Current Estimates from the Health Interview Survey: United States—1977. Vital and
               Health Statistics. Series 10, Number 126. Washington, D.C: National Center for
               Health Statistics.
12   Hoyt, Danny R., Marvin A. Kaiser, George A. Peters, and Nicholas Babchuck
       1980   Life satisfaction and activity theory: a multidimensional approach. Journal of Geron-
               tology 35:935–41.
8   Hoyt, George C.
       1954   The life of the retired in a trailer park. American Journal of Sociology 59:361–70.
     Hudson, Robert B.
19   1974   Rational planning and organizational imperatives: prospects for area planning in aging.
               Pp. 41–54 in Frederick R. Eisele (ed.), Political Consequences of Aging. Philadelphia:
               American Academy of Political and Social Sciences.
17   1978   The "graying" of the federal budget and its consequences for old-age policy. The
               Gerontologist 18:428–40.
17   1981   (ed.), The Aging in Politics: Process and Policy. Springfield, Ill.: Charles C. Thomas.
17   Hudson, Robert B., and Robert H. Binstock
       1976   Political systems and aging. Pp. 369–400 in Robert H. Binstock and Ethel Shanas
               (eds.), Handbook of Aging and the Social Sciences. New York: Van Nostrand Rein-
               hold.
5   Hughston, George A., and Sharon B. Merriam
       1982   Reminiscence: a nonformal technique for improving cognitive functioning in the aged.
               International Journal of Aging and Human Development 15:139–49.
5   Hulicka, Irene M.
       1967   Age changes and age differences in memory functioning. The Gerontologist 7(2, part
               2):46–54.
5   Hultsch, D. F., and R. W. Bortner
       1974   Personal time perspective in adulthood: a time-sequential study. Developmental Psy-
               chology 10:835–37.
5   Hunter, Kathleen I., Margaret W. Linn, and Rachel Harris
       1981–82 Characteristics of high and low self-esteem in the elderly. International Journal of
               Aging and Human Development 14:117–26.

Hunter, Woodrow W.
9   1968   A Longitudinal Study of Pre-Retirement Education. Ann Arbor, Michigan: University of Michigan Division of Gerontology.
9   1972   Leadership training for pre-retirement programs in religious communities. The Gerontologist 12:17–18.
7, 12 Hurst, Charles E., and David A. Guldin
       1981   The effects of intra-individual and inter-spouse status inconsistency on life satisfaction among older persons. Journal of Gerontology 36:112–21.
16   Hurwitz, Jacob C., and William L. Burris
       1972   Terminated UAW pension plans: a study. Industrial Gerontology 15:40–51.
5   Hussian, Richard A., and Sandra D. Hill
       1980   Stereotyped behavior in elderly patients with chronic organic mental disorder. Journal of Gerontology 35:689–91.
7, 12 Hutchison, Ira W., III
       1975   The significance of marital status for morale and life satisfaction among lower-income elderly. Journal of Marriage and the Family 37(2):287–93.
12   Hynson, Lawrence M., Jr.
       1975   Rural-urban differences in satisfaction among the elderly. Rural Sociology 40(1):64–66.
7, 9   Ingraham, Mark H.
       1974   My Purpose Holds: Reactions and Experiences in Retirement. New York: TIAA/CREF.
16   International Centre of Social Gerontology
       1971   Work and Aging. Second International Course in Social Gerontology. Florence—May 24–28. Paris: International Centre of Social Gerontology.
9   Irelan, Lola M.
       1972   Retirement history study: introduction. Social Security Bulletin 35(11):3–8.
9   Irelan, Lola M., and D. B. Bell
       1972   Understanding subjectively defined retirement: a pilot analysis. The Gerontologist 12:354–56.
8   Irelan, Lola M., and Dena K. Motley
       1972   Health on the threshold of retirement. Industrial Gerontology 12:16–19.
5   Isaacs, B., and A. J. Akhtar
       1972   The set test: a rapid test of mental function in old people. Age and Ageing 1:222–26.
8, 18 Ishizaki, Barbara, Leonard E. Gottesman, and Stacey Mong McBride
       1979   Determinants of model choice for service management systems. The Gerontologist 19:385–88.
13   Ivester, Connie, and Karl King
       1977   Attitudes of adolescents toward the aged. The Gerontologist 17:85–89.
       Jackson, Hobart C.
14   1971a   National caucus on the black aged: a progress report. Aging and Human Development 2:226–31.
19   1971b   National goals and priorities in the social welfare of the aging. The Gerontologist 11:88–94.
       Jackson, Jacquelyne J.
14   1967   Social gerontology and the negro: a review. The Gerontologist 7:168–78.
14   1971a   Sex and social class variations in black aged parent-adult child relationships. Aging and Human Development 2:96–107.
14   1971b   The blacklands of gerontology. Aging and Human Development 2:156–71.
14, 19 1971c   Negro aged: toward needed research in social gerontology. The Gerontologist 11(1, part 2):52–57.
14   1972a   Aged negroes: their cultural departures from statistical stereotypes and rural-urban dif-

ferences. Pp. 501–13 in D. P. Kent, R. Kastenbaum, and S. Sherwood (eds.), Research Planning Action for the Elderly: The Power and Potential of Social Science. New York: Behavioral Publications.

8, 14   1972b   Social impacts of housing relocation upon urban, low-income black aged. The Gerontologist 12:32–37.

14, 17   1974   NCBA, black aged and politics. Pp. 138–59 in Frederick R. Eisele (ed.), Political Consequences of Aging. Philadelphia: American Academy of Political and Social Sciences.

14   1975   Aging Black Women. Washington, D.C.: College and University Press.

14   1975–76   Plights of older black women in the United States. Black Aging 1(2,3):12–20.

5, 14   1976–77   Menopausal attitudes and behaviors among senescent black women and descriptors of changing attitudes and activities among aged blacks. Black Aging 2(1):8–29.

8, 14   1978   Special health problems of aged blacks. Aging 287–88:15–20.

12, 14   Jackson, James S., John D. Bacon, and John Peterson
    1977–78   Life satisfaction among black urban elderly. International Journal of Aging and Human Development 8:168–79.

8   Jackson, M. L., Jr.
    1972   Housing for older Americans. HUD Challenge 3(July):4–7.

    Jacobs, Jerry
9   1974   An ethnographic study of a retirement setting. The Gerontologist 14(6):483–87.
9   1975   Older Persons and Retirement Communities: Case Studies in Social Gerontology. Springfield, Ill.: Charles C. Thomas.

    Jacobs, Ruth H.
7, 8   1969   The friendship club: a case study of the segregated aged. The Gerontologist 9:276–80.
14   1976   A typology of older American women. Social Policy 7(3):34–39.

11   Jacobs, S., and A. Ostfeld
    1977   An epidemiological review of the mortality of bereavement. Psychosomatic Medicine 39:344–357.

9   Jacobson, D.
    1972   Willingness to retire in relation to job strain and type of work. Industrial Gerontology 13:65–74.

    Jaffee, A. J.
9   1968   Differential patterns of retirement by social class and personal characteristics. Pp. 105–10 in Frances M. Carp (ed.), The Retirement Process. Washington, D.C.: U.S. Department of Health, Education and Welfare.
9   1970   Men prefer not to retire. Industrial Gerontology 5:1–11.
9   1971a   The middle years: neither too young nor too old. Industrial Gerontology. September (Special Issue):1–90.
9, 16   1971b   Has the retreat from the labor force halted? A note on retirement of men, 1930–1970. Industrial Gerontology 9:1–12.
9   1972   The retirement dilemma. Industrial Gerontology 14:1–88.

9   Jaffe, A. J., and Jeanne Clare Ridley
    1976   The extent of lifetime employment of women in the United States. Industrial Gerontology 3:25–36.

5   James, William
    1890   Principles of Psychology. New York: Dover.

9   Janis, I. L., and Mann, L.
    1977   Decision Making. New York: Free Press.

5   Jarvik, Lissy F.
    1975   Thoughts on the psychobiology of aging. American Psychologist 30(5):576–83.

5   Jarvik, Lissy F., and J. E. Blum
      1971   Cognitive declines as predictors of mortality in twin pairs. Pp. 199–211 in Erdman Pal-
              more and F. C. Jeffers (eds.), Prediction of the Life Span. Lexington, Mass.: D. C.
              Heath.

19   Jarvik, Lissy F., and D. Cohen
      1974   Relevance of research to work with the aged. Pp. 301–31 in A. N. Schwartz and I. N.
              Mensh (eds.), Professional Obligations and Approaches to the Aged. Springfield, Ill.:
              Charles C. Thomas.

5   Jarvik, Lissy F., J. E. Blum, and A. O. Varma
      1972   Genetic components and intellectual functioning during senescence: a 20-year study of
              aging twins. Behavioral Genetics 2:159–71.

12   Jarvis, George K., R. G. Ferrence, F. G. Johnson, and P. C. Whitehead
      1976   Sex and age patterns in self-injury. Journal of Health and Social Behavior 17:145–54.

9, 12 Jaslow, Philip
      1976   Employment, retirement, and morale among older women. Journal of Gerontology 31:
              212–18.

11   Jeffers, F. C., C. R. Nichols, and C. Eisdorfer
      1961   Attitudes of older persons toward death: a preliminary study. Journal of Gerontology
              16:53–56.

13   Jeffreys-Fox, Bruce
      1977   How Realistic Are Television's Portrayals of the Elderly? University Park, Penn.: The
              Annenberg School of Communications.

13, 16 Jenkins, M. M.
      1972   Age discrimination in employment testing. Industrial Gerontology 12:42–46.

4, 13 Jensen, Gordon D., and Frederick B. Oakley
      1980   Aged appearance and behavior: an evolutionary and ethological perspective. The Geron-
              tologist 20:595–97.

10   Jericho, Bonnie J.
      1977   Longitudinal changes in religious activity subscores of aged blacks. Black Aging
              2(4,5,6):17–24.

     Jerome, Dorothy (ed.)
      1983   Aging in Modern Society. London: St. Martins Press.

8, 18 Jette, Alan M., Lawrence G. Branch, Richard A. Wentzel, William F. Carney, Deborah Dennis,
              and Maria A. Madden
      1981   Home care service diversification: a pilot investigation. The Gerontologist 21:572–79.

9   Jewson, Ruth H.
      1982   After retirement: an exploratory study of the professional woman. Pp. 169–82 in M.
              Szinovacz (ed.), Women's Retirement. Beverly Hills, Calif.: Sage.

7   Johnson, Colleen Leahy, and Donald J. Catalano
      1981   Childless elderly and their family supports. The Gerontologist 21:610–18.

     Johnson, Elizabeth S.
7   1978   "Good" relationships between older mothers and their daughters: a causal model. The
              Gerontologist 18:301–06.
7   1982   Role expectations and role realities of older Italian mothers and their daughters. Inter-
              national Journal of Aging and Human Development 14:271–76.

7   Johnson, Elizabeth S., and Barbara J. Bursk
      1977   Relationships between the elderly and their adult children. The Gerontologist 17:90–96.

17   Johnson, Gregory, and J. Lawrence Kamara
      1977–78 Growing up and growing old: the politics of age exclusion. International Journal of
              Aging and Human Development 8:99–110.

8   Johnson, S. K.
          1971   Idle Haven: Community Building Among the Working-Class Retired. Berkeley: University of California Press.

9   Jolly, J., S. W. Creigh, and A. Mingay
          1981   Age qualifications in job vacancies: an examination of British practice. The Gerontologist 21:251–56.

8   Jonas, Karen
          1979   Factors in development of community among elderly persons in age-segregated housing. Anthropological Quarterly 52:29–38.

5   Jones, Harold E.
          1959   Intelligence and problem-solving. Pp. 700–38 in James E. Birren (ed.), Handbook of Aging and the Individual. Chicago: University of Chicago Press.

17   Jones, Rochelle
          1977   The Other Generation; The New Power of Older People. Englewood Cliffs, N.J.: Prentice-Hall.

5, 7   Kaas, M. J.
          1978   Sexual expression of the elderly in nursing homes. The Gerontologist 18:372–77.

7   Kabrin, Frances, E.
          1981   Family extension and the elderly: economic, demographic, and family cycle factors. Journal of Gerontology 36:370–77.

       Kahana, Eva
8   1973   The humane treatment of old people in institutions. The Gerontologist 13:282–89.
8   1974   Matching environments to needs of the aged: a conceptual scheme. Pp. 201–14 in Jaber F. Gubrium (ed.), Late Life: Communities and Environmental Policy. Springfield, Ill.: Charles C. Thomas.

7   Kahana, Eva, and Boaz Kahana
          1971   Theoretical and research perspectives on grandparenthood. Aging and Human Development 2:261–68.

8   Kahana, Eva, Jersey Liang, and Barbara J. Felton
          1980   Alternative model of person-environment fit: prediction of morale in three homes for the aged. Journal of Gerontology 35:584–95.

15   Kahana, Eva, Jersey Liang, Barbara Felton, Thomas Fairchild, and Zev Harel
          1977   Perspectives of aged on victimization, "ageism," and their problems in urban society. The Gerontologist 17:121–28.

7   Kahn, Robert L., and Toni C. Antonucci
          1981   Convoys of social support: a life-course approach. Pp. 383–405 in Sara B. Kiesler et al. (eds.), Aging: Social Change. New York: Academic Press.

16   Kahne, Hilda
          1981   Women and Social Security: social policy adjusts to social change. International Journal of Aging and Human Development 13:195–208.

9   Kaiser, Marvin A., George R. Peters, and Nicholas Babchuck
          1982   When priests retire. The Gerontologist 22:89–94.

       Kalish, Richard A.
11   1963a   An approach to the study of death attitudes. American Behavioral Scientist 6:68–80.
11   1963b   Some variables in death attitudes. Journal of Social Psychology 59:137–45.
11   1966   A continuum of subjectively perceived death. The Gerontologist 6:73–76.
7, 8   1967   Of children and grandfathers: a speculative essay on dependency. The Gerontologist 7:65–69.
7, 8   1969   (ed.) The Dependencies of Old People. Ann Arbor, Michigan: University of Michigan, Wayne State University, Institute of Gerontology.

7, 8	1971	Sex and marital role differences in anticipation of age-produced dependency. Journal of Genetic Psychology 199:53–62.
11	1972	Of social values and the dying: a defense of disengagement. Family Coordinator 21:81–94.
5	1975	Late Adulthood: Perspectives of Human Development. Monterey, Calif.: Brooks/Cole.
11	1976	Death and dying in a social context. In Robert Binstock and Ethel Shanas (eds.), Handbook of Aging and the Social Sciences. New York: Van Nostrand Reinhold.
11	1981	Death, Grief, and Caring Relationships. Monterey, Calif.: Brooks/Cole.

12 Kalish, Richard A., and Frances W. Knudtson
    1976   Attachment versus disengagement: a life-span conceptualization. Human Development 19:171–81.

11 Kalish, Richard A., and D. K. Reynolds
    1976   Death and Ethnicity: A Psychocultural Study. Los Angeles: University of Southern California Press.

14 Kalish, Richard A., and Sam Yuen
    1971   Americans of East Asian ancestry: aging and the aged. The Gerontologist 11(1, part 2):36–47.

8, 18 Kamerman, S. B.
    1976   Community services for the aged: the view from eight countries. The Gerontologist 16:529–37.

Kane, Robert L., and Rosalie A. Kane
8, 18   1976   Long-Term Care in Six Countries: Implications for the United States. Washington, D.C.: U.S. Government Printing Office.

18   1980   Alternatives to institutional care of the elderly: beyond the dichotomy. The Gerontologist 20:249–59.

18   1981   Assessing the Elderly: A Practical Guide to Measurement. Lexington, Mass. D.C. Heath.

5 Kaplan, Howard B.
    1971   Age-related correlates of self-derogation: contemporary life space characteristics. Aging and Human Development 2:305–13.

8 Kaplan, Jerome, and Gordon J. Aldridge (eds.)
    1962   Social Welfare of the Aging. New York: Columbia University Press.

8 Kaplan, Jerome, Caroline S. Ford, and Harry Wain
    1964   An analysis of multiple community services through the institution for the aged. Geriatrics 19:773–82.

Kaplan, Max
10   1961   Toward a theory of leisure for social gerontology. Pp. 389–412 in Robert W. Kleemeier (ed.), Aging and Leisure. New York: Oxford University Press.

10   1972   Implications for gerontology from a general theory of leisure. Pp. 49–64 in Leisure in the Third Age. Paris: International Centre for Social Gerontology.

9 Kaplan, T. S.
    1971   Too old to work: the constitutionality of mandatory retirement plans. Southern California Law Review 44:150–80.

8 Kapnick, Philip L.
    1972   Age differences in opinions of health care services. The Gerontologist 12:294–97.

17 Kapnick, Philip L., Jay S. Goodman, and Elmer E. Cornwell
    1968   Political behavior in the aged: some new data. Journal of Gerontology 23:305–10.

7, 8 Karcher, C. J., and L. L. Linden
    1975   Family rejection of the aged and nursing home utilization. International Journal of Aging and Human Development 5:231–44.

8, 9   Karn, Valerie
  1980   Retirement resorts in Britain—successes and failures (England). The Gerontologist 20: 331–41.

9   Karp, David A., and Willilam C. Yoels
  1981   Work, careers, and aging. Qualitative Sociology 4:145–66.

8, 14   Kart, Cary S., and Barry L. Beckham
  1976   Black-white differentials in the institutionalization of the elderly: a temporal analysis. Social Forces 54(4):901–10.

Kasschau, Patricia L.

9   1974   Reevaluating the need for retirement preparation programs. Industrial Gerontology 1:42 –59.

19   1976a   The elderly as their planners see them. Social Policy 7(3):13–20.

9   1976b   Retirement and the social system. Industrial Gerontology 3:11–24.

14   1977   Age and race discrimination reported by middle-aged and older persons. Social Forces 55(3):728–42.

8   Kasteler, Josephine M., R. M. Gray, and M. L. Carruth
  1968   Involuntary relocation of the elderly. The Gerontologist 8:276–79.

Kastenbaum, Robert J.

5   1964a   Is old age the end of development? Pp. 61–71 in Robert Kastenbaum (ed.), New Thoughts on Old Age. New York: Springer.

11   1969   Death and bereavement in later life. Pp. 28–54 in A. H. Kutscher (ed.), Death and Bereavement. Springfield, Ill.: Charles C. Thomas.

12   1971   Getting there ahead of time. Psychology Today 5(December):52–58.

5, 11   1973   Loving, dying and other gerontological addenda. Pp. 699–708 in C. Eisdorfer and M. P. Lawton (eds.), The Psychology of Adult Development and Aging. Washington, D.C.: American Psychological Association.

11   1974   On death and dying. Should we have mixed feelings about our ambivalence toward the aged? Journal of Geriatric Psychiatry 7:94–107.

19   1978   Gerontology's search for understanding. The Gerontologist 18:59–63.

12   1980–81   Habituation as a model of human aging. International Journal of Aging and Human Development 12:159–70.

11   Kastenbaum, Robert J., and R. Aisenberg
  1972   The Psychology of Death. New York: Springer.

8   Kastenbaum, Robert J., and Sandra E. Candy
  1973   The 4% fallacy: a methodological and empirical critique of extended care facility population statistics. International Journal of Aging and Human Development 4:15–21.

Kastenbaum, Robert J., and Nancy Durkee

5   1964a   Elderly people view old age. Pp. 250–62 in Robert Kastenbaum (ed.), New Thoughts on Old Age. New York: Springer.

13   1964b   Young people view old age. Pp. 237–49 in Robert Kastenbaum (ed.), New Thoughts on Old Age. New York: Springer.

5, 11   Kastenbaum, Robert J., and A. D. Weisman
  1972   The psychological autopsy as a research procedure in gerontology. Pp. 210–17 in D. P. Kent, R. Kastenbaum, and S. Sherwood (eds.), Research Planning and Action for the Elderly: The Power and Potential of Social Science. New York: Behavioral Publications.

16   Katona, George
  1965   Private Pensions and Individual Saving. Ann Arbor, Michigan: University of Michigan Survey Research Center.

9   Katona, George, James N. Morgan, and Richard E. Barfield
  1969   Retirement in Prospect and Retrospect. Pp. 27–49 in Occasional Papers in Gerontology,

No. 4. Ann Arbor, Michigan: University of Michigan-Wayne State University Institute of Gerontology.

5   Katz, M. M.
     1974   The effects of aging on the verbal control of motor behavior. International Journal of Aging and Human Development 5:141–56.

5   Kay, D. W. K.
     1972   Epidemiological aspects of organic brain disease in the aged. C. M. Gaitz (ed.), Aging and the Brain. New York: Plenum.

8   Kaye, I.
     1973   Transportation problems of the older American. Pp. 86–109 in J. G. Cull and R. E. Hardy, The Neglected Older American: Social and Rehabilitation Services. Springfield, Ill.: Charles C. Thomas.

8, 12   Kayne, Ronald C.
         1976   Drugs and the aged. Pp. 436–51 in Irene M. Burnside (ed.), Nursing and the Aged. New York: McGraw-Hill.

13   Kearl, Michael C.
      1982   An inquiry into the positive personal and social effects of old age stereotypes among the elderly. International Journal of Aging and Human Development 14:277–90.

7, 9   Keating, Norah C., and Priscilla Cole
        1980   What do I do with him 24 hours a day? Changes in housewife role after retirement. The Gerontologist 20:84–89.

9   Keating, Norah, and Judith Marshall
     1980   The process of retirement: the rural self-employed. The Gerontologist 20:437–43.

13   Keith, Jennie
      1981   Old age and age differentiation: anthropological speculations on age as a social border. Pp. 453–88 in Sara B. Kiesler et al. (eds.), Aging: Social Change. New York: Academic Press.

      Keith, Patricia M.
17   1977a   A comparison of general and age-specific factors associated with political behavior. Experimental Aging Research 3:289–304.

13   1977b   An exploratory study of sources of stereotypes of old age among administrators. Journal of Gerontology 32:463–69.

6, 13   1977c   Life changes, stereotyping, and age identification. Psychological Reports 41:661–62.

17   1979   Sex differences in sources of political efficacy among the aged. The Cornell Journal of Social Relations 14:2:179–90.

9, 12   1982   Working women versus homemakers: retirement resources and correlates of well-being. Pp. 77–92 in M. Szinovacz (ed.), Women's Retirement. Beverly Hills, Calif.: Sage.

7   Keith, Patricia M., and Timothy H. Brubaker
     1977   Sex-role expectations associated with specific household tasks: perceived age and employment differences. Psychological Reports 41:15–18.

9   Kelleher, C. H., and D. A. Quick
     1974   Preparation for retirement: an annotated bibliography of literature 1965–1974. Industrial Gerontology 1:49–73.

11   Keller, John W., Dave Sherry, and Chris Piotrowski
      1984   Perspectives on death: a developmental study. Journal of Psychology 116: 137–42.

5   Kelley, George A.
     1955   The Psychology of Personal Constructs. New York: Norton.

5   Kelly, E. Lowell
     1955   Consistency of the adult personality. American Psychologist 10:659–81.

15   Kelly, Jim
      1977   The aging male homosexual: myth and reality? The Gerontologist 17:328–32.

Kent, Donald P.

8   1965a Meeting the Needs of Older People at the Community Level. Washington, D.C.: U.S. Government Printing Office.

17   1965b Government and the aging. Journal of Social Issues 21:79–86.

3   1968   Aging within the American social structure. Journal of Geriatric Psychiatry 2:19–32.

14   1971a The negro aged. The Gerontologist 11(1, part 2):48–51.

14   1971b The elderly in minority groups: variant patterns of aging. The Gerontologist 11(1, part 2):26–29.

8, 19   Kent, Donald R., R. Kastenbaum, and S. Sherwood (eds.)

1972   Research Planning and Action for the Elderly: The Power and Potential of Social Science. New York: Behavioral Publications.

13   Kent, K. E. M., and Peggy Shaw

1980   Age in time: a study of stereotyping. The Gerontologist 20:598–601.

Kerckhoff, Alan C.

7, 9   1964   Husband-wife expectations and reactions to retirement. Journal of Gerontology 19:510–16.

7   1965   Nuclear and extended family relationships: a normative and behavioral analysis. Pp. 93–112 in Ethel Shanas and Gordon F. Streib (eds.), Social Structure and the Family: Generational Relations. Englewood Cliffs, N.J.: Prentice-Hall.

7, 9   1966a Family patterns and morale in retirement. Pp. 173–92 in Ida H. Simpson and John C. McKinney (eds.), Social Aspects of Aging. Durham, No. Carolina: Duke University Press.

7   1966b Norm-value clusters and the strain toward consistency among older married couples. Pp. 138–59 in Ida H. Simpson and John C. McKinney (eds.), Social Aspects of Aging. Durham, No. Carolina: Duke University Press.

8   Kerr, John R.

1968   Income and expenditures: the over-65 age group. Journal of Gerontology 23:79–81.

5   Kesler, Mary S., Nancy W. Denney, and Susan E. Whitely

1976   Factors influencing problem solving in middle-aged and elderly adults. Human Development 19:310–20.

1   Kidder, Louise A.

1981   Research Methods in Social Relations, fourth edition. New York: Holt, Rinehart and Winston.

7   Kidwel, I. Jane, and Alan Booth

1977   Social distance and intergenerational relations. The Gerontologist 17:412–20.

9   Kiefaber, Mark

1977   Experimental approach to job redesign for oldler workers. Industrial Gerontology 4:119–24.

13, 19   Kiesler, Sara B.

1981   The aging population, social trends, and changes in behavior and belief. Pp. 41–74 in Sara B. Kielser et al. (eds.), Aging: Social Change. New York: Academic Press.

13   Kilty, Keith M., and Allen Feld

1976   Attitudes toward aging and toward the needs of older people. Journal of Gerontology 31:586–94.

Kimmel, Douglas C.

5   1974   Adulthood and Aging: An Interdisciplinary, Developmental View. New York: Wiley.

15   1978   Adult development and aging: a gay perspective. Journal of Social Issues 34:113–30.

5, 15   1980   Adulthood and Aging, second edition. New York: Wiley.

9   Kimmel, Douglas C., Karl F. Price, and James W. Walker

1978   Retirement choice and retirement satisfaction. Journal of Gerontology 33:575–85.

11   Kimsey, L. R., J. L. Roberts, and D. L. Logan
         1972   Death, dying and denial in the aged. American Journal of Psychiatry 129:161–66.

9   King, Charles E., and William H. Howell
         1965   Role characteristics of flexible and inflexible retired persons. Sociology and Social Research 49:153–65.

9   Kingson, Eric R.
         1981   Health of very early retirees. Aging and Work 4:11–22.

9   Kinn, J. M.
         1973   Unemployment and mid-career change: a blueprint for today and tomorrow. Industrial Gerontology 17:47–59.

5, 15   Kinsey, Alfred C., and P. H. Gebhard
         1953   Sexual Behavior in the Human Female. Philadelphia: W. B. Saunders.

5, 15   Kinsey, Alfred C., W. B. Pomeroy, and C. E. Martin
         1948   Sexual Behavior in the Human Male. Philadelphia: W. B. Saunders.

8   Kistin, H., and R. Morris
         1972   Alternatives to institutional care for the elderly and disabled. The Gerontologist 12:139–42.

7   Kivett, Vira R.
         1980   Perspectives on the childless rural elderly: a comparative analysis. The Gerontologist 20:708–16.

7   Kivett, Vira R., and R. Max Learner
         1982   Situational influences on the morale of older rural adults in child-shared housing: a comparative analysis. The Gerontologist 22:100–06.

5   Kivett, Vira R., J. Allen Watson, and J. Christian Busch
         1977   The relative importance of physical, psychological, and social variables to locus of control orientation in middle age. Journal of Gerontology 32:203–10.

7   Kivnick, Helen I.
         1982   Grandparenthood: an overview of meaning and mental health. The Gerontologist 22:59–66.

3   Klapp, Orinn E.
         1973   Models of Social Order. Palo Alto, Calif.: National Press Books.

5   Kleban, Morton H., M. Powell Lawton, Elaine M. Brody, and Miriam Ross
         1976   Behavioral observations of mentally impaired aged: those who decline and those who did not. Journal of Gerontology 31:333–39.

10   Kleemeier, Robert W. (ed.)
         1961   Aging and Leisure. New York: Columbia University Press.

19   Klegon, Douglas A.
         1977   Manpower in the Field of Aging. Oxford, Ohio: Scripps Foundation Gerontology Center.

9, 16   Klein, D. P.
         1975   Women in the labor force: the middle years. Monthly Labor Review 98(11):10–16.

5   Klein, R. L.
         1972   Age, sex and task difficulty as predictors of social conformity. Journal of Gerontology 27:229–36.

         Klemmack, David L., and Lucinda Lee Rof
13, 18   1980   Public support for age as an eligibility criterion for programs of older persons. The Gerontologist 20:148–53.

13, 17   1981   Predicting general and comparative support for government's providing benefits to older persons. The Gerontologist 21:592–99.

6, 12   Kline, Chrysee
　　　1975   The socialization process of women: implications for a theory of successful aging. The Gerontologist 15(6):486–92.

5   Kline, Donald W., and Frank Schieber
　　　1981   What are the age differences in visual sensory memory? Journal of Gerontology 36:86–89.

　　　Knapp, Martin R. J.
12   1976   Predicting the dimensions of life satisfaction. Journal of Gerontology 31:595–604.
12   1977   The activity theory of aging. An examination in the English context. The Gerontologist 17:553–59.

7   Knudson, Frances W.
　　　1976   Life-span attachment; complexities, questions, considerations. Human Development 19:182–96.

8   Kobasky, M. G.
　　　1974   Educational opportunities for the elderly. Pp. 80–85 in S. M. Grabowski and W. D. Mason (eds.), Education for the Aging. Syracuse, N.Y.: ERIC Clearinghouse Adult Education, Syracuse University.

8   Koff, Theodore H.
　　　1982   Long-Term Care: An Approach to Serving the Frail Elderly. Boston: Little, Brown.

　　　Kogan, Nathan
5   1974   Categorizing and conceptualizing styles in younger and older adults. Human Development 17:218–30.
5, 13   1975   Judgments of chronological age: adult age and sex differences. Developmental Psychology 11:107.
5   1982   Cognitive styles in older adults. Pp. 586–601 in T. M. Field et al. (eds.), Review of Human Development. New York: Wiley.

5   Kogan, Nathan, and Michael A. Wallach
　　　1961   Age changes in values and attitudes. Journal of Gerontology 16:272–80.

7   Kohen, Janet A.
　　　1983   Old but not alone: Informal social supports among the elderly by marital status and sex. The Gerontologist 23:57–63.

　　　Kohlberg, L.
5   1973a   Continuities in childhood and adult moral development revisited. Pp. 179–204 in Paul B. Baltes and K. Warner Schaie (eds.), Life-Span Developmental Psychology: Personality and Socialization. New York: Academic Press.
5   1973b   Stages and aging in moral development—some speculations. The Gerontologist 13:497–502.

9   Kohn, M. L., and C. Schooler
　　　1978   The reciprocal effects of the substantive complexity of work and intellectual flexibility: a longitudinal assessment. American Journal of Sociology 84:24–52.

9, 16   Kolodrubetz, Walter W.
　　　1970   Private and public retirement pensions: findings from the 1968 survey of the aged. Social Security Bulletin 33(9):3–22.

　　　Korim, A. S.
8   1974a   Older Americans and Community Colleges: An Overview. Washington, D.C.: American Association of Community and Junior Colleges.
8   1974b   Older Americans and Community Colleges: A Guide for Program Implementation. Washington, D.C.: American Association of Community and Junior Colleges.

8   Kornblum, S., and I. Kaufman
　　　1972   Choice and implications of models for working with active older adults. The Gerontologist 12:393–97.

8   Kosberg, Jordan I., and Joanna F. Gorman
        1975   Perceptions toward the rehabilitation potential of institutionalized aged. The Gerontologist 15(5, part 1):398–403.

8   Kostick, A.
        1972   A day care program for the physically and emotionally disabled. The Gerontologist 12:134–38.

8, 18   Kovar, Mary Grace
        1977   Health of the elderly and use of health services. Public Health Reports 92(1):9–19.

8, 18   Kowalski, N. Claire
        1981   Institutional relocation: current programs and applied approaches. The Gerontologist 21:512–19.

        Koyl, Leon
9   1970   A technique for measuring functional criteria in placement and retirement practices. Pp. 140–56 in Harold L. Sheppard (ed.), Industrial Gerontology. Cambridge, Mass.: Shenkman.
9, 16   1973   Employing the Older Worker. Washington, D.C.: National Council on Aging.
9   Krantz, David L.
        1977   The Santa Fe experience. Pp. 165–88 in Seymour B. Sarason (ed.), Work, Aging, and Social Change. New York: Free Press.

9   Kratcoski, P. C., J. H. Huber, and R. Gavlak
        1974   Retirement satisfaction among emeritus professors. Industrial Gerontology 1:78–81.

        Kreps, Juanita M.
9   1962   Aggregate income and labor force participation of the aged. Law and Contemporary Problems 27:51–66.
9   1963   (ed.) Employment, Income, and Retirement Problems of the Aged. Durham, No. Carolina: Duke University Press.
7   1965   The economics of intergenerational relationships. Pp. 267–88 in Ethel Shanas and Gordon F. Streib (eds.), Social Structure and the Family: Generational Relations. Englewod Cliffs, N.J.: Prentice-Hall.
16   1966a   Employment policy and income maintenance for the aged. Pp. 136–57 in John C. McKinney and Frank T. deVyver (eds.), Aging and Social Policy. New York: Appleton-Century-Crofts.
16   1966b   (ed.) Technology, Manpower, and Retirement Policy. Cleveland, Ohio: World.
16   1968a   Economic policy and the nation's aged. The Gerontologist 8(2, part 2):37–43.
9   1968b   Comparative studies of work and retirement. Pp. 75–99 in Ethel Shanas and John Madge (eds.), Methodology Problems in Cross-National Studies in Aging. New York: S. Karger.
9   1968c   Lifelong Allocation of Work and Leisure. Washington, D.C.: Social Security Administration.
9   1971a   Career options after fifty: suggested research. The Gerontologist 11(1, part 2):4–8.
9   1971b   Lifetime Allocation of Work and Income. Durham, No. Carolina: Duke University Press.

9, 16   Kreps, Juanita, and R. Clark
        1975   Sex, Age and Work: The Changing Composition of the Labor Force. Baltimore: Johns Hopkins University Press.

16   Krislov, Joseph
        1968   Four issues in income maintenance for the aged during the 1970s. Social Service Review 42:335–43.

9   Kroeger, Naomi
        1982   Preretirement preparation: sex differences in access, sources, and use. Pp. 95–112 in M. Szinovacz (ed.), Women's Retirement. Beverly Hills, Calif.: Sage.

4   Krohn, Peter L. (ed.)
     1966   Topics in the Biology of Aging. New York: Interscience.
14   Kronus, Sidney
     1971   The Black Middle Class. Columbus, Ohio: Merrill.
13   Kubey, Robert W.
     1980   Television and aging: past, present, and future. The Gerontologist 20:16–35.
     Kubler-Ross, Elizabeth
11   1969   On Death and Dying. New York: Macmillan.
11   1975   Death: The Final Stage of Growth. Englewood Cliffs, N.J.: Prentice-Hall.
     Kuhlen, Raymond G.
8   1963a   Psychological Background of Adult Education. Chicago: Center for the Study of Liberal Education for Adults.
5   1963b   Motivational changes during the adult years. Pp. 77–113 in Raymond G. Kuhlen (ed.), Psychological Backgrounds of Adult Education. Chicago: Center for the Study of Liberal Education for Adults.
5   1964a   Developmental changes in motivation during the adult years. Pp. 209–46 in James E. Birren (ed.), Relations of Development and Aging. Springfield, Ill.: Charles C. Thomas.
5   1964b   Personality change with age. Pp. 524–55 in Philip Worchel and D. Byrne (eds.), Personality Change. New York: Wiley.
11   Kunkel, Suzanne R.
     1979   Sex Differences in Adjustment to Widowhood. Unpublished M.A. thesis. Oxford, Ohio: Miami University.
     Kutner, Bernard
8   1956   Five Hundred Over Sixty: A Community Survey of Aging. New York: Russell Sage Foundation.
6   1962   The social nature of aging. The Gerontologist 2:5–8.
11   Kutscher, Austin H. (ed.)
     1969   Death and Bereavement. Springfield, Ill.: Charles C. Thomas.
     Kuypers, Joseph A.
5   1972a   Changeability of life-style and personality in old age. The Gerontologist 12:336–42.
5   1972b   Internal-external locus of control, ego functioning and personality characteristics in old age. The Gerontologist 12:168–73.
5   1974   Ego functioning in old age: early adult life antecedents. International Journal of Aging and Human Development 5:157–79.
12   Kuypers, Joseph A., and Vern L. Bengtson
     1973   Social breakdown and competence: a model of normal aging. Human Development 16:181–201.
5   Labouvie-Vief, Gisela
     1976   Toward optimizing cognitive competence in later life. Educational Gerontology 1:75–92.
13   Labouvie-Vief, Gisela, and Paul B. Baltes
     1976   Reduction of adolescent misperceptions of the aged. Journal of Gerontology 31:68–71.
5   Labouvie-Vief, Gisela, and Judith N. Gonda
     1976   Cognitive strategy training and intellectual performance in the elderly. Journal of Gerontology 31:327–32.
14   Lacklen, C.
     1971   Aged, black and poor: three case studies. Aging and Human Development 2:202–07.
5   Lakin, Martin, and Carl Eisdorfer
     1962   A study of affective expression among the aged. Pp. 650–54 in Clark Tibbitts and Wil-

ma Donahue (eds.), Social and Psychological Aspects of Aging. New York: Columbia University Press.

8   Lakoff, Sanford A.
      1976   The future of social intervention. Pp. 643–63 in Robert H. Binstock and Ethel Shanas (eds.), Handbook of Aging and the Social Sciences. New York: Van Nostrand Reinhold.

15   Lally, M., E. Black, M. Thornock, and J. D. Hawkins
      1979   Older women in single room occupant (S.R.O.) hotels: a Seattle profile. The Gerontologist 19(1):67–73.

9   Lambert, Edward
      1964   Reflections on a policy for retirement. International Labor Review 90:365–75.

    Lambing, Mary L. B.
10, 14   1972a   Leisure-time pursuits among retired blacks by social status. The Gerontologist 12:363–67.
14   1972b   Social class living patterns of retired Negroes. The Gerontologist 12:285–88.

8   Lando, Mordechai E.
      1976   Demographic characteristics of disability applicants: relationships to allowances. Social Security Bulletin 39(5):15–23.

8   Langford, Marilyn
      1962   Community Aspects of Housing for the Aged. Ithaca, New York: Cornell University Center for Housing and Environmental Studies.

7   Lansing, John B., and Leslie Kish
      1957   Family life cycle as an independent variable. American Sociological Review 22:512–19.

18   Lareau, Leslie S., and Leonard F. Heumann
      1982   The inadequacy of needs assessments of the elderly. The Gerontologist 22:324–30.

12   Larson, Reed
      1978   Thirty years of research on the subjective well-being of older Americans. Journal of Gerontology 33:109–25.

2, 3   Laslett, Peter
      1977   Societal development and aging. Pp. 87–116 in Robert H. Binstock and Ethel Shanas (eds.), Handbook of Aging and the Social Sciences. New York: Van Nostrand Reinhold.

5   LaTorre, R. A., and K. Kear
      1977   Attitudes toward sex in the aged. Archives of Sexual Behavior 6:203–13.

14   Laufer, Robert A., and Vern L. Bengtson
      1974   Generations, aging, and social stratification: on the development of generational units. Journal of Social Issues 30(3):181–205.

8   Lauriat, Patience
      1970   Benefit levels and socio-economic characteristics: findings from the 1968 survey of the aged. Social Security Bulletin 33(8):3–20.

13   Lawrence, Janet H.
      1974   The effect of perceived age on initial impressions and normative role expectations. International Journal of Aging and Human Development 5:369–91.

9, 12   Lawrence, Mary W.
      1961   Sources of satisfaction in the lives of working women. Journal of Gerontology 16:163–67.

8   Lawton, Alfred H.
      1965   Accidental injuries to the aged. The Gerontologist 5:96–100.

8   Lawton, Alfred H., and Gordon J. Azar
      1966   Consequences of physical and physiological change with age in the patterns of living

and housing for the middle-aged and aged. Pp. 19–26 in Frances M. Carp and W. M. Burnett (eds.), Patterns of Living and Housing of Middle-Aged and Older People. Washington, D.C.: U.S. Public Health Service.

Lawton, M. Powell

8, 12   1968   Social rehabilitation of the aged: some neglected aspects. Journal of the American Geriatrics Society 16:1346–63.

8   1969   Supportive services in the context of the housing environment. The Gerontologist 9:15–19.

8   1970   Planning environments for older people. American Institute of Planners Journal 36(March):124–29.

5, 8   1971   The functional assessment of elderly people. Journal of the American Geriatrics Society 19:465–81.

8   1972a   Assessing the competence of older people. Pp. 122–43 in Donald P. Kent, R. Kastenbaum, and S. Sherwood (eds.), Research Planning and Action for the Elderly. New York: Behavioral Publications.

12   1972b   The dimensions of morale. Pp. 144–65 in D. P. Kent, R. Kastenbaum, and S. Sherwood (eds.), Research Planning and Action for the Elderly. New York: Behavioral Publications.

5   1974   Psychology of aging. Pp. 73–83 in W. C. Bier (ed.), Aging. Its Challenge to the Individual and to Society. Pastoral Psychology Series, No. 8. New York: Fordham University Press.

8   1975a   Planning and Managing Housing for the Elderly. New York: Wiley.

12   1975b   The Philadelphia Geriatric Center Morale Scale: a revision. Journal of Gerontology 30:85–89.

8   1976   The relative impact of congregate and traditional housing on elderly tenants. The Gerontologist 16:237–42.

5   1977   The impact of the environment on aging and behavior. Pp. 276–301 in James E. Birren and K. Warner Schaie (eds.), Handbook of the Psychology of Aging. New York: Van Nostrand Reinhold.

10   1978   Leisure activities for the aged. Annals of the American Academy of Political and Social Sciences 438:71–80.

8   1981a   An ecological view of living arrangements. The Gerontologist 21:59–66.

14   1981b   To be black, poor, and aged in South Africa. The Gerontologist 21:235–39.

5, 12   1982   The well-being and mental health of the aged. Pp. 614–28 in T. M. Field et al. (eds.), Review of Human Development. New York: Wiley.

8   Lawton, M. Powell, Elaine M. Brody, and Patricia Turner-Massey
1978   Symposium on community housing for the elderly; the relationships of environmental factors to changes in well-being. The Gerontologist 18:133–37.

Lawton, M. Powell, and T. Byerts (eds.)

8, 19   1973   Community Planning for the Elderly. Washington, D.C.: The Gerontological Society.

8, 12   1974   The generality of housing impact on the well-being of older people. Journal of Gerontology 29:194–204.

8   Lawton, M. Powell, and L. E. Gottesman
1974   Psychological services to the elderly. American Psychologist 29:689–93.

8   Lawton, M. Powell, Maurice Greenbaum, and Bernard Liebowitz
1980   The lifespan of housing environments for the aging. The Gerontologist 20:56–64.

Lawton, M. Powell, and M. H. Kleban

8   1971   The aged resident of the inner city. The Gerontologist 11:277–83.

8   Lawton, M. Powell, M. H. Kleban, and D. A. Carlson
1973   The inner-city resident: to move or not to move. The Gerontologist 13:433–48.

8   Lawton, M. Powell, M. H. Kleban, and Maurice Singer
      1971   The aged Jewish person and the slum environment. Journal of Gerontology 26:231–39.

5, 15   Lawton, M. Powell, and Fay G. Lawton (eds.)
      1965   Mental Impairment in the Aged. Philadelphia: Philadelphia Geriatric Center.

8, 18   Lawton, M. Powell, Miriam Mass, Mark Fulcomer, and M. H. Kleban
      1982   A research and service oriented multilevel assessment instrument. Journal of Gerontology 37:91–99.

5, 6   Lawton, M. Powell, and L. Nahemow
      1973   Ecology and the aging process. Pp. 619–74 in C. Eisdorfer and M. P. Lawton (eds.), The Psychology of Adult Development and Aging. Washington, D.C.: American Psychological Association.

15   Lawton, M. Powell, Lucille Nahemow, Silvia Yaffe, and Steven Feldman
      1976   Psychological aspects of crime and fear of crime. Pp. 21–29 in Jack Goldsmith and S. S. Goldsmith (eds.), Crime and the Elderly. Lexington, Mass.: Lexington Books.

8, 19   Lawton, M. Powell, R. J. Newcomer, and T. O. Byerts (eds.)
      1976   Community Planning for an Aging Society. New York: Halsted Press.

12   Lawton, M. Powell, Beverly Patnaik, and Morton H. Kleban
      1976   The ecology of adaptation to a new environment. International Journal of Aging and Human Development 7:15–26.

7, 8   Lawton, M. Powell, and B. Simon
      1968   The ecology of social relationships in housing for the elderly. The Gerontologist 8:108–15.

15   Lawton, M. Powell, and Silvia Yaffe
      1980   Victimization and fear of crime in elderly public housing tenants. Journal of Gerontology 35:768–79.

       Lebowitz, Barry D.
5   1973   Age and fearfulness: personal and situational factors. Journal of Gerontology 30:696–700.

19   1979   The management of research in aging: a case study in science policy. The Gerontologist 19:151–57.

8, 17   Lebowtiz, Barry D., and John L. Dobra
      1976   Implementing an income strategy for the elderly: studies in organizational change. International Journal of Aging and Human Development 7:255–68.

2   Lee, Ann S.
      1974   Return migration in the United States. International Migration Review 8:283–300.

       Lee, Gary R.
7, 12   1978   Marriage and morale in later life. Journal of Marriage and the Family 40:131–39.

5, 15   1982   Sex differences in fear of crime among older people. Research on Aging 4:284–98.

7, 12   Lee, Gary R., and Eugene Ellithorpe
      1982   Intergenerational exchange and subjective well-being among the elderly. Journal of Marriage and the Family 44:217–24.

1   Lee, Gary R., and John M. Finney
      1977   Sampling in social gerontology: a method of locating specialized populations. Journal of Gerontology 32:689–93.

5   Lehman, H. C.
      1953   Age and Achievement. Princeton, N.J.: Princeton University Press.

8, 18   Lehman, Virginia, and Geneva Mathiasen
      1963   Guardianship and Protective Services for Older People. New York: National Council on the Aging.

5   Lehr, Ursula
      1967   Attitudes towards the future in old age. Human Development 10:230–38.

7   Leigh, Geoffrey K.
        1980   Kinship interaction over the family life span. Journal of Marriage and the Family 42: 197–208.

8, 18   Leinbach, Raymond M.
        1982   Alternatives to the face-to-face interview for collecting gerontological needs assessment data. The Gerontologist 22:78–82.

8   Lemke, Sonne, and Rudolph H. Moos
        1981   The suprapersonal environments of sheltered care settings. Journal of Gerontology 36: 233–42.

2   Lenzer, Anthony
        1965   Mobility patterns among the aged. The Gerontologist 5(1, part 1):12–15.

12   Leon, Gloria Rakita, John Kamp, Richard Gillum, and Brenda Gillum
        1981   Life stress and dimensions of functioning in old age. Journal of Gerontology 36:66–69.

5, 12   Leonard, Wilber M.
        1977   Sociological and social-psychological correlates of anomia among a random sample of aged. Journal of Gerontology 32:303–10.

8, 11   Lerea, L. Eliezer, and Barbara F. LiMauro
        1982   Grief among health care workers: a comparative study. Journal of Gerontology 37:604–08.

11, 12   Lester, D.
        1973   Suicide, homicide, and age dependency ratios. International Journal of Aging and Human Development 4:127–32.

13   Levin, Jack, and William C. Levin
        1981   Willingness to interact with an older person. Research on Aging 3:211–17.

5   Levin, Sidney
        1964   Depression in the aged: the importance of external factors. Pp. 179–85 in Robert Kastenbaum (ed.), New Thoughts on Old Age. New York: Springer.

        Levine, Martin
9, 16   1980a   Four models for age/work policy research. The Gerontologist 20:561–74.
13, 17   1980b   Research in law and aging. The Gerontologist 20:163–67.

7   Le Vine, Robert A.
        1965   Intergenerational tensions and extended family structure in Africa. Pp. 188–204 in Ethel Shanas and Gordon F. Streib (eds.), Social Structure and the Family: Generational Relations. Englewood Cliffs, N.J.: Prentice-Hall.

7   Levinger, George, and J. Diedrick Snoek
        1972   Attraction in relationship: a new look at interpersonal attraction. Morristown, N.Y.: General Learning Press.

5, 6   Levinson, Daniel J., C. M. Darrow, E. B. Klein, M. H. Levinson, and B. McKee.
        1978   The Seasons of a Man's Life. New York: Knopf.

9, 12   Levy, Sandra M.
        1981   The adjustment of the older woman: effects of chronic ill health and attitudes toward retirement. International Journal of Aging and Human Development 12:93–110.

5   Lewis, Charles N.
        1971   Reminiscing and self-concept in old age. Journal of Gerontology 26:240–43.

14   Lewis, Myrna I., and Robert N. Butler
        1972   Why is women's lib ignoring older women? Aging and Human Development 3:223–31.

14   Lewis, Oscar
        1961   Five Families. New York: Basic Books.

7   Lewis, Robert A.
        1978   Transitions in middle-age and aging families: a bibliography from 1940 to 1977. The Family Coordinator 27:457–76.

12   Liang, Jersey
    1982   Sex differences in life satisfaction among the elderly. Journal of Gerontology 37:100–09.

8   Liang, Jersey, Eva Kahana, and Edmund Doherty
    1980   Financial well-being among the aged: a further elaboration. Journal of Gerontology 35: 409–20.

15   Liang, Jersey, and Mary C. Sengstock
    1981   The risk of personal victimization among the aged. Journal of Gerontology 36:463–71.

8, 18   Libow, Leslie S.
    1982   Geriatric medicine and the nursing home: a mechanism for mutual excellence. The Gerontologist 22:134–41.

2, 8   Lichter, Daniel T., Glenn V. Fuguitt, Tim B. Heaton, and William B. Clifford
    1981   Components of change in the residential concentration of the elderly population: 1950–1975. Journal of Gerontology 36:480–89.

Lieberman, Morton A.
8   1969   Institutionalization of the aged: effects on behavior. Journal of Gerontology 24:330–40.
8, 19   1974   Relocation research and social policy. The Gerontologist 14:494–500.
12   1975   Adaptive processes in late life. Pp. 135–59 in Nancy Datan and Leon Ginsberg (eds.), Life Span Developmental Psychology: Normative Life Crises. New York: Academic Press.

14   Liebow, Elliot
    1967   Tally's Corner. Boston: Little, Brown.

11   Linn, Bernard S., and Margaret W. Linn
    1981   Late stage cancer patients: age differences in their psychophysical status and response to counseling. Journal of Gerontology 36:689–92.

Lipman, Aaron
7   1961   Role conceptions and morale of couples in retirement. Journal of Gerontology 16:267–71.
7   1962   Role conceptions of couples in retirement. Pp. 475–85 in Clark Tibbitts and Wilma Donahue (eds.), Social and Psychological Aspects of Aging. New York: Columbia University Press.
8, 12   1969   Public housing and attitudinal adjustment in old age: a comparative study. Journal of Geriatric Psychiatry 2:88–101.

11   Lipman, Aaron, and P. Marden
    1966   Preparations for death in old age. Journal of Gerontology 21:426–31.

12   Lipman, Aaron, and Kenneth J. Smith
    1968   Functionality of disengagement in old age. Journal of Gerontology 23:517–21.

7   Litwak, Eugene
    1960   Occupational mobility and extended family cohesion. American Sociological Review 25:9–21.

9   Liu, Y. H.
    1974   Retirees and retirement programs in the People's Republic of China. Industrial Gerontology 1:72–81.

5   Livson, Florine B.
    1976   Patterns of personality development in middle aged women; a longitudinal study. International Journal of Aging and Human Development 7:107–15.

5   Livson, N.
    1973   Developmental dimensions of personality: a life-span formulation. Pp. 97–122 in Paul B. Baltes and K. Warner Schaie (eds.), Life-Span Developmental Psychology: Personality and Socialization. New York: Academic Press.

13   Locke-Connor, Catherine, and Patricia Walsh
    1980   Attitudes toward the older job applicant: just as competent but more likely to fail. Journal of Gerontology 35:920–27.

12   Lohmann, Nancy
    1977   Correlations of life satisfaction, morale and adjustment measures. Journal of Gerontology 32:73–75.

7, 13   Long, Barbara H., Robert C. Ziller, and Elaine E. Thompson
    1966   A comparison of prejudices: the effects upon friendship ratings of chronic illness, old age, education and race. Journal of Social Psychology 70:101–09.

    Longino, Charles F., Jr.
8   1981   Retirement communities. Pp. 391–418 in F. J. Berghorn and D. E. Schafer (eds.), The Dynamics of Aging. Boulder, Colo.: Westview Press.
2   1982   Changing aged nonmetropolitan migration patterns, 1955 to 1960 and 1960 to 1970. Journal of Gerontology 37:228–34.

    Longino, Charles F., Jr., and Jeanne C. Biggar
2   1981   The impact of retirement migration on the South. The Gerontologist 21:283–90.
2, 18   1982   The impact of population redistribution on service delivery. The Gerontologist 22:153–59.

8, 10, 13   Longino, Charles F., Jr., and G. C. Kitson
    1976   Parish clergy and the aged; examining stereotypes. Journal of Gerontology 31:340–45.

7, 8   Longino, Charles F., Jr., and Aaron Lipman
    1982   The married, the formerly married and the never married: support system differentials of older women in planned retirement communities. International Journal of Aging and Human Development 15:285–97.

5, 6, 17   Longino, Charles F., Kent A. McClelland, and Warren A. Peterson
    1980   The aged subculture hypothesis: social integration, gerontophilia and self-conception. Journal of Gerontology 35:758–67.

    Looft, W. F.
5   1972   Egocentrism and social interaction across the life span. Psychological Bulletin 78:73–92.
6   1973a   Socialization in a life-span perspective: white elephants, worms and will-o'-wisps. The Gerontologist 13:488–97.
5, 6   1973b   Socialization and personality throughout the life span: an examination of contemporary psychological approaches. Pp. 25–52 in Paul B. Baltes and K. Warner Schaie (eds.), Life-Span Developmental Psychology: Personality and Socialization. New York: Academic Press.

    Lopata, Helena Z.
11   1970   The social involvement of American widows. American Behavioral Scientist 14(September-October):41–48.
11   1971a   Living arrangements of American urban widows. Sociological Focus 5:41–61.
11   1971b   Widows as a minority group. The Gerontologist 11(1, part 2):67–77.
7   1971c   Occupation: Housewife. New York: Oxford University Press.
9   1971d   Work histories of American urban women. The Gerontologist 11(4, part 2):27–36.
8   1972   Social relations of widows in urbanized countries. Sociological Quarterly 13(Spring):259–71.
7, 11   1973   Widowhood in an American City. Cambridge, Mass.: Schenkman.
7, 8   1975a   Support systems of elderly urbanites: Chicago of the 1970's. The Gerontologist 15:35–41.
11   1975b   On widowhood: grief work and identity reconstruction. Journal of Geriatric Psychiatry 8:41–55.
11   1975c   Widowhood: societal factors in life-span disruptions and alternatives. Pp. 217–34 in Nancy Datan and Leon H. Ginsberg (eds.), Life-Span Developmental Psychology;

Normative Life Crises. New York: Academic Press.

7, 11   1979   Women as Widows: Support Systems. New York: Elsevier.

Loughman, Celeste

13   1977   Novels of senescence: a new naturalism. The Gerontologist 17:79–84.

13   1980   Eras and the elderly: a literary view. The Gerontologist 20:182–87.

14   Louis, Arthur M.

1968   America's centimillionaires. Fortune 77:152–57.

5   Lowe, G. R.

1972   The Growth of Personality: From Infancy to Old Age. Baltimore: Penguin Books.

Lowenthal, Marjorie F.

5   1964a   Lives in Distress. New York: Basic Books.

5, 8   1964b   Social isolation and mental illness in old age. American Sociological Review 29:54–70.

5   1965   Antecedents of isolation and mental illness in old age. Archives of General Psychiatry 12:245–54.

12   1971   Intentionality: toward a framework for the study of adaptation in adulthood. Aging and Human Development 2:79–95.

12   1977   Toward a sociopsychological theory of change in adulthood and old age. Pp. 116–27 in James E. Birren and K. Warner Schaie (eds.), Handbook of the Psychology of Aging. New York: Van Nostrand Reinhold.

5   Lowenthal, Marjorie F., and Paul L. Berkman

1967   Aging and Mental Disorder in San Francisco. San Francisco: Jossey-Bass.

12   Lowenthal, Marjorie F., and Deetje Boler

1965   Voluntary versus involuntary social withdrawal. Journal of Gerontology 20:363–71.

Lowenthal, Marjorie F., and David Chiroboga

12   1973   Social stress and adaptation: toward a life-course perspective. Pp. 281–310 in Carl Eisdorfer and M. Powell Lawton (eds.), The Psychology of Adult Development and Aging. Washington, D.C.: American Psychological Association.

12   1975   Responses to stress. Pp. 146–62 in Marjorie F. Lowenthal, Majda Thurner, and David Chiriboga, The Four Stages of Life. San Francisco: Jossey-Bass.

7, 12   Lowenthal, Marjorie F., and Clayton Havens

1968   Interaction and adaptation: intimacy as a critical variable. American Sociological Review 33:20–31.

7, 8   Lowenthal, Marjorie F., and Betsy Robinson

1976   Social networks and isolation. Pp. 432–56 in Robert H. Binstock and Ethel Shanas (eds.), Handbook of Aging and the Social Sciences. New York: Van Nostrand Reinhold.

5   Lowenthal, Marjorie F., M. Thurnher, and D. Chiriboga

1975   Four Stages of Life. San Francisco: Jossey-Bass.

Lowy, L.

8, 19   1972a   The role of social gerontology in the development of social services for older people. Pp. 20–36 in D. P. Kent, R. Kastenbaum, and S. Sherwood (eds.), Research Planning and Action for the Elderly. New York: Behavioral Publications.

8, 19   1972b   A social work practice perspective in relation to theoretical models and research in gerontology. Pp. 538–44 in D. P. Kent, R. Kastenbaum, and S. Sherwood (eds.), Research Planning and Action for the Elderly. New York: Behavioral Publications.

Lozier, J., and R. Althouse

8, 13   1974   Special enforcement of behavior toward elders in an Appalachian mountain settlement. The Gerontologist 14:69–80.

9   1975   Retirement to the porch in rural Appalachia. International Journal of Aging and Human Development 6:7–15.

3   Lubove, Ray
        1968   The Struggle for Social Security: 1900–1935. Cambridge, Mass.: Harvard University Press.

5, 7   Ludeman, Kate
        1981   The sexuality of the older person: review of the literature. The Gerontologist 21:203–08.

5   Ludwig, Edward G., and Robert L. Eichhorn
        1967   Age and disillusionment: a study of value changes associated with aging. Journal of Gerontology 22:59–65.

5   Ludwig, Thomas E.
        1982   Age difference in mental synthesis. Journal of Gerontology 37:182–89.

5   Lynch, D. J.
        1971   Future time perspective and impulsivity in old age. Journal of Genetic Psychology 118:245–52.

5   Maas, H. S., and J. A. Kuypers
        1974   From Thirty to Seventy. San Francisco: Jossey-Bass.

7   MacIver, Robert M., and Charles H. Page
        1949   Sociology: An Introductory Analysis. New York: Rinehart.

5, 9   Maehr, Martin L., and Douglas A. Kleiber
        1981   The graying of achievement motivation. American Psychologist 36:787–93.

11   Maddison, David, and Agnes Viola
        1968   The health of widows in the year following bereavement. Journal of Psychosomatic Research 12:297–306.

        Maddox, George L.
10, 12 1963   Activity and morale: a longitudinal study of selected elderly subjects. Social Forces 42:195–204.

12   1964   Disengagement theory: a critical evaluation. The Gerontologist 4:80–82.

12   1965   Disengagement among the elderly: how common and with what effect? Pp. 317–23 in Frances C. Jeffers (ed.), Duke University Council on Gerontology Proceedings of Seminars, 1961–1965. Durham, No. Carolina: Duke University Regional Center for the Study of Aging.

9   1968   Retirement as a social event in the United States. Pp. 357–65 in Bernice L. Neugarten (ed.), Middle Age and Aging. Chicago: University of Chicago Press.

6   1970   Themes and issues in sociological theories of human aging. Human Development 13:17–27.

4, 5, 6 Maddox, George L., and E. B. Douglass
        1974   Aging and individual differences: a longitudinal analysis of social, psychological, and physiological indicators. Journal of Gerontology 29:555–63.

10, 12 Maddox, George L., and Carl Eisdorfer
        1962   Some correlates of activity and morale among the elderly. Social Forces 40:254–60.

14   Maldonado, David, Jr.
        1975   The Chicano aged. Social Work, 20:213–16.

11   Malinak, D. P., M. F. Hoyt, and V. Patterson
        1979   Adults' reactions to the death of a parent: a preliminary study. American Journal of Psychiatry 136:1152–56.

9   Mallan, Lucy B.
        1974   Women born in the early 1900's: employment, earnings, and benefit levels. Social Security Bulletin 37(3):3–25.

9   Mannheim, Bilha, and Josef Rein
        1981   Work centrality of different age groups and the wish to discontinue work. International Journal of Aging and Human Development 13:221–32.

Manton, Kenneth G.

2, 4   1980   Sex and race specific mortality differentials in multiple cause of death data. The Gerontologist 20:480–93.

2, 4,
14   1982   Temporal and age variation of United States black/white cause-specific mortality differentials: a study of the recent changes in the relative health status of the United States.
The Gerontologist 22:170–79.

8   Marden, Parker G., and Robert G. Burnight
1969   Social consequences of physical impairment in an aging population. The Gerontologist
9:39–46.

16   Margolius, S., P. S. Barash, V. Knauer, A. J. Jaffe, J. N. Morgan, and D. A. Peterson
1969   The Aging Consumer. Occasional Papers in Gerontology, Number 8. Ann Arbor,
Michigan: University of Michigan-Wayne State University, Institute of Gerontology.

7, 12,
14   Markides, Kyriakos S., Delia Saldana Costley, and Linda Rodriguez
1981   Perceptions of intergenerational relations and psychological well-being among elderly
Mexican Americans: a causal model. International Journal of Aging and Human Development 13:43–52.

4   Markides, Kyriakos S., and Charisse Pappas
1982   Subjective age, health, and survivorship in old age. Research on Aging 4:87–96.

5, 8   Markson, E., and P. Grevert
1972   Circe's terrible island of change: self-perceptions of incapacity. Aging and Human Development 3:261–71.

5   Markson, E. W., and G. Levitz
1973   A Guttman scale to assess memory loss among the elderly. The Gerontologist 13:337–40.

Markus, E., M. Blenkner, M. Bloom, and T. Downs
8   1971   The impact of relocation upon mortality rates of institutionalized aged persons. Journal
of Gerontology 26:537–41.

8   1972   Some factors and their associations with post-relocation mortality among institutionalized aged persons. Journal of Gerontology 27:376–82.

10   Marquis Academic Media
1978   Sourcebook on Aging. Chicago: Who's Who.

11   Marris, R.
1958   Widows and their families. London: Routledge and Kegan Paul.

5   Marsh, Gail R.
1980   Perceptual changes with aging. Pp. 147–68 in E. Busse and D. Blazer (eds.), Handbook of Geriatric Psychiatry. New York: Van Nostrand Reinhold.

Marshall, Victor W.
12   1974   The last stand: remnants of engagement in the later years. Omega 5:25–35.

11   1975   Socialization for impending death in a retirement village. American Journal of Sociology 80:1124–44.

11   1980   Last Chapters: A Sociology of Death and Dying. Belmont, Calif.: Wadsworth.

12   Martin, J. David
1971   Powers, dependence, and the complaints of the elderly: a social exchange perspective.
Aging and Human Development 2:108–12.

9   Martin, John, and Ann Doran
1966   Evidence concerning the relationship between health and retirement. Sociological
Review 14:329–43.

12   Martin, W. C.
1973   Activity and disengagement: life satisfaction of in-movers into a retirement community.
The Gerontologist 13:224–27.

12   Martin, W. C., V. L. Bengtson, and A. C. Acock
        1974   Alienation and age: a context-specific approach. Social Forces 53:266–74.

5   Mason, Evelyn
        1954   Some correlates of self-judgments of the aged. Journal of Gerontology 9:324–37.

9   Masse, B. L., S. Scheiber, M. L. Lovely, H. A. Schwartz, and R. Bragman
        1974   The experience of retirement. Pp. 167–83 in W. C. Bier (ed.), Aging: Its Challenge to
                the Individual and to Society. Pastoral Psychology Series, No. 8. New York: Fordham
                University Press.

5, 7   Masters, William H., and Virginia Johnson
        1966   Human Sexual Response. Boston: Little, Brown.

8   Mathis, Evelyn S.
        1973   Characteristics of residents in nursing and personal care homes: United States. June–
                August 1969. Vital and Health Statistics. Series 12, Number 19.

8   Matthews, Sarah H.
        1982   Participation of the elderly in a transportation system. The Gerontologist 22:26–31.

        Maves, Paul B.
8, 10   1960   Aging, religion, and the church. Pp. 698–749 in Clark Tibbitts (ed.), Handbook of So-
                cial Gerontology. Chicago: University of Chicago Press.

8, 10   1965   Research on religion in relation to aging. Pp. 69–79 in Frances C. Jeffers (ed.), Duke
                University Council on Gerontology. Proceedings of Seminars 1961–65. Durham, No.
                Carolina: Duke University Regional Center for the Study of Aging.

8   Mayer, Neil S., and Olsen Lee
        1981   Federal home repair programs and elderly homeowners' needs. The Gerontologist 21:
                312–22.

9, 16   Mcauley, William J.
        1977   Perceived age discrimination in hiring: demographic and economic correlates. Industrial
                Gerontology 4:21–28.

5   McCandless, B. R.
        1973   Symposium discussion: life-span models of psychological aging. The Gerontologist 13:
                511–12.

5   McCarthy, Sarah M., Ilene C. Siegler, and Patrick E. Logue
        1982   Cross-sectional and longitudinal patterns of three Wechster Memory Scale subtests.
                Journal of Gerontology 37:169–75.

8, 14   McCaslin, R., and W. R. Calvert
        1975   Social indicators in black and white: some ethnic considerations in delivery of service to
                the elderly. Journal of Gerontology 30:60–66.

8, 10   McClellan, R. W.
        1977   Claiming a Frontier: Ministry and Older People. Los Angeles: Ethel Percy Andrus
                Gerontology Center, University of Southern California.

        McConnel, Charles E., and Firooz Deljavan
2, 11   1982   Aged deaths: the nursing home and community differential: 1976. The Gerontologist
                22:318–23.

16   1983   Consumption patterns of the retired household. Journal of Gerontology 38:480–90.

16   McConnell, John W.
        1960   Aging and the economy. Pp. 489–520 in Clark Tibbitts (ed.), Handbook of Social
                Gerontology. Chicago: University of Chicago Press.

8, 16,
17   McConnell, Stephen R., and Patricia L. Kasschau
        1977   Income versus in-kind services for the elderly: decision makers' preferences. Social Ser-
                vice Review 51:337–56.

9, 16   McCormick, E. J., and J. Tiffin
        1974   Industrial Psychology. Englewood Cliffs, N.J.: Prentice-Hall.

5   McCrae, Robert R., Paul T. Bartone, and Paul T. Costa
        1976   Age, anxiety, and self-reported health. International Journal of Aging and Human Development 7:49–58.

5   McCrae, Robert R., and Paul T. Costa, Jr.
        1982   Aging, the life course, and models of personality. Pp. 602–13 in T. M. Field et al. (eds.), Review of Human Development. New York: Wiley.

5   McCrae, Robert R., Paul T. Costa, and David Arenberg
        1980   Constancy of adult personality structure in males: longitudinal, cross-sectional and times of measurement analysis. Journal of Gerontology 35:877–83.

8   McCraw, M. L.
        1976   Retired couple's budgets updated to autumn 1975. Monthly Labor Review 99:36–37.

5, 15   McCreary, Charles P., and Wan N. Mensh
        1977   Personality differences associated with age in law offenders. Journal of Gerontology 32: 164–67.

9   McEaddy, B. J.
        1975   Women in the labor force: the later years. Monthly Labor Review 98(11):17–24.

9   McEvan, Peter J. M., and Alan P. Sheldon
        1969   Patterns of retirement and related variables. Journal of Geriatric Psychiatry 3:35–54.

        McFarland, Ross A.
5   1968   The sensory and perceptual processes in aging. Pp. 9–52 in K. Warner Schaie (ed.), Theory and Methods of Research on Aging. Morgantown, W. Virginia: West Virginia University.

9   1973   The need for functional age measures in industrial gerontology. Industrial Gerontology 19:1–19.

8   McGlone, F. B., and E. Kick
        1978   Health habits in relation to aging. Journal of the American Geriatrics Society. 26:481–88.

8   McGuire, Marie C.
        1969   The status of housing for the elderly. The Gerontologist 9:10–14.

        McKain, Walter C., Jr.
8, 10   1967   Community roles and activities of older rural persons. Pp. 75–96 in E. Grant Youmans (ed.), Older Rural Americans. Lexington, Kentucky: University of Kentucky Press.

7   1969   Retirement Marriage. Storrs, Conn.: University of Connecticut Agriculture Experiment Station.

3, 13   McKee, Patrick L. (ed.)
        1982   Philosophical Foundations of Gerontology. New York: Human Sciences Press.

17   McKinney, John C., and Frank T. deVyvers (eds.)
        1966   Aging and Social Policy. New York: Appleton-Century-Crofts.

5   McLeish, John A. B.
        1976   The Ulyssean Adult: Creativity in the Middle and Later Years. Toronto: McGraw-Hill Ryerson Ltd.

13   McTavish, Donald G.
        1971   Perceptions of old people: a review of research, methodologies and findings. The Gerontologist 11(4, part 2):90–101.

12   Medinger, Fred, and Raju Varghese
        1981   Psychological growth and the impact of stress in middle age. International Journal of Aging and Human Development 13:247–63.

Medley, Morris L.

12   1976   Satisfaction with life among persons sixty-five years and older: a causal model. Journal of Gerontology 31:448–55.

7   1977   Marital adjustment in the post-retirement years. The Family Coordinator 26(1):5–11.

9, 16   Meier, Elizabeth L., and Elizabeth A. Kerr
        1976   Capabilities of middle-aged and older workers: a survey of the literature. Industrial Gerontology 3:147–56.

9   Meltzer, Michael W.
        1981   The reduction of occupational stress among elderly lawyers: the creation of a functional niche. International Journal of Aging and Human Development 13:209–19.

8, 18   Mendelson, Mary A.
        1974   Tender Loving Greed. New York: Knopf.

8, 18   Mendelson, Mary A., and David Hapgood
        1974   The political economy of nursing homes. Pp. 95–105 in Frederick R. Eisele (ed.), Political Consequences of Aging. Philadelphia: American Academy of Political and Social Sciences.

8   Menefee, John A., Bea Edwards, and Sylvester J. Scheiber
        1981   Analysis of nonparticipation in the SSI program. Social Security Bulletin 44(6):3–21.

12   Menninger, Karl
        1938   Man Against Himself. New York: Harcourt, Brace & World.

1   Mercer, Jane R., and Edgar W. Butler
        1967   Disengagement of the aged population and response differentials in survey research. Social Forces 46:89–96.

8   Merriam, Ida C.
        1966   Implications of technological change for income. Pp. 166–74 in Juanita M. Kreps (eds.), Technology Manpower and Retirement Policy. New York: World.

5   Merriam, Sharon
        1980   The concept and function of reminiscence: a review of the research. The Gerontologist 20:604–08.

        Merriam-Webster
        1981   Webster's Third New International Dictionary of the English Language Unabridged. Springfield, Mass.: Merriam-Webster.

5   Merritt, C. Gary, Joel E. Gerstl, and Leonard A. LoScuito
        1975   Age and perceived effects of erotica-pornography: a national sample study. Archives of Sexual Behavior 4(6):605–21.

9   Messer, Elizabeth F.
        1969   Thirty years is a plenty. Pp. 5–66 in Occasional Papers in Gerontology No. 4. Ann Arbor, Michigan: University of Michigan, Wayne State University, Institute of Gerontology.

5   Messer, Mark
        1968   Race differences in selected attitudinal dimensions of the elderly. The Gerontologist 8:245–49.

        Metropolitan Life Insurance Company
2   1965a   Accidental injury and death at the older ages. Statistical Bulletin of the Metropolitan Life Insurance Company 46(February):6–8.

2   1965b   International trends in survival after age 65. Statistical Bulletin of the Metropolitan Life Insurance Company 46(January):8–10.

2   1971   Mortality from accidents by age and sex. Statistical Bulletin of the Metropolitan Life Insurance Company 53(May):6–9.

2, 12   1972   Suicide—international comparisons. Statistical Bulletin of the Metropolitan Life Insurance Company 53(August):2–5.

2, 12   1973   Regional variations in mortality from suicides. Statistical Bulletin of the Metropolitan Life Insurance Company 54(August):2–4.

2   1974   Accident mortality at the older ages. Statistical Bulletin of the Metropolitan Life Insurance Company 55(June):6–:8.

12, 15   Meyers, Allan R., Eli Goldman, Ralph Hingson, Norman Scotch, and Tom Mangione
1981   Evidence for cohort or generational differences in the drinking behavior of older adults. International Journal of Aging and Human Development 14:31–44.

11   Meyers, D. W.
1973   The legal aspects of medical euthanasia. Bioscience 23:467–70.

7   Millard, Peter H., and Chris S. Smith
1981   Personal belongings—a positive effect? The Gerontologist 21:85–90.

17   Miller, Arthur H., Patricia Gurin, and Gerald Gurin
1980   Age consciousness and political mobilization of older Americans. The Gerontologist 20:691–700.

18   Miller, Dulcy B., and Janet T. Barry
1979   Nursing Home Organization and Operation. Boston: CBI Publishing.

19   Miller, Emily H., and Neal E. Cutler
1976   Toward a comprehensive information system in gerontology: a survey of problems, resources and potential solutions. The Gerontologist 16:198–206.

11   Miller, M. B.
1971   Decision-making in the death process of the ill aged. Geriatrics 26(5):105–16.

12   Miller, Marv
1978   Toward a profile of the older white male suicide. The Gerontologist 18:80–82.

13   Miller, Richard B., and Richard A. Dodder
1980   A revision of Palmore's Facts on Aging Quiz. The Gerontologist 20:673–79.

Miller, Sheila J.
8, 14   1978   Will the real older woman please stand up? Pp. 287–94 in M. M. Seltzer, S. L. Corbett, and R. C. Atchley (eds.), Social Problems of the Aging. Belmont, Calif.: Wadsworth.

8, 15   1982   Older women and disabilities. Unpublished manuscript. Oxford, Ohio: Scripps Foundation.

9, 10   Miller, Stephen J.
1965   The social dilemma of the aging leisure participant. Pp. 77–92 in Arnold M. Rose and Warren A. Peterson (eds.), Older People and Their Social World. Philadelphia: F. A. Davis.

8   Milliren, John W.
1977   Some contingencies affecting the utilization of tranquilizers in long-term care of the elderly. Journal of Health and Social Behavior 18:206–11.

3, 9   Mills, C. Wright
1951   White Collar: The American Middle Classes. New York: Oxford University Press.

8, 12   Mindel, C. H., and C. E. Vaughan
1978   A multidimensional approach to religiosity and disengagement. Journal of Gerontology 33:103–08.

7, 8   Mindel, Charles H., and Roosevelt Wright, Jr.
1982   Satisfaction in multigenerational households. Journal of Gerontology 37:483–89.

8, 18   Minkler, M., S. Frantz, and R. Wechsler
1982   Social support and social action organizing in a "grey ghetto": the tenderloin experience. International Journal of Community Health Education 3:3–15.

15   Minnigerode, F. A.
            1976   Age-status labeling in homosexual men. Journal of Homosexuality 1:273–76.
15   Minnigerode, F. A., and M. Adelman.
            1976   Adaptations of aging homosexual men and women. Paper presented at the Annual
                    Meeting of the Gerontological Society. New York. October.
            Mishara, Brian L., and Robert Kastenbaum
8, 12   1973   Self-injurious behavior and environmental change in the institutionalized elderly. Inter-
                    national Journal of Aging and Human Development 4:133–45.
12, 15   1980   Alcohol and Old Age. New York: Grune & Stratton.
8, 18   Mitchell, Janet B.
            1982   Physicians visits to nursing homes. The Gerontologist 22:45–48.
9   Mitchell, William I.
            1968   Preparation for Retirement. Washington, D.C.: American Association of Retired Per-
                    sons.
            Moberg, David O.
8, 10   1965a   The integration of older members in the church congregation. Pp. 125–40 in Arnold
                    M. Rose and Warren A. Peterson (eds.), Older People and Their Social World. Phila-
                    delphia: F. A. Davis.
8, 10   1965b   Religion in old age. Geriatrics 20:977–82.
8, 10   1965c   Religiosity in old age. The Gerontologist 5:78–87.
7, 8   1972   Religion and the aged family. Family Coordinator 21:47–60.
10, 12   Moberg, David O., and Marvin J. Taves
            1965   Church participation and adjustment in old age. Pp. 113–24 in Arnold M. Rose and
                    Warren A. Peterson (eds.), Older People and Their Social World. Philadelphia: F. A.
                    Davis.
9   Mohler, Stanley R.
            1981   Aircraft accidents and age. Aging and Work 4:54–57.
8, 18   Monahan, Deborah J., and Vernon L. Greene
            1982   The impact of seasonal population fluctuations on service delivery. The Gerontologist
                    22:160–63.
5   Monge, Rolf H.
            1975   Structure of the self-concept from adolescence through old age. Experimental Aging
                    Research 1:281–91.
            Monk, Abraham
9   1971   Factors in the preparation for retirement by middle-aged adults. The Gerontologist
                    11(4, part 1):348–51.
9   1972   A social policy framework for pre-retirement planning. Industrial Gerontology 15:63–
                    70.
8   1977   Education and the rural aged. Educational Gerontology 2:147–56.
5   Monk, Abraham, Arthur G. Cryns, and Kirsten Milbrath
            1976   Personal and social value concerns of Scandinavian elderly: a multivariate study. Inter-
                    national Journal of Aging and Human Development 7:221–30.
8   Monk, Abraham, and Lenard W. Kaye
            1982   The ombudsman volunteer in the nursing home: differential role perceptions of patient
                    representatives for the institutionalized aged. The Gerontologist 22:194–99.
            Montgomery, James E.
8   1967   Housing for the rural aged. Pp. 169–94 in E. Grant Youmans (ed.), Older Rural
                    American. Lexington, Kentucky: University of Kentucky Press.
8   1972   The housing patterns of older families. Family Coordinator 21:37–46.

8   Montgomery, James E., Alice C. Stubbs, and Savannah S. Day
    1980   The housing environment of the rural elderly. The Gerontologist 20:444–51.
7, 8   Montgomery, Rhonda J. V.
    1982   Impact of institutional care policies on family integration. The Gerontologist 22:54–58.
14   Moore, Joan W.
    1971   Mexican-Americans. The Gerontologist 11(1, part 2):30–35.
5   Moore, Loretta M., Christene R. Nielsen, and Charlotte M. Mistretta
    1982   Sucrose taste thresholds: age related differences. Journal of Gerontology 37:64–69.
15   Morella, Frank P.
    1982   Juvenile Crimes Against the Elderly. Springfield, Ill.: Charles C. Thomas.
    Morgan, James N.
8   1962   Income and Welfare in the United States. New York: McGraw-Hill.
8   1965   Measuring the economic status of the aged. International Economic Review 6:1–17.
    Morgan, Leslie A.
11   1976   A re-examination of widowhood and morale. Journal of Gerontology 31(6):687–95.
11   1980   Work in widowhood: a viable option? The Gerontologist 20:581–87.
7, 8   1981   Economic change at mid-life widowhood: a longitudinal analysis. Journal of Marriage and the Family 43:899–907.
7, 8   1983a   Intergenerational financial support: retirement-age males, 1971–1975. The Gerontologist 23:160–67.
7, 8   1983b   Intergenerational economic assistance to children: the case of widows and widowers. Journal of Gerontology 38:725–31.
10   Mori, Mikio
    1973   The elderly and leisure in Japan. Society and Leisure 5(4):109–25.
11   Morison, R. S.
    1971   Dying. Scientific American 229(3):54–62.
5   Moriwaki, S. Y.
    1974   The affect balance scale: a validity study with aged samples. Journal of Gerontology 29:73–78.
2   Moriyama, Iwao
    1964   The Change in Mortality Trend in the United States. Washington, D.C.: National Center for Health Statistics.
8   Morlok, E. K., W. M. Kulash, and H. L. Vandersypen
    1971   Reduced fares for the elderly. Effects on a transit system. Welfare Review 9(5):17–24.
12   Morris, J. N., and S. Sherwood
    1975   A retesting and modification of the Philadelphia Geriatric Center Morale Scale. Journal of Gerontology 30:77–84.
12   Morris, J. N., R. S. Wolf, and L. V. Klerman
    1975   Common themes among morale and depression scales. Journal of Gerontology 30:209–15.
19   Morris, Robert, and Robert H. Binstock
    1966   Feasible Planning for Social Change. New York: Columbia University Press.
8, 18, 19   Morris, Robert, and Ollie A. Randall
    1965   Planning and organization of community services for the elderly. Social Work 10:96–102.
    Morrison, Malcolm H.
9   1975   The myth of employee planning for retirement. Industrial Gerontology 2:135–43.
9   1976   Planning for income adequacy in retirement; the expectations of current workers. The Gerontologist 16:538–43.

16   1982   The Economics of Aging: The Future of Retirement. New York: Van Nostrand Reinhold.

8, 17   Morrissey, Maureen
          1982   Guardians ad litem: an educational program in Virginia. The Gerontologist 22:301–04.

14   Morse, Dean W.
          1976   Aging in the ghetto: themes expressed by older black men and women living in a northern industrial city. Industrial Gerontology 3:1–10.

9   Morse, Nancy C., and Robert S. Weiss
          1955   The function and meaning of work and the job. American Sociological Review 20:191–98.

6   Mortimer, Jeylan T., and Roberta G. Simmons
          1978   Adult socialization. Annual Review of Sociology 4:421–54.

10   Moss, Miriam S., and M. Powell Lawton
          1982   Time budgets of older people: a window on four lifestyles. Journal of Gerontology 37:115–23.

          Motley, Dena K.
8, 9   1972   Health in the years before retirement. Social Security Bulletin 35(12):18–36.
8   1975   Paying for health care in the years before retirement. Social Security Bulletin 38(4):3–22.
9   1978   Availability of retired persons for work: findings from the retirement history study. Social Security Bulletin 41(4):18–28.

3   Mott, Paul E.
          1965   The Organization of Society. Englewood Cliffs, N.J.: Prentice-Hall.

7, 12   Mueller, Daniel P.
          1980   Social networks: a promising direction for research on the relationship of the social environment to psychiatric disorder. Social Science and Medicine 14A:147–61.

8, 18   Mueller, Marjorie Smith
          1975   Private health insurance in 1973: a review of coverage, enrollment, and financial experience. Social Security Bulletin 38(2):21–40.

8, 18   Mueller, Marjorie Smith, and Robert M. Gibson
          1975   Age difference in health care spending, fiscal year 1974. Social Security Bulletin 38(6):3–16.

11   Munley, Anne, Cynthia A. Powers, and John B. Williamson
          1982   Humanizing nursing home environments: the relevance of hospice principles. International Journal of Aging and Human Development 15:263–84.

          Munnell, Alicia H.
16   1974   The Effect of Social Security on Personal Saving. Cambridge, Mass.: Ballinger Publishing Co.
16   1977   The Future of Social Security. Washington, D.C.: Brookings.
16   1982   The Economics of Private Pensions. Washington, D.C.: Brookings.

7   Munnichs, Joep M. A., and W. J. A. van den Heuvel (eds.)
          1976   Dependency or Interdependence in Old Age. The Hague: Martinus Nijhoff.

8   Murphy, B.
          1971   Finding the invisible elderly poor. Opportunity 1(8):2–10.

8   Murray, Janet
          1972   Homeownership and financial assets: findings from the 1968 survey of the aged. Social Security Bulletin 35(8):3–23.

9   Murray, J. R., E. A. Powers, and R. J. Havighurst
          1971   Personal and situational factors producing flexible careers. The Gerontologist 11(4, part 2):4–12.

16   Murray, Roger F.
       1968   Economic Aspects of Pensions: A Summary Report. New York: Columbia University
               Press.

5, 12 Murrell, S., S. Himmelfarb, and K. Wright
       1983   Prevalence of depression and its correlates in older adults. American Journal of
               Epidemiology 117:173–85.

7   Murstein, B. I., and P. Christy
       1976   Physical attractiveness and marriage adjustment in middle-aged couples. Journal of Per-
               sonality and Social Psychology 34:537–42.

12   Mussen, Paul, Marjorie P. Honzik, and Dorothy H. Eichorn
       1982   Early adult antecedents of life satisfaction at age 70. Journal of Gerontology 37:316–22.

9, 12 Mutran, Elizabeth, and Donald C. Reitzes
       1981   Retirement, identity and well-being: realignment of role relationships. Journal of
               Gerontology 36:733–40.

12   Myers, Jerome K., Jacob J. Lindenthal, and Max P. Pepper
       1975   Life events, social integration and psychiatric symptomatology. Journal of Health and
               Social Behavior 16:421–27.

12   Myers, J. K., J. J. Lindenthal, M. P. Pepper, and D. R. Ostrander
       1972   Life events and mental status: a longitudinal study. Journal of Health and Social Be-
               havior 13:398–406.

      Myers, Robert J.
9   1954   Factors in interpreting morality after retirement. Journal of the American Statistical As-
               sociation 49:499–509.
16   1975   Social Security and private pensions—where do we go from here? Industrial Gerontolo-
               gy 2:158–63.

      Myles, John F.
8, 14 1981   Income inequality and status maintenance: concepts, methods, and measures. Research
               on Aging 3:123–41.
16   1984   Old Age in the Welfare State: The Political Economy of Public Pensions. Boston: Lit-
               tle, Brown.

9   Nadelson, Theodore
       1969   A survey of the literature on the adjustment of the aged to retirement. Journal of
               Geriatric Psychiatry 3:3–20.

15   Nagi, Saad Z.
       1965   Some conceptual issues in disability and rehabilitation. Pp. 100–03 in Marvin B. Suss-
               man (ed.), Sociology and Rehabilitation. Washington, D.C.: American Sociological As-
               sociation.

7   Nahemow, L., and M. Powell Lawton
       1975   Similarity and propinquity in friendship formation. Journal of Personality and Social
               Psychology 32:205–13.

8   Namey, Christy, and R. W. Wilson
       1972   Age patterns in medical care, illness, and disability. Vital and Health Statistics, Series
               10, No. 70.

5   Nardi, A. H.
       1973   Person-conception research and the perception of life-span development. Pp. 285–301
               in Paul B. Baltes and K. Warner Schaie (eds.), Life-Span Developmental Psychology:
               Personality and Socialization. New York: Academic Press.

8, 18 Nardone, Maryann
       1980   Characteristics predicting community care for mentally impaired older persons. The
               Gerontologist 20:661–68.

8, 9   Nathanson, Connie
   1980   Social roles and health status among women: the significance of employment. Social Science and Medicine 14A:463–71.

National Center for Health Statistics
5   1959   United States National Health Survey. Health Statistics, Series B, No. 9. Washington, D.C.: U.S. Government Printing Office.

2, 7   1974   Vital Statistics of the United States, 1970. Volume 3: Marriage and Divorce. Washington, D.C.: U.S. Government Printing Office.

2   1977   Vital Statistics of the United States, Volume II—Mortality, Part A, Section 5—Life Tables. Washington, D.C.: U.S. Government Printing Office.

4, 8   1978   Conditions Causing Activity Limitation: United States, 1976. Vital and Health Statistics, Series 10, Number 123. Washington, D.C.: U.S. Government Printing Office.

2   1980   Vital Statistics of the United States, 1976, Volume II—Mortality, Part A. Washington, D.C.: U.S. Government Printing Office.

4   1982   Current estimates from the National Health Interview Survey: United States, 1981. Vital and Health Statistics, Series 10, Number 141. Washington, D.C.: U.S. Government Printing Office.

17   National Council of Senior Citizens
   1971   Legislative Approaches to Problems of the Elderly: A Handbook of Model State Statutes. Washington, D.C.: National Council of Senior Citizens.

National Council on the Aging
19   1970   The Golden Years—A Tarnished Myth. New York: National Council on Aging.

8   1971a   The Older Non-Professional in Community Service. Four Professional Viewpoints. Washington, D.C.: National Council on the Aging, Senior Community Service Project.

9, 14   1971b   Employment Prospects of Aged Blacks, Chicanos and Indians, Washington, D.C.: National Council on the Aging.

9   1971c   Guidelines for the Development of Employment Opportunities for Older People. Washington, D.C.: National Council on the Aging. Senior Community Service Project.

14   1972a   Triple Jeopardy: Myth or Reality. Washington, D.C.: National Council on the Aging.

8   1972b   Housing and Living Arrangements for Older People: A Bibliography. Washington, D.C.: National Council on the Aging.

16   National Industrial Conference Board
   1966   Expenditure Patterns of the American Family. New York: National Industrial Conference Board.

19   National Retired Teachers Association and American Association of Retired Persons
   1971   Proposals for a National Policy on Aging. Washington, D.C.: National Retired Teachers Association and American Association of Retired Persons.

13   Naus, P. J.
   1973   Some correlates of attitudes towards old people. International Journal of Aging and Human Development 4:229–43.

8, 10   Naylor, H. H.
   1973   Volunteerism with and by the elderly. Pp. 195–204 in R. R. Boyd and C. G. Oaks (eds.), Foundations of Practical Gerontology, second edition. Columbia, So. Carolina: University of South Carolina Press.

1   Nelson, Edward E., and Bernice C. Starr
   1972   Interpretation of research on age. Pp. 27–84 in Matilda White Riley and others (eds.), Aging and Society. Volume 3: A Sociology of Age Stratification. New York: Russell Sage Foundation.

12   Nelson, Franklyn L., and Norman L. Farberow
        1980   Indirect self-destructive behavior in the elderly nursing home patient. Journal of Geron-
                tology 35:949–57.
8, 18   Nelson, Gary
        1980   Social services to the urban and rural aged: the experience of area agencies on aging.
                The Gerontologist 20:200–07.
        Nelson, Gary M.
14, 17 1982   Social class and public policy for the elderly. Pp. 101–30 in B. L. Neugarten (ed.), Age
                or Need? Public Policies for Older People. Beverly Hills, Calif.: Sage.
8, 16   1983   Tax expenditures for the elderly. The Gerontologist 23:471–78.
8   Nelson, L. M., and M. Winter
        1975   Life disruption, independence, satisfaction, and the consideration of moving. The
                Gerontologist 15:160–64.
5, 8   Nelson, Martal Nadal, and Robert L. Paluck
        1980   Territorial markings, self-concept, and mental status of the institutionalized elderly.
                The Gerontologist 20:96–98.
1   Nesselroade, John R.
        1977   Issues in studying developmental change in adults from a multivariate perspective. Pp.
                59–95 in James E. Birren and K. Warner Schaie (eds.), Handbook of the Psychology
                of Aging. New York: Van Nostrand-Reinhold.
1   Nesselroade, John R., and Hayne W. Reese
        1973   Life-Span Developmental Psychology: Methodological Issues. New York: Academic
                Press.
5   Nesselroade, John R., K. Warner Schaie, and Paul B. Baltes
        1972   Ontogenetic and generational components of structural and quantitative change in adult
                cognitive behavior. Journal of Gerontology 27:222–28.
        Neugarten, Bernice L.
5   1963   Personality changes during the adult years. Pp. 43–76 in Raymond G. Kuhlen (ed.),
                Psychological Backgrounds of Adult Education. Chicago: Center for the Study of Lib-
                eral Education for Adults.
5   1964a   A developmental view of adult personality. Pp. 176–208 in James E. Birren (ed.), Rela-
                tions of Development and Aging. Springfield, Ill.: Charles C. Thomas.
5   1964b   (ed.), Personality in Middle and Late Life. New York: Atherton Press.
13   1966   The aged in American society. Pp. 167–96 in Howard S. Becker (ed.), Social Problems.
                New York: Wiley.
5, 6   1968   (ed.), Middle Age and Aging. Chicago: University of Chicago Press.
12   1970   Dynamics of transition of middle age to old age: adaptation and the life cycle. Journal
                of Geriatric Psychiatry 4:71–87.
12   1971   Grow old along with me! The best is yet to be. Psychology Today 5(December):45–48.
5   1972a   Personality and the aging process. The Gerontologist 12:9–15.
5   1972b   Personality changes in late life: a developmental perspective. Pp. 311–38 in Carl Eis-
                dorfer and M. Powell Lawton (eds.), The Psychology of Adult Development and Ag-
                ing. Washington, D.C.: The American Psychological Association.
19   1973   Patterns of aging: past, present, and future. Social Service Review 47:571–80.
2, 19   1974   Age groups in American society and the rise of the young-old. Pp. 187–98 in Frederick
                R. Eisele (ed.), Political Consequences of Aging. Philadelphia: American Academy of
                Political and Social Sciences.
19   1975   The future of the young-old. The Gerontologist 15(1, part 2):4–9.

5   1977   Personality and aging. Pp. 626–49 in James E. Birren and K. Warner Schaie (eds.), Handbook of the Psychology of Aging. New York: Van Nostrand Reinhold.

17   1982   (ed.), Age or Need? Public Policies for Older People. Beverly Hills, Calif.: Sage.

6   Neugarten, Bernice L., and Nancy Datan
        1973   Sociological perspectives on the life cycle. Pp. 53–69 in Paul B. Baltes and K. Warner Schaie (eds.) Life-Span Developmental Psychology: Personality and Socialization. New York: Academic Press.

6   Neugarten, Bernice L., and Gunhild O. Hagestad
        1976   Age and the life course. Pp. 35–55 in Robert H. Binstock and Ethel Shanas (eds.), Handbook of Aging and the Social Sciences. New York: Van Nostrand Reinhold.

6   Neugarten, Bernice L., and Joan W. Moore
        1968   The changing age-status system. Pp. 5–21 in Bernice L. Neugarten (ed.), Middle Age and Aging. Chicago: University of Chicago Press.

7   Neugarten, Bernice L., and Karol K. Weinstein
        1964   The changing American grandparent. Journal of Marriage and the Family 26:199–204.

12   Neugarten, Bernice L., Robert L. Havighurst, and Sheldon S. Tobin
        1961   The measurement of life satisfaction. Journal of Gerontology 16:134–43.

6   Neugarten, Bernice L., Joan W. Moore, and John C. Lowe
        1965   Age norms, age constraints, and adult socialization. American Journal of Sociology 70: 710–17.

4   Neugarten, Bernice L., Vivian Wood, Ruth J. Kraines, and Barbara Loomis
        1963   Women's attitudes toward the menopause. Vita Humana 6:140–51.

5   Newcomb, Theodore M., Ralph H. Turner, and Philip E. Converse
        1965   Social Psychology. New York: Holt, Rinehart, and Winston.

18   Newcomer, Robert J., and Charlene Harrington
        1983   State Medicaid expenditures: trends and program policy changes. Pp. 157–86 in Carroll L. Estes and R. J. Newcomer (eds.), Fiscal Austerity and Aging: Shifting Government Responsibility for the Elderly. Beverly Hills, Calif.: Sage.

8   Newcomer, Robert J., Susan R. Newcomer, and Louis E. Gelwicks
        1976   Assessing the need for semi-dependent housing for the elderly. The Gerontologist 16: 112–17.

13   Newell, David S.
        1961   Social structural evidence for disengagement. Pp. 37–74 in Elaine Cumming and W. E. Henry (eds.), Growing Old. New York: Basic Books.

8   Newman, Evelyn S., and Susan R. Sherman
        1977   A survey of caretakers in adult foster homes. The Gerontologist 17:436–39.

9   Newman, Evelyn S., Susan R. Sherman, and Claire Higgins
        1982   Retirement expectations and plans: a comparison of professional men and women. Pp. 113–22 in M. Szinovacz (ed.), Women's Retirement. Beverly Hills, Calif.: Sage.

5, 7   Newman, G., and C. R. Nichols
        1960   Sexual activities and attitudes in older persons. Journal of the American Medical Association 173:33–35.

18   Newman, H. F.
        1969   The impact of Medicare on group practice prepayment plans. American Journal of Public Health 59:629–34.

        Newman, Sandra J.
8   1976   Housing adjustments of the disabled elderly. The Gerontologist 16:312–17.
8   1981   Exploring housing adjustments of older people: the HUD-HEW longitudinal study. Research on Aging 3:417–28.

8, 14   Newton, Frank Cata-Rables
      1980   Issues in research and service delivery among Mexican American elderly: a concise statement with recommendations. The Gerontologist 20:208–13.

17   Nie, N., S. Verba, and J. Petrocik
      1976   The Changing American Voter. Cambridge, Mass.: Harvard University Press.

8, 18   Nithman, C. J., Y. E. Parkhurst, and E. B. Sommers
      1971   Physicians' prescribing habits: effects of Medicare. Journal of the American Medical Association 217:585–87.

5   Norris, Michael L., and David R. Cunningham
      1981   Social impact of hearing loss in the aged. Journal of Gerontology 36:727–29.

13   Nuessel, Frank H., Jr.
      1982   The language of ageism. The Gerontologist 22:273–76.

8, 18   Nuttbrack, Larry, and Jordon I. Kasberg
      1980   Images of the physician and help-seeking behavior of the elderly: a multivariate assessment. Journal of Gerontology 35:241–48.

12   Nydegger, C. N. (ed.)
      1977   Measuring Morale: A Guide to Effective Assessment. Special Publication No. 3. Washington D.C.: Gerontological Society.

8, 18   Oakes, C. G.
      1973   Sociomedical fit and misfit among the elderly. Pp. 77–102 in R. R. Boyd and C. G. Oakes (eds.), Foundations of Practical Gerontology, second edition. Columbia, So. Carolina: University of South Carolina Press.

8   O'Bryant, Shirley L.
      1982   The value of home to older persons: relationship to housing satisfaction. Research on Aging 4:349–63.

3   O'Donnell, C. F.
      1974   Aging in preindustrial and in contemporary industrial societies. Pp. 3–13 in W. C. Bier (ed.), Aging: its Challenge to the Individual and to Society. Pastoral Psychology Series, No. 8. New York: Fordham University Press.

5   Okun, Morris A.
      1976   Adult age and cautiousness in decision: a review of the literature. Human Development 19:220–33.

5   Okun, Morris A., and Cherin S. Elias
      1977   Cautiousness in adulthood as a function of age and payoff structure. Journal of Gerontology 32:451–55.

5   Okun, Morris A., Ilene C. Siegler, and Linda K. George
      1978   Cautiousness and verbal learning in adulthood. Journal of Gerontology 33:94–97.

    Oliver, David B.
8   1975   Nutrition and Health Care. Pp. 163–84 in Robert C. Atchley (ed.), Environments and the Rural Aged. Washington, D.C.: Gerontological Society.

10   1971   Career and leisure patterns of middle-aged metropolitan out-migrants. The Gerontologist 11(4, part 2):13–20.

5, 15   Ollenburger, Jane C.
      1981   Criminal victimization and fear of crime. Research on Aging 3:101–18.

9   Olsen, Henning, and Gert Hansen
      1977   Retirement from Work. Copenhagen: The Danish Institute for Social Research.

16   Olson, Laura K.
      1982   The Political Economy of Aging. New York: Columbia University Press.

8, 9   O'Rand, Angela, and John C. Henretta
        1982   Midlife work history and retirement income. Pp. 25–44 in M. Szinovacz (ed.),
                Women's Retirement. Beverly Hills, Calif.: Sage.
10   Orbach, Harold L.
        1961   Aging and religion: a study of church attendance in the Detroit metropolitan area.
                Geriatrics 16:530–40.
9   1969   (ed.), Trends in Early Retirement. Ann Arbor, Michigan: University of Michigan-
                Wayne State University Institute of Gerontology.
16   Orbach, Harold L., and Clark Tibbitts (eds.)
        1963   Aging and the Economy. Ann Arbor, Michigan: University of Michigan Press.
10, 12 O'Reilly, Charles T.
        1958   Religious practice and personal adjustment. Sociology and Social Research 42:119–21.
17   Oriol, William E.
        1981   Modern age and public policy. The Gerontologist 21:35–45.
17   1983   Redefining the New Federalism: Impact on Low-Income and Other Older Americans.
                Washington, D.C.: National Council on the Aging.
13, 19 1984   Getting the Story on Aging: A Sourcebook on Gerontology for Journalists. New York:
                Brookdale Institute on Aging and Human Development.
17, 19 Oriol, William, and David Affeldt
        1976   Federal directions for the aged. Social Policy 7(3):76–80.
9   O'Rourke, J. F., and H. L. Friedman
        1972   An inter-union pre-retirement training program: results and commentary. Industrial
                Gerontology 13:49–64.
7, 10,
12, 14 Ortega, Suzanne T., Robert T. Crutchfield, and William A. Rushing
        1983   Race differences in elderly personal well-being: friendships, family, and church. Re-
                search on Aging 5:101–18.
7, 10   Orthner, Dennis K.
        1975   Leisure activity patterns and marital satisfaction over the marital career. Journal of
                Marriage and the Family 37:91–102.
8, 18   Ouslander, J. G., and J. C. Beck
        1982   Defining the health problems of the elderly. Annual Review of Public Health 3:55–83.
9   Owen, John P., and L. D. Belzung
        1967   Consequences of voluntary early retirement: a case study of a new labour force phe-
                nomenon. British Journal of Industrial Relations 5:162–89.
        Owens, William A.
5   1953   Age and mental abilities: a longitudinal study. Genetic Psychology Monographs 48:3–
                54.
5   1966   Age and mental abilities: a second adult follow-up. Journal of Educational Psychology
                57:311–25.
        Palmore, Erdman
2   1964a   Work experience and earnings of the aged in 1962: findings of the 1963 survey of the
                aged. Social Security Bulletin 27(6):3–14.
9   1964b   Retirement patterns among aged men: findings of the 1963 survey of the aged. Social
                Security Bulletin 27(8):3–10.
9   1965   Differences in the retirement patterns of men and women. The Gerontologist 5:4–8.
9   1967   Employment and retirement. Pp. 89–108 in Lenore Epstein (ed.), The Aged Popula-
                tion of the United States. Washington, D.C.: U.S. Government Printing Office.
5, 6   1970   (ed.) Normal Aging: Reports from the Duke Longitudinal Study, 1955–1969. Durham,
                No. Carolina: Duke University Press.

9   1971a   Why do people retire? International Journal of Aging and Human Development 2:269–83.

13   1971b   Attidudes toward aging as shown by humor. The Gerontologist 11:181–86.

9   1972   Compulsory versus flexible retirement: issues and facts. The Gerontologist 12:343–48.

5, 12   1973a   Social factors in mental illness of the aged. Pp. 41–52 in E. W. Busse and E. Pfeiffer (eds.), Mental Illness in Later Life. Washington, D.C.: American Psychiatric Association.

2   1973b   Potential demographic contributions to gerontology. The Gerontologist 13:236–42.

13   1974a   The brighter side of four score and ten. The Gerontologist 14:136–37.

5, 6   1974b   (ed.) Normal Aging II: Reports from the Duke Longitudinal Study, 1970–73. Durham, No. Carolina: Duke University Press.

3, 13   1975a   The Honorable Elders. Durham, No. Carolina: Duke University Press.

13   1975b   What can the USA learn from Japan about aging? The Gerontologist 15:64–67.

13   1975c   The status and integration of the aged in Japanese society. Journal of Gerontology 30:199–208.

8   1976   Total chance of institutionalization among the aged. The Gerontologist 16:504–07.

13   1977   Facts on aging: a short quiz. The Gerontologist 17:315–20.

1   1978   When can age, period, and cohort be separated? Social Forces 57:282–95.

13   1980   The Facts on Aging Quiz: a review of findings. The Gerontologist 20:669–72.

13   1981   The Facts on Aging Quiz: part two. The Gerontologist 21:431–37.

13   1982   Attitudes toward the aged: what we know and need to know. Research on Aging 4:333–48.

12   Palmore, Erdman, W. P. Cleveland, J. B. Nowlin, D. Ramm, and I. C. Siegler
           1979   Stress and adaptation in later life. Journal of Gerontology 34:841–51.

5   Palmore, Erdman, and William Cleveland
           1976   Aging, terminal decline, and terminal drop. Journal of Gerontology 31:76–81.

9   Palmore, Erdman B., Linda K. George, and Gerda G. Fillenbaum
           1982   Predictors of retirement. Journal of Gerontology, 37:733:42.

8, 18   Palmore, Erdman, and Frances C. Jeffers
           1971   Health care in a longitudinal panel before and after Medicare. Journal of Gerontology 26:532–36.

12   Palmore, Erdman, and Vira Kivett
           1977   Change in life satisfaction: a longitudinal study of persons aged 40–70. Journal of Gerontology 32:311–16.

6   Palmore, Erdman, and George L. Maddox
           1977   Sociological aspects of aging. Pp. 31–58 in Ewald W. Busse and Eric Pfeiffer (eds.), Behavior and Adaptation in Late Life, second edition. Boston: Little, Brown.

           Palmore, Erdman, and K. Manton
14   1973   Ageism compared to racism and sexism. Journal of Gerontology 28:363–69.

3   1974   Modernization and status of the aged: international correlations. Journal of Gerontology 29:205–10.

3   Palmore, Erdman, and F. Whittington
           1971   Trends in the relative status of the aged. Social Forces 50:84–91.

8, 9   Pampel, Fred C.
           1981   Social Change and the Aged: Recent Trends in the United States. Lexington, Mass.: Heath.

3, 16   Pampel, Fred C., and Jane A. Weiss
           1983   Economic development, pension policies, and the labor force participation of aged males: a cross-national, longitudinal approach. American Journal of Sociology 89:350–72.

8   Papsidero, Joseph A., Sister Mary Honora Kroger, and Marilyn Rothert
        1980   Preparing health assistants for service roles in long-term care. The Gerontologist 20:534
                –46.

5   Park, Denise Cortis, J. Thomas Puglisi, and Robert Lutz
        1982   Spatial memory in older adults: effects of intentionality. Journal of Gerontology 37:330
                –35.

11   Parkes, C. M.
        1972   Bereavement. New York: International Universities Press.

11   Parkes, C. Murray, and Robert S. Weiss
        1983   Recovery from Bereavement. New York: Basic Books.

8   Parmelee, Patricia A.
        1982   Social contacts, social instrumentality, and adjustment of institutionalized aged. Re-
                search on Aging 4:269–80.

9   Parnes, Herbert S.
        1981   From the middle to the later years: longitudinal studies of the pre- and post-retirement
                experiences of men. Research on Aging 4:387–402.

        Parnes, Herbert S., Arvil V. Adams, Paul Andrisani, et al.
9   1975   The Pre-Retirement Years: Five Years in the Work Lives of Middle Aged Men. Man-
                power Research Monograph, Number 15. Washington, D.C.: U.S. Department of La-
                bor.

9   1976   Dual Careers; A Longitudinal Analysis of the Labor Market Experience of Women.
                Volume 4. Ohio: Ohio State University, Center for Human Resource Research.

9, 16   Parnes, Herbert S., and Randy King
        1977   Middle-aged job losers. Industrial Gerontology 4:77–96.

9   Parnes, Herbert S., and Lawrence Less
        1983   From Work to Retirement: The Experience of a National Sample of Men. Columbus,
                Ohio: Ohio State University Center for Human Resource Research.

4, 9   Parnes, Herbert S., and Gilbert Nestel
        1981   The retirement experience. Pp. 132–54 in Herbert S. Parnes (ed.), Work and Retire-
                ment: A Longitudinal Study of Men. Cambridge, Mass.: MIT Press.

        Parsons, Talcott (ed.)
6   1942   Age and sex in the social structure of the United States. American Sociological Review
                7:604–16.

11   1972   Death in American experience. Social Research 39:367–567.

8   Patnaik, B., M. P. Lawton, M. H. Kleban, and R. Maxwell
        1974   Behavioral adaptation to the change in institutional residence. The Gerontologist 14:305
                –07.

        Patterson, James
3, 16   1981   American Attitudes Toward Poverty. Cambridge, Mass.: Howard University Press.

9   Patton, Carl Vernon
        1977   Early retirement in academia: making the decision. The Gerontologist 17:347–54.

8, 10   Payne, Barbara P.
        1977   The older volunteer: social role continuity and development. The Gerontologist 17:355–
                61.

12   Pearlin, L. I., and J. S. Johnson
        1977   Marital status, life-strains and depression. American Sociological Review 42:704–15.

12   Pearlin, L. I., and C. Schooler
        1978   The structure of coping. Journal of Health and Social Behavior 19(1):2–21.

5   Pease, R. A.
        1974   Female professional students and sexuality in the aging male. The Gerontologist 14:153
                –57.

5   Peck, R. C.
     1968   Psychological developments in the second half of life. Pp. 88–92 in Bernice L. Neu-
             garten (ed.), Middle Age and Aging. Chicago: University of Chicago Press.

17   Pedersen, Johannes Thestrup
     1976   Age and change in public opinion: the case of California, 1960–1970. The Public Opin-
             ion Quarterly 40(2):143–53.

9, 10   Peppers, Larry G.
        1976   Patterns of leisure and adjustment to retirement. The Gerontologist 16:441–46.

9   Peretti, Peter O., and Cedric Wilson
     1975   Voluntary and involuntary retirement of aged males and their effect on emotional satis-
             faction, usefulness, self-image, emotional stability, and interpersonal relationships. In-
             ternational Journal of Aging and Human Development 6:131–38.

5   Perlmutter, Marion, and Judith A. List
     1982   Learning in later adulthood. Pp. 551–68 in T. M. Field et al. (eds.), Review of Human
             Development. New York: Wiley.

5, 12   Perrotta, Peter, and Meacham, John A.
        1981   Can a reminiscing intervention alter depression and self-esteem? International Journal
                of Aging and Human Development 14:23–30.

5   Peters, George R.
     1971   Self-conceptions of the aged, age identification, and aging. The Gerontologist 11(4, part
             2):69–73.

13   Petersen, M.
     1973   The visibility and image of old people on television. Journalism Quarterly 50:569–73.

     Peterson, David A.
8, 16   1972a   The Crisis in Retirement Finance: the Views of Older Americans. Occasional Papers in
                Gerontology, No. 9. Ann Arbor: Michigan: University of Michigan-Wayne State Uni-
                versity Institute of Gerontology.

8, 16   1972b   Financial adequacy in retirement: perceptions of older Americans. The Gerontologist
                12:379–83.

8   1975   Life-span education and gerontology. The Gerontologist 15:436–41.

13   Peterson, David A., and Donna Z. Eden.
     1977   Teenagers and aging; adolescent literature as an attitude source. Educational Gerontolo-
             gy 2:311–25.

13   Peterson, David A., and Elizabeth L. Karnes
     1976   Older people in adolescent literature. The Gerontologist 16:225–31.

19   Peterson, David A., Chuck Powell, and Lawrie Robertson
     1976   Aging in America; toward the year 2000. The Gerontologist 16:264–69.

7   Petrowsky, Marc
     1976   Marital status, sex, and the social networks of the elderly. Journal of Marriage and the
             Family 38(4):749–56.

9   Pfeffer, Jeffrey
     1981   Some consequences of organizational demography: potential impacts of an aging work
             force on formal organizations. Pp. 291–330 in Sara B. Kiesler et al. (eds.), Aging: So-
             cial Change. New York: Academic Press.

8, 10   Pfeffer, R. I., T. T. Kurosaki, C. H. Harrah, Jr., J. M. Chance, and S. Filos
        1982   Measurement of functional activities in older adults in the community. Journal of
                Gerontology 37:323–29.

5   Pfeiffer, Eric
     1977   Sexual behavior in old age. Pp. 130–41 in Ewald W. Busse and Eric Pfeiffer (eds.),
             Behavior and Adaptation in Late Life, second edition. Boston: Little, Brown.

Pfeiffer, Eric, and G. C. Davis

10   1971   The use of leisure time in middle life. The Gerontologist 11(3, part 1):187–95.

5   1972   Determinants of sexual behavior in middle and old age. Journal of the American Geriatric Society 20:151–58.

17   Philibert, Michel

1970   La politique nationale de la vieillesse en France. Gerontologie (November):10–13.

12   Phillips, Bernard S.

1957   A role theory approach to adjustment in old age. American Sociological Review 22:212–17.

2, 11   Phillips, D. P., and K. A. Feldman

1973   A dip in deaths before ceremonial occasions: some new relationships between social integration and mortality. American Sociological Review 38:678–96.

9   Phillipson, Chris

The Emergence of Retirement. Durham, England: University of Durham.

1982   Capitalism and the Construction of Old Age. London: Macmillan.

10   Pierce, Charles H.

1975   Recreation for the elderly: activity participation at a senior citizen center. The Gerontologist 15(3):202–05.

12   Pierce, R. C., and M. M. Clark

1973   Measurement of morale in the elderly. International Journal of Aging and Human Development 5:83–101.

11, 12   Pihlblad, C. Terence, and D. L. Adams

1972   Widowhood, social participation and life satisfaction. Aging and Human Development 3:323–30.

8, 12   Pihlblad, C. Terence, and Robert L. McNamara

1965   Social adjustment of elderly people in three small towns. Pp. 49–73 in Arnold M. Rose and Warren A. Peterson (eds.), Older People and Their Social World. Philadelphia: F. A. Davis.

8   Pihlblad, C. Terence, Richard Hessler, and Harold Freshley

1975   The Rural Elderly. Eight Years Later: Changes in Life Satisfaction, Living Arrangements and Health Status. Columbia, Missouri: University of Missouri.

7   Pineo, Peter

1961   Disenchantment in the later years of marriage. Marriage and Family Living 23:3–11.

19   Pinker, Robert A.

1980   Facing up to the eighties: health and welfare needs of British elderly (Great Britain). The Gerontologist 20:273–83.

17   Pinner, Frank A., Paul Jacobs, and Philip Selznick

1959   Old Age and Political Behavior: A Case Study. Berkeley, Calif.: University of California Press.

8, 18,
19   Pippen, Roland N.

1980   Assessing the needs of the elderly with existing data. The Gerontologist 20:65–70.

5   Plemons, Judy K., Sherry L. Willis, and Paul B. Baltes

1978   Modifiability of fluid intelligence in aging; a short-term longitudinal training approach. Journal of Gerontology 33:224–31.

5   Plutchik, R., H. Conte, and M. Bakur-Weiner

1973   Studies of body image, III. Body feelings as measured by the semantic differential. International Journal of Aging and Human Development 4:375–80.

8, 16   Polinsky, Ella J.

1969   The position of women in the Social Security System. Social Security Bulletin 32(7):3–19.

9   Pollak, Otto
         1956   The Social Aspects of Retirement. Homewood, Ill.: Irwin.

         Pollman, A. William

9   1971a   Early retirement: a comparison of poor health to other retirement factors. Journal of Gerontology 26:41–45.

9   1971b   Early retirement: relationship to variation in life satisfaction. The Gerontologist 11(1, part 1):43–47.

9   Pollman, A. William, and A. C. Johnson
         1974   Resistance to change, early retirement and managerial decisions. Industrial Gerontology 1:33–41.

3, 17   Polner, Walter
         1962   The aged in politics: a successful example, the NPA and the passage of the Railroad Retirement Act of 1934. The Gerontologist 2:207–15.

5, 12   Pope, Hallowell, and Miller Dwayne Ferguson
         1982   Age and anomia in middle and later life: a multivariate analysis of a national sample of white men. International Journal of Aging and Human Development 15:51–74.

2   Population Reference Bureau
         1979   World Population Data Sheet. Washington, D.C.: Population Reference Bureau.

8   Posner, J.
         1974   Notes on the negative implications of being competent in a home for the aged. International Journal of Aging and Human Development 5:357–64.

17   Post, J. M.
         1973   On aging leaders: possible effects of the aging process on the conduct of leadership. Journal of Geriatric Psychiatry 6:109–16.

         Powers, Edward A., and G. L. Bultena

1   1972   Characteristics of deceased dropouts in longitudinal research. Journal of Gerontology 26:530–35.

7   1976   Sex differences in intimate friendships of old age. Journal of Marriage and the Family 38(4):739–47.

9   Powers, Edward A., and Willis H. Goudy
         1971   Examination of the meaning of work to older workers. International Journal of Aging and Human Development 2:38–45.

7   Powers, Edward A., Patricia Keith, and Willis H. Goudy
         1975   Family relationships and friendships. Pp. 67–90 in Robert C. Atchley (ed.), Environments and the Rural Aged. Washington, D.C.: The Gerontological Society.

9   1980   A panel study of nonmetropolitan older workers. Aging and Work 3:163–74.

8   Pratt, Clara Collette, William Simonson, and Sally Lloyd
         1982   Pharmacists' perceptions of major difficulties in geriatric pharmacy practice. The Gerontologist 22:288–92.

         Pratt, Henry J.

17   1974   Old age associations in national politics. Pp. 106–19 in Frederick R. Eisele (ed.), Political Consequences of Aging. Philadelphia: American Academy of Political and Social Sciences.

17   1977   The Gray Lobby. Chicago: University of Chicago Press.

         Prentis, Richard S.

9   1975   National Survey of Fortune's "500" Preretirement Plans and Policies. Ann Arbor, Michigan: University of Michigan-Wayne State University Institute of Labor and Industrial Relations.

9   1980   White-collar working women's perception of retirement. The Gerontologist 20:90–95.

16   The President's Commission on Pension Policy
         1981   Coming of Age: Toward a National Retirement Income Policy. Washington, D.C.:
                 U.S. Government Printing Office.

3, 13   Press, I., and M. McKool, Jr.
         1972   Social structure and status of the aged: toward some valid cross-cultural generalizations.
                 International Journal of Aging and Human Development 3:297–306.

7   Presser, Harriet B.
         1975   Age differences between spouses: trends, patterns, and social implications. American
                 Behavioral Scientist 19(2):190–205.

5   Preston, Caroline E., and Karen S. Gudiksen
         1966   A measure of self-perception among older people. Journal of Gerontology 21:63–71.

8   Preston, Caroline E., and S. Helgerson
         1972   An analysis of survey data obtained by a service agency for older people. The Geron-
                 tologist 12:384–88.

11   Preston, Caroline E., and R. H. Williams
         1971   Views of the aged on the timing of death. The Gerontologist 11:300–04.

2   Preston, S. H.
         1974   Effect of mortality change on stable population parameters. Demography 11:119–30.

9   Price-Bonham, Sharon, and C. K. Johnson
         1982   Attitudes toward retirement: a comparison of professional and nonprofessional married
                 women. Pp. 123–38 in M. Szinovacz (ed.), Women's Retirement. Beverly Hills, Calif.:
                 Sage.

5   Prinz, Patricia N.
         1977   Sleep patterns in the healthy aged: relationship with intellectual function. Journal of
                 Gerontology 32:179–86.

        Puglisi, J. Thomas, and Dorothy W. Jackson
5   1981   Sex role identity and self esteem in adulthood. International Journal of Aging and Hu-
                 man Development 12:129–38.

5   1983   Self-perceived age changes in sex role self concept. International Journal of Aging and
                 Human Development 16:183–91.

9   Pursell, Donald E., and William D. Torrence
         1980   The older woman and her search for employment. Aging and Work 3:121–28.

9   Pyron, H. Charles, and U. Vincent Manion
         1970   The company, the individual, and the decision to retire. Industrial Gerontology 4:1–11.

12   Quayhagen, Mary P., and Margaret Quayhagen
         1982   Coping with conflict: measurement of age-related patterns. Research on Aging 4:364–77.

9   Quinn, Joseph F.
         1981   The extent and correlates of partial retirement. The Gerontologist 21:634–43.

        Quirk, Daniel A.
9   1974   Public policy note: age discrimination in employment—some recent developments. In-
                 dustrial Gerontology 1:77–80.

16   1975   Public policy note in defense of the Social Security System: the white paper. Industrial
                 Gerontology 2:164–66.

9   1976   Employment opportunities for the older adult: recent policy initiatives. Industrial
                 Gerontology 3:134–38.

9   Quirk, Daniel A., and J. H. Skinner
         1973   Physical capacity, age, and employment. Industrial Gerontology 19:49–62.

5   Rabbitt, Patrick
         1982   Breakdown of control processes in old age. Pp. 540–50 in T. M. Field et al. (eds.),
                 Review of Human Development. New York: Wiley.

12   Rabbitt, Patrick, and Subhash M. Vyas
        1980   Selective anticipation for events in old age. Journal of Gerontology 35:913–19.
12   Rabkin, J. G. and E. C. Streuning
        1976   Life events, stress and illness. Science 194:1013–20.
8   Raffaul, Paul R., James K. Capper, and David W. Love
        1981   Drug misuse in older people. The Gerontologist 21:146–50.
17   Ragan, Pauline K., and James J. Dowd
        1974   The emerging political consciousness of the aged: a generational interpretation. Journal of Social Issues 30:137–58.
8   Rakowski, William, and Tom Hickey
        1980   Late life health behavior: integrating health beliefs and temporal perspectives. Research on Aging 2:283–308.
3, 18   Randall, Ollie A.
        1965   Some historical developments of social welfare aspects of aging. The Gerontologist 5:40–49.
12, 14 Rao, V. Nandini, and V. V. Prakasa Rao
        1981   Life satisfaction in the black elderly: an exploratory study. International Journal of Aging and Human Development 14:55–65.
5   Reese, H. W.
        1973   Life-span models of memory. The Gerontologist 13:472–78.
8   Regan, John J.
        1978   Intervention through adult protective services programs. The Gerontologist 18:250–54.
14   Register, Jasper C.
        1981   Aging and race: a black-white comparative analysis. The Gerontologist 21:438–43.
8   Regnier, Victor, and Louis E. Gelwicks
        1981.   Preferred supportive services for middle to higher income retirement housing. The Gerontologist 21:54–58.
9   Reich, Murray H.
        1977   Group preretirement education programs: whither the proliferation? Industrial Gerontology 5:29–43.
        Reichard, Suzanne, Florine Livson, and Paul G. Petersen
5   1962   Aging and Personality, New York: Wiley.
9   1968   Adjustment to retirement. Pp. 178–80 in Bernice L. Neugarten (ed.), Middle Age and Aging. Chicago: University of Chicago Press.
8, 18   Reichstein, Kenneth J., and Linda Bergofsky
        1983   Domiciliary care facilities for adults: an analysis of state regulations. Research on Aging 5:25–44.
5   Reid, David W., Gwen Haas, and Douglas Hawkins
        1977   Locus of desired control and positive self-concept of the elderly. Journal of Gerontology 32:441–50.
12   Reid, David W., and Michael Ziegler
        1980   Validity and stability of a new desired control measure pertaining to psychological adjustment of the elderly. Journal of Gerontology 35:395–402.
5, 8, 15 Reifler, Burton V., Gary B. Cox, and Raymond J. Hanley
        1981   Problems of mentally ill elderly as perceived by patients, families, and clinicians. The Gerontologist 21:165–70.
8   Reingold, J., and R. L. Wolk
        1974   Gerontological sheltered workshops for mentally impaired aged: some tested hypotheses. Industrial Gerontology 1:1–11.

Reno, Virginia P.

9   1971   Why men stop working at or before age 65. Social Security Bulletin 34(4):3–17.

9   1972   Compulsory retirement among newly entitled workers: a survey of new beneficiaries. Social Security Bulletin 35(3):3–15.

8   1973   Women newly entitled to retired-worker benefits: survey of new beneficiaries. Social Security Bulletin 36(4):3–26.

8   Reno, Virginia P., and Carol Zuckert

     1971   Benefit levels of newly retired workers. Social Security Bulletin 34(7):3–31.

13   Reston, J.

     1971   On the nobility of old age. Journal of American Geriatric Society 19:460–61.

5   Reynolds, D. K., and R. A. Kalish

     1974   Anticipation of futurity as a function of ethnicity and age. Journal of Gerontology 29:224–31.

8   Reynolds, Frank W., and Paul C. Barsam

     1967   Adult Health: Services for the Chronically Ill and Aging. New York: MacMillan.

7   Rheinstein, Max

     1960   Duty of children to support parents. Pp. 442 in E. W. Burgess (ed.), Aging in Western Societies. Chicago: University of Chicago Press.

12   Ricciardelli, Sister R. M.

     1973   King Lear and the theory of disengagement. The Gerontologist 13:148–52.

16   Richards, Mary Lynne

     1981   The clothing preferences and problems of elderly female consumers. The Gerontologist 21:263–67.

     Riegel, Klaus F.

5   1959   Personality theory and aging. Pp. 797–851 in James E. Birren (ed.), Handbook of Aging and the Individual. Chicago: University of Chicago Press.

5   1973a   On the history of psychological gerontology. Pp. 37–68 in C. Eisdorfer and M. P. Lawton (eds.), The Psychology of Adult Development and Aging. Washington, D.C.: American Psychological Association.

5   1973b   Language and cognition: some life-span developmental issues. The Gerontologist 13:478–82.

5   1976a   A note on the modifiability and reversibility of development and aging. International Journal of Aging and Human Development 7:269–72.

5   1976b   The dialectics of human development. The American Psychologist 31:689–700.

5, 6 1976c Adult life crises: a dialectical interpretation of development. Pp. 99–128 in N. Datan and L. Ginsberg (eds.), Life Span Developmental Psychology: Normative Life Crises. New York: Academic Press.

5   Riegel, Klaus, F., and R. M. Riegel

     1972   Development, drop, and death. Developmental Psychology 6:306–19.

4, 8 Ries, Peter W.

     1979   Acute conditions: incidence and associated disability: United States, 1977–1978. Vital and Health Statistics, Series 10, Number 132. Washington, D.C.: U.S. Government Printing Office.

3   Riesman, David

     1950   The Lonely Crowd. New Haven: Yale University Press.

11   Riley, John W., Jr.

     1983   Dying and the meanings of death: sociological inquiries. Annual Review of Sociology 9:191–216.

     Riley, Matilda W.

13   1971   Social gerontology and the age stratification of society. The Gerontologist 11(1, part 1):79–87.

1   1973   Aging and cohort succession: interpretations and misinterpretations. Public Opinion Quarterly 37 (Spring):35–49.

13   1976   Age strata in social systems. Pp. 189–217 in Robert H. Binstock and Ethel Shanas (eds.), Handbook of Aging and the Social Sciences. New York: Van Nostrand-Reinhold.

Riley, Matilda W., and Anne Foner (eds.)
1968   Aging and Society. Volume 1: An Inventory of Research Findings. New York: Russell Sage Foundation.

13   Riley, Matilda W., Marilyn Johnson, and Anne Foner (eds.)
1972   Aging and Society. Volume 3: A Sociology of Age Stratification. New York: Russell Sage Foundation.

19   Riley, Matilda W., John W. Riley, Jr., and Marilyn E. Johnson (eds.)
1969   Aging and Society. Volume 2: Aging and the Professions. New York: Russell Sage Foundation.

1   Rives, Norfleet W., Jr.
1981   Designing census public use samples for aging research. Research on Aging 4:375–80.

2   Rives, Norfleet W., Jr., and William J. Serow
1981   Interstate migration of the elderly: demographic aspects. Research on Aging 3:259–78.

9, 10 Roadburg, Alan
1981   Perceptions of work and leisure among the elderly. The Gerontologist 21:142–45.

8   Robbins, Ira S.
1971   Housing the Elderly. Washington: D.C.: White House Conference on Aging.

5   Roberts, Jean
1968   Monocular-Binocular Visual Acuity of Adults. Vital and Health Statistics, Series 11, Number 30. Washington, D.C. U.S. Government Printing Office.

Robertson, Joan F.
7   1975   Interaction in three generation families: parents as mediators: toward a theoretical perspective. International Journal of Aging and Human Development 6:103–10.

7   1976   Significance of grandparents: perception of young adult grandchildren. The Gerontologist 16:137–40.

Robin, Ellen Page
5   1971   Discontinuities in attitudes and behaviors of older age groups. The Gerontologist 11 (4, part 2):79–84.

13   1977   Old age in elementary school readers. Educational Gerontology 2:275–92.

Rockstein, Morris
4   1968   The biological aspects of aging. The Gerontologist 8:124–25.

4   1975   The biology of aging in humans—an overview. Pp. 1–7 in R. Goldman and M. Rockstein (eds.), The Physiology and Pathology of Human Aging. New York: Academic Press.

2   Rogers, T. W.
1974   Migration of the aged population. International Migration 12:61–70.

5   Rokeach, Milton
1973   The Nature of Human Values. New York: The Free Press.

7   Rollins, Boyd C., and Kenneth L. Cannon
1974   Marital satisfaction over the family life cycle: a re-evaluation. Journal of Marriage and the Family 36:271–82.

7   Rollins, Boyd C., and Harold Feldman
1970   Marital satisfaction over the family life cycle. Journal of Marriage and the Family 32:20–28.

9, 12   Roman, Paul, and Philip Taietz
    1967   Organizational structure and disengagement: the emeritus professor. The Gerontologist 7:147–52.

15   Rooney, James F.
    1976   Friendship and disaffiliation among the skid row population. Journal of Gerontology 31:82–88.

Rose, Arnold M.
10   1960   The impact of aging on voluntary associations. Pp. 666–97 in Clark Tibbitts (ed.), Handbook of Social Gerontology. Chicago: University of Chicago Press.

13   1965a   The subculture of aging: a framework for research in social gerontology. Pp. 3–16 in Arnold M. Rose and Warren A. Peterson (eds.), Older People and Their Social World. Philadelphia: F. A. Davis.

8   1965b   Physical health and mental outlook among the aging. Pp. 201–09 in Arnold M. Rose and Warren A. Peterson (eds.), Older People and Their Social World. Philadelphia: F. A. Davis.

8   1965c   Mental health of normal older persons. Pp. 193–99 in Arnold M. Rose and Warren A. Peterson (eds.), Older People and Their Social World. Philadelphia: F. A. Davis.

17   1965d   Group consciousness among the aging. Pp. 19–36 in Arnold M. Rose and Warren A. Peterson (eds.), Older People and Their Social World. Philadelphia: F. A. Davis.

14   1966   Class differences among the elderly: a research report. Sociology and Social Research 50:356–60.

Rose, Arnold M., and Warren A. Peterson (eds.)
    1965   Older People and Their Social World. Philadelphia: F. A. Davis.

9   Rose, Charles L., and John M. Mogey
    1972   Aging and preference for later retirement. Aging and Human Development 3:45–62.

7, 8   Rosel, Natalie
    1983   The hub of a wheel: a neighborhood support network. International Journal of Aging and Human Development 16:193–200.

Rosen, Benson, and Thomas H. Jerdee
9, 13   1976a   The nature of job-related stereotypes. Journal of Applied Psychology 61:180–83.

9, 13,
16   1976b   The influence of age stereotypes on managerial decisions. Journal of Applied Psychology 61:428–32.

9   1982   Effects of employee financial status and social adjustment on employers' retention/ retirement recommendations. Aging and Work 5:111–18.

9   Rosen, Benson, Thomas H. Jerdee, and Robert O. Lunn
    1980   Retirement policies and management decisions. Aging and Work 3:239–46.

14   Rosen, Catherine E.
    1978   A comparison of black and white rural elderly. Black Aging 3:60–65.

Rosenberg, George S.
7, 8   1968   Age, poverty and isolation from friends in the urban working class. Journal of Gerontology 23:533–38.

8   1970   The Worker Grows Old. San Francisco: Jossey-Bass.

Rosenberg, Morris
5, 9   1964   Society and the Adolescent Self-Image. Princeton, N.J.: Princeton University Press.

1   1968   The Logic of Survey Analysis. New York: Basic Books.

5   Rosenberg, Stanley D., and Michael P. Farrell
    1976   Identity and crisis in middle-aged men. International Journal of Aging and Human Development 7:153–70.

10   Rosenblatt, Aaron
    1966   Interest of older persons in volunteer activities. Social Work 11(3):87–94.

9   Rosenblum, M.
     1975   The last push: from discouraged worker to involuntary retirement. Industrial Geron-
         tology 2:14–22.

7, 8,
16   Rosenfeld, Jeffrey P.
     1979   The Legacy of Aging: Inheritance and Disinheritance in Social Perspective. Norwood,
         N.J.: Ablex.

13   Rosenfelt, Rosalie H.
     1965   Elderly mystique. Journal of Social Issues 21:37–43.

7, 8,
18   Rosenheim, Margaret K.
     1965   Social welfare and its implications for family living. Pp. 206–40 in Ethel Shanas and
         Gordon F. Streib (eds.), Social Structure and the Family: Generational Relations. En-
         glewood Cliffs, N.J.: Prentice-Hall.

2   Rosenwaike, Ira
     1983   Accuracy of death certificate ages for the extreme aged. Demography 20:569–85.

     Rosow, Irving
13   1962   Old age: one moral dilemma of an affluent society. The Gerontologist 2:182–91.
7   1964   Local concentrations of aged and intergenerational friendships. Pp. 478–83 in P. From
         Hansen (ed.), Age with a Future. Copenhagen: Munksgaard.
7   1965   The aged, family and friends. Social Security Bulletin 28(11):18–20.
7, 8   1966   Housing and local ties of the aged. Pp. 47–64 in Frances M. Carp and W. M. Burnett
         (eds.), Patterns of Living and Housing of Middle-Aged and Older People. Washington,
         D.C.: U.S. Public Health Service.
7, 8   1967   Social Integration of the Aged. New York: Free Press.
9   1969   Retirement, leisure, and social status. Pp. 249–57 in Frances C. Jeffers (ed.), Duke
         University Council on Aging and Human Development: Proceedings of Seminars, 1965
         –1969. Durham, N. Carolina: Duke University Center for Study of Aging and Human
         Development.
5   1973   The social context of the aging self. The Gerontologist 13:82–87.
5, 6   1974   Socialization to Old Age. Berkeley, Calif.: University of California Press.

8   Ross, Hugh
     1968   Protective services for the aged. The Gerontologist 8(1, part 2):50–53.

     Ross, Jennie-Kieth
8   1974   Life goes on. Social organization in a French retirement residence. Pp. 99–120 in Jaber
         F. Gubrium (ed.), Late Life. Springfield, Ill.: Charles C. Thomas.
8   1977   Old People, New Lives. Community Creation in a Retirement Residence. Chicago:
         University of Chicago Press.

     Rowe, Alan R.
9   1972   The retirement of academic scientists. Journal of Gerontology 27:113–18.
9   1976   Retired academics and research activity. Journal of Gerontology 31:456–61.

11   Rowland, K. F.
     1977   Environmental events predicting death for the elderly. Psychology Bulletin 84:349–72.

     Rowles, Graham D.
8   1978   Prisoners of Space? Exploring the Geographical Experience of Older People. Boulder,
         Colo.: Westview.
8   1981   The surveillance zones as meaningful space for the aged. The Gerontologist 21:304–11.

     Rubenstein, Daniel
10   1971   An examination of social participation found among a national sample of black and
         white elderly. International Journal of Aging and Human Development 2:172–88.
15   1982   The older person in prison. Archives of Gerontology and Geriatrics 1:287–96.

Rubin, Isadore

5   1965   Sexual Life After Sixty. New York: Basic Books.

5   1968   The "sexless older years"—a socially harmful stereotype. Annals of the American Academy of Political and Social Sciences 376:86–95.

8   Rubin, Leonard

       1973   Late entitlement to retirement benefits: findings from the survey of new beneficiaries. Social Security Bulletin 36(7):3–20.

17   Rule, Wilma L. B.

       1977   Political alienation and voting attitudes among the elderly generation. The Gerontologist 17:400–04.

7, 8   Rundall, Thomas G., and Connie Evashwick

       1982   Social networks and help-seeking among the elderly. Research on Aging 4:205–26.

9   Rusalem, Herbert

       1963   Deterrents to vocational disengagement among older disabled workers. The Gerontologist 3:64–68.

11   Russell, Olive Ruth

       1975   Freedom to Die. Moral and Legal Aspects of Euthanasia. New York: Human Sciences Press.

7   Ryder, Robert G.

       1968   Husband-wife dyads versus married strangers. Family Process 7:233–38.

12   Ryff, Carol D.

       1982   Successful aging: a developmental approach. The Gerontologist 22:209–14.

10   Sainer, J. S., and F. K. Kallan

       1972   SERVE: a case illustration of older volunteers in a psychiatric setting. The Gerontologist 12:90–93.

8, 10 Sainer, J. S., and M. Zander

       1971   Guidelines for older person volunteers. The Gerontologist 11:201–04.

12   Sainsbury, Peter

       1963   Social and epidemiological aspects of suicide with special reference to the aged. Pp. 153 –75 in Richard H. Williams, Clark Tibbitts, and Wilma Donahue (eds.), Processes of Aging. Volume 2. New York: Atherton Press.

13   Salter, Charles A., and Carlota D. Salter

       1976   Attitudes toward aging and behaviors toward the elderly among young people as a function of death anxiety. The Gerontologist 16:232–36.

5   Salthouse, Timothy A.

       1982   Adult Cognition: An Experimental Psychology of Human Aging. New York: Springer-Verlag.

10   Saltz, R.

       1971   Aging persons as child-care workers in a foster-grandparent program: psychosocial effects and work performance. Aging and Human Development 2:314–40.

5   Sanford, A. J., and A. J. Maule

       1973   The concept of general experience: age and strategies in guessing future events. Journal of Gerontology 28:81–88.

9   Sarason, Seymour B.

       1977   Work, Aging, and Social Change: Professionals and the One Life-One Career Imperative. New York: The Free Press.

9   Sarason, S. B., E. K. Sarason, and P. Cowden

       1975   Aging and the nature of work. American Psychologist 30(5):584–92.

12   Sauer, William

       1977   Morale of the urban aged: a regression analysis by race. Journal of Gerontology 32(5):600–08.

11   Saunders, Cicely
        1976   St. Christopher's Hospice. Pp. 516–23 in E. S. Shneidman (ed.), Death: Current Per-
                spectives. Palo Alto, Calif.: Mayfield.
11   Saul, S., and S. R. Saul
        1977–78 Old people talk about—the right to die. Omega 8:129–39.
5   Savage, Robert D., P. G. Britton, N. Bolton, and E. H. Hall
        1975   Intellectual Functioning in the Aged. New York: Harper and Row.
5   Savage, Robert D., L. B. Gaber, P. G. Britton, N. Bolton, and N. Cooper
        1977   Personality and Adjustment in the Aged. New York: Academic Press.
        Schaie, K. Warner
1   1967   Age changes and age differences. The Gerontologist 7:128–32.
5   1977–78 Toward a stage theory of adult cognitive development. International Journal of Aging
                and Human Development 8:129–38.
5   1980   Intelligence and problem solving. Pp. 262–84 in J. Birren and R. B. Sloane (eds.),
                Handbook of Mental Health and Aging. Englewood Cliffs, N.J.: Prentice-Hall.
5   Schaie, K. Warner, and K. Gribbin
        1975   Adult development and aging. Annual Review of Psychology 26:65–96.
        Schaie, K. Warner, and I. A. Parham
5   1976   Stability of adult personality traits; fact or fable? Journal of Personality and Social Psy-
                chology 34:146–58.
5   1977   Cohort-sequential analyses of adult intellectual development. Developmental Psychology
                13:649–53.
1   Schaie, K. Warner, G. V. Labouvie, and T. J. Barrett
        1973   Selected attrition effects in a fourteen-year study of adult intelligence. Journal of
                Gerontology 28:328–34.
5   Schaie, K. Warner, G. V. Labouvie, and B. U. Buech
        1973   Generational and cohort-specific differences in adult cognitive functioning: a fourteen
                year study of independent samples. Developmental Psychology 9:151–66.
5   Scheff, Thomas J.
        1983   Toward integration in the social psychology of emotions. Annual Review of Sociology
                9:333–54.
5   Schemper, Thomas, Scott Voss, and William Cain
        1981   Odor identification in young and elderly persons: sensory and cognitive limitations.
                Journal of Gerontology 36:446–52.
10, 17 Schlesinger, Joseph A., and Mildred Schlesinger
        1981   Aging and opportunities for elective office. Pp. 205–239 in Sara B. Kiesler et al. (eds.),
                Aging: Social Change. New York: Academic Press.
9   Schlossberg, Nancy K.
        1975   Career development in adults. American Vocational Journal 50:38–41.
17   Schmidhauser, John
        1968   The political influence of the aged. The Gerontologist 8(1, part 2):44–49.
12   Schmidt, John F.
        1951   Patterns of poor adjustment in old age. American Journal of Sociology 56:33–42.
1   Schmidt, Mary G.
        1975   Interviewing the "old old." The Gerontologist 15:544–47.
9   Schneider, Betty V. H.
        1962   The Older Worker. Berkeley, Calif.: University of California Institute for Industrial
                Relations.
9   Schneider, Clement J.
        1964   Adjustment of Employed Women to Retirement. Unpublished doctoral dissertation,
                Cornell University, Ithaca, New York.

11   Schoenberg, Bernard, Arthur C. Carr, Austin H. Kutscher, et al.
        1974   Anticipatory Grief. New York: Columbia University Press.
16   Scholen, Ken, and Yung-Ping Chen (eds.)
        1980   Unlocking Home Equity for the Elderly. Cambridge, Mass.: Ballinger.
13   Schonfield, David
        1982   Who is stereotyping whom and why? The Gerontologist 22:267–72.
12   Schooler, Kermit K.
        1969   The relationship between social interaction and morale of the elderly as a function of environmental characteristics. The Gerontologist 9:25–29.
        Schorr, Alvin L.
7   1960   Filial Responsibility in the Modern American Family. Washington, D.C.: Social Security Administration.
7   1962   Filial responsibility and the aging, or beyond pluck and luck. Social Security Bulletin 25(5):4–9.
8   Schottland, C. I.
        1965   Poverty and income maintenance for the aged. Pp. 227–39 in Margaret S. Gordon (ed.), Poverty in America. San Francisco: Chandler.
8   Schreiber, M. S.
        1972   The multi-purpose senior center: a vehicle for the delivery of services to older people. Pp. 19–26 in Senior Centers: A Focal Point for Delivery of Services to Older People. Washington, D.C.: National Institute of Senior Centers, National Council on Aging.
9   Schreter, Carol, and Nadine Hudson
        1981   Investing in elder craftsmen. The Gerontologist 21:655–61.
        Schuchat, T.
9   1971   Postponed retirement under the Social Security Act. Industrial Gerontology 11:20–22.
16   1973   The impact of private pension plan terminations. Industrial Gerontology 17:72–74.
16   1974   Pension reform: limits and accomplishments. Industrial Gerontology 1:26–33.
12, 15 Schuckit, M. A.
        1977   Geriatric alcoholism and drug abuse. The Gerontologist 17:168–74.
13   Schuerman, Laurell E., Donna Z. Eden, and David A. Peterson
        1977   Older people in women's periodical fiction. Educational Gerontology 2:327–51.
        Schulz, James H.
8   1967   Some economics of aged home ownership. The Gerontologist 7:73–74.
8   1968   The Economic Status of the Retired Aged in 1980: Simulated Projections. Washington, D.C.: U.S. Government Printing Office.
16   1970   Pension Aspects of the Economics of Aging: Present and Future Roles of Private Pensions. Washington, D.C.: U.S. Senate Special Committee on Aging.
16   1973   The economic impact of an aging population. The Gerontologist 13:111–18.
9   1974   The economics of mandatory retirement. Industrial Gerontology 1:1–10.
8, 16   1976a   The Economics of Aging. Belmont, Calif.: Wadsworth.
8   1976b   Income distribution and the aging. Pp. 561–91 in Robert H. Binstock and Ethel Shanas (eds.), Handbook of Aging and the Social Sciences. New York: Van Nostrand-Reinhold.
8   1978   Liberalizing the social security retirement test: who would receive the increased pension benefits? Journal of Gerontology 33:262–68.
8   1981   Pension policy at a crossroads: what should be the pension mix? The Gerontologist 21: 46–53.
16   Schulz, James H., Guy Carrir, Hans Krupp, et al.
        1974   Providing Adequate Retirement Income. Hanover, New Hampshire: Brandeis University Press.

2, 8   Schulz, Richard, and Gail Brenner
    1977   Relocation and the aged: a review and theoretical analysis. Journal of Gerontology 32: 323–33.

9, 16   Schwab, Donald P., and Herbert G. Heneman III
    1977   Effects of age and experience on productivity. Industrial Gerontology 4:113–17.

5   Schwertz, Arthur N., and Robert W. Kleemeier
    1965   The effects of illness and age upon some aspects of personality. Journal of Gerontology 20:85–91.

11   Scott, F. G., and R. M. Brewer (eds.)
    1971   Confrontations of Death: A Book of Readings and a Suggested Method of Instruction. Eugene, Oregon: Oregon Center for Gerontology.

17   Scott, Richard W.
    1981   Reform movements and organizations: the case of aging. Pp. 331–45 in Sara B. Kiesler et al. (eds.), Aging: Social Change. New York: Academic Press.

8   Sears, D. W.
    1974   Elderly housing: a need determination technique. The Gerontologist 14:182–87.

5   Sears, David O.
    1981   Life-stage effects on attitude change, especially among the elderly. Pp. 183–204 in Sara B. Kiesler et al. (eds.), Aging Social Change. New York: Academic Press.

5   Secord, Paul F., and Carl W. Backman
    1964   Social Psychology. New York: McGraw-Hill.

13   Seefeldt, Carol, Richard K. Jantz, Alice Galper, and Kathy Serock
    1977   Using pictures to explore children's attitudes toward the elderly. The Gerontologist 17: 506–12.

7   Seelbach, Wayne C.
    1977   Gender differences in expectations for filial responsibility. The Gerontologist 17:421–25.

7   Seelbach, Wayne C., and C. J. Hansen
    1980   Satisfaction with family relations among the elderly. Family Relations 29:91–98.

7, 12   Seelbach, Wayne C., and William J. Sauer
    1977   Filial responsibility expectations and morale among aged parents. The Gerontologist 17(5):492–99.

7   Seguin, M. M.
    1973   Opportunity for peer socialization in a retirement community. The Gerontologist 13:208–14.

5   Seigler, Ilene C.
    1980   The psychology of adult development and aging. Pp. 169–221 in E. Busse and D. Blazer (eds.), Handbook of Geriatric Psychiatry. New York: Van Nostrand-Reinhold.

5   Sekuler, Robert, and Lucinda Picciano Hutman
    1980   Spatial vision and aging. I: Contrast sensitivity. Journal of Gerontology 35:692–99.

12   Seleen, Diane R.
    1982   The congruence between actual and desired use of time by older adults: a prediction of life satisfaction. The Gerontologist 22:95–99.

Seltzer, Mildred M.
19   1974   Education in gerontology: an evolutionary analogy. The Gerontologist 14:308–11.
1   1975a   The quality of research is strained. The Gerontologist 15(6):503–07.
1, 14   1975b   Women and sociogerontology. The Gerontologist 15:483.
13   1977   Differential impact of various experiences on breaking down age stereotypes. Educational Gerontology 2:183–89.

Seltzer, Mildred M., and Robert C. Atchley
13   1971a   The concept of old: changing attitudes and stereotypes. The Gerontologist 11:226–30.

9, 10   1971b The impact of structural integration into the profession on work commitment, potential for disengagement, and leisure preferences among social workers. Sociological Focus 5:9–17.

19   1974 Developing Educational Programs in the Field of Aging. Oxford, Ohio: Scripps Foundation.

12   Sendbuehler, J. M., and Goldstein, S.

1977 Attempted suicide among the aged. Journal of the American Geriatric Society 25:245–53.

9   Serwer, A. M.

1974 Mandatory retirement at age 65—a survey of the law. Industrial Gerontology 1:11–22.

8   Settin, Joan M.

1978 Some thoughts on diseases presented as senility. The Gerontologist 18:71–72.

Shanas, Ethel

7   1960 Family responsibility and the health of older people. Journal of Gerontology 15:408–11.

8   1962 The Health of Older People: A Social Survey. Cambridge, Mass.: Harvard University Press.

7, 8   1964 Family and household characteristics of older people in the United States. Pp. 449–54 in P. From Hansen (ed.), Age with a Future. Copenhagen: Munksgaard.

8   1965 Health care and health services for the aged. The Gerontologist 5:240, 276.

7, 14   1967 Family help patterns and social class in three countries. Journal of Marriage and the Family 29:257–66.

8   1968 A note on restriction of life space: attitudes of age cohorts. Journal of Health and Social Behavior 9:86–90.

8   1971a Measuring the home health needs of the aged in five countries. Journal of Gerontology 26:37–40.

9   1971b Disengagement and work: myth and reality. Pp. 109–19 in Social Gerontology, Paris: International Centre of Social Gerontology.

9   1972 Adjustment to retirement: substitution or accommodations? Pp. 219–44 in Frances M. Carp (ed.), Retirement. New York: Behavioral Publications.

7   1977 National Survey of the Aged: 1975. Chicago: University of Illinois, Chicago Circle.

7   1979 The family as a social support system in old age. The Gerontologist 19:169–74.

7   1980 Older people and their families: the new pioneers. Journal of Marriage and the Family 42:9–15.

2, 7   Shanas, Ethel, and P. M. Hauser

1974 Zero population growth and the family life of old people. Journal of Social Issues 30(4):79–92.

8, 18   Shanas, Ethel, and George L. Maddox

1976 Aging, health, and the organization of health resources. Pp. 592–618 in Robert H. Binstock and Ethel Shanas (eds.), Handbook of Aging and the Social Sciences. New York: Van Nostrand Reinhold.

7, 18   Shanas, Ethel, and Gordon F. Streib (eds.)

1965 Social Structure and the Family: Generational Relations. Englewood Cliffs, N.J.: Prentice-Hall.

8, 18   Shanas, Ethel, and Marvin B. Sussman (eds.)

1977 Family, Bureaucracy, and the Elderly. Durham, N. Carolina: Duke University Press.

7, 8, 9   Shanas, Ethel, Peter Townsend, Dorothy Wedderbum, Henning Friis, Paul Milhoj, and Jan Stehouwer

1968 Older People in Three Industrial Societies. New York: Atherton Press.

10   Shapiro, E.

1974 Guidelines for a creative newspaper written by and for residents of homes for the aged. International Journal of Aging and Human Development 5:365–68.

8, 18   Shapiro, Evelyn, and Noralou P. Roos
       1982   Retired and employed elderly persons: their utilization of health care services. The Gerontologist 22:187–93.

8, 18   Shapiro, Evelyn, Noralou Roos, and Steve Kavanagh
       1980   Long-term patients in acute care beds: is there a cure? (Canada) The Gerontologist 20: 342–49.

15   Shapiro, Joan H.
       1966   Single room occupancy: community of the alone. Social Work 11(4):23–33.
       1971   Communities of the Alone. New York: Association Press.

7, 8   Shaw, David L., and Judith B. Gordon
       1980   Social network analysis and intervention with the elderly. The Gerontologist 20:463–67.

8, 12   Shaw, Robert, and Lawrence Crapo
       1982   Emotional bondedness, subjective well-being, and health in elderly medical patients. Journal of Gerontology 37:609–15.

13   Sheehan, Robert
       1978   Young children's contact with the elderly. Journal of Gerontology 33:567–74.

13   Sheehan, Tom
       1976   Senior esteem as a factor of socioeconomic complexity. The Gerontologist 16:433–40.

5   Sheehy, Gail
       1976   Passages: Predictable Crises of Adult Life. New York: E. P. Dutton.

2   Sheldon, Henry D.
       1960   The changing demographic profile. Pp. 27–61 in Clark Tibbitts (ed.), Handbook of Social Gerontology. Chicago: University of Chicago Press.

8   Sheley, J. F.
       1974   Mutuality and retirement community success: an interactionist perspective in gerontological research. International Journal of Aging and Human Development 5:71–80.

13   Sheppard, Alice
       1981   Response to cartoons and attitudes toward aging. Journal of Gerontology 36:122–26.

9, 16   Sheppard, Harold L.
       1970   Industrial Gerontology. Cambridge, Mass.: Schenkman.

9   Sheppard, Harold L., and Michel Philibert
       1972   Employment and retirement: roles and activities. The Gerontologist 12(2, part 2):29–35.

9, 16   Sheppard, Harold L., and Sara E. Rix
       1977   The Graying of Working America: The Coming Crisis of Retirement Age Policy. New York: Free Press.

8   Sherman, Edith M., and Margaret R. Brittan
       1973   Contemporary food gatherers: a study of food shopping habits of an elderly urban population. The Gerontologist 13:358–64.

7, 8   Sherman, Edmund, and Evelyn S. Newman
       1977–78   The meaning of cherished personal possessions for the elderly. International Journal of Aging and Human Development 8:181–92.

8   Sherman, Sally R.
       1973   Assets on the threshold of retirement. Social Security Bulletin 36(8):3–17.

    Sherman, Susan R.
8   1971   The choice of retirement housing among the well-elderly. International Journal of Aging and Human Development 2:118–38.

7, 8   1975a   Patterns of contacts for residents of age-segregated and age-integrated housing. Journal of Gerontology 30:103–07.

7, 8   1975b   Mutual assistance and support in retirement housing. Journal of Gerontology 30:479–83.

10   1975c Leisure activities in retirement housing. Journal of Gerontology 29:325–35.

8   Sherman, Susan R., Wiley P. Mangum, Jr., Suzanne Dodds, Rosabelle Walkley, and Daniel M. Wilner

     1968 Psychological effects of retirement housing. The Gerontologist 8:170–75.

8, 18   Sherman, Susan R., and Donald A. Snider

     1981 Social participation in adult homes: deinstitutionalized mental patients and the frail elderly. The Gerontologist 21:545–50.

5   Sherwood, S., and T. Nadelson

     1972 Alternate predictions concerning despair in old age. Pp. 408–44 in D. P. Kent, R. Kastenbaum, and S. Sherwood (eds.), Research Planning and Action for the Elderly. New York: Behavioral Publications.

8   Sherwood, S., J. Glassman, C. Sherwood, and J. N. Morris

     1974 Pre-institutionalization factors as predictors of adjustment to a long-term care facility. International Journal of Aging and Human Development 5:95–105.

17   Sheufield, B. E.

     1957 Social Policies For Old Age: A Review of Social Provision For Old Age in Britain. Westport, Conn.: Greenwood Press.

5, 13   Shin, Ken E., and Robert H. Putnam, Jr.

     1982 Age and academic-professional honors. Journal of Gerontology 37:220–27.

     Shock, Nathan W.

4   1962 (ed.) Biological Aspects of Aging. New York: Columbia University Press.

4   1966 (ed.) Perspectives in Experimental Gerontology. Springfield, Ill.: Charles C. Thomas.

4   1977a Biological theories of aging. Pp. 103–15 in James E. Birren and K. Warner Schaie (eds.), Handbook of the Psychology of Aging. New York: Van Nostrand Reinhold.

4   1977b System integration. Pp. 639–65 in Caleb E. Finch and Leonard Hayflick (eds.), Handbook of the Biology of Aging. New York: Van Nostrand Reinhold.

4, 5   Shock, Nathan W., and A. H. Norris

     1970 Neuromuscular coordination as a factor in age changes in muscular exercise. Pp. 92–99 in D. Brunner and E. Jokl (eds.), Physical Activity and Aging. New York: S. Karger.

5   Shukin, Alexey, and Bernice L. Neugarten.

     1964 Personality and social interaction. Pp. 149–57 in Bernice L. Neugarten (ed.), Personality in Middle and Late Life. New York: Atherton Press.

5   Shulz, Richard

     1982 Emotionality and aging: a theoretical and empirical analysis. Journal of Gerontology 37:42–51.

7, 8   Shuttlesworth, Guy E., Rubin Allen, and Michael Duffey

     1982 Families versus institutions: incongruent role expectations in the nursing home. The Gerontologist 22:200–08.

9, 12   Siassi, Iradj, Guido Crocetti, and Herzl R. Spiro

     1975 Emotional health, life and job satisfaction in aging workers. Industrial Gerontology 2:289–96.

10   Sidney, Kenneth H., and Roy J. Shephard

     1977 Activity patterns of elderly men and women. Journal of Gerontology 32:25–32.

     Siegel, Jacob

2   1976 Demographic aspects of aging and the older population in the United States. Current Population Reports, Series P-23, No. 59. Washington, D.C.: U.S. Census Bureau.

2   1981 Demographic background for international gerontological studies. Journal of Gerontology 36:93–102.

2   Siegel, Jacob S., and Maria Davidson

     1984 Demographic and Socioeconomic Aspects of Aging in the United States. Current Population Reports, Series P-23, No. 138.

2, 10   Siegel, Jacob S., and Cynthia M. Taeuber
          1982   The 1980 census and the elderly: new data available to planners and practitioners. The Gerontologist 22:144–50.

2   Siegel, Jacob S., and William E. O'Leary
          1973   Some demographic aspects of aging in the United States. Current Population Reports, Seris P-23, Population Estimates, No. 43. Washington, D.C.: U.S. Bureau of the Census.

5   Siegler, Ilene C., Sarah M. McCarty, and Patrick E. Logue
          1982   Wechsler Memory Scale scores, selective attrition, and distance from death. Journal of Gerontology 37:176–81.

15   Sigrang, Tricia A.
          1982   Who should be doing what about the gay alcoholic? Journal of Homosexuality 7:4:27–36.

8   Silberstein, Joseph, Ruth Kossawsky, and Pnina Lilus
          1977   Functional dependency in the aged. Journal of Gerontology 32:222–26.

5, 12   Sill, John Stewart
          1980   Disengagement reconsidered: awareness of finitude. The Gerontologist 20:457–62.

11   Silverman, P. R.
          1972   Widowhood and preventive intervention. Family coordinator 21:95–102.

7, 8   Silverstone, B., and L. Wynter
          1975   The effects of introducing a heterosexual living space. The Gerontologist 5:83–87.

          Simmons, Leo W.
3   1945   The Role of the Aged in Primitive Society. New Haven, Conn.: Yale University Press.
3   1960   Aging in preindustrial societies. Pp. 62–91 in Clark Tibbitts (ed.), Handbook of Social Gerontology. Chicago: University of Chicago Press.

9   Simpson, Ida H.
          1973   Problems of the aging in work and retirement. Pp. 157–72 in R. R. Boyd and C. G. Oakes (eds.), Foundations of Practical Gerontology. Columbia, S. Carolina: University of South Carolina Press.

5, 7, 9   Simpson, Ida H., and John C. McKinney (eds.)
          1966   Social Aspects of Aging. Durham, N. Carolina: Duke University Press.

          Simpson, Ida H., Kurt W. Back, and John C. McKinney
9   1966a   Continuity of work and retirement activities, and self-evaluation. Pp. 106–19 in Ida H. Simpson and John C. McKinney (eds.), Social Aspects of Aging. Durham, N. Carolina: Duke University Press.
9   1966b   Exposure to information on, preparation for, and self-evaluation in retirement. Pp. 90–105 in Ida H. Simpson and John C. McKinney (eds.), Social Aspects of Aging. Durham, N. Carolina: Duke University Press.
9   1966c   Orientation toward work and retirement, and self-evaluation in retirement. Pp. 75–89 in Ida H. Simpson and John C. McKinney (eds.), Social Aspects of Aging. Durham, N. Carolina: Duke University Press.

4   Sinex, F. Marott
          1977   The molecular genetics of aging. Pp. 37–62 in C. E. Finch and L. Hayflick (eds.), Handbook of the Biology of Aging. New York: Van Nostrand-Reinhold.

6   Singer, E.
          1974   Premature social aging: the social-psychological consequences of a chronic illness. Social Science and Medicine 8:143–51.

7   Singh, B. Krishna, and J. Sherwood Williams
          1981   Childlessness and family satisfaction. Research on Aging 3:218–27.

6, 14   Sinnott, Jan D.
          1982   Correlates of sex roles of older adults. Journal of Gerontology 37:587–94.

8   Sirrocco, Alvin
       1972   Services and activities offered to nursing home residents: United States, 1968. Vital and Health Statistics, Series 12, No. 17.

13   Skoglund, John
       1977–78 A comparative factor analysis of attitudes toward societal relations of the elderly. International Journal of Aging and Human Development 8:277–91.

       Skolnik, Alfred
8   1976   Private pension plans, 1950–1974. Social Security Bulletin 39(6):3–17.

5   Slater, Philip E., and Harry A. Scarr
       1964   Personality in Old Age. Genetic Psychology Monographs 70:228–69.

9, 13 Slater, Robert, and S. Kingsley
       1976   Predicting age-prejudiced employers: a British pilot study. Industrial Gerontology 3:121–28.

9   Slavick, Fred
       1966   Compulsory and Flexible Retirement in the American Economy. Ithaca, N.Y.: Cornell University Press.

9   Slavick, Fred, and Seymour L. Wolfbein
       1960   The evolving work-life pattern. Pp. 298–329 in Clark Tibbitts (ed.), Handbook of Social Gerontology. Chicago: University of Chicago Press.

9   Slee, John L. F.
       1977   Career change: innovative approach to reemployment. Industrial Gerontology 4:137–39.

5   Smith, A. D.
       1975   Aging and interference with memory. Journal of Gerontology 30:319–25.

3   Smith, Adam
       1776   The Wealth of Nations. New York: Modern Library.

7   Smith, Harold E.
       1965   Family interaction patterns of the aged: a review. Pp. 143–61 in Arnold M. Rose and Warren A. Peterson (eds.), Older People and Their Social World. Philadelphia: F. A. Davis

7, 8   Smith, Joel
       1966   The narrowing social world of the aged. Pp. 226–42 in Ida H. Simpson and John C. McKinney (eds.), Social Aspects of Aging. Durham, N. Carolina: Duke University Press.

17   Smith, Joel, Herman Turk, and Howard P. Myers
       1962   Understanding local political behavior: the role of the older citizen. Law and Contemporary Problems 27:280–98.

       Smith, John M.
16   1969   Age and occupation: a classification of occupants by their age structure. Journal of Gerontology 24:412–18.

16   1973   Age and occupation: the determinants of male occupational age structures—hypothesis H and hypothesis A. Journal of Gerontology 28:484–90.

16   1974   Age and occupation: a review of the use of occupational age structures in industrial gerontology. Industrial Gerontology 1:42–58.

12   Smith, K. J., and A. Lipman
       1972   Constraint and life satisfaction. Journal of Gerontology 27:77–82.

5   Smith, Madorah E., and Calvin Hall
       1964   An investigation of regression in a long dream series. Journal of Gerontology 19:66–71.

13   Smith, Mickey C.
       1976   Portrayal of the elderly in prescription drug advertising; a pilot study. The Gerontologist 16:329–34.

9   Smith, P. C.
     1969   The Measurement of Satisfaction in Work and Retirement: A Strategy for the Study of Attitudes. Chicago: Rand McNally.

14   Smith, Stanley H.
     1967   The older rural negro. Pp. 262–80 in E. Grant Youmans (ed.), Older Rural Americans. Lexington, Kentucky: University of Kentucky Press.

8   Smyer, Michael A.
     1980   The differential usage of services by impaired elderly. Journal of Gerontology 35:249–55.

7, 8   Snider, Earle L.
       1981   The role of kin in meeting health care needs of the elderly. Canadian Journal of Sociology 6:325–36.

9   Snow, Robert B., and Robert B. Havighurst
     1977   Life style types and patterns of retirement of educators. The Gerontologist 17:545–52.

8   Snyder, Lorraine H.
     1973   An exploratory study of patterns of social interaction, organization, and facility design in three nursing homes. International Journal of Aging and Human Development 4:319 –33.

5   Snyder, Lorraine H., Janine Pyrek, and K. Carroll Smith
     1976   Vision and mental function of the elderly. The Gerontologist 16:491–95.

     Social Security Administration
8   1972a   Annual Statistical Supplement. Social Security Bulletin.
8   1972b   Current operating statistics. Social Security Bulletin 41(12):31–98.
8   1981   The income and resources of the elderly in 1978. Social Security Bulletin 44:12:3–11.
8, 16 1984   Current operating statistics. Social Security Bulletin 46:3:63–132.

     Sohngen, Mary
13   1975   The writer as an old woman. The Gerontologist 15:493–98.
13   1977   The experience of old age as depicted in contemporary novels. The Gerontologist 17:70 –78.
13   1981   The experience of old age as depicted in contemporary novels: a supplementary bibliography. The Gerontologist 21:303.

     Sokolovsky, Jay, and Carl Cohen
15   1981a   Being old in the inner city: support systems of the SRO aged. Pp. 163–84 in C. L. Fry (ed.), Dimensions: Aging, Culture, and Health. New York: Praeger.
1, 7,
10   1981b   Measuring social interaction of the urban elderly: a methodologial synthesis. International Journal of Aging and Human Development 13:233–44.

8, 19 Soldo, Beth
       1981   The living arrangements of the elderly in the near future. Pp. 491–512 in Sara B. Kiesler et al. (eds.), Aging: Social Change. New York: Academic Press.

5   Soliday, S. M.
     1974   Relationship between age and hazard perception in automobile drivers. Perception and Motor Skills 39:335–38.

8   Solomon, Barbara
     1967   Social functioning of economically dependent aged. The Gerontologist 7:213–17.

8   Solomon, Kenneth
     1982   Social antecedents of learned helplessness in the health care setting. The Gerontologist 22:282–87.

8   Sommers, Tish
     1975   Social Security: a woman's viewpoint. Industrial Gerontology 2:266–79.

9   Sommers, Tish, and Laurie Shields
    1979   Problems of the Displaced Homemaker. Pp. 86–106 in Ann F. Cahn (ed.), Women in Midlife—Security and Fulfillment. Washington, D.C.: House Select Committee on Aging.

8, 18   Sonne, Lemke, and Rudolph H. Moos
    1980   Assessing the institutional policies of sheltered care settings. Journal of Gerontology 35:96–107.

1   Sontag, Lester W.
    1969   The longitudinal method of research: what it can and can't do. Pp. 15–25 in Frances C. Jeffers (ed.), Duke University Council on Aging and Human Development: Proceedings of Seminars 1965–1969. Durham, N. Carolina: Duke University Press.

14   Sontag, Susan
    1972   The double standard of aging. Saturday Review 55(39):29–38.

10   Spain, Nola
    1969   Recreational programs for the elderly. Pp. 180–90 in Rosamonde R. Boyd and C. G. Oakes (eds.), Foundations in Practical Gerontology. Columbia, S. Carolina: University of South Carolina Press.

7   Spanier, Graham B., Robert A. Lewis, and Charles L. Cole
    1975   Marital adjustment over the family life cycle: the issue of curvilinearity. Journal of Marriage and the Family 37:263–75.

7   Spanier, Graham B., W. Sauer, and R. Larzelere
    1979   An empirical evaluation of the family life cycle. Journal of Marriage and the Family 41(1):27–38.

5   Sparks, P. M.
    1973   Behavioral versus experiential aging: implications for intervention. The Gerontologist 13:15–18.

8   Spear, Mel
    1968   Paramedical services for older Americans. Journal of the American Geriatrics Society 16:1088–94.

12   Spence, Donald L.
    1975   The meaning of engagement. International Journal of Aging and Human Development 6(3):193–98.

7   Spence, Donald L., and Thomas Lonner
    1971   The "empty nest": a transition within motherhood. Family Coordinator 20:369–75.

17   Spengler, Joseph J.
    1977   The aged and public policy. Pp. 349–66 in Ewald W. Busse and Eric Pfeiffer (eds.), Behavior and Adaptation in Late Life, second edition. Boston, Mass.: Little, Brown.

8   Spilerman, Seymour, and Eugene Litwak
    1982   Reward structures of organizational design: an analysis of institutions for the elderly. Research on Aging 4:43–70.

15   Spradley, James P.
    1970   You Owe Yourself a Drunk: An Ethnography of Urban Nomads. Boston: Little, Brown.

12   Spreitzer, E., and E. E. Snyder
    1974   Correlates of life satisfaction among the aged. Journal of Gerontology 29:454–58.

5   Staats, S.
    1974   Internal versus external locus of control for three age groups. International Journal of Aging and Human Development 5:7–10.

12   Stack, William A., and Morris A. Okun
    1982   The construct validity of life satisfaction among the elderly. Journal of Gerontology 37:625–27.

10   Stafford, Juliene L., and Robert G. Bringle
      1980   The influence of task success on elderly women's interest in new activities. The Gerontologist 20:642–48.

       Stagner, Ross
9, 16   1975   Boredom on the assembly line: age and personality variables. Industrial Gerontology 2:23–44.

12   1981   Stress, strain, coping and defense. Research on Aging 3:3–32.

       Stanford, E. P.
9   1971   Retirement anticipation in the military. The Gerontologist 11:37–42.

14   1974   (ed.) Minority Aging: Institute on Minority Aging Proceedings. San Diego: Center on Aging, School of Social Work, San Diego State University.

       Staples, Thomas G.
8   1973   Supplemental security income: the aged eligible. Social Security Bulletin 36(7):31–35.

8, 12   Starkey, P. D.
      1968   Sick-role retention as a factor in nonrehabilitation. Journal of Counseling Psychology 15:75–79.

5   Starr, Bernard D., and M. B. Weiner
      1981   Sex and Sexuality in the Mature Years. New York: McGraw-Hill.

       Stearns, P.
3   1977   Old Age in European Society. New York: Holmes and Meier.

3   1980   Old women: some historical perspectives. Journal of Family History 4:44–57.

7   Stehouwer, Jan
      1965   Relations between generations and the three-generation household in Denmark. Pp. 142–62 in Ethel Shanas and Gordon F. Streib (eds.), Social Structure and the Family. Englewood Cliffs, N.J.: Prentice-Hall.

8, 18   Steinberg, Raymond M., and Genevieve W. Carter
      1983   Case Management and the Elderly. Lexington, Mass.: Heath.

10   Steiner, Gary A.
      1963   The People Look at Television. New York: Knopf.

8   Steiner, Peter O., and Robert Dorfman
      1957   The Economic Status of the Aged. Berkeley, Calif.: University of California Press.

8, 18   Steinhauer, Marcia B.
      1982   Geriatric foster care: a prototype design and implementation issues. The Gerontologist 22:293–300.

6   Steitz, Jean A.
      1981   The female life course: life situations and perception of control. International Journal of Aging and Human Development 14:195–204.

       Stephens, Joyce
15   1974   Carnies and marks: the sociology of elderly street peddlers. Sociological Symposium 11:25–41.

15   1975   Society of the alone: freedom, privacy, and utilitarianism as dominant norms in the SRO. Journal of Gerontology 30:230–35.

15   1976   Loners, Losers, and Lovers: Elderly Tenants in a Slum Hotel. Seattle: University of Washington Press.

11   Stern, Karl, Gwendolyn M. Williams, and Miguel Prados
      1951   Grief reactions in later life. American Journal of Psychiatry 108:289–94.

14   Sterne, Richard S., James E. Phillips, and Alvin Rabushka
      1974   The Urban Elderly Poor: Racial and Bureaucratic Conflict. Lexington, Mass.: Heath.

5   Sterns, Harvey L., G. V. Barrett, R. A. Alexander, P. E. Panek, B. J. Avilio, and L. R. Forbinger.

	1977 Training and Evaluation of Older Adult Skills Critical for Effective Driving Performance. Final Report. Akron, Ohio: University of Akron, Department of Psychology.

5, 12   Steuer, Joanne, Lew Bank, Edwin J. Olsen, and Lissy F. Jarvik
   1980   Depression, physical health and somatic complaints in the elderly: a study of the Zung Self-Rating Depression Scale. Journal of Gerontology 35:683–88.

5   Steuer, Joanne, Asenath LaRue, June E. Blum, and Lissy F. Jarvik
   1981   "Critical loss": in the eight and ninth decades. Journal of Gerontology 36:211–13.

9   Stewart, C. D.
   1974   The older worker in Japan: realities and possibilities. Industrial Gerontology 1:60–75.

9, 16   Stewman, Shelby
   1981   The aging of work organizations: impact on organization and employment practice. Pp. 243–90 in Sara B. Kiesler et al. (eds.), Aging: Social Change. New York: Academic Press.

5   Stimson, Ardyth, Jane F. Wase, and John Stimson
   1981   Sexuality and self-esteem among the aged. Research on Aging 3:228–39.

7   Stinnett, Nick, Linda M. Carter, and James E. Montgomery
   1972   Older persons' perceptions of their marriages. Journal of Marriage and the Family 34:665–70.

9   Stokes, Randall G., and George L. Maddox
   1967   Some social factors in retirement adaptation. Journal of Gerontology 22:329–33.

6   Stone, K., and R. A. Kalish
   1973   Of poker, roles, and aging: description, discussion, and data. International Journal of Aging and Human Development 4:1–13.

5, 19   Storandt, Martha
   1983   Understanding senile dementia: a challenge for the future. International Journal of Aging and Human Development 16:1–6.

1   Storandt, Martha, and Walter Hudson
   1975   Misuse of analysis of covariance in aging research and some partial solutions. Experimental Aging Research 1:121–25.

13   Storck, Patricia A., and Marion B. Cutler
   1977   Pictorial representation of adults as observed in children's literature. Educational Gerontology 2:293–300.

5   Storck, Patricia A., William R. Looft, and Frank H. Hooper
   1972   Interrelationships among Piagetian tasks and traditional measures of cognitive abilities in mature and aged adults. Journal of Gerontology 27:461–65.

9   Strain, R. M.
   1974   Retirement among priests and religious. Pp. 145–63 in W. C. Bier (ed.), Aging: Its Challenge to the Individual and to Society. Pastoral Psychology Series, No. 8, New York: Fordham University Press.

4   Strehler, Bernard L.
   1977   Time, Cells, and Aging, second edition. New York: Academic Press.

Streib, Gordon F.
9, 12   1956   Morale of the retired. Social Problems 3:270–76.
7, 9   1958   Family patterns in retirement. Journal of Social Issues 24:46–60.
13   1965a   Are the aged a minority group? Pp. 311–28 in Alvin W. Gouldner (ed.), Applied Sociology. New York: Free Press.
7   1965b   Intergenerational relations: perspectives of the two generations on the older parent. Journal of Marriage and the Family 27:469–76.
12   1968   Disengagement theory in sociocultural perspective. International Journal of Psychiatry 6(1):69–76.

14   1976   Social stratification and aging. Pp. 160–85 in Robert H. Binstock and Ethel Shanas (eds.), Handbook of Aging and the Social Sciences. New York: Van Nostrand Reinhold.

9   1983   The social psychology of retirement: theoretical perspectives and research priorities. Pp. 202–14 in J. E. Birren et al. (eds.), Aging: A Challenge to Science and Society. Oxford: Oxford University Press.

1   Streib, Gordon F., and Harold L. Orbach
     1967   Aging. Pp. 612–40 in P. E. Lazarsfeld, W. H. Sewell, and H. L. Wilensky (eds.), The Uses of Sociology. New York: Basic Books.

9, 12   Streib, Gordon F., and Clement J. Schneider
     1971   Retirement in American Society. Ithaca, N.Y.: Cornell University Press.

8   Streib, Gordon F., and Ruth B. Streib
     1975   Communes and the aging. American Behavioral Scientist 19:176–89.

     Streib, Gordon F., and Wayne E. Thompson
9   1958a   Situational determinants: health and economic deprivation in retirement. Journal of Social Issues 14(2):18–34.

9, 12   1958b   (eds.) Adjustment in retirement. Journal of Social Issues 14(2):1–63.

7, 9   Streib, Gordon F., Wayne E. Thompson, and E. A. Suchman
     1958   Family patterns in retirement. Journal of Social Issues 14:46–60.

14   Stretch, John J.
     1976   Are aged blacks who manifest differences in community security also different in coping reactions? International Journal of Aging and Human Development 7:171–84.

     Struyk, Raymond J.
8   1977a   The housing situation of elderly Americans. The Gerontologist 17:130–39.
8   1977b   The housing expense burden of households headed by the elderly. The Gerontologist 17:447–52.

11   Sudnow, David
     1967   Passing On: The Social Organization of Dying. Englewood Cliffs, N.J.: Prentice-Hall.

8   Sullivan, D. F.
     1971   Disability components for an index of health. Vital and Health Statistics, Series 2, No. 42. Washington, D.C.: U.S. Government Printing Office.

2, 9   Sullivan, Deborah A., and Sylvia A. Stevens
     1982   Snowbirds: seasonal migrants to the sunbelt. Research on Aging 4:159–78.

15   Sundeen, Richard A., and James T. Mathieu
     1976a   The fear of crime and its consequences among elderly in three urban communities. The Gerontologist 16:211–19.

15   1976b   The urban elderly: environments of fear. Pp. 51–66 in Jack Goldsmith and S. S. Goldsmith (eds.), Crime and the Elderly. Lexington, Mass.: Lexington Books.

     Sussman, Marvin B.
7, 10   1955   Activity patterns of post-parental couples and their relationship to family continuity. Marriage and Family Living 17:388–41.

7   1965   Relationships of adult children with their parents in the United States. Pp. 62–92 in Ethel Shanas and Gordon F. Streib (eds.), Social Structure and the Family: Generational Relations. Englewood Cliffs, N.J.: Prentice-Hall.

     Sussman, Marvin B., and Lee Burchinal
7   1962a   Parental aid to married children: implications for family functioning. Marriage and Family Living 24:320–32.

7   1962b   Kin family network: unheralded structure in current conceptualizations of family functioning. Marriage and Family Living 24:231–40.

15   Sutherland, Edwin H.
        1949   White Collar Crime. New York: Dryden.
14   Suzuki, Peter T.
        1975   Minority group aged in America: a comprehensive bibliography of recent publications on Blacks, Mexican-Americans, Native Americans, Chinese, and Japanese. Council of Planning Librarians Exchange Bibliography. No. 816. Monticello, Ill.: Council of Planning Librarians.
11   Swenson, W. M.
        1961   Attitudes toward death in an aged population. Journal of Gerontology 16:49–52.
        Szinovacz, Maximiliane
9   1982a   Personal problems and adjustment to retirement. Pp. 195–204 in M. Szinovacz (ed.), Women's Retirement. Beverly Hills, Calif.: Sage.
9   1982b   Retirement plans and retirement adjustment. Pp. 139–150 in M. Szinovacz (ed.), Women's Retirement. Beverly Hills, Calif.: Sage.
19   Taber, Merlin
        1965   Application of research findings to the issue of social policy. Pp. 367–79 in Arnold M. Rose and Warren A. Peterson (eds.), Older People and Their Social World. Philadelphia: F. A. Davis.
2   Taeuber, Cynthia
        1983   America in Transition: An Aging Society. Current Population Reports, Series P-23, No. 128. Washington, D.C.: U.S. Government Printing Office.
9, 16   Taggart, Robert
        1973   The Labor Market Impacts of the Private Retirement System. Studies in Public Welfare, Paper Number 11. Washington, D.C.: U.S. Congress, Subcommittee on Fiscal Policy. Joint Economic Committee.
        Taietz, Philip
8   1966   Community structure and aging. Pp. 375–78 in Proceedings of the 7th International Congress of Gerontology, VI. Vienna: Wiener Medizinischen Akadamie.
8   1975a   Community complexity and knowledge of facilities. Journal of Gerontology 30:357–62.
8   1975b   Community facilities and social services. Pp. 145–56 in Robert C. Atchley (ed.), Environments and the Rural Aged. Washington, D.C.: Gerontological Society.
8   1976   Two conceptual models of the senior center. Journal of Gerontology 31:219–22.
5   Talland, George A. (ed.)
        1968   Human Aging and Behavior. New York: Academic Press.
8, 14   Tallmer, Margot
        1977   Some factors in the education of older members of minority groups. Journal of Geriatric Psychiatric 10:89–98.
13   Tallmer, Margot, and Bernard Kutner
        1969   Disengagement and the stresses of aging. Journal of Gerontology 24:70–75.
11, 12 Tate, Lenore Artie
        1982   Life satisfaction and death anxiety in aged women. International Journal of Aging and Human Development 15:299–306.
5   Taub, H. A.
        1975   Mode of presentation, age, and short-term memory. Journal of Gerontology 30:56–59.
8   Taube, Carl A.
        1965   Characteristics of patients in mental hospitals: United States, April–June, 1963. Vital and Health Statistics, Series 12, No. 3.
9   Taylor, Charles
        1972   Developmental conceptions and the retirement process. Pp. 75–116 in Frances M. Carp (ed.), Retirement. New York: Behavioral Publications.

8   Teaff, Joseph D., M. Powell Lawton, Lucille Nahemow, and Diane Carlson
    1978   Impact of age integration on the well-being of elderly tenants in pubic housing. Journal of Gerontology 33:126–33.

9   Tellier, R. D.
    1974   The four-day workweek and the elderly: a cross-sectional study. Journal of Gerontology 29:430–33.

    Templer, D. I.
11 1971   Death anxiety as related to depression and health of retired persons. Journal of Gerontology 26:521–23.

11 1972   Death anxiety in religiously very involved persons. Psychological Reports 31:361–62.

11 Templer, D. I., C. Ruff, and C. Frank
    1971   Death anxiety: age, sex, and parental resemblance in diverse populations. Developmental Psychology 4:108.

8   Terris, Bruce J.
    1972   Legal Services for the Elderly. Washington, D.C.: National Council on Aging.

7, 12 Tesch, Stephanie, Susan Krauss Whitbourne, and Milton F. Nehrke
    1981   Friendship, social interaction and subjective well-being of older men in an institutional setting. International Journal of Aging and Human Development 13:317–27.

5   Thaler, Margaret
    1956   Relationships among Wechsler, Weigl, Rorschach, EEG findings and abstract-concrete behavior. Journal of Gerontology 11:404–09.

    Theodorson, George A., and Achilles G. Theodorson
    1969   Modern Dictionary of Sociology. New York: Crowell.

15 Thio, Alex
    1983   Deviant Behavior, second edition. Boston: Houghton Mifflin.

    Thomae, Hans (ed.)
    1975   Patterns of Aging: Findings from the Bonn Longitudinal Study of Aging. New York: S. Karger.

13 Thomas, Elizabeth C., and Kaoru Yamamoto
    1975   Attitudes toward age; an exploration in school-age children. International Journal of Aging and Human Development 6:117–29.

2, 8 Thomas, G.
    1973   Regional migration patterns and poverty among the aged in the South. Journal of Human Resources 8:73–84.

9   Thomas, L. Eugene
    1977   Motivations for mid-life career change. Paper presented at the annual meeting of the Gerontological Society, San Francisco, California.

13 Thomas, William C., Jr.
    1981   The expectation gap and the stereotype of the stereotype: images of old people. The Gerontologist 21:402–07.

16 Thomasson, Richard F.
    1983   Old age pensions under Social Security. American Behavioral Scientist 26:699–723.

    Thompson, Gayle B.
9, 10 1973   Work versus leisure roles: an investigation of morale among employed and retired men. Journal of Gerontology 28:339–44.

8, 9 1974   Work experience and income of the population aged 60 and older, 1971. Social Security Bulletin 37(11):3–20.

8, 14 1975   Blacks and social security benefits: trends, 1960–1973. Social Security Bulletin 38(4):30–40.

8   1978   Pension coverage and benefits, 1972: findings from the retirement history study. Social Security Bulletin 41(2):3–17.

Thompson, Wayne E.

9   1956   The Impact of Retirement. Unpublished doctoral dissertation, Cornell University, Ithaca, New York.

9   1958   Pre-retirement anticipation and adjustment in retirement. Journal of Social Issues 14:35 –45.

9   Thompson, Wayne E., and Gordon F. Streib
    1958   Situation determinants: health and economic deprivation in retirement. Journal of Social Issues 14:18–34.

9, 12   Thompson, Wayne E., Gordon F. Streib, and John Kosa
    1960   The effect of retirement on personal adjustment: a panel analysis. Journal of Gerontology 15:165–69.

5   Thornbury, Julia M., and Charlotte M. Mistretta
    1981   Tactile sensitivity as a function of age. Journal of Gerontology 36:34–39.

13   Thorson, James A.
    1975   Attitudes toward the aged as a function of race and social class. The Gerontologist 15: 343–44.

13   Thorson, James A., Lynda Whatley, and Karen L. Hancock
    1974   Attitudes toward the aged as a function of age and education. The Gerontologist 14:316 –18.

5   Thune, Jeane M.
    1967   Racial attitudes of older adults. The Gerontologist 7:179–82.

8, 9   Thune, Jeanne M., Sebastian Tine, and F. E. Booth
    1974   Retraining older adults for employment in community services. The Gerontologist 4:5– 9.

5, 14   Thune, Jeanne M., C. R. Webb, and L. E. Thune
    1971   Interracial attitudes of younger and older adults in a biracial population. The Gerontologist 11:305–10.

Thurnher, Majda
5   1974   Goals, values, and life evaluations at the preretirement stage. Journal of Gerontology 29:85–96.

7   1975   Midlife marriage; sex differences in evaluation and perspectives. International Journal of Aging and Human Development 7:129–35.

5   Thurston, L. L., and T. G. Thurstone
    1949   Examiner manual for the SRA primary mental abilities. Chicago: Science Research Associates.

Tibbitts, Clark
    1960   (ed.) Handbook of Social Gerontology. Chicago: University of Chicago Press.
17   1962   Politics of aging: pressure for change. Pp. 16–25 in Wilma Donahue and Clark Tibbitts (eds.), Politics of Age. Ann Arbor, Michigan: University of Michigan Press.

Tibbitts, Clark, and Wilma Donahue (eds.)
    1962   Social and Psychological Aspects of Aging. New York: Columbia University Press.

4   Timiras, Paola S.
    1978   Biological perspectives on aging. American Scientist 66:605–13.

Tissue, Thomas L.
12   1968   A Guttman Scale of disengagement potential. Journal of Gerontology 23:513–16.
8, 14   1970   Downward mobility in old age. Social problems 18:67–77.
8   1971a   Old age, poverty and the central city. Aging and Human Development 2:235–48.
12   1971b   Disengagement potential: replication and use as an explanatory variable. Journal of Gerontology 26:76–80.
8   1971c   Social class and the senior citizen center. The Gerontologist 11:196–200.

12   Tissue, Thomas L., and L. Wells
         1971   Antecedent lifestyles and old age. Psychological Reports 29:1100.

8, 18   Tobin, Sheldon S. (ed.)
         1982   Current Gerontology: Long-Term Care. Washington, D.C.: Gerontological Society of America.

8   Tobin, Sheldon S., and Morton A. Lieberman
         1976   Last Home for the Aged. San Francisco: Jossey-Bass.

12   Tobin, Sheldon S., and Bernice L. Neugarten
         1961   Life satisfaction and social interaction in the aging. Journal of Gerontology 16:344–46.

7   Tognoli, Jerome
         1980   Male friendship and intimacy across the life span. Family Relations 29:273–79.

9   Tomika, K.
         1975   Counseling middle-aged and older workers. Industrial Gerontology 2:45–52.

14, 17   Torres-Gil, Fernando, and Rosina M. Becerra
         1977   The political behavior of the Mexican-American elderly. The Gerontologist 17:392–98.

         Townsend, Peter

7   1957   The Family Life of Old People: An Inquiry in East London. Glencoe, Ill.: Free Press.

3   1964a   The place of older people in different societies. Lancet 1:159–61.

8   1964b   The Last Refuge. New York: Routledge.

7   1965   The effects of family structure on the likelihood of admission to an institution in old age: the application of a general theory. Pp. 163–87 in Ethel Shanas and Gordon F. Streib (eds.), Social Structure and the Family: Generational Relations. Englewood Cliffs, N.J.: Prentice-Hall.

7   1968   Problems in the cross-national study of old people in the family: segregation versus integration. Pp. 41–60 in Ethel Shanas and John Madge (eds.), Methodology Problems in Cross National Studies in Aging. New York: S. Karger.

16, 17   Townsend, Peter, and Dorothy Wedderburn
         1965   The Aged in the Welfare State. London: Bell.

16   Tracy, Martin B.
         1978   Flexible retirement features abroad. Social Security Bulletin 41(5):18–36.

8   Travis, Georgia
         1966   Chronic Disease and Disability. Berkeley, Calif.: University of California Press.

         Treas, Judith

7   1977   Family support systems for the aged. Some social and demographic considerations. The Gerontologist 17:486–91.

2, 17   1981   The great American fertility debate: generational balance and support for the aged. The Gerontologist 21:98–103.

         Trela, James

10, 17   1971   Some political consequences of senior center and other old age group membership. The Gerontologist 11(2, part 1):118–23.

10, 17   1972   Age structure of voluntary associations and political self-interest among the aged. Sociological Quarterly 13:244–52.

10, 14   1976   Social class and association membership an analysis of age-graded and non-age-graded voluntary participation. Journal of Gerontology 31:198–203.

10, 14   1977–78 Social class and political involvement in age-graded and non-age-graded associations. International Journal of Aging and Human Development 8:301–10.

12   Trenton, Jean-Rene
         1963   The concept of adjustment in old age. Pp. 292–98 in Richard H. Williams, Clark Tibbitts, and Wilma Donahue (eds.), Processes of Aging. Volume 1. New York: Atherton Press.

Troll, Lillian

7   1970   Issues in the study of generations. Aging and Human Development 1:199–218.

7   1971   The family of later life: a decade review. Journal of Marriage and the Family 33:263–90.

5   1975   Early and Middle Adulthood. Monterey, Calif.: Brooks/Cole.

7   Troll, Lillian, and Jean Smith

1976   Attachment through the life span; some questions about dyadic bonds among adults. Human Development 19:156–70.

7   Troll, Lillian, Sheila J. Miller, and Robert C. Atchley

1979   Families in Later Life. Belmont, Calif.: Wadsworth.

5   Troll, Lillian, Rosalyn Saltz, and Aleksandra Dunin-Markiewicz

1976   A seven-year follow-up of intelligence test scores of foster grandparents. Journal of Gerontology 31:583–85.

Tuckman, Jacob, and Irving Lorge

13   1953a   Attitudes toward old people. Journal of Social Psychology 37:249–60.

9   1953b   Retirement and the Industrial Worker: Prospect and Reality, New York: Columbia University Teachers College.

13   1953c   When aging begins and stereotypes about aging. Journal of Gerontology 8:489–92.

13   1953d   When does old age begin and a worker become old? Journal of Gerontology 8:483–88.

5   1954   Classification of the self as young, middle-aged, or old. Geriatrics 9:534–36.

13   1956   Perceptual stereotypes about life adjustments. Journal of Social Psychology 43:239–45.

13   1958a   Attitudes toward aging of individuals with experiences with the aged. Journal of Genetic Psychology 1958:92:199–215.

13   1958b   The projection of personal symptoms into stereotyping about aging. Journal of Gerontology 13:70–73.

5   Tuckman, Jacob, and M. Lovell

1957   Self-classification as old or not old. Geriatrics 12:666–71.

5   Tuckman, Jacob, Irving Lorge, and F. D. Zeman

1961   The self-image in aging. Journal of Genetic Psychology 90:317–21.

8   Turbow, Sandra R.

1975   Geriatric group day care and its effect on independent living: a thirty-six-month assessment. The Gerontologist 15:508–15.

10, 17   Turk, Herman, Joel Smith and Howard P. Myers

1966   Understanding local political behavior: the role of the older citizen. Pp. 254–76 in Ida H. Simpson and John C. McKinney (eds.), Social Aspects of Aging. Durham, N. Carolina: Duke University Press.

17   Turner, Barbara F., and Robert L. Kahn

1974   Age as a political issue. Journal of Gerontology 29:572–80.

9, 16   Turner, R. G., and W. M. Whitaker

1972   The impact of mass layoffs on older workers. Industrial Gerontology 16:14–21.

9   Tyhurst, James S., Lee Salk, and Miriam Kennedy

1957   Mortality, morbidity, and retirement. American Journal of Public Health 47:1434–44.

11   Uhlenberg, Peter I.

1969   Study of cohort life cycles: Cohorts of native born Massachusetts women, 1830–1920. Population Studies 23:407–420.

2, 7   Uhlenberg, Peter, and Mary Ann P. Meyers

1981   Divorce and the elderly. The Gerontologist 21:276–82.

18   Ullmann, Steven G.

1981   Assessment of facility quality and its relationship to facility size in the long-term care industry. The Gerontologist 21:91–97.

United Nations

2	1973	Demographic Yearbook: 1973. New York: United Nations.
2	1975	The Aging: Trends and Policies. New York: United Nations, Department of Economic and Social Affairs.
2	1979	Demographic Yearbook: 1979. New York: United Nations.

United States Bureau of the Census

17	1965	Voter participation in the national election, November 1964. Current Population Reports, Series P-20, No. 143. Washington, D.C.: U.S. Government Printing Office.
2	1968	Lifetime migration histories of the American people. Current Population Reports, Series P-23, No. 25. Washington, D.C.: U.S. Government Printing Office.
2, 19	1970	Projections of the population of the United States, by age and sex (interim revisions): 1970 to 2020. Current Population Reports, Series P-25, No. 448. Washington, D.C.: U.S. Government Printing Office.
2, 19	1971a	Projections of the population of the United States, by age and sex: 1970–2020. Current Population Reports, Series P-25, No. 470. Washington, D.C.: U.S. Government Printing Office.
8	1971b	Characteristics of the low-income population, 1970. Current Population Reports, Series P-60, No. 81. Washington, D.C.: U.S. Government Printing Office.
2, 19	1972	Projections of the population of the United States by age and sex: 1972 to 2020. Current Population Reports, Series P-25, No. 493. Washington, D.C.: U.S. Government Printing Office.
17	1973a	Voting and registration in the election of November 1972. Current Population Reports, Series P-20, No. 253. Washington, D.C.: U.S. Government Printing Office.
9	1973b	Employment status and work experience. Census of Population: 1970. Subject Report PC(2)-6A. Washington, D.C.: U.S. Government Printing Office.
2, 14	1973c	Census of Population: 1970. Volume 1, Characteristics of the Population. Part 1, United States Summary, Section 1. Washington, D.C.: U.S. Government Printing Office.
7	1973d	Census of Population: 1970. Subject Reports, Final Report PC(2)-4B, Persons by Family Characteristics. Washington, D.C.: U.S. Government Printing Office.
14	1973e	Census of population, 1970. Subject Reports, Final Report PC(2)-7A, Occupational Characteristics. Washington, D.C.: U.S. Government Printing Office.
14	1973f	Census of population, 1970. Subject Reports, Final Report PC(2)-1G, Japanese, Chinese, and Filipinos in the United States. Washington, D.C.: U.S. Government Printing Office.
14	1973g	Census of population, 1970. Subject Reports, Final Report PC(2)-1F, American Indians. Washington, D.C.: U.S. Government Printing Office.
14	1973h	Census of population, 1970. Subject Reports, Final Report PC(2)-1D, Persons of Spanish Surname. Washington, D.C.: U.S. Government Printing Office.
2, 14	1973i	Census of population, 1970. Subject Reports, Final Reports PC(2)-8B, Earnings by Occupation and Education. Washington, D.C.: U.S. Government Printing Office.
2	1973j	Some demographic aspects of aging in the United States. Current Population Reports, Series P-23, No. 43. Washington, D.C.: U.S. Government Printing Office.
	1974	Statistical Abstract of the United States: 1974. Washington, D.C.: U.S. Government Printing Office.
8	1975a	Money income in 1973 of families and persons in the United States. Current Population Reports, Series P-60, No. 97. Washington, D.C.: U.S. Government Printing Office.
3	1975b	Historical Statistics of the United States: Colonial Times to 1970. Washington, D.C.: U.S. Government Printing Office.
	1976a	Statistical Abstract of the United States: 1976. Washington, D.C.: U.S. Government Printing Office.

2   1976b Demographic aspects of aging and the older population in the United States. Current Population Reports, Series P-23, Number 59. Washington, D.C.: U.S. Government Printing Office.

8   1977a Money income in 1975 of families and persons in the United States. Current Population Reports, Series P-60, Number 105. Washington, D.C.: U.S. Government Printing Office.

8   1977b Characteristics of the population below the poverty level: 1975. Current Population Reports, Series P-60, Number 106. Washington, D.C.: U.S. Government Printing Office.

2, 19   1977c Projections of the population of the United States: 1977 to 2050. Current Population Reports, Series P-25, No. 704. Washington, D.C.: U.S. Government Printing Office.

7   1977d Marriage, divorce, widowhood, and remarriage by family characteristics. Current Population Reports, Series P-20, No. 312. Washington, D.C.: U.S. Government Printing Office.

17   1978a Voting and registration in the election of November, 1976. Current Population Reports, Series P-20, Number 322. Washington, D.C.: U.S. Government Printing Office.

8   1978b 1976 survey of institutionalized persons: a survey of persons receiving long-term care. Current Population Reports, Series P-23, Number 69. Washington, D.C.: U.S. Government Printing Office.

         1979a Statistical Abstract of the United States. Washington, D.C.: U.S. Government Printing Office.

2   1979b Mexico. Current Country Demographic Profiles, IPS-DP-14. Washington, D.C.: U.S. Government Printing Office.

2   1980a Educational Attainment in the United States: 1979. Current Population Reports, Series P-20, No. 356. Washington, D.C.: U.S. Government Printing Office.

2   1980b Illustrative Projections of Money Income: 1980–1995. Current Population Reports, Series P-60, No. 122. Washington, D.C.: U.S. Government Printing Office.

8   1981a Characteristics of households and persons receiving noncash benefits: 1979. Current Population Reports, Series P-23, No. 110. Washington, D.C.: U.S. Government Printing Office.

2   1981b Money Income of Individuals: 1980. Current Population Reports, Series P-60, No. 127. Washington, D.C.: U.S. Government Printing Office.

2   1981c Money Income of Families and Persons in the United States: 1979. Current Population Reports, Series P-60, No. 129. Washington, D.C.: U.S. Government Printing Office.

         1981d Statistical Abstract of the United States. Washington, D.C.: U.S. Government Printing Office.

         1982a Statistical Abstract of the United States: 1982–83. Washington, D.C.: U.S. Government Printing Office.

17   1982b Voting and Registration in the Election of November, 1980. Current Population Reports, Series P-20, No. 370. Washington, D.C.: U.S. Government Printing Office.

2   1982c Marital Status and Living Arrangements: March, 1981. Current Population Reports, Series P-20, No. 372. Washington, D.C.: U.S. Government Printing Office.

2   1982d Projections of the Population of the United States. Current Population Reports, Series P-25, No. 922. Washington, D.C.: U.S. Government Printing Office.

2, 16   1983a America in Transition: An Aging Society. Current Population Reports, Series P-23, No. 128. Washington, D.C.: U.S. Government Printing Office.

14   1983b 1980 Census of Population, Vol. 1, Chapter B, United States Summary. Washington, D.C.: U.S. Government Printing Office.

United States Bureau of Labor Statistics

8   1976   Budgets for an urban family of four persons and budgets for a retired couple. Bulletin 1970–76. Washington, D.C.: U.S. Government Printing Office.

8   1981   Three budgets for a retired couple, Autumn 1980. News, U.S. Department of Labor 81:384.

United States Commission on Civil Rights

13   1977   The Age Discrimination Study. Washington, D.C.: The Commission.

13   1979   The Age Discrimination Study, Part II. Washington, D.C.: The Commission.

8   United States Department of Health, Education, and Welfare, Office of Aging

1965   Foster Family Care for the Aged. Washington, D.C.: U.S. Government Printing Office.

16   United States Department of Health, Education, and Welfare, Office of Consumer Affairs

1973   An Approach to Consumer Education for Adults. Washington, D.C.: Office of Consumer Affairs.

8   United States Department of Health, Education, and Welfare, Social Rehabilitation Service, Administration on Aging

1971   Transportation and Aging: Selected Issues. Washington, D.C.: U.S. Government Printing Office.

United States Department of Health, Education, and Welfare, Social Security Administration, Office of Research and Statistics

8   1971a   Resources after Retirement. Report No. 34 (By Edna C. Wentworth and Dena K. Motley.) Washington, D.C.: Office of Research and Statistics.

8   1971b   Resources of People 65 or Over. Washington, D.C.: Office of Research and Statistics.

8   1971c   Posthospitalization Use of Home Health Services under Medicare, 1967. H1-29. Washington, D.C. Office of Research and Statistics.

8   1972   Economic Resources of Institutionalized Adults: 1967 Survey of Institutionalized Adults. Report No. 3 (By Philip Frohlich.) Washington, D.C.: Office of Research and Statistics.

8   1973   Income of the Aged Population: 1971 Money Income and Changes from 1967. Note No. 14. (By Gayle B. Thompson.) Washington, D.C.: Office of Research and Statistics.

8   1974a   Earnings Replacement from Social Security and Private Pensions: Newly Entitled Beneficiaries, 1970. Report No. 13. (By Alan Fox.) Washington, D.C.: Division of Retirement and Survivors Studies.

8   1974b   Effects of the OASDI Benefit Increase in March, 1974. Note No. 14. (By Barbara A. Lingg.) Washington, D.C.: Office of Research and Statistics.

2   1975a   Demographic and Economic Characteristics of the Aged, 1968 Social Security Survey. (By Lenore E. Bixby, Wayne W. Kolodurbetz, Patience Lauriat, and Janet Murray.) Washington, D.C.: Office of Research and Statistics.

8, 18   1975b   Age Differences in Health Care Spending, Fiscal Year 1974. No. 6. Washington, D.C.: Office of Research and Statistics, Division of Health Insurance Studies.

18   United States Department of Health, Education, and Welfare, Welfare Administration

1966   Planning Welfare Services for Older People. Washington, D.C.: U.S. Government Printing Office.

United States Department of Housing and Urban Development

8   1968   Housing for the Physically Impaired: A Guide for Planning and Design. Washington, D.C.: U.S. Government Printing Office.

8   1972   Population, Housing and Income: The Federal Housing Programs. Washington, D.C.: U.S. Government Printing Office.

8   1973   Older Americans: Facts about Incomes and Housing. HUD 359-S. Washington, D.C.: U.S. Government Printing Office.

United States Department of Justice

15   1979   Crime in the United States: 1979. Washington, D.C.: U.S. Government Printing Office.

15   1983   Crime in the United States, 1982. Washington, D.C.: U.S. Government Printing Office.

United States Department of Labor

9   1965   The Older American Workers Age Discrimination in Employment. Washington, D.C.: U.S. Department of Labor.

9, 16   1975   Manpower Report to the President. Washington, D.C.: U.S. Government Printing Office.

9, 16   1979   Age Discrimination in Employment Act of 1967: Activities Under the Act During 1978. Washington, D.C.: U.S. Department of Labor.

9   1983   Manpower Report to the President, 1983. Washington, D.C.: U.S. Government Printing Office.

9   United States Department of Labor, Labor Management Services Administration

            1969   The 100 Largest Retirement Plans: 1960–1968. Washington, D.C.: U.S. Government Printing Office.

9   United States Department of Labor, Women's Bureau

            1977   Role and Status of Women Workers in the U.S. and Japan. Washington, D.C.: U.S. Government Printing Office.

18 United States General Accounting Office

            1982   The Elderly Should Benefit from Expanded Home Health Care But Increasing These Services Will Not Insure Cost Reductions. Washington, D.C.: U.S. General Accounting Office.

United States Senate Special Committee on Aging

15, 16   1965   Frauds and Deceptions Affecting the Elderly. Washington, D.C.: U.S. Government Printing Office.

19   1968   Long-Range Program and Research Needs in Aging and Related Fields, Part I. Washington, D.C.: U.S. Government Printing Office.

16   1969a   Health Aspects of the Economics of Aging. Washington, D.C.: U.S. Government Printing Office.

8, 16   1969b   Economics of Aging: Toward a Full Share of Abundance. Washington, D.C.: U.S. Government Printing Office.

8, 18   1971a   Trends in Long-Term Care. Parts 12 and 13—Chicago, Illinois. Hearings before the Subcommittee on Long-Term Care, 92nd Congress, 1st Session. Washington, D.C.: U.S. Government Printing Office.

14   1971b   Elderly Cubans in Exile: A Working Paper. Prepared for the Special Committee on Aging. United States Senate, 92nd Congress, 1st Session. Washington, D.C.: U.S. Government Printing Office.

19   1971c   Developments in Aging, 1970. Washington, D.C.: U.S. Government Printing Office.

19   1973   Training Needs in Gerontology. Washington, D.C: U.S. Government Printing Office.

18   1982   Health Care Expenditures for the Elderly: How much protection does Medicare provide? Washington, D.C.: U.S. Government Printing Office.

18, 19   1983   Developments in Aging: 1982. Washington, D.C.: U.S. Government Printing Office.

17   1984   Older Americans and the Federal Budget: Past, Present, and Future. Washington, D.C.: U.S. Government Printing Office.

7   Updegraff, Sue G.

            1968   Changing role of the grandmother. Journal of Home Economics 60:177–80.

5   Urberg, K. A., and G. Labouvie-Vief

            1976   Conceptualizaiton of sex roles: a life span developmental study. Developmental Psychology 12:15–23.

12 Vaillant, George E.

            1977   Adaptation to Life. Boston: Little, Brown.

8   Van Nostrand, Joan F.
      1981   The aged in nursing homes: baseline data. Research on Aging 3:403–16.
11   Van Tassel, David D. (ed.)
      1979   Aging, Death, and the Completion of Being. Philadelphia: University of Pennsylvania
             Press.
8   Van Zonneveld, Robert J.
      1962   The Health of the Aged. Baltimore, Md.: Williams and Wilkins.
2   Verbrugge, Lois M.
      1981   NCHS data and studies of differential morbidity and mortality. Research on Aging 3:
             429–58.
5   Verwoerdt, Adrian, Eric Pfeiffer, and Hsioh-Shan Wang
      1969   Sexual behavior in senescence: changes in sexual activity and interest in aging men and
             women. Journal of Geriatric Psychiatry 2:168–80.
4   Verzar, F.
      1957   The aging of connective tissue. The Gerontologist 1:363–78.
8   Vessey, Wayne
      1968   Organization of community social services for the aging. The Gerontologist 8(2, part
             2):54–56.
17   Vineyard, Dale
      1972   The Senate Special Committee on Aging. The Gerontologist 12:298–303.
7   Vinick, Barbara H.
      1979   Remarriage. Pp. 141–243 in R. H. Jacobs and Barbara H. Vinick, Re-Engagement in
             Later Life. Stamford, Conn.: Greylock.
9   Vogel, Bruce S., and Robert E. Schell
      1968   Vocational interest in late maturity and retirement. Journal of Gerontology 23:66–70.
8   Wachs, Martin
      1979   Transportation for the Elderly: Berkeley, Calif.: University of California Press.
7, 10 Wagner, Donna L., and Frederick Keast
      1981   Informal groups and the elderly: a preliminary examination of the mediation function.
             Research on Aging 3:325–32.
9, 16 Walerk, J. W., and K. F. Price
      1974   The impact of vesting, early retirement, rising cost of living and other factors on pro-
             jected retirement patterns: a manpower planning model. Industrial Gerontology 1:35–
             48.
5   Wales, Jeffrey B.
      1974   Sexuality in middle and old age: a critical review of the literature. Case Western Re-
             serve Journal of Sociology 6:82–105.
4   Walford, Roy L.
      1964   The immunologic theory of aging. The Gerontologist 4:195–97.
4   Walford, Roy L., and Gary M. Troup
      1966   Auto-immunity theories. Pp. 351–58 in Nathan W. Shock (ed.), Perspectives in Experi-
             mental Gerontology. Springfield, Ill.: Charles C. Thomas.
12   Walker, D. W.
      1968   A study of the relationship between suicide rates and age in the United States (1914 to
             1964). Pp. 408–20 in Proceeding of the Social Statistics Section. Washington, D.C.:
             American Statistical Association.
11   Walker, J. V.
      1968   Attitudes to death. Gerontologia Clinica 10:304–08.
9   Walker, James M.
      1977   A flexible retirement policy. Perspectives on Aging 6(5):21–25.

9   Walker, James W., Douglas C. Kimmel, and Karl F. Price
     1981   Retirement style and retirement satisfaction: retirees aren't all alike. International Journal of Aging and Human Development 12:267–81.

5   Walmsley, Sean A., and Richard L. Allington
     1982   Reading abilities of elderly persons in relation to difficulty of essential documents. The Gerontologist 22:36–38.

9   Wan, T.
     1972   Social differentials in selected work-limiting chronic conditions. Journal of Chronic Diseases 25:365–74.

7, 8, 18   Wan, Thomas T. H., and William G. Weissert
     1981   Social support networks, patient status, and institutionalization. Research on Aging 3: 240–56.

8   Wan, Thomas, T. H., William G. Weissert, and Barbara B. Livieratos
     1980   Geriatric day care and homemaker services: an experimental study. Journal of Gerontology 35:256–74.

4   Wantz, Molly S., and John E. Gay
     1981   The Aging Process: A Health Perspective. Cambridge, Mass.: Winthrop.

       Ward, Russell A.
12, 13   1977   The impact of subjective age and stigma on older persons. Journal of Gerontology 32: 227–32.

11   1980   Age and acceptance of euthanasia. Journal of Gerontology 35:421–31.

6   1984   The marginality and salience of being old: when is age relevant? The Gerontologist 24: 227–32.

13   Waring, Joan M.
     1975   Social replenishment and social change. The problem of disordered cohort flow. American Behavioral Science 19:237–56.

7, 12   Watson, J. Allen, and V. R. Kivett
     1976   Influences on the life satisfaction of older fathers. Family Coordinator 25(4):482–88.

5   Waugh, Nancy C., James L. Fozard, George A. Talland, and Donald E. Erwin
     1973   Effects of age and stimulus repetition on two-choice reaction time. Journal of Gerontology 28:466–70.

5   Webb, Wilse, B.
     1982   Sleep in older persons: sleep structures of 50-to-60-year-old men and women. Journal of Gerontology 37:581–86.

5   Webber, I. L., D. W. Coombs, and J. S. Hollingsworth
     1974   Variations in value orientations by age in a developing society. Journal of Gerontology 29:676–83.

13   Weber, Timothy, and Paul Cameron
     1978   Humor and aging—a response. The Gerontologist 18:73–75.

8, 16   Wedderburn, Dorothy
     1968   Cross-national studies of income adequacy. Pp. 61–74 in Ethel Shanas and John Madge (eds.), Methodology Problems in Cross-National Studies of Income Adequacy. New York: S. Karger.

7, 8   Weeks, John R., and Jose B. Cuellar
     1981   The role of family members in the helping networks of older people. The Gerontologist 21:388–94.

5   Weg, Ruth (ed.)
     1983   Sexuality in the Later Years: Roles and Behavior. New York: Academic Press.

5   Weiffenbach, James M., Bruce J. Baum, and Rosemary Burghauser
       1982   Taste thresholds: quality specific variation with human aging. Journal of Gerontology
               37:372–77.

8   Weihl, Hanna
       1981   On the relationship between the size of residential institutions and the well-being of
               residents. The Gerontologist 21:247–50.

15   Weinberg, M. S., and C. J. Williams
       1975   Male homosexuals. New York: Penguin.

8   Weinberger, Arthur
       1981   Responses to old people who ask for help: field experiments. Research on Aging 3:345–
               68.

13   Weinberger, L. E., and J. Millham
       1975   A multidimensional, multiple method analysis of attitudes towards the elderly. Journal
               of Gerontology 30:343–48.

9, 10 Weiner, Andrew I., and Sharon L. Hunt
       1981   Retiree's perceptions of work and leisure meanings. The Gerontologist 21:444–46.

8   Weinstock, C., and R. Bennett
       1971   From "waiting on the list" to becoming a "newcomer" and an "old timer" in a home
               for the aged: two studies of socialization and its impact upon cognitive functioning. In-
               ternational Journal of Aging and Human Development 2:46–58.

       Weisman, Avery D.
11   1972   On Dying and Denying. New York: Behavioral Publications.
11   1974   On death and dying. Does old age make sense? Decisions and destiny in growing older.
               Journal of Geriatric Psychiatry 7:84–93.

5   Weiss, Alfred D.
       1959   Sensory functions. Pp. 503–42 in James E. Birren (ed.), Handbook of Aging and the
               Individual. Chicago: University of Chicago Press.

8   Weiss, Joseph D.
       1969   Better Buildings for the Aged. New York: Hopkinson and Blake.

       Welford, Alan T.
5   1958   Ageing and Human Skill. London: Oxford University Press.
5   1959   Psychomotor performance. Pp. 562–613 in James E. Birren (ed.), Handbook of Aging
               and the Individual. Chicago: University of Chicago Press.
5   1964   Aging and personality: age changes in basic psychological capacities. Pp. 60–66 in P.
               From Hansen (ed.), Age with a Future. Copenhagen: Munksgaard.
5   1976   Motivation, capacity, learning and age. International Journal of Aging and Human De-
               velopment 7:189–99.
5   1977a   Motor performance. Pp. 450–96 in James E. Birren and K. Warner Schaie (eds.),
               Handbook of the Psychology of Aging. New York: Van Nostrand Reinhold.
9   1977b   Thirty years of psychological research on age and work. Journal of Occupational Psy-
               chology 49:129–38.

       Welford, Alan T., and James Birren (eds.)
5   1965   Behavior, Aging and the Nervous System. Springfield, Ill.: Charles C. Thomas.
5   1969   Decision Making and Age. New York: S. Karger.

2   Weller, Robert H., and Leon F. Bouvier
       1981   Population: Demography and Policy. New York: St. Martin's Press.

7, 8   Wells, Lilian, and Grant McDonald.
       1981   Interpersonal networks and past relocation adjustment of the institutionalized elderly.
               The Gerontologist 21:177–83.

8   Wendell, Richard F.
       1968   The economic status of the aged. The Gerontologist 8(2, part 2):32–36.
7, 12 Wentowski, Gloria J.
       1981   Reciprocity and the coping strategies of older people: cultural dimensions of network
               building. The Gerontologist 21:600–09.
9   Wentworth, Edna C.
       1968   Employment after Retirement: A Study of Post-Entitlement Work Experience of Men
               Drawing Benefits under Social Security. Washington, D.C.: U.S. Government Printing
               Office.
       Wershow, Harold J.
14   1964   The older Jews of Albany Park—some aspects of a subculture of the aged and its in-
               teraction with a gerontological research project. The Gerontologist 4:198–202.
5, 8   1977   Reality orientation for gerontologists: some thoughts about senility. The Gerontologist
               17:297–302.
15   West, D. J.
       1967   Homosexuality. Chicago: Aldine.
18   West, Howard
       1971   Five years of Medicare—a statistical review. Social Security Bulletin 34(12):17–27.
10   Whiskin, Frederick E.
       1964   On the meaning and function of reading in later life. Pp. 300–04 in Robert Kasten-
               baum (ed.), New Thoughts on Old Age. New York: Springer.
5   Whitbourne, Susan K., and Comilda S. Weinstock
       1979   Adult Development: The Differentiation of Experience. New York: Holt, Rinehart,
               and Winston.
5   White, Robert W.
       1959   Motivation reconsidered: the concept of competence. Psychological Review 66:297–333.
19   White House Conference on Aging
       1971   Report of the Delegates from the Conference Sections and Special Concerns Sessions.
               Washington, D.C.: White House Conference on Aging.
8, 14 Whittington, F.
       1975   Aging and the relative income status of blacks. Black Aging 1(1):6–13.
3   Whyte, William H., Jr.
       1956   The Organization Man. New York: Doubleday.
5   Wigdor, Blossom T.
       1980   Drives and motivations with aging. Pp. 245–61 in J. E. Birren and R. B. Sloane (eds.),
               Handbook of Mental Health and Aging. Englewood Cliffs, N.J.: Prentice-Hall.
11, 15 Wilbanks, William
       1981   Trends in violent death among the elderly. International Journal of Aging and Human
               Development 14:167–75.
11   Wilcox, Sandra G., and Marilyn Sutton
       1981   Understanding Death and Dying. Sherman Oaks, Calif.: Alfred.
       Wilder, Charles S.
8   1971   Chronic conditions and limitations of activity and mobility: United States, July 1965 to
               June 1967. Vital and Health Statistics, Series 10, No. 61.
8   1973   Limitation of activity due to chronic conditions: United States, 1969 to 1970. Vital and
               Health Statistics, Series 10, No. 80.
8   1974a   Acute conditions: incidence and associated disability: United States, July 1971 to June
               1972. Vital and Health Statistics, Series 10, No. 88.
8   1974b   Limitation of activity and mobility due to chronic conditions: United States—1972. Vi-
               tal and Health Statistics, Series 10, No. 96.

9   1977   Health characteristics of persons with chronic activity limitations: United States, 1974. Vital and Health Statistics, Series 10, No. 112. Washington, D.C.: U.S. Government Printing Office.

8   Wilder, Mary H.
     1972   Home care for persons 55 years and over: United States, July 1966 to June 1968. Vital and Health Statistics, Series 10, No. 73.

9, 10   Wilensky, Harold
     1964   Life cycle, work situations and participation in formal associations. Pp. 213–42 in Robert W. Kleemeier (ed.), Aging and Leisure. New York: Oxford University Press.

     Williams, Richard H.
6   1960   Changing status, role and relationships. Pp. 261–97 in Clark Tibbitts (ed.), Handbook of Social Gerontology. Chicago: University of Chicago Press.

11   1973   Propaganda, modification, and termination of life: contraception, abortion, suicide, euthanasia. Pp. 80–97 in R. H. Williams (ed.), To Live and To Die: When, Why, and How. New York: Springer.

12   Williams, Richard H., and Martin B. Loeb
     1968   The adult's social life space and successful aging: some suggestions for a conceptual framework. Pp. 379–81 in Bernice L. Neugarten (ed.), Middle Age and Aging. Chicago: University of Chicago Press.

12   Williams, Richard H., and Claudine Wirths
     1965   Lives Through the Years. New York: Atherton Press.
     Williams, Richard H., Clark Tibbitts, and Wilma Donahue (eds.)
     1963   Processes of Aging, Volumes 1 and 2. New York: Atherton Press.

17   Williamson, John B., Linda Evans, Lawrence A. Powell, and Sharlene Hesse-Biber
     1982   The Politics of Aging: Power and Policy. Springfield, Ill.: Charles C. Thomas

5   Willits, Fern K., Robert C. Bealer, and Donald M. Crider
     1977   Changes in individual attitudes toward traditional morality: a 24-year follow-up study. Journal of Gerontology 32:681–88.

8   Wilner, Daniel M., and Rosabelle P. Walkley
     1966   Some special problems and alternatives in housing for older persons. Pp. 221–59 in John C. McKinney and F. T. deVyver (eds.), Aging and Social Policy. New York: Appleton-Century-Crofts.

8   Wilner, Daniel M., Susan R. Sherman, Rosabelle P. Walkley, Suzanne Dodds, and Wiley P. Mangum, Jr.
     1968   Demographic characteristics of residents of planned retirement housing sites. The Gerontologist 8:164–89.

7   Wilson, Karen Brown, and Michael R. DeShane
     1982   The legal rights of grandparents: a preliminary discussion. The Gerontologist 22:67–71.

15   Wiltz, C. J.
     1978   The Influence of Age on Length of Incarceration. Unpublished doctoral dissertation. Ames, Iowa: University of Iowa.

8, 12   Windley, Paul G., and Rick J. Scheidt
     1982   An ecological model of mental health among small-town rural elderly. Journal of Gerontology 37:235–42.

13   Wingard, Joseph, Robert Heath, and Susan A. Himelstein
     1982   The effects of contextual variations on attitudes toward the elderly. Journal of Gerontology 37:475–82.

10   Wingrove, C. Ray, and Jon P. Alston
     1971   Age, aging, and church attendance. The Gerontologist 11(4, part 1):356–58.

8   Winiecke, L.
       1973   The appeal of age segregated housing to the elderly poor. International Journal of Aging and Human Development 4:293–306.

15   Wiseman, Jacqueline P.
       1970   Stations of the Lost: The Treatment of Skid Row Alcoholics. Englewood Cliffs, N.J.: Prentice-Hall.

9   Withers, W.
       1974   Some irrational beliefs about retirement in the United States. Industrial Gerontology 1:23–32.

8, 18 Witkin, E.
       1971   The Impact of Medicare. Springfield, Ill.: Charles C. Thomas.

8   Wittels, I., and J. Botwinick
       1974   Survival in relocation. Journal of Gerontology 29:440–43.

7   Woehrer, Carol E.
       1978   Cultural pluralism in American families: The influence of ethnicity on social aspects of aging. Family Coordinator 27:329–39.

9   Wolfbein, Seymour L.
       1963   Work patterns of older people. Pp. 303–12 in Richard H. Williams, Clark Tibbitts, and Wilma Donahue (eds.), Processes of Aging. Volume 2. New York: Atherton Press.

5, 12 Wolff, K.
       1971   The treatment of the depressed and suicidal geriatric patient. Geriatrics 26(7):65–69.

8   Wolk, R. L., and R. B. Wolk
       1971   Professional workers' attitudes toward the aged. Journal of American Geriatric Society 19:624–39.

8, 12 Wolk, S., and Telleen S.
       1976   Psychological and social correlates of life satisfaction as a function of residential constraint. Journal of Gerontology 31:89–98.

6   Wood, V.
       1971   Age-appropriate behavior for older people. The Gerontologist 11(4, part 2):74–78.

5   Woodruff, D. S., and J. E. Birren
       1972   Age changes and cohort differences in personality. Developmental Psychology 6:252–59.

16   Woodsworth, D. E.
       1977   Social Security and National Policy. Sweden, Yugoslavia, Japan. Montreal: McGill-Queen's University Press.

8   Woodward, H., R. Gingles, and J. C. Woodward
       1974   Loneliness and the elderly as related to housing. The Gerontologist 14:349–51.

       Wray, R. P.

8   1971a   An Interdisciplinary Non-Credit Community Course in Adult Development and Aging. Bethesda, Md.: ERIC Document Reproduction Service.

19   1971b   Gerontology: interdisciplinary and intercollegiate. The Gerontologist 11:261–63.

5   Wright, Ruth E.
       1981   Aging, divided attention, and processing capacity. Journal of Gerontology 36:605–14.

8   Wunderlich, Gooloo S.
       1965   Characteristics of residents in institutions for the aged and chronically ill: United States, April–June, 1963. Vital and Health Statistics, Series 12, No. 2.

13, 14 Wylie, R. W.
       1971   Attitudes toward aging and the aged among black Americans: some historical perspectives. Aging and Human Development 2:66–70.

8, 18,
19   Yordi, Cathleen L., Amelia S. Chu, Kathleen Ross, and Sylvia Wong
    1982   Research and the frail elderly: ethical and methodological issues in controlled social experiments. The Gerontologist 22:72–77.

7, 8   York, Jonathan L., and Robert J. Calsyn
    1977   Family involvement in nursing homes. The Gerontologist 17:500–05.

    Youmans, E. Grant
8, 9   1966   Objective and subjective economic disengagement among older rural and urban men. Journal of Gerontology 21:439–41.

7   1967a   Family disengagement among older urban and rural women. Journal of Gerontology 22:209–11.

    1967b   (ed.) Older Rural Americans: A Sociological Perspective. Lexington, Kentucky: University of Kentucky Press.

13   1971   Generation and perceptions of old age: an urban-rural comparison. The Gerontologist 11:284–88.

5   1973   Age stratification and value orientations. International Journal of Aging and Human Development 4:53–65.

5   1974   Age group, health and attitudes. The Gerontologist 14:249–54.

5   1977a   Attitudes: young-old and old-old. The Gerontologist 17:175–78.

    1977b   The rural aged. Annals of the American Academy of Political and Social Science 429:81–90.

12   Youmans, E. Grant, and Marian Yarrow
    1971   Aging and social adaptation: a longitudinal study of old men. Pp. 95–103 in Samuel Granick and Robert C. Patterson (eds.), Human Aging II: An Eleven-Year Followup. Washington, D.C.: U.S. Government Printing Office.

7   Young, Michael, and Peter Willmott
    1957   Family and Kinship in East London. London: Routledge and Kegan Paul.

5   Zard, Steven H., Kenneth D. Cole, and Rebecca L. Guider
    1981   Memory training strategies and subjective complaints of memory in the aged. The Gerontologist 21:158–64.

12   Zarit, S. H., and R. L. Kahn
    1975   Aging and adaptation to illness. Journal of Gerontology 30:67–72.

7   Zarit, Steven H., Karen E. Reever, and Julie Bach-Peterson
    1980   Relatives of the impaired elderly: correlates of feelings of burden. The Gerontologist 20:649–55.

5, 8   Zatlin, C. E., M. Storandt, and J. Botwinick
    1973   Personality and values of women continuing their education after thirty-five years of age. Journal of Gerontology 28:216–21.

10   Zborowski, Mark
    1962   Aging and recreation. Journal of Gerontology 17:302–09.

2   Zelinsky, Wilbur
    1966   Toward a geography of the aged. Geographical Review 56:445–47.

    Zepelin, Harold
5   1981a   Age differences in dreams. I: Men's dreams and thematic apperceptive fantasy. International Journal of Aging and Human Development 12:171–86.

5   1981b   Age differences in dreams. II: Distortion and other variables. International Journal of Aging and Human Development 13:37–41.

9, 16   Zillmer, Theodore W.
    1982   Age impact on employee benefit costs is not a major problem for employees. Aging and Work 5:49–53.

12, 15   Zimberg, Sheldon
    1974   The elderly alcoholic. The Gerontologist 14:221–24.
5   Zola, Irving K.
    1962   Feelings about age among older people. Journal of Gerontology 17:65–68.
8   Zube, Margaret
    1980   Outlook on being old: working class elderly in Northhampton, Massachusetts. The Gerontologist 20:427–31.
2, 13   Zuckerman, Harriet, and Robert K. Merton
    1972   Age, aging, and age structure in science. Pp. 292–456 in Matilda W. Riley, Marilyn Johnson, and Anne Foner (eds.), Aging and Society. Volume 3: A Sociology of Age Stratification. New York: Russell Sage Foundation.

Index